GLORIOUS BATTLE

GLORIOUS BATTLE

The Cultural Politics of
Victorian Anglo-Catholicism

John Shelton Reed

VANDERBILT UNIVERSITY PRESS
Nashville

Publication of this book was made possible partially through a generous grant from
the National Endowment for the Humanities.

First Edition 1996
First Paperback Edition 2000

Paperback ISBN 0-8265-1380-8

04 03 02 01 00   5 4 3 2 1

Cloth Edition Library of Congress Cataloging-in-Publication Data

Reed, John Shelton.
Glorious battle: the cultural politics of Victorian Anglo-Catholicism /
John Shelton Reed.—1st ed.
    p.   cm.   Includes bibliographical references and index
           ISBN 0-8265-1274-7 (alk. paper)

1. Anglo-Catholicism—England—History—19th century.
2. England—Church history—19th century. I. Title.

BX5121.R44 1996
283'.42'09034—dc20   95-52009

Made in the United States of America

For Dale, Elisabeth, and Sarah,
who have seen it start to finish,
with love.

Sing my tongue, the glorious battle,
Sing the winning of the fray.

Pange lingua,
tr. John Mason Neale

I pondered all these things and how men fight and lose the battle and the thing that they fought for comes about in spite of their defeat, and when it comes it turns out not to be what they meant, and other men have to fight for what they meant under a different name....

William Morris
A Dream of John Ball

In endeavouring to depict the characters of the persons of whom I write, I am to a certain extent forced to speak of sacred things. I trust, however, that I shall not be thought to scoff at the pulpit, though some may imagine that I do not feel all the reverence that is due to the cloth. I may question the infallibility of the teachers, but I hope that I shall not therefore be accused of doubt as to the thing to be taught.

Anthony Trollope
Barchester Towers

CONTENTS

ILLUSTRATIONS

The illustrations can be found following page 168

PREFACE

When I began this project nearly twenty years ago, I had no idea where it would lead, but I rather hoped it would lead back to Oxford, where my family and I had enjoyed a pleasant but too short visit in 1973. It eventually did that, thanks to the generosity of the John Simon Guggenheim Foundation, which awarded me a fellowship for 1977-78.

Our stay was made delightful and my work much easier by a great many people. St. Antony's College, Oxford, now occupies the former house of the Society of the Holy and Undivided Trinity: its warden (Raymond Carr) and fellows extended me the college's hospitality. The library at Pusey House was an indispensable resource, and the librarian, Father Peter Cobb, an accommodating host and guide. I also made extensive use of the Bodleian Library and of the British Library in London, and I thank the staffs of those two splendid institutions.

Bryan Wilson invited me to present an early version of this story to his sociology of religion seminar at All Souls; I am grateful to him and to Graham Simpson, a member of that seminar, both for their comments and for their kindness to a stranger in a strange land. Another gracious and helpful host was Professor David Martin of the London School of Economics.

I am indebted to the clergy and communicants of the dozens of churches throughout the south of England who showed me their buildings, unlocked their treasured vestments and plate, gossiped about old controversies, invited me to their services, and generally made me welcome. But the prize must go to our friends and neighbors in Great Missenden, Buckinghamshire, especially Geoff and Sue Clare, Betty Clemetson, Graham Leonard, and Father Donald Rydings, whose hospitality taught us Southerners a thing or two.

During our time in England, I did nearly all of the research for this book, but not (by a long shot) all of the writing I had so optimistically promised the Guggenheim Foundation. From time to time, as subsequent years went by, I was granted the leisure to return to this project, to read my way back into the world that existed in my notes—"a nostalgic country of the mind [to paraphrase Vincent Starrett on the Sherlock Holmes stories] where it is always 1870"—and to come back to the present with a few chapters in hand. Three of those journeys were made possible by the generosity of various benefactors, two of whom were supporting other projects altogether. I was privileged to receive the patronage of the Rockefeller Foundation, as scholar in residence at its Study and Conference Center in Bellagio in 1981; that of the National Humanities Center, as a fellow (supported by National Endowment for the Humanities grant #FC-2038-81) in 1983-84; and, that of the Center for Advanced Study in the Behavioral Sciences, as a fellow (under National Science Foundation #BNS-8700864) in 1990-91. I am deeply grateful to those institutions and to the staff of each, especially to Kathleen Much of the CASBS, who gave my manuscript the benefit of her editing talent. I am also thankful to the William R. Kenan, Jr., Trust Fund, which made possible a return trip to England in 1991 to tie up some bibliographic loose ends and to visit a few more churches.

In the mid-1980s a burst of accomplishment led to the publication of three articles based on this material. Chapters 8, 10, and 11 are adapted from, respectively, "'Ritualism Rampant in East London': Anglo-Catholicism and the Urban Poor," *Victorian Studies* 31 (Spring 1988): 375–403; "'A Female Movement': The Feminization of Nineteenth-Century Anglo-Catholicism," *Anglican and Episcopal History* 57 (June 1988): 199–238; and "'Giddy Young Men': A Counter-Cultural Aspect of Victorian Anglo-Catholicism," in Craig Calhoun, ed., *Comparative Social Research*, vol. 11, *Culture*, Greenwich, Conn.: JAI Press, 1989. They appear here by permission of the copyright holders. I thank the editors of those periodicals, and their anonymous reviewers.

This project has benefited from the observations of a great many people over the years, beginning with Sigmund Diamond and Herbert Hyman, my teachers at Columbia University. Stephen Tonsor and Martha Bohachevsky-Chomiak each made many good suggestions; the book is better for those I took, and would be better still if I had been up to the work required to take more. Other friends, colleagues, and scholars who have provided counsel and encouragement include Francis Absalom, Ward Allen, Joseph Altholz, Paul Betz, Timothy Breen, Craig Calhoun, Elizabeth Fox-Genovese, Eugene Genovese, Larry Griffin, Don Herzog, Walter Hooper, Robert Bernard Martin, Bruce Mullin, James Oakes, Denis Paz, Albert Reiss, Jr., David Riesman, the Triangle Area Religious Historians, Grant Wacker, and Nigel Yates. I am particularly grateful to one publisher's reader, of whom I know only that he is an Englishman and an ecclesiastical historian. Especially because I am neither, I appreciate his generous comments and helpful advice.

By publishing this book Vanderbilt University Press has demonstrated that the Age of Faith is not yet over. I am particularly grateful to Laurie Parker and to Charles Backus, director of the press, for their personal interest in the book, and for their confidence in me. Bard Young did a thorough, yet tactful, job of copyediting.

Finally, gratitude is the least part of what I owe my daughters and my wife. They have lived with this project for a long time, and this book's dedication is heartfelt. Elisabeth and Sarah probably cannot remember when I was not supposed to be working on it. Dale can, if only because she has been involved in it from the beginning, most recently as critic and editor of the semi-final draft. I believe she is even more glad to see it finished than I am.

INTRODUCTION

Ⅰt began in the universities. From the beginning, the movement had a special appeal to the young, and children of the privileged classes seemed to find it particularly attractive. Some observers took a tolerant view, seeing it as a harmless outlet for youthful high spirits; others argued that all could learn from its adherents' high-mindedness and seriousness, that they were recalling the nation to its own ideals; some said that the movement offered spiritual meaning and purpose in a crass and materialistic society. But these voices were drowned out by the chorus of condemnation. Many more saw the movement as an expression of hedonism and self-indulgence, an unfortunate sign of the times, a symptom of the nation's moral decay. On the fringe, a few even argued that the movement's leaders were agents of an alien ideology, covertly serving a foreign power and seeking to subvert the nation's constitution.

Certainly the movement's gatherings were sensual experiences, marked by vivid color and light, exotic costumes, the sweet aroma of incense, and music—powerful music. Many of its followers dabbled in the arts: with few exceptions their paintings and poetry were mediocre, but their music had an undeniable appeal. Few took seriously the warnings of Evangelical Christians that its words were often code for dangerous, soul-destroying doctrine, and it was played and copied by many who had no other use for the movement.

The religious views of the young partisans frequently did depart from their parents' conventional religiosity, toward an ornate and antirational mysticism that struck many observers as an anomaly in a scientific, rational, modern age. A few young people even ran away to join religious communities, where (it was said) some were held incommunicado, denied contact with their despairing families. Most of the movement's young adherents stayed at home, of course, but their beliefs, their mannerisms, and their like-minded friends often set parents' teeth on edge.

People with middle-class ideas of decency and respectability found much to be alarmed about, particularly in what they saw as the movement's casual attitude toward sexual morality—and, in their own terms, these critics were often correct. The movement was said to produce unladylike women and unmanly men, and there was some truth in this observation, too.

The movement's intellectual spokesmen were, for the most part, older men: university professors, clergymen, thinkers of greater or lesser significance. The movement held them in respect, quoted them, honored them in public, revered them for having shown the way earlier, when they had held their views almost alone. In truth, these men were sometimes distressed or dismayed at the way their self-styled disciples put their ideas into practice; sometimes, indeed, they were thoroughly out of patience with their hot-headed young followers, who in turn were privately impatient with their elders' caution. For the most part, though, the alliance held, cemented in large measure by the opposition's indiscriminate condemnation.

The politics of the movement ranged from support for state socialism to romantic communitarianism to apolitical otherworldliness, but its adherents were emphatically not commercially minded, narrowly "patriotic" imperialists, like so many of the men their fellow citizens continued to elect to high office. Many saw a community of interest with the poor and genuinely wished them well, although we may doubt that either they or the poor ever really understood the other. A few dedicated men and women went into the slums to work and to organize; their efforts were generally unavailing, but they alarmed some of the movement's less discerning opponents. Symbolically, too, their modest successes were important. Token poor people were sometimes produced at public gatherings of the movement; less innocently, toughs were sometimes recruited to provide an element of menace that the movement's leaders occasionally implied could explode at any time.

Most politicians returned the movement's contempt, with interest, and demanded "law and order." Blue-ribbon panels studied the problem. More than once attempts were made to put the movement down by law, and gangs of patriotic workingmen several times assaulted its gatherings. A concerted plan of civil disobedience resulted in the trials of several activists and the jailing of a few, and reinforced the movement's image of lawlessness. News of these trials and appeals for the defense funds were staples in the movement's newspapers.

The movement seemed to thrive on confrontation, even sometimes to seek it out. Its goals were many and various, never entirely agreed-upon or clear, apparently always expanding. The word "compromise" did not seem to be in its vocabulary; many of its leaders and followers seemed to enjoy putting their demands in the most outrageous terms they could find. One has to suspect that part of the movement's appeal, part of the story of its success, was that it offended the stuffy and the powerful, contradicting them and denying their cultural hegemony at every turn.

I have purposely left some details—among them, those of time and place—unspecified. In most respects, of course, the description could fit the American youth movement of the 1960s, but the movement I have described is the "Catholic Revival" or Anglo-Catholic movement in the nineteenth-century Church of England. I shall try to tell the story of that movement here, but juxtaposing the ferment of the 1860s with that of the 1960s may suggest that I have something more than straightforward narration in mind.

Both movements exemplify a phenomenon increasingly common in the cultural politics of modern industrial society; beneath their many obvious dissimilarities they share one definitive characteristic. Each stood in opposition to some of the dominant values of its time and place, appealing to people who were, for one reason or another, disaffected from those values. Both were, in short, "countercultural" movements.[1]

Perhaps a study of Victorian Anglo-Catholicism has some lessons for our own times, if only to demonstrate that the counterculture of the 1960s was less unprecedented than many of its participants supposed.[2] But that is not the point. Perhaps looking at Anglo-Catholicism in this uncustomary light can illuminate some of the dynamics of countercultural movements in general. But that is not the point either. This is not an attempt to construct or to test a theory of countercultures; rather, the value of the theory in this case lies primarily in the questions it leads us to ask, questions that have not often been asked of the Anglo-Catholic movement. If the answers suggest that its appeals were largely countercultural, we shall have learned something worth knowing about both the movement and the culture that spawned it.

The story of the rise of Anglo-Catholicism and the resulting conflict between High and Low Church in the Church of England is probably little known to modern readers other than some scholars and Anglo-Catholics. (Indeed, the *Masterpiece Theatre* adaptation of Trollope's Barsetshire novels simply omitted the party background of the story, making its central conflict wholly a matter of personalities.) Large parts of that account are only now being written in any systematic way, but that is a task for historians. I do not intend to write any more of that history than I have to, but I have had to write some, if only to indicate what it is that needs explaining.

In the next few chapters, we shall look at the roots of the revival in the Oxford Movement of John Henry Newman and his friends, an academic and mostly clerical effort to shore up the Church of England in its relations to the state—or, as its opponents would express the same facts, to strengthen the position of the clergy relative to the laity of the Church. We shall see how, as that movement spread into the parishes and acquired a lay following, its agenda expanded to include the revival of an ever-increasing number of beliefs and practices from the Church of England's pre-Reformation heritage. We shall examine in particular the simultaneous revivals of religious communities and the practice of confession. Throughout, my focus will be as much on the changes in worship, church furnishings, and extra-liturgical practices that Anglo-Catholics believed their doctrines licensed or required as on the doctrines themselves. (Those innovations were what the fuss was mostly about.) After describing these initial revivals, I shall examine the significant acceleration of ritual "advance" in the 1860s and 1870s, as Anglo-Catholicism became a full-blown social movement. We shall also look at the growing opposition to the movement's program, culminating in attempts to suppress it by law.

After telling the story in a fairly straightforward way—although with a great many examples and a few excursions too obvious to pass up—I shall turn to explanation. As the ecclesiastical historian John Kent has observed, "Somehow, the central problem remains untouched: why did a section of the nineteenth-century Anglican Church move so dogmatically and successfully back to a style of religious behaviour that had seemed so entirely abandoned in England?"[3] The answer will require some attention to the movement's context, both its institutional setting (in particular, its relation to the rest of the Church of England) and the broader social context, where nineteenth-century demographic and even technological changes made such a movement more likely. After that, I shall try to address Kent's question by asking the ordinary questions that sociologists ask about any social movement. Most obviously: What kinds of people took it up, who opposed it, and why?

Looking at Anglo-Catholicism as a countercultural movement can help us understand both its opposition and its support. It was no surprise, for instance, that stalwart Protestants opposed the movement. They found its theology objectionable and opposed practices said to symbolize or to follow from those beliefs. But many "commonsense" Englishfolk, men and women with little discernible interest in doctrine, also found the movement contemptible or infuriating. We simply cannot understand their opposition without reference to Anglo-Catholicism's broader cultural implications. But when we recognize that many of the practices the movement championed were symbolic affronts to central values of Victorian middle-class culture, and that a few were actual threats to those values, we can see that the movement's opponents were right to be offended—even that sometimes they were *supposed* to be offended.

Of course, as we shall see, other men and women found the same themes appealing. The sacerdotalism that so irritated the movement's opponents, for instance, offered a new and gratifying occupational self-image to clergymen, whose profession was manifestly declining in influence and social standing. It gave them a view of the priesthood as a calling like medicine or the law, with its own special (indeed, divinely ordered) authority and abilities.

Similarly, in the cities and watering-places of England, Anglo-Catholicism offered the fashionable (or aspirants to that description) a mode of religious expression associated with the avant-garde of culture and taste, one that distinguished them from stuffy, vulgar, pushing persons of the rising commercial classes (what we might call the Weberian middle class), allied with Anglican Evangelicalism or with Dissent. Politically, a few Anglo-Catholics flirted with socialism and most inclined to a sort of neo-feudalism: in either case the ideal was a society in which "trade" was subordinate.

To the urban poor, Anglo-Catholicism offered more tangible attractions: nursing for the sick, food and fuel, solace in times of hardship. But for some of them, too, it had a cultural appeal. At its best, it offered respect and friendship across the chasm of class. At the very least it took the poor seriously and was no more condescending to them than to any other laymen.

The movement took women seriously, too, consulting their tastes, offering them useful and important work, and even allowing a sort of silent protest against the oppressive authority of fathers and husbands. To the young of both sexes it also offered an attractive form of rebellion: one could be mildly daring, enjoy the comradeship of an embattled minority, and shock the merely respectable (in many cases, one's parents) in the service of unquestionably high and worthwhile ideals. Finally, men who were indifferent to the demanding Victorian ideal of manliness, or repelled by it, found in Anglo-Catholicism an alternative to "muscular Christianity," one that tolerated, even encouraged, personal sensitivity and sometimes extravagant aesthetic expression.

As we shall see, each of these constituencies contributed disproportionately to Anglo-Catholicism's early support; together they provided the bulk of the movement's adherents at the time when someone was an Anglo-Catholic only because he or she had chosen to become one. Each group can be seen as culturally subordinate or in decline—threatened, oppressed, or at least bored by the Victorian values that the movement challenged—and ready to hear subversive messages.

For later generations, of course, the situation was different. For those raised in Anglo-Catholicism, *it* was the conventional form of religion, and there was little daring, rebellious, or countercultural about it. This story's denouement comes toward the end of the century, when such people began to outnumber converts to the movement and Anglo-Catholicism itself had become respectable. By then it had also become clear that it could not be put down by law, and some former opponents had begun to doubt that putting it down was a good idea anyway. The movement had won its right to exist as a legitimate, tolerated party within the Church of England. Paradoxically, that victory removed some of its outlaw charm, although its fringes have retained some of the earlier flavor up to our own times.

When I began this inquiry, I did not think of Anglo-Catholicism as a countercultural movement. I came to that view of it only gradually, after immersion in the literature by and about the movement left me wondering how it could be so impolitic, so indifferent to the offense it gave in so many ways to so many people whose goodwill would seem to have been desirable. Eventually I had to conclude that the offensiveness was not just accidental, not just the result of shortsightedness or thoughtless lack of tact, that many were drawn to the movement precisely because it offended those whom they wished to offend. Anglo-Catholicism, in other words, thrived on opposition; it attracted adherents in part because of who opposed it. A movement like that has little to gain and much to lose from compromise.

I am overstating, of course. People often sincerely claim higher motives than a skeptical observer might be prepared to grant them, and the offense of Anglo-Catholicism was only sometimes calculated. In any case, some may rightly object that it is a distortion to treat a serious religious movement in terms almost exclusively social and cultural. But to say that Anglo-Catholicism was a countercultural movement is not to say that it was only that, and I, for one, would not want to say that it was even primarily that.[4] But that is part of its story, an important part, and a neglected one.

Certainly a number of the movement's otherwise puzzling characteristics become perfectly understandable when viewed in this light. I do not wish to belabor this point, but I have used it to organize my observations, and subsequently, to some extent, my chapters. There is little profit in arguing over whether Victorian Anglo-Catholicism was "really" a countercultural movement, but thinking of it as one has helped me to make sense of the movement, and it has helped me to tell this story.

I confess that I now find the movement less sympathetic, if more entertaining, than when I began. The Anglo-Catholics were often treated shamefully, to be sure, and there is no excuse for the narrow-mindedness and little for the shortsightedness of some of their opponents. Other opponents, notably Disraeli, were scandalously opportunistic. But many Anglo-Catholics asked for the treatment they got, and clearly they sometimes even enjoyed it. Piety and seriousness might suggest that I should call this a depressing tale of squabbling over sacred things, of tragic misunderstanding and martyrdom; honestly, though, I find it for the most part a delightful story, with a gallery of characters engaging, or outrageous, or often both. Whatever readers' views of my analytical tack may be, I hope they will find that to be true.

GLORIOUS BATTLE

I

The Seeds of Ritualism

The Church of England at the end of the nineteenth century was a very different institution from what it had been seventy or eighty years before.[1] Of course England was a different place, and many of the changes in the Church simply reflected that. The nation's population had more than doubled between the 1830s and the 1880s; that of London had nearly trebled. Hundreds of new churches had been built in an attempt to keep up with the growing urban and suburban population, and the numbers of clergymen and churchgoers had also greatly increased—if not as fast as the population.

The new clergymen struck many observers as more earnest, more hard working, more professional than their predecessors, and more of them had received theological training, in the new theological colleges founded during the period. Some of the worst abuses of patronage and plurality had been eliminated, and if anticlericalism was still widespread, it was at least less violent than it had been in 1830. The Church of England was a leaner, more efficient institution than ever before. The concentration of population in the cities and improved transportation in the countryside meant that clergymen could gather more often, and they did, in ruridecanal conferences, diocesan synods, annual church congresses, and meetings of innumerable groups for special purposes. The convocations of Canterbury and York had begun to meet again, giving the clergy of the Church a greater voice in its government, and the decennial Lambeth Conference had even begun to gather Anglicans from around the world.

Disturbingly, however, each of these improvements seemed to be matched by other, less encouraging changes. The proportion of the population actually attending Anglican churches—or any churches, for that matter—had declined steadily throughout the century. Particularly in the working-class areas of English cities, attendance had reached levels that contemporary observers thought alarmingly low. Some people did not much care for the new sort of clergymen, either, and pointed out that fewer had university degrees or were, in a word, gentlemen. Whether as cause or effect, the social standing of the clergy was markedly lower at the end of the century than it had been at the beginning.

Disestablishment was still a threat, and the Church had lost its monopoly in education. More and more, it seemed, decisions were being made without reference to the Church or the Church's law—decisions about social services, about divorce and remarriage, even about who could be buried in Anglican graveyards. Religious censuses had revealed what everyone already feared, that as many as half of English churchgoers were to be found in congregations other than those of the Church of England. Particularly in the cities, the parish system had pretty well broken down. Many parishioners stayed home on Sundays; others went to Dissenting or Roman Catholic churches; still others crossed parish boundaries to attend Anglican services more to their taste than those offered by their parish churches.

And by the end of the century there were many varieties of Anglican worship to choose from. (Some believed that this was an improvement, but many disagreed.) An ecclesiastical Rip Van Winkle roused from a seventy-year sleep in the 1890s would have noticed few changes in the Church of England more startling at first glance than those in the conduct of public worship. It would not have been immediately evident that those changes were bound up, one way or another, with all of the other changes in the Church, but they were.

Varieties of Anglican Worship

Suppose that our sleeper awoke to find himself in London, at Oxford Circus, on a Sunday morning.[2] Within a few blocks he would find a bewildering array of services ranging from some almost identical to those he had known seventy years before to some that he would not recognize as Anglican at all.

If he walked north along Regent Street, for instance, he would immediately enter the parish of All Souls, Langham Place. Soon he would come to the church itself, a fine neoclassical building dating from 1824, where he would find a service very much like what he was accustomed to. Most of the congregation would be seated in their family pews, rented by the year, and he would be directed by the verger to one of the "open" (i.e., public) seats at the rear of the church. The members of the choir, in their Sunday best, would also be in the back of the church.

The service would be the Prayer Book office of morning prayer, with a sermon. It would be read by the rector, in a white surplice with his M.A. hood; to preach the sermon, he would change to a black Genevan gown. Accompanied by Miss Bloomer on the organ, the congregation would sing

hymns from the *Hymnal Companion*; some would be new to him, but neither they nor the sermon would contain any novel doctrine (although he
might find both somewhat "methodistical" by the standards of the 1830s).
He would not be surprised to learn that there were to be two services of
evening prayer that same day, the second with another sermon. If it happened to be a communion Sunday, the service of Holy Communion would
follow morning prayer. The minister, wearing his surplice and hood, would
read the Prayer of Consecration standing to the left of the communion table,
sideways to the congregation, as the Prayer Book directed.

The observer would notice a few changes. Even at morning prayer, there
would be a collection, or "offertory." And he would be startled to learn that
there was a communion service every Sunday—if not after morning prayer,
then early in the morning, in the afternoon, or after evening prayer. He
would also find more weekday services than he was used to: morning prayer
on Wednesdays, Fridays, and saints' days; evening prayer on Wednesdays.
But, all things considered, he would not be alarmed by what he encountered
at All Souls.

If he turned south from Oxford Circus, though, he would enter the
parish of St. John the Baptist. A left turn on Argyll Place would take him in
a couple of blocks to the church, a small, recently constructed Gothic
Revival building on Great Marlborough Street. Entering, he would find all
but fifty of the 460 seats open to the public, and he could probably sit where
he pleased. Morning prayer would begin early, at 10:30, to allow a service
of Holy Communion to follow.

The service would begin with a procession from the back of the church:
the choir, in surplices, would take their place in the chancel, at the front of
the church. The ministers (there would probably be more than one) would
also wear surplices, but with brightly colored embroidered stoles rather than
academic hoods. The visual focus of the church would be the communion
table rather than the pulpit; it would be decorated with an embroidered
frontal, flowers, and candles, and would bear little resemblance to the plain
wooden table to which the visitor was accustomed. The psalms and canticles
would be sung, not read, with a rather florid setting, and some of the hymns
in *Hymns Ancient and Modern* might sound strangely "Romish" (for example, number 97: "Faithful Cross, above all other"). The sermon might puz-
zle the visitor, too: it might deal with some point of ecclesiastical history or
symbolism. He would notice that the preacher did not change to his black
gown for the sermon.

When morning prayer ended and the communion service began, he
would probably be struck by the celebrant's reading the Prayer of Consecration with his back to the congregation. He would certainly be startled to
learn that there had already been an early communion service that morning,
and that there was another every Thursday, as well as on holy days.

Our observer would recognize the words of the *Book of Common Prayer*,
but few of the accompaniments would be familiar unless he had extensive

experience in Anglican cathedrals. He would certainly be more struck by the changes than by the continuities. He might or might not be disturbed to learn that what he saw was becoming typical of Church of England services.

But if he walked a little farther down Regent Street to the next parish, St. Thomas, he would almost certainly be shocked. If he knew something of the Roman Catholic Mass, he would recognize what he saw at St. Thomas's Church, although he might wonder why the words were those of the Anglican prayer book. If he knew nothing of Catholicism he would be mystified.

The interior of the seventeenth-century building, redone in the 1860s by William Butterfield, would be filled with light and shadow and vivid color. Ornamental banding, encaustic tile, banks of flowers, many candles, embroidery, stained glass—all would contribute to an overwhelming impression, only heightened when the church was seen through the haze of incense, which would be liberally burned in procession and during the Mass that followed. With the thurifer in procession would come a surpliced choir, acolytes, and a number of priests, one of them (the preacher) wearing what our visitor might just possibly recognize as a cope, the others in gorgeous vestments of a sort nowhere to be found in the Church of England of the 1830s.

There would be no reserved pews. Some of the music would be Gregorian, and the Prayer Book communion service would be read with a great deal of crossing, bowing, and genuflecting. Not only would the congregation engage in mysterious signs of devotion from time to time, but some of them would be very strange-looking folk—especially some women dressed in the habits of sisters.

The sermon might be especially striking; if our visitor knew his history, he might observe that it was as if the Reformation had never taken place. The announcements would be equally strange, dealing with the activities of a number of parish guilds and perhaps exhorting the congregation to avail themselves of the opportunity for confession and absolution.

During the celebration of Holy Communion, the celebrant would face the altar, his back to the congregation, flanked by two other oddly vested clergymen. Some of the prayers would be virtually inaudible, and they would be punctuated by long intervals in which the celebrant appeared to be praying privately. After the consecration, the celebrant would himself consume the consecrated elements: probably our visitor would not be given the opportunity to receive communion. If he asked, he would be told that those who wished to do so had come to one of two earlier celebrations. There was a celebration every morning at St. Thomas's, two on Thursdays and saints' days, and five on great festivals.

Here, in a stroll of less than half a mile down Regent Street, on any Sunday in the 1890s, our observer could witness a range of Anglican worship that he would probably refuse to believe possible. At All Souls, an austere Evangelical service not very different from what he would have seen in most

English parish churches sixty years before. At St. John the Baptist, a lav-
ishly decorated choral service reminiscent, perhaps, of cathedral services
early in the century, but increasingly representative of "normal," middle-of-the-road parochial worship. At St. Thomas, Regent Street, a High
Mass almost indistinguishable save in language from that of any well-to-do
Roman Catholic church of the period. The same contrasts could be seen in
many other neighborhoods of London, in most large cities of the nation,
and in many smaller ones.

What had happened while our observer slept? The answer is that a
movement called "Anglo-Catholicism" had sprung up and, despite reversals,
had flourished. St. Thomas was among the churches in the vanguard of that
movement; they showed how far it had come since its beginnings. The worship at St. John the Baptist looked like Anglo-Catholic worship of an earlier day, but it was not an Anglo-Catholic church. It illustrated, rather, how
much the great central body of Anglican practice had been influenced by the
movement. Even All Souls, Langham Place, had been influenced by Anglo-
Catholicism, although in a reactive way. Its weekday services and weekly
communion had been Anglo-Catholic innovations, but Evangelicals alarmed
at their rivals' success had adopted those practices in self-defense.

In short, the Anglo-Catholics had not only won their right to toleration
within the Church of England, they had by their example and success influenced the practice and attitudes of all parts of the Church. How had this
come about?

The history of the Anglo-Catholic movement in the nineteenth-century
Church of England comes in two parts, one relatively well known, the other
largely forgotten, even by Anglo-Catholics. The first part, the story of the
Oxford Movement, is told in John Henry Newman's *Apologia pro Vita Sua*,
and it has often been told since, largely in the terms that Newman laid
down: as the story of his vision, his discouragement, his spiritual crisis, and
his conversion to Roman Catholicism. But the history of the movement
after Newman's secession has been much less thoroughly described.[3] In serious histories of Victorian Britain, even in most serious histories of Victorian
religion, the heroes and mock-heroes of the second, "Ritualist" phase of the
Anglo-Catholic revival are usually relegated to a becoming obscurity. The
movement's most important political ally, Gladstone, and its most effective
political adversary, Disraeli, are remembered for many things but seldom for
their opinions on Anglo-Catholicism. Its most significant clerical ally,
"Soapy Sam" Wilberforce, bishop of Oxford and then of Winchester, is
probably remembered today, if at all, for coming off second-best to T. H.
Huxley in an exchange concerning the theory of evolution.

Although some historians are now beginning to put this situation right,
for a picture of the movement in the second half of the nineteenth century
we still must turn to dusty Victorian and Edwardian biographies and memoirs, to hagiographies compiled to mark this or that centenary, or to

little-read novels by authors like Shane Leslie and Compton Mackenzie.

Foremost among the several reasons for the relative neglect of the movement's later period, I suspect, is one that is almost purely aesthetic. The story of the Oxford Movement is so compelling, so dramatically complete, that the rest comes as an anticlimax. To demonstrate that (and also to show that many of the later movement's characteristics and problems were present almost from the start) it may be appropriate briefly to recount what happened in Oxford in the years 1833-1845.[4]

Tracts for the Times

On July 14, 1833, John Keble preached a sermon on "National Apostasy" in the church of St. Mary the Virgin, Oxford. John Henry Newman later identified that sermon as the beginning of the Oxford Movement, and subsequent historians have generally followed his lead. On its face, the sermon protested parliamentary interference in the affairs of the Church, specifically a proposal by the Whig government to suppress some bishoprics of the Church of Ireland. Keble's point was not that the bishoprics were needed (they assuredly were not), but rather that Parliament was an assembly of laymen (including non-Anglican laymen) and had no business ordering the affairs of the Church as if it were merely a branch of government like the postal service.

Of course the movement did not spring up full-blown from that single sermon. But its message fell on fertile ground. Many churchmen were concerned about growing popular hostility to the Establishment, expressed not only in acts of Parliament but in the actions of mobs like those that stoned the carriage of the bishop of Bath and Wells, burned the bishop's palace in Bristol, and on Guy Fawkes Day in 1831 burned the bishop of Exeter himself, in effigy, after the bishops voted in the House of Lords against the First Reform Bill. In part, the movement was a reaction against lethargy and negligence in the Church (often overstated, to be sure, by sympathetic historians); in part it was merely an amplification and mobilization of the already-existing High Church tradition that Keble's poems in *The Christian Year* exemplified.[5] But even if Keble's sermon did nothing more than focus Newman's attention, it can serve as a convenient marker for the start of a dramatic twelve years.

The course of the movement in its Oxford home began with excitement and success. A series of ninety *Tracts for the Times* was begun shortly after Keble's sermon, with a tract by Newman defending the spiritual independence of the Church under bishops standing in the apostolic succession. Other tracts followed, arguing the case for orthodoxy in other respects.[6] The publication of the *Tracts* and Newman's sermons in St. Mary's won adherents to the cause, both enthusiastic undergraduates and distinguished High Church divines, notably E. B. Pusey, professor of Hebrew and fellow of Christ Church, who soon became identified as a leader of the movement, with Newman and Keble. Newman's brilliance, Keble's manifest holiness, Pusey's scholarship—all were put to the service of an exalted vision of the English Church and its ministry, a vision with obvious appeal to young men destined for that ministry and more subtle but no less potent attractions for others. Within a year of Keble's sermon, a declaration of "deep attachment to the apostolical doctrine and liturgy and polity of the Church of England" was drawn up, signed by seven thousand clergymen, and presented to the archbishop of Canterbury.[7]

But almost from the beginning the Tractarians (as they came to be known) faced external opposition. As long as the movement remained a donnish affair, its opposition was theologically based, but it was no less fierce for that. Three months after the first tracts appeared, the *Record*, an Evangelical newspaper, denounced the series and its writers for Romanism. This accusation would be incessant, and soon it would be made by others besides extreme Low Churchmen.

Also virtually from the beginning, there was internal division on matters of both policy and substance. On the one hand, the younger men—like Newman, Keble, and their friend Hurrell Froude—wanted to take a stand on principle and to make a commotion, not fearing even disestablishment if it came to that (Keble would have welcomed it). On the other hand was the group that Froude called the Z's, conservative High Churchmen like William Palmer and Hugh James Rose who valued Establishment and disliked enthusiasm, even in its support.[8] This group was responsible for the moderate tone of the declaration delivered to the archbishop, and was dubious at first about the *Tracts*.

Soon there followed what the conservatives saw as a series of disastrous blunders, feeding the suspicions of the movement's Evangelical opponents, alienating many potential supporters, and contributing to a growing impression in many quarters that the Tractarians were dishonest, disloyal, and too clever by half. In 1836 the Tractarians opposed the Prime Minister's appointment of Dr. Hampden, a divine of doubtful orthodoxy, as Regius Professor of Divinity. The protest was as much against the way in which such appointments were made as against Hampden's teaching, and the Tractarians had a legitimate point, but they succeeded only in denying the new professor the right to help select university preachers and laid the groundwork for future troubles by persuading many in Oxford, and elsewhere, that they were spiteful bigots.

In the Hampden controversy, the Tractarians had acted in concert with Evangelicals, but that uneasy alliance was soon shattered irreparably. When their beloved friend Hurrell Froude died of tuberculosis in 1836, Newman and Keble undertook to edit his letters and journals, and published them as a memorial in 1838. Opinions differ about whether this was an act of staggering innocence or a conscious attempt to polarize opinion, but even a sympathetic historian has observed that "to describe [the book's] publication as indiscreet is far too weak an expression."[9] Most readers would have found the harrowing self-discipline, spiritual minutiae, and anguished scruples revealed in the diaries unsettling enough, but what really confirmed Low Churchmen's worst suspicions were Froude's exuberant attacks on the English Reformers. One example sums it up: "Really, I hate the Reformation and the Reformers more and more."[10]

Thomas Arnold remarked of Froude's *Remains* that its "predominant character" was its "extraordinary impudence."[11] An indirect result of its publication was the erection of the Martyrs' Memorial in Oxford, to honor the Reformers, and a direct result was greatly heightened suspicion of a movement led by men who could publish such a work without dissociating themselves from it.

The next year saw another cause for suspicion. Isaac Williams, Keble's student and, for a time, Newman's curate, published Tract 80, "On Reserve in Communicating Religious Knowledge." Williams's argument for teaching religious truths only after adequate preparation was unremarkable, if not unexceptionable; taken out of context, however, he could be seen as arguing for practices that some Protestants liked to call Jesuitical. To the charge of disloyalty was added that of dishonesty, and Williams paid for his own lack of "reserve"; denounced by several bishops (including the bishop of Gloucester, who had apparently read only his title), he was denied the Professorship of Poetry at Oxford in 1842.

After 1838 the uneasiness that conservatives in the movement felt toward those who shared Froude's opinions or his temperament was exacerbated by the presence and activities of a number of unabashed Romanizers, such men as W. G. Ward, Frederick Oakeley, and F. W. Faber (all of them later to become Roman Catholics). In 1841, Newman's probably hopeless attempt to reconcile this group to the Church of England led to the disaster of Tract 90, in which he attempted to show that the Church's Thirty-Nine Articles were not incompatible with the formulations of the Council of Trent. This was the last straw for many churchmen, while for Hampden's friends and others it was the ammunition they had been waiting for. Four Oxford tutors, including the future Archbishop Tait, protested; the powerful Heads of Houses at the university, almost without exception, condemned the tract; one bishop allowed that he would not want to trust its author with his purse; and Newman, apparently bewildered by the firestorm he had provoked, agreed to put a stop to the *Tracts*, at the bishop of Oxford's request.

The movement's enemies were now in the ascendant. In 1843, without a hearing, an explanation, or the opportunity for a defense, Pusey was condemned for one of his sermons by an ad hoc committee of his enemies appointed by the vice-chancellor of the university, and he was suspended from preaching for two years. Pusey by all accounts accepted this punishment with humility and an absence of bitterness, but the message was not lost on his fellow Tractarians.

The year before, Newman had withdrawn from his rooms in college and retired to Littlemore, a village in the parish of his church of St. Mary's. Disturbed and unsettled by the response to Tract 90, as well as by his study of the Arian heresy (wherein he detected analogies to the Church of England) and by plans afoot for cooperation between Anglicans and Protestants (Lutherans) in the Holy Land, he converted some sheds into the semblance of a monastic establishment where, with some friends, he kept a schedule of worship and study.

In February of 1843 Newman preached his last sermon before the university. In September, after Pusey's condemnation in June, he resigned the living of St. Mary's. On September 25 he preached his last sermon as an Anglican, at Littlemore. The subject, "The Parting of Friends," was occasioned by the secession to the Roman communion of one of the young men of Littlemore, but its words left no room for doubt about what was to follow.

One blow remained. In the summer of 1844 W. G. Ward published *The Ideal of a Christian Church*, in which he made it plain that in his view only the Roman Catholic Church met that ideal, yet that he gloried in the "most joyful, most wonderful, most unexpected sight" that he and other English churchmen could believe everything that Roman Catholics believed, without being censured for it.[12] This provocation, surely intended, led the Heads of Houses to summon a meeting of Convocation. In February 1845 Oxford graduates gathered from all over England in the Sheldonian Theatre, solemnly condemned Ward's book (by a two to one vote), stripped him of his Oxford degrees (by a closer vote), and were prevented from condemning Tract 90 and, by implication, its author only by the proctors' exercise of their statutory veto. The drama of the occasion was somewhat undermined by the undergraduates who threw snowballs at the vice-chancellor as he entered the theater, and by the fact that Ward's witty defense of himself evoked what one observer called "one of the historical laughs of the world."[13]

But the condemnation of Ward and the knowledge that only a procedural stratagem had saved Newman from a like condemnation was no laughing matter at Littlemore. Newman was clinging to Anglicanism by a thread, and it was now apparent to him not only that his hopes for the Church of England were in vain but that there was no place for him in it. The steady flow of secessions continued, but still Newman hesitated. His friends watched breathlessly as the summer passed. On October 3, Newman resigned his fellowship at Oriel. Five days later a Roman Catholic priest, Father Dominic, came to Littlemore to receive Newman into the Church of Rome.

And there the story often ends. It is a great tale, when told well: early, heady success and excitement; internal division and growing opposition; the first reversals, then disaster piled on disaster; Newman's retreat to Little-more, the hushed anticipation of his conversion, his seclusion (reminiscent of Gethsemane); the inevitable calling in of the Passionist father to receive the great man's submission. At that point the Oxford Movement, properly speaking, was over. Disgraced in Oxford, its enemies' suspicions wholly con-firmed, abandoned by its greatest spokesman and by the many lesser figures who preceded and followed him—the curtain should fall, or we risk bathos.

The "Subtractarians"

Respect for the drama is surely one reason for the general neglect of the Anglo-Catholic revival's later history. But there is another. As one historian has written, rightly, "This second phase of the Oxford Movement compares, on the whole, unfavourably, at least in intellectual and spiritual interest, with its predecessor."[14] The post-Tractarians or (as they have been called fondly, but with full awareness of the implications) "subtractarians" were many things: pastors, organization-builders, hymn-writers, ecclesiologists, contro-versialists, and vestry-room lawyers.[15] But until the emergence of "Catholic modernism" at the end of the century, few who propelled the movement after 1845 were thinkers whose thought still commands attention.[16]

In 1874, one partisan, responding to the charge that "no men of genius or mark" were connected with the movement, simply granted the point and observed that Jesus' early disciples were an undistinguished lot as well; besides, he said, this lack was "one of many indications that the work is *not* from man."[17] If so, the Lord's ways were as mysterious as usual, because some of the movement's most conspicuous adherents lacked not just genius but common sense, and a few were clearly unhinged. At times one gets the sense that twentieth-century Anglo-Catholics who know of these figures at all find them a little embarrassing, a clutch of monomaniacal Uncle Tobies lurking in the family tree.

It is easy to forget that the Oxford Movement had its silly side, too—to forget, for example, J. B. Morris, who irritated Newman by arguing in a ser-mon at St. Mary's that the brute creation should fast and who, Mark Patti-son recalled, "passed his whole time up the tower of Exeter College, read-ing the Fathers and cutting jokes upon 'our step-mother, the Church of England.'"[18] But the leaders of the Oxford Movement were so patently un-silly, such imposing moral and intellectual presences, that the high jinks of lesser figures pale into insignificance, at least in retrospect.

The post-Tractarians, in contrast, could not be said to have had leaders. The only two who could have claimed that role were Pusey and Keble, and neither was willing to accept it. Not only was there no dominant figure to color the entire movement by force of personality or intellect, there was no one in a position to check the excesses of the more zealous partisans, or to expel from the movement those who eventually went too far. The result was that side by side with the movement's authentic saints walked some of the most colorful eccentrics of the age, and the story is complicated by the fact that some of the eccentrics had their saintly qualities, and some of the saints their eccentricities.[19]

Anglo-Catholics can take pride, for example, in a number of great slum priests, men of holy lives, who gave themselves in selfless service to the poor of Victorian cities.[20] But what is one to make of that other slum priest, the Reverend Dr. F. G. Lee of All Saints, Lambeth, who obtained bishop's orders from a mysterious source (allegedly on the high seas, to avoid jurisdictional difficulties), proclaimed himself pro-provincial of Canterbury, and went about secretly reordaining clergymen who had come to doubt the validity of Anglican orders?[21]

One can likewise admire many of the pioneers in the reestablishment of Anglican religious orders. Priscilla Lydia Sellon's iron will prevailed in the face of bitter prejudice against both her religion and her sex, and enabled her to found and to direct what became the Society of the Most Holy Trinity.[22] W. J. Butler was an exemplary parish priest as vicar of Wantage and combined his parochial duties with the oversight of the Community of St. Mary the Virgin, his foundation.[23] The delightful John Mason Neale annoyed his bishop and sometimes his friends by his immoderate enthusiasm for "the good old times of England," but that enthusiasm led him to establish the Society of St. Margaret, and to guide its early history, while pursuing the scholarship that made him perhaps Anglicanism's greatest hymn-writer and translator.[24] R. M. Benson's founding of the Society of St. John the Evangelist (the Cowley Fathers), the great preaching order of the Anglican Communion, is also an edifying and relatively well-known story.[25]

But these communities have survived to a respectable middle age. Less stable founders produced less stable communities, and there were many of these as well. For instance, J. L. Lyne, who preferred to be known as "Father Ignatius," set out single-handedly to revive the Benedictine Order in the Church of England, and was said by some of his admirers to have raised a young woman from the dead with a relic of the True Cross —conduct, Sir Shane Leslie remarked, thought by some to be uncalled-for in an Anglican curate.[26] Most Anglo-Catholics were so sympathetic to Lyne's aims that they kept their misgivings about this and other excesses to themselves, and the movement may have suffered in consequence.

Lyne's co-worker in the monastic revival, Father George Nugee, was less quixotic, but almost as odd. Quietly removed by Bishop Wilberforce from his family living in Hampshire on charges of "impropriety and immorality (especially but not exclusively with a person called Sister Agatha)," Nugee retired to South London and founded St. Austin's Priory, which one historian has called "a residential club for religious eccentrics."[27] No less an aesthete than Walter Pater was delighted by the gorgeous services at the prio-

ry: one of Nugee's proteges, Richard Jackson, a young clergyman and amateur painter also known as "Brother à Becket," was the original for Pater's
portrait of Marius the Epicurean.[28]

Dean Church and Canon Liddon of St. Paul's Cathedral, Benjamin
Webb of St. Andrew's, Wells Street, and scores if not hundreds of other clergymen in parishes across England maintained a sober Tractarian emphasis on
loyalty to the Church of England and decency and order in worship, but
others embraced ceremonial and decorative extravagances hard to defend as
the result of obedience to the Church's law.[29] Sometimes these excesses
seem to have been calculated to offend the movement's enemies; sometimes
they achieved the same result out of thoughtless exuberance—as in the case
of the Reverend John Purchas of Brighton, brought to trial in an ecclesiastical court on thirty-five counts of ceremonial irregularity, including hanging a stuffed dove over the altar at Whitsuntide.[30]

In Christina Rossetti the movement nurtured a remarkable poet, but the
aesthetic impulse elsewhere produced wackier results, as at the hands of the
Reverend Sabine Baring-Gould, author of "Onward, Christian Soldiers" and
collector of ghost stories, who thundered against Protestantism from his
remote vicarage and forbade his daughters to read the novels he wrote or to
mention the Reformation in his presence.[31] Even quainter was
Baring-Gould's fellow poet, Parson Hawker, vicar of Morwenstow in Cornwall for forty-one years.[32] Hawker designed his own yellow vestment (a
copy, he said, of St. Padarn's) and paced his parish in a purple cassock, a blue
jersey, high wading boots, and an assortment of headgear that included a
pink cap resembling a fez. Hawker kept a pet pig that followed him like a
dog, he believed that pixies were the souls of unbaptized children, and he
paid his parishioners ten shillings for every washed-up corpse that they
brought him, unrobbed, for proper burial.

Obviously, these flamboyant characters were hardly representative. Few
contributed to building the movement's institutional base; they were not
leaders or even reliable followers, and none was an intellectual figure of
much account. Some of their allies found them an embarrassment at the
time, and others perhaps should have. Still, they were as much of a presence
in the movement as the responsible, earnest, and quiet folk, and there is a
sense in which they should be taken as seriously. They belong in the movement's history not just for the sake of comprehensiveness, but because they
helped to shape the popular response to Anglo-Catholicism as much as the
others, and possibly more.

The Question of Continuity

Perhaps it is not surprising that it has suited some friends of
Anglo-Catholicism to emphasize the movement's early years, discreetly passing over its later, Ritualist phase. Other historians have gone further still,

arguing (like some of the movement's opponents at the time) that the later developments were a perversion of the earlier movement, or even a new and quite distinct phenomenon. Just after the turn of the century, Archbishop Davidson, testifying before the Royal Commission on Ecclesiastical Discipline, quoted liberally from Newman, Pusey, and Keble to show that they were relatively indifferent to "ritual" practices compared to those who claimed to be their successors, and Davidson was neither the first nor the last to distinguish invidiously between the intellectual and devotional contribution of the Oxford Movement, on the one hand, and the ceremonial froth it stirred up later, on the other.[33]

But even if Ritualism could be shown to be an alien or irrelevant growth, somehow grafted onto a serious movement by lesser men of a later generation, that would not be grounds for dismissing it as unworthy of serious attention. In any case, some recent historians have agreed with the Ritualists' own argument, that their program was a natural and inevitable result of Tractarian ideas planted in new and different circumstances.[34]

Certainly, as its name implies, the Oxford Movement was largely an academic affair; more than that, it was largely a clerical movement, and its concerns and its style reflected that fact. Its appeal was not wholly to the intellect—Keble's poetry, Newman's sermons, Pusey's personal example of sanctity and scholarship were persuasive in other ways—but as long as the movement was confined to Oxford common rooms and the studies of rural vicarages, its principal mode of expression was verbal (as its other label, "Tractarian," makes plain). When the movement went out from Oxford into the parishes and sought a lay following, however, it necessarily underwent some changes. In two respects, later developments in the movement were clearly in line with the wishes of the founders: both the establishment of religious orders and the revival of the practice of "auricular confession" had the explicit sanction of the movement's surviving leaders. As Archbishop Davidson's testimony shows, what sometimes unsettled, puzzled, or displeased the Tractarian elders who survived to the last third of the century was the growth and development of the Ritualists' distinctive ceremonial and decorative practices.

But even in this respect, those who have argued great discontinuity between the Oxford Movement and the Ritualists have overstated the case. Aside from the Ritualists' own denial, there are two answers to the charge that Ritualism departed from the ideals of the original Tractarians. One is to show that Newman, Pusey, and Keble themselves were sympathetic to ritual "advance," although with qualifications that the Ritualists did not share: any discontinuity, then, reflects the dropping of the qualifications, not the emphasis on ritual itself. The other response is to show that, from the first, lesser figures in the movement attached considerable importance to various controversial practices, as expressions of the doctrines they were absorbing.

Ritualism and the Leaders of the Oxford Movement

When comparing the attitudes of the Tractarians to those of the Ritualists, however, we must keep in mind that the meaning of the disputed practices changed as time passed. In the 1840s and 1850s services were disrupted in a number of places when clergymen followed the Prayer Book directions and preached in surplices rather than black gowns. Forty years later, that was the practice in nearly all except the most extreme Evangelical churches in London and was unexceptionable almost everywhere else in England. By then Protestant demonstrators were protesting, among other things, the distinctively Roman Catholic service of "Creeping to the Cross" on Good Friday. While Newman was still at Littlemore and still an Anglican, an altar cross and candles were as provocative as incense and images would be fifty years later. So in arguing, for instance, that Pusey would not have approved of incense in the 1840s (or for that matter in the 1870s), we should not lose sight of the fact that some of the things he very much wanted to introduce in the 1840s were as offensive to contemporary Low Churchmen as some of the things he later opposed as unnecessarily offensive. Pusey's views had not changed, but the times had, and his views were no longer so radical.

Of the three acknowledged leaders of the Oxford Movement the one least uneasy about the proto-Ritualists in the movement was probably Newman, less because he shared their enthusiasms than because he was not temperamentally opposed to controversy and did not oppose their activities on grounds of prudence. True, he referred to them as the "gilt-gingerbread school," and he was quite conservative in his own practice as long as he remained an Anglican. Pusey said, for example, that Newman always consecrated at the north end of the altar (sideways to the congregation), as the Prayer Book directed, unlike most Anglo-Catholics, who took the so-called eastward position (facing the altar, back to the congregation), which they held to be that of a sacrificing priest.[35] Still, Newman placed candles on the altar and mixed water and wine in the chalice at St. Mary's, both innovations that would later become the grounds for controversy elsewhere. And he did not object when his curate at Littlemore introduced a stone cross behind the altar, a crimson Bible and gilded wooden candlesticks on it, a credence table, litany desk, and wooden alms dish—decorations that produced an "indescribable horror" in Peter Maurice, chaplain of New College and author of *Popery in Oxford*. When Newman heard rumors that candles burned night and day at Littlemore and that his surplice was adorned with "a rich illuminated cross," he seems to have been more amused than alarmed.

No, Newman was not hostile to ceremonial and decorative innovation; he seems simply not to have been very interested in the subject. As Thomas Mozley observed, "Newman never went into architecture," and he criticized those like the ecclesiologists of the Cambridge Camden Society, who, he feared, were "making a fair outside, while within are dead men's bones." He added that "we shall do nothing until we have a severer religion."[36] His real interests lay elsewhere: in the grand project of editing the *Lives of the Saints*, for instance.

But if Newman was not a major innovator in the ornamentation of churches and ministers, some of the early distinguishing marks of the Tractarians may owe themselves to his example. At St. Mary's in 1834 he began daily morning prayer (as directed by a widely ignored Prayer Book rubric), and he instituted an early communion service on Sundays four years later. Until churchmen of other persuasions followed suit in later decades, such "multiplication of services" was almost a party badge for Anglo-Catholics. Newman read the daily office kneeling on the altar step, facing east, a practice that tended to accompany the restoration of the daily services, according to S. L. Ollard. (In 1835, Hurrell Froude wrote that it "seems to be striking all apostolicals [his preferred name for the less conservative adherents of the movement] at once," but it does not seem to have persisted.) Newman also used a small hand-held prayer book rather than the volume on the reading desk, a custom taken up by his young admirers, although the only reason for Newman's practice was that he was nearsighted. When Newman retired to Littlemore, he and the young men who joined him there were not surrounded by material beauty, but they did keep a schedule of prayer (basically the monastic hours) that would have been called Ritualistic a few years later. By that time, however, Newman had joined a communion where Ritualism was not at all controversial.

Although some of the Oxford Movement firebrands grumbled about Newman's timidity, there is little in his behavior or his writings to suggest that he was afraid of controversy, and certainly he was less cautious than other leaders of the movement.[37] He felt that the controversy stirred up by the *Tracts* could only be a good thing, since it at least drew attention to them. He called them "a dose of volatile salts, pungent but restorative." Of one of his poems he said, "Moderate and well-judging men will be shocked by it." At the Oxford Movement's high point he must have shared the opinions of his friend Froude: "Church principles, forced on people's notice, must work for good."[38] The young Newman would not have abandoned the Ritualists in their troubles on grounds of prudence alone.

It is idle to speculate about the possible development of Newman's views had he remained an Anglican, but he would probably have been sympathetic to the Ritualist impulse. While still a Church of England clergyman he wrote to his friend Manning: "You must make the Church more suitable to the needs of the heart.... Give us more services, more vestments and decorations in worship; ... give us the signs of an apostle, the pledges that the Spouse of Christ is among us."[39] And after his conversion he offered this description of his former Church before the Oxford Movement:

a ritual dashed upon the ground, and broken piecemeal; ... vestments chucked off, lights quenched, jewels stolen, the pomp and circumstances [*sic*] of worship annihilated; a dreariness which could be felt, and which seemed the token of an incipient Socinianism, forcing itself upon the eye, the ear, the nostrils of the worshipper; a smell of dust and damp, not of incense; a sound of ministers preaching Catholic prayers, and parish clerks droning out Catholic canticles; the royal arms for the crucifix; huge ugly boxes of wood, sacred to preachers, frowning on the congregation in the place of the mysterious altar; and long cathedral aisles unused, railed off, like the tombs (as they were) of what had been and was not.[40]

Many who stayed within the Anglican communion felt the same, and believed that there was only one course of action to be taken. Grant their premise, and no logician as astute as Newman could have quarreled with their conclusion.

Rather more to the point, however, are the views of Keble and Pusey, who stayed in the Church of England and witnessed the development of Ritualism from positions (undesired, to some extent) of leadership. Archbishop Davidson summarized Keble's position:

He never himself adopted vestments or other ritual usages of the kind. He continued to deprecate the practice of non-communicating attendance [on the grounds of primitive practice], and he strongly disapproved of any insistence upon a rule of fasting reception [on the grounds that it made things difficult for the aged and infirm and those who could not come to early services]. On the other hand, he was, on large principles, in favor of all that gave increased dignity to, and implied a deeper reverence for, the Holy Communion. And in this way he was constantly quoted by the younger school, who thought that their ritual usages were implicitly sanctioned by his teaching, though not part of his own practice.[41]

This summary seems fair enough. Keble believed that the so-called Ornaments Rubric of the Prayer Book, which stipulated that "such Ornaments of the Church, and of the Ministers thereof at all times of their Ministration, shall be retained, and be in use, as ... in the Second Year of the Reign of King Edward the Sixth," sanctioned most pre-Reformation ceremonial and usages. He believed that the neglect of that rubric was "a real blemish in our ecclesiastical practice [and] a contradiction to our theory." He thought that charity and pastoral considerations dictated a temporary inconsistency: "The time and manner of regaining the old paths must, under our circumstances, be a question of equity and charity, not of strict law alone." But, he added, "I, for one, rejoice whenever and wherever I see that kind of revival successfully and tranquilly accomplished."[42]

It would be wrong to say that Keble saw the usages for which the Ritualists were to fight as unimportant, but he did not see them as important enough to fight for, or about. It seems unlikely that he ever accepted the

Ritualists' argument that their ceremonial served an evangelistic function, first to draw people to church, then to instruct them in doctrine. It may be that his position of vicar of a village church, with an established tradition of churchgoing, colored his views; if he had been serving an East End slum church with no established congregation to upset, his opinions and practice might have been different. As it was, Keble's role in the ritual disputes that he lived to see was that of the pastor, urging charity, compromise, moderation, seeing the other side's point of view. He apparently did not always accept the Ritualists' claim that attacks on ritual were simply disguised attacks on doctrine —and, indeed, in a parish like his they almost certainly would not have been. But when he was convinced that doctrine was at stake, he was as forthright a partisan as anyone could ask.

The only Tractarian leader who stayed an Anglican and lived long enough to witness Ritualism full-blown was E. B. Pusey, and by the 1870s he was thoroughly put out with some of those who were seen as his successors, although he, too, stood by them loyally when persuaded that doctrinal questions were at issue.[43] "I have a thorough mistrust of the Ultra Ritualist body," he wrote in 1873. "[I] fear that the Ritualists and the old Tractarians differ both in principle and in object." The next year, he and his friend Liddon wrote the Ritualistic vicar of St. Alban's, Holborn, to ask whether some of "the exaggerated ceremonial and ill-considered language, which are sometimes to be found among (so-called) 'Ritualists'" could not be tempered, for political purposes. And in 1875 Pusey wrote: "There has been, and is, a good deal of infallibilism outside the Vatican decree. The whole extreme Ritualist party is practically infallibilist. 'We will not retreat because we are certainly right.' And so they must lay the whole blame on their opponents' hostility, as they think, to truth. Yet very much of their practice has no relation to the truth, or only so far as it makes the Eucharistic Service gorgeous."

These and many other quotations reveal that Pusey was out of sympathy with those who claimed to be his followers in the 1870s. And this was not a new development. In 1860, when rioters at St. George's-in-the-East were protesting the vicar's introduction of "Puseyite" practices, Pusey wrote Bishop Tait of London: "In regard to my 'friends,' perhaps I regret the acts to which your Lordship alludes, as deeply as you do. I am in this strange position, that my name is made a by-word for that with which I never had any sympathy, that which the writers of the tracts, with whom in early days I was associated, always deprecated; any innovations in the way of conducting the service, anything of ritualism, or especially any revival of disused vestments." If Pusey's report of what he and the writers of the *Tracts* "always deprecated" is correct, that would seem to settle the matter.

But was that his earlier view? Archbishop Davidson argued that it was and based his argument primarily on an exchange of correspondence between Pusey and the Reverend J. F. Russell in 1839, a correspondence that requires closer examination, particularly in the light of Pusey's own experience a short time after with the church he endowed in Leeds, St. Saviour's.

In his letters to Russell, Pusey certainly did attempt to discourage Russell and his friends from some practices they had adopted and were contemplating: "You will not mind my freely saying to you that I cannot hear without much anxiety of some practices of some friends of yours, e.g., the hanging a room with black velvet during Lent." Pusey gave several reasons for restraint, including prudence. Concerning a proposal that, on a given day, all Tractarian clergymen should reassume the eucharistic vestments, he wrote: "At present we have the surplice for a token of purity, and the scarf as an emblem of Christ's yoke. But beyond this I should deprecate anything which could serve as the badge of a party; at present, much as the opposed party speaks of it, they can find nothing; but the agreement to adopt a dress which would be peculiar would furnish them with what they want." Moreover, he argued, the change would be undesirable in itself: "Hardly anything, perhaps, has given so much handle as this subject of dresses; it has deterred many, made many think the questions at hand to be about outward things only, given occasion to scoffing, and disquieted many sober people."

A case could be made that Pusey simply did not regard such matters as important; certainly time and again he displayed an ignorance that, in anyone else, would have produced the suspicion that he was joking. "Please do tell me what a cope is," he is reported to have said one day to J. R. Bloxam.[44] In 1851 he wrote to a clergyman who was having trouble for (among other things) taking the eastward position for the Prayer of Consecration, "I was not ritualist enough to know till the other day that the act of turning had any special meaning in the consecration" and almost twenty-five years later he wrote of Charles Lowder's insistence on censing persons and things that "to the mass of the English people (and among them to me) it is an un-understood rite. Three different explanations of it have been given me by ritualists. As it does not concern me, I have not looked into books."

But in his letters, and especially in his practice, Pusey made a distinction among the disputed ornaments and usages that suggests that his attitude was more complicated than simple disapproval of disturbing innovations. He was especially opposed to those, like vestments, that had any tendency to exalt the person of the minister. He suspected the Ritualists of self-will, a characteristic that he greatly distrusted in others as in himself. This man who was later to set himself a course of penitential discipline harrowing even to contemplate, who wore a hair shirt until his death, vowed never to smile except at children, regarded himself as "scarred all over and seamed with sin, so that I am a monster to myself," and longed for "the discipline" (flagellation) that his poor health forbade—this man had little patience with those who, he thought, sought "occasion for distinction by the very means of Church practices" or made "an idol of self, while seeming to honour God and the Church."[45] To Russell he wrote that he had heard men argue that others should take up new practices at once, "for a few years hence they would be so common that there would be no distinction in them, or something to this effect." Such seeking after glory was wrong: "It is tricking up an idol, and that idol, self: not serving God. I must pain you by so writing, and I am sorry to do so; but I really feel I cannot write strongly enough, if by any means that veil could be torn off your friends' eyes and they taught to act ... reverently and soberly, not amuse themselves (for it is nothing better) with holy things."

That Pusey's letters to Russell were written shortly after the death of his beloved wife lends a poignant ambiguity to his words, "the garment of mourning was fitter for us than one of gladness." One might speculate that his wife's death affected Pusey's opinions on this subject. Certainly he had been a good deal more tolerant the year before. When Pusey's assistant lecturer in Hebrew began to wear an embroidered stole in his duties at St. Thomas's, Oxford, and the bishop wrote Pusey for an explanation, he replied that the stole was "very narrow" and the embroidered crosses "very unpretending," and that he had warned the young man "not to let his attention be distracted by these things from others of more moment," but "it seemed a very safe way for the exuberance of youth to vent itself in."[46]

Pusey apparently viewed his wife's death as punishment for his sins and was afterwards less willing to make allowances for youthful exuberance. "It seems beginning at the wrong end for the ministers to deck their own persons," he wrote Russell. "Our own plain dresses are more in keeping with the state of the Church, which is one of humiliation. It does not seem in character to revive gorgeous or even in any degree handsome dresses in a day of reproach and rebuke and blasphemy; these are not holiday times." Pusey wore eucharistic vestments himself only much later, and then rarely, in churches where their use was customary.[47]

But when a decoration was clearly for God's glory and not the minister's, Pusey could be as enthusiastic and (surely unintentionally) as provocative as any Ritualist. His advice to Russell was to do without vestments for the time. "As far as externals will contribute to greater reverence, it were far better and far more influential to begin with that which is furthest removed from self.... It were better far to begin with painted windows, rich altar cloths or Communion plate."

St. Saviour's, Leeds

Six years later, however, Pusey's attempt to follow his own advice led to the tragicomic events surrounding the consecration of St. Saviour's, Leeds.[48] The story is worth retelling, since it illustrates that Pusey was far from indifferent to the "externals" of worship. It also shows that beginning with painted windows, altar cloths, and communion plate—although it might avoid the spiritual dangers Pusey saw—did nothing to forestall the movement's enemies. And since Pusey's concern for externals led him in this case into painful conflict with a bishop, perhaps we can understand why he did not encourage others, later.

After his wife's death, Pusey, who viewed himself as a penitent, resolved to devote his private means to the building of a church. He wrote his friend W. F. Hook, the High Church vicar of Leeds, "I know a person who wishes in such degree as he may, if he lives, to make up a broken vow." He wrote that this "friend" wished to build a church in Leeds, the only condition being that it should display the inscription, "YE WHO ENTER THIS HOLY PLACE, PRAY FOR THE SINNER WHO BUILT IT." Hook accepted the offer, and plans went forward to build the church in one of the squalid slums of Leeds, an area housing approximately eleven thousand souls, in the shadow of the Black Dog Mill. Pusey desired that the church should be beautiful and edifying, and also that it should be served by a "college" of celibate clergymen living in community nearby. Both parts of his plan would involve him in difficulties.

Throughout the early 1840s Pusey, acting as "agent" of the donor, involved himself in planning the new church and recruiting its clergy. Apparently a plan to transport a building from Portugal (where the established church had just been dissolved and lovely old buildings could be picked up at bargain prices) was considered and rejected. Instead, Pusey chose a plan submitted by a student of the noted Gothic Revival architect (and convert to Roman Catholicism) A. W. N. Pugin, a plan true to Pugin's teachings about the importance of medieval principles in church architecture. Pusey's own wish, embodied in the design of the church and its furnishings, was that everywhere the worshipper looked, he should see the cross: the church itself was to be cruciform, and every window and fitting was to be embellished with the cross. It would be named Holy Cross Church.

For help with the windows and furnishings, Pusey turned to the Cambridge Camden Society, a newly formed group of Catholic-minded amateur church archaeologists and historians who were trying to rediscover and restore pre-Reformation patterns of church design and decoration. We shall return to this society in the next chapter, but because it is sometimes credited with independently raising the aesthetic issues that characterized Ritualism, it is important to note that Pusey turned to them voluntarily for advice and that the cooperation was, for the most part, an easy one. (The Camdenians were distressed that Pusey insisted on erecting the Ten Commandments at the front of the church, but he was determined to follow current practice in that respect.[49])

Meanwhile Pusey was interviewing candidates for the clergy of the church, making what use he could of the "old boy" network of Anglo-Catholic clergy, which was only beginning to be established. Among those considered were Keble's curate at his church in Hursley and the Reverend G. R. Prynne, later to become vicar of St. Peter's, Plymouth. Prynne was thought unsuitable because he would not promise that he would not marry.

Troubles began almost immediately, first with the bishop, then with Pusey's friend Hook, the vicar of Leeds. The bishop objected to the name Holy Cross Church. The Church of England, he said, did not accept the legend of the discovery of the Holy Cross, and it could not risk implying that it did. Reluctantly, Pusey changed the name to St. Saviour's. (In 1850, incidentally, Pusey laid the cornerstone for St. Saviour's Home, Osnaburgh Street, London, on Holy Cross Day, with the understanding that the words St. Saviour's were "code" for Holy Cross.[50]) The college arrangement of curates and vicar was too monastic, the bishop said (although, as Sabine Baring-Gould pointed out later, every college at Cambridge and Oxford was operated on similar lines); the plans for the vicarage made no provisions for housing a wife and children; Pusey's plan to allow the college to elect a successor on the death of the vicar was unacceptable; the institution must be called a community rather than a college (an obscure objection); the covered walk connecting the vicarage to the church was too much like a cloister and could not be permitted. Pusey yielded on all of these points. Anticipating trouble because of a recent dispute in Cambridge, Pusey took legal opinion on whether he could install a stone altar, or at any rate an altar with a stone slab set into it: he was told that the altar must be wooden and movable.

A west window had been designed for the church, incorporating an illustration of the Holy Face of Jesus, copied from the Cirencester parish church. The bishop rejected the plan as "Romish." A new plan was produced, approved, and executed, but shortly before the scheduled consecration of the church someone complained to the bishop that it showed a crowned Virgin and that angels were shown catching the blood of Christ in chalices. The bishop of Ripon was unimpressed by the argument that the seals of his brother bishops of Lincoln and Salisbury incorporated crowned Virgins, and the offending panels had to be replaced with plain glass for the consecration service. The altar linen also proved to be unacceptable, since it covered only the mensa rather than the entire table.

But the saddest conflict was over a set of communion plate. In 1844 Pusey's daughter Lucy, dying of tuberculosis at the age of fifteen, had expressed a wish that her jewelry and her inheritance should go to make up a set of plate, and the Camden Society's design for a chalice pleased her very much. After her death, her brother, sister, and friends saw to the completion of the service as a memorial. The six pieces incorporated over two hundred precious stones, including diamonds, rubies, pearls, and emeralds. Pusey himself had the plate inscribed, in Latin, "Have Mercy, Lord, on Lucy Maria." As the clergy were lining up for the procession into the church at its consecration service, Bishop Longley refused to go ahead if the plate were used: the inscription was a prayer for the dead (implying belief in Purgatory). One who was present when the gift was refused never forgot the sadness in Pusey's face.

But one more matter remained to be resolved. The bishop noticed the inscription over the west door, asking prayers for the donor of the building. He demanded that it come down, but relented when he was assured that the donor was still living and that he would be informed if the donor died while he was bishop. At last the troubled church, Pusey's self-denying and anonymous gift, was consecrated.

Its history, off to such a difficult start, was not to be easy. In keeping with Pusey's views, the ornaments of the clergy were relatively sedate; black scarves were replaced by white stoles at Christmas in 1849, but it was not until 1859 at the earliest that eucharistic vestments were introduced and the altar adorned with a cross and lighted candles. On the other hand, daily celebration of Holy Communion was begun during the 1849 cholera epidemic and continued more or less regularly after that. (At the same time, and apparently with the bishop's permission, the Catholic practice of reserving the Sacrament was introduced, ostensibly so it could be administered to the sick.) A community of laymen grew up around the clergy of St. Saviour's, and a new building was added to house the overflow from the clergy house. Although the clergy displayed sartorial restraint within the church, about 1850 they and these laymen began to wear cassocks and birettas as their ordinary dress—a development with which Pusey could hardly have been pleased.

These and other practices led the church's many critics to keep up a running chorus of complaints to the bishop. The atmosphere of distrust made any innovation suspect. Dr. Hook, for example, had no objection to splendid worship—he himself introduced choral services at the Leeds parish church. But he did take a less sanguine view than his friend Pusey of what he saw as "Romanism" at St. Saviour's, and he came to believe that the "hornet's nest" (as he called it) was more trouble than it was worth. In later years he joined those who complained to the bishop about the clergy's taking the eastward position, keeping the monastic schedule of prayer, carrying lighted candles in procession at baptism, and placing a cross over the chancel screen.

One practice was especially objectionable in itself, and it also somehow stood for all of the other objectionable developments. As Keble reported to Pusey, after an interview with Hook in 1848: "He did not specify any evil practice, so that, as far as it can be seen, his alarm resolves itself into an attack on the principle of private confession and absolution. I was, as you may suppose, delighted with St. Saviour's, and with the kind and earnest people there: surely they and their work will be blest." But Hook's suspicions were not entirely unfounded. Nine of the first fifteen clergymen associated with St. Saviour's became Roman Catholics, although it is impossible to say how much the attitude of the Diocese of Ripon had to do with this statistic.[51]

The point of all these details is simply that Pusey's distinction between ornaments of the minister and ornaments of the church, important to him though it may have been, was not one that the movement's opponents made. Those who were simply conservative and opposed to unsettling innovations opposed the two sorts indiscriminately. Those who disliked "Puseyism," for whatever reason, saw both sorts of change (rightly) as marks of that faction. And those whose real opposition was to the doctrines and the extraliturgical practices of the clergy of St. Saviour's viewed any innovation of theirs with deep suspicion.

Moreover, the distinction did not convince many of the movement's adherents, especially those who did not share Pusey's deep conviction of personal unworthiness. "What sense is there —" John Mason Neale wrote a few years later, "what sense can there be—in rejoicing that His inanimate creature, the altar, should be vested in the richest apparel; if you would forbid His not only animate, but especially consecrated, creature, the Priest, to wear any but the simplest vestments?"[52] At the very least, the same ecclesiological considerations that made it appropriate or even mandatory to ornament churches in pre-Reformation splendor applied to the dress of ministers. Pusey had conceded the propriety of a jewelled chalice: why should the priest who elevated that chalice be restricted to the mundane black and white of surplice and scarf?

Of the three early leaders of the movement, then, none could be said to have been a proto-Ritualist. Newman, perhaps the likeliest candidate by temperament, was more concerned with other things, and in any case removed himself from the controversy in 1845. Keble sympathized with the Ritualists, but also with laymen who were bewildered or annoyed by changes in familiar and beloved patterns of worship: he lacked the Ritualists' burning conviction that their changes were important, although he welcomed them when they were brought about happily. Pusey, at least after the death of his wife, was suspicious of the Ritualists' motives, but he too welcomed the changes they introduced when convinced of the humility of the innovators. None of the three could have objected in principle to the Ritualists' arguments for their changes, although each might have argued countervailing considerations in any particular case. And certainly none could have objected to the doctrines that motivated the Ritualists—for where, after all, had those doctrines been learned?

The "Gilt-Gingerbread School"

When the Ritualists claimed, as they did, that their ceremonial and decorative practices were somehow the natural expression of Catholic doctrine, they could certainly have made at least an empirical case for that argument. From a very early stage of the Oxford Movement, Tractarian doctrine often did lead to the revival of pre-Reformation usages or the adoption of contemporary Roman Catholic practice. We saw that Pusey as early as the 1830s was warning his followers about their innovations, and old-fashioned High Churchmen who had originally supported the movement found a good deal to be alarmed about as it progressed. Much of what concerned them was more serious than ceremonial or decorative exuberance, but they did object from time to time to such things as a curate in "a short surplice edged with lace and a stole with crosses, looking as like a Roman priest as possible" (the words are Hook's, in a letter to Pusey).[53] When Pusey's assistant lecturer took to wearing a "very narrow" stole (and Pusey, as we saw, defended him to the bishop of Oxford), a canon of Durham warned the clergy under his supervision against such practices, and the bishop of Oxford ventured in his charge of 1838, "I do not think it likely we shall hear of a repetition of this or of similar indiscretions." But, as S. L. Ollard pointed out, there was already a shop in Leicester where stoles could be purchased.[54]

Oddly enough, the groundwork for these developments and for the later revival of eucharistic vestments had been laid by one of the most conservative adherents of the Oxford Movement. The year before Keble's Assize sermon, William Palmer of Worcester College (who was later to urge that the *Tracts* should be approved by a committee and who grew very uneasy about the Romanizing tendencies of the movement) published *Origines Liturgicae*. In that work he described and illustrated the alb, chasuble, and stole, and asserted that the Ornaments Rubric ordered their use.

Palmer seems to have intended his book to be a work of liturgical archaeology, certainly not a guide for immediate application, but the book was undoubtedly read and assimilated by J. R. Bloxam, Fellow of Magdalen and Newman's curate at Littlemore from 1837 to 1840.[55] Bloxam was responsible for the decorations at Littlemore that horrified the chaplain of New College, and he was described some years later as "the father or grandfather of all ritualistics." In the late 1830s he wore a black silk stole over his surplice at Littlemore and in chapel at Magdalen, and another Fellow of Magdalen also wore a stole, crossed over his shoulder because he was only a deacon. The *Quarterly Review* and the *British Magazine* saw fit to comment.

Magdalen became something of a center for these activities as other Fellows followed Bloxam's lead. One of them, who doubled as rector of a parish in Lincolnshire, had by 1842 converted a tomb to make a stone altar and placed a cross and candles upon it. He had also begun to wear a maniple when celebrating Holy Communion and had painted the ceiling of the sanctuary blue, with gold stars. In 1839 another Fellow, who served a proprietary chapel, vested his choir in cassocks and surplices.[56]

This last innovator, R. W. Sibthorpe, was the first notable Tractarian convert to Roman Catholicism, "poping" (as it was later to be called) in 1841. He seems to have been unusually susceptible to conversion: he soon returned to the Church of England, went back to Roman Catholicism some years later, and was buried as an Anglican in 1879.[57] (Sibthorpe once compared the Church of England to "a stiff, cross, unattractive old maid by the side of a most fascinating adulteress."[58])

The tendency to ceremonial extremism seems to have been most marked among those given to doctrinal extremism—that is, to Romanizers like Sibthorpe. For some of these men the appeal to contemporary Roman Catholic usage was explicit, and not because it was "Catholic" (that is, medieval) but because it was Roman. W. G. Ward (or "Ideal" Ward, as he was called after the controversy over his *Ideal of a Christian Church*) was another one of these; yet another was F. W. Faber.

Faber wrote the life of St. Wilfrid in Newman's series of *Lives of the English Saints,* and his account of the seventh-century bishop of York who brought the Celtic Church of England into conformity with Roman practice was filled with little lessons for those disposed to seek them.[59] In Lindisfarne, "in the very stronghold of Scottish usages," the young Wilfrid grew uneasy. "Whether he had fallen upon some old books, or from whatever cause, he began to suspect that there was a more perfect way of serving God; that there were ancient traditions of Catholic customs which it was most dangerous to slight, and yet which were utterly neglected." Eventually, Wilfrid understood that "the one thing to do was to go to Rome, and learn under the shadow of St. Peter's chair the more perfect way." Faber observed that "to look Romeward is a Catholic instinct, seemingly implanted in us for the safety of the faith." For any readers who missed the point, Faber added that Wilfrid went first to the archbishop of Canterbury, "St. Honorious, a man who is described as particularly skilled in ecclesiastical matters.... But it was short of Rome." After Wilfrid learned the more perfect way in Rome, he introduced it to the British Church.

Faber's book concluded, oddly enough, with some pages critical of the ceremonial revival then taking place—a revival that had the effect, after all, of approximating Church of England practice to that of Rome—and an appeal to the young "who require some field for their zeal" to consider "the pursuit of Holy Virginity." These passages, so foreign to the burden of the preceding two hundred pages, were quoted against the Ritualists in a pamphlet of 1882 and attributed to Newman himself, and they may well have been added by him, as editor of the *Lives,* or at his suggestion.[60]

In any case, Faber did not himself stop at Canterbury, but not surprisingly went with Wilfrid, and Newman, to Rome. So did most of the other early Romanizers, and in fact there was a more or less constant trickle of converts from that wing of the Anglo-Catholic movement where "Roman fever" was endemic. From time to time, whenever the Church of England committed itself to what Anglo-Catholics regarded as some new and egregiously "Protestant" error, the trickle became a torrent, but a steadily increasing number of Anglicans were directed by their Catholic instincts to look Romeward for their liturgical models. And the more of them who did so, the less necessary it was for anyone actually to become Roman Catholic in order to find "the more perfect way."

True, there were other, less theological tributaries to the current of the ceremonial revival. Even without the Oxford Movement and the *Tracts* there would have been elaboration of the interiors of churches and of the services conducted in them. It could not have been otherwise, given Victorian taste, which would also have guaranteed a backward look to "antique" models. As early as 1823, well before Newman came to understand Keble, A. P. De Lisle, later a great friend of Bloxam's but then a dreamy fourteen-year-old, persuaded the vicar of his Leicestershire parish church to wear a cope and donated a French-style altar to the church, with a black wooden altar cross (the bishop of Peterborough ordered that it be removed).[61] Pugin, although he had become a Roman Catholic in 1834, was explicating his Gothic Revival architectural principles to an audience that included some grudgingly admiring Anglicans as early as 1836, and there were many other, lesser-known enthusiasts for reviving Gothic architecture, if not Gothic religion. The Cambridge Camden Society's more than seven hundred members included two archbishops, sixteen bishops, thirty-one peers and M.P.s, and sixteen architects. As Owen Chadwick has observed, a society with that membership was not Tractarian, and it consulted happily with both High and Low Church builders and restorers until its leaders' identification with Anglo-Catholicism led to its breaking up and re-formation as the Ecclesiological Society.[62]

But from early in the course of the Oxford Movement, the impulse to restore old churches and to build new ones on old models became identified in the public mind and in fact with Tractarianism. So did the impulse to ornament the ministers of those churches in pre-Reformation style, to restore the worship of the Church to old patterns, to reintroduce old practices like sacramental confession and old institutions like religious orders, to revitalize or (in some cases) to reintroduce old beliefs and doctrines—apostolic succession of bishops, the real presence of Christ in the Eucharist, the invocation of saints, Purgatory. All of this, as both the movement's opponents and its uneasy allies feared, was latent in the movement in its earliest years.

Only a few of the movement's adherents embraced full-blown "Anglo-Romanism," but those who did not found it extraordinarily difficult to criticize those who did, on any grounds other than those of prudence. When, years later, Pusey criticized some of the Ritualists for going too far down this path, Archdeacon Denison (no Ritualist himself, but a sympathizer) is said to have remarked: "If Pusey did not foresee how the fire would burn, he should not have lighted it."[63] Certainly the evidence was all around him from the first days of the movement.

II

Into the World

Well before the controversy at St. Saviour's—indeed, before Newman's secession—it had become clear that Oxford Movement theology and Cambridge Camden Society aesthetics were producing a new sort of parish clergyman. Young men who had listened to Newman's sermons in Oxford or waited for the latest number of the Tracts to reach Cambridge were being ordained and were spreading out around the country as curates and incumbents, determined to put their new ideas into practice. "For the last dozen years," wrote a journalist in the mid-forties, "a party has been growing up, waxing, spreading, the life and strength of which has been devoted to re-model the doctrine and entire theory of religion upon principles directly opposed to the articles of agreement." He estimated that there were over five hundred "Newmanite" clergy at large, and (he added ominously) "they have the care of parishes."[1]

Apparently not everyone knew how to identify the species. One tract, "Is Our Minister a Puseyite? A Dialogue for the Unlearned," offered a guide to the distinguishing characteristics.[2] Watch out, it said, for appeals to the "Fathers" ("As if men had not now the liberty nor the ability to judge for themselves as well as the fathers"). "Baptismal regeneration" and "apostolical succession" were also giveaway expressions, as were references to the Lord's table as an "altar" or to the Real Presence of Christ in the Eucharist, veneration of church buildings because they have been consecrated, or an emphasis on good works and fasting.

At this time most of the marks seem to have been doctrinal rather than ceremonial, although the tract went on to warn against the teaching "that there is much religion in bowing and kneeling, and observing the outward forms of worship" and against "pictures, and the crucifix, and candles."

Despite Evangelical journalists' and pamphleteers' warnings, the doctrines themselves did not seem to excite parishioners much one way or the other. A writer in the *Standard* lamented, "We hear from time to time that such and such parishes have Puseyite clergymen. But what then? It is thought a light matter."[3] And a disturbed layman, in an open letter to the bishops, complained that "the people ... know little and think little of Tractarianism. Few perceive the real bearing of the question." But, he added, the matter is "indeed of great importance, and to a truly Christian population would appear so; and it is high time to awaken from this lethargy."[4]

What did disturb people were the changes their clergymen started to make in the fittings of churches and the forms of worship. We have already seen that the "gilt-gingerbread school" in Oxford could annoy people with seemingly minor innovations; when these and other changes were introduced elsewhere they encountered even greater resistance. The Tractarian program came in several parts, although they were usually introduced gradually and few parishes encountered them all at once.[5]

The Tractarian Program

In the first place, there was a general impulse to clean up and brighten up neglected churches, to restore the fabric of the buildings and their furnishings, usually to a "Gothic" model. This might involve the introduction of new-old furniture: candlesticks and litany-desks (or "faldstools") were popular, as were credence tables like the one that occasioned comment at Littlemore. This impulse seized a great many clergymen and laypeople whose Puseyism was not otherwise remarkable, and it was shaped and nurtured, when it was not inspired, by the Cambridge Camden Society.

The Camden Society put forward "three leading principles" to guide church-restorers. The first "great canon" has a strangely modernist ring: "LET EVERY MATERIAL EMPLOYED BE REAL." No brick pretending to be stone; no cement or "other sham material." The second principle, "THE ABSOLUTE NECESSITY OF A DISTINCT AND SPACIOUS CHANCEL," and the third, "THE ABSOLUTE INADMISSIBILITY OF PUES and GALLERIES in ANY SHAPE WHATEVER," caused more trouble, as we shall see.[6]

From ornamenting the church, it was but a step (whatever Pusey might think) to ornamenting the ministers and the choir, and from that to ornamenting the service. "Cathedral" practices, about the only remaining Anglican examples of ornate worship, were introduced in parish churches. Chanted psalms and monotoned (or "intoned") prayers began to be heard in unlikely places. Choirs were surpliced and moved from the back of the church to the chancel. Ministers began to wear stoles over their surplices to distinguish themselves from the choir, and these stoles might be discreetly embroidered. The necessary process of moving the choir from vestry to chancel became the occasion for a procession. Various outward marks of reverence were revived: bowing to the altar (as it was indeed beginning to be called again) or at the name of Jesus or the Gloria Patri, turning east for the Creed, and the like.

Coupled with these developments was a new insistence on strict construction of the rubrics of the *Book of Common Prayer* and the canon law of the Church. In vain did one clergyman write that many of the rubrics should be treated as dead letters and that "the Rubric must give way, like the Statute-book, if it wishes to accommodate itself to the immense and nearly total changes of Society." In vain did he argue that some of the rubrics simply could not be enforced: "What clergyman, in the present time, for example, would venture, as the Rubric evidently intends by the words, breaking bread before the people, to substitute wafers for bread in the Communion, or to call the Lord's Supper the Mass; ... or to preach on the Seven Sacraments, or to place the table in the body of the church, or to read the Prayers in the chancel, all of which would be ... generally offensive." His crowning example of absurdity was the requirement that the curate inform the people on Sunday what holy days or fasts fall in the next week. "We may anticipate the effect on a congregation of the following notice—'Tomorrow being the Vigil of the Annunciation of the Blessed Virgin, is to be observed as a fast, and a day of abstinence.'"[7] But as he wrote in 1845 events were already overtaking him.

In 1843, the *Christian Remembrancer*, a Tractarian organ, carried a long article on "The Moral Effect of Irregularities in the Ritual of the Church," reminding its clerical readers of their solemn vows at ordination and urging complete conformity to the rubrics, enforced if need be. The writer listed a number of neglected rubrics, the non-neglect of which was becoming part of the program and a mark of Puseyite clergymen. The article scolded those who neglected the daily offices, allowed private baptism or sponsors who were not communicants, celebrated communion infrequently, did not observe "Holy-days," did not catechize children publicly, and the like. It called in particular for the restoration of a weekly "offertory," and it pointed out that the practice of changing from surplice to gown for preaching could be costly. Rather than following the sermon immediately with a collection, the minister "retires into the vestry [to remove his gown], and returns into church, as though a fresh service were about to commence, finds nine-tenths of his congregation gone ... ; and he collects five pounds, when he ought to have had fifty."[8] Although this sort of calculation might reassure clerical readers, it provided ammunition for cynics like the London lawyer who commented on the matter: "A nice picking for the parsons. I do not wonder at you high Churchmen being anxious to revive the Offertory, if they are to have the distribution of the funds."[9]

Not only did the rubrics appear to require a good many changes in the customary frequency and ordering of public worship, their newly strict construction also empowered—indeed, seemed to require—clergymen to exercise a good deal of judgment that they had often abdicated in the past. They were not to administer communion to an "open and notorious evil liver," for instance, or to bury the "unbaptized, or excommunicate." They were given considerable room for interpretation in such matters as the churching of women, the times and places of baptism, and the like. A conscientious clergyman could easily feel himself obliged to change the way a great many things were done; a pharisaical or power-hungry one could find easy justification for imposing his will on a reluctant congregation. In practice, the Tractarian emphasis on the authority of the Church was often experienced by laypeople as an increase in the power of the vicar.

For whatever reason, young clergymen of Tractarian leanings took the matter of obedience to the rubrics very seriously—so seriously that one of their many nicknames at this time was "ultrarubrician." Sometimes their scrupulous interpretation of their ordination vows led them to what seemed strange conclusions. In 1847, for instance, the incumbent of St. James's, Enfield Highway, preached to an apparently skeptical congregation on the topic "Obedience to the Church in Things Ritual." His vows, he said, "compelled [him] to make certain alterations in the conduct of the sacred worship of this sanctuary." "Strict obedience to the Prayer-book" was obviously required, he observed, and not even a bishop had authority to dispense a clergyman from that obligation—authority, that is, to order him not to make the changes.[10]

Conflict in the Parishes

It was in urban churches, especially those like St. Saviour's, Leeds, and St. Barnabas, Pimlico, in rough neighborhoods, that resentment against the Tractarians sometimes led to mob violence, as we shall see. But feelings were at least as intense and controversy could be just as bitter in smaller towns and villages, where the only alternative to the parish church might be the Dissenting chapel. Of course controversy was not the rule. Many parishes experienced no discord at all, because they were served by clergymen with no desire to remake the church. In others, tact and consideration—or timidity—on the part of an innovating clergyman were met with goodwill or indifference on the people's part.

In general, we hear about those clergymen who offended enough people to provoke petitions, if not riots, and it is fortunate for the historical record that someone thought to compile a chronicle of churches that did not explode: *The Oxford Church Movement: Sketches and Recollections* is a soothing (not to say soporific) account of "the gradual trickling of the stream through the quiet drowsy villages, washing away the dust of a century and a half." Although there is, as its author acknowledged, a "great deal of sameness in the narrative" of daily prayers established here, weekly communion restored there, a new altar cloth or reredos elsewhere, this collection of dog-bites-man stories reminds us that such was the rule, and it would be wrong to forget it.[11]

But conflict was frequent enough, and just as there was an ideal type of the Tractarian parish clergyman, so was there a typical course of parochial conflict, common enough to make its way into the fiction of the forties and fifties. As long as the Oxford Movement remained in Oxford it was almost completely ignored by novelists, testimony to its popular unimportance; when it began to trouble parishes, however, it proved so rich a source of story lines that one scholar has exhumed 128 Tractarian novels.[12] Most of these fictional treatments, whether sympathetic or opposed to Tractarianism, are dreary and didactic stuff, but some have their moments—as when the hero of *The Parish Rescued* chops down the Tractarian vicar's Maypole.[13]

A more intentionally entertaining treatment of the subject can be found in *A Paper Lantern for Puseyites*, a lengthy verse published in 1843, in which the young Reverend Hilary Oriel gushes about his plans to "stir up Squire Bradshaw, and all these dull people, / To restore the old church, and to rebuild the steeple." He vows

> To come once every day to the church, at the least;
> To keep strictly each fast-day, each vigil and feast;
> To refurnish the fald-stool, if not the sedilia,
> And with all the old rites to become quite familiar.

He forms a boys' choir to chant the services; gets a new altar, books, cushions, and altar-cloths; and has a new surplice made:

> This at least I will have. I may shortly, I hope,
> Bear a cross on my scarf, and most surely a cope.

He sets out to repair the images of saints that adorn the old screen:

> There is one wants a head and another a nose,
> St. Chad has no fingers, St. Crispin no toes.

When he tries to remove Squire Bradshaw's old enclosed family pew, however, the otherwise tolerant and humorous old man refuses to go along with him and accuses him of "New-mania." Oriel calms himself by reflecting on the apostolic succession and thinking dark thoughts about the squire's regicide ancestors. The story ends when Oriel falls in love with the squire's daughter, Miss Rachel, and they marry. He takes the Bradshaw name and arms, gives up his Newmaniac foolishness, and all live happily ever after.[14]

Although conflicts in real life seem seldom to have ended so agreeably, they often started in the same way. New clergymen, especially young ones enthusiastic to make great changes, had a way of irritating members of their congregations, who thereafter viewed every change with suspicion. When the young Reverend Frederick Oakeley went down from Oxford to London's Margaret Street Chapel in 1839 with the explicit intention of "trying the effect of Tractarian principles upon a practical scale," for instance, he announced that "a building with some pretensions to an ecclesiastical character [was] a sine qua non," demolished the old three-decker pulpit, stated his intention to remove the building's pews and gallery—and promptly found himself in conflict with the clerk, a veteran of fifty years' service.

After that, Oakeley was watched very closely, and correspondence flew back and forth from members of the congregation to the bishop of London, and from the bishop to Mr. Oakeley. He was accused of "importing candlelight, for instance, upon the back of a friendly fog," and told he could have candles on the "table" only if they remained unlit. He could have flowers on it, too, but only one bouquet, and white should not predominate on the feast of a virgin nor red on that of a martyr. He could have a weekly "offertory," but he must use the customary dish rather than an alms-bag to collect it—and a member of his congregation complained that he gazed too intently on the dish. He could preach in his surplice in the morning, if he "balanced" it by preaching in a gown in the evening.[15]

It is hard to discern the basis for the bishop's ad hoc judgments in these matters, but it is clear that Oakeley was consciously testing the limits of his bishop's tolerance, that Oakeley's adversaries were determined that he make no changes at all, and that the bishop found the whole matter trying and believed that he had better things to do. The conflict ended only when Oakeley was suspended by the ecclesiastical Court of Arches in 1845 for defending "Ideal" Ward's view of subscription to the Thirty-nine Articles.[16] (He subsequently became a Roman Catholic.)

Conflict with a congregation was especially likely when a new clergyman succeeded a popular, long-term incumbent. Then any changes in the way things had "always been done" implied a criticism of his predecessor, and explaining that the changes were to eliminate lawlessness or were required by elementary considerations of decency did not help at all. At Southam, Warwickshire, in the 1870s, for instance, Mr. Ridley, of The Abbey, complained to the bishop of Worcester about his new rector's innovations.[17] Mr. Ridley's complaints included objections to intoning, to a floral cross on the altar, to banners and processions, and to "obeisance" to the altar by "Acolytes, or members of the Choir." As the rector, M. W. Mayow, observed in a sermon, the real question was: "Why should not that which satisfied our late excellent and revered Rector satisfy his successor, and why should not all things continue as they were?"[18] The bishop ordered Mayow to resume one practice (wearing his academic hood at Holy Communion) and to cease five others, despite evidence that Mayow was supported by many members of the congregation. Mayow yielded, but with a poor grace, grumbling that he had become "the only unstoled priest in England"—which was more nearly true in the 1870s than it had been thirty years before.[19]

Sometimes a "ritual" dispute seems to have been simply a way for laymen to settle other scores with the vicar. When the churchwardens of Beaminster, in Dorset, protested the vicar's decorating the church with flowers at Easter, for example, it seems to have had something to do with his forbidding the ringing of the church bells at the annual Pleasure Fair.[20] In the context of the 1840s and 1850s, any sort of innovation could be tarred as "Puseyite," and those who disliked particular innovators had a convenient weapon at hand.

Often the original grounds for a clergyman's unpopularity could be found in his insistence on the letter of a rubric open to considerable interpretation. Shortly after Thomas Chamberlain became vicar of St. Thomas the Martyr, Oxford, for instance, he exercised what he understood to be his rubrical responsibility to refuse to bury a parishioner who had died, Chamberlain said, without repenting for a life of sin. Some other parishioners resented this. For several years Chamberlain walked from St. Thomas to his rooms in Christ Church in danger of stoning, and people protested when he removed some pews, installed a new altar, and introduced altar lights, the eastward position, and the mixed chalice. But after Chamberlain and the sisterhood he founded in 1847 endeared themselves to the parish by devoted nursing in the cholera epidemics of 1848 and 1854, he introduced eucharistic vestments and even experimented with incense (at the Feast of the Ascension in 1855) without arousing opposition.[21]

Helston, Cornwall, saw a similar case. The vicar was Walter Blunt, described by one historian as an "amusing and energetic" man, but "possessed of the passion for exact obedience to authority which was the mark of the age."[22] Blunt refused communion to a sick man who had long attended the church but had been baptized a Roman Catholic, refused to bury a young man baptized by a Wesleyan, and refused to marry those who could not prove that they had been baptized. After that, many of his parishioners found everything he did offensive.

In 1844 his churchwarden wrote Bishop Phillpotts of Exeter to complain. Blunt had begun to preach in a surplice, he prayed neither before nor after the sermon, and his sermons were extemporaneous: in the morning, a "dissertation on the Liturgy" or "a sort of lecture, on one of the lessons, ... more frequently historical than of any practical tendency." He required women to be churched while kneeling at the altar rail, rather than allowing them to remain in their appointed seats. He dismissed the choir from the organ loft (because they ate apples throughout the service, he said) and replaced them with a choir of boys in the chancel. He tried to persuade the churchwardens to refuse burial to Dissenters until after 8:00 P.M. And so forth.

The warden complained to the bishop that many had stopped coming to church altogether, and many who continued to come "are not able to rid themselves of the fear that some strongly exciting event is about to take place." He knew of many "ladies who have been incapacitated from performing their religious and other duties for the remainder of the day, in consequence of the excitement they have been subjected to at church."[23]

The irascible Bishop Phillpotts was one of the few bishops at all sympathetic to the Tractarians' program, but one must doubt whether his support was actually helpful. In the Helston case, he supported Blunt, and denounced the complaining churchwarden for his "lamentable delusion ..., little short of infatuation, which can discern nothing but popery in every attempt to restore sound Church principles"—although the charge of Romanizing was only a small part of the man's list of grievances, almost an afterthought.[24] Not only did Phillpotts exonerate Blunt; he promptly issued a pastoral letter to the other clergy of the diocese, directing them to wear the surplice for preaching as well.

This directive set off a flurry of meetings, petitions, and protests throughout the diocese, and Phillpotts withdrew it soon after issuing it. But at the parish church of St. Sidwell's, Exeter, already divided and suspicious because of an earlier conflict, the curate ill-advisedly wore the surplice for preaching anyway. Two-thirds of his congregation walked out, and he was mobbed on his way home by two hundred protesters. The next Sunday, he required a police escort to protect him from a mob of two thousand. The following Sunday, he relented, but five thousand people were on hand to see that he did.

Phillpotts's sympathies with the Tractarians made his diocese something of a center for this sort of conflict. Ultrarubricians in the Diocese of Exeter could obey the dictates of the Prayer Book without having to worry about their bishop's reaction. In the ensuing atmosphere of excitement and suspicion, however, congregations soon became wary and alert for signs of Puseyism. At St. John's Chapel in Torquay, for instance, the churchwardens (one of whom was Admiral Sir C. Dashwood), with forty-four of "the most respectable heads of families renting Pews," wrote Bishop Phillpotts to complain about "the interruption occasioned in our devotions by the unusual number of officiating Clergy," "the novel ceremonies," "genuflexions and turnings to the Communion Table"—all of these practices implying doctrines "as taught in the Romish Church." Moreover, they asked "that the Psalmody may be conducted with that simplicity which may enable the congregation to take their part; that the Service may not be unnecessarily lengthened by Chanting ...; and that our attention may no more be distracted from the vital substance of our Religion by ever-varying novelties in its external forms."

A long and tedious exchange of letters followed between the bishop (who was not sympathetic), the wardens, the admiral, the curate, and others, including some members of the congregation who supported the curate.

Bishop Phillpotts finally declined to continue the correspondence: "To say the truth—I am tired of the discussions in Torquay, and congratulate myself on the reflection that of the 6 or 700 parishes in my diocese, there are very few indeed equally prolific of disputes."[25]

One of those other troublesome parishes, however, was Woodbury, where, as in Torquay, the practice of intoning parts of morning and evening prayer led to conflict. The rubric directs that these passages should be "said or sung," and some rubrical scholars concluded that *said*, in this context, originally meant *intoned*.[26] In Woodbury, the Reverend J. Loveband Fulford received this argument with pleasure. Even before he understood the rubric, he asserted, "Nature dictated to me that, in offering Prayers to God, in the congregation, the voice should keep the same tone."

Most of his congregation understood nature's dictates and the rubric differently, and demanded that he stop intoning and "restore to your Parish that spirit of peace and good will which prevailed in it, during the time of your predecessor." The vicar refused, citing his duty to obey the rubric, and eventually a number of parishioners seceded to a chapel where the Prayer Book was *read*. In 1852, when the churchwardens complained to Bishop Phillpotts about their parson's "monotonous whine," Mr. Fulford responded to the bishop's inquiry by explaining his understanding of the rubric, and enclosing a letter of support signed by 200 persons, including 38 communicants. The churchwardens, in turn, circulated a petition claiming that "said" means *said*, and that making a "slow protracted Noise" was not saying. Their petition was signed "(with two exceptions) by every influential person in the parish," some 298 in number, including 92 communicants, a baronet, a clergyman, an admiral, and a captain. Bishop Phillpotts, wearying of the matter, replied that whatever the vicar was doing it was either saying or singing, and that he would not forbid it.[27] The parish seems to have settled into a grumpy stalemate; some years later Mr. Fulford was still in place, and presumably still intoning.[28]

The same practice continued to be the cause, or at least a pretext, for dissension in many other churches. R. W. Randall was a wealthy and well-connected clergyman who succeeded Archdeacon Manning at Lavington, when the future cardinal became a Roman Catholic. When Randall found himself at odds with his curate, the schoolmaster, the choirmaster, and most of his parishioners, his friend Samuel Wilberforce (bishop of Oxford and the patron of his living) advised him to dress less peculiarly, to be "less priestly and more like others" in his manner, and to read books other than Romish ones. When the trouble continued, Wilberforce wrote again: "The greatest objection by far of the people and what I especially dislike is your intoning.... It is a sort of falsetto which is very provoking to many ears, producing on them the same effect certain notes produce on dogs when they make them howl.... Read the service in the most unmistakable reading tone, and do not let them think you are going as near the wind as you can."[29]

The most strenuous objections to Puseyite innovation, however, were found at the London church of St. George's-in-the-East, where the rector's intoning was one of several practices that set off an eighteen-month-long series of riots that we shall examine later. For the record, when the archbishop of Canterbury finally engaged two prominent jurists to give their opinions on whether *say* could mean *intone*, they concluded that it could not—but by then it was 1867, and the battleground had shifted.[30]

Although collectively these disputes contributed to the generalized suspicion that the Tractarians were up to no good, few had any other importance outside the boundaries of the parishes involved, and the modern reader may find them as tiresome as Bishop Phillpotts claimed to (although one suspects the old warrior sometimes actually enjoyed them). As Owen Chadwick has pointed out, however, two had extra-parochial effects of some consequence.[31]

In the first, a weekly offering begun in 1844 in the Berkshire parish of Hurst had the entirely disastrous consequence for Anglo-Catholics of alienating the owner of the *Times* of London, a parishioner. A confidential memorandum on "Puseyites of London" was soon prepared for the *Times's* editor, ranking ninety-nine London clergymen from most to least Puseyite, and describing them in some detail.[32] (Tractarians were less likely than moderates or Evangelicals to be described as popular, influential, or "active.") Thereafter, the *Times*, which had formerly defended the Tractarians, harried them without mercy, pursued and printed news of troubled parishes throughout England, and denounced sacerdotalism in leader after leader for years.

The next year saw a dispute at Cambridge over whether a stone altar in the newly restored medieval church of St. Sepulchre was or was not a communion table as stipulated by the rubric. This conflict confirmed many people's suspicions of the Cambridge Camden Society and completed its identification with Puseyism. The society lost many moderate members, and was essentially destroyed as a broad-based archaeological society.

Elsewhere in England and beyond, the familiar pattern of parochial dispute repeated itself again and again. The built-in strains of parish life were exacerbated by clergymen determined to remake the fabric, the worship, and the discipline of the church. One or two particular acts might alienate some parishioners—parish notables accustomed to deference, friends or relatives of someone who was the object of discipline, members of a choir whose services were no longer needed, "Protestant" churchmen alarmed by stories of Puseyism and Romanism elsewhere, friends of the vicar's predecessor who saw any change as disloyal. As the classic downward spiral of community conflict was established, members of the congregation took sides and sought allies outside the parish—bishop, press, and other clergymen and lay churchmen with sympathetic views. What previously would have passed without comment now became cause for fresh complaint. Positions hardened, as people on both sides came to see principle involved in what was formerly, for most, a mere matter of taste.

Remodeling of parishes on Puseyite lines continued throughout the century and continued to produce conflict when it was not conducted with the utmost tact, and sometimes even when it was. From time to time, later in the century, remote parts of the realm were troubled by exactly the same sorts of innovations that had disturbed the south of England in the 1840s and 1850s. As late as 1898, for instance, flowers behind the communion table, the use of the word "altar," processions, and turning to the east for the Creed set off a riot at St. George's, Belfast—but that is Ulster, of course, and another story.[33] Well before then, the Anglo-Catholic avant-garde had moved on to contest other issues, and the nature of the conflict had changed as well. In the 1840s and 1850s, however, in the first early attempts to try "the effect of Tractarian principles upon a practical scale," we can discern a few general features.

The Importance of Ritual

In the first place, the ceremonial and decorative changes that came to be known as "Ritualism" appear to have been virtually inseparable from Anglo-Catholic doctrine. Looking back from 1869, one observer said, correctly, that "wherever Tractarianism was in any degree accepted, some alteration in the mode of performing the service marked the adoption of its opinions by the officiating clergyman." Here and there, other factors—charity or tact, for instance—intervened to weaken the connection: some clergymen hesitated to introduce changes that their congregations would find unsettling or irritating, and sometimes the change was only one of "tone and manner."[34]

But no clergyman who accepted the theological tenets of the Oxford Movement opposed the Tractarian program on principle or denied that it was a worthy goal (although some questioned the prudence of particular changes and were more willing than others to bide their time). Moreover, only rarely were changes of the sort we have examined introduced by clergymen who did not sympathize with the Tractarians. Quite early, these innovations were identified by all sides with Puseyism and became, in fact, party badges, and there was little reason to risk conflict and condemnation for changes that were only cosmetic. This close correlation between partisanship and behavior has a lucky consequence for the student of Anglo-Catholicism, because it means that the spread of the movement can be traced by examining the spread of its distinctive practices. And it is much easier to determine what particular clergymen were doing at any given time than to find out what they were thinking.

Eventually, most of the movement's adversaries came to that same conclusion—or at least they despaired of attacking successfully on doctrinal

grounds. In large part, this was because the courts proved singularly reluctant to condemn clergymen for doctrinal error. The Judicial Committee of
the Privy Council, the court of final appeal in matters of clergy discipline,
was a secular body, and it faced an insoluble dilemma. If it heard and decided doctrinal cases, it risked confirming the Tractarians' worst fears about the
Babylonish captivity of the Church: its very doctrine subject to determination by the State!

This lesson was learned the hard way in 1850 when the Judicial Committee overturned Bishop Phillpotts's refusal to institute to a living in his
diocese a clergyman named Gorham, who had denied the doctrine of baptismal regeneration.[35] The Gorham judgment led to a wave of secessions by
Tractarian clergymen who saw it as the State's imposing a heretical clergyman on an orthodox bishop. The opposite decision, of course, would have
alienated those who shared Gorham's Calvinist views, as well those who simply believed that such views should not be proscribed in the Church of England.

After Gorham, the Judicial Committee by and large avoided questions
of doctrine, a policy that protected deviants of all sorts. It refused to hear
the theological complaints against Bishop Colenso of Natal, who had questioned the historicity of the Pentateuch, and held only that his metropolitan
did not have the authority to depose him.[36] Earlier, it had dismissed on a
technicality the charges against G. A. Denison, archdeacon of Taunton, who
had preached (in apparent contradiction of Article XXXIX) the Real Presence
of Christ in the Eucharist.[37] The Judicial Committee's decisions protected
Evangelicals like Gorham, latitudinarians like Colenso, and Anglo-Catholics
like Denison, and thus contributed to the comprehensiveness of the Church
of England, but at the risk of implying that Anglican clergymen could
believe almost whatever they pleased. This situation was not wholly satisfactory, but it was preferable in the eyes of many to having a secular body determine Church doctrine.

Given the courts' reluctance to become involved in doctrinal matters,
the Anglo-Catholics' opponents turned to prosecution for the ceremonial
and decorative practices that usually accompanied the new theological
emphases. "Against false doctrine in the abstract there is *practically* no remedy," one pamphlet concluded, but it called on "the laity to exert their
undoubted power of checking ritual excesses."[38] The Church Association
was founded in 1865 to protect the Church from efforts "to assimilate her
services to those of the Church of Rome," and prosecution in the courts was
to be the means.[39] For many laymen these practices were the real ground of
offense, anyway; behavior was easier to establish than doctrine; and the
courts were less hesitant to say what was legal ceremonial than to say what
were legal beliefs. Perhaps they were less hesitant than they should have
been.

The Law of the Church

Whatever the ultrarubricians might say, the legal status of the Anglo-Catholics' innovations was not clear. "The ordinary every-day Englishman," said a writer in the *Contemporary Review*, found the whole of ecclesiastical law "a sort of Cabala—a thing to be revered or scoffed at, according to the turn of his mind and his politics, but in any case a thing incomprehensible."[40] Years later, after much litigation and learned inquiry, A. J. B. Beresford Hope observed that the situation had not changed: "The general conclusion at which a dispassionate man must arrive is that, irrespective of specific rites and 'ornaments,' the ceremonial law of the Church of England—as on the one hand a body whose continuous corporate existence ranges over nearly thirteen hundred years, and on the other a Reformed Church, the principles of whose Reformation have to be gathered out of statutes, rubrics, canons, articles, proclamations, advertisements, visitation articles, &c., dating from 1547 to 1662—is far from being a simple question."[41]

At first, the Puseyites' opponents generally assumed that the customary, established practices were not only legal but obligatory and that the problem was merely one of getting the courts to say so. As one put it, optimistically: "There is a common law in ecclesiastical as well as secular matters;... continuous usage, when not opposed to the rubrics, is a portion of that common law. Usage also is generally a safe interpreter of ambiguous rubrics."[42] By acknowledging the authority of the rubrics, however, this argument was on shaky ground. The Prayer Book, product of a Reformation compromise, was (as Shane Leslie put it, mixing metaphors) "the Anglican scrapbook ... full of fossils."[43] "While that precious jewel the Prayer Book remains, they cannot destroy or weaken Tractarianism," Pusey wrote in 1851, and he was right.[44] Appended to an act of Parliament, its rubrics given the force of law, the Prayer Book often did yield to a "Catholic" interpretation; Anglo-Catholic doctrine and practice were both sanctioned to a greater extent than most Anglicans had imagined.[45]

In some of their early criticisms of prevailing practice, the Tractarians were clearly in the right. Henry Phillpotts was not the only bishop to agree with their interpretation of the rubrics as obliging preachers to wear surplices (rather than changing to black gowns) and requiring that the (often omitted) Prayer for the Church Militant be read in the communion service. The archbishop of Canterbury himself wrote the clergy of his province in 1845 to regret that efforts to secure obedience in these two respects "should not have been received with unanimous acquiescence." Although he recognized that established custom made it difficult for many clergymen to comply and recommended that things be left as they were for the time being, he plainly favored uniformity on the basis of the rubrics—which meant, for many congregations, change—in the long run.[46]

The rubrical basis for other Tractarian innovations was more ambiguous, but the results of the first "ritual" case to come before the Judicial Committee of the Privy Council pleased most ultrarubricians and shocked their adversaries. In a case arising out of a dispute at St. Barnabas, Pimlico, and its parent church, St. Paul's, Knightsbridge, the Judicial Committee ruled in 1857 that a number of modest revivals were legal, among them credence tables, colored altar cloths, candles (if lit only when required for light), and a cross (but not a crucifix) behind (but not on) the altar (which must be movable).[47]

This decision did not satisfy the more extreme partisans on either side. A few Ritualists (not yet called that) announced their inability to comply with even these limitations and invited prosecution, and some of the Puseyites' opponents began to agitate anew for revision of the Prayer Book.[48] But the details of the so-called Liddell judgment were less significant than the fact that it was based on the Ornaments Rubric. A great deal of historical spadework had gone into establishing that the challenged "ornaments" were in use "in the Second Year of the Reign of King Edward the Sixth." By allowing that changes consistent with that criterion could be made in the face of established custom, the decision opened the way for the widespread introduction of many other "Ornaments of the Church, and of the Ministers thereof," the most provocative of which were the distinctive eucharistic vestments: alb and chasuble.

The Liddell judgment allowed Anglo-Catholics not only to defend their own practices as legal and to elaborate them further, but to attack their opponents' shortcomings even more vigorously. One pamphleteer was able eventually to list three doctrines denied and seven practices generally neglected by Evangelicals, all of them (he argued) required by the Prayer Book and all of which, save for the superior charity of High Churchmen, could have been grounds for legal proceedings.[49]

This argument threw at least some Evangelicals on the defensive and even enlisted ambivalent support from a few bishops. One Evangelical, writing to defend his use of the gown rather than a surplice for preaching, said that the Liddell judgment showed that "the double-edged sword had been unsheathed and it would be now seen that those who had challenged the issue had called down a judgement upon themselves."[50] Another exhorted his colleagues: "Let us endeavour, indeed, honestly to mold our practice in the conduct of Divine Service, and the management of our Churches upon the true spirit of the Rubrics and Canons. Let us give no occasion to any man to charge us with neglect of the material fabric, or with slovenly carelessness in the solemnities of the House of God."[51] The bishop of Chester, replying to an anti-Ritualist petition from 128 Liverpool clergymen, must have chilled them: "I have no sympathy with ceremonial innovations or revivals. But ... if the law is invoked for the suppression of errors on the side of excess, it must be expected that strict conformity to the Rubric will be insisted on whenever variations or omissions in any of the offices of the Church have come to have the sanction of custom."[52]

In the years to come, matters would become less clear than they seemed to be in 1857. The Ritualist pacesetters would move on to introduce ornaments and practices more difficult to justify by appeal to the Prayer Book, hostile lawyers and ecclesiological scholars would discover weak spots in the legal and historical arguments that underlay the Liddell judgment, ecclesiastical courts and the Judicial Committee would respond to those discoveries and to political pressure by reversing earlier decisions, and there was always the possibility that the ultrarubricians' position would simply be legislated into oblivion: many felt that if the Prayer Book said *that*, then the Prayer Book must be changed, and the threat of revision was always in the air.[53] But as the 1860s began, Anglo-Catholics were able to argue that their innovations were strictly legal, and sometimes legally required.

Symbolic Necessity and Other Rationales

Many of the innovators believed sincerely that they were only recalling the Church to practices that its own law required, and they were motivated by a spirit of obedience to an institution that the Tractarians had taught them to revere. Others, however, were more concerned to use the latitude that the Church's law allowed to serve values other than obedience and lawfulness; it was enough for their purposes that the law explicitly sanction some of their practices and be ambiguous with regard to others, and it did that.

When innovators felt the need of proof-texts, they favored Old Testament descriptions of Temple worship, or the Book of Revelation.[54] But Scripture was used primarily to argue with Evangelicals. Elaborate ceremony and decoration, to Anglo-Catholics, were more often attempts to imitate medieval or Continental than heavenly or Hebrew practice. Most arguments for what came to be known as ritual "advance" were variations on the theme that certain ornaments and practices were symbolically important, that they stood for "Catholic" beliefs and thus were not merely matters of taste or preference. From the early days of the Cambridge Camden Society, many changes had been justified on aesthetic or (much the same thing) antiquarian grounds, and this justification originally appealed to many who did not share the Tractarians' theological views. But in time it became clear that the decorative and liturgical links with pre-Reformation antiquity were valued by many of the innovators as symbols of a doctrinal continuity as well, and later borrowings from contemporary Roman Catholicism had a similar symbolic import.

At the very least, some argued, it was wrong to deny God's house sumptuous ornaments, wrong for worship to be other than gorgeous and "correct." One clergyman offered a hymn on the subject:

> Lord, bring home the glorious lesson
>   To their hearts who strangely deem
> That an unmajestic worship
>   Doth Thy Majesty beseem!...
>
> 'Tis for Thee we bid the Frontal
>   Its embroidered wealth unfold;
> 'Tis for Thee we deck the Reredos
>   With rich jewels and with gold;
>
> Thine the floral glow and fragrance,
>   Thine the vesture's fair array;
> Thine the starry lights that glitter
>   Where Thou dost Thy Light display.[55]

In addition, some said that the changes were needed to attract worshippers, especially the poor, and that once worshippers were assembled the symbolism of the new ceremonial and fittings of the church would instruct them in doctrine.[56] Symbolic explanations were devised for practically everything, and sermons and lectures explained the symbolism when it was not obvious, as it often was not. In 1855, a preacher at St. Barnabas, Pimlico, led his listeners from item to item around the church, explaining for example that the colored altar cloths were "nothing but the obvious fulfillment of the Church's order" that fasts and festivals be announced after the Creed, "through another sense, which is very susceptible and acute, and especially so among the poor."[57] The altar lights, he said, symbolized the "Light of the World" (although one critic suggested a few years later that clergymen's use of lights in the daytime might symbolize their "deep spiritual darkness" instead).[58]

In any case, in the 1850s, before the Denison case brought the doctrine of the Real Presence to center stage in the controversy between Anglo-Catholics and their adversaries, the "symbolic" argument was diffuse and undiscriminating. To read an 1857 pamphlet called *The Symbolism of Churches and Their Ornaments*, one would think that everything was as important as everything else: altar crosses and candles, flowers and colored altar cloths were defended as "symbolic," but so were such things as fonts, spires, bells, and doors.[59] Various well-meaning moderates tried to argue that many of these uses and ornaments were merely matters of taste, not worth disrupting a congregation over, and subject to amiable negotiation. W. F. Hook, the vicar of Leeds, for example, no doubt mindful of his problems with Pusey's church of St. Saviour's, argued in the early 1850s that "a Church should be a standing sermon to the neighborhood," and called for "decency and order" in worship and adherence to the rubrics. But he believed that many of the ultrarubricians' changes were not required by the rubrics or by doctrine, and he advised discretion in changing from accustomed usage. He urged tolerance and deference to local custom:

If we observe a ceremony [like turning to the East for the Creed] when others do not, or refuse to observe it when others do, we act indecently. Others will not be led right by the ill manners and disorderly conduct of an individual, whose conduct, offensive to others, should lead him to self-examination. Is not his proud heart thinking not of God's glory, but his own? Is he not seeming to say, See how much wiser I am than you? stand apart, I am holier than thou? I know better than not to do this; or, I am not superstitious, and therefore I abstain from what men wiser and more holy regard as a thing indifferent?"[60]

As we have seen, this was largely Keble's view as well, but it was not the view of most Puseyites. Investing every detail of ceremonial and decoration with symbolic importance had the effect of turning an attack on any aspect of them into an attack on the doctrine "symbolized." Nor was it the view of the ultrarubricians' opponents, who were as indiscriminate in their opposition to change as the innovators in their justification of it. These opponents were of two sorts: "Some say that it is new, and they do not like changes;" a pamphlet-writer observed, "others that it is old, and they are afraid of getting back to Popery."[61] The latter made most of the noise.

In the *Christian Guardian*, in 1850, for instance, one letter-writer complained that the "ultra high church party" was "turning our churches into imitations of mass-houses."[62] "The Church, with its commandments and observances, is preached," he said, "in place of the simple Gospel of the grace of God." His visits to several London churches had shown him that "candlesticks, crosses, flowers, intonings, superstitious practices, and perversions of the Protestant faith have found their way, and retain their hold, unchecked, within our churches." At Christ Church, Albany Street, he had found "forbidden vases of flowers," a credence table, and a sermon on baptismal regeneration. He observed that four different ministers took part, and found it a "blessing ... that the ministry of such men is limited to a single spot, instead of being diffused in four different spheres of action."

At St. Paul's, Knightsbridge, he found less to object to in the service (and Lord John Russell in the congregation), but noted the many "cross-bearing service-books," with their "party-coloured pages of red and black."[63] The Margaret Street Chapel was the worst: his list of objections there was lengthy, and included the collection of alms in "small velvet bags, after the approved Romish fashion"—the bishop's earlier instructions to use a dish now evidently being disregarded. There were no flowers (it was Lent), but "it almost made me rub my eyes, to see if my vision was not deceptive, when I beheld a genuine cross, of some inlaid metal, standing upon the altar, between the candlesticks." The "cloven foot of Romish teaching" was also evident in the sermon, on "the five sacred wounds of Jesus."

One of the most persistent no-popery vigilantes was the Reverend C. P. Golightly, Newman's former curate, and one of Golightly's perennial targets was the newly founded Cuddesdon Theological College, near Oxford.[64] With some reason, he saw it as a hotbed of Puseyism, with a "tendency ... to sow broad cast the seeds of Romish perversion in the counties of Oxfordshire, Berkshire, and Buckinghamshire." In 1858 he complained about the college's chapel, "fitted up with every fantastic decoration to which a party-meaning has been assigned." He found the "so-called Altar" to be "Romish," and the service of Holy Communion to be "conducted with genuflections, rinsings of cups in the piscina, and other ceremonial acts, foreign to the Ritual and usages of the Church of England." The college authorities denied some of the charges—that the service book in use contained the seven canonical hours of the Roman Catholic Church, for one— but others were true enough.[65] Twenty years later, Golightly was still attacking Cuddesdon: he complained that the 1876 Annual Record reported a "retreat" conducted by "the Reverend Father Benson," and found significance in the fact that 145 of the college's first 350 students were members of the (Anglo-Catholic) English Church Union, and seventeen were brothers of the Society of the Holy Cross.[66]

"What the laity require and demand," one letter-writer to *The Examiner* announced, "is, that the chancels and communion tables of our churches shall not be so decorated as to resemble the Romish churches; that intoning in our parish churches should be prohibited; that the crossings and genuflexions of the clergy, other than is stipulated for in the rubrics, shall likewise be forbidden—not that in themselves they are sinful, but because they approximate to and are practiced in the Church of Rome."[67] That was part of it, to be sure. But for every Protestant churchman who recognized that the Puseyites intended party warfare and that he was the enemy, there were other laymen who simply disliked what they saw as high-handed innovation. They had no love for Romanism, and if the changes were Romish, so much the worse. But whether the novelties were Romish or not, they were irritating, a matter (as one layman put it) of "uncouth singing, and bowing and turning this way and that way, to say nothing of a complex apparatus of reading-pews, and credences, and letterns [sic], and fald-stools."

Worse still, these changes were too often imposed by a "new race of clergymen," men "more laborious and strict in the externals of religion, but of a narrower, a more uncharitable, and more unenglish mind than heretofore." This new clergyman could be found "displaying [himself], in all the beauty and pomp of holiness, within the rails of the communion-table"; his sermons had "a new and peculiar character"; he was all "too deeply imbued with the legitimate deduction from his principles, that he is indeed a vessel made to honor."[68] We have enough similar testimony to recognize that this was a frequent response to a genuinely new phenomenon, although the Tractarians would, of course, interpret it differently.

"Auricular Confession"

Hand in hand with decorative and ceremonial change went two other developments that marked the spread of Anglo-Catholicism: the practice of private confession to one's priest or "spiritual director," and the founding of religious communities. Both were viewed by their proponents as revivals of legitimate Anglican institutions unwisely abandoned at the Reformation, and here the old Tractarians were as one with their disciples. Pusey might question the ultrarubricians' motives for ornamenting their churches, their services, and (especially) themselves; Keble might question their wisdom and charity; but both men explicitly and repeatedly endorsed spiritual direction and the revival of religious orders. When we try to assess the continuity between the authors of the *Tracts* and the Ritualists of a few decades later, their agreement in these areas is important; if nothing else, it helped to keep them allied despite friction over ceremonial matters.

The more controversial, though less visible, of the two innovations was the increasing practice of regular, private, sacramental confession—or, as it was sometimes called, "auricular" or "habitual" confession. The Prayer Book clearly implied in its forms of absolution and in the ordination service that Anglican clergymen were empowered to grant absolution to the penitent; and in the Order for the Visitation of the Sick, ministers were instructed to move the sick to confess their sins, if their consciences were troubled. This was one of the "fossils" that Evangelicals regretted or ignored and that Anglo-Catholics began early on to revitalize.[69]

Occasional confession was not unknown among old-fashioned High Churchmen, but it was the Tractarians and their successors who used the license the Prayer Book allowed to develop a high doctrine of the Sacrament of Penance. Pusey apparently began to hear confessions as early as 1838, defended the practice for the rest of his life, and translated a manual for the use of confessors. Keble, too, placed a high value on confession, and urged it on his parishioners at Hursley; it was the one way, he believed, that a parish clergyman could know what really troubled his flock and effectively exercise his duty of discipline. Both Pusey and Keble were greatly sought-after spiritual directors, as was Archdeacon Manning, before his secession.

Various explanations are available for the increasing centrality of confession in Anglo-Catholic doctrine and practice. One historian has suggested that it followed necessarily from the Tractarian emphasis on baptismal regeneration, as the only remedy for post-baptismal sin.[70] For those who looked to Rome for the ideal of a Christian Church, of course, Roman Catholic practice was reason enough to adopt it; those whose ideal was the pre-Reformation English Church drew the same conclusion. Certainly, like ritual, it served as a party badge, and, in a sense, an act of defiance.

When the practice came to light it provoked bitter controversy. In 1850, for example, the troublesome church of St. Saviour's, Leeds, was the scene of several conflicts involving confession, including one in which two clergymen were accused of compelling a female parishioner to confess and of asking her indelicate questions. Another well-publicized dispute took place at St. Peter's, Plymouth, where the Reverend George Rundle Prynne had been attacked for the usual Tractarian innovations—preaching in a surplice, intoning, and so forth—soon after he arrived in 1848. (Bishop Phillpotts supported Prynne, although he advised him to give up the alms-bags he had substituted for plates. The *Plymouth Herald* referred to them as "Judas bags" and said Prynne should "receive the sack.") Prynne's association with the Devonport sisterhood also offended his adversaries, and in 1852 Prynne was brought before Bishop Phillpotts on charges that he had compelled orphans in the sisters' care to confess and had asked them "corrupting questions." When it became clear that key witnesses were perjuring themselves, Bishop Phillpotts, who had defended the principle of confession in his charge of 1851 but discouraged "the general habit," exonerated Prynne, remarking, "I acquit him even of indiscretion, and I pray God that every clergyman in my diocese may do his duty as well as Mr. Prynne has done his." In the atmosphere of excitement, rumors circulated that Pusey had been seen going up a ladder to a room over St. Peter's to hear confessions, and a "monster meeting" sent protests to Parliament, to the Queen, and to the archbishop of Canterbury. When Bishop Phillpotts held a confirmation afterwards, the church was surrounded by a mob that threw stones at the bishop, broke the vicarage windows, and called for Prynne to be hanged from a lamppost.[71]

A few years later, in 1858, two other cases caused a momentary sensation.[72] When it was alleged that a female charity worker at St. Barnabas, Pimlico, had refused to give assistance to a woman unless she went to confession, and that the Reverend Alfred Pole had asked her improper questions when she did, Bishop Tait of London (whose predecessor had condemned private confession in a charge of 1842) suspended Pole and set off a four-year series of appeals that ended inconclusively. At Boyne Hill in the Diocese of Oxford, a similar complaint about improper questions in the confessional led Bishop Wilberforce to defend the practice of confession in extreme cases and to appoint a commission of inquiry; when it acquitted the accused curate, Wilberforce stood by the man and suffered much abuse in consequence.

But the wonder is that there were not more scandals and protests. With confession, as with sisterhoods and ritual, the Anglo-Catholics were feeling their way. As in those cases, the model nearest to hand was the Roman Catholic one—not a happy choice if they wished to avoid controversy. Add to the fact that the practice was "Romish" the widespread belief that (as a proponent wrote in 1854) "there are ... generally more sins to be found under this [the seventh] commandment than under any other."[73] Add also the (well-advised) secrecy that surrounded the confessional, and the Anglican confessors' complete inexperience and lack of training. Perhaps it is not surprising that few other Anglo-Catholic innovations elicited as much visceral opposition, even among the movement's allies and sympathizers.

The revivers were playing with fire, and they knew it. In this matter more than any other they displayed some measure of tact. Although guidebooks began to appear around 1860 listing churches with all manner of controversial and sometimes illegal ceremonial, I have been unable to find published before the turn of the century any guide to churches where confessions were heard.[74] As early as 1847 one observer claimed that confession was "practiced very extensively, and, as we believe, most beneficially, in the English Church," but he noted that it was "scarcely ever spoken of, even in the most confidential intercourse."[75] In 1850 a Roman Catholic priest, formerly a Tractarian, wrote an open letter to Pusey describing confession among Anglicans as a matter of "persons secretly received against the known wish of their parents, of Confessions heard in the houses of common friends, ... of clandestine correspondence to arrange meetings, under initials, or in envelopes addressed to other persons," and we have enough examples to know that the man did not exaggerate.[76] Pusey, Manning, John Mason Neale—all are known to have heard confessions with varying degrees of secrecy to keep the practice hidden from hostile parents, spouses, or bishops, and many lesser lights among the Tractarians did the same.

Some penitents found the need for secrecy distasteful and either discontinued the practice or became Roman Catholics, but E. A. Knox was certainly right when he observed that for others "a rite stigmatized as papistical [was] all the more alluring," and that "all the 'thrill' of mystery and of persecution for the faith [only] added to the joy of unburdening the conscience."[77] As the forties and fifties went on, more and more Anglo-Catholics came to regard confession "as a part of the spiritual life, and among religious duties."[78] In the words of one who knew the practice at first hand, it was one of the "secret privileges" of young Anglo-Catholics.[79]

Sisterhoods and Oratories

The revival of religious orders was only slightly less controversial than the practice of confession, but it was probably more important for Anglo-Catholicism in the long run. In the movement's adolescence, the higher reaches of Anglo-Catholic practice were not to be found in parish churches where most of the conflict occurred, but in the private oratories of the new communities, beyond the reach of hostile journalists and anxious bishops, unobserved by unsympathetic layfolk. In those communities spiritual direction was well-nigh universal, and forms of devotion, decoration, and cere-

monial that were practiced elsewhere only rarely and furtively were mat-
ter-of-fact, everyday realities—Anglican models for what some hoped would
become the norm of Church of England parish life.

The story of the revival of religious communities in the Church of England has been thoroughly and ably told elsewhere, but a brief review may be
in order here.[80] The founding of orders had the unqualified and enthusiastic support of all of the surviving elders of the Oxford Movement; unlike
confession, it also had the support of many High Churchmen—such men as
Hook of Leeds, whose suspicions of the Puseyites in other respects we have
already noted. Although most bishops deprecated life vows and distinctive
garb and hoped for some clearly Protestant form of deaconesses, a few gave
their cautious approval to the new sisterhoods.

Newman's establishment at Littlemore was the earliest manifestation of
the impulse to this revival, but that came to an end with Newman's conversion. Frederick Faber, the biographer of St. Wilfrid, began a similar brotherhood at about the same time in his parish of Elton, Huntingdonshire.
Midnight matins in the rectory, devotion to the Sacred Heart, the wearing
of hair-shirts, and use of "the discipline," or scourge, distinguished this
small band of self-styled "Anglican Papalists," and the brotherhood seceded
as a group in 1845. Some ten years later, while Edward Burne-Jones and
William Morris dreamt of establishing an order in Oxford dedicated to Sir
Galahad, Edward Steere (later bishop of Central Africa) founded the Brotherhood of St. James in a ruined chapel near Tamworth, but concluded within a year that his companions, although enamored of the romance of monasticism, had too much difficulty rising before 8:00 A.M. to make a go of it.

During this period a number of guilds and associations for men were
also founded. Characterized by varying degrees of secrecy, they were less
demanding than the brotherhoods, and some were more successful. Among
them were the Guild of St. Mary the Virgin (later the Brotherhood of the
Holy Trinity), founded in Oxford in 1844 for the study of Church art and
history under Pusey's guidance, and the Guild of St. Alban the Martyr,
founded in Birmingham in 1851 "to assist the Clergy in maintaining and
extending the Catholic Faith and to spread a knowledge of the True Doctrines of the Church." The latter soon spread to other parts of England, and
both organizations outlasted the century. But the time was not ripe for the
revival of religious orders for men.

For a variety of reasons, the story was different for women.[81] One historian has identified sixteen sisterhoods and communities for women founded in the fifteen years before 1860, only two of which have not survived to
the present.[82] Pusey himself served as advisor and spiritual director to several of these early communities, including the first, the Sisterhood of the
Holy Cross, founded in London in 1845 as a memorial to the poet Robert
Southey.[83] Pusey compiled that sisterhood's Rule and adapted the Breviary
for its use. He was also central to the foundation (ca. 1850) and oversight

of Marian Hughes's Society of the Holy and Undivided Trinity, in Oxford, and of Priscilla Lydia Sellon's Society of the Most Holy Trinity, established in Devonport in 1848.[84] (Miss Sellon's sisterhood absorbed the Sisterhood of the Holy Cross in 1856.)

Some of the early sisterhoods were notably independent. Miss Lydia Sellon and Miss Hughes had the support of Bishops Phillpotts and Wilberforce respectively, but these right-reverend gentlemen had no final control over the sisterhoods' activities. Bishop Blomfield of London knew almost nothing about the Holy Cross Sisterhood, and one gathers that he preferred it that way. Mother Lydia and Mother Marian were free to shape their communities—in fact, obliged to do so—as they went along, improvising or borrowing from whatever sources were at hand, as the need or the impulse arose.

The same was true of the other communities founded in this period, of course. There had been no sisterhoods in the Church of England since the Reformation; there was no living tradition save the Roman Catholic one observable on the Continent, in Ireland, and in a very few scattered British establishments. The only thing unusual about the Devonport sisters and Mother Marian's sisterhood was that they were governed by women, with Pusey's advice, to be sure, but otherwise independent of ecclesiastical and masculine authority. That was very unusual indeed.[85]

The more common pattern saw new, small religious communities attached to particular parish churches, engaging at first in good works of various sorts within the parish, under the supervision and direction of the clergy. When their activities were extended elsewhere, it was usually at the invitation of some other incumbent who needed help with education, nursing, or social work in his parish. Many of the leading Tractarian parishes soon had sisterhoods attached to them, and many Puseyite clergy doubled as chaplains or wardens or informal overseers of parochial sisterhoods.[86] Thomas Chamberlain of St. Thomas the Martyr, Oxford, for instance, founded the community of the same name in 1851. In that same year, T. T. Carter, rector of Clewer, founded the Community of St. John the Baptist, and Alfred Suckling oversaw the foundation of the Sisterhood of St. Michael and All Angels, attached to his church in Bussage, Gloucester. (Suckling's church had been built in 1846 by a group of undergraduate disciples of Keble and Pusey). Another early foundation was the Community of St. Mary the Virgin, established by W. J. Butler in 1848 to do "rescue work" in his parish of Wantage (not to be confused with the now-defunct community of the same name founded ten years later by the eccentric George Nugee, vicar and squire of Wymering).

The Society of St. Margaret, founded by John Mason Neale at East Grinstead in 1855, was not a parish sisterhood, strictly speaking: Neale's health kept him from accepting parish work and he was the warden of an old almshouse. But the sisterhood was soon called to extend its activities to

J. C. Chambers's parish of St. Mary's, Crown Street, Soho, a well-known center of Anglo-Catholic activity. The Community of the Holy Cross, founded in 1857, was associated with Charles Lowder, working with him first in the slums of St. George's-in-the-East, London, later in his new church of St. Peter's, London Docks. At All Saints, Margaret Street, the vicar, Upton Richards, aided and guided the Society of All Saints, founded about the same time. As the fifties ended, Arthur Douglas Wagner of St. Paul's, Brighton, founded the Community of the Blessed Virgin Mary; Canon John Sharp began the Community of St. Peter to work in his Yorkshire parish of Horbury; and two successive vicars of Coatham oversaw what would become the Community of the Holy Rood.

Many of these communities were administered by strong and able mothers superior, and sometimes it is difficult to assess the relative influence of the mother-foundress and the clerical sponsor. Harriet Monsell of the Clewer sisterhood, Elizabeth Neale of the Community of the Holy Cross, Harriet Brownlow Byron of the All Saints sisters—these women were as important in the histories of their communities as Lydia Sellon and Marian Hughes were in theirs. But sisterhoods that were parochial organizations under clerical supervision were less anomalous than those that Pusey sponsored. They were devoted to education, nursing, and work with orphans and prostitutes—all activities that usefully supplemented the work of parochial clergymen, and all activities that bishops and other observers could only approve.

It is not accidental that the revival of the enclosed, contemplative life first took place within Miss Sellon's community. As early as 1851, one sister began the life of an anchoress, under Pusey's spiritual direction, keeping a rule of perpetual silence for more than twenty-five years. In 1856, the Society established three Orders, or Rules, the second contemplative, "denominated of the Sacred Heart" and known as "The Englishe Nuns." In time, a contemplative emphasis came to characterize the Society as a whole. In the case of sisterhoods under the direct supervision of parochial clergymen, such developments came less often, and later. Some early sisterhoods simply extended the parish work of their clerical sponsors, and some seem to have been almost extensions of their founders' personalities. Their activities and their "culture" varied accordingly.

Nowhere were the founders' personalities more evident than in the sisterhoods' liturgical life. Conservative men sponsored conservative sisterhoods. T. T. Carter of Clewer, for instance, innovated only gradually in his parish church: as late as 1865 he still preached in a black gown. His sisterhood by and large presented the appearance that Bishop Wilberforce desired: "an assembly of pious women devoted to good works ... ladies boarded and lodged together, agreeing as a mutual convenience to observe certain regulations."[87] At the bishop's insistence, the sisters took no vows in the early days. Although their active program of penitentiary work (supplemented in time by teaching and nursing) was built around the recitation of the Divine Office, it was Carter's view that "Sisterhoods should be kept in harmony with Church order," and his sisterhood, at least, was.[88] The Prayer Book was supplemented by a relatively conservative and Anglican diurnal, *The Day Hours of the Church of England*, an 1858 adaptation of the pre-Reformation use of the Diocese of Salisbury (Sarum). Only Prayer Book holy days were observed, early editions omitted such practices as the invocation of saints, and several bishops were known to use the book for their private prayers.

The same book was used at Wantage, where the Reverend W. J. Butler maintained a sober, Tractarian style of worship for his Community of St. Mary the Virgin. Daily celebration was not introduced until 1886, and Butler always doubted the value of non-communicating attendance. Toward the end of his life, Butler described his sisterhood's principles thus: "simple, honest loyalty to the Church to which it belongs, that is the Church of England, the Church of our native land.... We believe that in her Prayer Book her teaching and will are found. We are not desirous to follow our own fancies, or to set forth doctrines and rituals which belong to the Church of Rome. We are satisfied with giving dignity and beauty to that which we have of our own."[89]

Several other sisterhoods organized their lives along similar lines, but a few founders were less determinedly "Church of England" than Butler and Carter, and their sisterhoods reflected it. In Oxford, Marian Hughes reportedly made one of the earliest nineteenth-century Anglican chasubles by sewing two Oxford M.A. hoods together, and it was worn by the Reverend Thomas Chamberlain at St. Thomas the Martyr. When Miss Hughes started the Society of the Holy and Undivided Trinity, she began a translation of the Roman Breviary (eventually completed by Pusey's son) for the use of her community. The Society of All Saints also worshiped with manuscript translations of the Breviary, and its mother-foundress later laid out a garden with shrines to the Virgin and to the Jesuit saint Aloysius Gonzaga. In Wymering, the Reverend George Nugee, a former member of the Cambridge Camden Society, concluded that "Sarum Use" was inconsistent with his hopes for the reunion of Christendom and produced an idiosyncratic adaptation of the "Latin Use" for his sisterhood.[90] (Nugee's Latinizing eventually reached full flower at St. Austin's Priory, for men, in South London.) Another sisterhood notably "Romish" from the outset was the Community of the Holy Cross, associated with Charles Lowder of St. Peter's, London Docks, and founded by Elizabeth Neale.

The liturgical pacesetter, however, was probably the order founded by Miss Neale's brother, the Society of St. Margaret, in East Grinstead. We have already encountered John Mason Neale as one of the undergraduate founders of the Cambridge Camden Society. Before that, he had shown a talent for twitting authority by attempting with some friends to shame the

Fellows of Trinity College into attending chapel, publishing lists of attendance and offering the prize of a handsome Bible for the best record, an
effort some dubbed the "Society for promoting Christianity amongst the
Dons."[91] After his ordination Neale devoted himself to ecclesiology: propagating the Camden Society's principles; editing an early seventeenth-century work that showed families who had taken Church lands at the Reformation cursed with strange accidents, loss of wealth, and failure of male heirs;
and writing a novel, *Ayton Priory*, which laid out his ideas on the monastic
life. The young novelist described the regime of Divine Office and observed
that "in an establishment of this kind, the re-introduction of copes would
come almost naturally."[92]

In 1846 Neale, then aged 28, went to be the warden of an almshouse
in the gift of Lord De La Warr, a fellow member of the Camden Society.[93]
Neale promptly equipped the establishment with what the local vicar called
"gew-gaw Popish chapel ornaments, and a fine belfry of bells, which annoy
me from morning till night." Neighboring Evangelical clergymen wrote the
bishop to complain about Neale's "fancy papistical mountebankism," and it
may not have been wise to set up a twelve-foot-high "Great Rood" in the
chapel and a screen inscribed "Pray for the Founders," or to leave a Roman
Breviary and a Vulgate Bible lying about (even if engaged in liturgical studies).[94]

The story of Neale's relations with his bishop is painful and tedious, but
the result was that Neale was soon inhibited from officiating in the Diocese
of Chichester, an inhibition that Bishop Gilbert accompanied with sorrow-
ful remarks about "spiritual haberdashery" and "imitation of the degrading
superstitions of an erroneous Church."

Neale remained at the almshouse, a private foundation, but he was more
or less continually involved in conflict with neighboring clergy, with inmates,
with assistant wardens, with the Brighton Protestant Association, and with
the Brighton *Gazette*, which editorialized about his "Puseyitical capers" and
attacked the bishop for not being sterner. The poisonous atmosphere was
much the same as that of the many parochial conflicts of the same period:
no accusation was too wild to be believed, and Neale was at one time or
another accused of mistreatment of inmates, forcing inmates to confess to
him, and even arson. There was a great uproar in the early 1850s over
Neale's use of a bier and ornamented palls in the conduct of funerals. The
low point was probably reached in 1851, when a dead woman's relatives and
a mob carried off her coffin to prevent her being buried by Neale, as she had
requested, stopping at an inn to open the coffin to make sure the body was
in it. When a mob of about 150 later tried to burn Neale's house down,
Bishop Gilbert urged him to leave the diocese, but he refused.

In 1855 Neale began the Society of St. Margaret, to provide nursing for
the rural poor. (Its activities soon expanded to include an orphanage in East
Grinstead as well as education and nursing at an outpost in London.) The

next year one of Neale's assistant wardens, at a meeting of the Brighton Protestant Association, accused him of using the almshouse chapel for "secret services with closed doors, the nature of which he refuses to disclose to the Assistant Wardens." "At such times," the man said, "voices are heard inside the chapel, and in looking up at the windows the glimmering of lights burning within is visible." His revelations of a "peculiar smell" like that of incense, of fragments of wafer bread found on the floor, and of "stains on the piscina of some coloured liquid" confirmed his audience's suspicions, and his denunciation of Neale was received with three hearty cheers.[95]

Whatever may have been going on in the almshouse chapel, it could hardly have been more offensive to Protestant sensibilities than what undoubtedly did take place in the Society of St. Margaret's oratory, opened in 1856 in a former carriage-house. Virtually from the beginning, the sacrament was reserved on the oratory altar and the distinctly Roman Catholic rites of exposition and benediction were practiced.[96] (As late as the 1890s these devotions were virtually unknown in parish churches. Even at an Anglo-Catholic stronghold like the Church of the Resurrection, Brighton, benediction was held behind locked doors on a weeknight.[97]) Also from the beginning Neale wore a chasuble to celebrate Mass in the oratory, and by 1858 he had installed the Stations of the Cross. Neale put his erudition to the sisterhood's service, producing service books for its use, taken primarily from the Sarum breviary but (Peter Anson tells us) with "many enrichments from other medieval English Breviaries and from Roman, French, and different continental Office Books."[98]

The sisters' day began with the Litany and Holy Communion (daily from 1856). Neale described the service in a letter as "unlike anything I ever saw in England," and he was certainly right. "At the Offertory of the elements they sing Pange lingua down to Sola fides suffict. Then, immediately after the Consecration, the Tantum ergo."[99] Katherine Warburton later described her first Good Friday at East Grinstead, in 1859. The sisters did not fast but had cross buns and coffee (Neale did not care for what he called the "pseudo-asceticism" of Lydia Sellon's sisterhoods). The oratory was stripped bare, its windows covered with black curtains, the crucifix draped with black. In the morning was the rite of the "Adoration of the Cross," taken from a Roman Catholic source; in the afternoon the sisters made the Stations of the Cross. That Easter, the future Mother Kate observed, Neale censed the altar, which bore four vases of flowers.[100] Sympathetic visitors were sometimes admitted to the sisterhood's services. One night an Orthodox clergyman and a Roman Catholic layman (both Neale's friends) were present.[101]

The founding of sisterhoods continued apace after 1860. The next decade saw a dozen more. There was another independent foundation under Pusey's inspiration (the Society of the Sisters of Bethany, founded by Ethelreda Anna Bennett, devoted from its beginnings to the holding of

retreats) and a bizarre Benedictine community associated with Father
Ignatius, but most followed the usual pattern: a priest-founder, incumbent
of an Anglo-Catholic church, enlisting devout women from his congregation in a sisterhood under his direction.[102] Holy Trinity, Brompton; St.
Michael's, Shoreditch; St. Peter's, Vauxhall; St. Alphege, Southwark—all in
London—as well as churches in Bristol and Exeter were foundations of this
sort. By the end of the century, according to Peter Anson's count, forty-nine
communities for women had been founded in the Church of England. Five
or six had failed or been absorbed by other sisterhoods, but by some reck-
onings there were more sisters in England in 1899 than there had been at
the Reformation.

But the early sisterhoods, those founded in the 1840s and 1850s, had
broken the ground and set the pattern. They were important for the
Anglo-Catholic movement, in two ways. First, those engaged in good works
were doing work that undeniably needed to be done, winning by their
self-sacrifice friends among those they helped and tolerance from others, not
just for themselves but for the form of Anglicanism to which they were so
conspicuously devoted. In the second place, they demonstrated by their very
existence what W. G. Ward had marveled at in Oxford: that one could
believe whatever Roman Catholics believed and do whatever Roman
Catholics did, and yet remain a member of the Church of England.

III

Ritualism Rampant

T he Reverend R. F. Littledale, a prominent Anglo-Catholic controversialist, friend of John Mason Neale and Christina Rossetti, and a fixture on the London Ritualist scene, was certainly in a position to know when he wrote that 1860 "marks the beginning of Ritualism."[1] That would date it from the disturbances at the old London parish church of St. George's-in-the-East, and although ultrarubricians in the provinces were still introducing their characteristic innovations (and getting in trouble for it) much later, it is convenient to let the troubles at St. George's mark the end of one era and the beginning of another.[2]

The Riots at St. George's

When the Reverend Bryan King came to St. George's in 1842, he set out to conform to what he took to be Tractarian standards, which promptly involved him in an utterly typical conflict with his parishioners, one of whom complained at a parish meeting that the rector had "at his mere pleasure disturbed and deranged the beautiful and solemn ceremonial." He compared the new services to a minstrel show, "a Jim Crow sort of buffoonery."[3] For the next seventeen years King struggled along with a parish that was sullenly hostile, when it did not ignore him. But the charge had been laid, and the explosion came in 1859, in a series of disorders that turned St. George's into a public spectacle every Sunday for more than a year.

The occasion for them was trifling. King's disgruntled parish elected a tub-thumping Evangelical to an old lectureship attached to St. George's. King tried and failed to veto the election. The preacher appeared, with a

large crowd, and preached an antagonistic sermon, afterwards reading the
Articles of Religion from the Prayer Book. Reports in the press brought out
the idle, hostile, and bored for the next week's lecture, and they stayed afterwards to disrupt King's evening service. Things went downhill from there.

As each succeeding Sunday brought fresh outrages, the beleaguered
King became an Anglo-Catholic martyr, and the fate of St. George's an
Anglo-Catholic cause. Several dozen High Church gentlemen from outside
the parish came to serve as a bodyguard for the rector; prominent figures in
the party put in an appearance to lend their moral support and to witness
the blasphemy at first hand. When F. G. Lee preached a guest sermon, he
had to contend with "shouting, stamping of feet, slamming of doors,
whistling and striking of lucifer matches." When he came back the next
month, he reported, "walnut shells, orange peels, and small detonating
crackers—some of which were let off during the service—were thrown at
me; and a row of boys to my left in the South gallery ... shot peas at my face
through pea-shooters, so that I was compelled to protect my eyes with the
sleeve of my surplice"—an unanticipated advantage of preaching in a surplice.[4]

Another visitor, Harry Jones, read prayers at the church during the disturbances. Fifteen years later, after he had become rector of St. George's
himself, Jones looked back and reported tongue-in-cheek that the "pervad-
ing sentiment of the assembly was keenly theological." He discovered that
the sight of the red edge on his hymn book could produce "a deep inartic-
ulate growl from all parts of the building." He tested this experimentally
several times: "When I lifted it up, apropos to nothing in the service, the
growl came as surely as sound follows the laying of the hand on the keys of
an organ in full wind." While the surpliced choir and their sympathizers
chanted the psalms at the top of their lungs, "the bulk of the congregation
preferred reading them, which they did in a sort of quarter-deck voice."[5]
Another observer reported that when the choir turned to the east at the
Creed, most of the congregation turned to the west.[6]

But these experiences were relatively mild. King complained in a letter
to the Home Secretary that on other occasions prayer books were thrown,
windows were smashed, carpets were torn up and burnt in the stove,
drugged dogs were turned loose, and someone "made use of a pew (No. 16
in the south aisle) as a water-closet."[7] For six weeks fifty uniformed police-
men were stationed in the church in an unsuccessful attempt to promote
reverence; then they were inexplicably withdrawn. For a month and a half
the bishop closed the church: other than that, every Sunday, month after
month, witnessed similar scenes.

Ostensibly, the quarrel was about King's refusal to abandon the
eucharistic vestments and the intoning of services—both changes demanded by his parishioners. King's initial refusal to comply was seen as pighead-
edness not only by Bishop Tait and a critical press, but even by many High

Churchmen, including Pusey.[8] When King eventually capitulated, however, and agreed to give up the objectionable practices, the riots did not stop. Peace returned to St. George's only when the rector, near collapse, left the parish for a prolonged holiday, leaving early in the morning to avoid the brass band his enemies had hired to escort him to the station.

He did not return. A quieter living was found for him in the peaceable village of Avebury, where, some years later, he consoled himself by reflecting that he had served the Catholic cause.[9]

A Period of Repose

And, in fact, he probably had. Those in the press and the government who had directly or indirectly encouraged the rioters had overreached themselves. The riots galvanized some of the movement's lukewarm allies and forced them into open support. The St. George's Church Defense Association, for example, enrolled a number of prominent High Churchmen not previously (and some not subsequently) identified with the movement.[10] That and other organizations formed at the time soon coalesced into the English Church Union, an institutional development of great importance for the movement.[11] One of the Union's very first resolutions was in support of Bryan King.[12]

Moreover, King believed that the riots shocked some of the movement's opponents into inactivity. Many clergymen told him, he said, that they had been able to make changes without opposition, because their congregations did not want to become "another St. George's."[13] Suspicious Evangelicals never ceased to cry "wolf," but some of the hostile scrutiny that had been directed against the movement was lifted, affording it several years' breathing space during which it could develop without encountering resistance at every turn. In addition, many people, including much of the press, were simply tired of the subject.

Their inattention was encouraged by the fact that, in the wake of the riots, the principal religious excitement was for a time provided by a newly vocal religious liberalism.[14] Individual liberals there always had been, but they began to come together as an organized body of opinion about this time. In 1859, for example, 460 clergymen petitioned for a Royal Commission to consider a number of changes in the Prayer Book, including the discontinuation of congregational use of the Athanasian Creed and observance of saints' days, and the elimination of passages that implied priestly absolution, baptismal regeneration, and "giving of the Holy Ghost by human hands" in ordination.[15] The next year, the publication of a volume called *Essays and Reviews* that questioned the literal inspiration of the Bible and the historicity of miracles led to calls for the resignation of several of its clerical authors.

Hard on the heels of *Essays and Reviews* came a commentary on Romans by Bishop Colenso of Natal, and soon after that, Colenso's commentary on the Pentateuch: the first made it plain that an Anglican bishop did not believe in eternal punishment; the second that the same bishop did not accept the literal truth of the Bible. The bishop of Capetown called a synod that deposed Colenso, but in 1865 the Privy Council, on Colenso's appeal, held the synod's proceedings to be null and void (on procedural, not doctrinal grounds).[16] The year before, hewing to its apparent policy of noninterference in doctrinal matters, the Privy Council's Judicial Committee had held in another case that the Articles of Religion did not require one to believe in the inspiration of "every part of the Scriptures," and that clergymen could legitimately express their hope that even the wicked may be pardoned.[17]

In the face of all this, High and Low Churchmen briefly put aside their differences and allied themselves to resist the inroads of latitudinarianism. After the Privy Council decision, for example, close to five thousand clergymen signed a "Declaration on the Inspiration of the Word of God and the Eternity of Future Punishment," affirming both. The committee that collected the signatures included both High Churchmen, like Pusey and Archdeacon Denison, and Low (the secretary, W. R. Fremantle, would soon become a member of the [anti-Ritualist] Church Association).[18]

The New Anglo-Catholicism

In the mid-1860s, however, public opinion suddenly awoke to find that something very strange had grown up within the Church of England. Seemingly overnight, politicians and journalists discovered that (as a writer in *John Bull* put it) "the most pressing Question of the Day" concerned "*Ritualism* under various aspects."[19] In 1867, the *Edinburgh Review* remarked on the movement's "sudden growth," describing it as "the work almost of the last three years," a development that had "taken the nation and Church by surprise."[20]

No-popery Evangelicals, of course, were not surprised. A writer in the *London Quarterly Review* remarked that the nation was merely seeing the "abundant fruit" of the Romanizing plot "laid in Oxford thirty years ago." He added, however, that now the "sappers and miners have made their way up to daylight, and are openly at work, breaching the defenses of our Protestantism, and tampering with the defenders."[21] Other Low Churchmen noticed the movement's newly aggressive tone. The *Patriot* warned that "England is in jeopardy of witnessing what is styled a Catholic revival."[22]

Anglo-Catholicism had indeed changed. It had become a fighting faith, with the form, apparatus, and program of a national movement; what observers now saw around them was quite different from the churchmanship of the ultrarubricians. On Christmas Eve of 1865 Benjamin Jowett wrote a friend, "If you walked abroad you would be greatly astonished at the

change which has come over the churches of London; there is a sort of aes-
thetico-Catholic revival going on."[23]

The most obvious changes, as usual, were liturgical and decorative, and
private oratories still set the Ritualistic pace. There the higher reaches of
sacramental devotion were being scouted; there could be found processions
with relics, and the Stations of the Cross; there Latin could be heard again
in worship; there the imitation of Roman Catholic practice was most patent.
South of the Thames, for example, at Father Nugee's eccentric St. Austin's
Priory, Jowett could have attended not just a gorgeous High Mass (the Mass
described in *Marius the Epicurean* is said to be an accurate representation of
the normal proceedings at St. Austin's) but a service of Benediction.[24] For
a short time in 1866, Jowett could have visited a Franciscan house in East
London, founded and overseen by Father Basil, otherwise the Reverend R.
Tuke. (The establishment was disbanded when Tuke became a Roman
Catholic the following year, but while it lasted the young men associated
with it wore Franciscan habits in the house, although some removed them
to commute to jobs in the City.[25]) Jowett might also have encountered the
Anglican deacon who called himself Father Ignatius, O.S.B., visiting London from Norwich to raise funds for his strange and ultimately pathetic
attempt to reestablish the Benedictine Order.[26] (An account of one of the
liturgical highlights in Norwich in 1865—the dedication, with incense, of a
cope presented by a Cambridge undergraduate—eventually reached the
floor of the House of Lords.[27])

But, as Jowett observed, extravagant Ritualism was increasingly evident
outside the semisecrecy of religious communities. Practices once confined to
oratories were beginning to appear in public worship. In the summer of
1865, the Marquess of Westmeath complained in the House of Lords about
what he had encountered in visits to several London churches, and the next
year his fellow peer Lord Shaftesbury ventured to one of them to see for
himself.[28] The earl's diary records the following impressions of his visit to
St. Alban's, Holborn:

A *high altar* reached by several steps, a cross over it—no end of pictures. The chancel very large, and separated from the body of the Church by a tall iron grille. Abun-
dance of servitors, &c., in Romish apparel. Service intoned and sung, except the
Lessons, by priests with white surplices and green stripes.... [T]hree priests in green
silk robes, the middle priest having on his back a cross embroidered, as long as his
body.... [S]uch a scene of theatrical gymnastics, of singing, screaming, genuflections,
such a series of strange movements of the priests, their backs almost always to the
people, as I never saw before even in a Romish Temple. Clouds upon clouds of
incense, the censer frequently refreshed by the High Priest, who kissed the spoon, as
he dug out the sacred powder, and swung it about at the end of a silver chain.... The
Communicants went up to the tune of soft music, as though it had been a melodra-
ma, and one was astonished, at the close, that there was no fall of the curtain.[29]

The clergy of St. Alban's even openly (although, of course, privately) heard confessions. An Evangelical minister from Islington had no difficulty finding the appointed time; when he appeared in the confessional and "confessed" to Father Mackonochie his failure to discharge his ordination vow "to banish and drive away all erroneous and strange doctrines," Mackonochie seems to have responded with a measure of dignity.[30]

This "new phase" of the movement "could hardly have been imagined as possible," wrote the *Quarterly Review* in the year of Shaftesbury's visit. Distressing enough were the ever-increasing "novelties of external worship." Worse was that they were "justified by the assertion of principles which [in the movement's early days] had not been discovered, or at least found no champion bold enough to maintain them."[31] The same year, the *Record* charged that Anglo-Catholic doctrines were now "asserted with a boldness at which most High Churchmen would have stood aghast twenty years ago," and the *Clerical Journal* claimed that "the movement has acquired a character likely to shake the Church of England to her foundations."[32]

The Tractarians had expressed their views largely in private or (almost the same thing) in scholarly works of ecclesiology, with the result that the informed theological opposition to Tractarianism had been limited for the most part to clerical, even to learned circles. The *Tracts for the Times* had quickly become "tracts" in name only: the last ten ran a total of nearly thirteen hundred pages.[33] Hurrell Froude's letters and diaries, however indiscreet, had at least been letters and diaries; even edited for publication, they made a book of limited circulation. The Tractarians' inadvertent reserve contributed to accusations of dishonesty when critics discovered what they actually believed, but it also reduced the scope of conflict and the occasions for it. What layfolk in conflict with ultrarubricians really disliked were the ceremonial and decorative changes and some of the cultural baggage that accompanied Puseyism; their complaints about the Puseyites' theological convictions were usually based on hearsay, and sometimes seemed almost an afterthought.

If some did not know what Anglo-Catholics believed, others apparently did not care. "It is not from its Doctrines mainly that the offence of Ritualism has arisen," wrote the Reverend E. W. Sergeant. "These, roughly stated or clumsily expounded, might indeed have startled old-fashioned congregations; there might have been here and there a complaint to the Bishop, or even a scene in church; but ... probably, if there had been no corresponding innovations in Practice, there would have been no riots, or public remonstrances, or suits in law-courts connected with Ritualistic teaching, and no Public Worship Regulation Act." Sergeant observed that it was almost as if Anglo-Catholics had been told, "Preach what you like, but don't show us that you believe it!"[34]

This was not a compromise satisfactory to those who wished to share their strongly held beliefs, and by the 1860s Anglo-Catholic theology was being expressed in forms harder for ordinary folk to ignore. Some of the movement's self-appointed spokesmen became as provocative in their language as in their liturgical practice. Disraeli would later accuse the Ritualists of importing "the mass in masquerade," but there was not much masquerade about it; in a public address in 1866, R. F. Littledale stated his party's position forthrightly: "It is perfectly true that in the case of the Ritualists it is the Mass which is being celebrated. Friends and foes are agreed on that head."[35] Similarly, to the charge that the "Tractarian school ... loses sight of the distinctive doctrines of the Reformation," the Anglo-Catholic *Church Times* replied, "We do not lose sight of them at all. We are busy in hunting them down, and have no intention of foregoing the chase until we have extirpated them."[36] The writer implicitly replied to the charge of dishonesty: "That is plain speaking enough, we trust."

Anglo-Catholics also became increasingly plainspoken and insistent about the symbolic linkage between their beliefs and ceremonial innovation. This, too, was partly in response to what some of them saw as indifference and inattention to their message. In a sermon of 1867, the Reverend John Edwards argued that "the restored Ritual of our own days is the natural and inevitable expression of that deep revival of faith and devotion which began in the University of Oxford about forty years ago." He observed that when the rising clergy had gone out from university, "they strove to teach what they themselves had learnt.... [Y]et it seemed that the response was hardly in proportion to the merits of the men, and that their influence was straitened. It seemed as though the movement were stayed.... [A]t length, it was seen that the Church's Ritual is the best exponent of Her Doctrine."[37] Archdeacon Denison spoke from his own experience when he wrote that he had found, "after many years experience, that Catholic Truth, however carefully taught in the Church, in the School, and from house to house, but not accompanied with its true and appropriate ceremonial, had failed to reach the hearts and influence the lives of my people." He had, he said, "made good the defect," and "the remedy has been largely blessed."[38]

The Popular Theology of the Movement

The "Catholic Truth" being asserted by symbolic ritual and increasingly forceful words was still that of the Tractarians: doctrines regarded as aspects of Catholicism from which the Church of England had unjustifiably fallen away, if not in its Reformation then in the course of its subsequent history. Like their predecessors, the new generation of Anglo-Catholics emphasized baptismal regeneration, the apostolic succession, the sacrament of penance (that is, confession and absolution), and—increasingly—the Real Presence of Christ in the Eucharist, and that sacrament's sacrificial character.

Belief in baptismal regeneration was a mark of High Churchmanship shared by Anglo-Catholics with others in that wing of the Church. That

belief was not required in the Church of England, even for clergymen; the
Gorham decision had established that, and some Anglo-Catholics had left
the Church in consequence. Those who remained were content to be
allowed to believe it themselves, but they believed it no less fervently as the
badge of a party than as a dogma of the Church. In 1850, at the time of the
Gorham case, a distinguished gathering that included Bishop Bagot of Bath
and Wells and many moderate High Churchmen as well as leading
Anglo-Catholics had signed a document reaffirming the Nicene doctrine
and denying the authority of the Privy Council in spiritual matters. When St.
Alban's, Holborn, was consecrated in the 1860s, the original copy of that
document was deposited above the baptismal font, behind the inscription:
"I acknowledge one Baptism for the remission of sins."[39]

Rather less was heard from the new generation than from the Tractarians on the subject of episcopal authority. The new generation of
Anglo-Catholics, like the old, combined high theoretical esteem for bishops
with an uncanny ability to provoke the ones actually existing in the Church
of England. Although an emphasis on the apostolic succession and the view
of holy orders that followed from it also remained hallmarks of High
Churchmanship, the practice of confession continued to spread, and to
some extent it came to replace episcopacy as a rallying-point for
Anglo-Catholics.[40] (Not incidentally, it was an institution that did not
require episcopal approval.) Like belief in baptismal regeneration and the
apostolic succession, confession served as a party badge; unlike those beliefs,
it set Anglo-Catholics apart not only from Calvinists and Liberals, but from
their High Church allies. The confessional, John Kent has written, "drew a
firm boundary round the Anglo-Catholic 'sect', marking off the priests who
heard confessions from those who would not do so, and the congregations
in which confession was possible from those in which it was impossible."[41]

But increasingly the distinguishing doctrinal marks of the movement
were its beliefs concerning the Eucharist, beliefs that were becoming central
to the very definition of Anglo-Catholicism. In 1866 the *Church Times*
remarked, "If there be one dogma which more emphatically than any other
marks off Catholicism from even the very best and purest forms which
Protestantism takes, it is that of the Holy Eucharist. The Real Presence and
the Unbloody Sacrifice are the two hinges of that mystic rite."[42] (Characteristically linking belief to ceremonial practice, the paper added that it was
"all but absolutely certain" that those priests who did not genuflect after the
Prayer of Consecration did not believe in the Real Presence and those who
did not take the eastward position did not believe in the unbloody sacrifice.)
Eucharistic doctrine united old Tractarians like Pusey and Keble with the
younger Ritualists like Mackonochie and Littledale: all four of those men
were among the twenty Anglo-Catholic clerical leaders who signed an 1867
declaration to the archbishop of Canterbury affirming that Christ is "really
and truly," if "spiritually and ineffably," present in the Eucharist, hence that

all who receive the consecrated bread and wine receive Christ's body and blood, and that adoration is due *him*, though not the elements per se.[43]

A number of events during the 1850s had foreshadowed this increasing emphasis on eucharistic doctrine. The titles of two treatises published during that decade, Pusey's *Real Presence* and Keble's *Eucharistical Adoration*, summed up the points at issue. In 1853, Pusey preached on the subject to the university; the same topic had led to his silencing ten years before, but this time it passed unreprimanded. In the same year, Archdeacon Denison began the course of sermons at Wells Cathedral that led to his prosecution, which dragged on until dismissed on a technicality in 1858. By that time, Bishop Forbes of Brechin was in trouble with the other bishops of the Scottish Episcopalian Church for an 1857 charge on the same subject.

Keble made the shift in emphasis explicit shortly before his death in 1866, when he changed the words of his poem on "Gunpowder Treason" in *The Christian Year*. Through ninety-four editions it had read:

> O come to our Communion Feast:
> There present in the heart,
> Not in the hands, th' Eternal Priest
> Will His true self impart.

After 1866, the word "Not" in the third line was replaced by "As."[44]

The point was taken by the movement's adversaries. A handbill offering "Twelve Reasons for Refusing to Join the English Church Union" listed the Union's teaching of the Real Presence as reason number three, and when the Protestant Evangelical Mission and Electoral Union attacked in verse what it saw as "cringing traitors, minions of the Pope, / Mumbling Bible-haters, clad in stole and cope," it asked and answered the question:

> Who consecrates the bread and wine,
> Then lifts them up as *The Divine*,
> And, eke, adores with nasal whine?
> —the Ritualist.

The battle lines were drawn.

It is not necessary here to examine in detail the sources to which the Tractarians and their successors turned in their quest for an authoritative witness to the components of the Catholic faith.[45] Their appeal to such Catholic-minded Anglican divines as Bishop Butler established in their own minds and for purposes of controversy the legitimacy of their views within the post-Reformation Church of England, as a part of the historic High Church party. (A satirical tract of 1842 bore the title "Bishop Butler An avowed PUSEYITE, & suspected CATHOLIC.") But for the Tractarians ultimate authority lay in the "undivided Church"—the Church of the Fathers, of the great Ecumenical Councils, of the undivided East and West, of the first several Christian centuries. This appeal allowed them to reject both the papal claims and the Protestantism that, in their view, was partly an overreaction to Roman errors.

In addition, however, as N. P. Williams has written, once the movement had opened up "the unknown wonder-world of Catholic devotion," it could hardly restrict its followers to the age of the Fathers and forbid them the "gothic romance of the Middle Ages and the barocco splendours of the Counter-Reformation."[46] Had not Tract 90 reconciled such beliefs and practices with the Prayer Book Articles of Religion? Accepting the central doctrines and practices of Catholicism led many to examine the more peripheral ones as well: the cults of the Virgin and the saints and the Sacred Heart, Purgatory and prayers for the dead, images and relics, shrines and pilgrimages.

Only a relative few looked exclusively to contemporary Roman Catholicism for a model. John Mason Neale and others flavored their teaching and practice with adaptations from the Eastern churches, and a large and influential segment of the movement deferred to pre-Reformation "English use" in such questions as whether to use six candles on the altar (Roman) or two (English).[47] (This distinction, of course, simply ignored the judicial decisions holding that any at all were illegal.) But from the days of the gilt-gingerbread school onward a small "advanced" element within the movement practiced, when it dared, what Williams describes as "a kind of truncated Roman Catholicism"—one complete, that is, save for submission to papal supremacy.[48] Opponents of the movement called them "Papists without the Pope," and some were content to accept that characterization.[49]

Some of those who copied Roman models defended what they were doing on ecumenical grounds; they hoped for eventual "corporate reunion" with the Vatican. Some said that they emulated Roman Catholicism because it preserved primitive or medieval practices unwisely or even unlawfully abandoned by the Church of England (and to those who said that nineteenth-century Romanism bore little resemblance to pre-Reformation Anglicanism, the irrefutable response was that Roman practice resembled what English practice would have become if the Reformation had not occurred). Even those who copied Roman models most exactly rarely accepted papal authority, however, and they were to that extent justified when they objected to charges of disloyalty.

The theological position of Anglo-Catholics was in fact hard to maintain consistently, as several tracts by converts to Roman Catholicism pointed out.[50] (Converts *from* Roman Catholicism wrote their own tracts, in reply.[51] And one author, the Reverend Edward Husband, contributed first a tract explaining his conversion to Rome, then one explaining why, a few weeks later, he became an Anglican again.[52]) Even the superficially attractive appeal to the undivided Church was less simple than it sounds. It often involved an element of circularity, as well as some reconstruction of history, and it may be significant that many of the keenest intellects of the movement gave it up, turning to religious liberalism or following Newman to a communion in which the source of authoritative teaching was less a matter for speculation and debate.[53]

But of course the movement's appeal was not entirely intellectual. Unlike the Tractarian leaders, most laypeople and priests with pastoral responsibilities lacked the time, the scholarship, or the inclination to deal seriously with the theological issues involved. A little hymn for children by John Mason Neale could summarize the beliefs of many adults:

> I am a little Catholic
> And Christian is my name,
> And I believe in Holy Church
> In every age the same.
>
> And I believe the English Church
> To be a part of her,
> The Holy Church throughout the world,
> That cannot fail or err.[54]

In practice, loyalty to the undivided Church usually meant little more than what the children of St. Mary Magdalene's, Munster Square, were taught to chant: "If it's new, it's not true."[55] Sabine Baring-Gould expressed the stalwart and serene fundamentalism of the Anglo-Catholic rank and file in "Onward, Christian Soldiers":

> What the Saints established
> That I hold for true.
> What the Saints believèd
> That believe I too.[56]

The new generation's relative indifference to the finer points of doctrine led one of their elders to resign from the English Church Union, complaining that too many in that organization regarded defending the faith of the Church as "a matter of policy or expediency."[57] What he objected to was evident in the attitude some took toward the Athanasian Creed, which the Prayer Book directed to be "sung or said" at morning prayer on thirteen appointed feast days each year (a rubric widely neglected, as for that matter were some of the feast days). Pusey thought the Creed—with its opening words, "Whosoever will be saved, before all things it is necessary that he hold the Catholick Faith"—an indispensable guardian of orthodoxy, and he campaigned tirelessly for its retention. But when a royal commission was established in the 1860s to look into Ritualism, the only Ritualist on the commission, the Reverend T. W. Perry, simply did not share Pusey's conviction that the matter was of vital importance: he was willing to see the Apostles' Creed substituted for it.[58]

Similarly, in 1869, when Pusey vigorously opposed Gladstone's nomination of Frederick Temple to the see of Exeter, it was not surprising that the moderate High Churchmen represented by the *Guardian* supported Gladstone rather than Pusey. But the Anglo-Catholic *Church Times* did not support Pusey either. It did not share his view that installing a contributor to *Essays and Reviews* as successor to Bishop Phillpotts would be a "frightful enormity," and declared Temple to be at least as orthodox as the archbishop of Canterbury (which was admittedly not meant as a compliment).[59] An orthodox bishop would have been delightful, but many Anglo-Catholics had become willing to settle for tolerant ones. More and more were at least temporarily abandoning the original goal of remaking the Church of England and fighting simply to be allowed to exist as a party within it.

The same change was evident in the party's shifting views on the rubrics of the Prayer Book. In 1843, the *Christian Remembrancer* had maintained that clergymen should be forced to observe them, that "uniformity, even without unity, is at least better than discrepancy added to disunion."[60] True to that view, in its first year of existence, 1860, the English Church Union protested (among other things) Evangelicals' irregular use of theaters for mission services and the neglect of the requirement that baptisms be public.[61] By the end of the 1860s, however, a new tone was evident, quite alien to that of dogged obedience to the rubrics. In 1869, for example, Father Mackonochie was pleading for "great latitude in all directions." His sort of churchman, he said, might revive the service of compline, but "why should we grudge to others the use of a prayer meeting, or extempore prayer in one form or other, by which they can best lay hold of the souls of their people?"[62] To be sure, Mackonochie's plea for latitude was not disinterested: he was being prosecuted for ritual irregularities at the time. But he and other Ritualists had indeed come to see the rubrics as unduly confining, even as irrelevant.

The Real Presence

In part, this reflected the increasing centrality of eucharistic doctrine in Anglo-Catholic thought. By the end of the sixties, the ceremonial and decorative changes for which the ultrarubricians had contended were well established. In 1850, only 56 of the 600 or so London churches had offered daily services; by 1870, 132 metropolitan churches obeyed the rubrics on that score. In the same year, 128 London churches offered at least one choral service on Sundays, 137 had a surpliced choir, and 83 had surpliced preachers.[63] Since these practices were generally found together, it appears that something on the order of one London church in five had adopted the outward marks of Tractarianism, although the proportion was certainly smaller elsewhere in England.

But many Ritualists had begun to regard these usages as, after all, relatively unimportant. "Do you not feel that our *daily* Morning and Evening Service as presented by the Prayer Book is comparatively speaking a lifeless and unprofitable task?" asked Edward Stuart of St. Mary Magdalene's, Munster Square. Stuart wanted the rubrics changed to allow solitary celebration of the Eucharist and reservation of the Sacrament.[64] Few in the movement were as eager as Stuart to tamper with the rubrics, recognizing that any change would likely be directed against them, but others certainly shared his sense of the relative importance of the daily offices and the Eucharist. In 1866 a writer in the *Church Monitor* observed that "a choral morning and evening service has become, to a certain extent, popular, and is so far tolerated, even when not enjoyed." But the Eucharist was the Church's central act of worship, and that was where ceremonial belonged, so "we *must* conduct the celebration of the Holy Eucharist with every accompaniment of ritual which our circumstances will permit of."[65]

This changing emphasis was not a matter of introducing new doctrine or discarding old; rather, it was a process of differentiation between important and unimportant. As the *Quarterly Review* observed in 1866, it was "no longer a question of surplice against gown as the dress of preachers in parish churches, of a weekly offertory, or of reading or omitting the prayer for the Church Militant." Instead, "vestures and ornaments are revived, ceremonies are practiced, which no one had ventured on [before]."[66]

The energies that once had gone to defend faldstools and intoned prayers were increasingly concentrated on the defense of eucharistic ceremonial. George Rundle Prynne's *Eucharistic Manual* of 1866, for instance, advocated vestments, two altar lights, incense, and a cross on or above the altar.[67] Many also saw wafer bread, the mixed chalice, and the singing of the Benedictus and Agnus Dei as necessary, or almost so.[68] Father Mackonochie held that altar lights, the eastward position, "some veils," and ceremonial ablutions were essential, and eucharistic vestments at least desirable; when he was taken to court in 1867, the charges against him included the use of incense and altar lights, mixing and elevation of the chalice, and "excessive kneeling" during the Prayer of Consecration.[69] (The case was heard before Sir Robert Phillimore, an urbane High Churchman, with much jocular discussion about degrees of inclination, puns about being "incensed," and so forth.)

Eventually, in 1875, the English Church Union adopted what came to be known as the "Six Points"—the eucharistic vestments, the eastward position, altar lights, the mixed chalice, wafer bread, and incense—thereby making formal what had become a consensus on the points of ceremony worth fighting for.[70] The legal status of these practices was unclear, and always subject to change; their advocates claimed, however, that all of them were linked symbolically to doctrine. As the Reverend James Skinner had put it a few years before, "Wheresoever the Blessed Eucharist has been restored to its due and fitting prominence in Christian worship, there it has become, or it is gradually becoming, *inevitable* to invest the Eucharistic worship with those accessories of ceremonial which are the appointed and fitting tokens of its grandeur."[71]

In fact, in the 1860s and 1870s, belief in some form of the Real Presence was far more widespread than the ritual that was said to symbolize it. As late as 1869 only fourteen London churches regularly employed the eucharistic vestments; only eleven had daily communion services; a mere eight burned incense.[72] But if practice lagged behind in all but a few flagship churches, theory advanced apace. Some began to argue that the Eucharist should be the principal service every Sunday. Attending a service of morning prayer and sermon, one writer argued, was a "shabby and selfish practice" of people who "think more of their own gratification"—that is, from hearing sermons—"than their duty as ransomed children of their Heavenly Father."[73] There should be a celebration at least weekly; daily, if possible.[74]

Communion, it was said, should be received fasting, as a sign of respect and a link with primitive and contemporary Catholic practice. Thus there should be early communion services on Sunday, and the principal service should be a High Mass, with few or no communicants other than the celebrant.[75] This, of course, was also consistent with the practice of the "Western Church."

If ritual were merely a question of taste and good order, compromise might be possible, or at least adjudication by secular authorities would not be sacrilege. So, again and again, well-meaning moderates tried to untangle ceremonial and doctrine. Many who held the doctrines, including Pusey himself, doubted that the link to ceremonial was really self-evident, and urged restraint. (On the other hand, at least one moderate High Churchman, a canon of Exeter, rather liked the ceremonial but had qualms about the doctrines; he appealed to the "mind and practice of the *first ages*" both to defend the use of eucharistic vestments and to deny Pusey's and Keble's views on the Real Presence.[76])

But the most fervent advocates of enhanced ceremonial were having none of it. "Ritual and ceremonial … are the signs of realities or they are nothing," said a former curate of St. Barnabas, Pimlico, in an 1865 lecture. "They are no mere accident to religion. They belong to the very substance of religion. They are not the mere adjuncts and decorations of religion. They are the natural and spontaneous exhibition of religion."[77] A popular expression had it that ritual was an "outwork," defending doctrine. The Reverend M. W. Mayow put it that way to a public meeting in Brighton, and he drew the implications: attacks on ceremonial amounted to attacks upon doctrine itself. As Mayow saw it, agitation to amend the rubrics against the Ritualists was intended "not merely to put down vestments, or put out candles, or extinguish incense; but to drive out of the Church of England the whole doctrine which those things represent; to expel every one, whether Ritualist or not, who holds and teaches it; to run riot in the destruction of every vestige of faith in the Real Presence, in the Priesthood, the Altar, and the Sacrifice."[78]

Mayow was certainly right about the movement's Evangelical opponents, who were quite candid about why they objected to the Ritualists' eucharistic practices. The principal of Cheltenham College said that he had to oppose the "external aspect" of Ritualism, despite its "accordance with the great aesthetic movement of our time," because "it is avowedly intended to assert a special form of doctrine, and on that assertion it must be judged."[79] Suppose the doctrine of the Real Presence to be true, another Evangelical said: "How consistently spring from and gather round that supposition the elaborate turnings to the East and repeated prostrations, the elevated altar and super-altar, with their gorgeous decorations and candles, the peculiar and strangely unnatural postures, the crossed arms and hands, the fear even to touch the elements, the elevation of the consecrated bread, and the silent pauses for adoration."[80]

The ultra-Protestant journal *The Rock* made a similar point, observing that

birettas, wafers, mixed chalice, elevation, prostration, eastward position &c., &c., ... do really involve the whole question for which the battle of the Reformation was fought. Is the Great KING objectively present on our "altars"—under whatever form—or is He not? If He *is* so present at the bidding of a "priest" then it behooves us to go softly and bow down in lowly adoration before His footstool. No service can be too solemn, no accessories too costly or magnificent for so august an occasion. Bring forth the royal vessels, and make the tabernacle of His feet glorious. Let clouds of incense ascend before His throne. Let us come into His courts with thanksgiving. Let the singers go before and the minstrels follow after. Let His priests be decked in the most sumptuous apparel, and let all things testify to our sense of the KING's condescension in visiting His people and to our desire to give Him the honour due unto His name. Such we know is the Roman (or sacerdotal) theory, perfectly consistent and coherent throughout, *if only it were true.*

(A Ritualist pamphlet reprinted this observation with statements on the Real Presence by sixteenth and seventeenth-century Anglicans, including Ridley and Latimer.[81])

Dean Close of Carlisle, an opponent of the movement since the days of the Cambridge Camden Society, preached in 1866 at St. George's, Bloomsbury: "There is not a dress, nor a decoration, nor a ceremony now revived among us, but it has a symbolic import, a *sacrificial* character!" he observed.

Why an *altar* ... if not for a sacrifice? Why incense, if no sacrifice? Why the veneration of the elements, the bowing and cringing and curtseying towards the holy table?
Why the superstitious reverence to the priest, if he be not a sacrificing, atoning, inter-
ceding, absolving priest?... The whole paraphernalia of modern Ritualism is but a
flimsy and transparent veil imperfectly concealing the deadly worship of the mystic
idol beneath—the *sacramental deity.*

The controversy, Close said, was not "a mere dispute regarding certain
ceremonies and decorations; above all, the question is, whether the Holy
Communion is or is not a repetition of the *real sacrifice of Christ's own body
and blood.*"[82] Give or take a nuance or two, his adversaries agreed that was
indeed the question. As the Broad Church author of *Orthodox London*
remarked, the Ritualist "does protest, and that with justice, against the idea
that ceremonial is everything, or even the principal thing, in his worship. Its
essence is the doctrine of the Real Presence in the Eucharist. Accept that,
and an ornate ritual follows as a thing of course."[83]

No, the problem was not one of misunderstanding. "On the one side,"
as Archdeacon Denison of Taunton observed, "are the 'Ritualists;' on the
other the denouncers of 'Ritualism.' It is surely contrary to reason, as to fact,
to say of either of these two classes of men that the active significance which
it attaches to 'Ritual' is *any other* than a 'doctrinal significance,'—or again,
that the doctrinal significance which they do attach is not to both of them
of the *deepest import.*"[84] The Ritualists could plausibly assert that opponents
of their eucharistic ritual were actually attempting to suppress their beliefs
because some of the most persistent and conspicuous certainly were. The
Ritualists themselves had ensured as much, by linking their ceremonial
securely to Anglo-Catholic doctrine.

As we shall see, many others, who cared very little what the Ritualists
believed, disliked both ritual and Ritualism. But to the considerable extent
that Anglo-Catholics were able to cast the issue as one of their right to their
beliefs, they won a measure of sympathy and support both from High
Churchmen who largely agreed with them and from others who simply felt
that those who held such beliefs should not be drummed out of the Church
of England.

A Working Religion

The movement's growing disaffection from the rubrics also reflected
many Ritualists' vital concern with evangelism. Father Mackonochie and
others like him were not at all indifferent to the Church's law (properly
interpreted, of course); for many, however, their genuine interest in services
that could lay hold of souls took precedence. They valued popular services,
whether contemplated by the Prayer Book or not. Some of the Ritualists'
unauthorized innovations were adapted from Roman Catholic sources and
were part of a larger pattern of imitation, but others were plainly devised and

adopted simply because they worked. The Harvest Festival (now almost universal in the Church of England) was apparently an Anglo-Catholic innovation, for example, as was the Three Hours' devotion on Good Friday.[85]

This concern with efficacy spilled over to cover the entire range of Ritualistic practice. As R. F. Littledale put it: "The religion we teach is an old one, and the condition of society round us is in many ways curiously like that old heathen Roman Empire which the small despised knot of Christians converted. The newfangled ways have all failed, and we think it worth while to try the old ones again. They succeeded thoroughly once, and they may not have lost their virtue yet."[86] With this argument, the Ritualists tried to enlist in their defense the national veneration of "common sense" that usually worked to their disadvantage. "We not only deny that Ritual is contrary to common sense," wrote C. J. LeGeyt, "but on the grounds of common sense we take our stand." He argued, in effect, that the "ways and customs of our fathers" were efficient tools.[87] By the sixties, Ritualists were offering oddly modern, pragmatic justifications for a great many of the old ways: for celibacy, as freeing men and women for mission work; for the sign of the cross, as a mechanism for autosuggestion; even for the rosary, as a mnemonic device.[88]

In pursuit of ways to bring people to church and to instruct them once they were there, the movement parted from its "High and Dry" heritage and did not hesitate to adopt even practices that would formerly have been scorned as "methodistical": indeed, Bishop Blomfield is said to have used that word when he censured Charles Lowder's curate, Henry Collins, for his hymns "Jesu, My Lord, My God, My All" and "Jesu, Meek and Lowly." (Blomfield, it is reported, found the hymns "contrary to the spirit of the Book of Common Prayer." Collins subsequently became a Roman Catholic and took the Trappist vow of silence.[89]) This new High Church methodism could also be observed in the rise and spread of Anglo-Catholic revivalism and in what even Bishop Ellicott, no friend of the movement, acknowledged was "almost a new tone of preaching," one of "home truths, set forth and enforced in soul-searching language."[90] A number of Ritualist clergymen, even (by some accounts, especially) Father Ignatius, were able and effective evangelists, resuscitating what could be seen as an Anglo-Catholic tradition since Newman, although one largely neglected by the ultrarubricians.[91]

But Bishop Blomfield picked the right target. Nowhere did the movement's evangelistic appeal find better expression than in its great hymns. It sometimes seems that almost every Ritualist clergyman had a go at hymn writing, and a number of them were remarkably good at it. Evangelicals protested the "sacerdotal error" their verses embodied (John Mason Neale's were accused of "administering popery in homeopathic doses"), and sometimes these critics had a point.[92] "The Fisherman's Song" by F. G. Lee, for example, published in 1866, contained the startling lines, "Mother of God, all pure, ... / Plead for us, pray for us."[93] (In 1879, Lee received an honorary doctorate from Washington and Lee College for his poems, although presumably not for that one.[94]) But Protestant objections were largely in vain: dozens of Anglo-Catholic hymns made their way into hymnals used by churchmen of all persuasions.

They are still there. The 1940 hymnal of the American Episcopal Church, for example, includes settings of verses from Keble's *Christian Year* ("New Every Morning is the Love," "Sun of My Soul, Thou Saviour Dear"); hymns by Newman ("Lead, Kindly Light") and Isaac Williams; and Frederick Oakeley's familiar translation of "O Come, All Ye Faithful."[95] But although these Tractarian elders set the pattern, the movement's second and third generations clearly surpassed their predecessors, in this one area at least. The same book includes single hymns by Henry Collins (the censured "Jesus, My Lord, My God, My All"), Benjamin Webb ("O Love, How Deep, How Broad, How High"), George Rundle Prynne ("Jesus, Meek and Gentle"), and Christina Rossetti ("In the Bleak Midwinter"); two by the American Anglo-Catholic John Henry Hopkins (one of them "We Three Kings"); three by Sabine Baring-Gould ("Through the Night of Doubt and Sorrow" and "Now the Day is Over," as well as "Onward, Christian Soldiers"); and four by R. F. Littledale (including his translation from a fifteenth-century source of "Come Down, O Love Divine").

But the largest individual contribution to the American hymnal is from the indefatigable John Mason Neale: his total of thirty-nine hymns includes his translations of sources ranging from St. John of Damascus ("Come Ye Faithful, Raise the Strain") to Peter Abelard ("O What Their Joy and Their Glory Must Be"). Many of these hymns and others are set to tunes by composers more or less closely associated with the movement: John Bacchus Dykes, for example, who wrote more tunes in the 1940 hymnal than any other single composer, and Richard Redhead, a major figure in the revival of plainsong.[96]

In hymnody, the "subtractarians" not only outperformed their predecessors, they simply overwhelmed their Low and Broad Church competitors. Against the Anglo-Catholic profusion, the 1940 hymnal includes only a scattering of hymns from Broad Churchmen (Charles Kingsley's "From Thee All Skill and Science Flow" is one, and Dean Stanley's "The Lord is Come! On Syrian Soil" another) and even fewer from Victorian Evangelicalism (one rare specimen is E. H. Bickersteth's "Peace, Perfect Peace").[97]

Anglo-Catholicism, as R. F. Littledale's obituary later put it, had "ceased to be a mere 'Oxford' Movement—an academical speculation, a luxury of culture, an entertainment of colleges and country parsonages, the possession of priests and clerical laymen—and [had become] the property of the crowd"—or, at any rate, *a* crowd.[98] It had become a working religion, an enterprise embodying a great deal more than simply a set of doctrines. What had begun as a school of theology, then an ecclesiastical faction, had finally emerged as a full-fledged social movement.

IV

Anglo-Catholicism as a Social Movement

In 1866 Bishop Ellicott of Gloucester and Bristol preached against Ritualism, condemning Anglo-Catholicism's "growing disloyalty to our Prayer Book." Nevertheless, he observed, the movement had come to be "shared in, and often very warmly shared in, by our Christian laity." He feared that "we can no longer conceal from ourselves that whole congregations are now clearly expressing their sympathies with the widening development, and by their very earnestness and devotion so far tending, not only to enhance, but to commend it."[1]

The support of these Anglo-Catholic laypeople was of great significance. Some brought money and political influence that could be mobilized on behalf of the movement, but at least as important is that all of them, by their very existence, helped to undercut the argument that the movement was a clerical conspiracy against the laity. Certainly Anglo-Catholicism emphasized clerical authority; just as certainly, some laypeople came to accept that authority, at least in principle, and even to glory in it.

Hand in hand with this increase in lay support went an elaboration of the movement's distinctive culture and the growth of a network of supporting institutions. Some argued that these developments were unworthy deviations from the serious theological and ecclesiastical concerns of the movement's Oxford fathers. That view requires us to ignore nearly all of the Tractarians some of the time and some of the Tractarians all of the time, but perhaps there is a sense in which it is true. Still, something of the sort appears to be necessary for the growth and success of any popular movement—certainly of any movement that defines itself as a movement of opposition.[2]

And Anglo-Catholicism did that. Many historians of the movement have remarked on its "sectarian" nature, on its members' "keen[ness] to create lines of demarcation between themselves and others, to speak of 'we' and 'they' even with reference to those within the Anglican Church."[3] At the time, the vicar of St. John's, Hammersmith, complained about those in his movement who "value particular practices just because [they are] party badges" and who constantly "devise some new fangled practice that shall serve to distinguish them as partisans." He assailed the "evil spirit that induces us to strain every nerve to maintain some distinctive practice, as long as it is disallowed by those from whom we choose to differ; but as soon as the point is conceded, [leads us to] seek out something new whereby to proclaim that we differ from our brethren."[4]

He meant well, but he rather missed the point. One of the movement's opponents came closer to understanding when he remarked that vestments and the like "represent the stern belief of those who uphold them, as truly as a scrap of fluttering silk upon a stick represents the sentiment and devotion of an army."[5] Such martial imagery was appropriate for a fighting faith, and by the 1860s it was perfectly evident that, for some time at least, Anglo-Catholics were to be an embattled band of partisans within the Church of England. Even Christian soldiers need badges, both as symbols of what they are struggling for and to identify one another in combat, and the emerging subculture of Anglo-Catholicism incorporated a great many practices that served—sometimes intentionally, sometimes not—to set Anglo-Catholics apart from other Anglicans.

Ritual as a Party Badge

As we have seen, Tractarian clergy and their successors could be easily and positively identified by what they wore and did in church. Time and again, seemingly insignificant practices took on meanings as badges of theological party (although which badges identified which party was subject to change). Lord Halifax, the longtime president of the English Church Union, was aware of this. "Lights and vestments, etc.," he said, looking back, "were only valuable as proofs that those who used them believed the same thing."[6] He overstated his case—the historical, ecumenical, and symbolic connotations of these practices were important, too—but they did identify Anglo-Catholic churches and clergy. Moreover, in time, the movement's most adamant opponents developed badges of their own, if only by resisting change.

As we saw, there were distinctive Tractarian insignia. In particular, as an early historian of the Oxford Movement observed, "one of the earliest notes of the practical results of the Church Movement" was the restoration of daily morning and evening prayer.[7] Some grumbled about "multiplication of services" when ultrarubricians began to implement the rubrics in this regard ("Too frequent repetition palls," said one critic); but since the Prayer Book clearly ordered such services, no one could argue that they were not doing their duty.[8] No one had to attend these services, and most of England did not. But attracting worshippers was not entirely the point: one reason for guides to churches where daily services were available (one such guide suggested) was that "the parish priest manfully standing alone in the practice of daily service in the midst of passive carelessness, or active opposition, will be encouraged to find how many of his brethren persevere in the same holy duty."[9]

Throughout the century, daily morning and evening prayer continued to distinguish Anglo-Catholic churches, although many churches of other complexions eventually followed suit, especially after lawfulness and obedience became weapons to be used against Anglo-Catholics rather than ones they could use effectively against their opponents. During the 1870s and 1880s, the practice spread to nearly a third of London-area churches, roughly the same proportion (and usually the same churches) as those with floral decorations on the altar.[10] The frequency of these relatively inoffensive Anglo-Catholic usages increased at a rate somewhat faster than the increase in the number of churches: the number of London churches with daily services doubled between 1860 and 1870.[11]

But the practice of celebrating Holy Communion at least weekly was spreading even faster, consistent with the movement's growing emphasis on eucharistic doctrine. In 1860, slightly fewer than half of the London churches with daily services also had weekly communion; ten years later, five out of six did so.[12] In fact, by the end of the sixties, weekly communion had become more common in London churches than daily morning and evening prayer, and in 1870 twenty London churches (nearly all Ritualist strongholds) celebrated the Eucharist *daily*.[13]

At the same time, a number of other practices clearly ceased to be infallible marks of Anglo-Catholicism. As late as 1870, special services on holidays, a surpliced choir, and an "offertory" every week were found almost exclusively in Anglo-Catholic churches, but soon after that these practices spread to moderate High Church congregations, many of which had already adopted the eastward position during the Prayer of Consecration, at least in part as a deliberate response to Evangelical attacks on the practice as symbolizing the Real Presence. By the 1870s one observer could specifically mention choral services and surpliced choirs as practices that had passed from the category of uses "of a contentious complexion" to "the class of self-adjusting questions" (that is, matters of taste and local custom), and another had caricatured the movement's opponents as saying, "Let us ... have choral services, but no tomfoolery."[14]

Not coincidentally, the younger Ritualists had little interest in such Tractarian innovations as these, in part because they had little relation to eucharistic doctrine, but also, we must suspect, because such things had become unexceptionable adjuncts to worship for all but the movement's most zealous opponents. By the 1880s these practices were found in a majority of Anglican churches in London and no longer served as reliable badges of Anglo-Catholic orthodoxy. Ironically, the *absence* of some was taking on a party significance—as a sign of extreme Evangelicalism.

Marks of Evangelicalism

For, of course, the Low Church had party badges, too: in most cases, simply practices that Evangelicals clung to longer than other churchmen. In 1880, E. H. Bickersteth, a prominent Evangelical soon to become a bishop, urged his brethren to adopt choral services, surpliced choirs, floral decorations, and more frequent communion, if their congregations desired them. These things were not un-Protestant, Bickersteth argued; they were, "as men say, in the air!"—evident even in Dissent and the Church of Scotland—and it was a mistake to identify them with Anglo-Catholicism. "May God grant us to try things that differ, and approve things that are excellent!"[15] Many Evangelicals, however, viewed all such innovations as tainted by their initial association with Puseyism and resisted them long after Anglo-Catholics had lost interest in promoting them.

This was notably the case with a practice that had been the subject of violent dispute in the 1840s and 1850s: preaching in a surplice rather than changing to a black gown. The antagonism that simple innovation once produced among Evangelicals is nonsensical if we do not recognize that the surplice was initially "the white badge of the Tractarian party" (as some aggrieved parishioners complained to Bishop Phillpotts).[16] "Nothing could be more indifferent in itself," Charles Wood's father observed—indeed, he recalled surpliced preachers from long before, but generally because they could not afford black gowns. He recognized, however, that, "as a symbol," the surplice had acquired a party meaning.[17] Evangelicals agreed: eleven Islington incumbents who declined to obey the bishop of London's 1842 injunction to wear the surplice were careful to point out that they had no intrinsic objection to the garment, but that it had become "a party badge, behind which were to be found all other objectionable innovations."[18] Anglo-Catholics were not the only members of the Church of England who believed that the surplice was clearly required by the rubrics of the Prayer Book, but even High Church bishops backed down in the face of opposition to it.

By the seventies, however, the surplice had lost most of its meaning of thirty years before, and consequently much of its appeal to younger Anglo-Catholics, who were likely by then to urge preachers to wear copes. It had no relation to the eucharistic doctrine that was increasingly the ground of conflict between the movement and its opponents, and the black gown was awkward garb for those who were calling for the Ritualists to obey the law; so when a different bishop of London called again for the use of the surplice, in 1871, his request was widely honored.[19] The number of London area churches where the surplice was worn for preaching more than trebled between 1870 and 1872. By 1876, a majority of London preachers complied, and one ecclesiastical journalist reported that "the academic gown of ancient times [had] ceased to be a symbol with any but very lag-behind Evangelicals."[20] By the 1880s, fewer than a third of metropolitan churches had begowned preachers.

That most of these churches were Evangelical strongholds is indicated by the fact that they also offered evening services of Holy Communion. That practice was the exception to the rule that Evangelicals resisted innovation: many took that one up enthusiastically, especially when, in time, it became highly offensive to Anglo-Catholics, who believed that communion should be received fasting. Ironically, although evening communion was, as one clergyman put it, "in fact, a Bible protest against the Ritualistic doctrine of the Real Presence," such services were initially introduced by High Churchmen.[21] In 1851, a committee of the Leeds Ruridecanal Chapter chaired by Dr. Hook, the High Church vicar of Leeds, had recommended such celebrations as convenient for the poor. At first, the practice had no party significance; indeed, the editor of the *English Churchman*, a Tractarian organ, specifically approved. The next year, evening celebrations were begun in Leeds and Birmingham, but the practice spread only slowly during the 1850s and 1860s. As late as 1869, only sixty-five of the 620 churches in London offered such services.[22]

Soon thereafter, however, the practice of evening communion became a party badge, and it must be said that the Anglo-Catholics made it one. In the early 1870s, Anglo-Catholic controversialists produced an enormous pamphlet literature opposing evening communion on every conceivable ground. Canon Bright wrote three articles in the *Literary Churchman*, reprinted as a pamphlet, "Evening Communions Contrary to the Church's Mind, and Why."[23] H. P. Liddon entered the fray with "Evening Communions Contrary to the Teaching and Practice of the Church in All Ages [etc.]."[24] For every Evangelical who pointed out that Jesus instituted the sacrament "after supper," there was an Anglo-Catholic scholar to argue that "it is, to say the least, more than probable that the Institution took place after midnight," or to point out that since the Jewish day begins at sunset the Last Supper took place first thing on Friday.[25]

One immediate result of the polarization produced by this controversy was that the number of London churches with evening communion doubled between 1869 and 1871, and doubled again by the end of the decade.[26] By then it had clearly become a mark of Evangelicalism, and an anti-Ritualist pamphleteer happily acknowledged that "the Evangelical party of the present day have wisely endeavored to restore the primitive practice," and affected to be disturbed by references to it in the Anglo-Catholic press as "this abomination," "this accursed thing," and "an offensive and profane badge of a party."[27]

Advanced Anglo-Catholics, of course, recognized that the established practice of communion at midday was also ordinarily inconsistent with fasting reception, and they began to insist that communion should be received at early morning services, with no communicants other than the celebrant at the later service. "All you who make midday Communions," a tract of about 1870 urged, "go to Churches where such a practice is common and encouraged. Don't come to our Catholic Churches to flaunt your Protestant spirit of disobedience."[28] By then, the nature of any given church could be precisely determined not only by the ornamentation and elaboration of its services but even by their scheduling.

The Culture of Anglo-Catholicism

Anglo-Catholics could also often be identified outside the liturgical setting. Many took pains to ensure that this was so. W. J. Conybeare wrote in 1853 that describing the Tractarian clergy would be a waste of time: "Their peculiarities have been made familiar to all, by the pen and pencil of innumerable satirists."[29] For a time, merely wearing black in one's ordinary dress—even just a black necktie—was a mark of Tractarianism. A broad-brimmed felt hat indicated similar tendencies.[30] But by the 1850s there was virtually a Puseyite uniform: "Who does not recognise, when he meets them in the railway or on the street, the clipped shirt-collar, the stiff and tie-less neckcloth, the M.B. coat and cassock waistcoat, the cropped hair and unwhiskered cheek?" Conybeare asked.[31] ("M.B." was ecclesiastical tailors' shorthand for "Mark of the Beast," a label taken up with amusement by Anglo-Catholics themselves.)

But the party significance of clergymen's garb, like that of their ritual practices, had a tendency to wander. By the end of the century, one observer tells us, the broad-brimmed hat had come to indicate "mild Anglican views," and the M.B. waistcoat had become "almost the badge of an Evangelical."[32] By then, many younger Anglo-Catholic clergymen had adopted long straight coats resembling cassocks, with jampot collars and the ordinary silk hats of English gentlemen—or Roman Catholic priests.[33] From its beginning the Society of the Holy Cross apparently required those attending its synod to wear cassock, surplice, and biretta, and in 1866 the Society's *Directory for Priests* included suggestions for the private dress of clergymen.[34]

Conybeare mentioned the unwhiskered cheeks of Anglo-Catholic clergymen, and, when he wrote, facial hair or its absence was indeed significant. In the 1850s, most Tractarians favored a clean-shaven, ascetic look. At the opening of Cuddesdon College, a young seminarian complained that the occasion was spoiled by the fact that an officiating priest was bearded and married; when the Reverend A. D. Wagner was beaten and thrown in a Brighton sewer during a controversy over confession, one of his adversaries observed with satisfaction that "Puseyites will poke their *smooth chins* into all kinds of filth."[35]

As late as the 1880s no-popery pamphlets retailed "The Song of the Ritualist Priest":

> With face all shaven and shorn,
> With crucifix over his head,
> The priest he stood in the Protestant church
> A-blessing his wafer bread....[36]

But by then whiskers, too, had lost their party meaning among Anglo-Catholics, becoming, if anything, a mark of generation and of faction within the movement. Dean Church believed that the younger men he encountered at Keble's funeral in 1866—"Mackonochie, Lowder, and that sort"—regarded his generation as "rather *dark* people, who don't grow beards and do other proper things."[37] As a matter of fact, neither Mackonochie nor Lowder wore a beard, but the point is clear enough.

From the start, Anglo-Catholic clergy not only looked different, but sounded different as well. After describing the Puseyite's appearance, Conybeare asked: "Who does not know that the wearer of this costume, will talk of 'the Holy Altar,' and 'the Blessed Virgin,' of 'Saint Ignatius Loyola,' and 'Saint Alphonso de Liguori?' And that he will date his letters on 'the eve of St. Chad,' or 'the Morrow of St. Martin?'"[38] Unlike clerical dress, this special vocabulary was something lay initiates could share with their clergy. As early as 1843, the novelist Francis Paget made fun of his fellow "disciples of the Tractarian school" who wrote notes to their tailors and greengrocers dated "The morrow of the Translation of the Bones of St. Symphorosa," and Conybeare even reported an unsuccessful attempt to rename the days of the week: "Ascension Day" for Thursday, "Passion Day" for Friday, and so forth.[39]

Liturgical terms, of course, offered ample opportunity for the display of esoteric knowledge, and simply knowing what some of them meant could be a sign of party affiliation. "Let any one take up a periodical devoted to 'High Church Matters,'" complained one self-described "Benighted Layman" in 1867,

and he will find terms and expressions ... with the very meaning of many of which he is altogether unacquainted. Instead of the old-fashioned morning and evening service, he will read of "Matins," "Evensong," and "Compline," with "High Celebration," and "Low Celebration." He will find himself in a most lamentable state of ignorance as to the "Vigils," and "Octaves," and festivals of saints whose names he never heard of; whilst the description of the "vestments" used for the getting up of the priests will almost take away his breath. [He] will find requisite at various times and for various purposes the "Albe," "Amice," "Cope," "Cassock," "Tunic," "Tunicle," "Chasuble," "Dalmatic," "Rochet," "Chimere," "Zucchetto," "Cotta," and "Maniple," with a "Stole," a "Cincture," and a "Biretta" to complete the ecclesiastical costume.[40]

Many of these terms, of course, like the ornaments and practices they designated, were borrowed wholesale from Roman Catholicism, and the borrowing seems to have begun quite early in the movement's history. One of the complaints leveled against Miss Sellon's Devonport Sisters in 1849, for instance, was that they addressed Pusey as "Father."[41]

Pusey himself was concerned about the effects of another common indicator of advanced views. Quoting his disciple H. P. Liddon, Pusey observed, "The use of the word 'Mass' [has] alienated thousands who ought to belong to us."[42] Other conservative Tractarians shared Pusey's misgivings, and some added an element of distaste. Charlotte Yonge, for example, in *The Three Brides* (1876), criticized the way certain "technically reverent" young ladies "discuss High Mass, as they are pleased to call it!"[43] Sometimes this phrasing could produce incongruous results, as when one fashionable young Anglo-Catholic gentleman spoke, to his friends' amusement, of "going to Mass" at one of the Chapels Royal.[44]

Yet the movement's avant-garde were prepared to suffer for their peculiar words. In the late seventies, when the membership list of the Society of the Holy Cross was purloined and published and many of the brethren were exposed to unwelcome attention, a committee of the society recommended removing words like "Mass" and "intention" from the society's statutes, but Mackonochie and others held their ground: the words remained, although about seventy of the society's three hundred or so members did not.[45]

In the matter of personal appearance, lay Anglo-Catholics did not have as much to work with as clergymen, but many did what they could to make themselves known to one another and to outsiders. We have already recorded complaints about "cross-bearing service-books"; Paget criticized those who wore "not crosses only, but crucifixes as conspicuously as possible."[46] Another observer claimed that Anglo-Catholics seemed "to parody the words of St. Paul, 'God forbid that I should glory save in the Cross.'" The sign had become so common among them, he said, "that it degenerates into brooches, eardrops, and book-markers."[47] Fifty years later, the vicar of Gorsley, Gloucestershire, was still complaining that "crosses have been introduced into Protestant churches and cemeteries, on the covers of Prayer Books, and elsewhere, by the Puseyites"—although by then that complaint was as passé as the word "Puseyite."[48]

Anglo-Catholics also set themselves apart from their fellow churchmen by their frequent fasting and conspicuous Lenten observance. The same gentleman who went to Mass at the Chapel Royal also vowed each year to give up something that he never ate again—partridges one year, oranges the next—which must have made him a troublesome dinner guest.[49] And, of course, the movement's lay adherents were even easier to identify in church than at dinner parties. In the 1840s Paget criticized those who made themselves "conspicuous in externals; bowing, and crossing, and performing all manner of notable antics."[50] The young ladies of whom Miss Yonge complained "startled the whole place with their curtsies and crossings in church, but they gabble up to the very porch."[51] For some, apparently, these externals were matters of arcane technique: one tract (apparently from about 1850) not only urged people to cross themselves, but gave instructions in a footnote for doing so.[52]

Genuflecting and crossing oneself, fasting, wearing a cross—all these had clear religious meanings. Like candles and vestments, these practices could be seen as following from doctrine or symbolizing it. Dating letters by the ecclesiastical calendar also conveyed a fairly clear message (especially when the holidays were not among those commemorated in the Prayer Book). But whatever pious motives prompted these newly revived signs of reverence, they also had significance and value as symbols of comradeship and markers of identity.

Some other practices had only that significance. What doctrinal import could there possibly have been, for instance, in the fact that Tractarians customarily abbreviated the word "Saint" as *S.* rather than *St.*?[53] But that abbreviation did have a party meaning, so much so that one wealthy donor helped to underwrite the publication of his vicar's sermons only on condition that the abbreviation *St.* be used throughout.[54]

Just as liturgical practice and clerical appearance were subject to a sort of semiotic shift as time passed, so Anglo-Catholics sometimes lost their commitment to practices that ceased to be distinctive. When a party marker diffused to wider circles or otherwise lost its meaning, either the matter became a subject of personal or local taste, or it became a sign of generation. In time, for instance, the more advanced among the younger churchmen returned to the traditional (and Roman Catholic) abbreviation for "Saint," just as they often abandoned Tractarian plainsong for the harmonized Anglican chant of the old High Church, or for continental Mass settings that the older generation found "operose."[55]

We can even see the process at work in patterns of given names. Tractarian parents revived names like Anselm, Aidan, Bernard, Theodore, and Hilda, but when these names spread into more general use (largely replacing the Old Testament names favored by Low Churchmen), High Church taste turned to medieval names like Guy, popularized by the novels of Charlotte Yonge.[56]

It is easy to poke fun at the affectations of most movements, particularly those of another age, but we should recognize that every living movement develops its own culture, and an important function of that culture is to give partisans symbols of their partisanship. Bishop Wilberforce wrote once of the theological students at Cuddesdon College: "I consider it a heavy affliction that they should wear neckcloths of peculiar construction, coats of peculiar cut, whiskers of peculiar dimensions—that they should walk with a peculiar step, carry their heads at a peculiar angle to the body, and read in a peculiar tone."[57] But we would have to worry about the morale of any school where students did not do something similar.

Development of an Institutional Base

During the same years that the distinctive culture of Anglo-Catholicism was being elaborated and clarified, a number of organizational developments were transforming the movement from an inchoate, decentralized, and largely clerical enterprise into an organized and articulated social movement, comprising laity as well as clergy and operating on a national scale as a force within the national Church. A complex, interlocking network of associations, guilds, newspapers, suppliers, publishers, and the like began to take shape, providing channels for communications and the mobilization of resources, focusing nationwide attention on particular trouble spots, coordinating campaigns of various sorts. Some of these developments also ensured that many people who were not themselves Anglo-Catholics would come to have a material interest in seeing the movement prosper.

Several institutions founded in the years before 1860 enlisted the support of Anglo-Catholics, usually in alliance, however uneasy, with more moderate High Churchmen. The Association for Making Known upon the Continent the Principles of the Anglican Church, better known as the Anglo-Continental Society, for instance, included both High Churchmen, like Bishops Phillpotts and Wilberforce, and Tractarians, like Gladstone and Keble, when it was founded in 1855 (although eventually its anti-Roman activities alienated many Anglo-Catholics).[58] Various associations for "Free and Open Churches" and "Freedom of Worship" allied a broad High Church constituency in the campaign against the pew rent system. Nathaniel Woodard's schools for the middle classes—the first of them, St. John's, Hurstpierpont, and St. Nicholas, Lancing, opened in the early 1850s—were not narrowly "movement" schools, but were linked to it closely enough to be characterized by one opponent thirty years later as "notorious institutions constitut[ing] a gigantic educational scheme conceived in the interests of priestcraft."[59]

Specifically Anglo-Catholic institutions were rare and often short-lived in these early years. The sisterhoods we have already examined were exceptions, as were various guilds, confraternities, and secret societies established as early as the 1840s. The Brotherhood of the Holy Trinity, founded in Oxford in 1844; the Guild of the same name established in Cambridge thirteen years later; the Guild of St. Alban, founded in Birmingham in 1851—these were typical organizations of the movement's first decades. Similar bodies continued to be founded as the movement diffused to other parts of the country: Durham University, for example, saw *its* Guild of the Holy Trinity established only in 1885.

A guild of this sort generally served two functions: it acquainted its members with Catholic services and devotions not found in the Prayer Book, and it encouraged such practices as fasting, confession, and frequent church attendance by incorporating them as rules.[60] Like many of the early sisterhoods, these guilds were often established by individual clergymen within their parishes, and consequently their influence tended to remain local. In the 1860s, however, the focus of organization, and of controversy, shifted to a higher level.

Two national groups that emerged in that decade largely defined the nature, direction, and progress of the movement. We have already encountered the English Church Union. Through its resolutions and other activities, the E.C.U. eventually came to speak for Anglo-Catholicism, insofar as any one voice (with the possible exception of the weekly *Church Times*) could be said to have done that.[61] The Society of the Holy Cross or (from its Latin initials) S.S.C., on the other hand, represented the extreme wing of legitimate Anglo-Catholic opinion, often acting independently. Despite its inflexibility—even sometimes because of it—the S.S.C. was often able to define the agenda or at least the timetable of the movement as a whole.[62] The two organizations were different in other ways as well.

Founded in 1857, but known to the public only a decade later, the S.S.C. was wholly clerical, based on "secrecy and absolute obedience," its members bound by vows, its polity "a very clearly marked electoral monarchy."[63] (Pusey wrote the vows and stood by the society in times of crisis, but did not himself remain a member.) All of this was in theory, of course; in practice, the society's longtime master, Father Mackonochie of St. Alban's, Holborn, sometimes had to remind his fractious brethren of these principles. The S.S.C. was a small group, with fewer than a hundred members in the mid-sixties and fewer than four hundred at its peak a decade later.[64]

The E.C.U., by contrast, was much larger and much more comprehensive. Formed at the time of the St. George's riots from the two hundred or so members of the Church of England Protection Society and a number of small, local bodies, its steadily increasing membership surpassed three thousand in the mid-sixties, seven thousand in 1870.[65] By the mid-seventies it had 205 local branches with 2420 clerical and 11,457 lay members, the latter both male and female.[66] By 1891 clerical and lay membership had reached 4000 and 29,000, respectively.[67] These members represented all shades of Anglo-Catholic opinion from old Tractarians like Keble and Pusey to the most extreme Ritualists.

Nine out of ten members of the S.S.C. (not always known to be such, before 1877) belonged to the E.C.U., and many were vigorously active in it; one, the Reverend T. O. Marshall, was the E.C.U.'s "Organizing Secretary." But they did not control the organization. Five out of six clerical members of the E.C.U. did *not* belong to the S.S.C.; many were relatively conservative Tractarians, often older and more influential than the firebrands of the S.S.C.[68] The E.C.U. was even sometimes defended (though seldom joined) by moderate High Churchmen, notably by Bishops Wilberforce and Hamilton in the Upper House of Convocation on one occasion in 1866.[69]

After 1862 the Church Union shared quarters with the Church Press (established that year to publish tracts) and with the *Church Review*. The latter was made nominally independent in 1862 so that the E.C.U. would not be responsible for its editorial views, but it remained the organization's "organ of communication" until the *Church Union Gazette* was established in 1870.[70] The E.C.U. also served as a speakers' bureau, providing lecturers for meetings of local branches. Probably its major concern, however, was to "afford counsel and protection to all persons, lay or clerical, suffering under unjust aggression or hindrance in spiritual matters." It pursued this objective vigorously, especially after 1868 under the presidency of Charles Wood (later Lord Halifax), by monitoring and publicizing discrimination and harassment, by bombarding Convocation and Parliament with resolutions, and by raising defense funds and providing legal advice and assistance to defendants in "ritual" cases.

Most importantly, however, the Church Union centralized the movement. The general hostility of the secular press, the well-established organs of Evangelical opinion, the interests of politicians who could capitalize on fears of Romanism—all of these factors had ensured that when parochial disputes received national attention it was unsympathetic. The Church Union changed that. Anglo-Catholic clergy in trouble, or anticipating trouble, with their congregations or their bishops or the Church Association or freelance no-popery agitators could look for support to a strong national body with influential connections and considerable resources. In addition, the E.C.U. began to impose at least some degree of uniformity on a movement that included partisans notable for their intractability. If its resolutions never really defined a party line, at least they made plain what the organization was prepared to defend.

In contrast, it is difficult to say whether the activities of the Society of the Holy Cross generally helped Anglo-Catholicism or hurt it. There is no question, however, that the S.S.C. shaped both the movement and the public perception of it. One early historian of Anglo-Catholicism anticipated the judgment of many later ones when he complained of a tendency to "extravagance instead of decency and order" and a "want of discretion" that cost the movement much support, and these characteristics were found double-distilled among the brethren of the S.S.C.[71] Time and again, the society displayed a remarkable lack of political sense, surpassing that of the most naive Tractarians. If Newman and his friends published Froude's *Remains* and Tract 90 with apparent indifference to likely reactions, their successors often seemed not so much indifferent as flatly uncomprehending.

The society's efforts to promote confession, for example, simply did not take account of many Englishmen's deep revulsion toward that practice. In 1873, the society was behind a petition to the bishops in Convocation requesting, among other things, "that, in view of the widespread and increasing use of Sacramental Confession, your Venerable House may consider the advisability of providing for the education, selection and licensing of duly qualified confessors in accordance with the provisions of Canon Law."[72] One member of the society later wrote that this was intended to be an exercise in political subtlety, a "prudent" attempt to offset efforts to amend the Prayer Book "by a counter-proposition to *raise* [its] teaching on certain points—the proposition itself, as I have the best means of knowing, being *simply intended as a check to alteration in any direction.*"[73] Be that as it may, "prudent" is hardly the word for the resulting petition, which even the society's official historian acknowledged was at least premature.[74] It alienated many moderate High Churchmen, the bishops condemned "the sacramental view of Confession" as "a most serious error," and the resulting furor helped to lay the groundwork for the passage of the Public Worship Regulation Act.[75]

A few years later, in 1877, a similar controversy ensued when a copy of *The Priest in Absolution*, a manual for confessors published by the society, made its way into the hands of Lord Redesdale, who read passages to the House of Lords.[76] (T. T. Carter had recommended that the manual be published in Latin, and that would probably have been a good idea: the Evangelical Reverend Hugh McNeile allowed that, if it were up to him, hearing confessions would be a capital offense in England.[77]) On that occasion, the bishops unanimously condemned any doctrine of confession that could be thought to make such a book necessary, and set up a committee to investigate the secret society that had produced it.[78]

Some Evangelicals pointed out, however, that if the bishops did not already know about the S.S.C.'s activities, they were about the only interested parties who did not.[79] In truth, the society's efforts to maintain its secrecy were often singularly inept. About this time, various Evangelical bodies began routinely to obtain and to publish the society's confidential membership rolls.[80] Once, when the society called a "Private Meeting, for mutual consultation, to include its own brethren, and others of like mind," it asked those invited to keep the matter confidential, but the plans were leaked to the newspapers—hardly surprising, since invitations went to nearly fifteen hundred clergymen.[81] On another occasion, Father Mackonochie felt it necessary to warn his brethren not to use postal cards for the society's confidential business.[82]

These efforts at secrecy served mainly to feed the suspicions of the society's opponents, contributing to the impression of underhandedness and conspiracy without in fact protecting its members or effectively disguising the nature of their activities.[83] It is hard to believe that a policy of total can-

dor would have been more harmful, although it might have been less deli-
cious than one that allowed secret greetings, symbolic rings, and cruciform
watch-fobs.

On the other hand, the S.S.C. did provide encouragement and social
support for its members, many of whom were engaged in grueling mission
work in the slums of England's cities; that work, as we shall see, eventually
won for the entire Anglo-Catholic movement a measure of tolerance and
even admiration from many who otherwise had little use for it. In addition,
although the society more or less continually annoyed and embarrassed
more conservative Anglo-Catholics, it may have served them, too, if only by
making them appear to be relatively reasonable and accommodating. So
long as Evangelical outrage and legal action were focused on the likes of
Father Mackonochie, less extreme and less intransigent churchmen were
likely to escape censure. Finally, the society served the larger movement by
providing it with what amounted to shock troops: in the legal cases that followed in the wake of the Public Worship Regulation Act, it is fair to say that
the E.C.U. provided the defense, but the S.S.C. supplied the defendants.

The brethren of the S.S.C., individually or collectively, were also active
in establishing an interlocking network of specialized organizations: "multiform agencies," one critic charged, that were "contingents of a great, united army"; a "division of labor" aiming at a "common object.... Like military companies told off for special duty—complete and definite in
itself—they yet stand responsible to a central, chief authority," namely, the
"promoters of the Ritualistic 'Conspiracy'" (the word had been used by the
archbishop of Canterbury), who intended "to 're-Catholicize the Church of
England,' and to 'liberate' it from the tyranny of the State."[84]

These new associations were indeed "multiform." Some were organized
for those in particular occupations: the Guild of St. Luke for the medical
profession, for instance; the Guild of the Holy Standard for soldiers; St.
Martin's League for postal workers; the Guild of the Holy Cross for the railway service.[85] Later, the Church of England Working Men's Society consolidated on the national level the activities of a number of local organizations.[86]

Other organizations addressed particular, limited concerns. The Ecclesiological Society, for example, carried on the mission of the Cambridge Camden Society in promoting archaeology, restoration, and "correct"
church-building; the Gregorian Society, founded in 1870, set itself a similar
task with respect to church music. The Society for the Maintenance of the
Faith, beginning in 1873, sought to acquire the patronage of livings, in
order to award them to Anglo-Catholic incumbents, and supported the
establishment of chapels and oratories where "the absence of Catholic privileges" or "the suppression of Catholic observances in edifices subject to
State interference" made it advisable. In 1876 all of the twenty clergymen
on the S.M.F.'s Council were members of the E.C.U., and thirteen were

brothers of the S.S.C.[87]

The Society of St. Alphege, Abp. & M. (that is, archbishop and martyr), established in 1864, was a more modest undertaking; its special task was the acquisition and distribution of vestments, ornaments, and needlework.[88] In 1868 the society reported that it had been "instrumental in introducing the use of the Eucharistic vestments in *nine*, coloured stoles in *seven*, and surpliced choirs in *three* churches," and it had also acquired a thurible and navicula for its own use, at a cost of one pound, ten shillings.[89] A prayer offered for the use of the society's members shows how they viewed their undertaking: "Strengthen our hands, O God, in the building of Jerusalem, and in the adorning of Thy holy place, that our enemies may not be able to hinder our work."[90] This was a small organization, with fewer than a hundred male associates in 1868, many of them undergraduates.[91] But at least nine of the twenty-three clerical members were or soon became members of the S.S.C., including two of the three clergymen among the society's officers.[92]

Some new organizations were devoted to propagating particular doctrines or practices. The Confraternity of the Blessed Sacrament, for instance, was established in 1862 to promote the "objective character" of the Eucharist, which it did by grants of vestments, plate, and altar linen, and by suggestions for "due and reverent celebration."[93] By the mid-seventies, the Confraternity circulated monthly "Intercession Papers" to a few hundred priests-associate and a few thousand lay members.[94] More than a third of the priests-associate and solid majorities of the clerical "wardens" and council members apparently were brethren of the S.S.C. (an exception was Canon Bright of Christ Church, Oxford, probably the most distinguished member of the council).[95]

As time passed, new organizations became more extreme, and correspondingly smaller. A clear trajectory can be traced from the Confraternity of the Blessed Sacrament, to the Guild of All Souls (formed in 1873 to encourage prayer for the departed and, by clear implication, to propagate the doctrine of Purgatory), to the Confraternity of Our Lady (established in 1880 to encourage Marian devotion), to (later still) the Union of the Holy Rosary and the Guild of the Sacred Heart of Jesus.

These organizations obviously had ecumenical implications, but others took ecumenism as their explicit concern.[96] In 1864, John Mason Neale and some of his friends established the Eastern Churches Association to encourage greater understanding of those churches and closer ties with them. Another group, the Association for the Promotion of the Unity of Christendom, founded in 1857, enrolled Anglo-Catholic, Eastern Christian, and Roman Catholic members to work and pray for reunion. The Romanism of the A.P.U.C. (which some unkindly translated as "A Plaster for Unquiet Consciences") led even such stalwart Catholics as Neale and Bishop Forbes of Brechin to protest, and some members—among them Father R. M. Benson of the Cowley Fathers and the Reverend Thomas Chamberlain of St.

Thomas, Oxford—to resign.[97] In 1864 the association's Roman Catholic members resigned, too, when the A.P.U.C. was condemned by the authorities of their communion.

What was left of the association remained in existence long enough, however, to repudiate one of its founders, the Reverend F. G. Lee, when, with two associates in the "Order of Corporate Reunion," he went outside the Church of England to be mysteriously consecrated as a bishop in 1877 and began secretly to reordain clergymen concerned about the validity of Anglican orders.[98] Lee was also expelled by the English Church Union for his activities, and even the Society of the Holy Cross condemned the Order of Corporate Reunion as "schismatical" and "sinning against Catholic obedience"—although we may suspect that a few of the brethren were among those reordained.[99]

Many other, smaller groups could be described. One of the most engaging, "the Anglican Crusade," did not appear until the 1880s, and did not enlist many members even then. Evidently a sort of Ritualistic scout movement (although it was open to adults as well as youths), the Crusade instructed its members to salute each other this way: "Point to your forehead with the forefinger of the left hand and trace the Cross of St. Andrew, x placing your right hand on your left breast; complete the signal with the other Cross + in responding, also using your left hand." The group's 111 "Facts and Principles" included the Six Points of the English Church Union, as well as unction, confession, fasting communion, and daily attendance at Mass.[100]

The *Church Times* and Its Advertisers

One other Anglo-Catholic institution of the 1860s must be mentioned. The *Church Times* was established in 1863 by George Palmer, Anglo-Catholic scion of a prominent Evangelical publishing family, and it quickly became the leading organ of Anglo-Catholic opinion. Within a year it was in the black; at the end of 1865 it had ten thousand subscribers and went from eight pages to twelve; in 1880 a Church Association member complained that the *Church Times*'s weekly circulation of twenty thousand was nearly twice that of all Evangelical papers combined.[101]

The movement had supported other periodicals in the past. The quarterly *British Critic* had expounded advanced Tractarian views from 1838 until 1843, under the editorship first of Newman and then of his brother-in-law, Thomas Mozley. After it was abandoned, the *Christian Remembrancer*, coedited by Thomas's brother, J. B. Mozley, filled the gap to some extent, although by the 1860s its brand of ultrarubricianism and sober Oxford Movement piety had become old-fashioned. A similar tone pervaded the *Monthly Packet*, founded in 1851 by Charlotte Yonge, who edited the journal until some time in the 1880s.

The *Church Times*, in contrast, was a popular, lively, and provocative weekly newspaper. And it did not attain its success by moderating its views: it was narrowly, determinedly partisan—much more so than, say, the *Guardian*, a moderate High Church weekly founded in 1846 by R. W. Church and others. There was nothing moderate about the churchmanship of the *Church Times*. It thundered anathema on Protestantism, rationalism, and moderate Anglicanism alike, week after week for decades. That there were enough possible readers left uncondemned to support the paper is powerful testimony to the movement's growing strength.

From time to time, more periodicals appeared—the *Church Review* in 1861, the A.P.U.C.'s *Union Review* two years later, the *Church Monitor* ("A Magazine Advocating Catholic Doctrine & Practice") in 1866, and others, but none rivaled the influence and importance of the *Church Times* as a notice-board for the movement, appealing for funds for worthy causes, announcing and subsequently "reviewing" functions of interest, rallying opinion, defining the party line, keeping laggards up to the mark, and providing a forum for internal debate.

The paper was also a medium for advertisements. Those in a typical issue indicate the number and variety of enterprises that had grown up within and around the movement—and, incidentally, the number of people whose livings had come to depend at least in part on Anglo-Catholic patronage.[102] In the issue of May 12, 1866, for example, fifteen different publishers and booksellers advertised their wares (which included a *Guide for Passing Holily Corpus Christi*—not a Prayer Book holiday).[103] Thomas Pratt and Son sold birettas for four shillings, chasubles from four guineas to twelve. Frank Smith & Co. dealt in similar goods, as did Mrs. Little's Ecclesiastical Warehouse (London), which advertised "Chasubles, Dalmatics, Copes, Albs, Surplices, Girdles, etc. Frontals, Stoles, Cases for visiting the sick and all Church requirements. Gothic laces in all widths.... Church Candlesticks, Vases, Crosses and Altar Plate. Gold and Silver Crosses. German prints of the Stations.... Altar Breads, Altar Wax, Incense, &c."

These are the sort of wares a Church Association writer had in mind when he complained of "the abominable things offered for sale in church shops."[104] That particular issue had no advertisements for the scourges and hair shirts that he said could also be found, but other advertisers did offer an array of products including harmoniums and clerical hats, needlework supplies and sewing machines, lamps and oil, soap and candles, wines, flower seeds, and religious jewelry. Still others offered plainsong instruction and plumbing services, hotel accommodations and household furniture, tonics, stoves, wallpaper, and coal. One advertisement offered small portraits of movement notables; another, sketches of Keble's church and parsonage. Positions were available for or were sought by sisters, clergymen, organists, tutors, and servants. A school in Plymouth advertised for the "DAUGHTERS OF GENTLEMEN, to be carefully trained in Catholic principles." There were appeals for contributions to the E.C.U. Defense Fund, to the (anti-pew) National Association for Freedom of Worship, to Father Ignatius's Benedictine enterprise, and to Father Lowder's new church of St. Peter's, London Docks. Finally, the undertaker to the Guild of St. Alban's advertised "Funerals conducted in proper form and with appropriate fittings approved of by the Ecclesiological Society, and patronized and recommended by the clergy of St. Paul and St. Barnabas and other churches."

Showing the Flag

Even in death Anglo-Catholics had their own distinctive way of doing things. Funerals had been important to the movement ever since the 1850s, when there was trouble in East Grinstead over ornamented palls. Once again, John Mason Neale proved to be only slightly ahead of his time. A decade later, during the York Church Congress of 1866, a lecturer on the ritual of Christian burials described the ideal funeral as one with a "Mass for the dead" with the "body solemnly incensed by the priest," and a procession with torchbearers and chanting.[105]

A few months earlier, Keble's funeral had not met that high standard, but innumerable movement figures, old and new, had marched in procession, and the *Church Times* noted that the coffin was covered by a violet pall with a full-length red cross.[106] Later that year, Neale's own funeral, appropriately, included a procession that the *Church Times* said was "unequalled in extent and picturesqueness by anything which has been seen in England (except perhaps at coronations) for three hundred years."[107] Some two hundred and fifty clergymen took part (including a Russian Orthodox priest), accompanied by the choirs of St. Alban's, Holborn; St. Matthias, Stoke Newington; Christ Church, Clapham; and St. Michael's, Brighton. The *Church Times* found the music not quite first-rate, but attributed its defects to lack of rehearsal; otherwise, it praised the High Celebration, conducted by five priests, three of them in "magnificent black silk vestments, ornamented with silver lace orphreys." At the grave, Vita Brevis was sung; characteristically, this was "in spite of the prohibition of the vicar."

Even modest funerals could be provocative: among the irritants that led to a lengthy correspondence in the *Hull and North Lincolnshire Times* in 1867 was a service involving a purple pall with a large cross, flowers cast in the grave, and an unannounced service of Holy Communion, at which the chalice was elevated.[108] But the funerals of leading figures in the movement were often public spectacles, almost rallies, that broadcast the faith to citizens who might otherwise have remained oblivious to what was going on inside Anglo-Catholic churches. The funeral of Thomas Combe, patron of pre-Raphaelite art and of the Ritualist church of St. Barnabas, Oxford, for instance, involved multiple processions through the streets with crucifer, clergy, and choir. Four celebrations were held before Combe's body as it lay in St. Barnabas, another procession carried it to the cemetery—and all of this elicited an annoyed pamphlet from "A High Churchman of the Old School."[109]

And funerals were not the only occasions on which the movement showed its strength in public. In 1873, the Reverend Edward Stuart published a pamphlet with the title *Choral Processions in the Streets*.[110] Such displays became a frequent adjunct to dedication festivals and holiday celebrations at many of the movement's showcase churches.

These conspicuous churches themselves indicated and extended the possibilities of ceremonial and doctrinal development. Stuart's church of St. Mary Magdalene's, Munster Square, and other strongholds of Ritualism encouraged Anglo-Catholics and outraged their opponents by their very existence. Many were in London, and *Mackeson's Guide* told the faithful or curious up from the country how to find them.[111] Even in London, they were not numerous—in 1870, fewer than a score of the 651 London-area churches employed the Eucharistic vestments, and only a third of those burned incense—but how many churches did these things was perhaps less important than the fact that they were done in the Church of England at all.[112]

And by 1870 there were enough of these exemplary churches that few in England had to go as far as London to see advanced Ritualism at first hand. Most English cities had at least one. Some were famous among Anglo-Catholics, and notorious among the movement's opponents. Father Wagner's church of St. Paul's, for instance, was one of the many attractions of Brighton for Ritualistic holiday-makers—including clergymen, who were allowed to assist at the church—and for aged and ailing Anglo-Catholics, who often retired there.[113] Plymouth had Father Prynne's church of St. Peter's, also known by reputation to any visitor likely to care.[114] And all readers of the *Church Times* would have known of St. Alban's, in Birmingham, where the Pollock brothers, "Father Pollock" and "Father Tom," faced disorders in 1867 that went on for weeks, worse in some ways than those at St. George's: on one occasion the police had to use sabers to hold off a mob that intended to tear the church down.[115]

Many other outposts of Ritualistic teaching and practice were well known outside their communities. But if reputation failed, the Anglo-Catholic traveler could turn to the *Tourist's Church Guide* to discover that in Bristol, for instance, All Saints, Clifton, offered daily eucharists, colored vestments, altar lights, free and open seating, the eastward position, and wholly Gregorian music. Sunday Masses were at 6:00, 7:00, 8:00, and 11:15, matins at 10:30.[116] (The *Guide* did not report it, but it was true that the most audible words in the communion service would be those of the Latin missal that the vicar used for "private prayer." He had excerpts bound with his prayer book, in red morocco.[117])

   All over England were churches where the Eucharist was celebrated frequently and received fasting, where "Catholic privileges" like confession
were openly available, where (in a line of John Mason Neale's) "banner,
cross and cope gleam[ed] thro' the incensed aisle."[118] Where had these
churches come from? Who went to them, and why?

V

The Context of Ritualism

"It will be the duty of the subsequent historian," remarked one contemporary observer, "to account for the fact that the same enlightened age which effected such marvelous discoveries in every department of science, also produced such things as Mormonism and Spirit-Rapping, Puseyism and Holloway's Pills."[1] Plainly, many Englishmen believed that Anglo-Catholicism was inconsistent with modern institutions, an anachronism in the Age of Steam. Yet, paradoxically, some nineteenth-century trends and institutions had made it easier for the movement to grow and to spread. Anglo-Catholicism began as an affair of debate in common rooms and obscure ecclesiastical periodicals; it might have remained that had it not been for the social, legal, and even technological context in which it developed.

In this chapter we shall examine three aspects of the movement's environment that contributed to its success. In the first place, the growth of Victorian cities subjected the Church of England's parish system to intolerable strains; it required that a great many new churches be built, giving the movement an opening that it exploited. Second, improvements in transportation and communication contributed to changes in the Church that allowed for mobilization at the national level, turning what might otherwise have remained parochial disputes into skirmishes in a larger conflict between parties in the national Church. Finally, the legal context, by its initial ambiguity and eventual heavy-handedness, gave the movement first space to develop, then a tolerable level of persecution that violated English standards of fair play without seriously inhibiting its activities.

The Breakdown of the Parish System

Just as Tractarian practice in the 1840s and 1850s had been most perfectly realized in new, urban churches like St. Barnabas, Pimlico, and St. Sav-

iour's, Leeds, so the flagships of Ritualism in the 1860s and 1870s were usually new churches in areas of rapid population growth.[2] Many of the most
"advanced" churches served new parishes (in the London borough of St. Pancras four old parishes quickly became thirty); others were missions nominally
attached to parish churches; still others were so-called district churches, independent of existing parishes, often built through private philanthropy.[3]

In an effort to keep up with urban growth, a great many such churches
were built.[4] English cities were ceasing to be a collection of neighborhoods,
each served by its parish church; a more fluid, pluralistic arrangement was
emerging, one in which churches competed for congregations on the basis
of proximity, the personal appeal of their clergy, the class composition of
their congregations, or the degree of Ritualism evident in their services.

This development evoked mixed feelings. Harry Jones, one of Bryan
King's successors at St. George's-in-the-East, hoped that it would attract the
working class to the Church of England by offering workingmen and their
families what were in effect their own churches. But Jones disliked the
resulting congregationalism and believed, with reason, that competition
encouraged churches to exaggerate their differences. Certainly the absence
of existing congregations, committed to customary forms of worship,
allowed them to do so.[5] Not even most of the new urban churches were
Anglo-Catholic in complexion, but, as Jones wrote, it was in such churches
that "opinion and practice have been pushed to an extreme" and that Ritualists "have struck such roots as they have."[6]

Anglo-Catholicism was indeed largely an urban phenomenon. Rural
conservatism may have contributed to that, but we can also explain it entirely in the language of ecology, or of marketing. Anglo-Catholicism never
appealed to more than a minority of Anglican layfolk; only in communities
with a number of churches could any one church succeed by catering to
their tastes. In many a village the parish church was the only place Anglicans
could worship; parishioners who disliked what was going on in their church
had no alternative but the Dissenting chapel. But in the cities there were
dozens—in London, hundreds—of Anglican churches. Those who did not
care for the ceremonies or the architecture or the sermons or the vicar at
their parish church seldom had far to go to find something more to their lik-
ing, and many used this freedom either to avoid Ritualist services or to seek
them out. An Anglo-Catholic clergyman in an English city stood a fair
chance of attracting enough sympathetic layfolk to fill his church; he could
also say truthfully that those upset by his innovations could go elsewhere.

If the church was new, of course, there was no established congregation
with settled habits to be upset, and the minister had an even freer hand. In
a new church, Harry Jones believed, "the tendency some clergymen feel
toward a development of their sacerdotal appetites" could go unchecked,
and "minute observance of ritual" and "sacerdotal direction" could flourish,
supported by congregations made up in part of Anglo-Catholics willing to

cross parish boundaries.[7] To be sure, there might be opposition from bishops, Evangelicals, the press, perhaps even mobs. But the supporters of such churches could say, as Pusey did in 1874, that objections came only from "bystanders, who are not hindered in their own devotion or indevotion."[8] Father Mackonochie put it well, in a letter to the bishop of London:

We are said to alienate as many as we draw, but where are they? It must be remembered that we came to a new Church without a congregation, so we could not alienate those in possession. We may have failed to attract some, but we have filled the Church, and that mostly with Parishioners. What could we do more? Then, again, the non-parishioners who come must have been repelled from somewhere. No one asks whence;—but whence can it be, except from the empty Church Association Churches round us?[9]

Ironically, high ritual could also be found in some very old churches—churches made obsolete by urban growth. The new churches began with no congregations; some of the old ones had lost theirs. By 1882, for instance, the medieval church of St. Ethelburga, Bishopsgate Street, in the City of London, offered an extensive schedule of Sunday services and an advanced ceremonial, but only 315 souls lived in the parish and ordinarily few of the church's 300 seats were occupied. The little fourteenth-century church at Perivale, near Ealing, served the smallest parish in the Diocese of London—only five houses, with thirty-three inhabitants. The church was closed from November to February, but it offered a very high service when open: a surpliced choir, vestments, and incense.

Obsolescence was not always proof against discord—Christopher Wren's church of St. Margaret Pattens, Rood Lane, served a total population of only 229, but its vicar, a member of the Society of the Holy Cross, celebrated in a chasuble, and contended with a vestry that wished to prosecute him for ritual irregularities.[10] Usually, however, the internal workings of the old, empty churches, like those of the new ones, were peaceable, if only because no one present was likely to complain.

Convocations, Colleges, and Congresses

Changes in the organization and operation of the Church at large also shaped the history of the movement. Some of these changes were made possible by improved transportation, and they made it easier for *any* movement to cohere: they allowed, even encouraged, the like-minded to come together to support one another and to oppose those they disagreed with. In particular, they had the effect (not always intended) of bringing clergy together, giving them a sense of themselves as a group with common problems and common interests, and providing them with opportunities to meet, to discuss, and to engage in ecclesiastical politics. First Anglo-Catholics, then their opponents, took advantage of these developments, turning what had been largely a matter of parochial disputes into party warfare at the national level.

In 1852, for example, thanks primarily to the efforts of High Churchmen, the Convocation of the Province of Canterbury met for the first time in 135 years, and it met regularly thereafter. Nine years later, the Convocation of York resumed. These bodies were entirely clerical, with separate houses for bishops and priests, and consequently they were viewed with suspicion by those who feared sacerdotalism. Some Anglo-Catholics distrusted them, too, because the lower houses included many cathedral clergy, rural deans, and the like, sitting *ex officio*, and these dignitaries were seldom sympathetic to the movement.

Nevertheless, in principle, the convocations gave the Church an organ for formulating and expressing its own mind on doctrine and ritual. Only the most extreme Anglo-Catholics ventured to doubt whether a "provincial synod" could overturn the rule of the "Western Church," and only the most extreme Erastians believed that the Church had no right to a mind of its own. By its very existence, Convocation did what its High Church supporters had hoped and its Low and Broad Church opponents had feared it would do: it implied that the government of the Church was (with Royal assent) the business of the Church, and it defined "the Church" as its clergy and bishops assembled.

Petitions to Convocation became a popular medium for expressing opinions and choosing sides, and Convocation became a forum for party conflict at a level not merely parochial or diocesan, but national (or nearly so). Because, in practice, the Convocations were never able to speak unequivocally on the matters at issue, a principal effect of reviving Convocation was to add to the legal confusion that the Ritualists exploited, which we shall examine later.

The more or less simultaneous multiplication of diocesan and ruridecanal conferences had similar premises and effects: all assumed that the Church was the business of the clergy; all brought clergymen together to deal with their common professional problems. These changes affected all clergymen, of course, but their affinity with the Anglo-Catholic view of the Church is obvious—as it was obvious to contemporary observers, both sympathetic and suspicious—and it is no accident that nearly all were introduced under High Church auspices.

The idea that the clergy were professional men, not mere gentlemen-amateurs or a branch of the civil service, was further reinforced by the establishment of theological colleges. From the first, these colleges were identified with the major Church parties. First Chichester, then Cuddesdon, later Wells, Leeds, and Ely trained prospective ministers in High Church principles, and offered a rich liturgical diet: the daily offices, some of the hours, a daily Eucharist. Evangelicals first opposed this trend, then emulated it by founding their own colleges: Ridley Hall, Wycliffe Hall, and

St. Peter's Hall, Oxford.[11]

The colleges' academic isolation encouraged the expression of their party character, nowhere more obviously than at Cuddesdon. We have already heard Bishop Wilberforce's lament about the peculiarity of Cuddesdon's students; even the college's vice-principal, H. P. Liddon, was said to resemble "an Italian ecclesiastic, glittering-eyed, with 'a white band for a collar and a black cassock with a broad belt.'"[12]

Similar in some of its consequences was another Anglo-Catholic innovation of this period, the practice of clergy retreats, which initially resembled nothing so much as party caucuses. The first, at Chislehurst in 1858, was conducted by the Reverend R. M. Benson of the Society of the Holy Cross, subsequently the founder of the Cowley Fathers; the second, the next year, was conducted by T. T. Carter, and its dozen participants included such prominent movement figures as Mackonochie, Lowder, G. Cosby White, and Bishop Forbes of the Scottish Church.[13]

National church congresses, begun in 1861, also contributed to the growth and consolidation of the Anglo-Catholic movement. The party flavor of these congresses had less to do with their programs than with their social aspects and some of the accompanying activities, but they were great occasions for the Anglo-Catholic parochial clergy, who could mingle, commiserate, and see what was being done elsewhere.

The 1866 Church Congress in York, for example, attracted a considerable number of clergymen, in a holiday mood despite what the *Church Times* called "the wretched insipidity of the programme" and the Great Northern Railway's refusal to issue reduced-rate tickets for congress-goers.[14] Anglo-Catholics were much in evidence in the audience, if not on the platform; they cheered the mention of John Mason Neale (recently deceased) and listened stonily to an address on Sunday observance by the Evangelical bishop of Ripon. When it became known that a lawyer scheduled to speak on the ecclesiastical courts had in a recent case referred to the mixed chalice as "grog," some of the audience shouted him down, then walked out when called to order.

Although Anglo-Catholics found little to their taste in the congress's program, there was a great deal for them to enjoy in an accompanying exhibit of ecclesiastical art, organized by a committee that included virtually every prominent Ritualist clergyman in England. The exhibition's eight patrons included five members of Parliament, an Irish peer, and the president of the English Church Union, but the most significant presence was that of E. B. Pusey, implicitly bestowing the blessings of Tractarianism on the enterprise. The catalog was partly the work of F. G. Lee, editor of the most recent version of the *Directorium Anglicanum* and not yet an *episcopus vagans*. It made the exhibition's orientation plain, asserting that "each week adds a fresh Church to those where the beautiful, the scriptural, the primitive, and the all-instructive Ritual of the Church of England is being restored."[15]

For a shilling, the curious could examine such items as a fifteenth-century Italian copper-gilt chalice with silver-gilt bowl, on loan from the architect G. Gilbert Scott, or a new "Chasuble of white silk, with Latin cross and pillar, richly embroidered with roses and foliage," provided by the Reverend Charles Walker of Brighton. From the chaplain of St. Augustine's Home, Bristol, came items (not antiques, either) hinting at practices in the oratory not even dreamed of in most parish churches: a brass thurible, an oak tabernacle, and a silver monstrance—for incense, reservation, and exposition, respectively. The exhibition also included a display of brass rubbings bearing on the interpretation of the Ornaments Rubric.

Hundreds of items were for sale, both by individuals and by clerical outfitting firms. A vicar's wife, for instance, offered banners ("S. Lawrence, white merino, with silk device," five guineas), proceeds to go to restoring her husband's church. An additional 6p admitted the visitor to one of the twice-daily lectures by well-known movement figures on various aspects of ritual. Undoubtedly the strangest was J. R. Lunn's discussion of "The Cloke Left by S. Paul at Troas," which argued that the garment in question must have been a chasuble.[16]

Representatives of the various Church parties responded to the exhibit in character: Evangelicals were appalled, Broad Churchmen were bemused, and even some of the Ritualists' Tractarian allies ventured to doubt whether such a flaunting display was wise. The *Christian Remembrancer*, for example, charged that "the chiefs of the new ceremonial" were putting the movement's accomplishments at risk and urged strict adherence to the letter of the Ornaments Rubric, "viz., a white alb, plain, with a vestment or cope," and caution in introducing even that in the face of opposition.[17]

For clergymen of all stripes, however, whatever their misgivings, attending church congresses became a popular annual activity—although another annual activity for some Evangelicals was debating whether Protestant churchmen should attend. One Low Churchman complained that congresses were primarily "a great advertising medium for Ritualistic opinions," but the Reverend J. C. Ryle replied that they served some useful purposes and should not be condemned because of "the restless energy of ecclesiastical-art tradesmen."[18] Ryle also argued that because congresses existed as a fact of life, Low Churchmen should not abandon the field to their adversaries, to which a fellow-Evangelical replied: "Well, dramshops also exist, and dancing saloons, and race-courses, and theatres, and many other things that Christians deplore."[19] Ryle was right, from his point of view (that of a man soon to become a bishop): the congresses did serve some useful functions, and in time they probably contributed to the diminution of party conflict, as we shall see. But in their early years, like the other institutional changes of the time, they sharpened the boundaries between parties and provided an arena in which they could contend.

The Legal Context

The growth of Ritualism was also made possible by the confused legal situation that we have already examined. In the movement's first decades innovators could appeal to the law at least as effectively as their opponents; both then and later, the absence of definitive liturgical standards and of any effective judicature to enforce them made it unlikely that any individual innovator would find himself in serious legal trouble. By the time the movement's opponents took steps to rectify this situation, in the 1870s, it was too late.

In the 1840s and 1850s, most advocates of a higher ceremonial could argue that they were merely recalling the Church to practices its own law required. Especially after the Liddell judgment, their legal position seemed strong; some disputed usages were held to be required by the Ornaments Rubric, and others were at least not explicitly forbidden. Even the extremists of the early period claimed only to be making use of the latitude that the law provided. Frederick Oakeley, for example, defended what Newman had called "the extravagances as they at present practise them at Margaret Street Chapel" by saying, "We are for carrying out the symbolical principle in our own Church to the utmost extent which is consistent with the duty of obedience to the rubric."[20]

As time went on, however, and Ritualists replaced ultrarubricians in the forefront of the movement, the predominant Anglo-Catholic attitude toward the law underwent a subtle change. It could not be said that Ritualists were indifferent to the legality of their practices—indeed, they devoted literally hundreds of tracts and sermons to the subject. But their efforts were devoted less to discerning the law in order to obey it than to devising legal formulas allowing practices held to be desirable, if not obligatory, on symbolic (that is, doctrinal) grounds.[21]

An extreme example of the sort of Prayer Book exegesis involved in this effort concerned the practice of taking the "eastward position" (back to the people) at the Prayer of Consecration in the Eucharist. Evangelicals and many others understood the rubrics to direct the celebrant to take the position customary in the Church of England, at the north end of the altar, sideways to the congregation, with the "manual acts" clearly visible. Anglo-Catholics preferred the eastward position, not simply because it was "primitive" (and Roman Catholic) practice but also because it was held to be the position of a sacrificing priest.[22] A lengthy controversy ensued, centering on whether the "north end" was the same thing as the "north side" and whether "before the table" could mean "beside the table."[23]

The courts were soon called on to decide these and other disputed matters, and from time to time disgruntled Low Churchmen proposed that Parliament intervene to settle them once and for all. For a variety of reasons, including the conservatism that usually worked against the movement, few were eager to tamper with the Prayer Book, but the threat was always in the air.[24] The bishop of Gloucester and Bristol was neither the first nor the last to suggest that "the ministerial dress" be established by "a simple and positive enactment" of Parliament; the "general temper of the country," he felt, demanded some such action.[25] In 1867, Lord Shaftesbury also proposed that Parliament outlaw vestments and incense; he was supported by Bishop Tait of London, who became archbishop of Canterbury the following year, but the prime minister postponed action by the time-honored expedient of appointing a royal commission to look into it. A decade later exasperated opponents of the movement were still calling for legislation to prohibit eucharistic vestments and the eastward position, arguing (as one clergyman put it) "that if these things have no significancy, they are silly, and unworthy of a Church to enact; if they have a meaning, it is essentially and emphatically Romish."[26]

But Prayer Book revision was only threatened. All but the most extreme Anglo-Catholics were confident that the law supported their position, but the movement's opponents were equally confident that it supported theirs. When the Church Association was formed in 1865, it undertook "to counteract the efforts now being made to assimilate [the Church of England's] services to those of the Church of Rome" through litigation, not new legislation. When the royal commission reported that it would be "expedient to restrain in the public services of the United Church of England and Ireland all variations in respect of vesture from that which has long been the established usage," the commissioners added, "We think this may be best secured by providing aggrieved parishioners with an easy and effectual process for complaint and redress"—implying that the variations would be found to be illegal.

Seven years later, when Parliament passed the only piece of legislation to be directed against the movement—Disraeli's "bill to put down Ritualism," the Public Worship Regulation Act—it, too, was based on the assumption that the objectionable practices were illegal and that the problem was simply one of making it easier for the courts to say so.[27] By that time some decisions had given some basis for this belief, but it was still mistaken.

Why the Law Did Not Work

Simple faith in litigation was misplaced because it proved extremely difficult to obtain authoritative rulings on the points at issue. The difficulty was due not only to the ambiguity of the law but to the structure of the courts that had to interpret it, a cumbersome hodgepodge that had grown up over the centuries. Linked to the Admiralty courts that interpreted naval law, they were often administered by men who knew little of the law they were interpreting. As a contemporary expert wrote: "The whole system of ecclesiastical Courts is to most people an unfathomable mystery. Their origins, their functions, their procedure, are equally obscure, and the only thing which repeated experiment has made clear about the Church judicature is that it will not work."[28]

There is no need to describe this unwieldy apparatus, or even the simpler system set up in 1874 by the Public Worship Regulation Act, or "PWRA." The act did in fact increase the number of prosecutions, but it did not seriously alter four important features of the system. First, even after the PWRA, obtaining a conviction was a long and expensive process. Second, final appeal was still to the Judicial Committee of the Privy Council, a wholly secular body. Third, the law itself remained ambiguous, and the courts produced conflicting, often political, and sometimes nonsensical judgments. Finally, the only way to enforce judgments on recalcitrant clergy was imprisonment, which proved to be unworkable. On balance, each of these features worked to the Ritualists' advantage.

Even after the PWRA's simplifications, prosecuting a clergyman for ritual offenses was a costly and complex undertaking. The most efficient prosecutions took years, not months, especially if the decisions were appealed, as they almost invariably were. In addition, the procedure was extremely complicated; the number of cases ending in acquittal on technical grounds is remarkable. Perhaps it is no surprise that, as one observer remarked, "nearly all, if not all, these ritual suits have been begun and carried on by that Society"—that is, by the Church Association; individual plaintiffs simply could not afford the legal costs.[29] The Association was indeed well-heeled, but even in the short run it had little to show for the forty thousand pounds it had spent on "advice and assistance" in Ritual cases by 1880.[30]

Of course, defendants had expenses, too, especially if they lost and had to pay the prosecution's expenses as well as their own. One clergyman's household effects went on the block to pay for the costs of convicting him, including wages for the Church Association witnesses ("spies," as the English Church Union saw them) who testified against him.[31] Another defendant cannily avoided that fate by signing everything over to his wife and claiming bankruptcy. The length of the proceedings was also surely a burden on some defendants, and Anglo-Catholic sources often speak of "harassment," not without reason. But the costs of defense were usually borne by the English Church Union, the *Church Times* was zealous in setting up defense funds, and it is plain that the well-publicized prosecutions provided rallying points for the movement. "The blood of the martyrs is the seed of the Church" was a favorite quotation.[32]

In any case, throughout this period the disputed practices continued to spread, prosecutions notwithstanding. It is obvious in retrospect that the Church Association simply could not prosecute fast enough to stem the tide, and as the practices became more common it became less likely that any given clergyman would have the bad luck to be brought to court. Prosecu-

tion was also ineffectual because of a widespread tendency to interpret decisions narrowly, as applicable only to the particular practice being challenged
or even to the particular defendant. It became clear that many priests did not
intend to give up the contested usages until they, personally, were ordered
to do so—if then.

The anti-Ritualists began by believing that a court decision against some
practice would put a stop to it, but that belief proved to be naive. Such a
decision might cause the prosecuted clergyman to give up the disputed practice. It might possibly inhibit some others who had not yet adopted it. But
once a usage had been introduced successfully in a given church, it was seldom abandoned just because some other church was ordered to stop it.
Moreover, the exact meaning of a decision was open to interpretation. In
1867 the English Church Union allowed that, in light of recent legal opinions, it could no longer defend "censing persons and things," but that it
would defend burning incense for "sweet fumigation" or as an "expressive
symbol."[33] When Father Mackonochie was ordered to remove the cross
from the altar of St. Alban's, Holborn, he did so—to a stand behind the
altar; when he was ordered to stop kneeling "excessively" at the Eucharist,
he began genuflecting instead; when he was ordered to stop genuflecting,
he began bowing—and his bishop lost his patience and removed him from
his church for a time.[34]

The judicial decisions were also marred by inconsistencies that raised
doubts about the courts' impartiality, sometimes even their competence. In
a bewildering series of judgments, every disputed practice but one was at
one time or another declared legal and then illegal, or vice versa.[35] (The
liturgical use of incense—which was, as Shane Leslie observed, the only
practice with any scriptural warrant—was consistently condemned).[36]

The principal problem for the litigators, however, stemmed from the
fact that the final court of appeal in ecclesiastical matters was the Judicial
Committee of the Privy Council, a lay body, and there was a growing belief
among Anglo-Catholics that a "secular court" had no right to regulate the
ceremonial of the Church. Even wholly ecclesiastical courts were compromised by the fact that their decisions could be appealed to the Privy Council. The Reverend John Purchas refused even to appear before the Court of
Arches, the supreme ecclesiastical court of the Province of Canterbury, on
that ground. (The ensuing "Purchas judgment" of 1871 declared the
eucharistic vestments and the eastward position to be illegal.) After the Public Worship Regulation Act, ritual cases were heard by a special court
appointed for the purpose by the archbishops, with the Queen's approval,
but appeal was still to the Privy Council. Moreover, some argued that any
court set up by an act of Parliament was unacceptably tainted since Parliament itself, of course, was a secular body.

Not long before, the view that Parliament and the Privy Council had no
right to regulate the Church had been voiced explicitly only by a few zealots,

but the ground had been laid as early as the Oxford Movement days for this new line of defense, as "legal" (or at least legalistic) as the Ornaments Rubric, but far more radical. H. P. Liddon, writing to the *Guardian* in the wake of the Purchas judgment, quoted Keble's remark, shortly before his death: "Depend upon it, we shall never have God's blessing on our work in the Church of England while we continue quietly to acquiesce in the present constitution of the Court of Final Appeal."[37] This had been an implicit theme of the movement's activities ever since Keble's protest against the suppression of Irish bishoprics in 1833, and beginning in the 1860s innumerable pamphlets and letters to the press argued that the Church should regulate its own affairs.

The argument was cogent, but one problem with it was that those who spoke of self-government for the Church invariably meant *clerical* government. The rector of Petershaw preached on the subject in 1865. In his text, I Corinthians xi, he found the clear implication that universal custom overrides local usage, as well as a warning against contentiousness and opposition to Catholic custom. "I do not mean, indeed," he said, "that the sound and laborious opinions of many laymen may not be accepted to inform and guide the minds of the clergy; but only this, that we [clergy] can never be called to submit to them as law, and that it is the vocation of the Clergy themselves to be lawyers in matters spiritual." On such a point as the Real Presence, "the humblest Presbyter of the Diocese of Ely [has] a greater right to speak with authority than the first lawyer in the land."[38]

What Might Have Been

Some Englishmen opposed clerical self-government in principle, and many more reserved the right to oppose it if it led to unsatisfactory results, but the argument was largely academic, since the clergy gave little indication that they were capable of governing themselves. However potent in principle, in practice Convocation failed miserably to articulate the Church's mind—or any coherent view at all—on the questions at issue between the Anglo-Catholics and their adversaries. It proved impossible to get both houses of both convocations to say what was permissible and what was not. Canterbury was usually more sympathetic to the movement than York, the lower houses more sympathetic than the upper. Time and again the bishops of the upper houses issued statements against the Ritualists, but the priests of the lower houses were unable to agree on anything much in the way of regulations. (The lower house of Canterbury's major effort in this direction was the "cope compromise" of 1877, which would have outlawed the eucharistic vestments but permitted the cope—a proposition that made no sense logically or historically, and was never taken seriously.) Nor were the bishops much more effective when acting on their own. Within their dioceses, bishops issued innumerable directives, so varied that it was difficult to

argue from them that the Church allowed or forbade anything in particular.
A practice allowed in Exeter might be winked at in Oxford and absolutely
forbidden in Manchester.

Had "the Church" been able to speak decisively through Convocation,
and had the bishops been willing to conform their own views to that declaration, perhaps some compromise could have been reached, satisfactory to
moderate churchmen of all parties, permitting more latitude than had been
the rule before, although less than was developing under the circumstances.
A clear-cut and uniform policy might have flushed the extremists, made it
plain just how extreme they were, and perhaps cut them off from their moderate allies.

But there would still have been trouble. No such compromise would
have placated either absolute Erastians like Shaftesbury or the no-popery
zealots of the Evangelical fringe. Nor would it have satisfied the advanced
wing of Anglo-Catholicism, where amateur canonists were already arguing
about the extent to which a "provincial synod"—that is, Convocation—
could alter the accepted use of the Catholic Church.[39] One marvelous exercise in vestry-room law, for example, was a pamphlet of 1877 that dealt with
the hypothetical question of "whether an English *parochus* is at liberty at the
present moment to act on a dispensation releasing him from the rubrical
obligation of wearing the eucharistic vestments." Actually, the question was
whether he should obey his bishop's order to stop, and the pamphlet concluded that such an order would be from a mere officer of the state; only the
implied dispensation from the Ornaments Rubric would come from the
bishop acting in his episcopal capacity. Since there is no requirement to use
a dispensation simply because one has it, the question becomes one of expe-
dience, and it would be inexpedient to abandon the vestments.[40] Q.E.D.

In other words, whether regulations had come from the courts or from
Convocation, from Parliament or from the bishops, some clergymen would
not have obeyed them. Nothing short of an ecumenical council would have
had the necessary authority. But, in the event, Anglo-Catholic extremists did
not have to fall back on that position. On balance, the indecisiveness of Convocation and the inconsistency of the bishops probably helped the movement, not only by contributing to the legal miasma that it exploited, but by
guaranteeing that the major attempt to clarify matters would come under
"secular" auspices, in the form of the Public Worship Regulation Act.

In the wake of that act, in 1874, Archdeacon Denison observed, "You
can't be burnt just now for disobeying the civil power. But you can be
deprived. Be deprived, then, rather than surrender one jot or tittle of your
Catholic inheritance, and then you will have done something for Christ."[41]
Denison was slow to adopt advanced ceremonial himself, but he had no
mixed feelings about the doctrines it was intended to symbolize or about the
clergy's right to adopt it even in the face of "secular" law. Three years later,
he was still breathing defiance:

Nothing may be surrendered to an authority which is no authority in the case. For his own and others' sake, let no Priest give way in any particular, either by way of resignation or by way of surrender of this or that detail of "Ritual," either before indictment, or during indictment, or after indictment brought to its *foregone* conclusion by sentence. Let no Priest give way. If he is to be dealt with "by law," let it be as by an external and hostile force only, not in any manner or degree, directly or indirectly, as by his own participation and concurrence.[42]

Denison spoke in 1877. That year, the Reverend Arthur Tooth of St. James's, Hatcham, was jailed for contempt of the court set up by the Public Worship Regulation Act, the first of five Anglican clergymen to be imprisoned for following Denison's advice.

VI

External Alliances and Internal Divisions

By the 1860s, three varieties of churchmanship had come to coexist uncomfortably on the right wing of the Church of England: a moribund remnant of the pre-Oxford Movement High Church known derisively as the "High and Dry," a new breed of "moderate High Churchmen" concerned with Church reform and influenced by Tractarianism, and of course the partisans of Anglo-Catholicism.[1] Some moderate High Churchmen and a handful of Laudians among the High and Dry might have described themselves as Anglo-Catholic, but they were at most allies of the movement, not part of it; indeed, comparison to the movement was what made moderate High Churchmen "moderate." Although in time Anglo-Catholics largely appropriated the High Church label for themselves, in the nineteenth century their right to it was never unchallenged, and their alliance with other High Churchmen was always a troubled one.

But that alliance was crucial. As one opponent saw it, "It is mainly on the misuse of this term [High Church] that Medievalists found their claim to be included in the comprehensiveness of our Church."[2] It is obvious why the movement's ecclesiastical allies were uneasy, less obvious why they remained allies.

The High and Dry

As Trollope put it, the High and Dry were what was left of "the high church as it was some fifty years since, before tracts were written and young clergymen took upon themselves the highly meritorious duty of cleaning churches."[3] Archdeacon Grantley in the Barsetshire novels exemplifies the type. Many observers believed that the concerns of this group were less religious than political; W. J. Conybeare wrote that "they sometimes talked of

Orthodoxy, at Visitation Dinners or University Elections; but they meant by Orthodoxy not any theological creed, but love of tithes and hatred of Methodists."[4] Their characteristic toast had once been to King and Church, but that old pairing, once so natural, was breaking up, as "King" was replaced by "Parliament" in the governance of the nation and its Church.

The High and Dry were socially respectable, often socially prominent, yet many observers had little use for them. In Conybeare's unsympathetic portrait, the most conspicuous were "the relatives or favourites of prelates long defunct," whose

youth was not fed with dreams of Catholic ideals, but inspired with more substantial visions of the comforts of an "establishment";
> "Wherein are various ranks and due degrees;
> The Bench for honour, and the Stall for ease."
Their fortune was often made for them before they left the nursery. No sooner had they quitted College, than they became dignitaries of the Church. Prebends, rectories, and archdeaconries seemed to have been created that these children of the purple might take their ease, eat, drink, and be merry.

Add to these High Church grandees a number of what Conybeare described as "country parsons, with fat rectories and fatter heads," and we have a recognizable, if mercilessly exaggerated, caricature of the High and Dry at mid-century.

But their day had passed; their once-formidable numbers and wealth were decreasing under the influence of religious revival and Church reform. Conybeare wrote:

One could almost pity the last survivors of that well-fed race, who are left bloated with pluralities and gorged with sinecures, to endure the indignant scoffs of a reforming age. They were but ordinary specimens of their breed, but their brethren have been swept away by the receding tide, and they lie stranded on the shore. By this perversity of fate they are doomed to gasp out their last breath under the harpoons of a crowd of satirists.[5]

In Conybeare's view, this was all that remained of the High Church party within which the Oxford Movement took shape in the 1830s, the party out of which both Pusey and Keble emerged. Among the original Tractarians, H. J. Rose and William Palmer represented this school of "High Church dignitaries, Archdeacons, London Rectors and the like," as Newman described them, and the differences of temperament and judgment between them and the younger Oxford men like Newman and his friend Froude were evident from the beginning. Newman described Rose, not quite approvingly, as a "practical man" for whom "existing facts had the precedence of every other idea, and the chief test of the soundness of a line of policy lay in the consideration whether it would work." When Froude called disestablishment "our only chance," Rose's comment was: "Very brilliant, very striking, very imaginative, but dreamy, theoretical, not practical." Palmer wanted the *Tracts* approved by a committee, and others must have regretted that they were not, especially after Tract 90, which was the last straw for many who had barely stomached Froude's *Remains*.[6]

The attitudes of High and Dry churchmen toward changes in the ornaments and services of the Church reflected their temperaments: they were not called *Dry* without reason. They disliked innovation and controversy (except for Phillpotts, who seemed to enjoy a good fight), they believed in the Establishment, and they were not Romanizers. They valued propriety. But they were not hostile to beauty, and although they sometimes viewed Anglo-Catholics' actions as imprudent or unbecoming, they seem often to have felt as Trollope's Mrs. Grantley did about her Tractarian sister:

A few high church vagaries [show] at any rate that her heart is in the subject; and [show] moreover that she is removed, wide as poles asunder, from that cesspool of abomination [marriage to the Evangelical Mr. Slope] in which it was once suspected that she would wallow and grovel. Anathema maranatha! Let anything else be held as blessed, so that that be well cursed. Welcome kneelings and bowings, welcome matins and complines, welcome bell, book, and candle, so that Mr. Slope's dirty surplices and ceremonial Sabbaths be held in due execration![7]

The High and Dry were not a theological party of consequence and they contributed only rarely to the revival of Anglo-Catholic thought, but in the movement's early years some bishops of this school gave the Tractarians a little support and somewhat more toleration. Bishops Phillpotts of Exeter and Hamilton of Salisbury defended sacramental confession in the early 1850s, a precedent greatly needed in the 1870s. Phillpotts's refusal to institute a clergyman who denied baptismal regeneration, of course, brought on the Gorham case, and Bagot of Bath and Wells also defended baptismal regeneration as the doctrine of the Church. Moreover, Bagot refused to prosecute Archdeacon G. A. Denison for his views on the Real Presence, even after Denison asked him to. (True, as bishop of Oxford, Bagot had condemned Tract 90, but it is clear that he appreciated the impulse behind the *Tracts* and believed they had done much good.) In addition, despite their declining importance, the High and Dry could still be roused to defend the Church's temporal rights and privileges, and in this matter they were usually allied with the rest of the High Church party, including the Anglo-Catholics.

Moderate High Churchmen

The High and Dry were largely a negative and inertial force linked to the rest of the High Church party by a common set of enemies, and it is hard to escape the conclusion that their enemies needed them more than their allies did. From the interaction between this school and the Tractarians, however, came a new sort of High Churchmen, a more vital and positive force in the life of the Church, who by thought and practice came by mid-century to occupy the center of the High Church party as a whole, relegating the remaining High and Dry to the position of fossils. These moderate High Churchmen—or simply "Anglicans," as they sometimes called themselves—had been affected by the Church revival and by the early teachings of the Tractarians, but they represented an old tradition in the Church of England, and they knew it. They took their stand squarely on the Prayer Book and the seventeenth-century Anglican divines, and in so doing revived an English tradition that had been largely dormant for a century and a half.

As Conybeare observed, in earlier generations many clergymen of this school would have been High and Dry as a matter of course; men "prejudiced by hereditary dislike against the doctrines and the persons of the Evangelicals" and not intellectually or temperamentally inclined to religious liberalism had nowhere else to go. But in the new climate provided by the circulation of Tractarian ideas they could, "under the name of orthodoxy and the banner of High Church," find a focus for loyalty as stirring and a field for work as demanding as anything the Low or Broad Church had to offer.[8]

Where many of the High and Dry found a high doctrine of the Church congenial because it rationalized their privileges, the new High Churchmen, like their Caroline predecessors, saw it as a challenge to make the Church an institution worthy of its founder, and they met the challenge with a characteristically Victorian combination of devoted pastoral work, personal piety, and moderate reform. Samuel Wilberforce, bishop of Oxford and subsequently of Winchester, was a leader of this faction, and his leadership accounted for many of its successes. The revival of Convocation at mid-century, a typical example of moderate High Church reform that restored a measure of "home rule" to the Church, as represented by its bishops and clergy, came about largely through his efforts and those of Lord Redesdale, a layman of the same persuasion.[9]

It is easy to overstate the difference between this body and the pre-Tractarian High Church, and Anglo-Catholic historians have often done so. But lately other historians may have overdone the necessary task of correction. It is not simply that the new generation took its religion seriously and the old generation did not; there are too many counterexamples for that generalization to stand. Moderate High Churchmen differed from the High and Dry chiefly in their vitality: where the old High Church party was passive, defensive, and isolated, the new was active, outgoing, and enthusiastic—a word and an attribute that the High and Dry found objectionable.

On the other hand, moderate High Churchmen differed from the Puseyites and Ritualists of the Anglo-Catholic movement in their pragmatism and sense of proportion. They were not pioneers, exploring and expanding the limits of acceptable belief and ceremonial, but they often sheltered those who were, and they were responsible for many of the most significant changes brought about in the course of the Church revival, if only because they were of greater political consequence than the more thoroughgoing Anglo-Catholics. Moderate High Churchmen did not feel themselves to be in opposition for the good and sufficient reason that they were not; they were part of the establishment against which the Anglo-Catholic movement contended.[10]

Doctrinal Unity

Whatever their differences, High Churchmen were united by common beliefs that set them off from Evangelicals and other Low Churchmen, on the one hand, and from the liberals and Erastians of the Broad Church party, on the other. In most respects, Anglo-Catholic theology merely emphasized doctrines that had always distinguished the High Church party from the rest of the Church of England. Conybeare wrote that the "characteristic tenets" of the High Church, its "watchwords," were "'*Judgment by works*,' '*Baptismal Regeneration*,' '*Church Authority*,' and '*Apostolical Succession*.'"[11]

R. F. Littledale was hardly a disinterested observer, but he was correct when he remarked, "It is very hard to say where Ritualism ends and where Anglicanism begins." Littledale argued that on the "diptychs" of the High Church "stand all the most illustrious names of the Anglican Communion— Hooker, Andrewes, Herbert, Laud, Taylor, Cosin, Pearson, Mede, Ken, Bull, Wilson, Butler, Horsley, Keble, Neale, and a host of other worthies." Some High Churchmen would have objected to Keble's inclusion, and many more to Neale's; as Littledale implied, however, all of these worthies embraced to one degree or another "the doctrines of Baptismal Regeneration, Apostolical Succession, the Priesthood, the Real Presence, the Eucharistic Sacrifice, Prayer for the Dead, and Auricular Confession."[12] Littledale's fellow Ritualist J. B. Dykes was not being disingenuous when, in a widely read essay on *Eucharistic Truth and Ritual*, he appealed to "my dear High-Church brethren" for support on the grounds that "we are one in heart, one in aim, one (in all essential points) in faith."[13]

This doctrinal continuity accounts for the fact that, as one critic observed in the 1870s, "thousands and tens of thousands both of clergy and laity ... stand neutral, or are on the side of toleration." He added,

Ritualism could not exist among us but for the protection it has received from High Churchmen.... Ritualists, who are covering the land with sisterhoods, confraternities, guilds; who are advocating confessions, masses, penances; who in schools, churches, and missions, teach the doctrines of the Church of Rome—all these style themselves

High Churchmen.... So long as the High Church party does not repudiate them, they derive a strength from this association to which they are in no wise entitled.

As this man observed, "The High Church party [was] often appealed to, but in vain."[14] Time and again, the movement's more politically astute opponents attempted to exploit the division between the Anglo-Catholic vanguard and the rest of the High Church party. As late as the turn of the century, an Evangelical writer called on his fellows to make distinctions, to "*discriminate*," urging "the great importance of *never* giving *the term of High Churchman*" to Ritualists.[15] But these efforts were almost always unsuccessful. To those who were genuinely concerned with such matters, supporters and opponents alike, the undeniable differences in practice between the movement and other High Churchmen were usually out-weighed in importance by equally undeniable doctrinal similarities. The Evangelical vicar of St. Luke's, West Holloway, for instance, contrasted "moderate Anglicans" with "Ritualists," but went on to aver that the distinction was immaterial because both groups held the doctrine of the Real Presence. Ritualists, he observed, "are not so guarded in their language. They tell us plainly what they mean, and so far, we have to thank them for their honesty."[16]

Anglo-Catholics complained about their allies' want of principle and readiness to compromise, while other High Churchmen denounced Anglo-Catholics' Romanism and lack of common sense; yet, in general, the alliance held. The underlying similarities of belief were emphasized and the alliance was strengthened by the indiscriminate opposition of those who did not share the beliefs in the first place. When push came to shove, High Churchmen could not repudiate Anglo-Catholicism without repudiating their own tradition.

Divisions in the High Church Party

This does not mean, however, that the strains in the relationship were unimportant. As the *Church Times* proclaimed in 1866, "No one is so heartily despised by the advanced Churchman as a moderate Anglican," and it was also true that many moderate Anglicans despised "advanced Church-men."[17] Their differences may have been matters of emphasis and practice rather than belief, but they were many and varied, and most were grounds for contention.

While moderates' opinions and practices often followed from their prin-cipled or prudential opposition to Romanism, the views of many (though not all) Anglo-Catholics reflected their tenderness toward their separated Catholic brethren. Most High Churchmen agreed, for example, that sister-hoods were a worthwhile experiment, but moderates usually wished that Anglo-Catholic sisters were less enthusiastic about life vows, distinctive habits, spiritual direction, and devotions adapted from Roman Catholic sources. Similarly, High Churchmen of all schools defended the doctrine of priestly absolution in principle, but the practice of "habitual confession" drew a sharp line between moderates, on the one hand, and even conservative Tractarians, on the other.

Bishop Wilberforce, so sympathetic in so many ways, so encouraging to the early sisterhoods, had a virulent distaste for Roman Catholicism (to which he had lost several relatives as converts), and he had a particular dislike for confession other than in exceptional circumstances. While advising the Clewer sisterhood in its early years, he warned against "a semi-Romanist system, with its *direction,* with its development of self-consciousness and morbid religious affection, with its exaltation of the contemplative life, its perpetual Confession, and its un-English tone."[18] In 1850 he inhibited Pusey from officiating in his diocese for nearly two years, writing, "I so firmly believe that of all the curses of Popery this [regular confession] is the crowning curse, that I cannot allow voluntarily within my charge the continuance of any ministry which is infected by it."[19] Dr. Hook, the vicar of Leeds, representative of old-fashioned High Church opinion in this respect as in others, felt much the same. During an 1850 conflict at St. Saviour's, Hook preached that confession is a means of comfort, not of grace, allowed by the Church of England only "as an extreme exception."[20]

The difference could also be observed in attitudes toward an organization called the Anglo-Continental Society. That respectable High Church bastion numbered archbishops and bishops among its patrons, and prominent laymen on the General Committee included A. J. B. Beresford Hope and J. G. Hubbard (later Lord Addington), the benefactors of All Saints, Margaret Street, and of St. Alban's, Holborn, respectively.[21] But the clergy of those two churches were not represented—not surprisingly, because most Anglo-Catholics came to disapprove of this enterprise.

The association's stated aim was to "to make the principles of the Church of England, her doctrine, discipline, and *status,* better known on the Continent of Europe," and some Tractarians (among them Keble and Gladstone) had worked with the association in its early days, in the 1850s.[22] By the 1870s, however, its "Special Operations" included "encouraging, developing, and helping to shape the Old Catholic movement throughout the world," and its agents in Italy were seeking priests and laymen "as may be disposed to a Reformation." Moderate High Churchmen regarded the Old Catholic movement and other "Primitive," anti-papal groups as similar in doctrine and polity to Anglicanism and as its natural allies, but Anglo-Catholics saw these bodies as schismatic. In Anglo-Catholic theory the legitimate diocesans on the Continent were the Roman Catholic bishops.

The so-called Maynooth controversy concerning support for a Roman Catholic seminary in Ireland had produced a similar division in 1845: the new Tractarians generally favored it; older High Churchmen with Establishment loyalties opposed it.[23] The Anglo-Continental Society's operations also bore an uncomfortable resemblance to Bishop Gobat's proselytizing in the Holy Land, which had upset the Tractarians.[24]

Moderate High Churchmen feared that Anglo-Catholics' Romanism and their emphasis on the independence of the Church endangered the Establishment, and they were probably correct.[25] Hubbard, Beresford Hope, Lord Redesdale, and other like-minded churchmen were active in the Church Defense Institution, an antidisestablishmentarian organization, but Anglo-Catholics repeatedly made it plain that (as the Reverend James Dunn observed offhandedly in an address to the Clifton branch of the E.C.U.) "there is not one amongst us who would not gladly welcome the disestablishment of the English Church" rather than see its "inherent spiritual power" surrendered to the state.[26] Such talk made other High Churchmen nervous, and had ever since the days of J. H. Rose and Hurrell Froude.

As usual, Anglo-Catholics distinguished themselves most conspicuously by their liturgical practices, which increasingly resembled those of Roman Catholics. In 1866, for instance, J. S. Pollock defended noncommunicating attendance at the Eucharist, and objected to what he called the "Protestant and High Church" practice of expelling noncommunicants.[27] A few years later, R. F. Littledale argued in the *Guardian* that Anglo-Catholics should not celebrate the Eucharist on Good Friday, since Roman Catholics took communion from the reserved Sacrament on that day, but reservation had been unambiguously forbidden in the Church of England. Littledale's "Anglican" critics replied that the Prayer Book provides a Gospel and Epistle for Good Friday, rather plainly implying that a celebration is intended.[28] (Of course, the argument was merely theoretical in those places where the Sacrament was reserved illicitly—as it had been for a quarter-century in the chapel of the Sisters of St. Margaret.[29])

In cases like these, where Anglo-Catholics were merely aping Roman practice, they received little sympathy from other High Churchmen. When they could argue that their practices symbolized High Church doctrine, however, they were far more likely to receive a measure of support; then they could argue that attacks on the practice were in fact attacks on the doctrine—as, indeed, they often were. This is shown clearly in the history of two practices said by their defenders to be intimately bound up with the doctrine of the Real Presence: the eastward position at the Prayer of Consecration, and the wearing of the distinctive eucharistic vestments.

The Vestments and the Eastward Position

The Liddell judgment, based on the Ornaments Rubric, had implied that the eucharistic vestments were legal, and many High Churchmen felt, as one wrote later, that the nature of the Eucharist might make special vestments for it appropriate; that perhaps they should be allowed in churches where the congregation approved; even that it might be desirable to restore them more generally when "circumstances and the general state of feeling in the Church allowed."[30] In practice, however, throughout the 1860s, their use was confined to those of extremely advanced views.

On the other hand, the eastward position, although it rested on some-what shakier legal foundations, had become widespread even among High Churchmen not otherwise given to Anglo-Catholic extravagance, including some of great influence and unimpeachable respectability. As Pusey observed, the eastward position was not "elaborate ritual"; like the mixed chalice and unlike the vestments, it could hardly "jar on the devotional feel-ings of persons really devout, but attached to simpler services."[31]

Both the vestments and the eastward position were under attack by Anglo-Catholicism's Evangelical opponents, but it was widely believed at this time that the law was on the side of the Anglo-Catholics; to change it, R. F. Littledale wrote, would be "against the feeling of the whole High-Church party, ranking from the most conservative of the old-fash-ioned Churchmen to the vanguard of advanced Ritualism" (as well as "the temperate and respectable Low-Church section, and all Broad churchmen who retain any feeling in favour of fair play").[32]

Be that as it may, many High Churchmen opposed any revision of the Ornaments Rubric. In 1866, when the English Church Union organized memorials on the subject, they were presented to the archbishop of Canter-bury by a delegation of approximately 150, led by the earl of Carnarvon, a moderate High Churchman who articulated his faction's point of view.[33] Lord Carnarvon said that he feared that "if Parliament legislates to-day on the Rubrics, to-morrow it may be legislating on the Articles of Faith." The "great bulk of the signatures," he insisted, were those of "moderate and sober-minded Churchmen." No doubt some approved of "those usages and ceremonials which have been introduced or restored in the Church, in cer-tain places," but

others there are (and, in justice to myself, I feel bound to state, distinctly, that I am amongst that number) who are unable to go along with the reasoning upon which these ceremonials are introduced; who are satisfied with the forms of public worship existing in the Church of England; who believe that those forms of worship are already sufficiently elastic; and who have learned to associate them for many years with the Services of the Church of England. [The transcript records murmurs of "Hear, hear."]

But, the earl continued, all who signed the memorials

deprecate any change in any part of the Prayer-book. [The transcript shows applause.] My Lord, so long as the law is not overstepped, we are not prepared by legislation, and still less are we prepared by *ex post facto* legislation [hear, hear], made for a special purpose, and directed against a particular set of individuals [hear, hear] to curtail that freedom ... which exists on either side; nor are we prepared to suffer any one party in the Church to put violence upon another.

The archbishop, largely unresponsive, stressed his desire for uniformity in the Church, and once again condemned "extreme Ritualism." He promised, however, that no change in the rubrics would be made without the "full concurrence of Convocation"—which was never forthcoming.[34]

Unable to outlaw Ritualism by ecclesiastical legislation, the Church Association and other hostile Evangelicals were more successful in their attempts to secure redress in the courts. In particular, the Judicial Committee of the Privy Council ruled in 1871 in the case of *Hebbert* v. *Purchas* not only that the eucharistic vestments were illegal after all, but that the eastward position was, too.

That decision caused some confusion among clergymen whose churches were not "oriented" with their altars at the eastern end; one complained to the bishop of Manchester that if he stood facing south as directed, his back would be to the people.[35] But more important was the resulting outcry from High Churchmen. Pusey's disciple, H. P. Liddon, a sober, scholarly, and respected cleric of Tractarian principles, wrote the *Guardian* to say that by condemning the eastward position the Judicial Committee had not only condemned the practice of such men as John Keble, but had attacked "the High Church school as a whole"; the eastward position, Liddon maintained, was a practice "cherished by the old-fashioned and learned churchmen of generations which preceded the Oxford Movement."[36] Liddon and another canon of St. Paul's asked the bishop of London to include them in any future prosecutions.

Pusey himself wrote the *Times* to argue that the judgment was without effect, since the case was not defended (Purchas had refused to recognize the authority of the Privy Council), and went on to point out why the matter was important. "The tumult has been, and is being, raised by [those] who wish to stamp out belief in the Real Presence and get rid of those who believe it," he wrote. Saying that he had himself taken the eastward position (although seldom in Christ Church) for "above thirty years"—that is, since the days of the Oxford Movement—he argued, "I do not think the High Church could, as a body, abandon it, without seeming to abandon the doctrine which it symbolizes."[37]

Other Anglo-Catholics repeated and elaborated the point. The eastward position, Malcolm MacColl observed, had been inherited by the High Church party; the Evangelicals were the ones who had given it a doctrinal significance. But once that significance had been attached to it, it could not be given up. Referring to an attack by the dean of Chester, MacColl asserted:

The programme which he has put out is a declaration of war upon the High Church party along the whole line; and the effect of such tactics will be, or rather has been, to make the entire body of High Churchmen close their ranks and present a united

front.... Surely he must see, on reflection, that his own book, if nothing else, has
made it quite impossible for the High Church party to give up the Eastward position. He condemns it on the very ground that it symbolizes an altar, a sacrifice, and
a priesthood. Very good. But these are doctrines which are inseparable from the history of the High Church party; and what the Dean of Chester modestly proposes
therefore is simply that the High Church party should turn its back upon a not inglo-
rious past and efface itself.[38]

The opponents of Anglo-Catholicism had clearly made a tactical error,
provoking reaction from a broad spectrum of High Church opinion. In a
fictional dialogue of 1877, the spokesman for moderation, allowing that he
sees no harm in restraining the clergy by law from "unauthorized and
unpopular changes," nevertheless criticizes the anti-Ritualists for their political stupidity; among other missteps, he says, "You have driven the old High
Church party *en masse* into the arms of the Ritualists by attacking the eastward position. You have raised the apprehensions of High Churchmen to
the highest pitch by allowing it to be believed, whether rightly or wrongly,
that it was intended to prevent the sacramental doctrines of Andrewes and
Laud, of Chrysostom and Augustine, from being any longer tenable in the
Church of England."[39]

It was apparently no accident that the Ridsdale judgment of that same
year reversed the Purchas decision on the eastward position, but upheld it in
the matter of vestments. "That is to say," Archdeacon Denison observed, "it
allows for what there may be some room for [legal] argument against, and
disallows what there is no room for argument against: repealing in the latter
case the Ornaments' [*sic*] Rubric."[40] It is difficult to escape Denison's conclusion that the decision was politically motivated, that the wiser of the Ritualists' opponents had belatedly adopted a divide-and-conquer strategy, protecting a use popular among moderate High Churchmen and concentrating
their fire on the extremists. A few years earlier, perhaps, that could have been
smart politics, but coming when it did (as a moderate High Church dean
put it) the Ridsdale judgment did not "satisfy and approve itself to (I do not
say the party against whose practices judgment was given; but) intelligent
and unprejudiced persons with no leaning whatever to Ritualism."[41] The
Spectator spoke for exactly such persons when it observed that "the judgments given in the Purchas and Ridsdale cases, though undeniably law, were
bad law," decided not "without regard to consequences."[42]

"The Gradual Effacement of Distinctions"

The taxonomy of High Churchmen with which we began—High and
Dry, moderate, Anglo-Catholic—points to real clusterings of sentiment and
practice, but it is misleading to think of the boundaries between the different types as fixed, sharply defined, and impermeable. (Recall Littledale's

observation about the difficulty of saying "where Ritualism ends and where Anglicanism begins.") Certainly we can identify figures who were representative of each of the categories, but others drifted back and forth across the boundaries, which were themselves constantly shifting and often very blurred. The bishop of Gloucester and Bristol identified a real problem when he said in an address to his diocese in 1878 that the presence of extremists working

for the express and scarcely concealed purpose of what is called "Catholicising" the Church of England certainly helps to contaminate and to compromise the loyalty of a more numerous body of men who, themselves quite free from the *mala fides* of the party to which I am alluding, cannot help sheltering them.... This large fringe has a still larger fringe around itself, and so on, until we have nearly arrived at that great and honourable party, the true and loyal High Church Party.

The bishop complained about the "gradual contamination of all the surrounding element, this obliteration of every break of continuity," and concluded that the "tendency to bring about the gradual effacement of distinctions is one of the evils connected with the existence of the extreme party."[43] The bishop's problem was not just conceptual but political: a strategy of divide-and-conquer is difficult to pursue without agreement about where the division should be made.

For some, this confusion was deliberate. Partisans of all colors sometimes stood to profit from effacing distinctions. Those who opposed Anglo-Catholicism root and branch could seldom resist the temptation to link its serious core to the ecclesiastical demimonde, and inhabitants of that fringe wished to legitimize their position by establishing the same link. Extreme Evangelicals, on a fringe of their own, saw little to choose between the movement and High Churchmen like Wilberforce; both believed in priestly absolution, did they not? As one put it, "The conflict against Ritualism merges itself into a wider and more portentous struggle," between those who hold "the doctrines of the Bible" and all those—not just Ritualists—who subscribe to "the doctrine of Eucharistic sacrifice."[44] The movement, for its part, saw the great advantage to be gained from that formulation.

All of this rhetorically useful confusion was made possible by the more or less continuous gradation that ran from Father Ignatius, Father Nugee, and Bishop Lee of the Order of Corporate Reunion, through the uncompromising hard core of the Society of the Holy Cross, the Tractarians and their successors in college and cathedral close, moderate High Churchmen in the House of Bishops and both Houses of Parliament, to the respected, powerful, and historically entrenched High Church party of Hook and Churton.

Confusion also came about because the movement was constantly changing, and those who did not change with it—those who merely staked out a position and held to it—sometimes awoke to find themselves in a different category. Innovation had its own dynamic. Looking back at the turn of the century, the longtime president of the English Church Union, Lord Halifax, pointed out that "those in the front of the battle have constantly been characterized and censured as extreme by those behind," but that "almost always what was condemned in the first instance has come to be accepted in the end." ("The lesson to be drawn from the fact," he added, "is too obvious to be insisted on."[45]) Sometime innovators became respectable merely by maintaining their original positions.

The result was a more-or-less constant generational tension. Old High Churchmen like Hook and Palmer viewed the young men of the Oxford Movement with some suspicion, but it was only a matter of time before the surviving Tractarians were feeling nervous about the rising generation of Ritualists, and eventually a Ritualist old-timer complained of the "meddlesome officiousness of a party of younger men" of *his* day, and urged restraint. (Restrict yourselves, he told them, to incense, vestments, and proper English usage; do not interpolate the Canon of the Tridentine Mass in the Prayer Book Communion service.[46])

It is not just that the old were more cautious than the young. That may have been generally true, although there were many exceptions (for instance, older men frequently became intransigent when the bishops or the courts finally went too far). But the point is that each generation in the movement was inclined to draw the boundary of legitimacy just beyond its own hard-won practice. As one member of the Society of the Holy Cross observed, every school of thought was opposed by "some, for the purpose of discrediting others just a little 'higher' than themselves," and this gradation often had a generational aspect to it.[47]

These line-drawing exercises are primarily of interest because of the way that practices defended as *not* extreme changed over time. In 1843, for example, one "ultrarubrician" defended the Church Militant prayer, the surplice in the pulpit, and some other minor innovations, but maintained that since the Prayer Book did not require such things as lit candles, altar flowers, bowing and genuflection, they should be avoided as "liable to give offense to tender consciences."[48] A generation later, in 1866, another High Church writer defended these practices (as well as weekly Communion and even eucharistic vestments), appealing to "the mind and practice of the *first ages* [as the] absolute standard of eucharistic duty"; he drew the line, however, when the "mediaeval and ultra-sacramental school" encouraged non-communicating attendance at the Eucharist, implied that the consecrated elements should be worshiped, or made what he considered superstitious use of crucifixes.[49] A few years later still, about 1880, an assistant master at Winchester College argued that most Ritualist practices were "reasonable expressions of moderate High Church doctrines, but criticized what he saw as mere imitations of Roman Catholic use, without doctrinal significance: "inaudible recitation" of the Prayer of Consecration, the "cele-brant's sitting down during the Nicene Creed," and "reluctant administra-tion" of the chalice.[50] By the turn of the century, the dean of Lichfield was maintaining that he and the "great majority of High Churchmen" did not hold with such practices as compulsory confession, absolution of departed souls, reservation of the Sacrament for purposes of adoration, candles before images, sprinkling Holy Water, devotions to the Blessed Virgin, and inter-polating the Latin Canon in the Prayer Book Communion service.[51]

Generational Tension within the Movement

As R. F. Littledale complained, many Anglo-Catholics had "remained all these several terms of years exactly at their starting point of 1828, 1838, 1848, and have never progressed an inch, even in power of comprehending the religious changes of the times."[52] By the late 1860s this dynamic had moved a number of extremists of the 1830s and 1840s to positions of rela-tive moderation. (In 1867 one Evangelical writer even used the phrases "moderate Anglican" and "Puseyite" synonymously, in contrast to the Rit-ualists—although he disapproved of all High Churchmen impartially, on doctrinal grounds.[53])

The result was exacerbation of the generational tension within the movement. One old Tractarian left behind by change and mellowed by age into a moderate High Churchman was the Reverend John W. Burgon, who in 1873 preached two widely noted sermons in Newman's former church of St. Mary the Virgin, Oxford, attacking Ritualist "extravagancies." He was, he said, no ally of those opposed to beauty and order, and he defended the doctrine of baptismal regeneration, the Athanasian Creed, and strict obser-vance of the rubrics. But, he complained, the new sort were not faithful to Anglicanism. "The Prayer-Book is felt to block the way. The vocabulary of the new sect is avowedly Roman." He found the latter development partic-ularly offensive in light of "the terrible position which the Church of Rome unmistakably occupies in unfulfilled Prophecy," and he sympathized with "aggrieved laymen" upset about Romanizing, so long as they were not of the Church Association stripe.[54]

Another clergyman, describing himself as a High Churchman, Anglo-Catholic, and Ritualist—"but one whose ritual lies within the words, 'The Rubrics of the Church of England, neither more nor less'"—remarked in a review of the Ritualist handbook, *Directorium Anglicanum*, "I have never risen from my present task without fervently thanking God for the Reformation."[55] Similarly, the *Christian Remembrancer*, a Tractarian organ, protested that "modesty and humble-mindedness are graces which are dis-tinguished by their absence from the Ritualist party—as a party," adding that "a Catholic-minded priest is, on inquiry, found to be a gentlemen of mod-erate abilities and limited information, who is distinguished for the fidelity of his adherence to the Roman sequence of colours, and [for] the correctness with which he wears and doffs his biretta." The *Remembrancer* feared that those "who organise Magnificats with incense and varied attitudes, who add Corpus Christi Day to the great festivals, and who strain all their energies to the converting of Sunday worship into non-communicant gazing on a high mass" were provoking middle-of-the-road opinion into sympathy with the extreme Evangelicals. The *Remembrancer* observed, "It is perfectly idle to contend that this class of ritualists is conservative of the Prayer-book," and took pains to dissociate "those who are determined to realise certain [illegal] practices because they think them Catholic, or because they like them" from "the great school of thought whose leaders have during the last thirty-four years conducted the Church revival."[56]

Earlier, the *Remembrancer* had provoked a storm by publishing an essay on "extreme men" by A. J. B. Beresford Hope, in which that one-time enthusiast, now a wealthy and influential High Church layman, called attention to "many small questions in which the Ritualists have shown themselves deficient in tact, and careless in ascertaining the drift of popular feeling." Even prejudice, he added, should "be taken into account by men whose duty and desire is to mould public opinion"—men, that is, like himself.[57] The extremists responded characteristically: the *Church Times* accused Beresford Hope of "open ratting from the party of which he had once been a useful subordinate, though not the redoubted champion which he thinks himself."[58] John Mason Neale also replied to his old friend and former colleague in the Ecclesiological Society, pointing out that the Prayer Book said little about "vestments of the altar," but "she does command [by the Ornaments Rubric] the use of the cope and chasuble, which is exactly what, by the code of your article, we are not to have. But we shall, though."[59]

In general, the Ritualists gave as good as they got. *Caught Napping*, for instance, an anonymous spoof of the Tractarian school, portrayed the rector of Grubbington-in-the-Clay, "where I have preached the doctrine of Baptismal Regeneration for fifteen years, ... where I always preach in a surplice and black stole, ... where I read the Church Militant every Sunday." Falling asleep over his *Guardian*, the good rector dreams he is in the catacombs with a group of early Christians, and he is horrified to discover that they act, look, and talk very much like Ritualists.[60] *Caught Napping* went through at least three editions, received favorable mention in the *Church Times* and the *Church Review* (the latter called it "downright fun"), and provoked an outraged open letter from the editor of the *Protestant Churchman* to the bishop of Oxford.[61]

In 1875 all but two of the bishops signed a pastoral letter repeating the by-then-familiar complaint about the "growing tendency to associate doctrinal significance with rites and ceremonies which do not necessarily involve it," and exhorting the clergy "not to disquiet their congregations by novel practices and unauthorized ceremonies." Almost immediately a pamphlet appeared that claimed to detect in the pastoral "a wish to draw off the one wing and centre of the High-Church Clergy from the one in danger, and, in propitiation of popular clamour, to sacrifice the one for the better safety of the other."[62] Whether this was an accurate assessment of the bishops' intentions or not, it is certainly true that from time to time opponents of the movement tried to exploit the continuing tensions between those (generally older) Anglo-Catholics whose emphasis on decency, order, and adherence to the rubrics of the Prayer Book was no longer so disturbing, and those (generally younger) responsible for the latest alarming and disloyal "extravagancies."

In 1873, for example, one Church Association writer claimed that his organization had not been necessary until the rise of Ritualism. He paid tribute to Keble's "erudition and high poetic talent" and to the "qualities of his heart"; he praised Newman's intellect and (referring to his *Apologia*) his honesty; he chided Pusey, but only for "shelter[ing] beneath the skirts of his vast learning the unworthy successors to the writers of the 'Tracts for the Times'—scholars whose highest literary efforts culminate in elaborate articles on the importance of receiving Holy Communion fasting, and whose thoughts are stirred by the colour of a stole, or the cut of a chasuble." The new generation, he said, did not have the "learning of Pusey and Keble, or the honesty of Newman and the Wilberforces"; they did not, in other words, go to Rome when their convictions led them there.[63]

Ironically, these Protestant observations were echoed a few years later by Orby Shipley, an extreme man indeed, who by 1880 had become a Roman Catholic. In an open letter to Pusey, Shipley compared the "vulgarised and degraded" Anglo-Catholicism of "so-called Ritualist[s]" with the faith of "the gentlemanlike, cultivated, pious and scholarly Oxford Tractarians."[64]

By 1881 Malcolm MacColl could write, with only a little exaggeration: "It is now, indeed, the fashion to pat the Tractarians on the back, praise their 'moderation,' glorify them as the 'old historical High Church party,' and then contrast them with the dreadful Ritualists." MacColl observed and demonstrated how "very different is the language that was applied to them forty years ago."[65]

Nevertheless, after the Purchas judgment and especially after the Public Worship Regulation Act of 1874, the breach between the two wings of Anglo-Catholicism threatened to become a chasm. The *Guardian*, maintaining as before "the rubric as the one rule of ritual observance," dismissed the view that the Ornaments Rubric required the eucharistic vestments as "a private opinion only," observing that "the only authority which has yet pronounced about it [is] flatly the other way."[66] The learned jurist Sir J. T. Coleridge allowed that his "feeling" favored the eastward position if not the vestments, but urged that the law should be obeyed, and many of the more conservative Anglo-Catholics agreed with him.[67]

The warden of Keble College, Oxford, for instance, opined that if God willed various improvements in the Church of England, they would not be hindered by strict obedience to the Church's law, and some other Anglo-Catholics who felt that way resigned from the English Church Union when the Union resolved in 1877 that the Judicial Committee of the Privy Council and courts subordinate to it had no spiritual authority.[68] The previous year Priscilla Sellon had written the Union's president to scold him for upsetting Pusey by an intransigent resolution on the Six Points: "The real doctrine of the Catholic Faith receives no let or hindrance," she wrote. Why then "force upon older people and the past generations outward observances which though very agreeable to your feelings are with a few individual exceptions new and foreign to them?"[69]

Patterns of signatures to a number of memorials, statements, and petitions reveal the differences not just between Anglo-Catholics and other High Churchmen but between the conservative and extreme wings of the movement. Soon after the Purchas judgment, for instance, a memorial to the Convocation of Canterbury was drawn up, protesting that the judgment was unfair, that it was bad law, and that it threatened the Church of England's continuity with "the Primitive and Catholic Church."[70] All of these opinions were widely held, but when the memorial went on to state that the signers were "unable consistently with our duty to God and the Church to acknowledge the authority in spiritual matters of the said Judicial Committee" of the Privy Council, it became more controversial. The 910 clerical signers included almost all the well-known Ritualists, most other members of the S.S.C., and many others from the English Church Union. Pusey, Liddon, and others of like mind, however, were notably absent from the list, and moderate High Churchmen were almost entirely unsympathetic.

The next month a more mildly worded "solemn remonstrance" was directed to the bishops, asking them on grounds of fair play and tolerance not to enforce the decision. It made no mention of the vestments, did not use the word "Catholic," hinted discreetly at danger to the Establishment, and received more than five times as many signatures. The signers included not only Ritualists but also an array of Tractarians including Pusey, and even many old-fashioned High Churchmen, including the former vicar of Leeds, Dr. Hook, now dean of Chichester and Chaplain-in-Ordinary to the Queen.[71]

Three years later a statement called the "Three Deans' Declaration" produced a similar division. Circulated by the dean of St. Paul's, it was signed by two other deans, six (retired, colonial, or coadjutor) bishops, and some 1467 other clergymen. It made no mention of doctrine, but deprecated "any attempt to enforce a rigid uniformity in the performance of divine worship," on the grounds that it would tend to "confusion."[72] The declaration asked that clergymen be protected from interference "in respect of the position which they may conscientiously feel it their duty to take at the holy table," and that "some liberty" be allowed for the vestments, at early celebrations or under such other restrictions as Convocation might deem appropriate, if both minister and congregation wanted them. Pusey and most of the old Tractarians were among the signers, as were a number of moderate High Churchmen like Benjamin Webb of St. Andrew's, Wells Street, and many other influential High Church archdeacons, canons, rural deans, prebendaries, and rectors.

This time, ironically, it was the "advanced Ritualists" who did not sign; they found the declaration's prudential argument unsatisfactory and its suggestion of limitations unacceptable. A meeting of Catholic clergy in Oxford produced a separate petition, addressed to both convocations and asking that "nothing be done to interfere with" the eastward position or the vestments, on the explicit grounds that interference, "especially at the present time, could not but be interpreted as striking at the doctrines of the Holy Eucharist and the Christian Priesthood handed down from the Primitive Church."[73] Pusey added a written "assent" in which he accepted the petitioners' reasoning; most of the several dozen signers, however, were Ritualists like Mackonochie, Littledale, and Lowder, many of them members of the S.S.C.

Soon after the passage of the Public Worship Regulation Act, the Society of the Holy Cross called a meeting (intended to be secret) of "those who are what are called 'the more extreme Ritualists,'" to decide upon a party line in preparation for an anticipated meeting to "embrace all the schools of the High Church Clergy," at which the extreme faction apparently feared that they would find themselves outgunned and outmaneuvered. The invitation list included, besides the Society's own members, priests-associate of the Confraternity of the Blessed Sacrament, clerical members of the English Church Union believed to be sympathetic, signers of the memorial to Convocation denying the spiritual authority of the Judicial Committee of the Privy Council and of the "licensed confessors" petition, and "certain [other] priests on whom reliance was placed."[74] The meeting clearly stated the points on which the extremists were not prepared to compromise: the court set up by the PWRA was without authority, and no revision of the Prayer Book rubrics or prohibition of the E.C.U.'s "Six Points" was acceptable.

In a show of reasonableness, the meeting allowed that arrangements that would serve the "necessities of congregations and peace of the Church" were acceptable (so long as no sacrifice of principle was involved) and that clergy had a duty to obey their bishops' "Godly judgments" (so long, that is, as "such judgments be not contrary to anything contained in the *Book of Common Prayer*, as revised in 1662, and to the principle of appeal to Primitive and Catholic doctrine and usage affirmed by authorities Ecclesiastical and Civil in the XVI. Century"). The escape clauses, of course, are more telling than the general propositions to which they are attached.

Pusey's attitude at this time was complex. He plainly sympathized with the Ritualists, but feared that they were jeopardizing the Anglo-Catholic cause with their lack of tact and judgment, and their unwillingness to compromise on what he regarded as inessentials. In 1874 he wrote the *Times* to deny that he was himself a Ritualist, although he confessed himself "bound to many Ritualists by affection and by their labour for souls."[75] In another letter that same year he wrote, "I never imagined myself as the head of any party, nor allowed myself to act as such"; consequently he could not order caution, only urge it. "In later times [after 1833] there was much which I thought unwise, and which, I feared would alienate rather than win the people of England.... When I could, I urged, *usque ad nauseam*, any I could influence, not to make any changes without having first won the people."[76]

Like Pusey, conservative Anglo-Catholics repeatedly complained that the activities of their more venturesome colleagues were imprudent, exciting opposition among those who would otherwise be sympathetic or at least indifferent to the movement's doctrine. For moderate High Churchmen, this was but one objection among many, but for Tractarians it was almost the only one. Ritualists have gone "too fast and too far," wrote one critic; rather than doing everything desirable in a few churches, they should have tried to move the generality up, more slowly.[77] Notice that the Ritualists' definition of the desirable was not questioned. "The too hasty adaptation of a highly ornate ceremonial, under our present circumstances, throws back the steady advance of Catholic truth, by creating prejudice, in those who dislike it, against the doctrines which it is intended to symbolize," wrote another critic. He had no quarrels with the Ritualists about the nature of "Catholic truth."[78]

And, indeed, he could not have, because, as one partisan remarked, "The main doctrines which are distinctive of Ritualists are in fact identical with those of their predecessors the Tractarians."[79] Both friends and foes of the movement acknowledged that fact, made plain in a "Declaration on the Doctrine of the Holy Eucharist" submitted to the archbishop of Canterbury in 1867. Responding to "imputations of disloyalty," the statement repudiated the "Corporal Presence of Christ's natural Flesh and Blood" in the Eucharist, the idea that any "fresh" sacrifice was involved, and adoration of the elements per se, but affirmed forthrightly that "Christ Himself, really and truly, but spiritually and ineffably, present in the Sacrament, is therein to be adored." The twenty-one signers ranged from Tractarians like Pusey and Liddon to Ritualists like Mackonochie and Littledale.[80] Six years later, the two factions came together again in a "Declaration concerning Confession and Absolution," asserting that confession was authorized by the Prayer Book and "may be, at least in some cases, of not infrequent occurrence"; Pusey called the statement "a rallying of the old school," but Mackonochie signed as a representative of the new.[81]

In neither of these cases were the Anglo-Catholic signers joined by moderate High Churchmen, but when it came to these points, the more conservative Anglo-Catholics were as unwilling to compromise as the most extreme Ritualist. The different factions and generations within the movement were, finally, held together by the same doctrinal unity in the face of indiscriminate opposition that cemented the High Church alliance as a whole. After saying that he had sometimes urged his colleagues to be more cautious, Pusey went on to say that, after the passage of the Public Worship Regulation Act, "now by gones are by gones." He said of the three thousand who attended an E.C.U. meeting at St. James's Hall in June 1874: "It seemed to me a welding together of those who hold the same truths into one compact body. Those who hold themselves the most 'advanced' seemed ready to retire into the main body; those who had hitherto held a middle position threw themselves heart and soul into the common cause—the cause, as we held, of God's truth, which is assailed." He claimed that "the Church Association has forced us into being a party. Even the brute creation will gather into one herd in the presence of those who seek their life."[82]

VII

The Appeal to the Clergy

"The Tractarians are essentially a clerical party, and have but few lay retainers," one well-informed journalist wrote in 1853.[1] This statement was not entirely accurate even then and it became less so in the following decades, but fifty years later another observer could still estimate that Anglo-Catholicism had the loyalties of one clergyman in six but of only one layman in twenty.[2] The movement always appealed disproportionately to the clergy, and it is not difficult to understand why. A. M. Fairbairn, a distinguished Congregationalist, observed that Anglo-Catholicism emphasized those aspects of the Church of England's heritage that set it off from Protestant Dissent—"And so [the Church's] authority was magnified, the apostolicity of its orders and doctrines was affirmed, its bishops were invested with a more awful dignity, and its priests with more sacred functions; its Prayer-book was filled with a deeper significance, its services were made to articulate a larger and lovelier faith."[3]

The Catholic view of the priest as a man set apart and endowed with special powers by virtue of his ordination was sanctioned, if not required, by the Anglican Prayer Book, and from the beginning Anglo-Catholics emphasized the distinction between priests and laymen, and championed the rights of ordained clergy against those of layfolk in parish, Parliament, and Privy Council. Also thoroughly understandable, if less theologically predictable, was the increasing assertion as time went on of the interests of priests against those of their nominal, consecrated superiors, the bishops of the Church.

A Calling in Decline

A movement articulating the clergy's interests and advocating its rights was quite naturally attractive to some who had chosen to devote their lives to the ministry, especially those who recognized that the clergy's secular influence and importance were decreasing. Among young men considering a clerical career, those who imbibed the Tractarian view of the priesthood were more likely to persevere and to take orders than those who saw only that the social standing and extrinsic rewards of the ministry were in decline and that other attractive careers were increasingly available for university graduates. Put another way, what John Kent has written about the revived practice of confession was true of nearly every distinctive Anglo-Catholic belief and practice: "By reintroducing the Confessional [the priest] hoped to retrieve some of the professional status which he had been losing during the century. The authority of the confessional, the expertise of spiritual direction, were to be set against the greatly increased professional prestige of other walks of life: the doctor, the surgeon, the teacher, the scientist and so on."[4]

It is clear that the movement's opponents were right when they accused Anglo-Catholics of sacerdotalism. Critics were fond of quoting Pusey's unapologetic observation, "Upon the principle of Sacerdotalism hangs the future of England's Church."[5] When the *Times* observed that the movement's sacramental doctrine meant that "the salvation ... of every man and woman in England, must be obtained, at least as a general rule, through the priesthood," few Anglo-Catholics would, or could, have disagreed.[6] That such doctrines found their strongest support among the clergy is perhaps not surprising. That they came to the surface when they did is not surprising either.

"Should the Government and Country so far forget their God as to cast off the Church, to deprive it of its temporal honours and substance," Newman had asked his fellow clergymen in the first of the *Tracts for the Times*, "*on what* will you rest the claim of respect which you will make on your flocks?"[7] The Oxford Movement's emphasis on the spiritual gifts transmitted by episcopal ordination exalted the spiritual importance and authority of the clergy at the very time when its secular influence and standing were clearly decreasing. The Anglo-Catholic view of the clergy's power and responsibilities was lofty and exhilarating, offering an occupational self-image worthy of a life's devotion. In any case, some of the alternative images, like that of "a resident gentleman in every parish," were increasingly untenable; others, like the Erastian view of the clergy as a superior sort of civil service, were becoming less tolerable as the extrinsic rewards of a clerical vocation declined.

Among the many indicators of this decline, the one most talked about at the time was the average income of the clergy. Throughout the century, the church authorities multiplied parishes in an effort to keep up with the growth of England's population, but the new parishes hardly provided comfortable, much less Trollopean, livings. Built and furnished on the cheap, most provided no money for assistants and bare livings for their incumbents.[8] Growing even faster than the number of underpaid incumbents, however, was the population of unbeneficed clergy, curates who could look forward to serving as assistants for twenty years, thirty years, or all of their lives. Despite the efforts of a number of funds and societies to alleviate the situation, half of all incumbents received less than two hundred pounds a year, and thousands of curates earned much nearer one hundred pounds annually.[9]

Hand in hand with this development went a decrease in the social standing of clergymen. Although most were still Oxford and Cambridge graduates, fewer each year came from the two universities, and a steadily increasing number were taken directly from the new theological colleges. The colleges' supporters claimed that this made for a better-trained and more professional clergy, but many observers (among them Anthony Trollope) believed, and regretted, that the new men were less likely than university graduates to be gentlemen.[10] Be that as it may, this trend certainly meant that the Church of England was dipping deeper into the middle classes for its recruits, and the class differences between Anglican and Nonconformist ministers were growing smaller with each decade.[11]

Young men without the social connections to obtain well-paid livings (many still in the hands of private patrons) could hardly ignore these facts, if they thought about becoming clergymen at all. Their prospects had been deteriorating for decades, and there was no end in sight. In addition, alternatives to clerical careers were opening up for bookish or socially-minded or impecunious young gentlemen, especially, after the 1870 Education Act, in teaching.[12] In 1866 J. E. T. Rogers summed it up:

With less to hope for, and more work to do, with the knowledge that other professional avocations are better paid, and perhaps as much esteemed socially, and that the clerical office is scantily compensated and is gradually occupying an inferior social status, it is no wonder that men hesitate before they enter on Holy Orders. It is altogether unreasonable to expect the devotion of an Apostle from an unbeneficed clergyman, and to reward him with less wages and less liberty than a domestic servant.[13]

Certainly it was unreasonable to expect apostolic devotion in those circumstances from anyone who did not consider himself as, in some sense, an apostle. In any case, the number of candidates presenting themselves for ordination failed to keep pace with population growth throughout the century, and toward the end of the century actually began to decline.

All of this suggests an unintended interpretation of a scornful observation by *Fraser's Magazine*: "The so-called Catholic revival means merely that intelligent men have withdrawn from participation in the whole matter, and enthusiasts, dreamers, knaves, and fools now have the field to themselves."[14] For merely intelligent men there were in fact many careers with greater worldly rewards than that of the average late Victorian clergyman. For some, the Anglo-Catholic view of the priesthood could compensate; if that view appealed to ambition at all, however, it was to ambition of an unconventional—some would have said foolish— sort. No doubt some fools were drawn to Anglo-Catholicism; certainly many enthusiasts and dreamers were. But *Fraser's* was probably wrong about the knaves. As R. F. Littledale observed about the movement of which he was part, "It may have fools in its ranks—every great party has them, and even fools have souls to be saved—but it is not likely to have rogues, for Tractarianism is a very bad pecuniary speculation indeed."[15] Increasingly that could have been said about the ministry in general.

Who Were the Ritualist Clergy?

These considerations help to explain why Anglo-Catholicism was more attractive to young clergymen than to old ones, and (the same thing, to some extent) more to unbeneficed clergy than to better-off incumbents, canons, prebends, deans, and other ecclesiastical dignitaries. As an American bishop put it, ingenuously: "The rising generation of the clergy will favor [Ritualism], because it adds so much to the solemn character of their Office, and the interest of their service in the House of God."[16]

One of the movement's opponents saw the same thing, but took a less sunny view: "Who are the Puseyites?" he asked. "For the most part mere boys, ... mightily pleased to find that, by a clever piece of Episcopal magic, they have become, if useless members of society on earth, at least very important personages on the way to heaven—nay, altogether indispensable!"[17] R. F. Littledale acknowledged the "constant assertion that the movement is entirely that of young, hot-headed men, actuated by a desire of notoriety, and by personal vanity," but, characteristically, he turned that argument back on the movement's critics, observing that "it is certain that the Evangelical party, at any rate, draws few or no recruits from [the young], nor, confessedly, the religious section of the Latitudinarians."[18] Another partisan, an anonymous "Priest of the Church of England," also acknowledged that there was some basis for the charge that Ritualism was "the hobby of the younger clergy," but pointed out that they would, in time, become older clergy.[19]

Contemporaries were more reticent about the possible contribution of blocked aspirations or dashed hopes to young clergymen's enthusiasm for Anglo-Catholicism. Although both friends and foes were ready enough to acknowledge that Ritualists were overrepresented in ill-paying and ill-regarded positions, their opponents took the fact to indicate their lack of importance and talent, while the movement's friends argued that it was a sign either of their dedication and self-sacrifice or of discrimination against them. Littledale put the Ritualists' own view well:

To be a pronounced Ritualist now is voluntarily to abandon all hopes of professional advancement; to be pelted with defamatory epithets by Bishops, newspapers, and parliamentary orators; ... to be the sport of biased Tribunals ...; to give his days and nights for many years together to unremitting and unrewarded toil, and in a great proportion of instances to derive either nothing at all or the barest pittance from his calling."[20]

No, Littledale wrote,

the curled and scented clerical dandies— the men of fine broadcloth, delicate cambric, varnished boots, lavender gloves, and generally faultless get-up— are not to be found in the Ritualistic churches. You may find them simpering over Evangelical tea-tables, or dawdling in Broad-Church salons, or flirting in High-and-Dry croquet-grounds; but not saying Low Mass in a Chasuble for a tiny company before light on a cold winter morning.[21]

Littledale exaggerated (there were some very fashionable Anglo-Catholic parishes indeed), but he built on a basis of fact. The Ritualists and their clerical allies were less likely than their opponents to be in responsible and rewarding positions, in part because they tended to be younger. A sample of clerical members of the anti-Ritualist Church Association in the 1870s shows that most were middle-aged and older men; similar samples reveal that ministers who belonged to the English Church Union were a decade younger, on the average, and brethren of the Society of the Holy Cross were younger still.[22]

Nearly all of the Church Association subscribers could remember a world without Ritualism; some remembered the world before the Oxford Movement. Half had begun their careers by mid-century, when fewer than a quarter of the future E.C.U. members and only one in sixteen S.S.C. brethren were out of college. Anglo-Catholic clergy belonged to a different generation, with a different collective experience: half of *them* had been graduated or ordained after the riots at St. George's-in-the-East in 1859, and a third had been clergymen for twelve years or less; only three Church Association members in fifty were that new to their profession.

Most Anglo-Catholics had entered the clergy, that is, after Anglo-Catholicism had become a party, a serious alternative, with recognized parishes that offered models for emulation and curacies for training. They had also entered the clergy at a time when it was becoming clear that the profession was declining in influence and respect.

There is no evidence in the sample data that Anglo-Catholic incumbents held poorer livings than their opponents, but Anglo-Catholics were less likely to be incumbents in the first place. Nearly all of the Church Association members held livings (or were retired from them), but a quarter of E.C.U. members and more than a third of S.S.C. brethren did not. (Nor, it appears, did a majority of clerical converts to Roman Catholicism.[23])

Consequently, while Church Association subscribers' median income from livings was closer to three hundred than to two hundred pounds, that for E.C.U. members was somewhat lower and that for S.S.C. members barely exceeded one hundred pounds a year. In large part, this difference reflected the relative ages of the three groups: older clergy had entered their profession at a time when the chances of obtaining an incumbency were greater, and had also had more time to work their way up. The data also suggest, however, that extreme Anglo-Catholics were unlikely to be found in remunerative positions. Whatever the explanation, it appears that Anglo-Catholic clergy were less dependent on the Establishment than their opponents.

Ecclesiastical Politics

The complicated relationship between theological party and standing or prospects within the Church was reinforced by the unimportance in Anglo-Catholic sacramental theology of the worldly and even the ecclesiastical distinctions among the clergy. Ill-paid curates and wealthy incumbents, mission priests and sinecured cathedral dignitaries, unemployed amateur ecclesiologists and rural deans— all had received orders from a bishop in the apostolic succession, and the differences among them were relatively insignificant. This view underlay much Anglo-Catholic political activity, activity interpreted by the movement's opponents as simply self-serving.[24]

Consider, for example, the English Church Union's incessant agitation on behalf of unbeneficed clergymen. In the Union's first year (1859-60), it set up a committee to examine bishops' powers to dismiss and to suspend curates. Two years later, a resolution urged that curates should have the same protection against arbitrary dismissal as incumbents. In 1865 the E.C.U. again expressed concern about curates' insecurity, in a letter to Convocation; it returned to the subject the next year, and again in 1873, when another letter argued that withdrawing a curate's license was not an appropriate punishment for ritual irregularities.

The E.C.U. also urged that Convocation be reformed to provide greater representation for parochial clergy, curates as well as incumbents, with fewer cathedral clergy, rural deans, and so forth seated ex officio.[25] By 1885, the Union had sent seven memorials on this subject to the archbishops, to all the bishops, or to Convocation itself. An 1872 resolution also proposed that cathedral representatives be elected by the cathedral chapter, including honorary, nonresident members— that is, parochial clergy.

In 1863, a revealing resolution called for removing the disabilities on Scottish Episcopal clergy in England, which disabilities, the resolution stated, "cast a slur on the undoubted validity of Scottish orders."[26] Although the old High Church tradition of the Scottish Episcopalians no doubt commended their clergy to the E.C.U., as did the fervent Catholicism of Bishop Forbes of Brechin, here again the argument had a theological base: the important distinction was between those with orders and those without, not between different types of clergymen with equally valid orders.

Occasionally this theme of clerical equality conflicted with other Anglo-Catholic values, overriding, for example, the movement's early emphasis on incumbents' authority within their parishes. In 1875-76, a majority of the E.C.U.'s local chapters endorsed a bill that would have allowed bishops to license clergy to function within a parish even against the will of the incumbent and would have relaxed a law that forbade nonresidents to attend services in private oratories. The E.C.U.'s support obviously reflected the desire to establish Anglo-Catholic worship in Evangelical parishes, but the proposed legislation would also have diminished the authority of incumbents relative to other clergy, increased the number of positions available for unbeneficed clergy, and secured the independence of those positions.

It could be said that the E.C.U. was serving the interests of its clerical constituency, but it could also be said that it was working out the implications of its theological position—and perhaps attracted its constituency in consequence.

Role of the Laity in Church Governance

The Anglo-Catholic emphasis on the rights of ordained clergymen, as such, was accompanied by an insistence on the distinction between clergy and laity. In general, Anglo-Catholics opposed *any* lay role in Church governance, and certainly any expansion of that role. In 1868 the English Church Union unanimously passed a resolution against admitting laymen to diocesan synods; soon after, a writer in the *Church Review* observed, "The Government of the Church does and ought to belong to Bishops and Priests; and it seems to me a fatal pandering to the anarchical and democratic spirit of the day to invite the laity to sit on equal terms with the clergy in their new Synods."[27] Virtually all Anglo-Catholic clergy and even most Anglo-Catholic laymen shared that view. (One layman who had reservations—Gladstone—was suspect for it.[28]) But even a few of the faithful laity may have had misgivings when the Reverend Luke Rivington, S.S.C., told the E.C.U. that he did not undervalue "the office of *the laity, whose high and noble prerogative it was to LISTEN and OBEY*."[29] One fears that Rivington (who subsequently became a Roman Catholic) may not have been joking.

As in other matters, the problem was not one of misunderstanding. Despite the efforts of well-meaning moderates to compromise and cloud the issues, Anglo-Catholics and their opponents understood one another all too well. Lord Shaftesbury, Evangelical in religion and Erastian in politics, was perhaps the most consistent and surely the most prominent of the Anglo-Catholics' lay opponents. In the years leading up to the Public Worship Regulation Act, Shaftesbury argued repeatedly that "the order of the service, or what vestments are to be worn" was "essentially a question for the laity," not for the minister, not for the bishops, not even for a "mere majority of the congregation"; rather, "it is for the great mass of the congregation to determine whether they will go on in those usages which their fathers have practiced for 300 years," and even then they must decide "consistently with the law of the land."[30] Earlier, when Convocation had been revived in the 1850s, Shaftesbury had opposed it or any other "clerical Parliament that will make the laity of this Church and of these realms mere 'hewers of wood and drawers of water' to a select knot of sacerdotal dignitaries," and had called for a form of governance "in which the laity of the Church will have not only a great, but a dominant share."[31]

There was obviously no common ground between Shaftesbury and, say, the Reverend A. D. Wagner of Brighton, who maintained that obedience to the Privy Council's judgments "subordinates the Spiritual and Divinely given powers of the Clergy to the powers of this world, degrades the Church to a mere department of the State, and ignores the Divine basis and supernatural character of Christianity."[32] That self-government for the Church meant government by the clergy followed logically from the assumption that (as one Ritualist put it) "our Church is, after all, the English body of Bishops and Priests providing those who live in England with the grace of the Sacraments."[33]

This position had the wholehearted support of the surviving Tractarians, and even, in principle, that of many old-fashioned High Churchmen.[34] When the bishop of London called in 1865 for the creation of a Royal Commission to look into the question of ritual, John Keble objected: "Today, at your request, the State new-models your Ritual; tomorrow, at the request of some one else, or of its own free judgement, it will be new-modeling your Creeds and Prayers."[35] "The Acts of the Church," Pusey had written earlier, "cannot be rescinded, nor explained, nor expounded authoritatively, by any authority less than the Church"; consequently, he regarded the American Episcopal Church as seriously compromised by lay participation in its governance, and expressed his concern that the institution of Lambeth Conferences would not establish "a precedent for Bishops of the United States taking part in what relates to matters of our discipline."[36]

Even the royal supremacy grated on some Anglo-Catholics. At an 1870 meeting of the Taunton branch of the English Church Union the chairman denounced "the pernicious and exploded fallacy that a layman, however exalted, can by any stretch of the imagination become the Head of the Church." (The critic who extracted that quotation from the *Church Union Gazette* reprinted it with the annotation, "E.C.U. sneers at the Queen."[37]) Anglo-Catholics were usually more guarded in their public observations, but a few years later the Reverend T. T. Carter argued a novel constitutional point: "In matters of State, the power of the Crown is limited by the two Houses of Parliament: in the affairs of the Church, it is limited also by the two Houses of Convocation."[38])

What Anglo-Catholics saw as the Church of England's problems, of course, reflected its status as the established church of the realm. Absent that, the State would have no voice in regulating public worship or revising the Prayer Book or appointing bishops, there would be no appeal from ecclesiastical courts to secular ones, and there would be no reason to define "the laity" as mere parishioners rather than communicants. Although a divorce would certainly have secured the independence of the Church, however, the cost would have been measured in more than buildings and income, and disestablishment was vigorously opposed not only by Low and Broad Churchmen, but by moderate High Churchmen (including J. G. Hubbard, the benefactor of St. Alban's, Holborn), and even by most Anglo-Catholics.[39]

There was no reliable correlation between support for disestablishment and liturgical or doctrinal extremism. F. G. Lee, for instance, whose Romanizing activities had evoked protests even from John Mason Neale, was a Jacobite, a fervent Tory, and a tireless defender of Establishment.[40] Not even among the zealous brethren of the Society of the Holy Cross could a majority be found to support it; the proposition was debated by the S.S.C. Synod twice, in 1876 and 1877, and lost, although by a close margin, each time.[41] (One opponent offered to receive the income from the endowments of those who were troubled in conscience; he observed that when St. Augustine came to convert England "he went straight to the king, and used the world's power for God."[42])

Nevertheless, ever since the Oxford Movement days, prominent Anglo-Catholics had advocated the Gordian solution to the Church's compromising entanglement with the State. Especially after the passage of the Public Worship Regulation Act, many, including even Gladstone, came to sympathize with the crusty archdeacon of Taunton, Anthony Denison, who declared himself "thoroughly persuaded that the Establishment is in its nature hurtful to true Religion; and has more particularly for some time past been filled with active injury to it," and announced that he "would gladly, if it so please God, see it done away."[43]

A. H. Mackonochie and Arthur Stanton, vicar and curate respectively of St. Alban's, Holborn, and Denison's brothers in the Society of the Holy Cross, went so far as to join with Dissenters and freethinkers in the (anti-establishment) Liberation Society, and helped to form the Church League for promoting the separation of Church and State.[44] Stanton told an English Church Union gathering that "the union of the temporal and spiritual orders" had been "the parent both of *Protestantism* and *Infidelity*," and Mackonochie put it this way: "Let the State send forth the Church roofless, and penniless, but free, and I will say 'Thank you.'"[45]

This political position had roots both social and theological. Even among Anglo-Catholics it remained the view of a minority, but it is significant that the movement provided most of the clerical support for it.[46] It was a manifestation, albeit an extreme one, of deep uneasiness about the blurring of distinctions between clerical and lay prerogatives.

The Campaign against Pews

That same concern, accompanied by a subtle attack on "worldly" rank, was symbolically evident in two architectural changes that tended to accompany the movement's remodelling of old churches and building of new ones: the abolition of private pews and the elevation of chancels. As opponents of these changes suspected, there was more to them than met the eye.

When the Oxford Movement began, most chapels and parish churches maintained a system of "appropriated" seats: private pews for particular families, often paid for by annual subscription. Sometimes these seats were enclosed, high-sided "box" pews, occasionally shut off entirely from view and fitted out to the occupants' taste. Those parishioners without appropriated seats were assigned to what seating remained: less comfortable, less well situated, and definitely regarded as inferior.[47] Pew-rents were an important part of many churches' revenues, but opposition to the pew system became a mark of Tractarian tendencies as early as the 1830s.[48]

At first the case for reform was made in archaeological or aesthetic terms. As the Cambridge Camden Society pointed out repeatedly, pews were late additions to ancient churches, and cluttered up the nave.[49] This sort of concern was characteristic of young clergymen of the ultrarubrician stamp; pews often figured in their conflicts with their parishes, and in fiction those conflicts inspired. Two novels among many of the 1840s were *The Church Restorers: A Tale Treating of Ancient and Modern Architecture and Church Decoration*, by F. A. Paley, the secretary of the Camden Society, and *Milford Malvoisin: Pews and Pew-holders* by Francis Paget, a member of the Oxford Architectural Society.[50] In *A Paper Lantern for Puseyites*, pew-removing was one of the Reverend Hilary Oriel's many projects; he announced: "The Bishop, I hope, will encourage my views, / And I mean, by his help, to get rid of the pews"—although he dropped those plans when he married the squire's daughter.[51]

Other pew-removers were more persistent. The campaign was not merely a matter of promoting good medieval taste. It was widely believed that the pew-rent system contributed to the alienation of the poor from their parish churches. "*The Prevalence of the Pew System is the main Cause why the Church of England is not the Church of the People in our Towns,*" wrote one abolitionist in 1865, adding, "Few thinking persons will deny this."[52] One pamphlet, probably by John Mason Neale, offered twenty-three reasons for doing away with pews. The first reason (characteristic of Neale) was that there were no pews "in the good old times, when churches were first built," but the list also noted that the poor, lacking pews, were tempted "to leave off going to church, and to go to meeting instead: thus becoming guilty of the fearful sin of schism."[53]

In this campaign, perhaps more than anywhere else, the Tractarians and their successors found influential support. Hilary Oriel's hope that his bishop would encourage him was not entirely misplaced; the bishop of Lincoln, speaking in 1855 at the reopening of a Newark church after its restoration, said that the many restorations in his diocese had been "a great element in giving our Church a proper energy and force, in winning back and retaining the affections of our people." (The record shows murmurs of "Hear, hear, hear.") "I recollect very well," the bishop continued, "a parish where the circumstance that so many of the poor went to the chapel instead of the Church was accounted for by the fact, that at the chapel they gave them seats covered with red baize. (Laughter.)"[54]

De-emphasizing secular distinctions of rank within the congregation was surely a useful first step toward making the poor feel more comfortable in Anglican churches. In this as in so much else, however, Anglo-Catholic theoreticians came to see the changes they desired not only as useful, fitting, and aesthetically pleasing but as symbolic of doctrine— indeed, practically *de fide*. As one writer on "The Symbolism of Churches" put it, "free and open" churches were symbolic of the fact that "God is no respecter of persons."[55]

The vicar of St. Matthias, Stoke Newington, C. J. LeGeyt, argued that a "principal object in the ordering of the Ritual of the Church, is to mark off the Worship of the Sanctuary from the ordinary actions of the world, and to sever between it and common life." "The world is to be left without," he said, "put off at the church door"— and worldly distinctions of social class were among those things to be put off.[56] On another occasion, LeGeyt protested "the perpetuation of absurd anomalies and time-honoured privileges of bumbledom and beadledom, and parochial dignitaries, and strange vested rights of freedom and irreverence," which make "un-Christian distinctions, even before the very altar, when 'all equal should be within the Church's gate.'"[57]

But beadles, and squires, and parish clerks, and other parochial dignitaries were sometimes strongly attached to these distinctions, and they often had powerful allies. As late as 1886 Archbishop Thomson of York threatened legal proceedings against the churchwardens of St. Mary's, Beverley, who wished to open the seats in their church; the archbishop invited parishioners to inform him of their social standing so that he personally could allocate seats "according to their degree."[58] Twenty years earlier, Christina Rossetti had parodied the conservatives' attitude, and mocked what she saw to be its basis:

We have borne with chants, with a surpliced choir, with daily services, but we will not bear to see all our rights trampled under foot, and all our time-hallowed usages set at nought. The tendency of the day is to level social distinctions and to elevate unduly the lower orders. In this parish at least let us combine to keep up wise barriers between class and class, and to maintain that fundamental principle practically bowed to all over our happy England, that what you can pay for you can purchase.[59]

Other opponents of pews attacked not just the motives of pew-holders, but their religious beliefs and even their ancestry. John Mason Neale's *History of Pues* condemned the furniture as "the offspring of indolence and pride" and "abortions of a puritanick age."[60] (Other Nealean epithets included "cattleless pens" and "distractors of devotion.") Another of the twenty-three reasons for getting rid of pews was that "they were invented at first by people who thought themselves too good to pray by the side of their neighbours: and who were in those days too proud to join in the service of God with such as were poorer than themselves."[61] The criticism of latter-day pew-holders was left implicit, but was plain enough, and if they could not be educated up to their responsibilities— well, the irrepressible Father Ignatius took an ax to the box pews of St. Lawrence, Norwich.[62]

By whatever means achieved, "free and open" churches were common by the 1870s. The working classes did not flock to fill them, as we shall see, but when the London Free and Open Church Association polled the clergy of such churches (to show, among other things, that the replacement of pew-rents by a weekly "offertory" did not adversely affect receipts), they found some consensus about who liked the new arrangement and who did not. One clergyman reported that "servants, shopmen, and young people" approved, another that "the working class" did, but others said that "every one wishes to be accommodated [in a pew] who is above the poor in station," and that "the few persons of the middle-class who come would prefer seats appropriated and would be willing to pay." A rural incumbent reported that "the farmers, as a rule, like a family pew because it keeps up their dignity"; another vicar said, "The system has been unpopular with some of the higher classes." One respondent claimed that the change to open seating had "somewhat affected the social character of the congregation," while several others reported that the change was acceptable "to the present worshippers," implying that there had been some turnover.[63]

By that time all of the well-known centers of advanced ritual had unappropriated seating, but by no means all free and open churches were Ritualist, or even "high." The arguments against pew-rents clearly had merit, and they had been influential, especially in the construction of new churches where there was no established pew-holding interest to be offended. Open seating was no longer a badge of party, and the conflict between Anglo-Catholics and their opponents had moved on to other issues.

Even these petty and seemingly trivial disputes over seating arrangements, however, illustrate themes in Anglo-Catholicism that recur in other contexts. In the campaign against pews we can recognize challenges to existing distinctions of worldly rank and attempts to reach out to the poor and the working classes that became more explicit in the activities of Ritualist priests and sisters in the slums of English cities, activities that eventually led some who engaged in them to embrace outright Christian socialism.[64]

The Meaning of Elevated Chancels

"All equal should be within the Church's gate" referred, of course, only to equality among members of the congregation. Although secular rank was to be put aside at the church door, it was to be replaced by stratification of a different order. The symbolic obliteration of worldly distinctions was accompanied by a heightened emphasis on ecclesiastical status, symbolized architecturally by the distinction between nave and chancel.

At the end of the century, one opponent of the movement wrote, "It has somewhat humorously been said that one reason why Ritualistic priests love to have their so-called 'altars' elevated on high is that the laity, being so far below, may thus humbly realise their proper level."[65] But his joke was not far from the truth. Sixty years earlier, the theoreticians of the Cambridge Camden Society had been quite candid about it. John Mason Neale and Benjamin Webb wrote, "The worshippers who are to assemble in our church are not all on equality. There are some who are endowed with high privileges as being those consecrated to the immediate service of the sanctuary." At the Reformation, they observed, "The great distinction between Clergy and Laity became lost or undervalued," and they proposed to put that right. Since the Camden Society taught that the distinction between nave and chancel "preach[es] to posterity the sacredness of Holy Orders, and the mutual duties arising from the relation in which the flock stand to their shepherds," the "ABSOLUTE NECESSITY" of a "DISTINCT AND SPACIOUS CHANCEL" followed. The society even argued that the medieval rood-screen was an appropriate symbol of the distinction, although its campaign to restore rood-screens was not particularly successful.[66]

For those who missed the architectural point, there were, as usual, preachers to explain. "We separate the clergy from the rest of the people," said one at St. Barnabas, Pimlico, "because S. Paul tells us that God has set divers orders in His Church; and where there are divers orders, they should be distinguished by their *position*." He pointed out that "God's priests have ever stood between Him and His people; as their 'Ministers,' and 'His Ambassadors,' acting in 'His stead;'— yea, in 'His Person.'"[67] Another preacher observed that the Book of Revelation shows that even in Heaven the Church has different ranks with different functions, "some to sing, some to worship, some to say Amen," and all with "the use of the highest Ritual." (Of those who found ritual distracting or annoying, he asked: "May they not be willing to make some efforts to conform their wills to the will of God?"[68])

Although ordinary social distinctions between laymen were to be disregarded in the Church's services, proper ritual would recognize "different ranks" based on liturgical function and proximity to the altar. The choir, for instance, should be relocated to the chancel and its members put in surplices. To get the lay and ordained "clerks" to the chancel would require a procession, during which the congregation should be encouraged to stand. In a tract of the period, "Mrs Protestor" grumbled that "a minister is only a man, and I don't see why we should treat the clergy as if they were so much better than other people." "Mr Explainer" told her patiently that "reverence" was due only to the priest's *office*: standing showed merely "common respect" for the man himself.[69]

At St. Alban's, Holborn, Father Mackonochie's practice of reading the lessons himself reflected his "invincible repugnance to lay readers of lessons," a view that may have been shared by other priests jealous of their privileges.[70] In general, however, Ritualism, like Tractarianism before it, resulted in a proliferation of choristers, lay-readers, subdeacons, acolytes, servers—what one critic called "mongrel ministers"—all of whom shared to some degree in the clergy's prerogatives, and who commonly shared their views as well.[71]

The choir, too, was often to be found on the vicar's side in conflicts over questions of ritual advance; occasionally, a vicar even found himself attempting to negotiate between an enthusiastic choir and a resistant congregation. Such was the case, for instance, at St. Mary's, East Fairleigh, where the choir threatened to resign en masse in 1852 when a new vicar was too responsive to the vestry's wishes that (among other things) the chants not be changed too often.[72]

Pusey's warnings about the dangers of self-will and self-glorification might well have been directed to some of the clergy's lay assistants. Occasionally reflected glory turned the heads even of lowly ushers. In 1873 the *Church Times* reported "frequent complaints" about the "uncouthness" of "those entrusted with the arrangement of the sittings" at St. Alban's, Holborn, and other Ritualist churches, and a correspondent wrote to agree, offering his opinion that a major cause of the disturbances at St. George's-in-the-East had been parishioners' dislike of being "poked about by officious young persons in cassocks," and urging that a curb be placed on such "arbitrary and uppish youths (not quite sufficiently educated perhaps to be in the choir)."[73]

But the differences between various lay functionaries and mere members of the congregation paled next to the grand distinction between clergy and laity. That, too, seemed to require ever-increasing symbolic expression. Once clergy were no longer distinguished from the choir by cassock and surplice, they added stoles to their attire, often embroidered and colored to mark the liturgical season. The chancel, no longer the exclusive preserve of those in orders, was subdivided; the sacrarium immediately around the altar was often set off by being still further elevated, or by an altar rail. With the increasing emphasis in the 1860s on the doctrine of the Real Presence, the

symbolic markers of that doctrine became increasingly important; among
them were the distinctive eucharistic vestments, which not only honored the
Sacrament and identified Anglo-Catholic congregations but (we can note in
this context) distinguished priests and deacons from choristers, acolytes, and
each other.

Like the ultrarubricians' reassertion of clerical authority in the ordering
of parish life, like the increasingly common practice of regular confession
and spiritual direction, the Ritualists' emphasis on different ranks and functions in the Church's worship (especially when combined with a willful
blindness to secular rank) was often experienced as an assertion of the clergy's personal power and, implicitly, of their superiority. But Edward Garbett,
one of the Ritualists' ablest opponents, conceded that Anglo-Catholic practice followed from their beliefs. If Anglican ministers were indeed sacrificing
and absolving priests of the Catholic Church, he told a meeting of Evangelical clergymen, "how natural become the many coloured and gorgeous vestments to symbolize their mysterious powers, the burst of music to welcome
their very appearance, and all the parade of successive dresses and ceremonial processions."[74]

Garbett, like other Evangelicals, denied the premise; so did Broad
Church and some High Church clergy, and many, many laypeople. Others
did not understand it, which came to the same thing. But for devout
Anglo-Catholics, of course, glorifying clergymen was not the point at all.
Honor *was* due to the office, not the man, and that honor both reflected and
announced to the world deeply held beliefs about the nature of the priesthood.

What to Do about Bishops

For good reason, Anglo-Catholics became even more insistent on the
distinction between the man and the office in the case of bishops of the
Church of England. The Tractarian doctrine of the Church placed a great
emphasis on the historic episcopate. Indeed, Newman's theory had been
that "when we were separated from the Pope, his authority reverted to our
Diocesans"; therefore, "our Bishop is our Pope."[75] No Anglican bishop
would have acknowledged as much, of course, and Newman's conclusion
was too extreme even for most who shared his high doctrine of the apostolic
succession. One party historian later characterized Newman's view as "prela-
cy run mad," and even Pusey, looking back, reflected that "at least I never
leant on the bishops; I leant on the Church of England."[76]

Nevertheless, the Tractarians' assessment of episcopacy required them to
respect the office and inclined them to respect the persons of the apostles'
successors in England. So when we find a *Church Times* editorial a generation later complaining that "the Archbishop of Canterbury offends one
every time he acts, speaks, or in any way lets us know of his existence," we
can conclude that the intervening years had not been happy ones for the

relation between the movement and the episcopate.[77]

In 1866 Anthony Trollope observed, "The chances are now that in meeting a bishop one meets an enemy of the Oxford movement."[78] Certainly, by that time, when one met an Anglo-Catholic chances were that one met someone who held most English bishops in contempt. One opponent of the movement remarked "the presbyterian and anti-episcopalian bias" of most Ritualist clergymen, quoting one to the effect that "the worst of episcopacy is, that it involves the necessity for bishops!"[79] Another Ritualist complained that the bishops were unlearned; they "do not even know their own side of the controversy, much less the opposite side." Worse was the bishops' lack of sanctity: many "may fairly pass muster as good ordinary Christians," of course, but

in no case does their devoutness rise to such a pitch as to clash with the conventional usages of society; in very few instances is it in the least degree likely that any person labouring under deep religious depression would think of going to one of our present Bishops for advice or comfort; in none, that any one aspiring to saintliness would deliberately model himself on any one of them as an example.[80]

The Anglo-Catholic laity usually shared their clergy's distaste for the men who were their bishops. In some advanced circles, it was even rumored that Archbishop Tait was unbaptized.[81] More common was the "widespread feeling" voiced by one layman "that to the incapacity of the Bishops many of the evils which affect the Church are to be attributed." A bishop, he wrote, was likely to be a man of "narrow intellect and mediocre attainments," someone "chosen by the State because he is a pious nonentity." Many, he added, were "feeble and senile."[82] The sad truth, this man concluded, was that "amongst Catholics, whose whole faith and system inclines them to the profoundest reverence for the Episcopal *office*, our Bishops—as men—have come to be regarded as little more than institutions for interfering arbitrarily with the peace of congregations, and as machines for propagating the priesthood, and for conferring Confirmation."[83] Small wonder that one Roman Catholic fishing for converts among Anglo-Catholics held out as a powerful attraction "Bishops whom you can respect, love, and *obey*, instead of bishops whom you distrust and are often conscientiously obliged to disobey."[84]

To be sure, as we have seen, not every bishop treated Anglo-Catholics harshly. In a letter to the *Times* in 1874, Pusey argued that the bishops, with a few exceptions, had been "very forbearing": "where they have known Christ to be preached, and souls rescued from Satan, they have rejoiced at the good work done, and not interfered[;] where the Congregation was at one and happy in its devotions, they have left them in peace."[85] Pusey's letter, though politic, seems a fair summary. But the old man was also right when he added that Anglo-Catholics had come—regretably, in his view—

to class the bishops as antagonists, a development that he attributed to the actions of only a few.

In other words, Father Mackonochie may have been exaggerating, but he was expressing a belief widely held among Anglo-Catholics when he claimed in 1875 that "the Bishops [have] consistently, for at least forty years, done all that they could to alienate the only section of the Church that cares a straw for their sacred office."[86] Certainly R. F. Littledale spoke for many in the movement when he asserted that "every step in [its] long triumphal advance was won in the teeth of the most strenuous opposition, of the loudest censure, invariably led on by members of the Episcopal Order."[87]

Pamphlets and sermons offered extensive catalogues of mistreatment, ranging from prosecution and deprivation to the bishop of Durham's refusal to consecrate new churches with more than three steps between nave and altar.[88] After the Church Association began to publish lists of the brothers of the Society of the Holy Cross, it was commonly reported that only three bishops—Winchester, Oxford, and Worcester—were willing to license them to serve in their dioceses. It was also said that "the bishops" pressed the Society for the Propagation of the Gospel to refuse S.S.C. men as missionaries and the Additional Curates Society to deny them grants.[89]

Of course, bishops did have reason to resist Anglo-Catholics' demands for toleration. Like most administrators in every time and place, they disliked unruly and defiant subordinates, which many Ritualist clergymen unquestionably were.[90] Moreover, those who protected or defended Anglo-Catholics, like Phillpotts or, later, Wilberforce, were likely to be denounced by the movement's opponents in Church, State, and the press. But few were inclined to protect them in the first place, since many had been chosen with that consideration in mind. Victorian prime ministers (other than Gladstone) either shared the Queen's distaste for the movement or were willing to affect it. Of the fourteen bishops appointed by Lord Palmerston, for example, seven were Evangelicals, two Broad Churchmen, three "non-party men," and two perhaps High Churchmen, though distinctly of the older, conservative school. None was sympathetic to the movement.[91] (It is not incidental that Palmerston's brother-in-law was Lord Shaftesbury.)

And even those bishops who more or less tolerated the movement got little thanks for it. Pusey's irenic letter was a rare expression of appreciation; the more usual Anglo-Catholic attitude was that when a bishop was obliging he was only doing his duty. As usual, R. F. Littledale gave pithy expression to the Catholic view: bishops are given their privileges, he wrote, so "they may be independent, and may confront the rich and noble of secular society on equal terms, in defence of the Church and the clergy." (As Littledale saw it, "In practice they treat these privileges as retainers on behalf of the laity, in return for which they are to act as spies and whippers-in over the clergy: to dragoon them into submission whenever, on whatever ground, any of the laity choose to disapprove of their conduct."[92]) Few bishops, if any, shared the common Anglo-Catholic view that martyrdom was an appropriate climax to an episcopal career. Keble's "National Apostasy" sermon of 1833 had suggested as much, in dead earnest; decades later the president of the English Church Union echoed it: "I cannot conceive of anything more splendid than that your Grace should be executed on Tower Hill," Lord Halifax told his friend and sometime adversary, the archbishop of York. "Nothing but the martyrdom of an Archbishop can save the Church of England. I crave the honour of it for you and that I should live to be there, so that I might plunge my handkerchief in your blood, and pass it on ... as the most precious of heirlooms."[93]

In truth, only unqualified championship of the movement—indeed, adherence to it—would have satisfied some of its partisans. Archdeacon Denison complained about the "good men" who were not "'denouncers of Ritualists,' except after a mild, expostulatory and deprecatory fashion, intimating plainly, if they do not say so, that they think them foolish and extravagant and troublesome people; speaking of them with good humoured but very unmistakeable contempt; and all the time representing themselves as their best defenders and truest friends."[94] Such men, Denison observed, made up "the great *present* majority of 'High Churchmen'"—and he could easily have had Bishop Wilberforce in mind.

Scorn for the persons of bishops presented no real theoretical problem for Anglo-Catholics, who knew enough history to realize that the Church had suffered such trials before. But disobedience did require some justification. Sometimes, for the sake of argument, Anglo-Catholic controversialists appealed to their opponents' Protestant principles: "If authority be in no case or in no wise to be resisted," one asked, "what justification could there possibly be in the 16th Century for the Reformation? Is not [the bishop of London's] occupancy of the Episcopal throne in S. Paul's Cathedral a standing witness to his belief that resistance to authority may in some cases be a duty?"[95]

But Anglo-Catholics could hardly use liberty of conscience as an excuse to defy successors of the apostles. It was necessary to distinguish between bishops acting as such and the same men acting in other, lesser capacities. "Catholic churchmen," one Ritualist observed, "have a wholesome dread of Bishops acting as mere tools of the civil power or ruling by their mere private judgments," and in such cases appeal could be made to some arguably higher authority.[96] As a speaker at an E.C.U. meeting put it, if the bishops ask "When will the clergy obey their Bishops?" the reply is "*My lords, when the Bishops obey the Church.*"[97] This pattern could be observed as early as the era of the ultrarubricians, "those [as one put it] who think it their duty to obey the plain law of the Rubric (with or without episcopal permission), instead of a so-called interpretation of it."[98] Wherever higher authority was to be found—in the rubrics of the Prayer Book, the ecumenical councils of the undivided Church, or the "Catholic Church of the West"—we have seen that Anglo-Catholics were ingenious in finding it and dogged in their obedience to it, once found.

Although the historian of the Society of the Holy Cross claimed that the S.S.C. had "done more, probably, than any other agency to promote the Catholic and true conception of Episcopal Authority in the English Church, while never yielding to private episcopal opinions that were Erastian, uncatholic, and unepiscopal," there was no shortage of both Protestant and Roman Catholic critics to point out the difficulty: for an English churchman, determining when episcopal opinions were unepiscopal required something that looked very much like private judgment.[99] "The nineteenth century has seen personal infallibility claimed by others besides the Bishop of Rome, and by much younger men," one scoffed.[100] But this theoretical difficulty affected Anglo-Catholic practice hardly at all. Even cautious and moderate Anglo-Catholics reserved the right of disobedience (or of higher obedience) under certain circumstances. As Pusey put it once, "It is everyone's duty to maintain Catholic truth, even if unhappily opposed by a bishop."[101] Pusey and those like him differed from the movement's extremists only in being less likely to see Catholic truth at stake in every disagreement.

It is plain that Anglo-Catholics' combination of official deference and personal defiance sometimes disconcerted their bishops. On one occasion, when Charles Lowder appeared before Bishop Tait of London for a reprimand, Tait confided to his diary, "I feel that I did not produce on him the impression I desired." As Lowder was leaving he asked for Tait's blessing. "I was so taken aback," Tait wrote, "that I only gave him half the blessing."[102] But half was more than John Bacchus Dykes got when he was installed as rector of St. Oswald's, Durham. At the end of the ceremony, Dykes knelt before his bishop; when no blessing was forthcoming Dykes asked for one, but his bishop (who was deeply suspicious of the new rector's ritualistic tendencies) replied: "Oh no, I do not give Blessings."[103]

Anglo-Catholics made it clear that they could do without the authority of the Church's bishops, at least when that authority was tainted, but they could hardly do without bishops as such. In the Anglo-Catholic view, the existing bishops served the episcopal functions of ordination and confirmation adequately, if uninspiringly, but a more thorny problem was posed by the sacrament of unction. The anointing of those near death, one of the seven sacraments of the pre-Reformation English and contemporary Roman Catholic Church, requires oil blessed by a bishop. That no diocesan of the Church of England was willing to bless oil for that purpose (or presumably any other) meant that a convert to Roman Catholicism could jeer at Anglo-Catholics' "six-Sacrament Church."[104] Unction was, as Bishop Forbes of the Scottish Episcopal Church put it, "the lost pleiad of the Anglican firmament."[105]

But Anglo-Catholics did have a few of their own bishops who were willing to do the necessary in such matters as unction and to represent the episcopal order in various ceremonies and observances. One opponent of the movement complained about the way that Anglo-Catholics "catch a Missionary Bishop to make him a novel element in a procession," and in fact the movement's episcopal sympathizers usually were missionary bishops, or Scottish, or American—at any rate, men who came with no territorial jurisdiction in England, but also with no compromising ties to Parliament or responsibility to the English laity.[106]

At the consecration of St. Barnabas, Oxford, for instance, Bishop Wilberforce declined to join a procession through the streets to the new building, but the bishops of Nassau and Minnesota did not hesitate.[107] (It must have been a difficult day for Wilberforce: when he insisted on celebrating at the north end, the design of the elaborate altar made him effectively invisible.) In 1862 the bishop of Honolulu took part in an elaborate ceremony to lay the cornerstone for a mission chapel in Plymouth.[108] By 1868 he and two other bishops—Nassau and Dunedin—had joined the Society of the Holy Cross, and in 1883 the bishop of Argyll and the Isles was appointed from the Society's ranks.[109]

These bishops filled a void for the movement, allowing it almost to act as a Church in its own right within the Church of England. Equally important was their standing affirmation of the recurrent theme that spiritual distinctions outweigh worldly ones. A Scottish bishop, a missionary or colonial bishop, a retired bishop, even an American one—each had the same sacramental powers as His Grace the archbishop of Canterbury, Primate of All England, and the Anglo-Catholic view was that questions of jurisdiction, authority, and temporal standing paled beside that great fact. Like the movement's other egalitarian messages—that priests were of equal standing and that laymen were, too—that conclusion was unwelcome in many quarters. If it was not mere foolishness, it was profoundly subversive.

VIII

Ritualism and the Urban Poor

Almost from the beginning, Anglo-Catholicism had a special relationship to East London and to the slums of other English cities; many of the movement's best-known churches were located there, and many of its best-known figures served those churches. As early as 1843, a sympathetic observer was writing to a friend, "Altogether in the east of London, in Bethnal Green, Stepney, Shoreditch, and that neighbourhood, the Church is doing wonders; and here the Morning Chronicle says Puseyism is all but universal. You and I know what this means."[1] Fifty years later, an anti-Ritualist pamphlet headlined "Ritualism Rampant in East London" described "the 'goose-step' of idolatry" ("Stand." "Kneel." "Be very attentive.") evident in an instructed children's Mass at St. Augustine's, Stepney.[2]

In time the Ritualist slum-priest became a figure well known to the point of stereotype, and the hagiography of the movement is amply provided with examples: Father Mackonochie of St. Alban's, Holborn, in and out of the courts for fourteen years on a succession of "Ritual" charges, and working tirelessly for the poor of Central London; Father Stanton, a great preacher in an age of great preachers, who loved the "undeserving poor" and spent his whole working life as an unpaid assistant curate at St. Alban's; Father Lowder of St. Peter's, London Docks, who founded the Society of the Holy Cross for mission work in English cities, and whose funeral was for East London what Stanton's had been for Central; "Father Bob" Dolling of St. Agatha's mission to sailors, Landport, "mucking in" with "the lads," boxing the ears of a young aesthete who criticized his posture at Mass, deposed by his bishop for saying Masses for the dead; Stewart Headlam, founder of the Christian Socialist Guild of St. Matthew, who defended the "pure and beautiful" dancing in London theaters and music halls and took a party of ballet girls to Fulham Palace to meet the bishop (who was not amused).[3]

These men, others like them, and the Anglican sisters who shared their work were there, among the poor. Some went voluntarily, as others went to Africa or the South Seas, agreeing with Lowder that "in the presence of such utter destitution, it was simply childish to act as if the Church were recognised as the mother of the people" and that the Church "must assume a missionary character ... to stem the prevailing tide of sin and indifference."[4] No doubt others went less willingly, because to be an Anglo-Catholic clergyman was often to suffer the displeasure of bishops and patrons. In either case, the slums of nineteenth-century England provided a laboratory for experimenting with what seemed to many a new and startling form of Anglicanism—as Lowder put it, "a new adaptation of Catholic practice to the altered circumstances of the nineteenth century and the peculiar wants of the English character."[5]

In time, a popular conception of slum Ritualism emerged, a conception shared in large measure even by many of the Ritualists' antagonists. Building on a base of undeniable fact—that these clergymen and sisters were hard-working, self-sacrificing, and devoted to the physical and spiritual welfare of the poor—this conception was of great symbolic and strategic importance to the movement. Ritualism's defenders argued, and some of its opponents came to believe, that the Ritualists were succeeding among classes of Englishmen where other sorts of Anglicanism had failed. Their forms of worship, it was argued, were uniquely adapted first to attract and then to instruct the poor and unlettered, and they were, in consequence, unusually successful in their mission work. Although the movement's bitterest enemies were disturbed by what they believed was its success in winning the poor, others, including many who found Anglo-Catholic doctrine and ceremonial offensive, were prepared to offer a measure of tolerance and even respect to men and women apparently able to reach a population largely untouched by the national Church, or indeed by religion in any form.

Like many stereotypes, this one had some truth in it, mixed with some exaggeration, some oversimplification, and some confusion about cause and effect. It was certainly true that many of the leading centers of Ritualism were located in poor and sometimes downright noisome parts of English cities; true also that the clergy and sisters associated with many of these churches worked tirelessly, often for decades, on behalf of the poor in their neighborhoods; and true that the poor frequently responded to these efforts with affection and respect. But it is less clear that they responded by adopting the religion of their benefactors, even to the extent of going to church. To be sure, the Ritualists had a theory about why they should, arguing the particular attraction of their services for the poor, but the poor did not respond as they should have, and when they were drawn to Ritualist churches it seems to have been more often despite the services than because of them.

The real attraction of some Ritualist churches, and the explanation for the differences among them, lay in the lives and persons of the clergy, not in the doctrines they preached or the ritual they practiced. The appeals of Ritualism as such were not to the poor but to a different sort of Englishman—and Englishwoman—altogether. There were attempts at the time to define these issues and to sort them out. We can review some of them and see whether anything can be added in retrospect.

Ritual as an Evangelical Device

It was almost an article of faith among the Ritualists that the ignorant found beautiful services unusually attractive. Once the poor were attracted, the argument continued, they stayed to be instructed, and the services were well-suited for that function, too.[6] Some observers were willing at least to consider the possibility. As the *Fortnightly Review* put it: "The Ritualists have laid hold of a great and powerful principle, and they find that it draws immensely. That principle is to make worship dramatic, and to teach religion by object lessons." Given the failure of the Church of England to reach the urban poor, the *Review* denied "that those men who are bent on trying a new principle deserve to be either insulted or repressed."[7]

R. F. Littledale was probably the most effective—and certainly the most forceful—proponent of this "principle." Other varieties of Christianity had failed among the "lower strata," Littledale argued, because they were "too intangible."[8] He urged that "a lesson may be learnt, by all who are not too proud to learn from the stage. For it is an axiom in liturgiology, that no public worship is really deserving of its name, unless it be histrionic."[9] (That comparison was calculated to affront the puritan, and Lord Shaftesbury quoted it, angrily, in the House of Lords.[10]) Even London gin-palaces, Littledale went on, warming to his subject, competed in "internal decoration, abundant polished metal and vivid colour, with plenty of bright light."[11] If spectacle and music were necessary to promote drink, he asked, how much more so to persuade people to take up something, religion, that they have never learned to care for and may, indeed, actively dislike?

In another essay, noting that the last joint protest of the bishops had been against Sunday excursion trains, Littledale (who approved of the trains) argued that "Ritualism is a sort of excursion train on the Sunday, to bring the poor man out of his dull, squalid, every-day life into a land of beauty, colour, light and song." (He added wickedly that the bishops, "having pictures, musical wives, spacious rooms, curtains and gilding in profusion, and being perfectly free from religious enthusiasm, do not see what the creatures can want with it."[12]) Another priest put the case less provocatively, this way: "The house of God, fittingly adorned, and the worship of God, solemnly, yet attractively rendered, is the poor man's only opportunity of rising above the dead level of his monotonous life."[13]

According to its defenders, ritual also had a didactic purpose. "In their efforts to teach Catholic doctrine to illiterate congregations," Mack-onochie's biographer has written, "the Ritualists resorted increasingly to what nowadays might be called 'visual aids.'"[14] As early as 1852, A. D. Wagner of St. Paul's, Brighton, defended his distribution of "pictorial crucifixes" (pictures of the crucifixion) on evangelistic grounds.[15] (He had been reproved, at the urging of the Brighton Protestant Association, by Bishop Gilbert of Chichester, who cited the Second Commandment and the danger of superstitious use.[16]) Two years later, H. P. Liddon, then chaplain to the workhouse at Wantage, defended his introduction of religious pictures in the sick wards on their "intrinsic common-sense merits." "A small proportion of the sick inmates can read," he argued; "their minds are simply tabulae rasae and they offer the Devil and the Gospel equal opportunities. The Gospel can only get at their hearts through their senses: and to treat them as purely intellectual beings is simply to ignore the facts of the case."[17] (The Guardians nevertheless ordered the pictures removed.)

In 1858, a preacher in the parish church of Clifton Campville combined the ultrarubricians' appeal to decency and order with the needs of evangelism, telling his listeners:

Your soul, perchance, may be able to rise to God in a place where well-nigh all these externals are away; in a place where God's Altar is represented by an old painted board, stuck nakedly on four legs, and which looks as if, in its better days, it had held an inferior position among somebody's household furniture; in a place, where the Service of God is familiarly talked-out, with every-day voice, in the form of a stupid dialogue between the Priest and Clerk; in a place, where Fast and Festival, Christmas and Good Friday, appear just alike, being submitted alike to this one dreary law of meagreness and desolation.... But let us remember that Christ's religion is not to be simply a religion for the well-trained minds of the educated few.

He called for a church and a service that would "strike home to a soul that is all ignorant and blind,—a soul, that cannot see into and understand words and verbal statements of religion, as, it may be, you can."[18]

Evangelicals might argue (one did) that Ritualism, "viewed in its most innocent light as an appeal to the imagination, as a means of representing truth to the soul, is far inferior to language," but Littledale proposed a practical experiment: "Take two street-Arabs, perfectly ignorant of Christianity. Read to one of them the Gospel narrative of the Passion, and comment on it fully as may be. Show the other a crucifix, and tell him simply what it means. Question each a week afterwards, and see which has the clearer notions about the history of Calvary."[19]

Tractarianism had come a long way from its common-room origins; as another Ritualist put it, "To the poor, a worship which appeals only to the intellect, requires an effort of which they are not capable."[20] This argument is plausible enough, and historians sympathetic to Anglo-Catholicism have generally accepted it. "The evangelistic necessities of work in the slums," one has written, "amongst bullies, criminals, and prostitutes, demanded a religion instinct with emotional appeal and converting power, with warmth, light, colour, and majesty, and, above all, with the tingling sense of the intimate nearness of the Sacred Humanity of Christ."[21]

No doubt these appeals of sacramental worship in its Ritualistic form were important for the priests and sisters at work in the slums, keeping up their morale and sustaining them in their grueling and, humanly speaking, unrewarding regime. But it is less obvious that the evangelistic theory was correct—less clear that large numbers of the poor were drawn to Ritualistic services, less clear even that those who did come were attracted by the services.

As was often the case, some of the Ritualists' most bitter opponents were in an odd sort of agreement with them. A Church Association writer, for instance, said that the Ritualists were "wiser in their generation" than the older Tractarians had been, precisely because they recognized that "most minds receive impressions more readily through the eye and ear than directly from the brain."[22] But others of their contemporaries were skeptical. As one wrote at the turn of the century: "So far as the working man is concerned, he seldom feels at home in a church with a highly ornate ritual.... The working classes prefer a simpler sort of worship, not too elaborate or symbolic."[23]

The extent and nature of Ritualism's appeal to the poor and the working class would seem to be empirical questions. We can subject the Ritualists' evangelical theory to a test, keeping in mind, however, that whether the theory actually worked may be less important for explaining the movement's eventual outcome than that many people believed that it did.

At first glance, the solution would seem easy enough. For London, for example, we can turn to *Mackeson's Guide* to identify Ritualist churches and to Charles Booth's maps in *Life and Labour of the People in London* to identify slums, and report, say, that of the thirty-six Greater London churches in which eucharistic vestments were being used in 1882, seven were located in the slums of East London and two in equally unsavory neighborhoods of Lambeth and Vauxhall, south of the Thames, and that another half-dozen were in somewhat more comfortable working-class neighborhoods or in "mixed" areas.[24] We can turn to the religious census of 1886 and to the reports of visiting journalists and observers and discover that some of these churches, particularly the best-known ones, consistently attracted large Sunday congregations.[25] But of course it is not that simple.

Defining a "Slum Church"

Pusey's endowment of St. Saviour's, Leeds, consecrated in 1845, set a pattern.[26] The most "advanced" Ritualist churches were almost always new establishments, and often they were missions or "district" churches (within the territory and under at least the nominal supervision of existing parish churches) in poor areas of English cities, where overcrowding made the need for new churches most evident and poverty made the need for social services most acute. By the 1880s perhaps a dozen Ritualist churches ministered to the slums of East and South London, and other well-known examples served the poorer neighborhoods of Oxford and Birmingham, Plymouth and Portsmouth, Leeds, Leicester, and elsewhere. Such churches always made up an appreciable proportion of Anglo-Catholic strongholds. What that proportion might be, however, is a problem.

The movement's critics argued, again and again, that the admittedly large congregations of some Ritualist slum churches were not made up of bona fide poor or working-class people, implying that the Ritualists were wrong in their assertion that their forms of worship were peculiarly suited for mission work among the poor and even that the Ritualist effort was a failure in its own terms—that it did not attract the poor to sacramental worship in any appreciable numbers. An Evangelical curate who somehow found himself in an Anglo-Catholic parish complained, "Whilst some rich and fashionable people eagerly embrace an opportunity of pampering a morbid taste for ecclesiastical millinery and sumptuous worship, the poor are conspicuous by their absence [and] prefer a simpler service."[27]

Many people who disliked Ritualism agreed with him that the poor shared their tastes. These critics asserted, first, that many "slum" churches were not actually in the slums at all, but rather in decent or at least socially heterogeneous neighborhoods; second, that churches in "mixed" neighborhoods drew their congregations from the well-to-do rather than from the poor; finally, that Ritualist churches, by their notoriety, attracted crowds of curiosity-seekers from considerable distances rather than congregations from the immediate neighborhood.

These ambiguities were evident even in the case of the first, and in some ways prototypical, London slum church, St. Barnabas, Pimlico, consecrated in 1843.[28] W. J. E. Bennett, vicar of the wealthy and fashionable church of St. Paul's, Knightsbridge, raised the money to build St. Barnabas in a poor and isolated corner of his parish. Bennett led the *Times*'s private list of "Puseyites of London" (which said he was "As near Romanism as possible"), and his new church's ceremonial quickly became the focus of unfavorable attention.[29] When, in 1850, riotous disorders broke out, Bennett resigned, at the bishop's request, and took a living at Frome (which he always spelled "Froome," as it is pronounced, perhaps in an unsuccessful attempt to forestall jokes about dropping the "F").

From the beginning, it was evident that the congregation at St. Barnabas was not wholly or even primarily made up of the poor from the neighborhood. St. Barnabas was only a short walk, or carriage ride, from some very fashionable West End addresses indeed, and Charles Lindley Wood, the future Viscount Halifax, was not the only parishioner of St. Paul's who preferred the more advanced services at the mission church.[30] After the riots of 1850 brought the church notoriety, it attracted even more outsiders.

So when we find that St. Barnabas held 382 worshippers on the morning of the religious census in 1886, and 683 (standing room only) in the evening, we cannot know what sorts and conditions of men and women they were. Some years before, in 1867, the vicar had testified before the Royal Commission concerning the ceremonial at his church.[31] He acknowledged that the morning services attracted chiefly the upper classes (necessarily from outside the neighborhood), but argued that the Sunday evening services were attended primarily by the "lower and middle classes." The extensive questioning he received on this subject suggests that the commissioners were skeptical, and Mr. White may have been somewhat misleading in his responses. When he asserted that a majority of the congregation came from within a three-quarter-mile radius, his interrogators surely knew that such a radius included Belgrave Square, not to mention Buckingham Palace.

In any case, by 1867 St. Barnabas was no longer in the forefront of ritual advance. By then, the baton had been passed to other churches, the most notorious being Mackonochie's church of St. Alban's, Holborn.[32] Consecrated in 1863 to serve the residents of a poor neighborhood in Central London, St. Alban's has always been considered a test case of Anglo-Catholicism in the slums, by both the movement's defenders and its detractors, and from the church's early days its critics repeated the familiar arguments. There were overflow congregations at the church, to be sure, but (1) Holborn was not a real slum, (2) St. Alban's worshippers were not poor, and (3) they were not from Holborn.

No one could deny that the church was full. On the census day in 1886 its congregations numbered 767 in the morning and 533 in the evening, in a building with seats for 600. But, Mackonochie's critics argued, in the first place Holborn was not as vicious and depraved as he and his friends claimed—no more to be compared for badness with parts of East and South London, as one put it, "than Bloomsbury is to be compared for fashion with Belgravia."[33] Booth's maps indicate that the critic was right: the neighborhood of St. Alban's runs Booth's color gamut from a touch of black ("Lowest Class") to red ("Well-to-do"), lacking only the yellow of the truly wealthy. Nevertheless, there were certainly poor people aplenty quite nearby: the blue of "Very Poor" predominates.

But were they found in the congregation as well as in the neighborhood? When Charles Wood went to St. Alban's in 1864, he found the church "beautiful, filled to overflowing, full of poor people, all kneeling about everywhere, and, what reminded me much of Rome, the fleas were very active."[34] But when a correspondent for the *Times* attended, in 1866, he reported that the congregation contained many (like Charles Wood) from "decidedly fashionable society, while scarcely any are below a respectable middle class." Father Mackonochie, stung, wrote to protest that, first of all, the morning service was not the place to find the poor in large numbers, and, besides, the congregation contained "many who, although dressed to pass muster, I know to be living by hard daily labour."[35] This moved another observer to report his count at six different Sunday and weekday services: at most, something on the order of 10 percent were poor, and the congregations came from the west: "Upwards of forty private carriages, and numerous cabs, convey the fashionable world on a Sunday morning to St. Alban's."[36]

This last testimony, unfortunately, came from the complainant in *Martin v. Mackonochie,* hardly a disinterested party. When we do find an impartial observer, a fair-minded Broad Churchman who visited the morning service a few years later, he reports that "the poor were decidedly in the ascendant, and fully on a par with the rich"—but it was a snowy morning, which might have kept those from outside the neighborhood away.[37]

When the resolution of a question hinges on the possible effects of London's weather on a particular Sunday in the 1870s, some measure of analytical humility seems called for. Perhaps we should leave the question of St. Alban's unresolved and seek other churches for our test.

East London's "Biretta Belt"

To the east lay some of those areas to which Holborn was being favorably compared. They were areas, moreover, remote enough from "the fashionable world" that few from those precincts would have been tempted to make a Sunday morning excursion there. The two registration districts of Shoreditch and Bethnal Green were home to some quarter-million Londoners in the 1880s, and, with the areas immediately to the south, were the heart of the East End.[38] They were characterized, Booth said, by "rough English poverty": the men employed as car-men, costermongers, and bootmakers, and in furniture making, silk weaving, glassblowing, and "gas-work"; the women in cardboard and matchbox making. Booth noted the "great want of open spaces" and "the number of beerhouses," but called the area's poverty "sturdy" rather than "wastrel," and noted that the criminal areas were highly localized.

This was an area in which the Anglo-Catholic missionary effort was concentrated. In 1882, six churches in the two districts were employing the eucharistic vestments, and four of the six were also using incense ceremonially, which indicated that they were very advanced indeed for the time. All six were new churches—one still in a temporary structure, the other five consecrated between 1865 and 1872. They had been built largely through the efforts of a surgeon named Robert Brett, convert from Nonconformity and author of *Devotions for the Sick Room,* whose involvement with most of the new Anglo-Catholic London churches in this period earned him the affectionate sobriquet "the Pope of Stoke Newington."[39]

Each of these churches had from the beginning been equipped with all of the apparatus of a complete Ritualist establishment. *Mackeson's Guide* for 1882 describes one, for instance, as follows:

225. COLUMBA, S., HAGGERSTON, Kingsland Rd. (L.)—V., J. Vodin Walters, M.A., (1872), Vicarage. C., J. B. Johnson, M.A., (1875), 75, De Beauvoir Road, N.; W. H. Browne, Ll.B., 75, De Beauvoir Road, N. Sacristan, E. Norton, 72, Foulden Road, Stoke Newington, N. Org., W. A. Smith, (1874), 28, Lidfield Road, Stoke Newington. **Services: Sun., +H.C., 7.0, 8.0, †11.15 (choral); m. 10.15; Lit., 10.45; Children's Services, 3.30; e. 7.0. Holy Days, H.C., 7.30, 9.0; m. 8.15, e. 7.30. Daily, H.C., 7.30; m. (plain), 8.15; e. 7.30 Wed. and Fri., Lit., 12.0. Hymnal, "Noted," with an App. Music, Gregorian (Doran and Nottingham). Choir, surpliced; vol. Seats, 1000, free. Offertory, weekly. Eucharistic Vestments, Cope, Incense. Complete Ritual according to Sarum Use. Altar Lights. Surplice in pulpit. Open for private prayer daily from 7.30 to 9.30. Architecture, Early English (J. Brooks); cons., July 7, 1869. Organ, by Allen, of Bristol, 1874. Patrons, Trustees, for forty years, afterwards Bp. and Crown, alt. Income, from Eccl. Comm., 300 and house. P., 8000. Flor. Dec. Ded. Fest., July 7. Sisters from St. Peter's Sisterhood, Kilburn, work in parish; Guilds for Boys and Girls; Ward of C.B.S. Working Men's and Youth's Club.

Translated, this gives us the names, addresses, degrees, and dates of appointment of the vicar, two curates, sacristan, and organist. The clergy lived in the neighborhood, the curates in what was undoubtedly called the "Clergy House," the vicar in the house provided by the Ecclesiastical Commissioners. The total income of the living was three hundred pounds a year, plus whatever the weekly offering brought in—certainly not much. No doubt the curates were celibate by choice, but unless they were independently wealthy, they could hardly have afforded to marry. The organist and the sacristan, of whom less was expected, commuted from somewhat more salubrious surroundings in Stoke Newington.

Except for weekday matins, the daily offices (morning and evening) were "fully choral" (**), a demanding regime for the organist and the volunteer choir of men and boys. The Sunday services were almost continuous, with two early celebrations of the Holy Communion, followed by matins, the litany, and a choral celebration, the last three separated (†) so that people could enter and leave after each part. Sunday afternoon was occupied with a children's service and choral evensong. On other days, an early communion service preceded matins ("said"), and there was a choral evensong. On saints' days (almost certainly more numerous than those appointed in the *Book of Common Prayer*), there was an additional communion service, and matins were sung by the choir. At all communion celebrations the priest faced the east (+). On Wednesdays and Fridays, the litany was read at noon.

The hymnbook was John Mason Neale's, one of several favored by Ritualist churches, with an appendix of introits and graduals. The hymnal consisted entirely of translations from the Latin, and the chants were Gregorian rather than Anglican—a mark of faction within the Ritualist party.[40] The choir was surpliced, of course, as was the preacher—except when he wore a cope. There were floral decorations and lights on the altar—the latter illegal, unless required for light, but then so were the eucharistic vestments, the eastward position, and the incense required by the "Sarum Use" (that of the pre-Reformation Diocese of Salisbury).

There were no pew rents at St. Columba's; all one thousand seats were free and open to the public. (Consequently, although *Mackeson's* does not mention it, the sexes were separated at some services.)[41] The church was left open fourteen hours a day for those who wished to pray—in a parish of eight thousand where thieves were probably more common than worshippers. The church was built in the Early English style, regarded by the Cambridge Camden Society as next best to Decorated, to the plans of a popular church architect of the day.[42] (The same architect had designed two of the other five Ritualist churches in Shoreditch and Bethnal Green.)

The church was associated with the Confraternity of the Blessed Sacrament, and other sources indicate that the vicar and one of his curates were priests-associate of the C.B.S. The vicar was also a member of the English Church Union and was (or would soon become) a member of the Society of the Holy Cross.[43]

St. Columba's had guilds for children and a club for young men, and sisters from Kilburn worked in the parish, but a few years later Booth observed that "the social agencies" were less important at St. Columba's than at most of the other Ritualist churches in the vicinity, and that the clergy tried to draw people into more distinctively religious activities. Processions around the neighborhood were something of a specialty, and Booth noted that "the roughest lads take their places as 'altar servers.'" "Confession is practically insisted upon," he observed, "and is made the very corner-stone of the system."[44] This emphasis was not new: the vicar had signed the controversial petition to Convocation asking for the licensing of confessors, a quarter-century before.[45]

Give or take a detail or two, and the same description would apply to the rest of the Ritualist churches in Shoreditch and vicinity; differences were only in what might be called "character." At St. Chad's, St. Augustine's, and St. Stephen's, Haggerston, where John Mason Neale's Sisters of St. Margaret were active, a more ambitious welfare program was undertaken: free dinners for the unemployed, half-penny dinners for schoolchildren, dinners sent out to the sick, doctors' prescriptions compounded and sold at cost, tickets given out for food and fuel, employment found for women.[46] The sisters' London priory was in the parish of St. Augustine.[47]

At St. Michael's, Shoreditch, the ceremonial was perhaps even more advanced. *Punch* was present in 1867 for a dedication festival: "Romanising commenced at eight o'clock with a procession," Bishop Gray of Capetown preached, and Father Ignatius put in an appearance.[48] Twenty-five years later, a Church Association pamphlet was still denouncing the "Mass and Mariolatry at St. Michael's": their scout had observed that four of the five hymns at a service during "the Octave of the Feast of the Assumption" were addressed to the Blessed Virgin.[49] The social work at St. Michael's was extensive, Booth reported, and largely unconditional: "The clubs are freely open to all, and it is averred that the poor who are relieved are not even asked to come to church."[50]

Even less demanding was nearby Holy Trinity, Shoreditch, located next to a particularly squalid slum portrayed (if not exactly immortalized) in Arthur Morrison's novel *A Child of the Jago*.[51] In 1882 Holy Trinity was in a temporary structure, but the Reverend Osborne Jay later built his church over a social club and spent most of his time in the latter, not shrinking (Booth reported) from associating even with criminals. He also ran a lodging house for men. Some of his clerical neighbors did not approve of his methods, but Booth observed that they were "a very real effort to take the Church to these people since they certainly will not come to the Church."[52]

In Bethnal Green and Shoreditch, the 1886 religious census indicated that the Ritualists' colleagues (more often viewed as competitors) in their mission efforts included thirty other Anglican churches and chapels, ranging from almost-as-high to very low indeed, one Roman Catholic church, and twenty-five dissenting Protestant congregations.[53] (In the 1890s, the last included a United Methodist Free Church mission built in the form of a lighthouse, which offered a revolving light, a brass band, and working-class evangelists.)[54]

Attendance in 1886

Here, if anywhere, we find (as Booth put it) "an excellent test of the results and value of the work of the High Church, better in many ways than can be obtained from any single isolated parish."[55] But let us be clear about our measure of "results and value": we are asking simply whether the Ritualist churches attracted any considerable number of the poor to sacramental worship; in other words, whether any appreciable proportion of Anglo-Catholic laypeople were drawn from the poor. Whether the Ritualists' good works did or did not effectively help the poor is not the question, unless those good works brought the poor into the churches.

It must be said that no form of Christian worship was particularly successful in East London, a fact that has often been remarked before.[56] Of the quarter-million inhabitants of Bethnal Green and Shoreditch, something under 12 percent were in one of the churches in the area on the Sunday of the 1886 census. The census-takers counted 30,936 persons at principal morning services and at evening services combined; since some of these were present at both, it is likely that the actual figure is nearer to 9 or 10 percent.[57] Of these churchgoers, 17,001 were counted in Church of England congregations, not counting 280 in the chapel of the workhouse. Anglicans of any sort, in other words, were only a bare majority of the minority who were churchgoers.

The problem was not lack of seating, despite a great deal of contemporary attention to that issue.[58] The thirty-six Anglican churches had seats for more than 31,000 worshippers, of which fewer than 4000 were "appropriated."[59] This number was a small fraction of the population of the area, but a substantial multiple of the number actually present. They held 7192 worshippers at the principal morning services on census Sunday, 9809 that evening. Only one church was more than half full that morning, and only six that evening.

The 4290 seats at the six Ritualist churches held only 1251 worshippers at the principal morning services, and only 980 that night. At the morning service, in other words, these churches attracted 29 percent of capacity, about 17 percent of the Anglican churchgoers and about 9 percent of all churchgoers in two districts, and about 0.5 percent of the total population. In the evening, attendance at the Ritualist churches decreased, reflecting an emphasis on the Mass as the principal Sunday service; attendance at all other sorts of churches was greater in the evening.

Making every allowance for the fact that the Ritualist churches had earlier morning services whose congregations went uncounted, the figures must still be regarded as disappointing. St. Columba's 1000 seats held only 132 worshippers that morning. St. Michael's 800 seats held 159; St. Stephen's 600 held 116. Tiny Holy Trinity had 41 worshippers in 150 seats. St. Chad's and St. Augustine's were relatively full, with congregations of 400 and 403 respectively, but only St. Chad's, with 800 seats, was as much as half full, and that barely.

The situation was much the same at other Ritualist slum churches in London. To the south, at St. Peter's, London Docks, the 600 seats of the church were occupied by 226 that morning. Things could have been worse—and were at All Saints, Lambeth, where the erratic rector, Dr. Lee, ministered to a congregation of 41 in a church built to seat 1500.

Nor was this a temporary phenomenon. The *Daily News* census of 1902 and 1903 revealed a decline in total attendance of 22 percent for the five surviving churches of the six.[60] This decrease was not much worse than the decline in attendance at all kinds of religious institutions in London (14 percent) and was actually somewhat better than the decline in Anglican attendances (26 percent), but the later census, unlike the earlier, counted congregations at all services between 9:30 and 11:45 A.M. and should have increased the count for Ritualist churches.[61]

Of course it could be argued that even if attendance at the Ritualist

churches in East London never reached the levels their founders and benefactors had hoped for, at least they did as well as those other Anglicans who
were working the same territory. Of the fifty people per thousand of population who were in church that morning, only twenty-seven were in the
churches and chapels of the Establishment: five in Ritualist churches, ten at
"low" services (almost certainly morning prayer and sermon), and twelve at
churches best characterized as middle-of-the-road.[62] But this largely reflects
the distribution of churches. With 14 percent of the total number of Anglican sittings, the Ritualist churches attracted 13 percent of the Anglican
churchgoers that Sunday in 1886. The middle-of-the-road churches did
somewhat better (38 percent of the seats and 49 percent of the worshippers), the Evangelical churches did worse (48 percent of the seats and 38
percent of the churchgoers).

So the Ritualist churches as a group were not conspicuously unsuccessful in attracting the poor. But neither were they unusually successful.
Although their failure to fill their large new churches must be seen as part
of a larger pattern of failure by the Church of England (indeed, by organized Christianity of all sorts), the churches were nevertheless largely
empty. In general, the situation seems to have been as Booth reported it at
St. Mary Magdalene's, Paddington, in the nineties: "The clergy are devoted to their work, and the people, they say, are full of gratitude, respect and
love; 'there is no unwillingness to come to church'—only they do not
come."[63] As the warden of Mansfield House put it at the turn of the century, reviewing these figures and his own experience in East London: "The
High Church—or at least the Ritualist section of the High Church—does
not seem to have made the progress that everybody anticipated."[64] That
seems a fair conclusion.

Working-Class Anglo-Catholics

And yet some poor men and women were in the pews. They were only
a small proportion of the working class of England's cities, but they were
there. They numbered only in the thousands, not the scores of thousands
envisioned by the builders of churches. But the working-class
Anglo-Catholic was not simply a creature of Ritualist propaganda.

"The congregations are not large," Booth observed of St. Columba's,
but "amongst such as these whom it serves, [the church's program] may
have power to interest, to sustain, and even to awaken a divine response in
their poor souls."[65] At Holy Trinity, the vicar's unorthodox methods did
not lead many men to climb the stairs from the club to the church above,
but the church had a large Sunday school and its services—"very high, very
bright, very short"—attracted a few worshippers, "a genuine congregation
of quite poor people," according to Booth.[66] At St. Alban's, Birmingham,
the baptismal register indicated the "Quality, Trade, or Profession" of the

father; an alphabetical list begins "baker, barman, basketmaker, bedstead polisher, blacksmith, bone turner, boot-finisher," and concludes with "tin-plate worker, tube drawer, upholsterer, venetian blind maker, vice maker [sic], warehouseman, wiredrawer, wire weaver, wood paviour."[67] We cannot know whether these men came to church other than for baptisms, but that is at least a start. The only professional man on the list—a surgeon—appears to have been a churchwarden, but at St. Peter's, London Docks, at least one of the wardens was a working man, "a well-respected lighterman."[68]

One observation, intended at the time as a criticism, does not seem to be well-founded. When Charles Booth remarked that the small congregations at St. Augustine's, Haggerston, were "mostly women and girls, or young persons of the lower middle and working classes of the district, together with a considerable number of children," he was implying what many others stated: that parents might send their children, but did not go themselves, and that Ritualism was particularly attractive to women—or unattractive to men.[69] We shall look at the truth of this observation in more fashionable districts later. In East London, however, it was not a fair accusation, at least not to judge from the results of the Daily News census at the turn of the century.

To be sure, some of the slum churches had large numbers of children in attendance. St. Peter's, London Docks, in particular, showed 584 children and only 300 adults at the morning services the census-takers attended.[70] But this ratio reflected a conscious mission strategy established by Father Lowder and followed faithfully by his successor, Father Wainwright.[71] Children from the parish schools were required to attend a special children's Mass, before the principal morning celebration. But elsewhere the Ritualists' congregations were less lopsidedly juvenile. In the five surviving Ritualist churches in Shoreditch and Bethnal Green, for instance, children made up 55 percent of their morning congregations and 36 percent of those in the evening, compared to 60 percent and 36 percent respectively for all Anglican churches and missions in the two boroughs. When these figures are compared to those for all of "inner," non-suburban, London (40 percent and 26 percent), it is clear that a relatively high proportion of children was characteristic of neighborhood and class, and not restricted to Ritualist congregations.[72]

Nor were women strikingly overrepresented in these congregations. Although most of the adult worshippers at the five East London churches were female, this was true in general for the Church of England in London. (Dissenters had a much more nearly even sex ratio in their congregations.) In fact, in the morning, the five Ritualist churches had a lower proportion of women in the congregation (57 percent) than the total for Anglican churches in the two boroughs (59 percent) or in all of inner London (64 percent), although the proportion of women was higher at the evening service (71 percent, compared to 65 percent for Shoreditch and Bethnal Green and 67 percent for inner London as a whole).

In other words, whatever the case in the West End, Ritualist churches in East London do not seem to have attracted congregations that were demographically different in any startling way from those of other Anglican churches serving the same area, except (as in the case of St. Peter's and the schoolchildren) by design.

But if they were not demographically different, members of these small but established working-class congregations were different from their neighbors by virtue of that fact itself. They were practicing Anglo-Catholics, and they were devoted to their forms of worship; they were, as we shall see, ready to fight for them. As early as 1851 the bishop of Exeter had remarked, "Few occurrences have affected me more than the lamentations of the poorer worshippers in one of the districts of the metropolis, when they saw, or thought they saw, at the dictation of a riotous and lawless mob, the approaching surrender of the ritual which they loved, and which was their weekly—to many among them the daily—solace to that poverty to which the providence of God had consigned them."[73] In the case of long-established congregations, where people had grown accustomed to high ceremonial, perhaps even grown up with it, the conservatism that elsewhere was an obstacle for the Ritualists became an asset. When a new vicar at St. Mary's, Crown Street, Soho, "lowered" the services there in 1874, the churchwardens, accompanied by four parishioners (a carpenter, a greengrocer, a coach-plater, and a printer), called on the bishop and asked him "to let them have their old services again."[74]

But it seems that the Ritualists' evangelistic theory was not correct, even for the few working-class men and women who were attracted to their churches. Their affection for their form of worship seems to have come after and because of commitment to a particular congregation and acceptance of the Ritualists' sacramental doctrines. The ceremony was not itself the original attraction, as the theory would have had it; rather, it came to express cherished beliefs and to serve as a badge of faction.

In all of the argument back and forth at the time and since, the workingman himself has scarcely been heard from. As we have seen, most voted with their feet, and avoided Ritualist services as impartially as they avoided other sorts of organized worship. But even those who came have left little testimony about why they came, and they have few spokesmen other than their priests, whose theories about their own success and failure must be taken with a grain of salt. There was often a great gulf fixed between them and their flocks, and some of them anguished over it. One clergyman in a working-class district of Kentish Town, for example, told Booth: "I would die for the workingman, but I do not really understand him; I cannot speak his language, and I cannot think his thoughts."[75]

The Church of England Working Men's Society

We can begin to sort out the appeal of Anglo-Catholicism for its working-class adherents by looking at the Church of England Working Men's Society. Early on, the principal Ritualist slum churches developed an apparatus of clubs and guilds as an adjunct to their missionary and relief work, and these almost always included a "working men's club." In Holborn, the St. Alban's Club offered a place for workingmen to dine, drink, and play cards: it offered no social improvement classes, religious newspapers were not allowed on the premises, and it had two hundred members by 1871.[76] At St. Peter's, London Docks, the St. Saviour's Working Men's Club ran a loan society, a sick benefit association, a soup kitchen, and a coal club. At its meeting in January of 1868, a hundred members partook of a hot supper and "two huge bowls of punch."[77]

In 1876, the English Church Union, anticipating trouble in the wake of the Public Worship Regulation Act, supported the organization of a national body, based on these existing clubs. By its second anniversary, the Church of England Working Men's Society, or C.E.W.M.S., claimed 101 branches and had a full-time general secretary (a former night watchman) with offices in Holborn, near St. Alban's and its active and supportive staff of curates.[78] By 1880 the society reported 216 branches, with 3766 members, in nearly all of the Ritualist strongholds in England; by 1888 it claimed 285 branches with 10,000 or so members.[79]

In the late seventies and early eighties, the society's activities were reported almost every week in the pages of the *Church Times*. The branches memorialized Parliament and the bishops to repeal the Public Worship Regulation Act, to oppose remarriage of the divorced, and on other favorite Anglo-Catholic topics. The branches also sponsored guest lecturers, distributed leaflets supplied by the English Church Union, and organized special services for the working classes.

Occasionally we get a glimpse of something more interesting. From time to time the society seems to have provided bodyguards for Ritualist clergymen and protection for meetings and services threatened with disruption. As the society's president said in 1880, "wherever there is a branch of the Church of England Working Men's Society, there will be found a band of ready defenders when [the clergy] and their services are attacked, and cordial co-workers when there is peace within their borders."[80] Sometimes the workingmen did not limit their activities to defensive ones. The *Church Times* noted with satisfaction the disruption of a Church Association lecture at Dorchester, observing that "this meeting is another indication of how strong a hold the Catholic movement is taking on the working classes."[81] Another Church Association lecture, in Brighton, was interrupted, an officer complained, when the lecturer was "violently assaulted by a well-known Ritualistic butcher."[82]

On both sides, violence and the threat of it emanated from the working class (although they were sometimes encouraged by their social betters). According to one observer, for instance, the anti-Ritualist rioters at Father Tooth's church, St. James, Hatcham, were "members of a Protestant Working Men's League, and all of them Orangemen of the worst type."[83] Perhaps the possibility of a dust-up added some zest to the work of handing out leaflets and listening to guest lecturers.

An organization of Ritualistic workingmen presented a threat of another sort as well. As the *Church Times* warned in 1877, "Depend upon it, if the Church of England Working Men's Society should add Disestablishment to its programme, its progress would be rapid indeed."[84] Again and again the society's spokesmen denied that they sought the disestablishment of the Church of England, but again and again they said that they would prefer that to the suppression of Ritualism.

It is difficult to say how seriously this threat was taken, but when a delegation from St. Alban's, Holborn, presented the archbishop of Canterbury with a petition in support of Father Mackonochie, signed by "525 bona fide working men parishioners," the following exchange was recorded:

Charles Powell, leader of the delegation: "This is a working man's question, and, when the working classes of this country become aware of the manner in which their heritage in Church matters was being attacked, they would rise up, and the Church of England, as an established Church, would fall; the working men of themselves could cause the whole fabric to fall about your ears."

The archbishop (smiling): "Oh, nonsense, nonsense."[85]

On the other hand, a mass meeting organized by the Working Men's Society in 1877 to support the imprisoned Father Tooth may have been taken more seriously. The two thousand in attendance (including the delegates from St. Cyprian's, Marylebone, a bootmaker and a coach-builder) were congratulated by the speakers on their restraint in not resorting to violence and in continuing to support Establishment.[86] Reports in the Anglo-Catholic press made plain the implication, however, that patience was wearing thin. Be that as it may, within three days of the meeting Tooth was released, and at least one historian has attributed his release to the authorities' concern in the wake of the meeting.[87] Father Tooth seems to have shared this view: two hours after his release he called on the secretary of the C.E.W.M.S. to thank him for his support.

Surely part of the society's appeal was that it allowed its members to be menacing, in a respectable sort of way. At its 1880 meeting, several speakers opposed a bill then before Parliament that would have allowed Noncon-

formist ministers to conduct burial services in parish churchyards. Many had
hard things to say about Nonconformists, and two of the speakers urged
that if the bill passed, "the Clergy, backed up by the working men" should
forcibly prevent "dissenting Ministers" from entering churchyards to conduct services.[88]

As we have seen, of course, workingmen were not the only Ritualists
whose views of the laws of Heaven licensed or even required them to break
the laws of the State, and throughout its history the Working Men's Society
had close ties with those clergymen who were in trouble with the courts. At
its fourth anniversary meeting, for instance, eighty delegates were led in procession by a brass band from the pier to St. Peter's, London Docks, where
Father Enraght preached. They then returned to Father Mackonochie's
church, St. Alban's, Holborn, for another procession, with banners and
incense. Another service for the society was held at St. Columba's, addressed
by the Reverend Mr. Pelham Dale. At the Members' Meeting, the news that
the flowers on the table had been sent by Father Tooth was greeted with
"loud applause."[89] Father Tooth, of course, had been in jail not long before.
Mackonochie, Enraght, and Pelham Dale were all in the courts as defendants at the time of the meeting, and the last two would be jailed within the
year.

Workingmen who embraced Anglo-Catholicism seem to have been an
exceptionally convinced or hardy lot, perhaps because prevailing working-class sentiment was against them. They seem to have had a particular
animus toward Dissent, and some valued ritual because it distinguished
them from their opponents. As the rector of Falmouth reported, "Where
there is any Church feeling at all [among the poor], it is a strong one. It is
a feeling antagonistic to Dissent; because being brought into daily communication with Dissent, it naturally takes a contrary character." Poor
Anglo-Catholics would oppose "any approximation to Dissent" in the
Church's services because they valued "the distinctive characters and features which now tell us we are of the true Church, and not aliens from that
Church."[90]

But the appeal of Ritualism for its working-class adherents is still not
clear. The bishop of London thought he knew. "My belief," he wrote to
Mackonochie in 1867, "is that the acknowledged earnestness and devotion
of your congregation spring, not from the peculiarities of the ceremonial
you have used or the doctrines you have preached, but in spite of these, from
God's blessing on the deep sense of the real Christian verities, and the anxious love to save souls, which are daily shown in the preaching and lives of
yourselves and others who cooperate with you."[91] But since Bishop Tait's
distaste for the Ritualists' ceremonial and doctrines was well-known, perhaps
the testimony of the president of the C.E.W.M.S. will carry more weight.

We may suspect a clerical hand behind the society's organization and its
subsequent resolutions and other actions, but the president's speech to the

society's 1880 meeting must have been heard with mixed feelings by some
of the clergymen in attendance. Mr. William Inglis (the society's officers
were all "Mr." in the official report; two of the three nonmember trustees
were "Esq." and the third "Lt. Col.") spoke of Ritualism's appeal as follows:

I am not now counselling zealous struggles for the introduction of extreme ritual
and elaborate music into your parish churches, these things are good in their way,
but not always advisable, for they are often not understood. My experience has
taught me thoroughly that there is no greater check to the Catholic movement, and
no greater assistance to our opponents, than a Church with an extreme ritual and
elaborate music, but without any parochial organization to win the people; the consequence is it forms a ritualistic Cave of Adullum, to which skin-deep Catholics flock
from all parts to the "functions," but the parishioners are to be found anywhere but
in their parish church.
   Think you St. Alban's, Holborn, St. Peter's, London Docks, and many others,
would ever have laid hold upon the people, and christianised the heathen around
them as they have done, with ritual only, or won the waifs and strays to the feet of
Christ with Schubert, Gounod, and Cherubini. Nay, there was a real, active, systematic work, a following the example of the Divine Master, a going among the publi-
cans and sinners, a seeking for the lost sheep.... Much as we love ritual and have
clung to it and those who used it ... let us shew pity upon the weaker brethren....
Let us aid the clergy in educating the bulk of the working class up to what is decent
and necessary, fully assured that as men understand and accept the doctrines, so in
like ration they will demand the ritual.[92]

   Here is impressive testimony that supports a number of observations we
have encountered from other sources, with quite different axes to grind.
Inglis acknowledged that some Ritualist churches were full of "skin-deep
Anglo-Catholics from all parts," rather than the poor of their parishes. He
argued, like Bishop Tait, that "extreme ritual" did not appeal to "the bulk
of the working class," and that working-class Anglo-Catholics were attracted, in the first instance, by the devoted pastoral work of the Ritualist clergy.
It seems that the Ritualists' evangelistic theory was simply unfounded when
it argued that "beauty, colour, light and song"—at least in the
Anglo-Catholic mode—drew crowds of worshippers. The ritual appealed to
those who had been educated up to an understanding of the "decent and
necessary," not to "weaker brethren" who did not yet understand and
accept the doctrines that underlay the ceremonial. Father Lowder, of St.
Peter's, London Docks, always maintained that ritual was an effective
teaching device—the poor, he said, are "taught by the eye and ear, as well
as by the understanding"—but he did not claim that the worship at St.
Peter's was attractive to the uninitiated. It was not "a mere aesthetic
embellishment," he said, "but the outward expression of a great reality. It
exactly meets the wants of *those who have been taught* to value their Lord's

Sacramental Presence."[93]

Nevertheless, Inglis's speech is further testimony to the fact that some *had* been taught. There was at least a small body of convinced and dedicated working-class Anglo-Catholics. The congregations of Ritualist slum churches were not composed only of slumming aesthetes and a few of the poor who were bribed to be there. Many working-class families had been won, as Inglis said, and they had been won by the clergy's labors in their behalf.

The Character of the Slum Ritualists

The "entire goodwill of the people," Father Lowder said, alone made ritual advance possible, and the most successful of the slum priests and sisters won that goodwill.[94] At the least, they wore themselves out by scrupulous attention to providing the rites and ceremonies of the Church for those who wanted them and otherwise would not have received them. At their best, they managed, as Father Stanton of St. Alban's put it, to throw "a bridge of friendship across that gaping chasm that separates the clergy from the working classes."[95] Father Stanton, Charles Lowder, Robert Dolling, and many others won the devotion of the poor—even of many who were never moved to come to church—by that "anxious love to save souls" that Bishop Tait had acknowledged, and a genuine concern for their welfare. At the turn of the century, Percy Alden, who disapproved of the Ritualists' ceremonial and doctrines as much as Bishop Tait had, nevertheless granted that some had made an impact, "because they put the man before the priest. They call nothing common or unclean, and are willing to share all that they possess with the people whom they serve."[96]

Certainly the Anglo-Catholics' style of pastoral work must often have been a pleasant contrast to that of Evangelicals working the same territory. We have already heard R. F. Littledale's views on Sunday excursion trains and noted the unusual rules of St. Alban's Club for workingmen, but there are other examples. One curate at St. Alban's noted in a memoir, for instance, that "Father Mackonochie ... was of opinion that Teetotalism was Manichaean. Large numbers of our parishioners seemed to share that opinion."[97] A temperance tract by another Ritualist urged a "*via media*" between teetotalism and drunkenness.[98]

Father Dolling's interpretation of the Incarnation, it is reported, led him not only to be enthusiastic for gymnastics and swimming baths, but to encourage dancing "as helping the lads and girls he worked among to be less hulking and awkward in their movements and rude or suspicious in their manners."[99] When the Reverend Osborne Jay of Holy Trinity, Shoreditch, built his church over the social club, "Mother Kate" of the Society of St. Margaret approved heartily—and went to the club one time to watch a boxing match.[100] Mother Kate (surely one of the most attractive figures the movement produced) founded the Men's and Lads' Home, in Brighton; she let the men smoke as much as they wished, "for I do believe in Thackeray's axiom, 'A man can't be doing much harm when he is smoking his pipe.'"[101]

Smoke was also on the agenda and in the air at Father Stanton's "S. Martin's League," for London postmen. Stanton joked that when asked "What good has the League done? Have you made the members High Church?" he had to reply, "No! Talk as I will, I cannot get incense substituted for tobacco." If all of the League's six hundred members had become ardent Anglo-Catholics, no one would have been more pleased than Stanton, but the League's reason for being was simply to bridge the gap between clergyman and workingman and to make comfortable those "whose duties involve great discomfort." "Are you content with this?" Stanton asked himself. "I am; and more than content."[102]

Not all of the Ritualists at work in the slums were as engaging as these, nor were all equally successful in winning the affection of their neighbors. "Here and there an able, devoted man has built up a strong and flourishing church," Percy Alden acknowledged, "but there are many instances of ineffectiveness and incapacity." Alden argued that when the East Londoner did support a Ritualist church, perhaps even attended it, "it is because he approves of the Socialist leanings of the parson and finds in him a real friend and brother."[103]

One is forced to the conclusion that Ritualist slum churches won the support of their people only when they were brought into being by saintly men. Where such men were absent, the same doctrines and the same ceremonial were simply ignored, or worse. Two adjoining East London parishes—St. George's-in-the-East and Charles Lowder's church of St. Peter's, London Docks—provide an almost classic demonstration.[104]

Most observers in the press and the government understood the provocation for the St. George's riots of 1859-60 to be the liturgical practices of the rector, Bryan King, especially his intoning and use of eucharistic vestments. Fifteen years after the riots even a new rector of St. George's wrote that his predecessor's trials had resulted from what "the bulk of the parishioners, rightly or wrongly, believed to be illegal sacerdotalism," which made their grievances "intelligible enough, and some form of resentment on their part defensible."[105]

It is true that King's Puseyism was extreme: in 1844 it had put him in a tie for fifth place in the *Times*'s private ranking of 99 London clergymen. But the *Times*'s intelligence report had also observed that "in private life he is as remarkable for his extreme pride & hauteur, as he is notorious for want of propriety & discretion in the administration of the duties appertaining to his public function," and the fact that the riots continued after he agreed to give up the disputed practices, and stopped only when he left the parish, suggests that the issue was as much the rector himself as his ritual.[106] For most of the protesting parishioners, the innovations were an excuse to protest, a stick to beat an unpopular clergyman with.

BROTHER À BECKET
(Mr. Richard C. Jackson)

HARRIET MONSELL

SABINE BARING-GOULD

ROBERT STEPHEN HAWKER

T. T. CARTER

JOHN BACCHUS DYKES

EDWARD STUART

PRISCILLA LYDIA SELLON

ARTHUR STANTON

JOHN MASON NEALE

GEORGE RUNDLE PRYNNE

CHARLES LOWDER

ENGLISHMEN !!

ANOTHER CLERGYMAN SENT TO PRISON.

REV. T. P. DALE

IS NOW IN

HOLLOWAY PRISON,

NOT FOR STEALING, OR CUTTING AND WOUNDING, NOT FOR BREAKING THE LAW,

But for obeying his conscience, and doing his duty, as an English Parson should who loves his Prayer Book!

Clergymen who neglect this duty, or who are Traitors enough to Marry Adulterers in their Churches, against all Laws of God and His Church, are promoted; Infidels may sit in Parliament and make Laws to harass Christian Clergy : but good men like Mr. DALE, who hurt no one, and who work hard as best they can for GOD and Souls, are to be put in Jail with common felons.

HOW LONG will Englishmen stand this UNFAIR, UN-ENGLISH and COWARDLY BULLYING of hard-working Clergymen ?

ISSUED BY THE

CHURCH OF ENGLAND WORKING MEN'S SOCIETY,

69, HIGH HOLBORN, W.C.,

C. POWELL, Secretary.

W. KNOTT, Printer, 26, Brooke Street, Holborn.

WORKING MEN'S SOCIETY HANDBILL

ARTHUR TOOTH
Vanity Fair, Feb. 10, 1877

A. H. MACKONOCHIE
Vanity Fair, Dec. 31, 1870

E. B. PUSEY
Vanity Fair, Jan. 2, 1875

J. L. LYNE (Father Ignatius)
Vanity Fair, April 9, 1887

FASHIONS FOR 1850; OR,

Punch, 1850

A PAGE FOR THE PUSEYITES.

Punch, June 26, 1858

RELIGION À LA MODE
Mr. Bull: "No, no, Mr. Jack Priest! After all I have gone through, I'm not such a fool as to stand any of this disgusting nonsense!"

Punch, November 3, 1866

"PERNICIOUS NONSENSE"
Mr. Bull: "I pay your reverences to look after my establishment, and if you neglect your duty, I shall see to it myself."

Punch, October 9, 1858

SAUCE FOR THE GANDER

Pusey—Pusey—Gander,
Whither would he wander,

Upstairs, down-stairs
And to My Lady's Chamber.

But Bull and *Punch* declared they wouldn't
Stand such priestly airs—

So took him by his shoulders,
And kicked him down-stairs.

Punch, 1850

THE PUSEYITE MOTH AND ROMAN CANDLE
"Fly away *Silly* Moth."

East End of St. Alban the Martyr, 1863

EDWARD KING

A. H. MACKONOCHIE

H. P. LIDDON

ARTHUR TOOTH

Mackonochie's biographer has written of King, sadly: "He was not without courage; he showed patience and forbearance, and behaved with considerable dignity in some trying situations. But it is difficult to escape the impression that he was something of a noodle."[107] At the time of King's greatest troubles, the *Daily Telegraph* was less temperate; it called him a "silly, effeminate, carnal man."[108]

Something of King's pastoral style can be gleaned, alas, from his memoirs. After describing the horrible state of affairs in the parish of St. George's when he arrived, he reports that "beyond the exercise of something like discipline in regard to a few extreme cases—such as the refusal to give Christian burial to unbaptized children, or to permit the bodies of some who had died in open sin to be taken into the Church for that portion of the Burial Service, and the refusal to Communicate one or two notorious evil livers— I was never able to make any attempt at anything like active aggression upon the seething mass of evil and sin by which I was encompassed."[109]

Perhaps it is not surprising that King neither won the affection of the small existing congregation nor attracted admirers from the parish's nonchurchgoers. When the riots began in 1859, his allies came almost entirely from outside the parish.

Outsiders also played a role in King's downfall, of course, but Charles Lowder's happier experience at St. Peter's shows that they could not have done so if King had enjoyed the support of his parishioners. Make every allowance for the fact that St. George's was an established parish church, where some churchgoers had fixed ideas, while Lowder was working in virgin territory; still, King's failure must be attributed to his personal qualities, and Lowder's success to his.

St. Peter's cannot be imagined apart from its founder. As a student at Oxford, Lowder had heard Newman preach; he then went to work as a priest in the slums of London. He was at St. Barnabas, Pimlico, in 1850, during the "no-popery" disturbances there. To his lasting regret, he organized some of the choirboys to throw eggs at one of the more obnoxious demonstrators: the "ovation" became a cause célèbre for the press, and Bishop Blomfield suspended Lowder for six weeks. He spent his enforced vacation in France, where he read the life of St. Vincent de Paul, and returned to found in 1855 the Society of the Holy Cross. Joining the staff of St. George's-in-the-East, he was assigned to work at a mission in the parish, which he soon built up to a position where it was consecrated as the independent church of St. Peter's, in 1866. St. Peter's under Lowder is universally acknowledged to have been an example of slum Ritualism at its best.[110]

Lowder and his associates undertook an extensive program of social work, reaching parishioners of every kind, and over the years they built up a small but devoted congregation from the poor and the working-class people of the parish. Lowder and his successor Father Wainwright were particularly known for their work with children.

One of Lowder's curates tells a revealing story. When two agents of the Church Association appeared one day and started taking notes during the service, a churchwarden—the "well-respected lighterman" we have already encountered—went up to them and whispered: "If you go on with this 'ere, there's half a dozen men behind you will crack your heads."[111] The story indicates not only that workingmen were to be found in positions of responsibility at St. Peter's, but that its ceremonial had the congregation's approval. Indeed, the eucharistic vestments were a gift to Lowder from the churchwardens, choir, and congregation.

We have already seen Lowder's views on the proper relation between doctrine and ceremonial; his belief that those who understood the doctrine would demand the ceremonial modestly understated his own role in producing that "entire goodwill of the people" that certainly existed at St. Peter's and that would probably have indulged him in whatever ceremonial he wanted. The final, touching tribute to Lowder came at his funeral, in the 1880s, when the poor of East London lined the streets; eight hundred parishioners rode a special train and many more walked the nine miles to Chislehurst, where the burial took place.

The Importance of Slum Ritualism

In one important respect, the Ritualists' hopes and their opponents' fears were not realized. The movement did not succeed in evangelizing the slums of Victorian England. What Booth observed of St. Augustine's, Haggerston, might in truth have been said of many other slum churches: "The influence of the church may be deep, but is certainly restricted."[112] Other churches could not even claim that. At nearby St. Stephen's, by the 1890s, the clergy had effectively given up: its services were "entirely neglected by the public," the vicar was most un-Ritualistically condemning the "multiplication of services," and he had abandoned the daily offices because no one came.[113]

When slum priests did succeed, their success was measured less by large numbers of communicants than by small but devoted congregations, and a large penumbra of goodwill and affection from people whom they served in other ways. Whatever the movement's theorists might say, when the poor responded to Anglo-Catholicism it was less a response to ceremonial or to doctrine than to some remarkable personalities. As one historian has put it, "the poor understood the meaning of sacrificial love—and men like Lowder, Goulden, Mackonochie, Stanton, and Talbot lived long enough among them that they could not fail to recognize its presence."[114]

These were not the only Christian ministers at work in the slums, of course: think only of the Salvationists. They were not even the only Anglicans. But they were new enough, devoted enough, numerous enough, and, yes, conspicuous enough that even their opponents could not fail to notice their good works. There were enough men like these, and women like Mother Kate, to win for the entire movement a measure of tolerance and eventually goodwill in circles far removed from the slums. We have already seen Bishop Tait's generous acknowledgment of their devotion, coupled with his condemnation of their doctrine and ceremonial. Many shared his ambivalence, including some of his brothers in the episcopate. In a sermon in Bristol Cathedral, Bishop Ellicott anathematized the Ritualists for their "disloyalty," but on the way to that conclusion he allowed that the leading Ritualists were "men of eminently pure and holy lives," who had shown "true Christian courage and a love for souls" in a recent cholera epidemic and had revitalized Anglican preaching. Perhaps he can be forgiven for the weary remark, "This movement, though at present it seems too much to hope for, may still gradually cease."[115]

Others felt the same. One curate, for example, thought it "highly probable that, had it not been for the zeal of the Ritualists, their system would have collapsed long ago, and been by this time a thing of the past, worthy of a place in the limbo of the Middle Ages." Yet he had to acknowledge that no one, "to whatever shade of opinion he may belong, denies the palpable fact that Ritualists are animated with unbounded zeal and ardour in the cause which they advocate; that they are proverbially distinguished for their restless activity and their wonderful self-denial"; moreover, "their attention upon the sick is unremitting; they labour among the poor with unwearied energy; they have increased, to an unparalleled degree, opportunities of resorting to the means of grace; they have made their churches free and unappropriated; they are earnest, warm, and impressive in the pulpit."[116] But this man, too, wished that these troublesome zealots would simply go away.

All of these observations were made in the 1860s. Some time later, when it was becoming clear that the movement was not going to abate, that the Public Worship Regulation Act was not going to work, and that the choice was toleration or expulsion, a new note began to be heard, an argument that it was worth putting up with the Ritualists' excesses for the sake of their good works. One pamphlet from 1877 presented the new, moderate view: "Whatever their faults, Ritualists are men of earnest, self-denying lives and there must be some good in them which compensates for their mistakes. They almost invariably go to the lowest and most crowded districts in our great towns, and there they labour without thinking of reward. It is to me more than disappointing, it is in the highest degree shocking, to find people who have not a tithe of their zeal and self-devotion, clamouring to have them put down by legal processes."[117]

This writer believed that "Ritualism seems to be gaining a hold on classes whom no one else can touch," a view not entirely accurate, as we have seen. But neither was it entirely without foundation, and the vicar of St. Giles, Durham, may have been right when he confessed himself "bound in justice to say" that the Ritualists' strongest point was "personal holiness" and to conclude that "we cannot afford to lose them."[118] He described himself as a "neutral with Evangelical leanings," and by then he was far from the only person of that description to feel that way.

In that fact, Ritualism as a movement could point to an undeniable and important accomplishment, and for the Ritualist priests and sisters in the slums of England it was a very real success—if not the one they most desired.

IX

Who Were the
Anglo-Catholic Laity?

Given license to hoot an aloof or pharisaical vicar, some slum-dwellers might well have seized the opportunity to dispel the boredom of a Victorian sabbath, but the cry of "No popery" would not have moved people like the costermonger who told Henry Mayhew, "I don't know what the Pope is. Is he in trade?"[1] One reason so many of the new Anglo-Catholic churches were located in the slums is that the most determined opponents of Anglo-Catholicism lived elsewhere.

But the movement's most enthusiastic supporters also came from other neighborhoods. The bodyguard of gentlemen that protected Bryan King during the St. George's-in-the-East riots was not recruited in the parish; neither, as we have seen, were many in the congregations of St. Alban's, Holborn, St. Barnabas, Pimlico, and other convenient and well-known centers of advanced ritual.[2] And many of the real strongholds of Anglo-Catholicism were not slum churches at all.

The documents of the period sometimes give the impression that the movement's lay support was socially if not numerically negligible—the movement's leaders often exaggerated the odds against it and its opponents often portrayed it as a clerical conspiracy against the laity—but as time passed some Ritualist clergymen in fashionable neighborhoods found themselves surrounded by congregations that shared their beliefs and their liturgical tastes. Who were these people?

The Class Basis of Ritualism

In the 1860s, R. F. Littledale summarized the social composition of the Church of England's various factions. The old "High and Dry" school, he said, appealed principally to the squirearchy. Its only influence with the poor came from "the natural weight of feodal pressure" in the countryside; in the towns it lacked even that, and it had no appeal to the lower-middle class at all. Littledale saw the Broad Church as even more class-bound, supported almost exclusively by the educated. It appealed, moreover, to "one age and sex alone": the very word "manly," of which it was so fond, showed its "neglect of the other aspects of Christianity." ("It is not easy to conceive the idea of a Broad-Church lady [and] the mind refuses to contemplate a Broad-Church boy or girl except in the light of an intolerable prig.") The Low Church, finally, was middle-class; it did not appeal to "the highest or the lowest strata of society" because its "merely subjective" character was "too intangible" for the lowest and its "deficiency of culture" alienated the highest.[3] Littledale went on to draw his conclusion: "All the sections of the English Church, save one, have stood their trial, and have failed.... The Tractarian now claims his turn."

But the appeal of Anglo-Catholicism was not universal, either. We can locate its constituency quite precisely with the aid of Charles Booth, who at the turn of the century described the relation between religion and social class in London.

First, it is important to recall that for the movement's first several decades one became an Anglo-Catholic only by choosing to become one, abandoning some other form of religion, or irreligion. The great families of the nation, consequently, were not especially vulnerable to the movement's appeals; as Booth observed, they had "easy and confident" relations with their inherited Church, whether Anglican or Roman, and their conservatism led them to avoid extremes.

Nor was the conventional upper-middle class susceptible. Members of that class—"legal and other professional men, some civil servants, men of business, wholesale traders and large retailers"—also had untroubled relations with their inherited religion. That was more often Nonconformity than Anglicanism, but Booth said that even the Anglicans took their religion in "a very simple, unquestioning, wholesome spirit."

The breeding ground for Anglo-Catholicism could be found between these two strata in the social hierarchy of the Victorian city, among university-educated professionals, higher civil servants, journalists, artists, intellectuals, the lesser nobility, and the urban gentry. Men and women of this class were gentlemen and ladies, they were not "in trade" (although their parents might have been), and they were distinguished from the commercial upper-middle class less by wealth than by taste or breeding or education.[4]

The rapid growth of this class in the nineteenth century meant that many of its members were new to it, and Booth observed that the upwardly mobile had "by the very law of their advancement shared to the full in the stress of worldly life, and in the characteristics it produced." People of this class were "mostly members of the Church of England, and supply the

Church with many of her clergy"; newcomers who were not already Church of England (and many were not) often converted, a form of "conventional development" that Booth found distasteful.

Booth remarked that members of this class were less "calm" in their religious attitudes than those above or below them in the social structure. Their religion was less a matter of duty than the aristocracy's, and their "religious anchorage" was less secure than that of the commercial class. "Men of business," Booth said, might be troubled by a personal sense of sin, but not by the weariness of life "nor by any doubts as to the foundations upon which the whole structure of organized religion is based." Among this intermediate class, however, religious feeling often took "the shape of reaction and revolt from the stress of worldly existence, which is apt otherwise to be the law of their being." In this state they, "especially the women," were liable to "rush into extremes of religious doctrines and practices."

Booth claimed that these were the natural recruits for occultism, new religions, new forms of old ones, or conversion to Rome, giving a new twist to R. F. Littledale's observation (quoting "an indiscreet votary") that Anglo-Catholicism was a "religion for gentlemen."[5] Several postgraduate members of the Society of St. Alphege did list their address as the Junior Carleton Club—and it is difficult to imagine men of business (or for that matter poor Anglo-Catholics in the slums) concerning themselves with the validity of Anglican orders.[6]

Empirical support for these observations comes from an odd source: scorecards kept by Roman Catholics of converts to their communion. Most of these converts at least passed through "advanced" Anglo-Catholicism on their way to Rome; one Roman Catholic journal stated as a notorious fact that three out of four did so, and the only surprise is that the estimate was not higher.[7] One list of secessions during the early 1850s noted that all of the converts belonged "more or less to the educated classes such as would be likely to be affected by the Oxford Movement"; they included a bishop's daughter, a duke's nephew, and a good many clergymen.[8] (One such clergyman, the "late Protestant curate of Bawdsey, Suffolk," compiled his own list of converts in 1861.[9])

In 1878, the *Whitehall Review* began to publish extensive lists of "Rome's Recruits," a project taken over by a Roman Catholic named Gordon Gorman, whose book *Converts to Rome* went through several editions. The fourth listed more than four thousand converts "since the Tractarian Movement to May 1899," ranging from "Newman, His Eminence the late John Henry, B.D., M.A., and Fellow of Trinity College Oxford [etc.]," through "à Beckett, Gilbert, sub-editor of *Punch*," to "Lean, Mrs., of London." (A twenty-page appendix listed American converts.) Because Gorman's compilation came primarily from newspapers and from converts and their friends, those from "a particular section of the community"—that is, the well-connected—were probably overrepresented. (Gorman tried to be more systematic, but a request for information sent to five hundred priests brought only thirty replies.) Still, it is striking that the list included 27 peers, 417 members of the nobility, and 32 baronets. It also included 205 Army officers (but only 39 from the Royal Navy); 162 authors, poets, and journalists; 129 lawyers, 60 physicians and surgeons, and 90 "public officials," as well as 446 Anglican clergymen and 37 Anglican sisters.[10]

An Oxford Movement, Still

To a surprising extent the movement retained its early identification as "the invasion from Oxford."[11] Quite late in the game opponents were still describing Ritualism as a species of "religious fanaticism which is generally picked up at the University of Oxford," and its enthusiasts as mostly "empty-headed and shallow-brained striplings, fresh from Oxford."[12] Anglo-Catholics themselves recognized the linkage, and sometimes this identification gave a varsity flavor to ecclesiastical conflict. When R. F. Littledale caught the Ritual Commission report of 1867 in a logical error, for instance—they had been directed to look into securing uniformity in "such matters as shall be deemed essential" and had recommended that vestments be suppressed because they were *not* essential—he attributed it to "the large Cambridge element on the Commission."[13]

The stereotype was not without foundation. Ever since the days of the Camden Society, Cambridge men had made notable contributions to the movement (and one wrote an entire book to document that fact), but they always remained a minority.[14] In a sample of fifty clerical members of the English Church Union in 1877, for instance, Oxford graduates outnumber Cambridge men by thirty to thirteen; Cantabrigians predominate, twenty-three to eleven, in a similar sample from the anti-Ritualist Church Association. (The "ultra" Society of the Holy Cross was more evenly balanced, but in a sample of fifty members Oxonians have a twenty-one to sixteen majority.[15])

The Oxford connection also seemed to hold for laymen. Gorman's statistical breakdown of converts to Roman Catholicism (which included them) found a ratio similar to that for clerical members of the E.C.U.: of 721 university graduates, 445 were from Oxford and 213 from Cambridge.[16] Oxford in the 1840s enrolled slightly more than four hundred new undergraduates a year, so it seems that something over one year's intake of students had succumbed to "Roman fever." Cambridge, on the other hand, which admitted more than five hundred new undergraduates a year, had provided only about 40 percent of a year's matriculations.[17]

Converts with degrees from other British universities were relatively rare, or at least rarely recorded. As might be expected of an Anglo-Irish institution, graduates of Trinity College, Dublin, were even less susceptible to conversion than Cambridge men: its twenty-three converts would have been only 7 percent or so of yearly new matriculations in the 1840s. London University provided only eleven identified converts; Durham and King's College, London, ten apiece; and all of the Scottish universities together, only nine.

Oxford college traditions also seem to have been important.[18] If we ask how many years' worth of undergraduates from each college had "gone over," Magdalen heads the list. The home of Bloxham and other proto-Ritualists, Magdalen possessed in Dr. Routh the only Head of House sympathetic to the Tractarians, and five years' worth of its matriculants had become Roman Catholics.

Magdalen was followed by New College, which had given up nearly three years' worth of converts. New College was not itself closely associated with the movement (indeed, its chaplain was conspicuous among the Tractarians' adversaries), but many of its students came from Winchester College, which was greatly affected by the revival.

After New College came Merton, Oriel, and St. Mary Hall, an Oriel dependency; at each, more than a year and a half's intake of undergraduates had converted. Merton came to be identified with the movement by the late 1850s: its chaplain introduced a choral communion with a surpliced choir, and prominent High Churchmen among its fellows included the future warden of Keble College and Father Mackonochie's spiritual director.[19] Oriel, of course, was the setting for the famous Common Room, home to many of the early Tractarians.

Keble College was founded, under Anglo-Catholic auspices, only in 1870, after the great waves of secession that swept the movement at mid-century. Even so, in its first thirty years it supplied more converts than seven other Oxford colleges in twice the time—testimony, if any were needed, to the connection between Anglo-Catholicism and secession to Rome.

Anchoring the other extreme at Oxford was Wadham College, where converts numbered only about a third of the average annual new enrollments during the 1840s. Wadham had longstanding Whig and Low Church connections, and was known throughout the nineteenth century as markedly Evangelical. (Its warden, one of the Tractarians' bitterest opponents, gained notoriety by spying on Newman's "monastery" at Littlemore.) The only other Oxford college with proportionately fewer converts than Cambridge was Pembroke, although Jesus College—whose principal in the 1860s and 1870s was a member of the Church Association—had a ratio almost as low.[20]

College traditions and cultures seem to have been less influential at Cambridge. Trinity College, home of the Camden Society, produced many Ritualists and sympathizers, and it also had a relatively high ratio of converts to matriculations, tied for third among fifteen Cambridge colleges.[21] The highest ratio at Cambridge was that for Jesus College, home to a half-dozen members of the Society of St. Alphege in the 1860s.[22] But these colleges' ratios were high only for Cambridge: all would have been well below average at Oxford.

The figures for Cambridge colleges—despite small numbers and resulting random variation—are notably uniform. Ratios of conversions to annual matriculations for Cambridge colleges range only from 22 percent to 68 percent; thirteen of fifteen are below 51 percent. These figures do not reveal the extreme variation that both feeds and feeds upon conflict. The storm that drove men and colleges at Oxford into factions apparently produced only ripples at Cambridge; with less pressure to take sides, it appears that those Cambridge men disposed to Catholicism took it up, and those who were not ignored it.

"Members of Evangelical Families"

In 1866 the *Church Times* cheerfully observed that the "movement is gaining strength in the rising generation, and the very children of our opponents, brought up to hate us, will, in future years, be our warmest defenders."[23] Certainly the movement had a special attraction for young layfolk, just as it did for young clergymen. Everyone agreed that young people were conspicuous in Ritualist congregations, and that in "mixed" congregations, where some were engaged in Anglo-Catholic devotional practices and others were not, it was usually the young who set the Ritualistic pace. Even the original Oxford Movement, as Raymond Chapman has observed, "was in its essentials a movement for the young."

Its first leaders were comparatively young men, who could ride about pressing the Tracts on bewildered parish clergymen. Hurrell Froude, and later W. G. Ward, brought gaiety, ebullience—and instability—into the theological issues. It was a movement hostile to the conformist Establishment, questioning the accepted values of contemporary society, reactionary in its appeal but charmed by a romantic nostalgia and the element of "Charlie over the waterism" which sent its opponents into paroxysms.[24]

Most Evangelicals simply denounced the "giddy young men and women" who were attracted to Ritualism, but a few, like a preacher at Camden Church, Camberwell, wondered how their own worship could be made more appealing to "the young and enthusiastic" whom Ritualists "attracted to their side and enlisted in the service of their cause by appeals to the fancy, the imagination, and the finer instincts; by poetry and art."[25] (It would not do, of course, to make Evangelical worship "fantastic, tawdry, full of flimsy conceits, a thing of tinsel, gew gaw, and glitter" like Ritualism.)

We shall return to the subject of the movement's attraction for the young.[26] Here, just note that it often led to conflict with the older generation. Mark Pattison's family was not the only one where parents watched with alarm as a son took up Newmanite ideas at Oxford, daughters hid Tractarian books, and young relatives embarked on courses that led some of them eventually to Rome.[27] Francis Lyne, the unbalanced and probably insane father of the almost equally erratic "Father Ignatius," wrote a series of pathetic tracts and articles in Evangelical newspapers to lament the loss of his son. Amid incoherent digressions on the descent of Queen Victoria from King David, and asides on how the use of slang expressions like "awful jolly" showed "how the High Church party by insulting their bishops have lowered the moral tone of society," Mr. Lyne blamed Pusey himself for leading his son astray, and claimed that "the Ritualists are robbers of children, and weeping parents proclaim the fact."[28]

Even the royal family displayed this generational tension, although in suitably restrained form. The queen's distaste for Ritualism and Ritualists was well known, but Charles Wood (later Viscount Halifax), long-time president of the English Church Union, was a good friend and Groom of the Bedchamber to the prince of Wales, who reportedly once remarked, "If ever I become religious, I should be of Charley Wood's religion." Later, in fact, the prince often went with Princess Emily to evensong at All Saints, Margaret Street.[29]

Conflict with parents was especially likely when the parents were Evangelicals or Nonconformists, and partisans on every side agreed that children from such families were conspicuous in the movement. W. J. Conybeare speculated that they might have been driven there by the shortcomings of the Evangelical clergy. His unflattering portrait of the smug and vulgar Evangelical clergy in one fashionable town would be completely familiar to anyone acquainted with Trollope's Mr. Slope, in *Barchester Towers*, and Coneybeare surmised that young people exposed to such clergymen could easily "fall victims to the first infidel publication which might happen to come into their hands" or "receive Christianity under its Tractarian form." Their "hatred of the Low Church" might even "possibly transfer them as easy converts to the Church of Rome."[30]

Before we jump to accept Conybeare's conclusion, we should recall that members of a new and expanding movement must come from *somewhere*. It would have been surprising had no Anglo-Catholics been raised as Evangelicals or Nonconformists, and naturally converts from "Protestantism" occasioned comment in all quarters. It does seem, however, that such converts were disproportionately represented in the "advanced" wing of the movement. An unsympathetic Paddington curate observed, for instance, that "amongst the extreme people here, those are most extreme who have emerged from Dissent and become Churchmen and Churchwomen: thus verifying the saying, 'Extremes meet.' They are the red-hot Ritualists *par excellence*."[31]

In any case, Anglo-Catholics claimed that converts from Evangelical or Nonconformist backgrounds were especially numerous among those who advanced right into the Church of Rome. Archdeacon Denison ventured an estimate that "about four-fifths" of those who converted to Romanism had begun life as Evangelicals.[32] R. F. Littledale (himself the son of a sturdily Protestant Orangeman) explained that converts to Roman Catholicism were usually those who had never been "properly grounded in Church of England principles." Rome, he said, "seldom attracts those who have been always brought up as High Churchmen."[33]

Even in the Tractarian days, a Protestant background had been used to explain extremism or instability. In 1842, Pusey wrote the archbishop of Canterbury that "such as have actually gone over to Rome, and such as have been endangered yet retained, and those for whom one has immediate fears [are] mostly out of Ultra-Protestantism, not at all from among us."[34] Pusey may well have had his friend Newman in mind: that former Evangelical was soon to go over himself. Twenty-five years later, James S. Pollock quoted Pusey, and explicitly applied his observation to Newman—and to several other early converts as well. Pollock complained that Tractarians "are not fairly accused of Popery by Protestants, because some Protestants choose to make Tractarianism a convenient half-way house in their progress from one extreme of disloyalty to another. It is not Catholic doctrine, but Protestant instability that is at fault."[35]

These observations have at least a superficial plausibility. They are consistent with a phenomenon frequently observed among converts, and it is certainly possible that those uprooted from Protestantism were likely to drift to an extreme position and to experiment with doctrines and usages alien to historic Anglicanism. Many observers were ready to note that they were less measured in their faith, less compromising, than those "always brought up as High Churchmen," who experienced Anglo-Catholicism as a deepening and elaboration of doctrines already held.

The hypothesis (if we may call it that) works well, at least when applied to the leading clerical figures of the movement. In general, those from High Church backgrounds—Pusey and Keble, for instance—seem to have remained more undeniably "Anglican" than those raised as Evangelicals or Nonconformists, who more often staked out extreme positions within the Church, like Mackonochie, Littledale, or Neale, or left it altogether, like Newman, Manning, Sibthorpe, and the Wilberforces.[36] (The extremist Charles Marriott might seem to be an exception, but his High Church father died when he was young, and he was raised a Calvinist by his family's servants.[37])

For ladies and gentlemen in the cities and towns of England—perhaps especially for those who wished to put Evangelical origins behind them—Catholicism had potent attractions over and above its doctrine. Three in particular were so closely intertwined that they are almost inseparable: the movement's aesthetic allure, its hostility to the rising commercial bourgeoisie, and the fact that it was, for a time, almost fashionable.

The Aesthetics of Catholicism

In the movement's early stages, R. F. Littledale observed, "so soon, at any rate, as it had passed out of common-rooms into parsonages," it attracted principally "persons of high rank and station," because "to them, and to their supposed monopoly of aesthetic perceptions, Anglo-Catholicism, with its black-letter learning, its pretty aestheticisms, and its religious bric-a-brac in the shape of antique calf-bindings, velvet faldstools and prie-Dieus, and engravings after Overbeck, seemed eminently adapted."[38] This observation was echoed by the journalist W. J. Conybeare, who remarked that the High Church's "system" gave "freer scope to the feelings of reverence, awe, and beauty, than that of their opponents." Anglo-Catholics "endeavour, and often successfully, to enlist these feelings in the service of piety," Conybeare believed. "Music, painting, and architecture they consecrate as the hand-maids of religion." Thus Anglo-Catholicism attracted "an order of men found chiefly among the most cultivated classes, whose hearts must be reached through their imagination rather than their understanding."[39]

Notice the odd resemblance between Conybeare's analysis and the argument for high Ritual in the slums. When Ritualists defended their practices on evangelistic grounds they usually had the poor in mind, but the theory may actually have worked better when applied to the cultural elite.

The movement's opponents, of course, argued that this was an unworthy and untrustworthy attraction. The rector of Pettaugh testified: "I know that Ritualism *does* gather congregations. Good music is very attractive, and the solemn notes of the organ have the effect of producing a sort of simulative devotion; but I fear that much of this religious activity is the spasmodic action of the dead corpse under galvanic influence."[40] An Evangelical curate regretted that "some rich and fashionable people" in his congregation "eagerly embrace an opportunity of pampering a morbid taste for ecclesiastical millinery and sumptuous worship."[41] And still another Evangelical chastised his fellows for adopting "Ritualistic" practices themselves, arguing that "we are disposed to copy feebly what we find to be attractive to popular taste, thus losing the dignified simplicity of our own service without gaining the showy parade of our neighbour's."[42]

Even Gladstone, a sympathetic observer, remarked that the wealthy "have a preference for churches and for services with a certain amount of ornament," and feared that many "improvements in fabrics and in worship may be due simply to the demands of the rich man for a more costly article," thus representing "not the spiritual growth but the materializing tendencies of the age."[43] But to acknowledge that Ritualism's appeal was largely aesthetic was not to imply that it was simply secular; after all, Gladstone asked, why should a people who decorated their homes ornately do less for their places of worship?

At least one reader objected to Gladstone's offhand remarks about the dress of English women ("reputed to be the worst in the European world") and the taste of the ancient Greeks ("a nation of Wedgwoods"): the Englishwoman, this Evangelical replied, "is the highest type of the truly good, the domestic, the affectionate, and, therefore, the beautiful," and Greece "one of the most impractical of nations; to philosophize; cultivate her senses and revel in the sensuous—if not the sensual—seem ever to have been her highest behests."[44] This critic was also not pleased with Gladstone's suggestion that the innovations had any other than a doctrinal basis, and some Anglo-Catholics agreed with him about that.[45] Others, however, rejoiced in the harmony between contemporary taste and the half-understood implications of Anglo-Catholicism, both dictating a "Gothic" style in religious ornamentation and ceremonial.[46]

As the nineteenth century wore on, tastes changed, and some Anglo-Catholics turned from pre-Reformation English ornaments and usages to more Italianate models (a development paralleled in both secular taste and the theology of the movement's "advanced" wing): by 1874, for example, Van Leems and Wheeler, clerical outfitters, were advertising "Zuchettas [*sic*] made on Roman principle."[47] Others stayed with the earlier patterns, and the more or less amiable division that developed between "English" and "Western"—that is, Roman Catholic—usage lasted well into this century.[48]

Of course, intentional and explicit Romanizing was especially outrageous to Protestant opinion, and among those who followed post-Tridentine Roman practice there must often have been an element of naughtiness about what they were doing, a sense of tasting forbidden fruit, teasing and provoking their rather grim adversaries. The pamphlets, letters, and memoirs of Victorian Ritualists are largely silent on the matter, but a scene from a Barbara Pym novel set in the 1950s conveys this mood well:

The procession round the church with lighted candles reminded me of a scene from an Italian opera—*Tosca*, I suppose. There was something daring and Romish about the whole thing which added to one's enjoyment. It should have been followed, I felt, by a reception in some magnificent palazzo, where we would drink splendid Italian wines with names like Asti Spumante, Lachryma Christi and Soave di Verona.[49]

The character adds, "That it seemed to go equally well with the tea and sandwiches and cakes in the church hall was perhaps a tribute to the true catholicity of the Church of England."

Ritualism and the World of Fashion

Be that as it may, for what one of the movement's historians called "the cultured despisers of the Evangelical bourgeoisie" Catholicism served more than purely aesthetic—or religious—functions.[50] For some it was a vehicle of protest against the rising commercial middle class and its culture, against what one Anglo-Catholic called "the low, calculating utilitarians, the mere nineteenth-century men."[51] Littledale, writing in the 1860s, argued that the class basis of Anglo-Catholicism was changing, as Ritualists began to work among the poor, but what he called the movement's "Tory stage" was far from over. In the same year in which he wrote, an Anglo-Catholic lady gave her view of the movement's appeal: "Activity, progress, beauty, refinement, and devotion, are allying themselves with the Catholic side, and Protestantism finds its chief adherents among the vulgar and money-gaining classes."[52]

When a small but conspicuous minority of Anglo-Catholics turned to socialism in the 1870s and 1880s, some were simply responding in a practical way to what they had encountered in the slums of England; for others the choice was more theological—socialism, one remarked, could be seen as merely "mediaeval Catholicism turned inside out."[53] Whatever their motives, however, Anglo-Catholic socialism remained largely an affair of aesthetes and intellectuals, and their antibourgeois sentiments were shared by their Tory brethren.[54] Scott Holland somehow consolidated the various themes with his appeal to Oxford undergraduates: "Come down and be the squires of East London!"[55]

Like many others offended by capitalism and its culture, at that time and since, Victorian Anglo-Catholics juxtaposed the mean, money-grubbing present with a happy, imagined, preindustrial past. To John Mason Neale and other enthusiasts for the good old days of England, life before the Reformation was "a sort of Utopia" (as the architect A. W. N. Pugin described it, mockingly), "—pleasant meadows, happy peasants, merry England—... bread cheap and beef for nothing, all holy monks, all holy priests—holy everybody. Such charity, and such hospitality, and such unity, when every man was a Catholic."[56]

While Evangelical novels like Anne Howard's *Mary Spencer: A Tale for the Times* exemplified what Anglo-Catholics despised—one character in Miss Howard's novel, for instance, argues that building railroads that spread the Gospel is better than adorning cathedrals—Anglo-Catholic novels like Charlotte Yonge's *The Daisy Chain* were doing much to popularize the view of High Churchmanship as "an elevated species of good manners."[57] Small wonder that, as early as 1844, Miss Howard's Evangelical heroine was observing regretfully that "Evangelical" was becoming a term of reproach, and that "Churchman" or "Catholic" was more fashionable.

Consider the circumstances surrounding the founding of All Saints, Margaret Street, an Anglo-Catholic "Model Church" founded under the patronage of Alexander Beresford Hope, rising Conservative M.P., former chairman of the Cambridge Camden Society, husband of Lady Mildred Cecil, proprietor of the *Saturday Review*, and one of what R. W. Franklin has identified as "a circle of well placed figures and politicians who provided the financial support for the Puseyites."[58] In 1845 Hope wrote that he wanted a church of "foreign character, lofty and apsidal" that would rebuke "the haughty and Protestantized shopocracy" of London; after the church was consecrated in 1859 he observed ingenuously: "The Church this week seems the great fashionable fact. Ever so many people were talking to me about it at Lady Derby's ball last night."[59]

Fashionable Anglo-Catholics like Beresford Hope gave their adversaries a great deal to work with. In one Ritualist publication, for instance, a book-seller's advertisement offered both translations of Roman Catholic devotional works and something called *The Continental Fish Cook; or, a Few Hints on Maigre Dinners*; another merchant advertised "'Monastery Wine' for the Altar" of "a Delicate Muscatel Flavour."[60] And one exasperated old-fashioned High Churchman objected to a letter in the church press about how to cross oneself while carrying a muff.[61]

Clearly, Anglo-Catholicism as a "religion for gentlemen" could serve Oxford graduates and others who moved in the same social circles as a mark of social distinction, almost of good taste. Emma Warboise, a Low Church novelist, mocked this sort of snobbery in *Overdale*, published in 1869. One of her characters says: "I do not think the eclat of going over to Rome is at all in good taste," but

I assure you it is quite *ton* now to be *very High*! In the best circles, there is just a certain clique that is Low Church, but the people who compose it are nobodies.... One might as well be a Methodist or Plymouth Brother as one of those dreadful, vulgar-minded Evangelicals. Eustace ought to be "high"; it is due to his rank that he should be so. It is the natural development of his aesthetic tastes and his Oxford training.[62]

Miss Warboise was writing satire, but something of the same attitude could be found week after week in the pages of the *Church Times*. An 1866 account of an anti-Ritualist meeting at Exeter Hall, for instance, invited readers to observe "the miserable thing Protestantism has become." "I do not suppose there were half-a-dozen really intelligent people in the body of the hall," the correspondent wrote. "A more contemptible, unintellectual-looking, seedy set of men and women I never saw collected together."[63]

In 1877, the Reverend J. C. Ryle, a prominent Evangelical soon to become bishop of Liverpool, delivered some equally contemptuous observations about the sorts of laypeople attracted to Anglo-Catholicism:

Shallow-minded members of the aristocracy—ill-taught ascetics—self-willed and half-instructed members of Evangelical families who want to mix ball-going and worldliness with religious formalism, and to compound for the one by supporting the other—idle young ladies and thoughtless young men, who love anything gaudy, showy, sensational, and theatrical in worship, or like to show their independence by disagreeing with their parents—all these may stick to Ritualism and stoutly support it.[64]

Ryle's view of Anglo-Catholics may have been almost as unfair as the *Church Times*'s view of his party, but, decoded, it offers some undeniably accurate generalizations. Many Anglo-Catholics had themselves emerged from the commercial class; others felt that the growing influence of that class threatened their social standing. In either case, their new mode of religious expression distanced them from the world of commerce, rebuked that world's pretensions, and subverted many of its values. The historian John Kent has identified "the dominant mood of an important section of the governing elite" of Victorian England as "rejection of the coming world, of resistance to the processes of 'modernization' and 'secularization.'"[65] Anglo-Catholicism was one expression of that mood. As we shall see, however, it was not simply a movement of reaction.

Women and Anglo-Catholicism

In the course of a diatribe against Ritualist clergymen, the rector of St.
Mary-le-Port, Bristol, indicated what he, and many others, believed to
be the composition of the Ritualists' flocks: the Anglo-Catholic priest,
he claimed, "rules with despotic sway over ever so many young ladies, not a
few old ones, some sentimental young gentlemen, and one or two old men
in their dotage."[1] The sentimental young gentlemen are the subject of the
next chapter; here, let us examine Anglo-Catholicism's appeal to women.

Many saw a practically self-evident harmony between Ritualism's ornamented worship and authoritarian doctrine, on the one hand, and feminine
tastes and character, on the other. This observation was seldom meant as a
compliment. Neither were generalizations like the rector's, about the pre-
ponderance of women in Anglo-Catholic congregations.

There was some truth in them, as we shall see. Women were overrepresented in Ritualist congregations, although not to the extent the movement's critics implied. Moreover, it seems likely that women made up an
even larger majority of those laypeople for whom Anglo-Catholicism was an
all-consuming interest, those in whose lives religion and the church were
central, those who were (in Max Weber's phrase) religious virtuosi within
the larger body of Anglo-Catholic layfolk.[2]

Several aspects of Victorian England virtually ensured that women
would be a large and conspicuous part of the active laity within almost any
religious movement. In the first place, men for whom religion was of central importance could become clergymen, a career not open to women.
More important, a number of demographic and cultural characteristics of
Victorian society produced a large pool of unmarried women, and of idle
married women, with the time and resources to devote to "church work."

If Anglo-Catholicism had recruited only its share of these laywomen, they would have been a noteworthy feature of the movement. But it probably received even more than its share. Certain aspects of Anglo-Catholicism had a special appeal for women; some were remarked at the time, and others became more evident in retrospect.

"A Female Movement"

The Ritualists were sensitive to "the scoffing censure that our churches are filled and our Altars crowded with women" (as the Reverend J. C. Chambers put it), and some (like Chambers) tried to deny that it was so.[3] In 1866 the English Church Union presented a memorial to the Archbishop of Canterbury, opposing change in the Ornaments Rubric. Of 36,008 signatures, the Union observed, "24,133 are MEN, thus furnishing an answer to an assertion sometimes made (if, indeed, any were needed, even on the supposition of the allegation being true), viz. that the Ritual movement in the Church of England finds few or no defenders, much less sympathizers, save among the female portion of the members of the Church."[4] Nine years later, Father Mackonochie of St. Alban's, Holborn, was implicitly responding to the same common assertion when he presented the Bishop of London with a memorial signed by "3,350 persons of whom 1450 are men," and the author of *Orthodox London* was doing the same when he reported of his visit to St. Alban's at about the same time that "the women were in excess that snowy morning, it is true; but the congregation was more evenly balanced than in most London churches."[5]

But these voices were dissenting from the much more common view that women predominated. Indeed, one misogynist even believed that women were behind the whole enterprise. This young curate, unhappy and out of his element in an Anglo-Catholic parish, denied that Ritualism was a clerical movement at all. "The Ritual movement is a lay movement;" he wrote, "but it is more than that; it is a female movement." There were many stories of clergymen forcing disturbing changes on their congregations, he acknowledged, but there was another side to it: "The Ritualistic clergyman is led, or rather misled, by a few ladies, who have time and taste for ornamental work, for embroidering coloured stoles, chasubles, &c., and they allow themselves no rest until they have persuaded him to wear these things ... to the intense gratification of a few zealots and the unbounded annoyance of many sensible people."[6]

Few of the Ritualists' opponents were as ready to hold the clergy blameless, but many were prepared to admit that innovating clergy were often supported and encouraged by women who were (as a Laymen's Defense Association pamphlet put it) "personal devotees of the Priest himself."[7] In this, no less a figure than Pusey had established the pattern; an early student of the Oxford Movement pointed to his influence with "a certain class of devout, benevolent, and enthusiastic women" (who, he added, "have great influence over other women sympathetic with themselves").[8] One leading Ritualist almost granted the point: in the early days of the movement, R. F. Littledale wrote, its worship had only limited appeal "outside the circle of clerics and their female adherents." But he argued that the Ritualist missionary effort in the slums of English cities had changed that.[9]

We saw evidence in chapter 8 to support Littledale's view that in so far as slum Ritualism attracted anyone at all, it did not attract disproportionate numbers of women (or at least no more than other varieties of Anglicanism did). But in West London, in areas more fashionable than Holborn, Shoreditch, Lambeth, and Bethnal Green, overrepresentation of women in Anglo-Catholic congregations was not wholly a fabrication of the Ritualists' opponents. To be sure, the problem (if that is what it was) was only a slight exaggeration of a pattern shared with Evangelical and middle-of-the-road Anglicanism. Even as late as the time of the *Daily News* census, however, just after the turn of the century, Anglo-Catholic congregations in West London tended to contain relatively more women, fewer men, than other Anglican congregations nearby.[10]

In Westminster, for instance, where women made up 66 percent of all congregations at Anglican morning services (excluding those of two Guards' chapels), they were 75 percent at St. Barnabas, Pimlico, and 71 percent at St. Thomas, Regent Street. In Paddington, they were 75 percent of all Anglican morning worshippers, but 82 percent of the congregation at St. Mary Magdalene's. (In both boroughs, the differences between Anglo-Catholic churches and others were roughly the same at evening services.) In St. Pancras, the percentage of women in the morning congregation at St. Mary Magdalene, Munster Square, was so low (51 percent, compared to 62 percent for the borough as a whole) that it suggests a reporting or counting error of some sort, but the usual difference appears when we examine the evening congregations (78 percent female at St. Mary Magdalene; 68 percent female for all Anglican congregations in the borough).

These differences are not large, to be sure. They tend to be smaller than those between Anglican congregations of any sort and Nonconformist ones. In Marylebone, where women made up 73 percent of Anglican congregations, for instance, 59 percent of Baptist, 58 percent of Wesleyan Methodist, and 57 percent of Congregationalist worshippers were female. But the differences are consistent. Women were 75 percent of the congregation at All Saints, Margaret Street, and 90 percent at St. Cyprian's, Dorset Square—although the little church of St. Cyprian's held only fifty-nine persons on the census Sunday to begin with.

Combine the overrepresentation of women with the fact that (as we shall see in the next chapter) Ritualism evidently attracted many single young men as well—that is, men who were not husbands or fathers of the women present—and we have to conclude that Ritualist churches attracted relatively large numbers of single women or unaccompanied married ones. Why were these women there?

Ritualism's Appeal to Women

At the time it was simply assumed that Ritualism's aesthetic aspects had a special appeal to women, particularly those of the cultivated classes. Some observers took an easygoing, if condescending, view of the matter. When some citizens complained about the Devonport Sisterhood, for instance, Bishop Phillpotts replied that he "could wish the cross and flowers had not been placed on the altar in the Oratory. But ladies were ladies."[11] A later advocate of tolerance observed that

a million girls and women [he surely exaggerated], who might be far less innocently engaged, find one of the sweetest pleasures of their life in decorating chancels, and working vestments, and helping to make the service of the altar as splendid as they know how. What senseless theorist, what narrow-minded bigot, would propose to sweep this joy of theirs away?[12]

Even one prominent Evangelical implied that this aspect of Ritualism was harmless enough, and suggested that his party indulge such tastes. "We have lost many young men, both lay and clerical, and more young women still from our Evangelical ranks because some of us have set ourselves against certain tastes of the age."[13] But others viewed those tastes with contempt. "Is it not a well-known fact," asked another Evangelical, "that any gorgeous show will attract people, especially the female portion of the community?"[14] An Evangelical broadside attacked the Ritualist clergyman, "leading captive silly women" by means of "his trumpery childish toys, his millinery, his candlesticks, his incense pots, his mystifying and nonsensical 'genuflexions.'"[15]

Certainly the picture of ladies of the parish embroidering things was not just a figment of an exasperated curate's imagination. In 1859, an Oxfordshire magistrate complained that embroidery was part of the Puseyites' program, that innovating clergymen appealed at first "to the hearts and feelings—ever open to kind and generous impressions—of our fair Countrywomen." In this effort he wrote, "particular attention is paid to 'ladies of a certain age,' and most particular attention to the younger and more impulsive and impressionable branches." Soon, "our kind-hearted and amiable female bevy are working, with the utmost assiduity, in producing ornamental altar-cloths, carpets, fauld-stools, &c. &c." He suggested a remedy: "namely, an early entrance into the holy state of matrimony, as being the best preservative against all spurious customs and factitious fancies; as the new duties and pleasing cares which arise therefrom, would imperceptibly release them from the clerical trammels which might otherwise cling to them through life."[16]

Here again the pattern was common enough to make its way into stereotype and popular culture.[17] In *A Paper Lantern for Puseyites*, the comic verse about the travails of the Reverend Hilary Oriel that we examined earlier, for instance, Squire Bradshaw's spinster daughter, Miss Leah, embroidered cushions for Mr. Oriel's new sedilia (although the ingrate later married her younger sister, Rachel).[18]

There was no need to abandon these labors once one's own church and minister were properly fitted out: the Society of St. Alphege took donations of needlework and distributed them to needy parishes; "sister associates" were "to assist and promote the work of the Society by handiwork of embroidery or other ornaments required."[19] When the churchwarden of St. Mark's, Bishopwearmouth, conducted a tour of his church in 1873, he called special attention to a variety of embroidered bookmarkers, kneelers, mats, hangings, and so forth, supplied "by the liberality of ladies of the congregation and others who, though outside our actual pale, have a very warm corner in their hearts for us."[20]

But women's attraction to Anglo-Catholicism was not always regarded as an innocent matter of aesthetics. As the Oxfordshire magistrate suggested, "clerical trammels" might have a particular fascination for women, especially those without the companionship and guidance of husbands. As a Church Association pamphlet put it, "Men, and still more women, need in religion to be directed, to be told what to do, and to be assured confidently that, in doing this, they are safe."[21]

The view that some women were attracted to Anglo-Catholicism because it offered authoritative dicta from clerical "fathers" was not one that Anglo-Catholics often expressed, but it can sometimes be read between the lines of their writings.[22] An anonymous sketch of "La Femme Dévote," by "A Lady," published in the *Church Review* in 1876, poked gentle fun at a social type that its readers evidently knew from their own experience:

The femme dévote knows all about priests, and brotherhoods, and convents; is the bosom friend of Sister MARY AUGUSTINE and the aunt of Brother AMBROSE; works altar-cloths for Saint Aloysius; stipples religious photographs for the sisters of Saint Mary Magdalene's, and is herself associate of half-a-dozen orders, and connected in some mysterious manner with several guilds, the outward manifestation of which connection crops out in numerous little medals and crosses with Latin inscriptions: some worn at special times, which no uninitiated observer can ever succeed in fixing, while there are never less than three or four worn all at once, and hints of others hidden away under her dress.

This pious lady's talk is largely ecclesiastical gossip, and she "lives in church": she is "the dryad of the sacred building." Her dependence is evident in the fact that "she goes to confession not less than once a-month, and would do so more frequently if permitted." She constantly asks, "Is this book 'correct' and that 'safe'?"[23]

The "femme dévote" is apparently unmarried and of "a certain age"—that is, quite possibly without either husband or father. We should not reject out of hand the argument that some women, trained and accustomed to submit to male authority, sought in the church the direction that they could not find in their families.

In addition, though, a *lady* without a husband or father (that is, a woman with independent means, however small, and no domestic obligations) had another problem—namely, what to do with herself. Anglo-Catholicism offered a solution for that as well. Even the *Church Review*'s caricature shows that the movement extended the possibility of what was virtually a full-time occupation, with a variety of useful and (in their own terms) important activities to engage in. It offered this to everyone, of course, but those with few alternatives were undoubtedly most likely to respond.

Middle-aged spinsters were not the only ladies of Victorian England troubled by boredom and feelings of uselessness; some younger, unmarried women suffered from the same ennui, and so did many married women of the higher classes, freed by servants from some household duties but without the civic and social obligations of the aristocracy. It is not surprising that the "multiplication of services" that was everywhere a sign of the movement received its greatest support from women of the middle and upper classes, who had the time and inclination to attend twice-daily (or more) services.[24]

But the problem must have been especially acute for older women who were unmarried and had no prospects—women like the "femme dévote." Unfitted by their lack of education and precluded by the constraints of respectability from any life save that of wife and mother, regarded (as one scholar has put it) as "an object of pity" and "an unsuccessful human being," such a woman made a natural recruit for a movement that filled her days with useful and transcendentally important occupations.[25] That the movement also explicitly valued virginity was almost too much to ask. There were a great many such virgins in Victorian England.[26]

The Demographics of Spinsterhood

As many recognized at the time, a monogamous society that views marriage as the only satisfactory occupation for women must regard an excess of women as a problem, and the feminist Anna Brownell Jameson pointed out that the 1851 census had counted half a million more women than men in Great Britain, 104 women for every 100 men.[27] Moreover, the imbalance was increasing. Twenty years later, there were 105 women for every 100 men in England and Wales; by 1891 there were 106.[28] English men and women of marriageable age faced a sex ratio even more unbalanced. In 1851, there were 110 women for every hundred men between the ages of 20 and 24, and the same ratio held for those between 25 and 29.

Even these statistics understate the problem, from the point of view of young women seeking husbands. The situation was exacerbated by the tendency of men to marry women younger than themselves. Britain's population was increasing by 12 to 14 percent each decade; as in any growing population, there were relatively fewer older people (including older men) compared to younger people (including younger women). Thus, there were 125 women between twenty and twenty-four for every 100 men between twenty-five and twenty-nine, and 125 women between twenty-five and twenty-nine for every 100 men between thirty and thirty-four. Moreover, many men did not marry: 18 percent were unmarried at thirty-five, and 11 percent at fifty.[29]

Consequently, at any specific time during the second half of the nineteenth century, nearly a third of women aged twenty-five to thirty-five were unmarried. Many would eventually marry widowers (given the high mortality rates among married women), but roughly half would still be unmarried ten years later. In some respects their situation was shared by widows, 10 percent or so of the female population at age forty-five.

One result was a change in the composition of the British labor force. The percentage of women employed increased from 25 percent to 34 percent in the fifty years after 1841, and the number employed increased by 2.7 million. But three-quarters of the new jobs were in the traditional areas of domestic and personal service, textiles, and clothing.[30] The sex ratio may have been most unbalanced among the working classes (male emigration, more common there, was thought to be a contributing factor), so these new jobs may have been where they were most needed, but they did little to alleviate the situation of unmarried women of the higher classes, who were not disposed to become servants, textile workers, or milliners.

These changes in the population and labor force of Britain obviously do not explain the growth of Anglo-Catholicism or the role of women in the movement, but they provide a necessary context for any explanation (and indeed for any discussion of the changing place of women in Victorian society).[31] Not only were there many unmarried women "of a certain age" available to do needlepoint for the church and attend the daily offices, but younger women could hardly have failed to recognize that spinsterhood was a serious statistical possibility. If they believed what they were told incessantly—that their only happiness lay in marriage and a family—the shortage of potential husbands must often have produced anxiety, and a readiness to hear other messages. If they did not believe that in the first place, or came to disbelieve it with experience, Anglo-Catholicism also had something to offer them.

Anti-Patriarchal Themes

Perhaps, as the movement's opponents claimed, Anglo-Catholicism offered some women a sort of patriarchal authority that they desired. Others, however, may have seen in it a challenge to the existing authority of fathers and husbands. Certainly many fathers and husbands saw it in that light.

Even by catering to women's tastes in decoration, the movement implied that those tastes should be consulted. By providing idle women with occupations, however humble, it implied that they had contributions to make. By its sometimes studied disregard for conventional standards of manliness and its revaluation of celibacy (which we shall examine in the next chapter), the movement issued a series of subtle but continual challenges to received patriarchal values. That these challenges were heard and understood by the movement's opponents is evident in their denigration of women's part in the movement, and in the alarm and contempt evoked by the movement's "effeminacy."

A challenge to patriarchal authority was even evident in an early innovation in the arrangement of seating for public worship. We speculated earlier that Anglo-Catholic worship in West London attracted a disproportionate number of unaccompanied women and single young men. For Anglo-Catholics, that is, churchgoing was less often a family affair than for other Anglicans and, especially, for Nonconformists. This was made explicit in some Ritualist churches, where those families that were present were not allowed to sit together.

Separating the sexes for worship had been on the Ritualist agenda since the days of the Cambridge Camden Society. In the 1840s its publication, *The Ecclesiologist*, had urged "the propriety and necessity of dividing the sexes during the publick office of the Church."[32] By the early 1860s this new custom was finding its way into practice. The *Church Times* remarked, for example, that it was observed at the consecration of St. Alban's, Holborn, in 1863.[33] By the mid-1870s a survey of London-area churches identified twenty-four where it was followed. Nearly all were well-known centers of Ritualism, and nearly all such centers were on the list.[34]

As usual, the rationale for the change was a curious mixture of the practical, the antiquarian, and the symbolic. "One great object of separating the sexes," a *Church Times* correspondent asserted, was "to afford protection to girls and young women who go to church alone."[35] A later writer in the same paper argued that, "in these free and easy days, it is better that men should sit and kneel with men, and women with women."[36] And the situation was complicated by considerations of social class. The campaign against private pews had been largely successful, but removing them worked best, one minister observed, with "the people being all of one class."[37] Oth-

erwise, as another commentator put it, a lady might find herself in uncomfortable proximity to some "rude fellow."[38] Indeed, Robert Brett wrote to
the *Church Times*, unless separation was effected, this possibility would lead
to the return of the "vile, detestable pew system," especially in large
towns.[39]

In fact, this argument was largely a pretext. By the 1870s, "free and
open seating" was by no means confined to Ritualist churches and Ritualists
had no monopoly on propriety—quite the contrary. That they were virtually the only churchmen even to consider separating the sexes suggests that
their reasons lay elsewhere.

The argument from antiquity was also widely heard, but not wholly persuasive. Although the survey did find some country churches that had apparently separated the sexes from time immemorial, the *Church Times*'s letters
column in the summer of 1875 witnessed a spirited discussion of just how
old and widespread the practice actually was.[40] (It ended inconclusively.)

The one unanswerable argument for this practice, as for others, was that
it was somehow of symbolic import. But what did it symbolize? One
woman thought she knew: "The spirit of the movement," in this respect as
in others, she wrote the *Church Times*, was "the Oriental principle of
women's inferiority."[41] And, indeed, a letter-writer the week before had
complained about women usurping male prerogatives, pointed out that
women did not accompany their menfolk to work, and suggested that the
appropriate division of the sexes was not women on the left and men on the
right, but men in front and women in back.[42] That there was an element of
misogyny among some Anglo-Catholic men cannot be denied, but both of
these writers were missing the point. Women were not the target at all.

As everyone recognized, separating the sexes broke up and dispersed
families. Some regarded this as an unfortunate accident. Others, however,
did not value "the British and teapot notion that families ought to sit
together in church" to begin with. The *Church Times* letter-writer who put
it that way went on to argue that "personal domestic feelings are out of place
in the House of God."[43] Just as removing pews had effaced the most obvious signs of rank among the congregation, so this Ritualistic practice
attacked the ties and distinctions within and between families, further reduc-
ing the extent to which the community's social structure was modeled and
reproduced within the nave of the church, further turning the individuals
who made up the congregation into an undifferentiated mass of
autonomous worshippers.

In particular, fathers of families were no longer to be known as such.
"The only husband you may recognize [in church] is Jesus Christ," this let-
ter continued; "the only father you may think of is the common Father to
Whom you are all common children." A member of the Society of the Holy
Cross had made it explicit earlier, in a sermon addressed to those who
wished to sit as families: "You do not come here, during the hours of ser-

vice, for private or for family worship," he said. "We are not to be thinking here of our families, but of God, the Father of us all." Let those who want to worship as families do so at home, he concluded. "Here let us know ourselves only in the God-given order of sons and daughters of the Everlasting."[44]

Being told not to think of their families was not something to which Victorian ladies were accustomed. To be told that in the God-given order human fathers are unimportant was even more startling. But that is what they were told, not only in sermons and letters to the *Church Times*, but by the seating arrangements they encountered at many Ritualist churches.

The Confessional and Patriarchal Privilege

Nowhere was the conflict between Anglo-Catholic practice and Victorian family ideology clearer than in the matter of confession. We have already seen the almost reflexive hostility that the revival of confession evoked, not just from the movement's usual adversaries, but from many of its allies and defenders as well. Coming as it often did from people not otherwise moved by "no-popery" appeals, that hostility is unintelligible without reference to the deep cultural implications of the practice.

It is remarkable how much of the polemic against confession was directed to the male relatives of women, warning them to protect their wives, daughters, and sisters. Men were almost never exhorted to avoid the confessional themselves (perhaps because the advice was thought to be unnecessary) and women were seldom addressed directly on the subject at all, but again and again preachers and pamphlet writers told Englishmen of the dangers to their womenfolk and to themselves, should the women resort to confession.[45] Many of the appeals amounted to candid warnings that male privilege was threatened, but to get to them we must pick our way through confession's alleged offenses against etiquette and morality.

From the beginning of the revival of the practice in Anglican parishes, its opponents assumed that it had a particular concern with sexual relations, and there was some basis for that belief. For all that the Reverend T. T. Carter denied that "the one most distressing form of sin coloured the whole atmosphere of the ministry of penance," they could support their belief with excerpts from the Ritualists' own manuals for penitents and confessors.[46] An Evangelical magazine pointed to the "manner in which the interrogatories of this new Confessional cluster around the seventh commandment," and a pamphlet offered extracts from the danker portions of *The Priest in Absolution*, "with a view [the extended title said] to expose and make known to fathers of families, belonging to the Church of England, the debasing and demoralising extent to which that body of Romanizers, known as Ritualist Priests are practicing 'sacramental auricular confession,' a doctrine strongly denounced by the Church of England in her Articles, Homilies, and teaching, and preparing themselves, by the study of filthy and obscene literature, to pollute the purity of our wives, daughters, and little children, by questions and suggestions on the most indecent subjects."[47]

If the association of confession with sins of the flesh needed any reinforcement in the public mind, it received that reinforcement from several early scandals arising out of the Ritualists' war on the "social evil," prostitution. Confession played a central part in that campaign, for (as one campaigner put it): "Yes—to women specially, the confessional is a haven in their sorrows, if they have fallen; it reclaims them, and saves them from utter ruin." "Oh!" he asked, "who can tell how many women have been saved from a life of open infamy, by the timely admonition and gentle guidance of a good priest."[48]

Some opponents of confession seem to have believed that rescue work was its most common application. A canon preached in Bristol Cathedral, for instance, that "the victims on whom [the confessional] first fastens, and whom it leads captive, chiefly are those whom the apostle, in writing to Timothy describes as 'Silly women, laden with sins, led away with divers lusts; ever learning and never able to come to the knowledge of the truth.'"[49] The Oxfordshire magistrate we have already heard from asked, "Who have been the victims but a few poor, sick, uneducated females?" He doubted that he would ever hear of a male penitent, "for a very few of the questions poured into the reluctant ears of the poor females above alluded to, would, if applied to the other sex, be most probably followed by rendering the 'Father Confessor' a candidate for the 'Army of Martyrs.'"[50]

But these gentlemen were deluding themselves. They were undoubtedly right that the great majority of penitents were women (consistent with women's numerical dominance among the lay virtuosi of Anglo-Catholicism), but it was not only or even especially fallen women and those at risk—not only poor, sick, uneducated women—who availed themselves of confession. The uncharacteristic discretion of the Ritualists in this matter somewhat concealed the fact that many others went to confession as well, including many who moved in the same circles as canons and magistrates. It will be recalled that the femme dévote went as often as she was allowed. So, according to one critic, did some "morbid young men" and a good many "hysterical young women."[51] It was, after all, one of the "secret privileges" of young Anglicans.[52]

Let an anonymous Cambridge graduate tell who went, as he saw it, in a typical Ritualist parish church. *The Ritualist's Progress* (1878) describes satirically, in 113 pages of verse, the ministrations of the new vicar of St. Alicia, Slumbertown.[53] Much of it sounds very much like the *Paper Lantern for Puseyites* published thirty years before ("When to 'born of Virgin Mary' / The choristers have got, / You'd think some twenty persons / Had suddenly been shot!"). The vicar's followers in the parish, a churchy clique of enthusiasts, worry about Anglican orders and flirt with Romanism; three of

them, "charitable spinsters," actually convert, "for a little mild excitement."
Unlike the ultrarubrician in *Paper Lantern*, however, the Ritualist Mr. Alban
explicitly preaches the duty of confession. When he first does so,

> For a first endeavour
> By pre-concerted plan,
> Some half-a-dozen ladies,
> And an invalid young man,
> And that fussy, vulgar "server,"
> In his hideous monkish dress,
> Assembled in the vestry,
> 'Tis stated, to "confess!"

The worldly narrator pooh-poohs the alarm of Evangelicals, however,
arguing that the vicar is too innocent to be any threat to liberty, and adds
that

> By the way, it's always ladies,
> Or nearly so, that seek
> This priestly "absolution"
> (Unless it's for a freak).

The men of the parish go around bragging that *their* sins would shock the
poor vicar.

Part of the opposition to confession was based simply on the familiar
themes of anti-Romanism and antisacerdotalism. To take two examples
almost at random from hundreds, Lord Shaftesbury, in the House of Lords,
denounced the 1873 petition to Convocation requesting the licensing of
confessors as "this pollution of the red one of Babylon," and an Evangelical
magazine spoke of "the pretended priest [who], forsooth, sits in the confessional as God, hearing and forgiving sins."[54] But objections to Romanism
and to sacerdotalism also figured in the complaints about many of the Ritualists' ceremonial practices. Overlaid on them in the case of confession was
this additional element of prurience, fueled on both sides by the fetid sort
of preoccupation with impurity that has given the word "Victorian" some of
its present-day connotation.

"Trifle if you will," said the preacher in Bristol Cathedral, "and play—if
such pastime is agreeable to you—play with processions, vestments, genuflexions, incense, and all the tinsel and mummery, and man-millinery of imitation Popery. These things are, though silly, but comparatively harmless.
Oh! I pray you, trifle not with the Confessional; it is a mighty power for evil,
and must not be trifled with."[55]

The danger, to many, was obvious. "The very reduction of sins of impurity to language ... must result in making them the fuel of fresh sin, and in

fanning the flame of a more dangerous temptation," an Evangelical magazine warned, concluding that "it becomes us never to mention such subjects, ... but to pass by them in silence."[56] In a later issue, unable to pass
by in silence, it reverted to the subject of "the instinctive horror" provoked
by "the idea of bachelor priests prying into all the inmost feelings and most
secret thoughts and acts of maidens and wives."[57] The folklore of anti-
Romanism provided a variety of salacious stories of the confessional—this
"fountain of filthiness," as one pamphlet called it—and one archdeacon
claimed (by the 1890s) to know of three Anglican clergymen who had "fall-
en into habits of immorality" with women who had come to them for guidance.[58]

Actually, it may be surprising how little seduction there actually was,
beyond rumor and conjecture, but for a woman even to talk about "impurity" with a man was sinful, not just improper. "Are not impure thoughts to
be counted as sin?" asked the Reverend S. A. Walker. "Does not the confessor, then, instigate to sin in himself and his penitent, when he deals in las-
civiousness of thought and expression under circumstances calculated to
quicken a corrupt imagination, and stimulate the vilest passions?"[59]

Not only might women be corrupted (if not seduced) in the confessional, they would also necessarily disclose details of their family relation-
ships that husbands and fathers felt were no business of a clergyman's. As
the Reverend Mr. Walker observed, "No one can make a disclosure of all the
acts of their daily life without at the same time betraying the secrets of other
parties without their consent." He asked if husbands and fathers were "satisfied that the privacy of their domestic life should be invaded by the prying
curiosity" of the confessor, and said that he was astonished "that fathers and
husbands have tolerated for an hour a system by which the purity of their
wives and daughters is so grossly outraged, and even the secrets of their own
domestic life are extracted from the female members of their family under
the moral rack of the Confessional."[60]

Walker was not alone in his assumption that Englishmen shared his outrage. "Habitual confession to Priests," the *Times* remarked, "is a practice
which English husbands and parents in general will never endure to have
inculcated upon their families."[61] The vicar and rural dean of Greenwich
told a Church Association gathering in 1867: "As husbands, as fathers, as
brothers, we will have none of it. We will protect the sanctities of our homes
and the purity of our wives, our children, and our sisters from this moral
inquisition, this thumb-screwing of the conscience."[62] Ten years later, after
Lord Redesdale read passages from *The Priest in Absolution* to the House of
Lords, Archbishop Tait commented, "I cannot imagine that any right-mind-
ed man could wish to have such questions addressed to any member of his
family."[63] Twenty years after that, an M.P. told the House of Commons, "If
there is any one thing that the people [read: men] of this country detest it
is the Confessional. They hate the idea that their wives and daughters are

to be questioned by a priest as to their inmost secret thoughts."[64]

The secrecy that so often surrounded confession was perhaps understandable, given the extent and ferocity of the opposition to it. But the secrecy itself compounded the offense, and fired the suspicions of its opponents. One such opponent, a man less unhinged by the subject than many others, expressed a common attitude. When the petition asking that confessors be licensed said that something of the sort was necessary because of the "widespread and increasing use of sacramental confession," he remarked that "when one hears not only of confessions in Churches and vestries, and parsonages; but of confessions of young women being heard by young Curates in their private lodgings, by day and by night: certainly it is high time to do something to meet an emergency like this: whatever that something may be."[65]

Perhaps some of the opponents of confession were reassured—they were surely meant to be—by one laywoman's account of her relations with her confessor, published in 1867. Nothing could have been less titillating. Throughout the account runs a strand that will be familiar to any student of the Oxford Movement: the anonymous author warned that the movement's chief danger lay in "defective self-denial; admiring the lives of the Saints, but reading them in an easy chair; admitting the blessings of celibacy, and marrying as soon as the opportunity offers; recommending fasting to everybody—except themselves."[66]

But the *Pall Mall Gazette* was not reassured. It found the essay to be "an illustration of the true character and pernicious effects of the superstition which is spreading widely and silently among some parts of the population and especially among ladies." The *Gazette* said the "painful" story showed the effects of "piety, refinement, and education" on those not "accustomed from infancy to independence, self-reliance, and the habit of recognizing the moral duty of the honest avowal of doubt on subjects on which you have imperfect information."[67] On the other hand, some readers must have been disturbed precisely by the lady's "independence": she made her first confession without the knowledge of her father (an Evangelical clergyman). Although the priest to whom she went required her to tell her father, the fact that she went without permission in the first place—and was heard—would have been alarming to many Englishmen.

Nor were all confessors even as deferential to paternal rights as hers. One notorious example involved the Reverend John Mason Neale, whom we have already encountered in several connections. When Miss Emily Ann Elizabeth Scobell, the daughter of an Evangelical clergyman of some importance in Sussex, took up music lessons at the age of eighteen, she fell in with a group of young people associated with St. Paul's, Brighton, and became in time a devout Anglo-Catholic. A few years later, she arranged to meet Neale, and made her first confession to him, in the schoolroom of her father's parish. She became a regular penitent and carried on a clandestine correspondence with Neale through the schoolmistress. Neale's biographer says that Neale seems to have feared that she would become a Roman Catholic if he did not oblige her. In any case, she did not tell her father any of this, although Neale urged her to do so. When her father learned about it (through the schoolmistress), he was outraged.

We will pick up this story later, but for now something of the nature of this father-daughter relationship can be inferred from the Reverend Mr. Scobell's description of his daughter a couple of years later. She was, he wrote, "an overwrought, dissatisfied and disobedient child, yielding herself to undue spiritual influence." She was thirty years old at the time.[68]

Here we draw close to the heart of another objection to confession, one implicit in much of what we have already seen: the belief that it was an attempt to undermine the authority of husbands and fathers and to destroy the patriarchal structure of the Victorian family. "I say, then, to you fathers, husbands, brothers," Canon Edward Girdlestone preached in a sermon on confession, "I say to you, beware lest these, the weaker vessels, be the means in the end—as Adam was driven out of Paradise—of driving you out of the Eden, the happy, the very happy Eden of an English Christian home."[69]

The problem was, as the *Times* put it, that confession meant that "a priest is to interfere in every household, to direct a wife in the discharge of her duties to her husband, children in their relations to their parents and their schoolfellows, girls in their relations to their mothers, their fathers, and at length, their lovers, and so on through every intimate relationship."[70] Bishop Wilberforce explained it this way to the archdeacons and rural deans of Winchester: "Then in families it [confession] introduces untold mischief. It supersedes God's appointment of intimacy between husband and wife, father and children; substituting another influence for that which ought to be the nearest and closest, and producing reserve and estrangement where there ought to be perfect freedom and openness."[71] Lord Sandon put it more forthrightly at the Wolverhampton Church Congress in 1867: the confessional meant, he said, "the establishment of another master in every household, by every hearth, in the place of the husband and father." (The transcript shows cries of "No No" and "Shame.")[72] An Evangelical novel of 1879 painted a stark picture of what confession's opponents feared. In Mrs. Lynn Linton's *Under Which Lord?*, the Reverend Launcelot Lascelles uses confession to dominate his "spiritual harem" and tries to turn a lady against her anti-religious husband.[73]

The values that underlay these objections were so ingrained that even the defenders of confession argued in their terms. In 1858 (in a passage that could be read as an appeal to seducers and domestic tyrants) one early proponent wrote, "If [women] are injured, it teaches them patience, and warns them against exposing their wrongs."[74] Forty years later, an advocate of toleration said merely that he saw nothing wrong with a clergyman's easing sinners' troubled consciences and that there was no need for legislation to control confession. If it became an excuse "for suggesting evil, or for tampering with innocence, or for the betrayal of confidence, or for meddling between husband and wife or between mother and daughter"—well, then "the father, or the brother, or the husband should know how to deal with the confessor."[75] When T. T. Carter conceded that "the main prejudice against confession arises from an apprehension of its interference with the confidence and relative duties of family life" (he added that "the feeling is that on this account it is contrary to the genius of the Church of England, which has always very specially loved to cherish the sacredness of home"), he did not challenge those "relative duties" at all, but merely asserted that in his extensive experience, confession did not so interfere.[76]

The prevalence of attitudes like these cannot be ignored in assessing what confession meant to those who took up the practice. A woman who made her confession could be seen—and could see herself—as engaged in an act of considerable daring. No doubt the more feverish imaginings of confession's opponents were well wide of the mark, but for a woman simply to meet alone with a man could be questionable conduct, especially if both were young and unmarried. To meet in secret was highly improper, and meeting secretly with a man to disclose one's sinful thoughts and actions was morally dangerous, if not worse. And to do this without the approval of one's husband or father was an act of rebellion.

So, at least, most husbands and fathers saw the matter, and women could hardly help knowing that they saw it that way. Most women undoubtedly shared that view themselves. Much of the opposition to confession and to the movement that preached it reflected those views, and I am suggesting that some of its support did, too. Here, as elsewhere in this study, we know what the movement's opponents thought, and we can be sure that its supporters were aware of that response. How many Anglo-Catholics understood their opponents' outrage and (like T. T. Carter) regretted it, how many achieved an otherworldly indifference, how many (for whatever reason) welcomed and enjoyed it we cannot say. But we can be certain that there were some of each. What the movement's adversaries found an offense and some of its allies a stumbling block—the symbolic, if not actual, threat to domestic authority—must surely have appealed to those who found parental and husbandly authority stifling. It is not accidental that the confessional had a particular allure for the young of both sexes, and for women of all ages.

Sisterhoods and the "Silent Rebellion"

We saw in an earlier chapter that the newly established Anglican sisterhoods, like confession, made many Englishmen uneasy. Naturally, sisterhoods evoked the automatic hostility of those who objected to anything "Romish." There was more or less constant controversy over such issues as

whether sisters were to be bound by vows, what their garb and their liturgical practices were to be, whether they were to practice "habitual confession," whether enclosed, contemplative orders of "nuns" were to be coun-
tenanced, and so forth.[77] In general, it is fair to say that most sisters wished
to assimilate entirely to pre-Reformation or current Roman Catholic models, while their supporters among the bishops and influential laity usually had
a more modest innovation in mind, something not unlike the Evangelical
district missionaries, but of a higher social class. It is also fair to say that the
sisters' wishes, in time, prevailed: they came less and less to resemble district missionaries, Lutheran deaconesses, or simply assemblies of pious
women devoted to good works.

Consequently, much of the opposition to sisterhoods (and probably
most of the verbiage directed against them) was, as in the case of confession,
recycled anti-Romanism. The usual stories of convent horror were trotted
out, and some of the less lurid ones seem actually to have been true. Little
accounts of the genuinely unpleasant life of "Sister Dora" (Dorothy Pattison) were, for a time, favorite prizes in Evangelical Sunday schools.[78] Much
of this is now rather distasteful: harrowing courses of fasting and penance;
the widespread use of "the discipline," or scourge; the autocratic manner of
some early mothers superior, who were necessarily strong-willed and not ter-
ribly concerned with others' opinions.

But the opposition, too, was a product of its age. Walter Walsh, in his
Secret History of the Oxford Movement, compiled some true stories and many
more doubtful ones, and speculated darkly about the uses to which the private graveyards of religious communities were being put.[79] An advertisement for a book called *The Phantom Railway* called attention to "a capital
illustration of a Nun in Chains," and *The Armoury* ("A Magazine of
Weapons for Christian Warfare") poeticized about "prisons of darkness all
over the land, / Their keepers unseen and their doings unscann'd." Alluding to the "twin-tyrants," abbess and priest, *The Armoury* lamented:

> ... woe to the nuns disobedient then,
> To the tempers of women and passions of men,
> Where anything foul can be done in the dark,
> Unstruck by Truth's spearpoint's electrical spark![80]

But it was not only champions of Protestantism, or those who feared the
Protestant reaction, who viewed the sisterhoods with suspicion, and that
needs to be explained, because few denied that they did valuable work. Like
the slum priests with whom they were often associated, the early Anglican
sisters undertook tasks of real significance in education, nursing, "penitentiary" work with prostitutes, and administration. (The only real objection
to the work itself came from the no-popery fringe, who saw it as a cover for
religious propaganda.) Most thoughtful observers recognized not only that

there was work to be done, but that there were women who needed work. Like Anglo-Catholicism in general, only more so, sisterhoods gave unmarried women new and meaningful things to do.

Some believed it was worth indulging them for the sake of their good works. One writer in the *Pall Mall Gazette*, for instance, argued that "unmarried and cultivated women of the middle and upper classes" could be expected to undertake the grueling work of hospital nursing only if doing so gave them "something like a real and permanent home for themselves." He found it inconceivable that such a community of women could exist "without some distinctly recognized religious bond," since "clerical advice, clerical companionship, and clerical ministrations are essential to the happiness of the large majority even of highly educated women," and argued that it was "the merest bigotry to refuse the services of a community of devoted women because they are under the guidance of a clergyman who wears a chasuble and feel a pleasure in seeing clouds of incense floating in their private chapel." Given the appalling conditions of the poor, he asked, was it not wise "to set aside our dislike of clerical pretensions and of the eccentricities of devout women, and to encourage the vast body of unmarried Englishwomen to come forward to the relief of the destitute on their own terms?"

But the *Gazette* (speaking no doubt for many of its readers) rejected this writer's attempt to put the best face on what was happening. The chasuble and incense, it said, represented "superstitions as degrading to the mind as habitual drams are to the body," and someone who requires "one or the other stimulant" in order to work is unfit to work in the first place. Moreover, to the writer's suggestion that sisterhoods provided suitable occupation for unmarried women, the *Gazette* replied that "the domestic and social ideal is, practically speaking, the one generally recognized by Englishwomen as the highest to which they can aspire. To be a good wife, mother, daughter or sister, is, so to speak, the highest ambition of a woman." One whose circumstances unfortunately shut her off from that ideal might well turn to "charitable pursuits," but should do so "without cutting herself off from society at large, or removing or weakening those ties which everyone possesses more or less." A "sensible person" would be able "to take a proper measure of charitable occupations, to think of them in their true light as occasional pursuits forming a part of life, and not as an absorbing profession taking up the whole of it."[81]

Here we begin to see why there was such widespread uneasiness about the development of sisterhoods. The answer surely lies in the affront to Victorian family values that sisterhoods—even more explicitly than confession—presented. Prebendary Gresley of Lichfield, a sober Tractarian, remarked matter-of-factly that "home and comfort have been too long the idols of Englishmen, a settlement and establishment in life the summum bonum of Englishwomen. It is a great point to have it admitted that there may be something nobler and more desirable than these acknowledged blessings; at any rate, that those who believe themselves called to a higher life are to be commended as praiseworthy, and not condemned as mere enthusiasts."[82] But few outside of Anglo-Catholic circles agreed that the religious life was nobler and more desirable than the life of an ordinary household. Even those non-Anglo-Catholics who were proponents of sisterhoods tended to see them as a salvage operation for women who had failed to realize "the highest ambition of a woman," and shared the *Pall Mall Gazette*'s views about what that ambition was, or should be.

Some argued that women who persisted in their aspirations to the religious life were going against nature. One anonymous writer, evidently a clergyman, argued that life in a religious community was even worse for "woman" than for "man": "God having given her a nature that looks to the other sex for support, she is less self-sufficient; ... with stronger sympathies and susceptibilities, and a warmer heart, to be severed without hope from the sphere of her natural influence does infinite violence to her, and she sooner becomes morbid, and deteriorates more rapidly though less grossly than man." Besides, "protracted silence frets her."[83]

The rise of sisterhoods can be seen as part of a larger "silent rebellion" against attitudes like these.[84] Sisterhood life took women out of their homes, gave them important work and sometimes great responsibility, and replaced their ties to fathers, husbands, and brothers by loyalties to Church and sisterhood. It demonstrated that there were callings for women of the upper and middle classes other than those of wife, daughter, and "charitable spinster." And it at least suggested that the religious life was the higher calling. Each of these aspects of the revival evoked opposition, and each appealed to at least some of the women drawn to the sisterhoods.

The *Pall Mall Gazette* and others might argue that charity should not become an "absorbing profession" for unmarried women, but a demanding and permanent commitment of some sort was exactly what many sought; it was, in a sense, what they had been brought up to seek. Becoming a Bride of Christ, often in a ceremony deliberately evocative of Holy Matrimony, provided that commitment.

In any case, charity was only part of the life of Anglican sisters (although often the most time-consuming part); the differences between their lives and those of unmarried women outside the sisterhood were smaller than many supposed, and lay principally in what they did with the time *not* devoted to good works. Aside from charitable duties and domestic chores, sisters spent their time largely in collective worship and private devotions.

The alternatives in private households were often less attractive. Single young women, if they were fortunate and so inclined, could pass the time developing and practicing the social graces. Spinsters often functioned as unpaid domestic servants in the households of their parents or of their married brothers or sisters. But what appeal would either of those lives have had to a well-educated and intensely intellectual woman like Philippa Meadows? Described as "an oddity, a woman of about thirty with a total absence of feminine softness or charm," Miss Meadows concluded that "the exaltation of the family is contrary to the genius of true religion," and became a Roman Catholic in the 1840s.[85] Twenty years later, she might well have entered an Anglican sisterhood.

Sisterhoods offered an alternative to a life of idleness or drudgery—exotic, but not *too* exotic, and cloaked at the same time in the respectability of religion. Prebendary Gresley wrote that there was "something romantic in the idea of being a Sister of Mercy, which is likely to captivate the weak-minded."[86] Be that as it may, many women outside sisterhoods certainly found little romance in their everyday circumstances, and sisters were objects of curiosity and flattering attention as well as of hostility, especially in the early years when there were so few of them. Keble warned in 1845 that sisters "may very easily think too much of themselves and be made too much of," and hoped that an increase in their numbers would remove that danger.[87]

But the actual life of a sister was not, in fact, especially romantic, and if some recruits were disappointed, others were no doubt pleased to be able to combine a romantic idea with a reality that was often merely a concentrated version of what Anglo-Catholic laywomen were already accustomed to. From daily Mass, matins, and evensong at church, and private devotions as well, it was not far to keeping a full schedule of hours in a sisterhood's oratory. From working embroidery for the parish church and the Society of St. Alphege to doing church needlework as a sister was only a small step, too (although that from Christmas baskets and parish visiting to cholera nursing, to penitentiary work, or to the Crimea with Florence Nightingale was larger).

Often, it seems, joining a sisterhood was also just a small extension of an existing pattern of rebellion against parental authority. Philippa Meadows's household was not the only one where daughters hid Tractarian books under their beds.[88] John Mason Neale's penitent, Miss Scobell, was not the only daughter whose confession was heard against her father's wishes.

Let us pick up Miss Scobell's story again. After her father discovered that she had been going to confession, he forbade her to continue. She compounded her offense by asking to test her vocation with the Sisterhood of St. Margaret, and he forbade that, too. She soon ran away, presented herself at the sisterhood in East Grinstead, and asked to be received. Neale said later that he was reluctant to accept her without her father's permission, but hearing what she "suffered at home, and more especially [about] the paroxysms of anger, to which even her presence seemed sometimes to excite her father," he consulted an "eminent divine," who said she should be allowed to try the life of the sisterhood. Miss Scobell subsequently took vows, and the name Sister Amy.

So far the story presents merely an exaggerated version of the father-daughter conflict present in many decisions to join the early sisterhoods. But (as so often happened with Neale) events took a bizarre turn that made the situation not just exaggerated, but grotesque. A month after entering the Society of St. Margaret, Sister Amy contracted scarlet fever while nursing and two months after that she was dead. Her alienation from her father was made explicit in her will, which appointed Neale and the superior of the society as executors and left four hundred pounds to the society (the balance of some five or six thousand was left to a favorite brother). The Reverend Mr. Scobell accused Neale of exposing his daughter to disease in order to inherit her money.

At Sister Amy's funeral, Neale and the sisters of St. Margaret were assaulted by a stone-throwing crowd chanting "No Popery" and "Remember, remember the fifth of November," and Neale had to scale two nine-foot walls to escape. In another fracas the next day, Neale was hit by a stone; the stone-thrower was arrested, tried, acquitted, and serenaded by the town band. The judge called Neale's conduct—he had "bowed to the crowd [from the train] in a manner indicative of contempt and derision"—"very injudicious." Sister Amy's aggrieved father published a pamphlet with the self-explanatory title, "Painful Account of the Perversion and Untimely Death of Miss Scobell, the Stolen Daughter of the Revd. J. Scobell, inveigled from her home, persuaded to become a Puseyite Sister of Mercy, and through threats of eternal damnation to her soul, plundered of her property by a crafty band of Puseyite Jesuits for the support of Popery: also the Crimes in Convents revealed by Father Gavazzi."[89]

Miss Scobell's story shows in its starkest form what the opponents of sisterhoods feared, and the sort of personal situation from which many early recruits to sisterhoods were drawn. Prebendary Gresley warned that young women who "would be glad to go anywhere to escape the troubles and annoyances of Home" did not make good sisters, and he instructed "young ladies who have a will of their own, and live uncomfortably with parents who are exacting and oppressing" that "persons must never leave duties to which they are obviously called, in order to undertake others to which the call is doubtful."[90] But not all heard or heeded such advice: a few years later a supporter of sisterhoods was writing, "No Postulants turn out more unsatisfactory than those who offer themselves for community life because they cannot have their own way at home, or cannot live in unity with their own kindred…. These are they who cause most annoyance in a Sisterhood, and most scandal in the World."[91]

Even if a sister was not seeking to escape an unpleasant situation at home, her decision to enter a sisterhood may well have produced one. "Nearly every novice," one sister attested, "had to undergo much opposition, if not petty persecution, before she had succeeded in entering the Sisterhood."[92] Whether embodied in the alienation of property or not, whether the pull of sisterhood life or the push of an unhappy domestic situation was more effectual, joining a religious community necessarily subordinated family ties and responsibilities to new ones, outside the home. Those who felt that they were losing a daughter, or a sister, or a widowed mother were not entirely mistaken.

Although the image of headstrong, rebellious, and flighty young women had some foundation in fact, as did that of tyrannical, overbearing, dictatorial fathers, not all tyranny was gross, nor all rebellion flagrant. As Florence Nightingale wrote privately in 1851: "I have known a good deal of convents. And of course everyone has talked of the petty tyrannies supposed to be exercised there. But I know nothing like the petty grinding tyranny of a good English family." She added that "the only alleviation is that the tyrannised submits with a heart full of affection."[93] When that affection was lacking, the life of a religious community must have seemed an attractive alternative.

Women in Authority

All sisters had important and worthwhile things to do—social work, domestic tasks, and a full round of worship—but some took on demanding administrative tasks as well, and this provided further ammunition for the sisterhoods' opponents. A woman, one critic asserted, "is scarcely ever fitted to rule, so that there are ten chances to one in favour of a Mother Superior, who is caged for life with her own sex, becoming a capricious, little-minded tyrant."[94]

Stories of domineering superiors, abusing the young women under their supervision while living luxuriously themselves, were staples of anti-sisterhood propaganda. Such stories tended to cluster especially around Mother Lydia (Sellon) of the Devonport Sisterhood, especially after the publication of several books written by disaffected ex-sisters, some of them demonstrably dishonest or unstable.[95] There is no question that Mother Lydia was strong-minded and sometimes ill-advised, but she did not deserve to be called a "petty despot," or likened to a "crafty old owl" preying on "poor little mice … imprisoned in a tree." The clerical lecturer who said that was closer to the mark, though, when he called her "unladylike": by definition, a woman with Mother Lydia's determination and responsibilities was not behaving like a lady, as that word was commonly understood.[96]

Even some of the warmest admirers of sisterhoods shared these misgivings about putting them under the more-or-less autonomous administration of women, and those clergymen who founded sisterhoods as adjuncts to their parish ministry tended to keep them on a short leash. This may, however, have been less an expression of masculine prejudice than a defense of clerical privilege. There was a revealing correspondence on the subject between Pusey and Arthur Stanton, who had been offered the position of vicar at St. Saviour's, Leeds, in 1865. Pusey objected to Stanton's plan to start a parochial sisterhood, and wished to have the Devonport Sisterhood work in the parish instead. Stanton replied that "Miss Sellon's work ... is hardly the help we wish," adding, "We feel we want lady helpers—bona fide 'Sisters of Mercy'." He distrusted the Devonport sisters' independence and "monastic" tendencies. Pusey exploded at the implied criticism of Mother Lydia, and accused Stanton of being "very much wedded to the modern idea of the Clergy, to have everything in their parishes under their own control." For the clergy "to interfere or check or wish to control any work, which religious women wish to set about in their parish [would] be most horrible tyranny."

Pusey probably had a sharper insight into Stanton's motives than his own. More than anything else, Pusey's response reflected his personal loyalty to Miss Sellon, but he offered a variety of reasons for disapproving of Stanton's plan. Aside from opposition to tyranny, he mentioned medieval precedent, considerations of efficiency, the "anomaly" of young clergymen directing women old enough to be their mothers, and—when Stanton made it clear that he proposed to start with younger women—the "worse evil" of that. Mixed in with this farrago, however, were some important statements of principle that ran counter to the received wisdom of the times. "I think that it is a wrong ambition of men, to wish to have the direction of the work of women. I should fear that it would be for the injury of both. Women ought to understand their own work, the education and care of young women [in this case]; or they would not be fit for it at all." With a "sensible head" like Miss Sellon, Pusey concluded, "the interference of the Clergy would be not only superfluous, but time-wasting and mischievous."[97]

Anglo-Catholicism and Feminism

For whatever reason, in this exchange Pusey echoed both the tone and substance of a species of High Church feminism that was also evident in the works of Charlotte Yonge—novelist, disciple of John Keble, and editor of the Tractarian *Monthly Packet*.[98] A. M. Allchin has described Miss Yonge's views: "At no time has she any use for women who set themselves up in competition with men. But, on the other hand, she urges to the full the rights and duties of women in their own particular sphere." Like the woman doctor in one of Miss Yonge's later novels, like the women's colleges at Oxford (in two cases headed by bishops' daughters who were Miss Yonge's friends), sisterhoods represented an extension of woman's sphere.[99] The opponents of sisterhoods realized that, and their opposition often reflected it.

A less radical, less threatening alternative was available. The office of deaconess offered (as one of its proponents put it) a "happy medium" of helpful service, between the family and conventual life. Becoming a deaconess filled a woman's time with good works, but did not demand the same commitment or make the same statement as joining a sisterhood. That this possibility was virtually ignored, Michael Hill has observed, is "evidence of the predominantly virtuoso and feminist motivation behind the development of sisterhoods."[100] Certainly something of the sort is necessary to account for Allchin's observation that the usual pattern of development in Christian monasticism—contemplation first, activity second; men first, women second—was reversed in the nineteenth-century Church of England.[101] By 1900 there were only a handful of communities for men, but dozens of sisterhoods enlisted two to three thousand women.[102] The simplest explanation for this disparity is that the life of a religious community offered something to women that it did not offer to men—or something that men could find elsewhere.

It would be a mistake to link the Anglo-Catholic movement too closely with Victorian feminism. It embodied some of the same values, but in such a limited and tentative way, and incorporating so many of the patriarchal assumptions of the time, that it might be better to regard it as an *alternative* to feminism. But there is no question that the movement responded to and benefitted from some real strains resulting from the prevailing views of appropriate activities for women.

Those views were held nowhere with greater intensity than among the movement's theological adversaries, the Evangelicals. In her despair, Florence Nightingale overstated it, but she saw clearly: "What I complain of the Evangelical party for, is the degree to which they have raised the claims upon women of 'Family'—the idol they have made of it. It is a kind of Fetichism.... They acknowledge no God, for all they say to the contrary, but this Fetich."[103] It was almost inevitable that a movement shaped in opposition to Evangelicalism should challenge that idolatry, and Anglo-Catholicism did so: symbolically in forms of worship and in confession, and institutionally in the newly established religious communities.

Such a movement should have appealed, and it seems that it did appeal, to those who felt themselves oppressed or affronted by the existing ideal. Some of these were men, and we shall look at them in the next chapter. More were women.

Young Men and Ritualism

Some men could be found in Ritualist congregations, but they were likely to be young. In 1865 R. F. Littledale wrote, "Wherever 'Tractarian' ritual is in the ascendant, young men throng the choir and frequent the services."[1] Another Ritualist claimed that "multitudes of young people, especially of young men, who have never concerned themselves with the Church or with religion, have been attracted ... by the Church's reformed and animated services."[2] The *Times* reported from St. Alban's, Holborn, in 1866, that "the spirit of devotion which pervades the whole assembly is remarkable, and foremost, perhaps, among the devotees are young men of 19 or 20 years of age, who seem to have the intricacies of ritualism at their fingertips."[3] A few years later, another visitor to St. Alban's also reported the presence of "young men in plenty."[4]

What sort of young men were these? The movement's opponents plainly did not regard them as the cream of British youth, or even as a wholesome cross section. Distaste and impatience shine through innumerable references to "strange millinery," to "babyish buffooneries," to "glittering baubles of a sensuous satisfaction"—those who saw Ritualism in that light could hardly be expected to think highly of its young adherents, and they did not.[5] We find a reference here to the "giddy young men," there to the "morbid young men" attracted to the movement.[6] Fictional accounts were equally harsh; some Anglo-Catholic choristers in Charles Kingsley's *Alton Locke*, for instance, are described as "exceedingly ill-looking men, whose faces bespoke principally sensuality and self-conceit."[7] Some who were willing to make allowances for women believed that in men such tastes were "silly and effeminate," and possibly worse.[8]

The charge of unmanliness was recurrent. *Fraser's Magazine* assailed the "effeminate fanatics" attracted to Ritualism, and one pamphlet writer suggested that they were not really men at all, but women—"for it must be remembered that the latter sex is as often to be found 'breeched' and with whiskers, as not."[9] Many shared the views of an opponent of incense and altar lights who argued that "spectacles of this kind" appealed only to "sentimental ladies and womanish men—youths of a lachrymose turn of mind."[10]

Ritualists' styles of controversy and exposition were suspect, too. In 1873, Bishop Tait wrote Gladstone, who had nominated Edward King, principal of Cuddesdon, to be professor of pastoral theology at Oxford, "I fear the Ultra High Church Party foster a womanly defence instead of a manly faith."[11] King, later Bishop of Lincoln, was a man with whom the word "saintly" is now almost reflexively associated, and Owen Chadwick has observed that Tait's misgivings demonstrate how Christian meekness can be misunderstood.[12]

But misunderstanding (if that is what it was) did not come only from irritated opponents of Ritualism. Bishop Wilberforce, who supported the movement in many ways, wrote a friend in 1858 that some of the young seminarians at Cuddesdon were "too peculiar." He complained of their "tendency to crowd the walls with pictures of the Mater Dolorosa, etc., their chimney-pieces with crosses, their studies with saints," and of the "habit of some of our men of kneeling in a sort of rapt prayer on the steps of the communion-table, when they cannot be alone there; when visitors are coming in and going out and talking around them." Wilberforce lamented the "want of vigour, virility, and self-expressing vitality of the religious life in the young men."[13] These surely were the sort that maverick Anglo-Catholic Sabine Baring-Gould said were most liable to become Roman Catholics: "not conspicuously virile men who delight in tinsel and paper flowers."[14]

It is obviously difficult to document the existence of a fringe of rather precious young men attached to Anglo-Catholicism other than by quoting amused or annoyed observers, but occasionally we hear their voices in the controversy of the period. It is usually more a matter of tone than of substance. Consider, from a colonial lay reader given to Victorian emphases: "The writer looks upon *the use of Incense* in her services as *one of the marks of the true Church*."[15] Or, from a church newspaper: "It is simply dreadful to contemplate the fact that Low Churchmen do as they do about Evening Communions.... Again and again that wretched print the Rock urges the introduction of Evening Communions everywhere."[16]

Young Devotees in Literature

Young men of this sort seem to have been attracted to Anglo-Catholicism from its beginnings in the Oxford Movement days. The "gilt-gingerbread school" was largely made up of them, and Newman's novel *Loss and*

Gain (written soon after his conversion to Roman Catholicism) offers this specimen of their conversation:

They entered [the church]; an old woman was dusting the pew as if for service. "That will be all set right," said Willis; "we must have no women, but sacristans and servers." "Then, you know, all these pews will go to the right about. Did you ever see a finer church for a function?" "Where would you put the sacristy?" said Willis; "that closet is meant for the vestry, but would never be large enough." "That depends on the number of altars the church admits," answered White; "each altar must have its own dresser and wardrobe in the sacristy." "One," said Willis, counting, "where the pulpit stands, that'll be the high altar; one quite behind, that may be Our Lady's; two on each side of the chancel—four already; to whom do you dedicate them?" "The church is not wide enough for those side ones," objected White. "Oh, but it is," said Willis; "I have seen, abroad, altars with only one step to them, and they need not be very broad. I think, too, this wall admits of an arch—look at the depth of the window; that would be a gain of room." "No," persisted White; "the chancel is too narrow" and he began to measure the floor with his pocket-handkerchief.[17]

Newman's description of Willis's rooms in college sounds very much like the sort of thing Bishop Wilberforce would later protest at Cuddesdon:

A large ivory crucifix, in a glass case, was a conspicuous ornament between the windows; an engraving, representing the Blessed Trinity, as is usual in Catholic countries, hung over the fire-place; and a picture of the Madonna and St. Dominic was opposite to it. On the mantel-piece were a rosary, a thuribulum, and other tokens of Catholicism of which [the visitor] did not know the uses; a missal, ritual, and some Catholic tracts lay on the table; and [Willis was] sitting in a vestment more like a cassock than a reading-gown, and engaged upon some portion of the Breviary.[18]

This image of the sort of young men attracted to Anglo-Catholicism has been remarkably persistent. Novelists writing eighty years after Newman, in the 1920s, painted very similar pictures of the movement's young devotées. In *The Anglo-Catholic*, by Shane Leslie, for example, we read of Edge, who "clung to his hopes [of reunion with Russian Orthodoxy] and kept Ikons blessed by Colonial Bishops," and of "various secret societies [which] used to bicycle from Cambridge to Fenny Magna to attend special services" with Father Whalley, a Roman priest who had defected to Anglicanism and whose orders were therefore undisputed. "His ritual was simple: two lights, Sarum Use and Sarum colours with simple vestments of linen."[19]

The early novels of Compton Mackenzie are full of such characters (particularly his "Altar Steps" trilogy, about a young Anglo-Catholic priest). In *Sinister Street*, Michael Fane's new friend shows Michael his room (the man is a young bank clerk, not an undergraduate—a sign of the social direction

Anglo-Catholicism had taken since Newman's day):

"That's St. Bernardine of Sienna," he explained, pointing to a coloured statuette. "My patron, you know. Curious I should have been born on his day and be christened Bernard. I thought of changing my name to Bernardine, but it's so difficult at a Bank. Of course, I have a cult for St. Bernard, too, but I never really can forgive him for opposing the Immaculate Conception. Father Moneypenny and I have great arguments on that point. I'm afraid he's a little bit wobbly. But absolutely sound on the Assumption. Oh, absolutely, I'm glad to say. In fact, I don't mind telling you that next year we intend to keep it as a Double of the First Class with Octave which, of course, it is. This rosary is made of olive wood from the Garden of Gethsemane and I'm very anxious to get it blessed by the Pope. Some friends of mine are going to Rome next Easter with a Polytechnic tour, so I may be able to manage it. But it's difficult. The Cardinals—you know," said Mr. Prout vaguely. "They're inclined to be bitter against English Catholics. Of course, Vaughan made the mistake of his life in getting the Pope to pronounce against English Orders. I know a Roman priest told me he considered it a fatal move. However—you're waiting for your tea."[20]

Arcana to Be Mastered

The element of one-upmanship that more or less inevitably accompanied immersion in the Anglo-Catholic subculture and the acquisition of detailed ritual knowledge may have had a particular appeal to the young. *A Ceremonial Guide to Low Mass*, compiled by two Ritualist clergymen from a Roman Catholic original, offered such guidelines as this: "As is remarked by St. Liguori, it is a mistake, on making a genuflection, to raise the tips of the fingers upwards."[21] A guide for acolytes and choristers urged its readers to be charitable: "When in quire, be careful to observe all the ritual customs of the place.... If some of the customs be ritually wrong it is no concern of yours.... If [the ceremoniarus] is wrong in his directions, and you cannot put him right with a word or two, let it pass; nothing is more unseemly than a wrangle upon some point of ceremonial just before leaving the sacristy or in quire."[22]

The incumbent of Christ Church, Surbiton, a prominent Evangelical, sneered at the "learned mysteries of chasubles and burses and veils, dalmatics and tunicles, ... their varieties far too abstruse for ordinary male knowledge; with plain orphreys or brocatelle, embroidered symbols and crosses, or cloth of gold and silver, false semifin or real, plain or moire." He added that "I confess myself wholly out of my depth, and have copied the words out of an Ecclesiastical millinery list."[23]

A fictitious dialogue presented a seasoned clergyman who complained about "presumptuous and ignorant young men and women, prating about 'Catholic' custom, and ready to instruct a grey-haired priest of years and experience on the strength of the last article in their favourite newspaper or review." Their religion, he asserted, "consists chiefly in gadding about after 'functions,' criticizing clergymen, processions, ritual, music, and the like, and making themselves as conspicuous as possible by the most absurd postures and gestures."[24] Another clergyman (this one real enough) denounced as the "most objectionable of lay helpers" one who sees it as his duty "to keep his clergyman up to the mark, or force him up to it, or abuse him in no measured language for refusing to move up to it." Pointing to "the way in which things are done at St. ——————'s" and drawing on "his researches in the *Church Times*, which is usually his sole library of Catholic Theology," such a helper "feels constrained either incessantly to worry his parson into adopting the practices of St. ——————'s, or, failing that, to deplore aloud the want of Catholic feeling in his parson and the parish at large."[25]

Nor did such "volunteer advisers" confine their efforts to their own churches. At St. Luke's, Berwick Street, about 1870, the vicar observed the activities of "a migratory brotherhood" going about to "push 'Catholic usage,' as it is called." He was not unsympathetic to Anglo-Catholicism, but was not pleased when his church was "invaded by a gang of these devotees, who scattered themselves here and there in the congregation and by studiously devout bowings and crossings tried to promote what they conceived to be improved gestures of reverence among the people."[26] (The people were not to be moved, however, and the Ritualist flying squad moved on after a month or so.)

Some young Ritualists did not stop at merely setting a good example. One young Etonian not only crossed himself before meals, but hid his housemates' breakfasts so that they would be obliged to communicate fasting.[27] In 1880, a Church Association officer complained that an anti-Ritualist lecture in Camberwell had been utterly disrupted by "a knot of young men—doubtless members of some Ritualistic guild in the neighborhood."[28]

At the turn of the century, an Evangelical historian, a man who had been at Oxford in Newman's day, adduced a number of factors to account for the movement's success, among them the "subtle attractions which found their expression in the too-evident self-complacency with which young people learned to speak of their elders as well-meaning persons who were ignorant of Church teaching and devoid of Church principles."[29] One of those elders, an Anglo-Catholic himself, complained in 1883 about the "meddlesome officiousness" of younger men, who he believed were jeopardizing the movement's progress: "We should all of us be sorry indeed to think that an affectation of superiority in Ritual knowledge or a fancy of special ceremonial experience ... could have the effect of annulling long labours, disappointing long-nursed hopes, quenching glorious aspirations, rendering nugatory the fruits of hard-won victories"—and so forth.[30]

Even a lifetime of service to the cause was not proof against young critics. The Reverend George Rundle Prynne of St. Peter's, Plymouth, was once told by a young curate, "Well, it is usual in Catholic churches for altars to be made of stone, and not wood with only a stone slab like ours." "I have always understood," Prynne replied, "the greatest of all sacrifices was offered on the wood of the cross."[31]

Father Dolling, the great slum priest of St. Agatha's Mission to Sailors, reportedly dealt with his critics even more forthrightly. Here is Compton Mackenzie's fictionalized account of one such episode:

[A] pietistic young creature, who brought with him his own lace cotta but forgot to bring his nightshirt, begged to be allowed the job of serving Father Rowley [Dolling] at early Mass next morning. When they came back and were sitting around the breakfast table, this young man simpered in a ladylike voice: "Oh, Father, could-n't you keep your fingers closed when you give the Dominus vobiscum?" "Et cum spiritu tuo," shouted Father Rowley. "I can keep my fingers closed when I box your ears." And he proved it.[32]

Some Anglo-Catholics took pleasure in mocking others' ignorance. The movement's folklore was full of examples, some of them even true. Apparently a journalist reporting on the consecration of St. Michael's, Shoreditch, really did describe the verger's cassock as "a long Roman-looking coat, buttoned from the neck to the feet." Other stories, less reliable, had newspapers reporting that curates practiced "celibacy in the open streets," that a cleric carried "the Vatican" to the dying, that a bishop appeared "with his tonsure in his hand," that "Acolytes [were] suspended from Rood-screens" and "Thurifers swung in procession."[33]

Again and again we find friends and foes urging young Ritualists to be more considerate, especially of their elders, and sometimes their superior airs and condescension were indeed unattractive.[34] But the young partisans could be wickedly funny, too, as in a pamphlet called *Directorium Puritanicum* (a take-off on the Ritualist manual *Directorium Anglicanum*) that satirized Low Church practice. The black Geneva gown, it said, "symbolizes the great act of preaching, by its length, its fulness, and its colour." When donning his furred academic hood, the minister may say, "Though my sins be as scarlet yet shall they be like wool."[35]

Like cricket, Anglo-Catholicism offered its young enthusiasts a heady blend of partisanship and arcana to be mastered. Indeed, the sporting analogy can be extended even further: advertisements in the *Church Times* in the 1860s offered the equivalent of American baseball cards, "carte de visite portraits" of Pusey, Keble, F. G. Lee, T. T. Carter, John Mason Neale (choice of cassock or alb and chasuble), George Nugee (cassock and biretta), R. M. Benson, Mackonochie, Lowder, and a dozen other Ritualist all-stars.[36] Add the movement's call to high-mindedness, its aesthetic attractions, and its capacity to shock the stuffy, and perhaps its appeal to some young men—and some high-spirited young women, too—can begin to make sense.

Some non-Ritualists felt this was all harmless enough. One observer argued that "an imperfect Christianity" is better than none at all. If Ritualism made young people "pert and conceited," he said, "they had better be that than vicious or abandoned."[37] But others disagreed. One critic likened Ritualism to an addiction: once people "acquired a taste and appetite for novelties," he said, "that taste and appetite must be gratified by fresh and incessant supplies." If they do not find it in their own church, "they go to another, in which the ministers give them stronger food and more exciting worship." Sometimes even this "does not satisfy their cravings, and we know what becomes of them *then*: they tumble into the Church of the Seven Hills."[38]

An Evangelical magazine suggested that Ritualism was one of the many temptations that could lead adolescents astray. It published a warning testimonial in which a young man told of falling in with bad companions who introduced him to Ritualism. Soon, "as I had Ritualistic friends and used regularly to read the *Church Times*, I began to desire something of a more developed character, my church 'not going far enough' for me." When the narrator hit bottom—attending Benediction at a Roman chapel and praying to an image of the Virgin in his sitting room—he happened by chance to hear an Evangelical sermon, and was saved.[39]

Sensuality and Aestheticism

Ritualism, Evangelicals believed, was tainted by the twin evils of sensuality and insincerity. Many others had the same perception, but did not feel as strongly about it. And some believed there was something to be said for sensuality, a few even for insincerity.

As early as the Oxford Movement days Isaac Williams had written: "Both soul and body took the Son of man, / Both soul and body must in him serve God."[40] In 1856, an Anglo-Catholic preacher at Tenbury argued that "the true notion is, that the body is the necessary companion and minister of the soul; that the senses ... may materially assist and even heighten the holiest exercises of those who worship God in spirit and in truth."[41] A decade later, the combative R. F. Littledale attacked the Evangelical view as Manichean, arguing that

because our bodies are to rise again, this world must be the place of training and probation for them as well as for our souls. We cannot give God half our nature, and refuse Him the other half. Therefore the body must worship Him as well as the soul. And the body can do this only by voice and gesture. Vocal prayer and song, bowings, kneelings, prostrations are the obvious ways of using the body in worship. To deny or to stint these is to refuse God his due.[42]

(Littledale went on to add that "it is hard to imagine any thing more unwelcome, unfamiliar, and distressing than Heaven, with all its elaborate liturgy, and the total absence of sermons, might fairly be expected to prove to the popular Protestant preacher, trained to such a widely different idea of Divine Service.")

Evangelicals could not have been expected to agree, of course, and their suspicions were fed by the existence of a few devotées of Anglo-Catholicism who saw in it primarily a source of exquisite sensations. These aesthetes might have been, for instance, disciples of J. H. Shorthouse, the author of *John Inglesant*, who argued that "enjoyment must be the end of all (real) existence," and urged agnostics to receive communion for the "thrill" of it.[43] G. S. Street satirized this attitude in his novel, *Autobiography of a Boy*, published in 1894: "From a purely aesthetic point of view," a character remarks, "there is much that is acceptable in the Church's ritual and surroundings. Why trouble about the import of her teachings? I never listen to them, or merely smile when some fragment of quaint dogmatism breaks in on my repose. But I love to sit in some old cathedral and fancy myself a knight of the middle ages, ready to die—dear foolish fellow!—for his simple faith."[44]

Something of the same attitude, although less jaded, underlay the undergraduate scheme of William Morris and Edward Burne-Jones for a brotherhood under the patronage of Sir Galahad.[45] But the confusion of art and religion probably reached its height in the life and work of Walter Pater.[46] As a youth, Pater was an avid Ritualist; toward the end of his life, he again became a regular communicant and immersed himself in religious literature, although he apparently never returned to orthodoxy. Even in his years of unbelief, when he was something of a high priest himself in his own cult of beauty, he continued to attend church regularly at outposts of advanced Ritualism like St. Alban's, Holborn, and Father Nugee's priory in Walworth.[47] Since Pater was at the time anti-Christian, sometimes offensively so, we must presume that he valued in Ritualism "not the fruit of experience, but experience itself"; that he found it a way of "maintaining ecstasies" and of getting "as many pulsations as possible" from life —all phrases from his teachings on the general value of aestheticism.[48]

W. H. Mallock may not have been far off the mark in his novel *The New Republic*, in which "Mr. Rose" (Pater) tells Lady Ambrose, an enthusiastic Anglo-Catholic, that "when in the weary mood for it," he attends Ritualist services. Rose says he often finds that

the whole thing is really managed with surprising skill. The dim religious twilight, fragrant with the smoke of incense; the tangled roofs that the music seems to cling to; the tapers, the high altar, and the strange intonation of the priests, all produce a curious old-world effect, and seem to unite one with things that have been long dead. Indeed, it all seems to me far more a part of the past than the services of the Catholics.

"Yes," Rose continues, "there is a regretful insincerity about it all, that is very nice, and that at once appeals to me, '*Gleich einer alten halbverklungen Sage.*' The priests are only half in earnest; the congregations, even—" (He is interrupted by the lady's protests.[49])

Later, Rose tells another character, Mrs. Sinclair, that he sees as a symbol of the age a "marble-white and swan-soft" figure of a woman, "couched delicately on cushions before a mirror, and watching her own supple reflection gleaming in the depths of it…. Such a woman do I see whenever I enter a ritualistic church—"

"I know," Mrs. Sinclair replies, "that very peculiar people do go to such places."[50]

Pater, those under his spell, and other, similar young men floated in and out of the Ritualist orbit. There was a good deal of overlap and more or less continuous exchange between the circles of advanced Anglo-Catholicism and the secular avant-garde. The young hero of *Sinister Street* traded his religious images for "Della Robbia reliefs and terra-cotta statuettes of this or that famous Greek youth"; no doubt other young men did the same, and vice versa.[51] Certainly the *Methodist Magazine* saw the two circles as intersecting. Ritualists, it said, were "men whom the languor of hereditary luxury has unmanned, and who, if they were not High-Church devotees, would be lisping exquisites." Both phenomena were "abortions of our modern civilization."[52]

And each could be a source of humor. We are told that W. S. Gilbert, in the 1870s, intended to lampoon curates, but was persuaded instead to ridicule "perceptively intense and consummately utter" young aesthetes, on the sound commercial calculation that there were fewer of them. *Patience*, the result, nevertheless indicates what Gilbert might have done to Anglo-Catholics, had he persevered in his original plan:

> Though the Philistines may jostle
>   you will rank as an apostle
>   in the high aesthetic band,
> If you walk down Piccadilly
>   with a poppy or a lily
>   in your medieval hand.

Gilbert's character Jane could easily have been a young man discussing an altar frontal when she called for the Heavy Dragoons' new uniforms to be "a cobwebby grey velvet, with a tender bloom like cold gravy, which, made Florentine fourteenth-century, trimmed with Venetian leather and Spanish altar-lace, and surmounted with something Japanese—it matters not what—would at least be Early English!"[53]

Muscularity and Masculinity

To hold the Ritualists responsible for the excesses of the Aesthetes is hardly fair. R. F. Littledale protested that many "practical men, perfectly free from effeminate sentimentality" regarded ceremonial as useful in their parochial and mission work, and even Father Nugee complained about "mere sightseers" and reproached his friend Pater for his lack of seriousness.[54] But there is no doubt that some of the same types—indeed, some of the same individuals—were drawn into the two movements, and the movements had some of the same attractions.

Moreover, the popular reaction to Ritualism was colored by the presence in its ranks of this sort of young man. Kipling's self-made merchant, Sir Anthony Gloster, Bart., sent his son to Trinity College, but it could as well have been Cuddesdon:

> The things I knew was proper
>   you wouldn't thank me to give,
> And the things I knew was rotten
>   you said was the way to live.
> For you muddled with books and pictures,
>   an' china an' etchin's an' fans,
> And your rooms at college was beastly—
>   more like a whore's than a man's—[55]

If Evangelicalism was Anglo-Catholicism's theological antithesis, its cultural antithesis is found here. In its religious expression, that antithesis was "muscular Christianity," of the variety associated with Charles Kingsley. This was also the Christianity of Thomas Hughes, the author of *Tom Brown's Schooldays*, a book advertised as "vigorous, manly, and thoroughly English"—everything its admirers thought Ritualism was not.[56] Unlike the Evangelicals, muscular Christians like Kingsley did not chide the Anglo-Catholics for their sensuality, exactly; rather, they felt that some were not sensual enough, or that their natural sensuality, suppressed, worked itself out in unhealthy ways. David Newsome has summarized Kingsley's views of Anglo-Catholicism:

To him, manliness was an antidote to the poison of effeminacy—the most insidious weapon of the Tractarians—which was sapping the vitality of the Anglican Church. Young men came to the church for spiritual nourishment: they went away perverted. Their enthusiasm was diverted into unnatural, un-English pursuits. They were encouraged to think of themselves as beings set apart from other men, their minds bent on other-worldliness, the beauty of holiness and the satisfaction of self-denial.

Scorning all earthly loves, they released their frustrated emotions upon saints long dead and upon the Holy Mother of God; renouncing the love of women, they clung to each other, casting aside all manly reticence by confessing to each other their secret temptations, and seeking solace in their own passionate attachments which seemed to a normal healthy male (such as Kingsley liked to think of himself) undesirably high pitched.[57]

Kingsley's views were not unusual, but they were expressed with unusual clarity and force. Roman Catholicism, he wrote to a clergyman who was thinking of converting, was for an "effeminate shaveling"; a Catholic saint was a "prayer-mongering eunuch." In fact, as his biographer has remarked, Kingsley thought Catholicism was "really satisfactory for no one except a sex-starved woman."[58] And Anglo-Catholics had even less excuse for themselves than Romanists; Kingsley found them "radically un-English," by which he meant unmanly. "In all that school," he wrote, "there is an element of foppery—even in dress and manner; a fastidious, maundering die-away effeminacy, which is mistaken for purity and refinement; and I confess myself unable to cope with it, so alluring is it to the minds of an effeminate and luxurious aristocracy."[59]

For Kingsley, the heart of the matter was celibacy. It was an affront to his most deeply held beliefs about the holiness of marriage and family life. More than that, it was a crime against nature. Any system that encouraged it—indeed, any system that did not discourage it—was offensive to him.[60] Anglo-Catholicism, with its revival of sisterhood and monastic life, with its strong and conspicuous minority of celibate priests, with its explicit teaching from the Oxford Movement days onward that "the pursuit of Holy Virginity" was a high calling, could not have been expected to win his approval.[61]

Although many Anglo-Catholic priests were married, many others, including most of the best-known slum Ritualists, were not. The highest "Rule" (the White) of the three that Pusey helped to devise for the Society of the Holy Cross was reserved for celibates, and at least one married priest, J. C. Chambers of St. Mary's, Crown Street, Soho, voluntarily separated from his wife, and the two lived celibate lives apart.[62] Lord Halifax, long-time president of the English Church Union, expressed an attitude common among advanced Anglo-Catholics when he remarked, "Of course if clergy have wives, they ought not to be ashamed of them, but I think it is a regrettable fact, and that they ought to be kept in the background."[63]

Dean Church defended the pursuit of celibacy paradoxically, as a manly act: "To shrink from it was a mark of want of strength or intelligence, of an unmanly preference for English home life, of insensibility to the generous devotion and purity of the saints."[64] But that renunciation did not require great strength from those like Newman's character Charles Reding, in *Loss and Gain*. When he encountered a young clergyman and his pretty bride,

"Charles had a faintish feeling come over him: somewhat such as might beset a man on hearing a call for pork-chops when he was sea-sick."[65] Nor, one suspects, would celibacy have been a manly choice for the "gushing and enthusiastic" Cuddesdon student we met earlier, the one who rushed into Oxford the day before the college was to be opened in the 1850s, "declaring that the whole thing was spoiled and must be a miserable failure" since one of the officiating clergymen wore whiskers and was married.[66]

Sexuality and Sublimation

As David Newsome has observed, Dean Church's view of celibacy would have astounded Kingsley if he had lived to encounter it.[67] We have seen that Kingsley's quite different views on the matter were maintained with unusual vehemence. His biographer has speculated that Kingsley's detestation of effeminacy and exaltation of manliness had its sources not only in his own robust heterosexuality and contented domestic life but in the possibility that his brother was homosexual.[68] And this raises a question as unanswerable as it is unavoidable: To what extent was the religious atmosphere of nineteenth-century Anglo-Catholicism colored by the presence of homosexuals among its adherents?

David Hilliard has argued that, historically, "a homosexual sensibility has expressed itself within Anglo-Catholicism," and that from its beginning this form of religion has attracted more than its share of homosexuals.[69] Hilliard acknowledges that his argument is limited not only by the secrecy that shrouded nineteenth-century homosexuality, but also by the fact that putting it that way is somewhat anachronistic. Until late in the century, to ask whether a man known to be chaste was homosexual would have been almost meaningless. The Victorians certainly knew about homosexual *acts* (the death penalty for sodomy was on the books until 1861), but the idea of homosexuality as a *condition* was not widespread until later—and, one might add, that of anything like a homosexual *sensibility* had currency only in some very rarefied circles.

Still, the question is insistent. Certainly the movement was now and again vexed by revelations of homosexual behavior. As early as 1850, for example, the troubled and troublesome church of St. Saviour's, Leeds, a paradigm in so many ways, was the scene of a scandal involving a Sunday school teacher and a choirboy.[70] Father Ignatius's Benedictine establishment in Norwich was more or less continually disturbed by similar liaisons, the most notorious of which ended when the *Norfolk News* published the text of a silly love letter from the choirmaster, Brother Augustine, to a young member of his choir.[71]

Indeed, Father Ignatius's most recent biographer has suggested that the entire Ignatian enterprise "offered what could be called in modern terms a sublimation of homosexual tendencies. Ignatius himself, with that delicate physique, that devotion to his mother, that love for his fellow men and that sympathy with lonely women, appeared to be the homosexual made Holy."[72] But if this is in any way a useful observation, the key word in it is sublimation. No one has suggested that Ignatius himself was a practicing homosexual. He was, to be sure, very strange, in ways that a more knowing generation than his would say had psychosexual origins. (Only read his account of the solemn, almost liturgical caning of the nine-year-old "Infant Oblate," Baby Ignatius, which ends with the observation, "It is a wonderful thing, this monastery life."[73]) But if he was aware of his "baser instincts" at all, he was zealous and utterly sincere in finding ways to devote them to the service of God.

Obviously nineteenth-century behavior had psychological roots that today we can confidently—perhaps too confidently—pigeonhole. We must remember, however, that these interpretations were seldom available to those involved. When Sister Katherine of the Park Village Sisterhood fasted to death during Lent of 1850 there was no modern diagnostician on hand to pronounce it anorexia; instead, Bishop Forbes of the Scottish church was there to administer Holy Unction (the first use of that sacrament in the English Church since the reign of Edward VI).[74] When the young ushers at St. Alban's, Holborn, habitually displayed "incivility ... to worshippers, and more specially ladies," there were comments on their breeding, but not on their motives.[75] Obviously no one could have rendered a Freudian accounting for the bizarre penances devised by a few spiritual directors, for Pusey's extravagant self-mortification, for Father Ignatius's devotion to his mother, or Edward King's devotion to his. No contemporary of Newman's could have interpreted his dreams as Geoffrey Faber did in 1933.[76] No one at the time read Kingsley's attacks on effeminacy in quite the way that modern readers must.

The fact that the movement's critics did not regard homosexuality as a condition makes the too-easy equation of male effeminacy and sexual inversion even less reliable for the nineteenth century than for our own.[77] A cultural assumption that such a connection exists makes for an obvious self-fulfilling prophecy, but those who assailed Anglo-Catholicism as effeminate did not even usually mean to imply that the movement nurtured homoeroticism. If they had meant that, they would not have stopped at verbal abuse. We must understand, though, that in their view effeminacy was bad enough.

There is simply no way to know whether the level of overt homosexuality in the Anglo-Catholic movement was higher or lower than that in the public schools, the Royal Navy, or the Brigade of Guards. But the movement's high valuation of virginity and celibacy, its emphasis on confession and direction, its concerns with ornament and attire and music—all were seen to be, and therefore were, unmanly. Ritualism's opponents did not know about sublimated homosexuality, but many did sense that there was something not quite *right* about some young Anglo-Catholics. They believed that the movement often attracted and nourished young men who were indifferent to or repelled by the Victorians' rigorous standards of manliness, and they were correct.

The Opposition

S oon after the passage of the Public Worship Regulation Act, the Reverend R. W. Enraght complained that "a small body of Churchmen at the present time are the target at which the shafts of all sects and parties, degrees and persuasions, are being directed from all sides at one and the same moment." He went on to catalogue the newspapers that had denounced the Ritualists, and to document opposition both from Roman Catholics and from virtually every Protestant denomination.[1]

We might suspect Enraght of exaggerating—he would soon be jailed for his contumacy—but another witness, a layman and no Anglo-Catholic, saw it much the same way: not only do all other Church of England folk dislike the Ritualist, this anonymous observer said, but "Roman Catholic and Protestant dissenters will join hands in his abuse" and "the unbiased sceptic" sees him as "an exceptionally besotted specimen of Christianity." No one but a "handful of Old Catholics [and] two or three urbane, but bewildered metropolitans from the Levant will give him a civil word." Otherwise, "he is alone—a pariah of religions, an ecclesiastical Ginx's baby."[2]

Certainly an impressively broad spectrum of British public opinion found Anglo-Catholicism dangerous or ludicrous or both, and responded to the movement in its early and middle years with a remarkable level of scorn and even hatred. The movement's main result in the public eye, Shane Leslie remarked, was the strife it produced: "Riots, liturgical brawls, and lawsuits followed endlessly."[3]

Odium Theologicum

To the extent that this conflict reflected doctrinal disagreement, the disposition of forces was largely given by the Church of England's tripartite structure of High Church, Low Church, and Broad Church. The High and Low Church parties antedated the Oxford Movement, as did the liberal and latitudinarian elements that would eventually form the Broad Church, but the controversies that followed in the movement's wake brought these factions into sharper definition and higher contrast.[4] Many from each camp opposed Anglo-Catholicism, but, as our anonymous observer remarked, "The mode of attack adopted by critics of different schools varies widely."[5]

In general, Broad Churchmen viewed Ritualism "with a mixture of pity and contempt, becoming sardonic as Erastianism more or less strongly predominates." A movement born in opposition to what one of the *Tracts* called "the shallow and detestable liberalism of the day" could hardly expect sympathy from liberal churchmen, most of whom viewed the movement as anachronistic and obscurantist.[6] As F. D. Maurice put it, Anglo-Catholics opposed "the child-like spirit of the Fathers against the intellectual spirit of these times—the spirit of submission to Church authority against the spirit of voluntary association."[7] A few Broad Churchmen urged fair play for the movement, but usually just as an extension of their party's principles of tolerance and comprehensiveness. And their support for toleration may not have been entirely disinterested: Disraeli spoke for many others when he claimed to view "Rits and Rats"—Ritualists and rationalists—with equal loathing.[8]

Low Churchmen were less philosophical about it. "The staunch upholder of 'inexpugnable Protestantism' is vehement almost to insanity," our anonymous observer wrote; "yet, while his vocabulary is insufficient to express his detestation of Ritualism, he does not attempt to disguise that he is profoundly afraid of it." Most of the ink spilled in the battle against Anglo-Catholicism came from Low Church, "no-popery" clergymen and laymen.[9] The legal effort that led eventually to the imprisonment of Enraght and four other Ritualists—"the Five Confessors," as they were known to their admirers—was almost entirely financed and carried out by the Church Association, the principal organizational arm of this school (whose solicitor bore the fine Dickensian surname "Droop").[10]

As we have seen, anti-Romanists could be driven to frenzy by what they saw in nominally Anglican churches. One more, late example will suffice: John Kensit, a bookseller who founded the Protestant Truth Society, notorious for disrupting Anglo-Catholic services at the turn of the century, wrote his M.P. to tell about a "Creeping to the Cross" ceremony he had attended in Holy Week of 1899. "I went up to the figure," Kensit wrote, speaking of a crucifix, "and taking it into my left hand, facing the people, I said, 'In God's name I denounce this idolatry in the Church of England, God help me.'" He was "then fiercely struck, and had to call murder."[11]

However far from the usual modes of theological disputation the movement's quarrels with Low and Broad Churchmen might stray, they were rooted in serious, longstanding, and well-defined doctrinal disagreements.

High Churchmen of various sorts, on the other hand, were necessarily more ambivalent about a movement that continually outflanked and embarrassed them. Some eventually cut their ties to the Ritualists, amid denunciations on both sides, but their condemnation of Anglo-Catholicism could be based only marginally on doctrine—after all, in most important respects they agreed. What other High Churchmen disliked about Anglo-Catholics was their lack of prudence, or their style.

To call on our anonymous observer one last time: "The strict and ortho-dox Anglican," he said (meaning the old-fashioned High and Dry or moderate High Churchman), tended to regard Ritualists "with less fear [than did the Evangelical], but equally decided repugnance. To the Protestant he is a dragon, to the Anglican a viper." A representative voice is that of the dean of Chichester, J. W. Burgon: "There is wondrous little of the Gospel of Jesus Christ in this miserable resuscitation of effete Medievalism," he said. "It is of the earth, earthy, an unspiritual, an unwholesome, a mawkish, a wholly un-English thing."[12]

The Party of Common Sense

In putting matters this way, hostile High Churchmen were articulating cultural objections to the movement that were more widely shared and more damaging than the theological concerns of alarmed Evangelicals or unsym-pathetic liberals. The movement's conflicts with the Low and Broad remained ecclesiastical, conducted almost exclusively by clergymen and cleri-cized (or at least theologically engaged) laymen. But the opposition to the movement, like its support, was by no means entirely a matter of doctrine. We cannot begin to understand that opposition without recognizing that Burgon's view of the movement was shared by an influential body of opin-ion, a "party more numerous by far than [the] three theological ones," a body so numerous "whether among the clergy or the laity, that the word 'party' is scarcely adequate."

The words are those of John Henry Newman, looking back at his for-mer Church and describing what he called "the party of order."[13] This party—if we may follow Newman and call it that—"is not a religious party, not that it has not a great number of religious men in its ranks, but because its principles and its *mots d'ordre* [watchwords] are political or at least eccle-siastical rather than theological." This was the party of the Establishment, embodying "the principle of Erastianism," distinguished by "its confidence in the protection of the civil power and its docility in serving it," its mem-bers "more zealous for the preservation of a national Church than solicitous for the beliefs which that national Church professes."

For practical purposes, this body included the less theologically inclined clergy of all three historic Church parties, as well as the vast majority of lay-men of the type likely to be found in the House of Commons. In religious

matters Disraeli and Archbishop Tait spoke for them. "John Bull" personi-
fied them. Newman, writing for a French audience, observed that "this great
assembly of men" truly represents "that English common sense which is so
famous for its good as for its evil consequences."

These churchmen were not Anglo-Catholics, Evangelicals, or liberals,
Newman observed—"or, if they are, it is in a very mild and very unaggres-
sive form." In fact they viewed all theology with suspicion. "In the seven-
teenth century they combated the Puritans; at the close of that century they
combated the Latitudinarians; in the middle of the eighteenth century they
combated the Methodists and the members of the Evangelical party; and in
our own times they have made an energetic stand at first against the Tractarians, and to-day against the Liberals."

Their own religious beliefs were simple: the sufficiency of scripture and
the ability of individuals to interpret it, Christ as the only mediator, redemp-
tion by his death, renewal by his spirit, and the necessity of good works. The
most generous assessment of them is probably Pusey's: "One could not but
see," he wrote, "amid all that prejudice against P——ism, that there was a
good deal of real attachment to the Church. And, after all, the dislike of
innovation is a good principle: for there ought not to be innovation in matters of religion."[14]

It is here, among what we might call the commonsense party, that secular opposition to Anglo-Catholicism was most widespread and effective.
The movement had attractions for women and for the young, for "the cultured despisers of the bourgeoisie," and even for some among the poor and
the working classes, but it profoundly offended many of those who were
none of those things: that is, men, especially those middle-aged or older, of
the commercial middle class.

We have heard a great deal from such men in earlier chapters. Year after
year, specimens could be found harrumphing their way through the letters
columns of the *Times*, and fictional examples abound in the novels of the
Tractarian period. When a character in *Tom Brown at Oxford* describes the
Oxford Movement as "all Gothic-mouldings and man-millinery business,"
we recognize the voice of the commonsense party; we hear it again in *The
Warden of Berkingholt*, when a gentleman complains of undergraduates
down from Oxford "full of crude crochets of nonsense, which they call
Catholicism, but which, for aught I can see, is as like Popery as one thing
can be to another."[15]

These were the men Lord Sandon had in mind when he called the attention of the 1867 Wolverhampton Church Congress to the absence of "a
large class of laymen whom we see taking the lead at the ordinary business
meetings which abound in this our prosperous and active county of
Stafford," and blamed it on the rise of Anglo-Catholicism.[16] A decade later,
the Reverend J. C. Ryle argued that "Ritualism is gradually robbing our
Church of some of its best members among the laity." "Not a few bankers,

lawyers, doctors, and merchants are dropping off and leaving the ship," Ryle observed. "Their confidence is thoroughly shaken," their "common sense" affronted by "Popish novelties," so "some join the Dissenters, and some stand aloof altogether, and refuse to take any part in the Church's affairs."[17]

Apparently a gentleman named John Clabon spoke for many others when he complained in 1869 that "an unsophisticated member of the Church of England may go into one of these churches and find a Prayer Book useless." Clabon grumbled that a layman attending his parish church might well find changes "added by degrees, one on one Sunday, and another on another Sunday; until a year quite alters the character of the services"—yet "the progress is still onward." "Purple vestments, and scarlet banners, smoking incense, and banks of bright flowers find their way into the Service.... Every Sunday increases the feeling of distress, for it brings some new change." Finally, "the common-sense of the average layman is bewildered"; "weary and unhappy, he looks out for a Church where the desire of change has not mastered common-sense."[18] And why? Another gentleman grumbled that sometimes one gets "the idea that the whole thing has been got up for the glorification of the priests and the exhibition of ecclesiastical vestments."[19]

The Church and the World

Opponents of all varieties responded predictably and vociferously to the publication of a book called *The Church and the World: Essays on Questions of the Day in 1866*. Edited by the Reverend Orby Shipley, what came to be called "the Ritualistic Papers" comprised essays by Anglo-Catholic clergy and layfolk on eucharistic doctrine, Gothic architecture, nursing, positivism, clerical celibacy, religious vows, infanticide, the Prayer Book of 1549, and other topics reflecting the movement's many theological, aesthetic, and social concerns. Shipley's brother in the Society of the Holy Cross, the ubiquitous R. F. Littledale, contributed an article on "The Missionary Aspect of Ritualism."[20] Characteristically, Shipley appended to the book's third edition a selection of reviews, mostly hostile, of the first.[21]

Low Church reviewers, of course, were appalled. The *Record*, probably the principal organ of Evangelical opinion, allowed that the essays were "written with great earnestness and much ability," but concluded that the book was "replete with insolence and presumption, and bears a thorough Romish face." The *Clerical Journal* called on the bishops to condemn the book, and complained that "Ritualism and ritualists have been petted and caressed and complimented, treated with such weak and amiable indulgence, regarded as such models of correct Churchmanship." The reviewer for the *Christian Advocate and Review* was somewhat calmer, though no less antagonistic, predicting that "Rome will appropriate a portion of the body; the law will frighten another portion into moderation; and common sense will persuade others to adopt a form of religion more in accordance with the Bible."

Although the secular press was hardly more hospitable, a few reviewers called for toleration and one or two even expressed admiration for some aspects of Anglo-Catholicism. The *Morning Post*, for instance, tried once again to distinguish between improved church architecture and religious music, on the one hand, and "the personal decoration of the clergy" and "distinctive Romish doctrines," on the other. The *Edinburgh Review* observed that Ritualism put the Church's comprehensiveness to the test, but that it was entitled to that comprehension; in any case, the *Review* predicted, "The fashion [will] probably pass away with the present generation." And the *British Quarterly Review* even found itself "constrained to say that, in spite of its priestly assumption, its ritual frippery, and its ecclesiastical exclusiveness, our religious feeling is strongly appealed to by the spirituality and moral goodness, and by the ministerial devotedness of the [Anglo-Catholic] party."

But in the 1860s these were dissenting voices. More typical was the *London Quarterly Review*, which denounced "the plot for Romanizing the Church of England," or the *Daily News*, which found that even the title of *The Church and the World* revealed "the calm confusion ... of religious and secular concerns, and the bland assumption of ... clerical superiority to civil obligations, which characterize the party it represents." Several reviewers responded to the book with disdain for the kinds of layfolk who might find such a religion attractive. *The Patriot* condemned "the indolent and frivolous 'rich' [who] are allured by the aesthetics, the antiquity, and the authority of the Catholic Church"; it was "with the gravest sense of the evil of rationalism," *The Patriot* said, that it denounced Ritualism as "inconceivably more portentous and hateful." The *Christian Advocate and Review* reassured its readers that "the people who make the most disturbance in the world are by no means of the greatest importance," and reminded them that the Ritualists were "a small [though] energetic and aggressive party, drawing fresh accessions to their ranks from very young men and women."

The movement's appeal to women again drew negative comment. The *Pall Mall Gazette* observed that "the superstition ... is spreading widely and silently among some parts of the population and especially among ladies." Similarly, *Fraser's Magazine* remarked that the "infection" was "spreading in the dark," but took comfort from the fact that "adult males" were not attracted to Ritualism, because "grown men, even the most foolish of them, do not generally show much favour to the pretensions of the clergy." "The intelligence of the nineteenth century," *Fraser's* concluded, "is not about to give way before a handful of effeminate fanatics."

Others agreed that Anglo-Catholicism was either a passing or a trivial phenomenon. To the *Westminster Review*, for instance, the book proved that Ritualism was not a matter of "mere ribbons and millinery" but a "system ... from which a great growth of priestcraft and fetishism might grow up 'while men sleep'"; nevertheless, the *Review* asserted, it would "prove unworkable in the long run." And the *Athenaeum* revealed itself to be better at polemic than at counting, when it remarked of "the—what shall we call them?—Puseyites, Tractarians, Anglo-Catholics, Ritualists, or—just to make up the half-dozen—Irrationalists" that they "will catch a few, and give the rest rational amusement."

"Rational Amusement"

Among the urbane, such "rational amusement" was indeed a frequent response. The author of *Orthodox London*, for instance, was a Broad Churchman who admired the Ritualists for their social work and was generally sympathetic to the impulse behind their ceremonial, but even he could be moved to poke fun. He described a tenebrae service at St. Matthias, South Kensington, this way: "Every now and then a sudden thought appeared to strike a young man in a surplice, who went with an extinguisher at the end of a pole and put out one candle, returning to his stall with the air of a person who had done his duty."[22]

Most commonsense Englishmen mixed their amusement with stronger doses of contempt. One Ritualist observed that ridicule was "one of the most popular of the weapons levelled at the advancing ranks" of his party: "Folly, trifling, childish nonsense, man-millinery, effeminacy—these are the style of epithets with which it is sought to laugh men out of the cause which Ritualism represents."[23]

The movement's treatment in the pages of *Punch* was typical. As Roger Lloyd has observed, that humor magazine articulated and shaped the views of "the real rulers of England," and it was consistently Erastian when not downright anticlerical.[24] *Punch* had little use for Evangelicals, Nonconformists, or Romanists, but it always reserved a special vitriol for Anglo-Catholics.[25] Soon after its founding in 1841, *Punch* burlesqued Newman's *Lives of the Saints*, and it was particularly and consistently merciless toward Pusey, advising him to go to Rome. During the disturbances at St. Barnabas, Pimlico, a cartoon portrayed the embattled clergyman, W. J. E. Bennett, as a "Puseyite Moth" fluttering about a "Roman Candle"; when Bennett left London, *Punch* was among those who happily punned on the name of his new living at Frome. A similar play on words was at the heart of an 1850 parody of "Home, Sweet Home": "Though crosses and candles we play with at home, / To go the whole gander there's no place like Rome."[26] Mock advertisements offered "Achromaticon, for blanching the complexion and imparting to the face that delicate pallor which is the recognised indication of severe thought and study," and "Macerative Elixir warranted to produce in the space of a few days a personal appearance not to be distinguished from the result of years of abstinence." In 1851, nine of the magazine's first thirteen cartoons were anti-Puseyite.[27]

Punch found an enduring source of humor in the fact that (in its words) "reverend gentlemen of extreme High Church proclivities are very fond of dressing up like ladies."[28] A typical cartoon from 1866 shows a clergyman admiring his vestments in a mirror as another exclaims, "Oh, Athanasius! it's charmingly becoming!" A poem addresses "Flirts of the chancel! ye Milliner priests, / Decked in your laces and satin bound hems." And any doubt about *Punch*'s view of confession was removed by a cartoon that showed John Bull about to horsewhip cringing Jack Priest, who holds a copy of *The Priest in Absolution* and has come to hear Britannia's confession.

After the magazine acquired a Roman Catholic editor, its anti-Roman tone moderated, but it still had no use for *Anglo*-Catholics. It applauded Archbishop Tait's efforts to bring them under control ("The Church should thank you, Tait—in time it will, / For your sagacious Public Worship Bill"), and it dealt sharply with Lowder, Mackonochie, Purchas ("the Brighton Professor of Ritualism"), and the imprisoned Arthur Tooth ("the unsound Tooth that must be stopped"), among other Ritualists.[29] R. F. Littledale complained of those "whose theological views are perhaps most clearly and consistently set forth in the learned and devout pages of *Punch*," but there can be no question that many shared the magazine's opinion that the movement, in Littledale's summary, was "the monkey-tricks of a few school-boy curates, and sillier, because less educated, choristers and young ladies."[30]

The Movement and the *Times*

Anglo-Catholics fared no better with another influential font of common sense, what one of their opponents called in 1845 "an organ of incalculable power and extent to preserve and support the creed of their forefathers": the *Times* of London.[31] (That characterization, by the way, was quoted approvingly by the *Times* itself.) In the 1840s and 1850s, the paper relentlessly assailed ultrarubricians and any bishop who seemed at all sympathetic to them. Again and again the newspaper endorsed what it saw as the laity's "strong repugnance" to "obnoxious novelties." During the "surplice riots" at St. Sidwell's, Exeter, the *Times* called the offending clergyman "a common nuisance" and "the cause of all the mischief," observed that "the indignation of the people is certainly excusable," and asked, "How long is the public patience to be abused by the impertinence of such men?" When the rector of St. Leonard's, Shoreditch, agreed to give up chanted psalms but proposed to chant a bit after the third collect, the *Times* responded: "Does he? Then we hope he will be hooted out of the church immediately."

The *Times* cared even less for the thoroughgoing Ritualists of the 1860s and 1870s. Its review of *The Church and the World* observed that "the real meaning of the banners, the gew-gaws, the incense, and the lights with which [Ritualists] decoy the sentimental and dazzle the foolish" was sacerdotal, and it urged the bishops to stamp out this "gross perversion of the spirit of the English Church."[32] The true spirit, in the *Times*'s view, was Erastian: "It seems to be generally felt," the paper observed in 1867, "that all classes of the clergy should be more amenable to the public than they have been."[33] The *Times* strongly supported the Public Worship Regulation Bill, writing of the need for "protecting the sober majority of the Church from a mediaeval delirium."[34]

As late as 1881, the *Times* still remembered the black gown in the pulpit fondly, although that fight had been lost a decade earlier. When Dean Church proposed that eucharistic vestments be tolerated, the newspaper allowed that for every million churchmen willing to endure those garments, five million would wish to see the gown restored. The writer described the sort of service the Church of England should offer:

After a hymn, given out by the minister in a black gown, a scripture-reader rises in his everyday coat and reads a selection from the Prayer-book, with a short lesson, and with the relief of several more hymns. The minister ascends the pulpit, offers a long extempore prayer, and then talks to the people very pleasantly for half an hour.[35]

"All this," he added, "is charming to small shopkeepers, humble citizens, cooks, and housemaids." Obviously, there was little common ground between this service and that urged by the ultrarubricians, much less between it and the full-blown Ritualism of the 1880s.

"The Spirit of Sacerdotalism"

It should be evident that a particularly offensive aspect of Catholicism, whether Roman or Anglican, was its elevated view of the priesthood. At least one critic believed that "the great mass of opposition" to the movement was due not to "dread of ceremonial, or ideas of illegality" but to "dislike of what is called 'Sacerdotalism,'" and when Lord Sandon lamented the absence of businessmen from the Wolverhampton Church Conference he blamed especially the rise of "a priestly feeling" among the clergy.[36] Plainly, the Anglo-Catholic view of the Church tapped a strong native streak of anti-clericalism among influential laymen who suspected that they were to be subject to the Church's newly magnified authority, particularly those who believed that it encouraged clerical arrogance. One Ritualist writer both lists and illustrates what many layfolk disliked, observing that

it seems monstrous to many old-fashioned people that the clergy should arrogate to themselves the title of Priests, with the powers of absolving, consecrating, and blessing. They deem it an impertinence if a steward of the mysteries of the Gospel should rebuke a member of his flock for neglect or misapprehension of these mysteries. They resent any assertion of the right of the shepherd to warn his flock against schismatical acts and heretical opinions. They hardly allow him to arrange or beautify his church, or increase the number of his services. If he restores to activity rubrics which they declare to be obsolete, ... they resent it. If he endeavours to invest the most awful Act of public worship with due solemnity by means of music, and liturgical postures, and sacrificial vestments; if he presume to adopt a distinctive dress to remind others and himself of his sacred office; if, in fact, he does or says any thing beyond their own narrow experience, this class ... is straightway offended.[37]

Anglo-Catholic priests did view themselves as men set apart. They could hardly do otherwise, but that fact seemed especially to infuriate some of their opponents. The Evangelical dean of Carlisle spoke for many when he offered this prayer:

Oh, Lord, we pray Thee, lift the veil of hypocrisy from these faces! We pray Thee, strip them of that meretricious sanctity, of that assumed form and garb of superior holiness, which is but the cover and concealment of the paganism and popery of the heart which lies within!"[38]

No doubt some who objected to sacerdotalism felt nostalgia for the fox-hunting gentleman-parsons of the not-too-distant past. As Anthony Trollope saw it: "The man who won't drink his glass of wine, and talk of his college, and put off for a few happy hours the sacred stiffnesses of the profession and become simply an English gentleman,—he is the clergyman whom in his heart the archdeacon does not love."[39] But for others the bias was frankly nineteenth-century, liberal, and Erastian. One critic accused Anglo-Catholics of promoting "a theory of the priestly office which all experience has shown to be incompatable [sic] with the existence of modern institutions," and the Pall Mall Gazette, condemning "the spirit of sacerdotalism" as "the most serious enemy of the Church of England," urged that "if the Church of England were made once for all to renounce the notion that there is anything supernatural in a clergyman, it would stand on an intelligent basis, and might communicate freely with other Protestant bodies."[40] Whether their views were nostalgic or forward-looking, however, many freeborn Englishmen were ready to detect and to resent the least hint that their vicar considered himself to be (in one such man's words) "a superhuman priest, and only incidentally an Englishman."[41]

Dishonest and Disloyal

Added to the well-founded charge of sacerdotalism, early and late, was what one observer called "the galling imputation of unfaithfulness, Jesuitry, and conscious fraud."[42] Newman was accused on all three counts at the time of Tract 90; later, the ultrarubricians were seen as rather too adept at reading new meanings into the Prayer Book, and the Ritualists, of course, were no improvement. A speaker at an E.C.U. chapter meeting acknowledged that nothing was more damaging to Englishmen than the charge of under-handedness. "It is for this reason, probably, that the charge of dishonesty is brought with such frequency and such pertinacity against the party in the Church of England to which we belong. It is heard on every side."[43] And it certainly was.

The movement's innovations were widely believed to violate the spirit of the law, if not its actual letter. Often, innovators' attempts to find legal warrant for what they were doing contributed to a general impression that they were devious, or at least unduly clever. One critic wrote that "minute and perhaps pettifogging knowledge" of such matters "is evidently suited to the meagre capacity of the Ritualist mind"; another took Anglo-Catholics to task for their "intellectual subtlety" (usually associated, he said, with "more southern nations").[44] That the north end of the altar was not the north "side," that intoning was "saying," that a stone altar weighing a ton and a half was "moveable," that incense was for "fumigation," that genuflecting was not "kneeling"—these and similar assertions gave substance to the accusation that the Ritualists displayed "a spirit of evasion ... which bears a very close resemblance to what in worldly language is termed 'shuffling,' and is at any rate unworthy of the teachers of even the lowest system of morals."[45]

And when the search for authority took Anglo-Catholics outside Anglican formularies, they invited a charge of disloyalty like that leveled by the bishop of Bath and Wells in 1873: "For an English Churchman to disobey his Prayer Book, on the plea of a so-called Catholic usage which his Church has rejected, and to endeavor, by sheer obstinacy, to over-rule the provisions which he had sworn to obey, and to substitute others for them, is to my apprehension a plain act of immorality."[46] That opinion was echoed even by Newman himself, who wrote to a Tractarian friend from his new home in the Roman communion, "When you propose to return to *lost* Church of England ways you are rational, but when you invent a *new* ceremonial which never was, when you copy the Roman or other foreign rituals, you are neither respectable nor rational."[47]

The charge of disloyalty was also fueled by Anglo-Catholics' reservations about "secular authorities," which were sometimes understood to be insults to the judiciary, to Parliament, or to the sovereign herself. The impression of dishonesty was inflamed by the often clandestine nature of confession and by the ineffectual attempts of some Anglo-Catholic organizations to keep their activities secret.[48] By 1899, 32,000 copies of a volume called *The Secret History of the Oxford Movement* were in print; when the author was reproached by the *Church Times* for publishing "the private papers of gentlemen who intended them to remain private"—that is, extracts from the proceedings of the Society of the Holy Cross—he replied that, of course, "men who work in the dark always hate the light."[49]

The word "conspiracy" turns up again and again in the pamphlets and tracts of the opposition, and sometimes the Ritualists' adversaries slipped over the edge of reason. The author of *Secrets of Ritualism*, for instance, believed that when Anglo-Catholic layfolk attended "what they call a Protestant church," they were ordered by their priests "either to withdraw as soon as the sermon begins, or to read a book as long as it continues." He said he saw both "frequently done in my own church, by visitors who attend it during their visit to Blackpool in the season."[50]

Popery Unmanly and Un-English

When Charles Lowder told the brethren of the Society of the Holy Cross in 1874 that they "must be prepared to show that Confession is neither unmanly nor un-English," he identified what commonsense Englishmen found so disagreeable not just about confession but about the movement as a whole: the opponents of Anglo-Catholicism often used those very words to describe it.[51] The charge of unmanliness we have already examined; here, let us take up the accusation that, as Dean Burgon put it, the movement was "a wholly un-English thing."

Characteristically, some Ritualists responded to that accusation by acknowledging its truth and flaunting it. R. F. Littledale, for instance, observed that "Christianity itself is eminently unEnglish."

It was cradled in Palestine, amidst Aramaic-speaking Jews; it was published in the East by Greek-speaking Hellenists; it was brought to our shores by Latin-speaking Italians. The most solemn of its rites cannot be celebrated without a liquor which England does not produce. Druidism may, perhaps, have been indigenous to Britain in some particulars, but Christianity in none.[52]

The *Church Times*, for its part, denounced the "excessive national self-conceit to which Englishmen are so prone," and suggested that the movement's critics recite the Nicene Creed with the phrase "one Protestant and English Church." (Anyway, the newspaper continued, it was Protestantism that had originated on the Continent.[53])

But what many commonsense Englishmen meant by "un-English" was, simply, "Romish"; their opposition to Catholicism picked up where that of Evangelical churchmen left off, and to them "popery" represented everything foreign and vile.[54] At the time of the Gorham controversy in 1849 Gladstone observed, "Such is the antipapal feeling of the country that, if a man would vent enough of that, he might well nigh preach the Koran."[55] Thus "the popular aversion to coloured Vestments," for example, was (as one M.P. remarked) "sincere, deeply rooted, and easily explicable": "Englishmen are quite as conservative in religious as in other matters; they dislike novelties even apart from their meaning, but they dislike coloured Vestments because they remind them of the Vestments used in the Roman Church."[56]

More cultural than strictly religious, anti-Romanism was bound up with feelings toward the nation, toward honesty, loyalty, decency—toward "common sense" itself.[57] "Let any impartial and unprejudiced person travel through any country whatever in which Popery is paramount, and confession an obligatory institution," one layman wrote, "and he must, he cannot fail to observe the degradation, moral and physical, of the inhabitants." Just compare Ireland to Scotland, he urged. Reunion with Rome would mean "decadence, moral and material, the utter abnegation of all moral virility, the encouragement of vice, filth, and idleness, the declension of patriotism, and the death of all vital personal Religion." It would mean that "all the more ignorant portion of the nation would be reduced to a state of the most abject and groveling superstition; and the entire intellectual part of it to black Infidelity."[58]

To those who believed that, of course, *Anglo*-Catholics were worse than bona fide Papists. If Romanists were enemies, Anglo-Catholics were traitors; Dr. Arnold of Rugby was reported to have said that the first was a French soldier in his own uniform, but the second was a French soldier in English garb, and he would honor one and hang the other.[59]

As late as the turn of the century, Bishop Stubbs of Oxford said that opponents of Anglo-Catholicism professed to regard it as "a reactionary, disloyal, underhand, intriguing conspiracy of a few not very able but very pertinacious traitors to lead us on, or lead us back to the state of sacerdotalism, Jesuitry, antiquarian dogmatism, effete ritualism, immoral dependence on exploded ordinances, false morality, and venal repentance, and that system of direction and discipline which ages of corruption had devised to make the world comfortable in sinning."[60] Bishop Stubbs went on to exonerate Anglo-Catholics, but, as we have seen, he was describing the feelings of a great many Englishmen.

We have also seen that few representatives of the movement gave them much reason to change their minds. Many Anglo-Catholics seemed indifferent to the offense they gave; others even seemed to enjoy it. But, as the *London Review* remarked, they were "playing with fire."[61] The attitudes of commonsense Englishmen dominated the popular press and dictated the actions of Parliament. Prince Albert and the Queen herself shared them. So did many bishops—and those who wished to become bishops. Such men did not themselves make up the mobs that disrupted Ritualist services, but their sympathy made disruption almost inevitable. As the *Times* put it at the time of the St. George's riots: "The discontent of the respectable gives scope to the passions of the vulgar."[62] The illogical judicial decisions that eventually undercut the ultrarubricians' strong legal position probably revealed the hostile influence of the men that the movement offended.

The effort to suppress Anglo-Catholicism peaked in 1874 with the passage of Disraeli's "bill to put down Ritualism," the Public Worship Regulation Act. Introduced by the prime minister, the bill was strongly supported by the archbishop of Canterbury. Queen Victoria wrote privately that "the defiance shown by the Clergy of the High Church and Ritualistic party is so great that something must be done to check it and prevent its continuation."[63] An eyewitness said that after Disraeli's speech in favor of the bill the scene in the House of Commons was "frenzied" and that "if it had been proposed to cut off the hands of all the offending clergymen, they would have carried it."[64] Disraeli's somewhat milder bill was passed by an overwhelming majority.

XIII

The Attempt to "Put Down Ritualism"

The Public Worship Regulation Act was popular not just with Parliament and the press, but with most commonsense Englishmen. In 1874 nearly 150,000 signed a Church Association petition in favor of such legislation, almost twice the number who signed an opposing memorial.[1] One man expressed the general opinion when he wrote, "The questions of doctrine and of ritual, now in dispute, must be settled.... They can only be settled by that tribunal, before which we are accustomed as Englishmen and as Churchmen to bow, the Law Courts provided by our Constitution."[2] This man was optimistic about the outcome: "Arguments, fairly admissible on either side so long as the law is interpreted in diverse ways, must 'hold their peace forever' when once the authoritative decision has been pronounced."

But the party of common sense had misjudged the Anglo-Catholics. Ironically, it had overestimated their reverence for law and order and their willingness to compromise—in short, their "Englishness." When it became clear that Ritualism could not simply be put down, the end of the story was in sight.

Ill-Considered Legislation

The most obvious immediate effect of the PWRA was to mobilize Anglo-Catholics.[3] Although one source listed seventy-seven clerical members of the English Church Union who defected to Roman Catholicism in the wake of the PWRA, most Anglo-Catholics took Father Mackonochie's motto, "No surrender, no desertion," for their own, and they organized for battle.[4] In the six months after the act's passage, the E.C.U. gained fourteen hundred new members; in the three years after 1874, its membership of slightly over ten thousand was swelled by nearly seven thousand more.[5]

Even moderate High Churchmen disliked what they saw as the animus behind the act. Bishop Wilberforce, caught in the middle, remarked of the "great wish to condemn lights, incense, etc." that "I *hate* them as novelties, but I see so plainly that the party who hate all real Church progress are the people who object to them, that it makes me very doubtful how far we can go in repression without repressing that development of real Church life which is our hope." He added, "What a plague it is that people cannot have common sense as well as earnestness."[6]

By the 1870s, the objectives of the PWRA were perhaps unattainable in any case, but this legislation was especially ill-designed for its purpose. The PWRA did not say what was permissible and what was not; it simply attempted to make prosecution less cumbersome. Any three "aggrieved parishioners" could bring charges against a clergyman; unless proceedings were vetoed by the bishop of the diocese, the charges would be heard by a new court appointed by the archbishops for the purpose. Even aside from its aims, the act gave Anglo-Catholics much to deplore.

Those who were concerned for clergymen's prerogatives disliked the provision that allowed laymen to initiate proceedings. As H. P. Liddon observed in 1877, "The pettiest resentment of a social or even a commercial origin, [has] sufficed to create the aggrieved parishioner, who forthwith became constant in his attendance at the Parish Church, not simply with a view to worshipping Almighty God, but in order to collect materials for a law-suit."[7]

Many others, not all of them sacerdotalists or even High Churchmen, pointed out that the word "parishioners" reflected the old understanding that a parish church served all the residents of its parish; it did not recognize that many parishioners were unchurched, or worshipped elsewhere. They argued that only a church's "communicants"—that is, those who attended its services—should have a voice in what those services were to be. Moreover, one clergyman complained, allowing any parishioners to bring charges would give "a swindler, an adulterer, and a profane swearer ... absolute power to prevent the use of vestments, incense, or lights, in their own parish church, though the remaining 996 parishioners should desire their use to be continued."[8] The *Christian Remembrancer* said that such a provision amounted to repeal of the Ornaments Rubric, since it was obvious that the Church Association stood ready to subsidize whatever number of aggrieved parishioners might be required, and one minister complained of "three non-communicant parishioners" who could be found in every parish: "the World, the flesh, and the Devil."[9]

Even more important, the act did not change the fact that final appeal was still to the Judicial Committee of the Privy Council, a wholly lay body—and insult was added to injury, from Anglo-Catholics' point of view, when a former divorce judge was appointed to head the new court. The English

Church Union, after debating whether supporting the defense in ritual cases amounted to recognizing the legitimacy of "secular courts" (a phrase that included ecclesiastical courts bound by the Judicial Committee's decisions), eventually decided it did not, but its president made it clear that "we go ... before the courts, not to ascertain the law of the Church, but to *defend* it."[10]

The most important shortcoming of the legislation, however, was that it made no provision for dealing with those who simply ignored the court's decisions, which is exactly what some Ritualists determined to do.

Civil Disobedience

In the words of a sympathetic historian, "Among other outstanding characteristics of the Revival has been reckoned a certain intransigence throughout."[11] Never was this intransigence more evident than in the movement's response to the PWRA. Shortly after the act was passed, an anonymous priest, probably a member of the Society of the Holy Cross, printed and circulated a pamphlet entitled "The Coming Campaign: How It Will Be Won."[12] His plan was followed almost to the letter.

Observing that the enemies of "the great Church Revival of the last forty years" demanded surrender "in the name of Parliament," the pamphlet's author urged his fellow Ritualists to stand fast, neither to give up their ritual nor to "desert the Church of England, where battle is offered." "Can we win it?" he asked. "We can: and without striking a blow." He called for "patient, passive resistance." Martyrs had never suffered for a nobler cause; there was never a better occasion. "Now is the time for the world to see what is the faith and endurance of the saints, and by its impotence to learn its own presumption."

The writer urged priests to transfer their property to wives, children, or trustees, to put it out of reach of adverse judgments. "Then, abiding at our post, let the Act do its worst."

Our churches cannot be carted away, they cannot be permanently closed, our flocks cannot be driven off, our mouths cannot be stopped.... If we are deprived [i.e., removed from office], let the sentence be reckoned null and void.... If another priest is intruded, he can take only what the law gives—the empty vicarage and the endowment; the faithful flock will not receive him; the church-door which opens for him and them stands open also to us, let us quietly take our accustomed place therein. Let him, if he insists, say "*Dearly beloved*," and then the choir will follow your voice, not his.

True, the police might be called to remove the offending clergyman, but his congregation would follow him out. Then, "you may be led off to the police-court, under the flourish of the policeman's baton. You can pay no fines: 'Silver and gold,' you will say, 'I have none.' In default of payment you will then be committed to prison."

What happened after that was left unclear (a crucial omission, as it turned out), but when "released from honourable detention, you will at once return to your post, and take up your work as before." As for ecclesiastical discipline: "If the Bishops are compliant, you may be deposed—it can take no effect, and excommunicated—it will not be ratified in the High Court of Heaven."

This plan would not work, obviously, for "the timid, and those not backed up by their people"; they should "make the best terms they can in face of the enemy, and bide their time." But "the stout of heart who lead the faithful flock ... need not, will not flinch." From this struggle "the Church will come out infinitely stronger than she went in; and our children, and our children's children, will come to tell of the brave confessors of eighteen hundred and seventy-five."

At a meeting in 1876, the English Church Union implicitly endorsed this program, with a resolution that "any sentence of suspension or inhibition pronounced by any court sitting under the P.W.R. Act is *spiritually* null and void," and a pledge to support any priest who disregarded such a sentence. A "Sustentation Fund" was set up to support priests whose livings had been taken away, and money was raised for the defense of several clergymen already in the courts as a result of the PWRA. The E.C.U. appealed to Tractarian authority and precedent by quoting John Keble's remark at the time of the Gorham judgment, "Let us protest that the Privy Council cannot represent the Church, and that we will not be bound by it; and let us be forward in offering our goods for the support of those whom our Master shall call out from among us, if so be, to suffer for the liberties of the Church."[13] (At the same time, the E.C.U. also carried the distinction between "parishioners" and "communicants" to its logical conclusion, by urging that assemblies of lay communicants be set up, since Parliament itself no longer represented the views of "churchmen.")

The movement was ready. Father Conrad Noel, the genial vicar of St. Barnabas, Oxford, whose hobby was tooth extraction, was told by his friend H. P. Liddon: "My dear Noel, you will have to go to prison, and then all the schoolchildren will give you sugar-plums through the bars."[14]

The "Five Confessors"

In the first four years of the PWRA the Church Association initiated proceedings against seventeen Ritualist clergymen.[15] A typical case was that of the rector of Donhead St. Andrew, whose practices—altar lights, illegal stoles, the mixed chalice, unleavened bread, and so forth—occasioned a representation to the bishop of Salisbury.[16] The rector, Horace Chapman, told the bishop that the complaint had been signed by perhaps eight communicants, some of them only under pressure from local notables like Sir Thomas

Grove. The other signers, he said, included Dissenters and even nonparishioners. Chapman submitted his own petition signed by 103 communicants; he acknowledged that they did not own as many acres as the complainants, but said that some were socially important.

Chapman pointed out that since coming to the parish he had restored the church (without a contribution from Sir Thomas), doubled the number of communicants, quadrupled Sunday school attendance, and begun twice-daily services. He admitted the truth of most of the charges, although he quibbled about a few (he said that he did not elevate the paten and cup above his head). The bishop vetoed the prosecution, but asked the rector to give up the candles and the mixed chalice. Chapman defended the practices, but submitted. The bishop acknowledged his submission and, significantly, added that the mixed chalice was in his opinion a good practice and that it was a "grave misfortune and wrong" that it was forbidden.

Most of the PWRA cases were resolved by this sort of negotiation, a few when clergymen simply capitulated or resigned their benefices. But four cases (and, later, a fifth) proceeded to the end that the Ritualist pamphleteer had envisioned in 1874: imprisonment for contempt.[17]

In January 1877, Arthur Tooth went to jail, where he remained for twenty-eight days, until the promoters of the suit against him intervened to secure his release.[18] In October of 1880, Thomas Pelham Dale of St. Vedast's, Foster Lane, was jailed; a month later, R. W. Enraght of Bordesley, Birmingham, joined him. Pelham Dale and Enraght were released after a few weeks, but when S. F. Green, of St. John's, Miles Platting, Manchester, went to jail in March 1881, he stayed there for over a year and a half. He simply refused to back down, and no one knew how to get him out. The E.C.U. asked the queen to pardon Green, but could not have been distressed when she did not: Father Green was far more useful to the cause in prison than out of it.[19] An Evangelical historian later concluded that "probably no one event in the history of the past half-century has done so much to foster the Romanizing movement, and to injure the Evangelical cause, as the imprisonment of Mr. Green."[20]

In the language of a later generation, the movement "created facts." As the *Church Review* observed, referring to Arthur Tooth, "A minister of Christ has been put in prison in England for his religion in the reign of Queen Victoria. No amount of special pleading can explain away this fact, or qualify it, or put it in another guise."[21]

Apparently many supporters of the PWRA had simply never thought of disobedience as a possibility. When the bishop of Gloucester and Bristol discussed the new act in an 1874 visitation address, for instance, he gave no hint that he expected anyone to disobey it, much less to go to jail; his only fear was that it might lead to secessions, especially to the Old Catholics.[22] A few years later, the complainant in *Martin v. Mackonochie* wrote the bishop of London, "I can only say that when proceedings were originally under-

taken it was understood that their object was simply to ascertain authoritatively the law of the Church on certain points, which, when ascertained,
would be acquiesced in by both sides, and obeyed. It never occurred to me,
nor, I suppose, to anyone else, that the judgements of the courts of law
would be set at defiance, and that obedience could only be enforced by
imprisonment."[23]

"Had such a result been foreseen," Martin went on, "I should not have
allowed my name to be used as promoter." This was not mere tender-heart-
edness on his part. By the time he wrote, there had been what Halifax's
biographer called a remarkable "*volte face* of public opinion." Many who
"had demanded energetic action against Ritualists, ... directly the Ritualists
began to go to prison, demanded their release." This was, he commented
complacently, "all quite illogical and very English."[24]

Be that as it may, the movement viewed its imprisoned firebrands as
martyrs; more important, many others had concluded, illogically or not, that
they were at least victims of injustice. A decade earlier George Rundle
Prynne had observed that "Englishmen are said to have in their characters a
strong sense of justice," that "injustice and persecution generally produce a
reaction in favour of the persecuted," and he had called on his fellow "so-
called Ritualists" to "wait patiently" for that result.[25] By the 1880s, thanks
to the PWRA and the Church Association, it had almost been attained.

It did little good to explain that the "confessors" had been jailed for
their actions in contempt of court, not for their beliefs. As Bishop Jackson
of London later observed, when clergymen are jailed, "public feeling
receives a shock, and sympathy is enlisted on the side of the sufferer. Imprisonment as the result of an ecclesiastical suit *looks* like persecution for religious opinions, and there is at least an apparent incongruity, when a more
severe and degrading penalty is the consequence of a broken rubric, than
would have followed on a moral offense."[26] Late in the game, an opponent
of the movement finally concluded that "to enforce a 'judgment' now may
well try the courage of a Bishop or of any plaintiff. Public opinion is not
convinced, and condemns penalty, suspension, and deprivation."[27]

Some of the older Tractarians had misgivings about this tack; Pusey, for
instance, wrote a friend that the Ritualists' imprudence and lack of consideration for others' legitimate objections meant that "we have no right to
assume that character of suffering merely for truth's sake."[28] But whether
the imprisoned clergymen were entitled to sympathy or not, they received
it—even if it was sometimes tinged with exasperation.

Clerical Opinion

Clerical opinion in particular was sharply divided, as, forced by the PWRA
to choose sides, most High Churchmen chose to stand with their doctrinal
allies, the Anglo-Catholics.[29] When Archbishop Tait asked the clergy in

1880 to let him know what sort of court they wanted, roughly five thousand approved the existing arrangements, but approximately the same number called for tolerance in questions of ritual and urged that the ecclesiastical courts be reformed so as to "secure the conscientious obedience" of High Churchmen.[30]

This surprising level of support represented a substantial victory for the movement, confirming R. F. Littledale's assertion a few years earlier that the Ritualist faction was "a very much larger one than is commonly supposed, not only in its own special numbers, but in its allies."[31] Nowhere in England were Anglo-Catholics a majority, but by the 1880s, if they could enlist the support of moderate High Churchmen, they could rally a near-majority of the Church of England's clergy, and even small majorities in several dioceses.

In greater London, for instance, the proportion of Anglo-Catholic churches had been increasing slowly, but even by a generous definition such churches made up no more than a third of the total by 1880 (and only some five percent were true centers of Ritualism).[32] But another 20 percent or more of London-area churches could be characterized liturgically as "Anglican," or moderate High Church. (At the other end of the spectrum, 25 to 30 percent of London churches were determinedly Evangelical, and the remaining 15 to 20 percent moderately Low Church.)

Elsewhere in England, especially in the North, the Anglo-Catholics' opponents were stronger, but London was not unique. When Christopher Wordsworth, the High Church bishop of Lincoln, polled the clergymen of his diocese in 1875 on a number of the points at issue, he found a similarly close division. Approximately three-quarters responded; of those, 58 percent were willing to tolerate the eastward position and 44 percent some "distinctive vestment" other than the surplice for celebrating the Eucharist.[33]

Plainly, Robert Gregory was correct when he told the lower house of the Convocation of Canterbury in 1881, "If the policy of coercion is to be continued, if every one who determines to use the Vestments ... is to be prosecuted, we shall have to deal with no inconsiderable numbers of our brother clergy."

It is manifest that those who sympathise with these persons form no small portion of the ranks of the clergy of the Church of England. It is quite clear that there are thousands—certainly there are many hundreds—who sympathise with them; men who do not practice the ritual themselves, but who, if those who do are to be put in prison, will feel that the position is intolerable, and will consider themselves called upon to stand by their suffering brethren. If we are to stamp out ritualism to the extent that would be necessary in order to eliminate it from the borders of the Church of England, it will require a very formidable amount of persecution indeed.[34]

The house adopted Canon Gregory's resolution urging the bishops to "discountenance so far as possible legal proceedings in these matters." The bishops, for their part, unanimously resolved that "litigation in matters of ritual is to be deprecated and deplored, and if possible to be avoided"—preferably by the clergy's submitting to the judgments of their bishops.[35]

The political situation was deadlocked.[36] Parliament was unwilling to revise the PWRA, except in ways that would have driven even more clergymen to acts of defiance and put even more of the defiant in jail, though possibly for shorter terms. (A piece of legislation called the Contumacious Clerks Bill, for instance, would have canceled the bishops' veto and restricted imprisonment to six months.[37]) As the Church Association continued to bring new suits, the bishops, sensitive to public opinion and concerned for the peace of the Church, began to use their statutory vetoes more freely. In one of the most significant instances, Archbishop Tait vetoed the proceedings against Charles Lowder of St. Peter's, London Docks, without a single concession from Lowder.

In 1881, Tait denied in the House of Lords that the bishops had agreed to veto ritual cases. For the most part, however, they acted as if they had—with one exception. When charges were brought in 1884 against the Reverend J. Bell-Cox of St. Margaret's, Liverpool, his bishop, J. C. Ryle, formerly an enthusiastic supporter of the Church Association, believed he could not conscientiously employ his veto; to those who objected to "secular courts" he replied, "I have no Court to which I can send it [except the one set up by the PWRA]. When you and your friends can provide me with another Court instead, I shall be happy to use it."[38] Even many prominent Evangelicals opposed the proceedings, but in May 1887 Bell-Cox was imprisoned for sixteen days.

The bishops allowed no more priests to be prosecuted under the PWRA in the nineteenth century. Even the Evangelical Bishop Bickersteth of Exeter used his veto, explaining that "in the present state of the law, I fear that prosecutions in the courts on such matters of ritual only aggravate the evils they are intended to suppress."[39] A few years later, J. A. Froude observed wryly that "this disease [of Ritualism] has not been checked; acrimonious lawsuits promoted by a few antediluvian Protestant parishioners have failed, and will continue to fail, because public opinion refuses to support the promoters; suffering priests ... pose as martyrs, and there is an unwillingness to punish them."[40]

Too Little, Too Late

The failure of the PWRA was not due simply to the illogicality of English public opinion. One observer remarked that "any sort of persecution which falls short of absolute extermination invariably produces the opposite effect to that which is intended," and it may be that he was right, at least in this case.[41] Certainly by the 1870s measures that might have worked well twenty years earlier were no longer suitable.

As we have seen, the situation had changed. The problem was no longer the excesses of individual, innovating clergymen. The clerical party had become a social movement, organized for defense at the national level. Its network of open and semisecret associations could turn a parish conflict into a national cause overnight. The movement's lay supporters included some (like Lord Halifax) with wealth and political influence, and others (like the Church of England Working Men's Society) who implicitly threatened violence and disestablishment.

No change was more important than this growth of lay support. After the PWRA, the Church Association chose to focus its attack on churches where ritual efflorescence was especially egregious and provocative. They could hardly have done otherwise: after all, why attack a clergyman for illegal candles on the altar when incense was being deployed across town? But it was neither accidental nor inconsequential that the highest ritual was usually found in churches with enthusiastically supportive congregations. The cases that went to trial were also almost always those of urban churches, which drew appreciative congregations from across parish lines, and where the disaffected parishioners did not have far to go to find "lower" services.

Bell-Cox's church, for instance, was a new one, with only a nominal parish; it had been founded expressly to serve Liverpool Anglo-Catholics. In London, Charles Lowder's church was a former mission and a model of congregational involvement. Mackonochie's congregation at St. Alban's, Holborn, even produced a petition in 1874 asserting that "the ritual that has been gradually developed has been requested at each successive stage by the laity, so that there is no pretence for saying that it has been forced upon an unwilling congregation," and asking "only that liberty and toleration which is extended to all other schools in the Church."[42]

Moreover, in most of the churches involved, high ritual was an established fact—often long-established: the Church Association was no longer attacking innovations. Some years before, John Bacchus Dykes had prophesied:

People will become as used to the sight of a Chasuble as to a surplice, to a Cope as to a black gown, to a coloured stole as to a funeral scarf. They will begin to like beauty as well as ugliness, cleanliness as well as squalor; to be no more frightened at the sight of a Cross than of the Ten Commandments, of a stately Altar than of a stately Pulpit, of the sculptured figures of Saints, than of the superstitious images of the Lion and Unicorn; they will learn to think it no more strange to see a clergyman turning *from* them when addressing God, than turning *to* them, when reading or preaching to themselves.[43]

That was not yet true of the Church of England as a whole, but it was true for many of its congregations. This gave the Ritualists a new debating point: as Dean Liddon observed, "the practical difficulty of giving up a beautiful and elaborate ceremonial, associated in thousands of devout minds with recognition of Truth and with inward reverence and love, is so great as to be almost insuperable."[44] W. J. E. Bennett even put a new twist on an old argument, remarking that "to abolish or mutilate ceremonial observances to which the eye has been accustomed, cannot pass unobserved by the most illiterate."[45]

The ground had shifted. Once the Church Association had defended the rights of congregations to worship in their accustomed way; now it wished to prevent Anglo-Catholic congregations from worshipping in theirs. Once ultrarubricians had insisted on obeying the Prayer Book despite their congregations' wishes; now an Evangelical protested that "neither a majority of the congregation, nor the whole congregation, have any right, moral or legal, ... to influence the minister to gratify their personal prejudice or tastes. The Book of Common Prayer has settled that question."[46] Memorials to bishops had once complained about strange and unwelcome practices forced on unwilling congregations; now one complained that "from every quarter large numbers [are] attracted by the peculiarity of the Service"—this at fashionable Christ Church, Clifton.[47]

Common Sense on Ritualism

True, from the memorialists' point of view, what was found at Christ Church was "doctrine and ritual at once unscriptural and disallowed by the Church of England," but that complaint was getting stale. As J. C. Ryle (not yet bishop of Liverpool) lamented in 1877, "Many now-a-days regard the subject of Popery as a 'bore.'"[48]

Ryle was right. He went on to complain that many "well-meaning and simple-minded Churchmen" believed it "unkind and naughty to interfere with such earnest, devoted men" as the Ritualists, and to regret that the Church Association had become "very unpopular, and greatly disliked in many quarters," "too often regarded as a mischievous, intolerant, persecuting body."

He was right about that, too. In 1877, an anonymous author produced a fictional dialogue that laid out the various views of Ritualism then current. The spokesman for common sense in this exchange observed that the prosecutions had "made the Act appear as an engine of persecution, instead of a vindication of the rights of justly aggrieved parishioners," adding that "it is such an obviously unfair thing to put every parish clergyman at the mercy of any three ill-conditioned people who may happen to live in his parish." (The author seems to have been a clergyman, and thus perhaps more sensitive on this point than most laymen.)

The character tells an anti-Ritualist that he would have seen no harm in the PWRA if it had only been used "to restrain the clergy from unauthorized and unpopular changes."

But you have begun at the wrong end. You have commenced by attacking churches with a long-established ritual, and with congregations deeply attached to it, who have felt their liberty to worship according to their conscience assailed through their clergyman. And whether anti-Ritualists believe it or not, the laity in these congregations are very often more attached to the ritual than the clergy.... And then, instead of interfering in cases where the dissatisfied were unable to attend another church, you have begun with churches in great centres of population, where the objectors had only to go into the next street to get exactly what they wanted.[49]

Even confession, the sticking point for many of the movement's opponents, had few terrors for this man. "Among the degraded, the badly brought-up, and even among those who crave for guidance, it will usually do more good than harm," he argued; "and as long as Englishmen and Englishwomen possess common sense, it is never likely to become universal."[50] In the year of the *Priest in Absolution* controversy, this character was probably more tolerant than most English laymen, but some at least had come to share his views, and more would in time.

Many simply concluded that toleration was preferable to continued strife. In 1880, for instance, Lord Selbourne wrote that, despite his personal distaste for Ritualism, he was ready to put up with it "for the sake of peace in the Church and to prevent the evils which I should apprehend from Disestablishment." Later, Selbourne wrote that it was better to tolerate Ritualists "than either to break up the Church, or to drive out of it [those] who are otherwise good men, good Christians, and doing good work." As for the law, he said, "they have too strong a body of opinion on their side ... to make the strict enforcement against them of the law which they refuse to obey practicable, if it were expedient."[51]

And those who had always tried to resolve differences by obscuring them were still trying. The bishop of Winchester, for example, wrote that much of the dispute was merely about *words*, that the two sides understood phrases like "Real Presence" and "sacrifice" differently. "Let us agree," the bishop said, "that neither vestments nor attitude have in themselves any doctrinal meaning whatever—and this is the only common-sense view of the matter, the only view that can be taken by reasonable men."[52] As statements of fact, these were dubious propositions, but many were ready to entertain them for the sake of peace.

By 1880 several bishops had become more outspoken for toleration than for conformity. Christopher Wordsworth of Lincoln, whose survey we looked at earlier, opposed the PWRA, and was ready to allow both the eastward position and eucharistic vestments.[53] In a charge of 1879 he concluded that the Ornaments Rubric rendered the vestments "Legal, But Not Obligatory."[54] (His conclusion was notable especially for the fact that he reached it with no reference at all to the Purchas and Ridsdale judgments.)

The bishop of Ely told some anti-Ritualist clergymen in his diocese that the Ritualists were not simply "a few ignorant fanatics breaking the peace of a great community by individual eccentricities," but rather "part of a vast religious movement which has made itself felt through the whole Anglican Communion at home and abroad." It was a mistake to go to law, he said.

> The Church of England cannot, without violence to her character as a National and Historical Church, refuse to find place for that section of her members which, although embracing many shades of feeling and practice, is comprehended under the term "Ritualists." To crush or drive out (if it were possible) a body consisting of both laity and clergy which has manifested not only a love of high ceremonial, but a fervent zeal for the spiritual welfare of the people, which has succeeded in awakening a sense of religion and a love for the ordinances of Christ among classes of the population which the English Church had utterly failed to reach, would inevitably be followed by a feeling of discouragement issuing in utter spiritual apathy.[55]

The new, irenic approach of these bishops was echoed by many parish clergymen. The rector of East Bergholt, for instance, wrote in 1881 that "even among those who practise eccentricities of which most of us would disapprove, the number who hold doctrinal views which may not loyally be held by Churchman [sic] is extremely small. Deduct those who act from a mere sentimental affection for antiquity or mere aesthetic predilections, and the residuum of disloyalty will certainly not be large."[56]

From the no-popery point of view, this attitude was either disingenuous or naive, but its currency suggested that middle-of-the-road Anglicans' definition of doctrinal views that could loyally be held by churchmen was changing. Even the vicar of St. Giles, Durham, author of *Hearty Services* and a man who described himself as "neutral with Evangelical leanings," wrote that although he did "not for a moment contend that *all* the members of the Ritualist Party are loyal and true men," nevertheless "the Party *as a whole*" was "loyal and devoted," and thus "fully entitled to [a] carefully limited measure of toleration." He said that "the attacking party have lost their heads," and went to scripture for Gamaliel's wait-and-see advice about Christianity, a text increasingly cited in this context.[57]

By the 1890s, this had become the dominant view among the clergy. The vicar of Humberstone, Leicester, for instance, a self-described "moderate" who took pains to deny the doctrine of the Real Presence, acknowledged that "almost any doctrine on the Sacrament short of Transubstantiation" seemed to be legitimate in the Church of England, and that therefore the Ritualists were as entitled to toleration as anyone else.[58] And the vicar of St. Mary's, Huntingdon, himself a "liberal Broad Churchman," wrote to a parishioner that "the High Churchman has, as I think, deserved to win. Very patiently, very courageously has he worked. Most of the opposition he has met with has been fatuous to the last degree. The High Church position is very largely warranted by our Church's formularies. It is, so it seems to me, only malice and ignorance that can determine otherwise."[59]

In 1895, the archbishop of York reflected this new clerical consensus when he wrote some aggrieved parishioners of Christ Church, Doncaster, including the mayor and the head of the family that had built the church, to say that he had attended to their complaints. But he went on to urge that the aggrieved, "in the spirit of true Christian charity, ... endeavour to put the most favourable construction on the actions of your clergy, even if you should feel it more profitable for yourselves to worship in some of the other churches which are close beside you in the town of Doncaster."[60]

Moderate Evangelicals

In the wake of the PWRA, even many Evangelicals began to take a more conciliatory approach. They may still have disliked and feared Anglo-Catholicism, but they had at least come to agree with one of their number who had written in 1868 that, although toleration might be "a sad evil—a great undoing of the mighty work of the Reformation," Ritualism was an "accomplished fact"; that, "for better or worse it must in future claim its place of importance in the Protesting community."[61] By the 1880s the leaders of the Evangelical party were treating Anglo-Catholics less as enemies than as competitors, sometimes even as colleagues. A gradual acceptance of Anglo-Catholicism, or at least a determination to combat it by means other than prosecution, had spread to affect nearly all but the most extreme Low Church clergy.

The "neo-Evangelicals," as the newly moderate were called, even began to borrow from their adversaries.[62] As early as 1868 A. W. Thorold had written in the *Contemporary Review* that "to confound good music or even a surpliced choir with either Romanism or Ritualism is foolish."[63] By 1880, E. H. Bickersteth, then dean of Lichfield, subsequently bishop of Exeter, was urging Evangelicals to adopt such Anglo-Catholic innovations as harvest festivals and the Three Hours' devotion on Good Friday, if congregations wanted them.[64] Bickersteth also found nothing objectionable in fasting, the weekday offices, observing all the Prayer Book holidays, and a number of other practices that would once have been suspect because of their Tractarian sponsorship.

Three years earlier Bickersteth had published a pamphlet called *Counsels of Peace*. It was remarkable primarily for its charitable tone. Bickersteth acknowledged the "deplorable condition" of the Church before the Oxford Movement, and praised "the effort, inspired (can we doubt it?) by the Holy Spirit, to recover what we had lost, or, at all events, to strengthen what remained." Within a context of sober and temperate opposition to "foreign usages [which] have too frequently been made the vehicle of corrupt teaching, which our Church repudiated at the Reformation," he allowed that differences were unavoidable in a comprehensive national church and urged "kind constructions of the opinions or practice of others," for "the sake of the great interests which are at stake, and which infinitely outweigh the question of a posture or a vestment."[65]

That same year, J. C. Ryle, still vicar of Stradbroke, Suffolk, and not yet bishop of Liverpool, was still saying that "Ritualism is the highway to Rome," and calling on all Evangelicals to "beware of Ritualism, and to do all you can to resist it"—in particular, to support the Church Association. The Ritualists' "ceremonial novelties," he said, "have *all* been as un-Protestant as possible": they were "*all* borrowed or imitated from Popery," and these "mischievous Popish revivals" have "*all* shown one common systematic determination to un-Protestantize, as far as possible, the simple worship of the poor old Church of England, and to assimilate it as far as possible to the gaudy, theatrical, and sensuous worship of Popery."[66] But the next year even Ryle was protesting the "*unwillingness of some to allow that any truth is preached, or any good done, except by Evangelical clergymen* and members of our own school."[67]

Soon after that, the Islington Clerical Meeting, a center of Evangelical influence since its founding in the 1820s, denounced the prosecutions of Ritualists under the PWRA.[68] At the same time, the principal Evangelical newspapers, faced with declining circulations, adopted a new, moderate tone.[69] The once doggedly anti-Ritualist *Record* became a sober four-penny weekly on the lines of the High Church *Guardian* and began to oppose litigation as counterproductive.[70] Even the firebreathing *Rock* came under the control of moderates, which prompted the remaining ultras to acquire the *English Churchman* for their organ. A number of Evangelical organizations began a process of consolidation that would finally result in the National Protestant Church Union (subsequently renamed the National Church League), a body whose principal purpose was education, not defense.[71]

Only a few years later the *Record* could be found arguing that "the repression of illegal practices is the duty of the authorities; their responsibility will be more readily recognized and more easily discharged when it is not attempted to be shared by volunteers."[72] In another article, the newspaper observed that "it became obvious years ago that Evangelical Churchmen as a body were not in sympathy with the Church Association."[73]

Given these developments, it is not surprising to find the Church Association's *Report* lamenting "the waning love and dubious attitude of once familiar friends."[74] In 1880, James Bateman, a member of the Church Association's council, blamed its problems not only on the "timidity, vacillation, and unfaithfulness of the Bishops," but also on the "half-heartedness of a considerable number of the Evangelical Clergy," which was due, he said, to the "deleterious influence of Church Congresses."[75]

Church congresses were an old sore spot for some Low Churchmen, many of whom had boycotted them in the early years.[76] After 1866, however, with the backing of other Evangelical leaders, J. C. Ryle had attended, to uphold Low Church principles. When the *Rock* denounced him for it, Ryle brought the matter up at a Church Association meeting in 1869 and carried his point.[77] After that Evangelical attendance was substantial, but ultra-Protestants still objected. When Ryle served on a panel to discuss the best way of "promoting united action and mutual toleration between different schools of thought within the Church," for instance, some members of his party observed that the panel begged the question of whether action with and toleration of "sceptics and Romanizers" was desirable.[78]

Bateman took an especially dark view of what happened at these meetings. Evangelicals who attended them, he said, associated with "law-breaking, wafer-worshiping" Anglo-Catholics, and caught "the plague of sacerdotalism, which is quite as contagious as the measles or the small-pox."[79] They "become 'churchy,' and speak of 'The Church,'" and "not a few of those who go to Congress as 'ministers' return as 'priests.'" Some even began to call themselves "*moderate* High Churchmen." ("As well might we speak of 'moderate chastity' as of 'moderate High Churchism.'")

No doubt Bateman exaggerated, but it is clear that Church congresses did, in time, promote civil discourse among the contending factions. On one occasion Ryle did not deliver an anti-Ritualist address that he had prepared, saying that the "deep religious feeling and loving kindness which pervaded the Congress" made it inappropriate.[80] The *Church Times* observed that at the Leicester Congress of 1880, despite such potential irritants as a speech by Canon King on the faithful departed, "the language of the Catholic School appeared to cause not the slightest uneasiness." The *Morning Post* complained of "the tiresome monotony" of the same gathering, "at which all the speakers seemed to be in a conspiracy to use none but conciliatory language toward their opponents, and to order themselves decently and reverently towards their betters."[81]

It may be significant that the proportion of London churches with evening communion services peaked at 32 percent in 1882; thirteen years later only 22 percent had such services.[82] Evening communion had always been as much a symbolic weapon as a service of worship, and for whatever reason—cooptation by the leaders of the Church, the failure of repression, their party's declining influence, even Christian charity—many Evangelicals, including most of the party's clerical leaders, were losing their combative zeal. They had evidently come to a conclusion expressed a few years later by the *Record*, namely that "it is by doing good, rather than preventing evil, that the Evangelical body exerts a real influence in the Church."[83]

No-Popery's Last Stand

The opposition to Anglo-Catholicism had always included the no-popery zealots that Henley Henson was later to call "the Protestant underworld," but they had been curbed, or at least overshadowed, by influential and relatively sober figures like Ryle and Bickersteth and Lord Shaftesbury. Now that the leading Evangelicals were making peace with Anglo-Catholicism and many members of the public were concluding that common sense dictated toleration, the extremists were increasingly on their own.

Anti-Ritualist activities did not cease (quite the contrary), but they became even more intemperate, and may have served primarily to alienate the commonsense majority. The Birmingham *Daily Post*, for example, had no use for Ritualism, but after quoting from a number of immoderate or unintelligible speeches to a Church Association meeting, it observed that "such speeches ... are much more calculated to help the Ritualists than to hurt them."[84] When a Church Association pamphlet in the 1890s warned Englishmen about the priestly boast, "I have your god in my hand, and your wife at my feet," one could anticipate Henson's remark from the 1920s: "I do not desire for that party anything worse than a keener interest in the things of the mind, and a more adequate sense of humour."[85]

The outright loonies were as active as ever. At St. Paul's Cathedral on Easter Eve of 1883, according to H. P. Liddon, one of them, a "well-dressed man,"

rushed into the choir during the anthem, then put his hat on, ran at an astonishing pace, jumped catwise upon the altar and in a moment had dashed the Cross, Candles, flowers, etc., on the floor of the Sanctuary. He was pursued by a little crowd of persons, surpliced and unsurpliced, who with zeal and difficulty got hold of him by various limbs and gave him up to the Police. Among his captors was Canon Gregory, ... who, as the man was shouting "Protestants to the rescue," at the top of his voice, put his pocket-handkerchief with great decision into his mouth. Altogether the scene was astonishing.[86]

Some who confined their activities to print were no less outlandish. A Norfolk clergyman, for instance, wrote an open letter to let Parliament know that some members of the Society of the Holy Cross were the illegitimate children of monks and nuns, raised as Jesuits and sent covertly to English public schools. (Two of them were at Charterhouse when he was there, he said.) He also claimed that Archbishop Benson was "either knowingly the willing agent, or unknowingly the efficient tool of the Jesuits and the Church of Rome."[87]

This man was peculiar by any standard, but even those no-popery activists who were not actually deranged tended toward his conspiratorial view of ecclesiastical politics. Their grim, uncompromising lack of judgment became even more evident, and their confrontational tactics even less productive, as they lost ground steadily during the 1880s and 1890s. Three episodes were particularly telling.

In the first, in 1879, a consecrated wafer was taken from the altar of

Father Enraght's church and introduced as evidence in court, where it was marked with pen and ink, and filed.[88] Even many Englishmen who did not share the Anglo-Catholic conviction about what—or What—had been abducted regarded the act as unbecoming and ungentlemanly, and Anglo-Catholics were understandably outraged. After three months of continual clamor about the "Bordesley Sacrilege," the Host was turned over to Archbishop Tait; when he reverently consumed it, there was a special service of thanksgiving, with a solemn Te Deum, at St. Faith's, Stoke Newington.[89]

In 1888, an ornate marble reredos was installed behind the altar at St. Paul's Cathedral. Designed by a prominent ecclesiastical architect, its central crucifix—the largest in any Church of England place of worship since the Reformation—was not exactly what the chapter or Dean Liddon had had in mind, but the dean had come to think it appropriate.[90] One retired clergyman promptly denounced the "image-worshippers" at St. Paul's, and the Church Association filed suit under the PWRA, charging that "the Image of the Blessed Virgin Mary and Child and the Crucifix at St. Paul's Cathedral tend, and each of them tends, to encourage ideas and devotions of an unauthorized, idolatrous, and superstitious kind."[91]

The suit was vetoed by Bishop Temple of London, and when his right to veto was challenged, it was upheld unanimously by the House of Lords. Legally, Owen Chadwick has observed, this meant that "even if a bishop thought that a law was being broken, he might still refuse leave to prosecute considering the general circumstances; and the general circumstances include the undesirable nature of litigation on such a subject."[92] Politically, it meant that Anglo-Catholicism was thoroughly entrenched, with powerful defenders; opponents of the movement were now the marginalized outsiders.

That point was made again, and decisively, when the Church Association brought charges in 1888 against Edward King, the bishop of Lincoln, not for using his veto, but for his own ritual irregularities.[93] The charges were relatively minor: the eastward position, lighted altar candles, the mixed chalice, the sign of the cross in absolution and blessing, and the like. King, the first Anglican bishop since the Reformation to wear a mitre, also wore eucharistic vestments in churches where their use was customary.[94] He was decidedly an Anglo-Catholic, but not a thoroughgoing Ritualist, and he was a saintly man, beloved in his diocese and widely respected by other churchmen. During the proceedings, one of King's opponents observed that only two bishops had commented publicly on the case, both of them only to praise King's character, and he remarked bitterly that "it is no doubt a delicate matter to condemn a brother prelate."[95] Certainly it was a delicate matter to condemn this one.

Archbishop Benson evoked an ancient precedent to convene his own "court," a procedure approved by the Judicial Committee, although Bishop Stubbs of Oxford remarked that "it is not a Court; it is an Archbishop sitting in his library."[96] Benson asked King to discontinue the sign of the cross and using the mixed chalice, but acquitted him on the other charges in what everyone recognized was a victory for Anglo-Catholicism. The *Church Times* remarked that the archbishop of Canterbury appeared to be making "considerable progress in the acceptance of Catholic truth."[97] In 1892 the substance of the decision was upheld by the Judicial Committee, and the relatively permissive Lincoln judgment itself became a precedent.[98]

Left with no recourse in the courts and little sympathy from the ecclesiastical establishment, the Church Association ceased its prosecutions and was reduced to petulance. Its pamphlets of "Advice to Protestants" began to include such items as "Don't stand up when choir boys march into church" and "Don't accept ... wafers of gluten bread."[99] The struggle was over, and the Anglo-Catholics had won the right to worship as they pleased.

True, not all of their opponents recognized that. The next fifteen years saw renewed disruption of Anglo-Catholic services, this time by John Kensit and his Protestant Truth Society.[100] Walter Walsh's *Secret History of the Oxford Movement* was published in 1897 and went through several printings; many were genuinely shocked by its revelations of semicovert Romanizing. In the House of Commons, Sir William Harcourt and others denounced both Ritualism and tolerant bishops, and in 1903 a hundred M.P.s waited on the new archbishop of Canterbury to demand that he do something.

But what the archbishop did was to calm the situation by appointing another royal commission. When the commission reported in 1906, after 118 meetings, its 1524 pages of evidence, gathered from 8689 of the Church of England's roughly 14,000 benefices, revealed that a third were tainted by some illegality (41 percent, if the eastward position is included), and it concluded that, "as thousands of clergy, with strong lay support, refuse to recognize the jurisdiction of the Judicial Committee, its judgments cannot effectively be enforced."[101] The commission's report had no discernable effect on Anglo-Catholic practice.

"The Tendency of Modern Intelligence"

Andrew Martin Fairbairn, a Congregationalist and one of the first historians of the movement, summarized its story this way:

In 1833 the first issue of the *Tracts* began, breathing the courage, defiance, and furious despair of a forlorn hope. In 1890 the men who have replaced the old leaders are within the citadel, victorious, proposing their own terms of peace. It were a curious question, why, in what is fancied to be a critical and sceptical age, so extraordinary a revolution has been achieved.[102]

Ironically, however, the skeptical nature of the age contributed to the movement's victory. By the turn of the century, it should have been clear that British public opinion had been largely enlisted on behalf of toleration, but this was not altogether—perhaps not even mostly—for reasons pleasing or complimentary to Anglo-Catholics.

As his title indicates, for instance, the anonymous author of *Bombastes Religioso or The Protestant Pope of 1899* did not so much appreciate Anglo-Catholicism as despise its opponents. Deprecating equally "enthusiasts on the one side and bigots on the other," he said that "an overwhelming majority of the English people [were] perfectly well satisfied to live and let live, and they care no more what amount of ritual is permitted in any given place of worship within the Queen's dominions than they care how many times the Sultan of Turkey prostrates himself next Friday."

He defended Ritualism against the then-current agitation explicitly "on the ground of common sense—for it is utterly senseless and stupid to interfere with any man's religion." "The whole tendency of modern intelligence and enlightenment and common sense—perhaps one should add of modern indifference—is flatly opposed to any interference with any man's religion, upon any pretence whatever," he continued. "Bigotry is the attitude of a savage, and intolerance the temper of a fool."

He also defended Ritualism "on the ground of simple justice" (tracing its growth, he called it "ungenerous and untrue to pretend that the clergy are one atom more responsible for this phenomenal development than the laity") and "on the ground of British dignity and independence," because it was absurd to think that the pope was a threat to England.

"To read the daily papers," he wrote, "one would imagine that the whole country was stirred to its very depths by the exposure of Papal intrigues, and that a great Protestant nation was on the point of rising as one man in defence of the fondly cherished principles of the glorious Reformation." But he detected not the "faintest sign of any such excitement or commotion." Like many others, he said, he was bored by the subject.

As a matter of fact, everybody is thoroughly sick of the whole controversy, and would welcome Home Rule, or another Fashoda incident, or even so silly a thing as a Peace Conference, for the sake of getting rid of it. Only stump orators and agitators, and played-out politicians in search of an opportunity, have any wish that the discussion should be prolonged.

So he urged that the Ritualists be left alone. "Let a handful of foolish Romanizers play their foolish pranks, and we can afford to look on and laugh at them," he said. "The best way to treat these harmless lunatics is to give them rope enough, and let them stumble onwards to their own confusion.... The *worst* way to treat them, beyond all question, is to make their absurdities the excuse for a senseless cry of 'No Popery'."[103]

That many had come to share this view represented a sort of victory for the movement.

The Irony of
Anglo-Catholicism

In 1879, in the preface to the fourth edition of the eucharistic manual *Directorium Anglicanum*, the Reverend F. G. Lee observed that "the Catholic type of service ... is now quite common and current in the Established Church," that the "high standard of previous centuries" had actually been reached in every diocese, and that, "at length," Church authorities "tacitly approve." He added, "The few points still in dispute, as past experience teaches, many be easily won by zeal, patience, and determination."[1]

As if taking this advice to heart, "advanced" Anglo-Catholics continued to advance throughout the last decades of the century, and after the Lincoln judgment the pace accelerated. By 1895 eucharistic vestments were being worn in 142 London churches, more than one out of every eight.[2] Meanwhile, the Ritualist pacesetters were inexorably pursuing the logic that led the bishop of London to complain that "almost every doctrine and practice is [being] reproduced which at the Reformation was renounced and laid aside":

Seven Sacraments are again taught; prayers for the dead, not without reference to Purgatory, practised and supplied; the invocation of the Virgin and of Saints recommended and introduced both in hymns and manuals of devotion; a doctrine of the Real Presence in the Eucharist maintained, which but verbally, if verbally, differs from Transubstantiation; and Auricular Confession explained in accordance with the definitions of Trent, and enforced as essential to peace and pardon on all who would live holily and die happily.[3]

Close behind the pioneers came the great central bulk of the movement, as represented by the English Church Union. Progress was being made on all of the points about which the bishop complained, but one example will suffice. When the archbishop of Canterbury wrote in 1870 to Greek Orthodox authorities (who had approached him on the subject) that the Church of England does not pray for the dead, the E.C.U., many of whose members did just that, protested vigorously.[4] In 1885 the Union held its first annual solemn requiem Mass for departed members, at St. Mary Magdalene's, Munster Square; seven years after that, the annual report of the Guild of All Souls listed 328 churches that offered Mass for the departed at least monthly.[5]

Despite the PWRA and the ensuing prosecutions, despite the furor and temporary setback over *The Priest in Absolution*, the Ritualist vanguard never lost sight of higher things. In a marvelously (if unintendedly) insouciant gesture, just as the PWRA was going into effect in 1875, the Society of the Holy Cross recommended to its members "the general rule of Western Christendom, which has since become a practice in these Provinces and is now printed in Church Calendars, that when Lady Day falls in Holy Week its observance should be transferred until the Octave of Easter."[6]

"Private Judgment in Gorgeous Raiment"

Beneath this apparent continuity, however, the movement had changed in many ways.[7] Almost without noticing, for instance, it had lowered its sights. Anglo-Catholics still pined for the reunion of Christendom, but they no longer seriously sought a unified, "Catholic" Church of England. They said their beliefs were those of the Church, but had become content to see them tolerated as the mark of a party.[8]

It had not always been so. The Tractarians were champions of doctrinal orthodoxy, and their ultrarubrician followers extended the principle of conformity and regularity to the worship of the Church. True to this heritage, the English Church Union in its first years appealed to Parliament for a law "to facilitate the bringing to trial of priests for heresy and breaches of Church discipline" and protested the "profanation of public worship," specifically by "the consorting of certain clergymen of the Church of England with Dissenting preachers in the use of theatres for public worship in London and elsewhere."[9]

But the Gorham decision had implicitly sanctioned doctrinal pluralism, and those Anglo-Catholics who remained in the Church of England had accepted that, if sometimes grudgingly. Pusey remarked, "It is one thing under an emergency to bear, for love's sake, with those who believe or teach erroneously, lest a greater evil should ensue; quite another that it should be declared that the Church meant, in an article of the faith, to leave it as an open question, for the priests to believe and teach, as they, in their individual opinions, held to be right."[10] Nevertheless, as one critic put it at the time, all parties had effectively agreed "to abandon zeal for the faith of the Church, if they are but allowed to exhibit zeal for their own faith."[11]

Moreover, as Anglo-Catholics ventured beyond the liturgical constraints of the rubrics and the doctrinal bounds of the Thirty-Nine Articles, and especially as it became clear that any move toward uniformity would likely be at their expense, they began to see the advantages of pluralism. Increasingly, Anglo-Catholics insisted that all they asked was "tolerance and forbearance" for themselves.[12] As early as 1867, for example, the Reverend Charles Walker had urged that Anglo-Catholic congregations be allowed to use their own "Directorium" and that other congregations be released from any obligation to observe the Ornaments Rubric, suggesting to the Royal Commission on Ritual that peace could be found in the recognition *"that the National Establishment embraces in its bosom two separate religions."*[13] Soon after the PWRA went into effect, another Anglo-Catholic asserted that "we only claim for ourselves liberty of conformity [to law and Catholic tradition], whilst we are willing to cede to the utmost to others an inherited liberty of non-conformity."[14] This appeal for toleration became increasingly effective when clergymen started going to jail, as we saw, and in time the efforts of Anglo-Catholics effectively extended the Church's new pluralism to include ceremonial.

A movement that originally championed orthodoxy had come to defend freedom; begun in opposition to religious liberalism, the movement now appealed to liberal values for its survival. Cardinal Manning, once an Anglo-Catholic clergyman himself, saw the irony, and maintained that "Ritualism is private judgment in gorgeous raiment, wrought about with divers colours." He declared that "every fringe in an elaborate cope worn without authority is only a distinct and separate act of private judgment; the more elaborate, the less Catholic; the nearer the imitation, the further from the submission of faith."[15] Although some denied it, Manning had a point.

The "Anglo" in Anglo-Catholicism

Not all Anglo-Catholics denied it. Although most still paid lip service to authority, some were beginning to speak out for individual rights. Sabine Baring-Gould, for one, declared in 1872 that "Rome is as bad as Geneva. The latter denies truths, the former denies rights. We want, and will have, both truths and rights."[16] Baring-Gould's observation was an early outcropping of the "liberal Catholicism" later associated with Charles Gore and *Lux Mundi*, a development that would trouble and divide the movement in the 1890s.[17]

It also illustrated the movement's decreasing tenderness toward Roman Catholicism. Anglo-Catholics' attempts to explain why they were not Romanists had often done little to calm the fears of English Protestants. One pamphlet, for instance, pointed out that devotions to the Sacred Heart of

Jesus in an Anglo-Catholic manual were directed to *Jesus*, not to *the heart*, as in Roman practice, and although Anglo-Catholics asked God for the prayers of the saints, saints were not *invoked* (that is, addressed directly).[18] It is fair to say that most Anglo-Catholics were, if not Romanists, at least anti-anti-Romanists.[19] In 1865, the English Church Union voted a resolution expressing a pious hope for the reunion of Christendom; when the Reverend Archer Gurney proposed an amendment critical of the Roman Church, he was shouted down and his amendment received only three votes.[20]

The movement would always include an "Anglo-papal" element, and attempts to rein it in—which included two royal commissions and twenty-two bills in Parliament between 1880 and 1906—would never be successful. But especially after the definition of the doctrine of papal infallibility in 1870, some prominent figures in the movement began to give greater emphasis to the "Anglo" in Anglo-Catholicism, and the extremists were increasingly isolated. By 1887, for example, the *Church Times* had become sufficiently anti-Roman that one brother of the S.S.C. privately accused it of supporting "the ritualistic Protestant," while portraying "Catholics as a tiny sect."[21] But that is what his sort of Catholics had always been.

Perhaps the most surprising anti-Romanist was R. F. Littledale, fervent Anglo-Catholic, brother of the Society of the Holy Cross—and, at least in print, an increasingly jingoistic British patriot. Implicitly responding to the charge that Anglo-Catholicism was "un-English," Littledale argued in widely-read pamphlets like *Why Ritualists Do Not Become Roman Catholics* and *Ritualists not Romanists* that the Church of England as a national church bore more resemblance to Eastern Orthodoxy than to Roman Catholicism.[22] (Characteristically, Littledale turned his new Englishness against old enemies: if Protestant doctrines were true, he wrote, then "it would be the bounden duty of the whole English people to sit at the feet even of foreigners and learn them, as many have been content to do."[23])

Liturgically, too, there was an attempt to turn to native models. Littledale was one of a dozen Anglo-Catholic elders who undertook to "moderate ... the evil of unnecessary Diversity in Ritual, as practised in various Churches aiming at the maintenance of Catholic doctrine and usage in the Church of England" by issuing a set of recommendations for worship.[24]

The movement's Romanizers opposed this project from the outset. Father Mackonochie spoke for many of them when he wrote a friend to say that such a conference "would be very desirable when peace is established." Meanwhile, he wrote, "I doubt whether the ground is not being better broken up for a final order, by the irregular and often mistaken efforts of individuals—however eccentric—than by a too hasty effort at organization." Mackonochie appealed to the movement's history, concluding that "the time will come for rule and discipline, and the sooner the better if the ground has been sufficiently broke."[25]

Nevertheless, the group assembled at All Saints, Margaret Street, for forty-eight meetings in the course of 1880 and 1881. Besides Littledale, it included Thomas W. Perry, the Ritualists' representative on the Ritual Commission in the 1860s, and Christopher Wordsworth, the bishop of Lincoln. Most participants were members of the E.C.U.; Littledale and two others were brothers of the S.S.C.[26]

Although the conference refused to take "legal decisions" (the quotation marks were in its report) as "guides or helps," relying instead on "true and loyal adherence to the spirit of the Prayer-Book," while avoiding dependence on "the mere abstract meaning of the words employed, without any reference to the circumstances under which the book had been written," its recommendations were unmistakably moderate and "Anglican." The group concluded, for example, that one should only incline the "head and body" at the words "and was incarnate" in the Nicene Creed, since "ancient English precedent furnishes no defence for prostration, or such exaggerated marks of reverence." The report garnered the support of a number of distinguished Anglo-Catholic laymen and clergy (among them Archdeacon Denison), but there is no indication that it had any effect on the practice of Mackonochie and his fellow innovators.

Middle-class Anglo-Catholics

Perhaps the most surprising change of all was the growing support for Anglo-Catholicism among the middle classes. In the 1860s, Ritualism was (as a contemporary critic wrote) "Puseyism dressed up to suit the tastes and to attract the attention alike of the gay and frivolous classes on the one hand and of the mob on the other," but by the Oxford Movement's semicentennial in the 1880s it was becoming evident that its future lay elsewhere.[27]

Anglo-Catholicism was penetrating the middle classes from both directions: both trickling down from the "frivolous classes" and percolating up from the "mob." Sir William Harcourt once challenged the Anglo-Catholics to show him a Ritualistic grocer, regarding such a creature as almost a contradiction in terms, but by the 1890s that idea did not seem very outlandish.[28] In her novel *David Grieve* (1892), for instance, Mrs. Humphry Ward showed how the daughter of a small tradesman took up Ritualism to escape the drab environment of Manchester.[29] Meanwhile, although the personalities, good works, and radical politics of individual priests and sisters attracted some of the "undeserving poor" whom Father Stanton loved, those who responded to Ritualism as such were more often young men and women who aspired to be, and almost were, of the lower-middle class. One observer indicated as much when he appealed for tolerance by arguing that "clerks and milliners' apprentices have souls, and they are better at a Ritualistic Church than at a music hall or a dancing saloon."[30] Michael Fane's friend the bank clerk, in *Sinister Street*, was apparently not unusual.

Nowhere was the growing middle-class support for Anglo-Catholicism more evident than in London's new suburbs, both north and south of the Thames. By 1882, a third of London's Ritualist churches formed a ring near or beyond the outskirts of the city.[31]

The Ritualist churches of South London ran virtually the entire gamut of middle-class possibilities. By the 1880s, some, like St. Peter's, Vauxhall, and F. G. Lee's church of All Saints', Lambeth, had seen better days. St. Peter's adjoined the London Gas Works; All Saints was on the river, its parish bisected by railway yards; both were in slums as unpleasant as anything East London had to offer. Nearby, and slightly up the social scale, was Christ Church, Clapham, long a center of advanced ritual, boasting that it was one of the first London churches to use the eucharistic vestments. In the 1890s Christ Church's services attracted what Booth called "Kensit riots and other strenuous forms of public notice."[32] Cut off from more well-to-do areas by the London and South West Railway, by the end of the century Christ Church had become "poorer than it looks."[33]

To the south, rapid population movement had first created and then transformed the neighborhood of St. John the Divine, begun as a mission amid brickfields and strawberry beds in the 1860s. Thirty years later, the vicar, ten curates, a nurse, and eight sisters served a parish of "doctors, shop-keepers, theatrical and musical people, much shabby gentility and many lodgers; medical students; clerks, artisans and some labourers."[34] The neighboring parish of St. Agnes was similar. Like Christ Church, Clapham, on Booth's maps these parishes were mostly the pink of "fairly comfortable": pink neighborhoods could be middle-class, Booth said, but "these people usually keep no servant."

St. Peter's, Streatham, and St. Stephen's, Lewisham, showed the Ritualist colors in more solidly suburban settings, further to the south. But beyond this world of "little gardens and ornamented villas" the social range of South London did not extend. As one observer put it "wealth and culture do not form disturbing elements" south of the Thames. When wealth accumulates, it usually "gathers together its goods and departs to the squares and terraces of the west, endeavouring there to forget that it once inhabited a suburban villa."[35]

North of the Thames, the social setting of Ritualism was much the same. St. Augustine's, Kilburn, formed in 1871 by a group who seceded from St. Mary's when a new incumbent "lowered" the services there, adjoined some truly wealthy neighborhoods in Maida Vale, but with that exception, none of the Ritualist churches of Outer London even pretended to fashion.[36] Like their South London counterparts, they served neighborhoods that tended to be, on the average, just "fairly comfortable."

St. Matthias, Stoke Newington, one such church, had been a center of the movement since its founding in the early 1850s. Its first vicar was a convert to Rome, and its practices reached a crescendo of vestments and incense in the 1860s and 1870s under the Reverend C. J. LeGeyt, S.S.C., C.B.S.[37] St. Matthias was the home parish of Robert Brett, surgeon and church-builder, the "Pope of Stoke Newington" whom we have already encountered. When LeGeyt's successor abandoned some of his practices in the 1880s, they could still be found at nearby St. Faith's, built through Mr. Brett's benefactions in 1873.

All of these were new churches, and they were full. On the Sunday morning of the 1886 religious census, only one of the nine churches for which we have attendance figures was less than half full (the median was almost two-thirds). Of the ten Ritualist slum churches in East and South London, *none* was as much as half full; in half of them, less than a quarter of the seats were occupied.[38] In the evening the disparity was even greater. At the morning service St. Augustine's, Kilburn, had a congregation of 866; St. John the Divine, Kennington, held another 817; St. Peter's, Streatham, was full to overflowing with 588. These three churches alone held more worshippers that morning than all of the slum churches in East and South London put together.

After the next religious census, that of 1902-3, Charles F. G. Masterman confessed himself surprised to see "the progress of ritualism and 'advanced' doctrine" still further along in suburban South London. Echoing a stereotype by then long outdated, he said,

I had thought its energies mainly exhibited amongst the rich who were attracted by its ceremonial and the poor who welcomed its gospel of Socialism and fellowship, but here are strong churches among the middle classes—churches built mostly in recent years, and by the worshippers themselves without external assistance—evidently providing something which their congregations desire.[39]

And here is the final irony. What had begun as a fashionable form of religious expression was, following what Thorstein Veblen would later identify as the natural history of all fashions, moving down through the class structure. A movement that had once protested bourgeois values was itself becoming middle-class, even suburban.

"Things Now Accepted"

The life of the Reverend George Rundle Prynne of St. Peter's, Plymouth, illustrates in miniature the history of the movement. In the 1850s, Father Prynne's Romanizing inspired both riots and legal proceedings; once, when preaching in a hostile church, he required a bodyguard of friends to get him from the chancel to the pulpit. He never altered or disguised a single one of his advanced opinions. Yet in 1882, the bishop of Exeter preached at the consecration of a new nave for the church, and later proposed a toast to its vicar. In 1885, by a large majority, the clergy of his diocese elected Father Prynne to represent them in Convocation. In 1889, he was elected to the Plymouth school board.[40] As an early historian of the movement wrote in 1897, "it is perfectly marvellous to observe how things are now accepted which once provoked suspicion and even actual rebellion."[41]

This sort of acceptance, the movement's new patriotism, its new liberalism, its growing support in the middle classes—all of these changes meant that Anglo-Catholicism had become increasingly conventional, almost respectable. By the 1890s most Anglo-Catholics plainly regarded this fact as a triumph. But it could also have been seen as the ultimate indignity.

APPENDICES
NOTES
GLOSSARY
WORKS CITED
INDEX

APPENDIX 1

Trends in Disputed Practices
1869–1884

In 1884 *Mackeson's Guide* reported statistics from the preceding sixteen years for a number of contentious practices. The steady increase in the number of churches covered by *Mackeson's* (from 620 in 1869 to 953 in 1884) was due both to the building of new churches and to the inclusion of old ones in towns and villages that had become London suburbs. This changing base makes the absolute numbers of churches reporting various practices misleading, but we can use Mackeson's figures to compute the percentage of metropolitan churches in which each practice was found.[1]

Between 1869 and 1884, several of what had once been distinctively Tractarian practices spread to a majority of London churches. The increasing proportions of churches with surpliced choirs (19 percent to 57 percent), services on saints' days (32 percent to 52 percent), and communion services at least weekly (26 percent to 58 percent) reflect the waning party character of those practices. The most dramatic increase was in the proportion of churches in which the surplice was worn for preaching; the change from 13 percent in 1870 (data for 1869 are not available) to 75 percent in 1884 reflects the bishop of London's belated request that clergy obey the rubric in that matter.

Other Tractarian innovations were less widely copied, but also became somewhat more common as the years went by. Daily services of morning and evening prayer spread from 19 percent of London churches in 1869 to 32 percent in 1884; that they were not offered at a majority of churches probably reflects the resources they required. On the other hand, flowers on the altar retained some party flavor; consequently, that practice spread more slowly and was seldom found outside relatively "high" churches (21 percent of London altars in 1874—the first year that information was collected—and 29 percent ten years later).

Two other early marks of Tractarianism, "free and open" seating and a weekly "offertory," also became more prevalent in this period. Although free seats became almost universal in Anglo-Catholic churches and quite common in new churches of all persuasions, old ways died hard: nearly two-thirds of London churches still had at least some rented pews in 1884. A weekly offering almost always accompanied open

---

1. The figures reported are percentages of Mackseon's "corrected" totals (the number of churches reporting on a majority of the practices in question). This number ranged from 95 to over 99 percent of all London churches.

seating, to make up for lost pew-rents, but was more common than open seating alone can account for. By the 1880s neither practice was a reliable mark of party.

The distinction between practices with doctrinal significance and those without it is evident in the difference between choral communion celebrations and choral services of morning and evening prayer. Both became more common during this period: choral communion celebrations spread from only seven percent of London churches to 22 percent of them, choral offices from 21 percent to 42 percent. But the latter were always roughly twice as common. Choral offices, like the surpliced choirs that sang them, came to be found at many middle of the road churches, while a sung eucharist remained a mark of Anglo-Catholicism.

Even in the metropolis the number and proportion of clearly Ritualist churches remained quite small, increasing only slowly during the 1870s and 1880s. Nevertheless, the movement at least held its own. Daily communion services, a mark of Anglo-Catholic devotion not subject to litigation, showed a slow but steady increase, from two percent of London churches in 1869 to five percent in 1884. Lit candles on the altar were also allowed (if required for light), and that practice spread from five percent of London churches in 1874 to ten percent a decade later.

The least ambiguous indicators of Ritualism were its eucharistic practices. In the wake of the Public Worship Regulation Act, the proportion of London churches in which the eucharistic vestments were worn leveled off at approximately four percent (although the number of such churches went from thirty in 1874 to forty ten years later). The proportion where incense was employed also held steady, at one or two percent. (In 1895, after the Lincoln judgment and under a more tolerant bishop, incense could be found in 35 London churches and the vestments in 142—that is, in three percent and 13 percent, respectively.)

Evening communion services, a distinguishing practice of the movement's Evangelical adversaries, increased sharply (from 11 percent to 24 percent) in the years leading up to the passage of the PWRA in 1874. In the middle and late 1870s, however, the spread of that observance slowed. It peaked at 32 percent in 1882; in that year the proportion of such churches began to decline, and the next year the actual number began to decrease, dropping from 289 to 282. By 1895, only 229 churches, or 22 percent, offered such services.) Meanwhile, the eastward position, a mark of the movement—or at least of High Church sympathy for it—increased dramatically, going from 10 percent in 1874 (the first year it was recorded) to 36 percent in 1884. After 1883, the eastward position was more common in London churches than evening communion.

APPENDIX 2

Comparison of clerical subscribers to Church Association
(1875), clerical members of English Church Union (1877),
and brothers of the Society of the Holy Cross (1877)[1]

	C.A.	E.C.U.	S.S.C.
B.A. (or deacon) before 1840	24%	4%	4%
B.A. (or deacon) before 1850	58%	22%	6%
B.A. (or deacon) less than 13 years	6%	32%	32%
Median date of B.A.(or diaconate)	1847	1859	1860–61
Approximate median age[2]	48	38	36–37
Median gross income (pounds) from livings (estimated)[3]	286	228	109
Incumbents or cathedral clergy (including retired)	94%	72%	62%[4]
Median gross income from livings for incumbents	300	300	300
Oxford graduate	22%	60%	42%
Cambridge graduate	46%	26%	32%

1. Data from *Crockford's Clerical Directory for 1883: Being a Statistical Book of Reference for Facts Relating to the Clergy and the Church* (London: Horace Cox, 1883) for systematic samples of fifty from each organization. Church Association subscribers from *Clergy Directory and Parish Guide*; English Church Union and Society of the Holy Cross members from *The Ritualistic Conspiracy* (23d ed., 1877; PH 6018). Clergy sampled but not located in *Crockford's* (12 C.A. subscribers, 3 E.C.U. members, and 9 S.S.C. members) were replaced with others selected similarly.
2. Assuming median age of twenty when B.A. received or deacon's orders conferred.
3. Non-incumbents' incomes from livings assumed to be zero.
4. Another two cases (4 percent) were incumbents in the Scottish Episcopal Church.

APPENDIX 3

Average matriculations in the 1840s and secessions to Roman Catholicism 1833–1899, for Oxford and Cambridge colleges with significant undergraduate enrollments.[1]

Oxford	Average yearly matriculations (A)	Converts to Roman Catholicism (B)	Ratio (B/A)
Keble	(founded 1870)	13	—
Magdalen	4.4	22	5.0
New	6.0	16	2.7
Merton	9.6	19	2.0
Oriel	18.0	33	1.8
St Mary Hall	7.0	11	1.6
Balliol	24.8	30	1.2
Exeter	39.6	45	1.1
Unversity	17.8	20	1.1
Christ Church	53.2	55	1.0
St Edmund Hall	8.2	8	1.0
Corpus Christi	5.8	5	0.9
St John's	18.6	15	0.8
Queen's	22.6	18	0.8
Brasenose	28.2	22	0.8
Trinity	22.4	14	0.6
Magdalen Hall (Hertford)	24.0	14	0.6
Lincoln	14.0	8	0.6
Worcester	31.0	16	0.5
Jesus	14.0	6	0.4
Pembroke	23.4	9	0.4
Wadham	25.6	9	0.4

1. Converts from W. Gordon Gorman, *Converts to Rome: Since the Tractarian Movement to May 1899* (London: Swan Sonnenschein, 1899), xi–xiii. Enrollments from *English Parliamentary Papers* (1850) 42:450–52. Oxford figures in Column A are averages of reported figures for 1845–49; Cambridge figures are averages for 1844–48.

Cambridge

Jesus	16.2	11	0.7
Downing	4.6	3	0.6
Pembroke	7.8	3	0.5
Trinity College	153.4	79	0.5
Trinity Hall	12.0	6	0.5
St Peter's	20.2	10	0.5
Sidney Sussex	11.4	4	0.4
Emmanuel	27.8	8	0.3
Christ's	25.6	7	0.3
Queen's	34.8	9	0.3
Clare	16.2	4	0.2
Caius	32.6	8	0.2
St John's	116.0	28	0.2
Corpus Christi	26.6	6	0.2
Magdalene	18.4	4	0.2

NOTES

Citations to pamphlets at Pusey House, Oxford University, include their Pusey House catalogue number (e.g., PH 1316), by which they are listed in the the the bibliography. For a general description of the collection, see Father Hugh, S.S.F., *Nineteenth Century Pamphlets at Pusey House: An Introduction for the Prospective User* (London: Faith Press, 1961).

INTRODUCTION

1. For the best general discussion of such movements, see Milton Yinger, *Countercultures: The Promise and the Peril of a World Turned Upside Down* (New York: Free Press, 1982).

2. See, for example, the treatment in Theodore Roszak, *The Making of a Counter Culture* (Garden City, N.Y.: Doubleday, 1969), or the uncritical celebration in Charles A. Reich, *The Greening of America* (New York: Random House, 1970).

3. John Kent, "The Study of Modern Ecclesiastical History Since 1930," in J. Daniélou, A. H. Couratin, and John Kent, *Historical Theology, Pelican Guide to Modern Theology*, vol. 2. (Baltimore: Penguin Books, 1969), 324.

4. A treatment of the spiritual side of the movement, relating it to similar, simultaneous movements on the Continent, can be found in R. W. Franklin, *Nineteenth-Century Churches: The History of a New Catholicism in Württemberg, England, and France* (New York: Garland Publishing, 1987). See also Frederick Houk Borsch, "Ye Shall Be Holy: Reflections on the Spirituality of the Oxford Movement," in *Tradition Renewed: The Oxford Movement Conference Papers*, ed. Geoffrey Rowell (London: Darton, Longman & Todd, 1986).

CHAPTER 1

1. Owen Chadwick's masterful two-volume *The Victorian Church*. (London: Adam & Charles Black: 1971, Part I, 3d ed.; and 1972, Part II, 2d ed.) examines the changes. Also valuable is Desmond Bowen, *The Idea of the Victorian Church: A Study of the Church of England, 1833–1889* (Montreal: McGill University Press, 1968); S. C. Carpenter's earlier treatment, *Church and People, 1789–1889: A History of the Church of England from William Wilberforce to "Lux Mundi"* (London: SPCK, 1933); and M. A. Crowther, *Church Embattled: Religious Controversy in Mid-Victorian England* (Newton Abbot, Devon: David & Charles, 1970). Roger Lloyd provides useful material on the Victorian Church as background in *The Church of England, 1900–1965* (London: SCM Press, 1966).

2. The information in the following paragraphs is from *Mackeson's Guide to the Churches of London and its Suburbs for 1894–5* (London: Metzler, 1866 *et seq.*). This annual publication by Charles Mackeson will be cited hereafter as *Mackeson's*, with the date.

3. Nigel Yates, *The Oxford Movement and Anglican Ritualism*, General Series 105 (London: Historical Association, 1983), offers a short, recent survey. Geoffrey Rowell, *The Vision*

Glorious: Themes and Personalities of the Catholic Revival in Anglicanism (Oxford: Oxford University Press, 1983), is also useful. Other recent works have treated specific aspects of the movement, conflicts in particular locales, or the life and work of individual figures. See especially the Oxford Prophets series, which includes, for instance, Peter Cobb, *Doctor Pusey* (London: Church Literature Association, 1983); Roger Greenacre, *Lord Halifax* (London: Church Literature Association, 1983); and John Newton, *Edward King* (London: Church Literature Association, 1983). There has, however, been no recent general history like those published to mark the Oxford Movement centenary (e.g., W. J. Sparrow Simpson, *The History of the Anglo-Catholic Revival from 1845* [London: George Allen & Unwin, 1932]; Herbert Leslie Stewart, *A Century of Anglo-Catholicism* [London: J. M. Dent & Sons, 1929]; T. Dilworth-Harrison, *Every Man's Story of the Oxford Movement* [London: Mowbray, 1932]). W. S. F. Pickering's recent *Anglo-Catholicism: A Study in Religious Ambiguity* (London: Routledge, 1989) is a valuable treatment of the movement in the twentieth century.

4. Histories of the Oxford Movement that treat it as finished after Newman's secession begin with his own *Apologia pro Vita Sua*, first published serially in 1864. Any listing would also have to include R. W. Church's influential *The Oxford Movement: Twelve Years, 1833–1845*, 3d ed. (London: Macmillan, 1892). E. A. Knox, *The Tractarian Movement, 1833–1845*, 2d ed. (London: Putnam, 1934), and Geoffrey Faber, *Oxford Apostles: A Character Study of the Oxford Movement* (New York: Charles Scribner's Sons, 1934), give us inter-war Evangelical and modernist views, respectively, and a good recent history is Marvin R. O'Connell, *The Oxford Conspirators: A History of the Oxford Movement, 1833–45* (London: Macmillan, 1969), but all three follow the dramaturgical conventions laid down by Newman and Church. One "standard" history that violates this convention is S. L. Ollard's charming *Short History of the Oxford Movement*, 2d ed., ed. A. M. Allchin (1932; reprint, London: Faith Press, 1963), which does devote 98 of its 188 pages to the post-Newman movement. My brief account here borrows heavily from Ollard and from Chadwick, *Victorian Church*, 1:64–211. A recent study critical of the Newman-centered account is George William Herring, "Tractarianism to Ritualism: A Study of Some Aspects of Tractarianism Outside Oxford, From the Time of Newman's Conversion in 1845, Until the First Ritual Commission in 1867" (D. Phil. thesis, Oxford University, 1984), which shows that many Tractarians outside Newman's circle greeted his secession with relief (24–35).

5. On this tradition in Anglicanism, see George H. Tavard, *The Quest for Catholicity: A Study in Anglicanism* (New York: Herder & Herder, 1964), and Richard Sharp, "New Perspectives on the High Church Tradition: Historical Background, 1730–1780," in *Tradition Renewed: The Oxford Movement Conference Papers*, ed. Geoffrey Rowell (London: Darton, Longman & Todd, 1986). On its particular relation to the Oxford Movement, see Peter Nockles, "The Oxford Movement: Historical Background, 1730–1780," in *Tradition Renewed: The Oxford Movement Conference Papers*, ed. Geoffrey Rowell (London: Darton, Longman & Todd, 1986).

6. Selections, with a useful introduction, can be found in Owen Chadwick, ed., *The Mind of the Oxford Movement* (Stanford, Calif.: Stanford University Press, 1961). Representative documents with helpful commentary can also be found in Elizabeth Jay, ed., *The Evangelical and Oxford Movements* (Cambridge: Cambridge University Press, 1983), and in Eugene R. Fairweather, ed., *The Oxford Movement* (New York: Oxford University Press, 1964).

7. Chadwick, *Victorian Church*, 1:75–77. His characterization of the address is quoted from p. 76.

8. On the difficult relationship of these men to Tractarianism, see Peter Nockles, "Continuity and Change in Anglican High Churchmanship in Britain, 1792–1850" (D. Phil. thesis, Oxford University, 1982), 429–528, 602–35 (recently published, much revised, as *The Oxford Movement in Context: Anglican High Churchmanship, 1760–1857* [Cambridge: Cambridge University Press, 1994]); and Reginald H. Fuller, "The Classical High Church Reaction to the Tractarians," in *Tradition Renewed: The Oxford Movement Conference Papers*, ed. Geoffrey Rowell (London: Darton, Longman & Todd, 1986). On their particular uneasiness with the

movement's sympathy for Rome, see Robert H. Greenfield, "Attitude of the Tractarians to the Roman Catholic Church, 1833–1850" (D. Phil. thesis, Oxford University, 1956).

9. Ollard, *Short History*, 53. Piers Brendon, "Newman, Keble and Froude's *Remains*," *English Historical Review* 87 (October 1972): 697–716, makes a strong case that the editors expected a hostile response and may even have intended to alienate the movement's merely lukewarm supporters. Certainly neither ever conceded that the publication was a mistake.

10. Quoted in Ollard, *Short History*, 54.

11. Quoted in Raymond Chapman, *Faith and Revolt: Studies in the Literary Influence of the Oxford Movement* (London: Weidenfeld & Nicolson, 1970), 47.

12. Quoted in Church, *Oxford Movement*, 374.

13. J. B. Mozley, quoted in Ollard, *Short History*, 79.

14. J. Lewis May, *The Oxford Movement: Its History and its Future, A Layman's Estimate* (New York: Dial, 1933), vii.

15. "Subtractarians" is Athelstan Riley's coinage, according to J. G. Lockhart, *Charles Lindley, Viscount Halifax* (London: Centenary, 1935), 1:92.

16. Many have made this point. See, for instance, Yates, *Oxford Movement and Anglican Ritualism*, 21; May, *Oxford Movement*, vii. Marcus Donovan, *After the Tractarians*, (London: Philip Allan, 1933), 29, also notes the accusation but is less ready to admit its truth.

17. John B. Dykes, *Eucharistic Truth and Ritual: A Letter to the Right Reverend the Lord Bishop of Durham* [etc.], 2d ed. (1874; PH 1631).

18. This faction (which included W. G. Ward) is described in C. P. S. Clarke, "The Genesis of the Movement" in *Northern Catholicism: Centenary Studies in the Oxford and Parallel Movements*, ed. N. P. Williams and Charles Harris (New York: Macmillan, 1933), 23–26 (quotation from 25). See also C. P. S. Clarke, *The Oxford Movement and After* (London: Mowbray, 1932), 88–97.

19. For sketches of a number of these figures see, for example, B. C. Boulter, *The Anglican Reformers* (London: Philip Allan, 1933), or Desmond Morse-Boycott, *Lead, Kindly Light: Studies of the Saints and Heroes of the Oxford Movement* (London: Centenary, 1932).

20. See below, chapter 8.

21. Henry R. T. Brandreth, *Dr. Lee of Lambeth: A Chapter in Parenthesis in the History of the Oxford Movement* (London: SPCK, 1951).

22. Thomas Jay Williams, *Priscilla Lydia Sellon: The Restorer after Three Centuries of the Religious Life in the English Church* (London: SPCK, 1950); Peter F. Anson, *The Call of the Cloister: Religious Communities and Kindred Bodies in the Anglican Communion* (London: SPCK, 1955), 259–79.

23. Anson, *Call of the Cloister*, 244–51.

24. A. G. Lough, *The Influence of John Mason Neale* (London: SPCK, 1962); Anson, *Call of the Cloister*, 337–47.

25. M. V. Woodgate, *Father Benson, Founder of the Cowley Fathers* (London: Geoffrey Bles, 1953); Anson, *Call of the Cloister*, 75–83.

26. The comment is from Shane Leslie's *The Oxford Movement, 1833 to 1933* (London: Burns Oates & Washbourne, 1933), 126. This account, by an Anglo-Irish novelist and convert to Roman Catholicism, is not the most reliable history of the movement, but it is certainly the most amusing. On Father Ignatius, see Peter Anson, *Building Up the Waste Places: The Revival of Monastic Life on Medieval Lines in the Post–Reformation Church of England* (Leighton Buzzard: Faith Press, 1973), and *Call of the Cloister*, 419–24. Beatrice de Bertouch, *The Life of Father Ignatius, O.S.B., The Monk of Llanthony* (London: Methuen, 1904), is a remarkable work by a charmingly uncritical admirer, but Donald Attwater, *Father Ignatius of Llanthony: A Victorian* (London: Cassell, 1931), is more reliable, and Arthur Calder-Marshall, *The Enthusiast: An Enquiry into the Life, Beliefs and Character of The Rev. Joseph Leycester Lyne alias Fr. Ignatius, O.S.B., Abbot of Elm Hill, Norwich, and Llanthony, Wales* (London: Faber & Faber, 1962), is probably the last word on the subject.

27. Wilberforce's correspondence with Nugee has only recently come to light, and the

charge should probably be regarded as not proven. See Nigel Yates, *Ritual Conflict at Far-lington and Wymering*, Portsmouth Papers no. 28 (Portsmouth: Portsmouth City Council, 1978), 11–21 (correspondence discussed, 15; Peter Anson quoted, 17). See also Anson, *Call of the Cloister*, 90–103.

28. Thomas Wright, *The Life of Walter Pater*, 2 vols. (London: Everett, 1907), 2:31–48 (photograph of Jackson as Brother à Becket opposite 52).

29. On the dean of St. Paul's, see B. A. Smith, *Dean Church: The Anglican Response to Newman* (London: Oxford University Press, 1958).

30. So far as I can determine, Purchas has not been the subject of a biography. Omitted even from compilations of short, admiring biographical sketches, he is a rare bird indeed among Victorian ecclesiastical celebrities.

31. Chapman, *Faith and Revolt*, examines the literary impact of Anglo-Catholicism; Rossetti is treated, 170–97. William Purcell, *Onward Christian Soldier* (London: Longmans, Green, 1957) and Bickford H. C. Dickinson, *Sabine Baring-Gould: Squarson, Writer and Folklorist, 1834–1924* (Newton Abbot, Devon: David & Charles, 1970), are recent biographies of the squire and parson ("squarson") of Lew Trenchard.

32. Piers Brendon, *Hawker of Morwenstow: Portrait of a Victorian Eccentric* (London: Jonathan Cape, 1975).

33. Royal Commission on Ecclesiastical Discipline, *Report of the Royal Commission on Ecclesiastical Discipline* and *Minutes of Evidence Taken before the Royal Commission on Ecclesiastical Discipline*, 3 vols. (London: H.M.S.O., 1906), 2:340–74. (Hereafter, this source will be cited as *Minutes of Evidence*.) A recent argument for discontinuity is Herring, "Tractarianism to Ritualism."

34. See, for example, Yates, *Oxford Movement*, especially 21–23.

35. Information on Newman's practice from Ollard, *Short History*, 116–18.

36. Mozley and Newman quoted in James F. White, *The Cambridge Movement: The Ecclesiologists and the Gothic Revival* (Cambridge: Cambridge University Press, 1962), 21–24. White says that Newman's decision to build the chapel at Littlemore in Gothic style seems to have been "almost accidental."

37. On criticism of Newman's "timidity," see Clarke, *Oxford Movement and After*, 94.

38. Newman and Froude quoted in Clarke, "Genesis of the Movement," 15–16.

39. Quoted in P. T. Marsh, *The Victorian Church in Decline: Archbishop Tait and the Church of England, 1868–1882* (London: Routledge & Kegan Paul, 1969), 112–13.

40. Quoted in E. A. Down, "Pastoral Ideals and Methods of the Movement: The Tractarian Tradition," in *Northern Catholicism: Centenary Studies in the Oxford and Parallel Movements* ed. N. P. Williams and Charles Harris (New York: Macmillan, 1933), 265.

41. *Minutes of Evidence*, 2:343.

42. Quoted in *Minutes of Evidence*, 2:343.

43. The following quotations from Pusey and this summary of his views are from *Minutes of Evidence*, 2:343–46, unless otherwise indicated. See also Leonard Prestige, *Pusey*, new ed. (1933; reprint, London: Mowbray, 1982), especially 142–59.

44. This story sounds unlikely on its face, but it is given in Clarke, "Genesis of the Movement," 26.

45. On Pusey's self-mortification, see Faber, *Oxford Apostles*, 399–400.

46. Quoted in Ollard, *Short History*, 120. Chadwick suggests that Maria Pusey's death left her husband a changed man (*Victorian Church*, 1:198), but David Forrester argues, in "Dr. Pusey's Marriage," *Ampleforth Journal* 77 (1973): 33–47, that Pusey's conviction of his own depravity dates from as early as 1835—that is, practically from the beginning of his association with the movement.

47. Carpenter, *Church and People*, 213.

48. The following account of the early history of St. Saviour's is adapted from Stephen Savage and Christopher Tyne, *The Labours of Years: The Story of St. Saviour's and St. Hilda's, Leeds* (Cowley: Bocardo & Church Army Press, n.d.), 266–89; and Nigel Yates, *The Oxford*

Movement and Parish Life: St Saviour's, Leeds, 1839–1929, Borthwick Papers no. 48 (York: University of York, Borthwick Institute of Historical Research, 1975), and *Leeds and the Oxford Movement: A Study of "High Church" Activity in the Rural Deaneries of Allerton, Armley, Headingley and Whitkirk in the Diocese of Ripon, 1836–1934*, Publications of the Thoresby Society, vol. 55, no. 121 (Leeds: Thoresby Society, 1975). For an early account by the church's senior curate, see George Peirce Grantham, *A History of Saint Saviour's, Leeds* (1872; PH 13499).

49. White, *Cambridge Movement*, 22.

50. Thomas Jay Williams and Allan Walter Campbell, *The Park Village Sisterhood* (London: SPCK, 1965), 73–74.

51. Carpenter, *Church and People*, 178.

52. J. M. Neale, *Extreme Men. A Letter to A. J. B. Beresford Hope* (1865; PH 6002).

53. Quoted in Clarke, "Genesis of the Movement," 27.

54. Ollard, *Short History*, 121.

55. Ibid., 117–19.

56. Ibid., 123.

57. Ibid., 77n. Pauline A. Adams, "Converts to the Roman Catholic Church in England, *circa* 1830–1870" (B.Litt. thesis, Oxford University, 1977), 178–80, offers several other examples of back and forth conversion. She concludes that Tractarian converts were of greater symbolic than numerical importance; see especially 9–29.

58. Quoted in Clarke, *Oxford Movement and After*, 84–85.

59. [F. W. Faber], *St. Wilfrid, Bishop of York* (James Toovey, 1844), 3–5, 204–8.

60. The attribution to Newman is in *Animadversions by Distinguished Divines and Others, on the False Position of the Ritualistic Clergy in the Church of England* (London: Hamilton, Adams, 1882).

61. Ollard, *Short History*, 115–16.

62. Chadwick, *Victorian Church*, 1:213.

63. Quoted in Boulter, *Anglican Reformers*, 60.

CHAPTER 2

1. "A Provincial," *The Helston Case: Twelve Letters on the Rubric and Ritual Innovations. Reprinted from The Standard.* (n.d., but ca. 1844; PH 70690).

2. *Is Our Minister a Puseyite? A Dialogue for the Unlearned* (n.d., but ca. 1845; PH 5569).

3. "A Provincial," *The Helston Case.*

4. *A Letter to the Bishops of the Church of England on the Necessity of Liturgical Adjustment Arising from the Principles and Practice of the School of Tractarian Theology* (London: Seeley, Burnside, & Seeley, 1843), 8–9.

5. An important study is George William Herring, "Tractarianism to Ritualism: A Study of Some Aspects of Tractarianism Outside Oxford, From the Time of Newman's Conversion in 1845, Until the First Ritual Commission in 1867" (D. Phil. thesis, Oxford University, 1984), which examines the first generation of parochial Tractarianism, emphasizing its differences from both the Oxford Movement proper and the Ritualism which followed it.

6. James F. White, *The Cambridge Movement: The Ecclesiologists and the Gothic Revival* (Cambridge: Cambridge University Press, 1962), 98–102.

7. H. Barry, *Letter to Lord Wharncliffe, on Innovations in the Services of the Church* (1845; PH 9254).

8. *The Moral Effect of Irregularities in the Ritual of the Church* (1843; PH 5993).

9. *Puseyism in London* (1843; PH 5852).

10. John Fuller Russell, *Obedience to the Church in Things Ritual: A Sermon* (1847; PH 11923).

11. G. Wakeling, *The Oxford Church Movement: Sketches and Recollections* (London: Swan Sonnenschein, 1895); quotations from 8, 214.

12. Joseph Ellis Baker, *The Novel and the Oxford Movement*, Princeton Studies in English,

no. 8 (Princeton: Princeton University Press, 1932); see p. 6 on novelists' ignoring the movement in the 1830s and early 1840s. See also Andrew L. Drummond, *The Churches in English Fiction* (Leicester: Edgar Backus, 1950), especially 42–104, and Margaret Maison, *Search Your Soul, Eustace: A Study of the Religious Novel in the Victorian Age* (London: Sheed & Ward, 1961), especially 11–168.

13. *The Parish Rescued*, by W. F. Wilkinson, was published in 1845.

14. "Will O' the Wisp," *A Paper Lantern for Puseyites* (1843; PH 5846).

15. Frederick Oakeley, *Historical Notes on the Tractarian Movement* (London: Longman, Green, Longman, Roberts, & Green, 1865), 61–66.

16. Ibid., 95–97.

17. M. W. Mayow, *A Reply to a Memorial on the Subject of Ritual* (1872; PH 1556).

18. M. W. Mayow, *Remarks upon Certain Principles of Ritual* (1872; PH 1566).

19. M. W. Mayow, *A Letter to the Right Reverend the Lord Bishop of Worcester* (London: James Parker, 1873).

20. Alfred Codd, *Easter Decorations. A Letter to the Parishioners of Beaminster* (1859; PH 12687).

21. "Centenary of the Oxford Movement, 1833 to 1933." Supplement to *St. Thomas the Martyr Parish Magazine* [Oxford], June 1933.

22. Owen Chadwick, *The Victorian Church*, 3d ed. (London: Adam & Charles Black: 1971), 1:218. I have drawn from Chadwick's account of the Helston case and the ensuing troubles at St. Sidwell's, Exeter, on 218–20. See also G. C. B. Davies, *Henry Phillpotts, Bishop of Exeter, 1778–1869* (London: SPCK, 1954), 181–91.

23. *Observance of the Rubric—Burial of Schismatics, &c. Report of Proceedings under a Commission Issued by the Lord Bishop of Exeter to Inquire into Certain Charges Preferred against the Rev. Walter Blunt, Curate of Helston* [etc.] (n.d., but 1844; PH 5855).

24. Ibid.

25. *Correspondence on the Subject of Innovations Introduced in the Celebration of Divine Worship in St. John's Chapel, Torquay* [etc.] (1845; PH 5853).

26. *Memorial of the Churchwardens of the Parish of Westbourne, to the Right Reverend the Lord Bishop of Chichester* [etc.] (1851; PH 5859). For a negative view see John Spurgin, *Intoning the Services in Parish Churches Contrary to the Directions of the Church of England* (n.p.: [n.d., but 1864])

27. *Intoning: or the Possibility of "Saying" Prayers without Making "a slow protracted noise," Duly Considered* [etc.] (1852; PH 5860). For an account of a similar contretemps in Westborne, Diocese of Chichester, in 1850, see *Memorial of the Churchwardens of Westbourne*.

28. *Crockford's Clerical Directory for 1883: Being a Statistical Book of Reference for Facts Relating to the Clergy and the Church* (London: Horace Cox, 1883) still lists him as vicar.

29. Quoted in J. F. Briscoe and H. F. B. MacKay, *A Tractarian at Work: A Memoir of Dean Randall* (London: Mowbray, 1932), 110, 117.

30. *Are Choral Services in Parish Churches Lawful?* (1867; PH 10144)

31. Chadwick, *Victorian Church*, 1:217, 221.

32. "The principal Clergy of London classified according to their opinions on the great Church question of the day" (1844), Bodleian MS. Add. C 290. This manuscript is labelled "for the private use of the Editor of the Times," and its cover bears the note "Puseyites of London."

33. Carlile M'Donnell, *Are We Ritualists?* (1898; PH 8841).

34. *Thoughts on Some Questions of the Day* (1869; PH 3656).

35. Chadwick, *Victorian Church*, 1:250–59; Davies, *Henry Phillpotts*, 230–63.

36. Owen Chadwick, *The Victorian Church*, 2d ed. (London: Adam & Charles Black, 1972), 2:90–95.

37. Chadwick, *Victorian Church*, 1:491–95.

38. Church of England Layman's Defense Association, *The Layman's Remedy against Ritualism* [etc.] (n.d., but ca. 1867; PH 10050). *Church Reform: and the Report of the Royal Com-*

mission on Ritual [etc.] (1868; PH 10254) indicates that the Church of England Laymen's Defense Association worked in close cooperation with the Church Association during the 1860s (see below).

39. On the Church Association's founding, see William Jesse Fong, "The Ritualist Crisis: Anglo-Catholics and Authority with Special Reference to the English Church Union, 1859–1882" (Ph.D. thesis, University of Toronto, 1978), 70–72.

40. Benjamin Shaw, *Ritualism and the Ecclesiastical Law* (n.d.; PH 9888).

41. A. J. B. Beresford Hope, *Hints toward Peace in Ceremonial Matters* (1874; PH 1642). On the confusing law of the Church, see Fong, "Ritualist Crisis," which reproduces an 1899 summary by the *Westminster Gazette*, 487–95, nine pages of small print.

42. C. H. Davis, *Remarks upon the Ritualistic "Memorial" of 12th. January, 1869* (1869; PH 1442).

43. Shane Leslie, *The Oxford Movement, 1833 to 1933* (London: Burns Oates & Washbourne, 1933), 19.

44. Quoted in "A High Churchman," *Common Sense: About the Church* (London: Hatchard, 1860), 8.

45. For a Baptist's observations on "the presence of Ritualism almost everywhere" in the *Book of Common Prayer,* see W. Landels, *Ritualism: A Speech Delivered at the Autumnal Meeting of the Baptist Union of Great Britain and Ireland* (1873; PH 71618).

46. William [Howley], Lord Archbishop of Canterbury, *A Letter Addressed to the Clergy and Laity of his Province* [etc.] (1845; PH 5849).

47. Chadwick, *Victorian Church,* 1:496.

48. Paul Thureau-Dangin, *The English Catholic Revival in the Nineteenth Century* (New York: E. P. Dutton, n.d.), 2:439.

49. George Rundle Prynne, *Treachery; or, Ritualism and Evangelicalism Brought to the Standard of the Teaching of the Church of England. Dedicated to the Church Association* (London: Masters, 1870).

50. Albert Augustus Isaacs, *The Rubrics and Ritual of the Church of England* (London: W. MacIntosh, 1869).

51. Edward Garbett, *What are Our Duties in the Present Circumstances of the Church?* (London: William Hunt, 1867).

52. Quoted in James S. Pollock, *Romanizing. The Substance of a Lecture delivered in the Town Hall, Birmingham, January 23, 1867* (London: Masters, 1867), 32.

53. See, for instance, "A High Churchman," *Common Sense*; Arthur Wolfe, *A Plea for Revision of the Prayer-Book and of the Authorized Version of the Bible* (Cambridge: Deighton, Bell, 1866); or A Layman of the Church of England, *An Address to the Laity of the Church of England upon the Errors and Abuses which Exist in that Church, with Suggested Reforms* (London: Effingham Wilson, 1860).

54. See, for instance, Colin Lindsay, "The Ritual Law of the Church of England," in *The Church and the World: Essays on Questions of the Day in 1867,* ed. Orby Shipley (London: Longmans, Green, Reader, & Dyer, 1867), 434–35; *Ritual: A Plea in Its Behalf, Grounded on Scripture and Reason. By One Who Has Viewed Both Sides of the Questions* (n.d.; PH 70681).

55. *Ritual: A Plea in Its Behalf.*

56. See below, chapter 8.

57. James Skinner, *Why Do We Prize Externals in the Service of God?* [etc.] (1856; PH 10036).

58. Davis, *Remarks on the Ritualistic "Memorial".*

59. Walter A. Gray, *The Symbolism of Churches and their Ornaments* (1857; PH 9224).

60. Walter Farquhar Hook, *Discourses Bearing on the Controversies of the Day* (London: John Murray, 1853), 82, 104.

61. *A Few Words on the Prayer for the Church Militant* (n.p.: [n.d., but 1864]).

62. "A Churchman of the Reformation," *Tractarian Practices in Protestant Churches: Three Letters Reprinted from the "Christian Guardian"* [etc.] (1850; PH 5851).

63. Charles Westerton, *A Letter to the Right Reverend the Lord Bishop of London, on the Popish Manner in which, Contrary to the Rubrics, Divine Service is Performed on Sunday Mornings at the Parish Church of St. Paul's, Wilton Place, Knightsbridge* (1853; PH 5863) suggests, that Bennett's successor, Liddell, briefly interrupted the objectionable practices at St. Paul's. But he had resumed them by 1853, under the influence of Bennett's former curate, George Nugee—or such was the belief of Charles Westerton, whose proceedings against Liddell would later lead to the "Liddell judgment."

64. Owen Chadwick, *The Founding of Cuddesdon* (Oxford: Oxford University Press), 1954.

65. Quotations from *Correspondence Relating to Cuddesdon Theological College, in Answer to the Charges of the Reverend C. P. Golightly, and the Report of the Commissioners Thereon* (Oxford: J. Vincent, 1858).

66. See his *A Solemn Warning Against Cuddesdon College* (London: Simpkin, Marshall, [n.d., but 1879]).

67. "E. J. T." [Troughton], letter in the *Examiner*, January 21, 1860.

68. *Letter to the Bishops on the Necessity of Liturgical Adjustment*, 8–9, 21.

69. For a call to remove these "few ill-judged expressions," see Association for Promoting the Revision of the Prayer-Book, *The Confessional and the Prayer-Book* (London: Wyman & Sons, 1877).

70. E. A. Knox, *The Tractarian Movement, 1833–1845*, 2d ed. (London: Putnam, 1934), 240.

71. This account is taken from A. Clifton Kelway, *George Rundle Prynne: A Chapter in the Early History of the Catholic Revival* (London: Longmans, Green, 1905), 29–35, 70–108.

72. Chadwick, *Victorian Church*, 1:503–4.

73. From *The Ministry of Consolation*, quoted in Walter Walsh, *The Secret History of the Oxford Movement* (London: Swan Sonnenschein, 1897), 402.

74. For a much later example, see English Church Union, *The E.C.U. Church Guide for Tourists and Others* (London: Mowbray, 1924).

75. This passage was quoted in Walsh, *Secret History*, 89.

76. William Maskell, *Protestant Ritualists* (1872; PH 1584), quoted in Walsh, *Secret History*, 86–87.

77. Knox, *Tractarian Movement*, 240.

78. W. Maskell, quoted in Walsh, *Secret History*, 87.

79. *From Oxford to Rome, and How It Fared with Some Who Lately Took the Journey*, quoted in Walsh, *Secret History*, 89.

80. Unless otherwise noted, material in this section is taken from Peter F. Anson, *The Call of the Cloister: Religious Communities and Kindred Bodies in the Anglican Communion* (London: SPCK, 1955), 29–51 (on the early communities for men) and 220–376, 528–30 (on sisterhoods). Also extremely useful are A. M. Allchin, *The Silent Rebellion: Anglican Religious Communities, 1845–1900* (London: SCM Press, 1958), and Michael Hill, *The Religious Order: A Study of Virtuoso Religion and Its Legitimation in the Nineteenth-Century Church of England* (London: Heinemann Educational Books, 1973).

81. See below, chapter 10.

82. Anson, *Call of the Cloister*, 509–94.

83. See also Thomas Jay Williams and Allan Walter Campbell, *The Park Village Sisterhood* (London: SPCK, 1965).

84. Thomas Jay Williams, *Priscilla Lydia Sellon: The Restorer after Three Centuries of the Religious Life in the English Church* (London: SPCK, 1950), is an instructive biography of one of these remarkable women.

85. See Allchin, *Silent Rebellion*. The Holy Cross Sisterhood's initial connection with Christ Church, Albany Street, was a personal one with the vicar, Charles Dodsworth, and did not survive Dodsworth's secession to Roman Catholicism.

86. Pusey is quoted in Anson, *Call of the Cloister*, 333.

87. The description is from Mary Frances Cusack, *Five Years in a Protestant Sisterhood,*

quoted in Anson, *Call of the Cloister*, 310n.

88. Quoted in Anson, *Call of the Cloister*, 315n.

89. Ibid., 248. Butler and Carter were, of course, only relatively conservative; both encouraged the practice of confession not only in their sisterhoods but in their parishes.

90. Nugee is listed as a Camden Society member in 1843, in Edward Jacob Boyce, *A Memorial of the Cambridge Camden Society* (London: G. Palmer, 1888).

91. Desmond Morse-Boycott, *They Shine Like Stars* (London: Skeffington & Son, [1947]), 121.

92. A. G. Lough, *John Mason Neale—Priest Extraordinary* (Newton Abbot, Devon.: privately published, [1975]), 57–58; and Lough's *The Influence of John Mason Neale* (London: SPCK, 1962), 42–51 (quotation from p. 49).

93. De La Warr is listed as a member in 1843, in Boyce, *Memorial of the Camden Society*.

94. Lough, *John Mason Neale*, 73–97 (quotations from 97, 85).

95. Quoted in Lough, *John Mason Neale*, 93–95.

96. Anson, *Call of the Cloister*, 345.

97. Ibid., 337n.

98. Ibid., 346.

99. Quoted in Lough, *John Mason Neale*, 103.

100. [Katherine ("Mother Kate") Warburton], *Memories of a Sister of S. Saviour's Priory* (Oxford and London: Mowbray, 1903), 27–28. Neale's remark about "pseudo-asceticism" is quoted in Anson, *Call of the Cloister*, 343.

101. Warburton, *Memories of a Sister*, 35.

102. Anson treats these later communities in *Call of the Cloister*, 377–431.

CHAPTER 3

1. Richard Frederick Littledale, *Ritualists not Romanists* (n.d.; PH 1504). (For a memoir of Littledale, see [Katherine Warburton], *Memories of a Sister of S. Saviour's Priory* [Oxford and London: Mowbray, 1903], 188–206; on his association with Rossetti, see Mackenzie Bell, *Christina Rossetti: A Biographical and Critical Study*, 3d ed. [London: Hurst & Blackett, 1898], 49.) The earliest date for the origins of Ritualism is 1837, suggested by Paula Schaefer, in *The Catholic Regeneration of the Church of England* (London: Williams & Norgate, 1935), 121–47, apparently identifying it with the first parochial manifestations of Tractarianism; Francis Penhale, *The Anglican Church Today: Catholics in Crisis* (London: Mowbray, 1986), 5, dates it from 1845. Most observers, however, have followed contemporary practice and reserved the term for a later phase of the movement. George William Herring, "Tractarianism to Ritualism: A Study of Some Aspects of Tractarianism Outside Oxford, From the Time of Newman's Conversion in 1845, Until the First Ritual Commission in 1867" (D. Phil. thesis, Oxford University, 1984), 286, has it beginning with the publication of *Directorium Anglicanum* in 1858. At the turn of the century, Archbishop Davidson dated the new phase from the beginnings of public concern about it, around 1866; so did the anonymous "Widow of a Clergyman," in *Ritualism and the Touchstone* (Southampton: A. Randle, 1877), 1.

2. For accounts of the St. George's riots, see, for instance, Michael Reynolds, *Martyr of Ritualism: Father Mackonochie of St. Alban's, Holborn* (London: Faber & Faber, 1965), 50–70; Owen Chadwick, *The Victorian Church*, 3d ed. (London: Adam & Charles Black, 1971), 1:497–501; Phillip T. Smith, "The London Police and the Holy War: Ritualism and St. George's-in-the-East, London, 1859–1860," *Journal of Church and State* 28 (1986): 107–19.

3. Quoted in Malcolm MacColl, *Tractarianism and Ritualism* (1881; PH 4033).

4. Quoted in Henry R. T. Brandreth, *Dr. Lee of Lambeth: A Chapter in Parenthesis in the History of the Oxford Movement* (London: SPCK, 1951), 6.

5. Harry Jones, *East and West London: Being Notes of Common Life and Pastoral Work in Saint James's, Westminster and in Saint George's-in-the-East* (London: Smith, Elder, 1875), 62–63.

6. Sabine Baring-Gould, *The Church Revival: Thoughts Thereon and Reminiscences* (Lon-

don: Methuen, 1914), 233.

7. Quoted in Reynolds, *Martyr of Ritualism*, 57.

8. Chadwick, *Victorian Church*, 1:499–500.

9. Bryan King, *The S. George's Mission, with the S. George's Riots and their Results* (London: Rivington's, 1877).

10. The full name was the "St. George's Church Defense Association, for the maintenance of law and order in the parish church of St. George's-in-the-East." For a list of prominent members, see G. Wakeling, *The Oxford Church Movement. Sketches and Recollections* (London: Swan Sonnenschein, 1895), 160–61.

11. On the founding and early days of the E.C.U., see William Jesse Fong, "The Ritualist Crisis: Anglo-Catholics and Authority with Special Reference to the English Church Union, 1859–1882" (Ph.D. thesis, University of Toronto, 1978), 10–22.

12. G. Bayfield Roberts, *The History of the English Church Union, 1859–1894* (London: Church, 1895), 10–12, 19.

13. King, *S. George's Mission*.

14. Paul Thureau-Dangin, *The English Catholic Revival in the Nineteenth Century* (New York: E. P. Dutton, n.d.), 2:442–43.

15. F. B. Woodward, *Remarks on a Petition Presented to Her Majesty, for a Revision of the Liturgy* (1860; PH 651).

16. For an account of the *Essays and Reviews* and Colenso controversies, see Owen Chadwick, *The Victorian Church*, 2d ed. (London: Adam & Charles Black, 1972), 2:75–97.

17. For one reaction, see "A Worcestershire Vicar," *The Church as it is* [etc.] (London: Whittaker, [1864]).

18. *Declaration on the Inspiration of the Word of God and the Eternity of Future Punishment* (1864; PH 1134). *Clergy Directory and Parish Guide* (London: Thomas Bosworth, 1875) lists Church Association members as of 1875, and Fremantle was among them. This coalition came together again in 1870, when a Unitarian was allowed to receive communion in Westminster Abbey; the resulting protest was signed by a galaxy of both High and Low Church luminaries (*Protest against the Communion of a Unitarian in Westminster Abbey on June 22, 1870* [1870; PH 1468]). Another rare example of interparty cooperation can be found in the establishment of the Church of England Purity Society in the 1880s (see the society's *Second Annual Report* [1885; PH 2357]).

19. Quoted in *The Church and the World: Essays on Questions of the Day in 1866*, ed. Orby Shipley, 3d ed. (London: Longmans, Green, Reader, & Dyer, 1867), 530.

20. Quoted in James Bentley, *Ritualism and Politics in Victorian Britain: The Attempt to Legislate for Belief* (Oxford: Oxford University Press, 1978), 20.

21. Quoted in Shipley, *Church and World: 1866*, 545.

22. Ibid., 543.

23. Quoted in Thureau-Dangin, *English Catholic Revival*, 2:444.

24. Andrew L. Drummond, *The Churches in English Fiction* (Leicester: Edgar Backus, 1950), 96. The description is in Walter Pater, *Marius the Epicurean: His Sensations and Ideas* (Garden City, N.Y.: Doubleday, Doran, 1935 [1885]), 254–61. "An Ex-Member of the Congregation of S. Bartholomew's, Brighton," refers to Nugee's practice of Benediction, in *Are You Safe in the Church of England? A Question for Anxious Ritualists* (London: R. Washbourne, 1878), 24.

25. Warburton, *Memories of a Sister*, 91–93.

26. See Arthur Calder-Marshall, *The Enthusiast: An Enquiry into the Life, Beliefs and Character of The Rev. Joseph Leycester Lyne alias Fr. Ignatius, O.S.B., Abbot of Elm Hill, Norwich, and Llanthony, Wales* (London: Faber & Faber, 1962); also Peter Anson, *Building Up the Waste Places: The Revival of Monastic Life on Medieval Lines in the Post–Reformation Church of England* (Leighton Buzzard: Faith Press, 1973) and *The Call of the Cloister: Religious Communities and Kindred Bodies in the Anglican Communion* (London: SPCK, 1955), 419–24.

27. Earl of Shaftesbury, *Speech in the House of Lords ... on moving the Second Reading of*

the Clerical Vestments Bill (London: Church Association, 1867).

28. Westmeath's comments were quoted twelve years later by Lord Ebury, who claimed that matters had not improved—as, indeed, they had not (Lord Ebury, *Quis Custodiet Custodes? or, 'Tis Twelve Years Since* [1877; PH 4245]).

29. Edwin Hodder, *The Life and Work of the Seventh Earl of Shaftesbury, K.G* (London: Cassell, 1886), 3:213.

30. James Ormiston, *A Protest against the Ritualists' Confessional* [etc.] (n.d., but probably 1867; PH 6144).

31. Quoted in Shipley, *Church and World: 1866*, 550.

32. Ibid., 527, 534.

33. Tract 81 alone was 424 pages long, but even the shortest of the last ten (no. 82) was a monograph of 42 pages.

34. E. W. Sergeant, *Ritualism: How Far Reasonable?* (n.d., but ca. 1879; PH 3975).

35. Disraeli quoted in Bentley, *Ritualism and Politics*, 69; Littledale in W. Vincent, *Report of the Proceedings at the Ecclesiastical Art Exhibition, Held at York, on the 9th, 10th, 11th, & 12th October, 1866* (1866; PH 12880), quoted against the Ritualists in G. Albert Rogers, *The Real Presence the Basis of Ritualism* (n.d., but ca. 1867; PH 10055).

36. *Church Times*, January 28, 1870; quoted, somewhat inaccurately, in Thomas Howard Gill, *A Letter to the Right Reverend the Lord Bishop of Manchester, touching "Ritualism,"* (London: Hatchards, 1878), 7.

37. John Edwards, *Catholic Ritual the Exponent of Catholic Truth* (1867; PH 11809).

38. G. A. Denison, *Loyalty to the Church of England. A Letter to the Lord Bishop of Bath and Wells* [etc.] (1873; PH 7258).

39. Desmond Morse-Boycott, *The Secret Story of the Oxford Movement* (London: Skeffington & Son, [1933]), 149.

40. John Kent, *Holding the Fort: Studies in Victorian Revivalism* (London: Epworth, 1978), 285.

41. Ibid., 284.

42. *Church Times*, November 10, 1866.

43. Quoted in C. S. Grueber, *A Reply to the "Remarks" of the Rev. C. A. Heurtley* [etc.] (1868; PH 1336).

44. The Society for the Propagation of Christian Knowledge dropped *The Christian Year* from its list of publications (John W. Burgon, *The Oxford Diocesan Conference; and Romanizing within the Church of England* [etc.] [Oxford: James Parker, 1873], 32–33n).

45. For an interpretation of the Anglo-Catholic "revolution by tradition," see Michael Hill, *The Religious Order: A Study of Virtuoso Religion and Its Legitimation in the Nineteenth-Century Church of England* (London: Heinemann Educational Books, 1973) 85–138. For a general discussion of Victorian appropriation of the past, see A. Dwight Culler, *The Victorian Mirror of History* (New Haven: Yale University Press, 1985), especially 90–121 (on the Oxford Movement).

46. N. P. Williams, "The Theology of the Catholic Revival," in *Northern Catholicism: Centenary Studies in the Oxford and Parallel Movements*, ed. N. P. Williams and Charles Harris (New York: Macmillan, 1933), 138.

47. The continuing tendency to look to Constantinople rather than Rome is evident in, for instance, J. F. Kershaw, *The Reunion of Christendom. The Anglican and the Eastern Churches* (London: J. Masters, 1896). On "English" or "Sarum" use, see, for instance, Marcus Donovan, *After the Tractarians*, (London: Philip Allan, 1933), 129–30.

48. The full development of this school within Anglo-Catholicism took place well into the twentieth century. See Nigel Abercrombie, "Some Directions of the Oxford Movement," *Dublin Review* 193, no. 386 (July–September 1933): 78.

49. Ibid., 141; "Papists without the Pope" from, for instance, "A High Churchman," *Common Sense: About the Church* (London: Hatchard, 1860), 6.

50. See, for instance "An Ex-Member of the Congregation of S. Bartholomew's," *Are You*

Safe?; George Akers, *A Letter to My Late Flock* (1868; PH 8587); William Maskell, *Protestant Ritualists* (1872; PH 1584).

51. E.g., Willis Nevins, *Why I Left the Church of Rome* (n.d., but ca. 1870; PH 8082).

52. Edward Husband, *Why I Left the Church of England* (1869; PH 8586) and *What Will Dr. Newman Do? A Letter to the Very Rev. J. H. Newman, D.D.* (1870; PH 8080).

53. A satirical treatment that nicely illustrates the difficulties can be found in *Church Defence: Report of a Conference on the Present Dangers of the Church* (London: R. Washbourne, 1873).

54. [John Mason Neale], *Collected Hymns, Sequences and Carols of John Mason Neale* (London: Hodder and Stoughton, 1914), 398–99. The hymn was written for the children of St. Matthew's, Ipswich.

55. Joyce Coombs, *One Aim: Edward Stuart, 1820–1877* (London: Stanhope Press, 1975), 25.

56. This is from the song's "missing" fourth verse, omitted from the version in the appendix to *Hymns Ancient and Modern.*

57. G. Bayfield Roberts, *The History of the English Church Union, 1859–1894* (London: Church, 1895), 58.

58. P. T. Marsh, *The Victorian Church in Decline: Archbishop Tait and the Church of England, 1868–1882* (London: Routledge & Kegan Paul, 1969), 49. A similar laxity is evident in Maxwell Julius Blacker, "Religious Toleration," in Shipley (ed.), *Church and World: 1867,* 253. On the royal commission and its four reports, see Fong, "Ritualist Crisis," 84–88, 120–35.

59. Chadwick, *Victorian Church,* 2:86–87.

60. *The Moral Effect of Irregularities in the Ritual of the Church* (1843; PH 5993).

61. Roberts, *History of the English Church Union,* 19; G. R. Balleine, *A History of the Evangelical Party in the Church of England,* new ed. (London: Church Book Room Press, 1951 [1908]), 181.

62. Quoted in Reynolds, *Martyr of Ritualism,* 158.

63. Figures for 1850 are from [Joseph Masters], *Masters's Guide to the Daily Prayers of England, Wales, & Scotland,* 4th ed. (London: Joseph Masters, 1850); those for 1870 are from *Mackeson's* (1871).

64. "The Editor of the Protestant Churchman," *Ritualist Caricature of the Bishops* (n.d., but ca. 1866; PH 10088); for a similar view, see F. G. Lee, *The Beauty of Holiness. Ten Lectures on External Religious Observances* (2d ed., 1866; PH 10564).

65. *The Church Monitor, A Magazine Advocating Catholic Doctrine & Practice* 1, no. 6 (August 1866): 71 (PH9906. What the appropriate accompaniments should be is detailed in, for instance, "A Catholic Priest," *An Explanation of the Parts of a Catholic Church, and the Ornaments and Ceremonies Used in the Holy Sacrifice* (1866; PH 10096) or F. G. Lee, *Directorium Anglicanum,* 4th ed. (London: John Hogg, 1879).

66. Quoted in Shipley, *Church and World: 1866,* 550.

67. Bentley, *Ritualism and Politics,* 21.

68. See, for instance, *Reasons for Ritual. Christ Church, Wolverhampton, Leaflet No. 7* (n.d., but 1876; PH 3379).

69. Reynolds, *Martyr of Ritualism,* 78, 133–43.

70. Roberts, *History of the English Church Union,* 174.

71. James Skinner, *A Plea for the Threatened Ritual of the Church of England* (1865; PH 7871).

72. *Mackeson's* (1871).

73. *The Congregation in Church: A Plain Guide to Reverent and Intelligent Participation in the Public Services of Holy Church, with Brief Information Concerning the Six Points* (etc.) (London: Wyman and Sons, [1885]), 11. For a similar statement, see C. S. Grueber, *A Primitive and Catholic Ritual with Primitive and Catholic Usage the Inheritance of the Church of England* [etc.] (1874; PH 1621); see also Skinner, *Plea for the Threatened Ritual.*

74. Robert Liddell, *On the Daily Celebration of Holy Communion* (1868; PH 8206), is a

sermon preached on the beginning of daily celebration at St. Paul's, Knightsbridge—"encouraged by the example of others, more devout neighbours"—in 1868.

75. *Congregation in Church.* See also Littledale in Vincent, *Report of the Proceedings.*

76. Philip Freeman, *Rites and Ritual; A Plea for Apostolic Doctrine and Worship* (1866; PH 7875).

77. Skinner, *Plea for the Threatened Ritual.* Many others argued the same point; see, for example, C. S. Grueber, *A Primitive and Catholic Ritual with Primitive and Catholic Usage the Inheritance of the Church of England* [etc.] (1874; PH 1621); John Edward Field, *Some Principles of Christian Ceremonial* (1874; PH 71691).

78. M. W. Mayow, *Remarks upon the First Report of the Royal Commission on Ritual* [etc.] (1868; PH 7858). For the similar views of Lord Halifax, see his remarks in the *Church Review* of June 24, 1865, quoted in Walter Walsh, *The Ritualists: Their Romanising Objects and Work* (London: James Nisbet, 1900), 32.

79. Alfred Barry, *The Church Questions of the Day* (etc) (London: Longmans, Green, 1868), 14–15.

80. E. Garbett, *Extreme Ritualism* (1866; PH 72876).

81. Church of England Working Men's Society, *Doctrine and Ritual* (n.d.; PH 8130).

82. Francis Close, *Ritualism and Scepticism, Being Two Sermons* [etc.] (1866; PH 9905).

83. C. Maurice Davies, *Orthodox London: or, Phases of Religious Life in the Church of England*, revised ed. (London: Tinsley Brothers, 1876), 143.

84. George Anthony Denison, *The Law of God and the Law of Man* [etc.] (1875; PH 2144).

85. Donovan, *After the Tractarians,* 128–29.

86. Richard Frederick Littledale, *Innovations: A Lecture Delivered in the Assembly Rooms, Liverpool, April 23, 1868* (1868; PH 1363).

87. Vincent, *Report of the Proceedings.*

88. *A Dissertation on the 32nd Article of the Church of England Prayer Book* (n.d., but 1890s; PH 7336); *The Sign of the Cross Defended* (1875; PH 14076); Sabine Baring–Gould, *The Golden Gate*, summarized in William Purcell, *Onward Christian Soldier* (London: Longmans, Green, 1957), 96–97.

89. Donovan, *After the Tractarians,* 17–18. Donovan's account is "based on the recollections of Athelstan Riley," and of uncertain reliability.

90. Kent, *Holding the Fort,* 236–94; Charles John Ellicott, *Ritualism. A Sermon Preached in Bristol Cathedral, Sunday, November 4, 1866* (1866; PH 10266). J. W. Bonham, *The Great Revival in the Church of England* (New York: T. Whittaker, 1875), describes the Ten Days' Mission of 1874 in London, which enlisted representatives of all Church parties. Bonham reports that some missioners prepared by a retreat with the Cowley Fathers, and among the services described are those at the Anglo-Catholic church of St. Augustine's, Kilburn.

91. Donovan, *After the Tractarians,* 101–12.

92. Quotations from Church Association, *Church Hymnals. The Special Need of Care in Selection* (n.d.; PH 10909), and Donovan, *After the Tractarians,* 117. For more Evangelical warnings, see *Ultra-Ritualism. Extracts from the Hymn Books Used in St. Alban's, Holborn, London* (1867; PH 10077); James Ormiston, *Hymns Ancient and Modern, and Their Romanizing Teaching. Church Association Tract No. XXI* (n.d.; PH 12498).

93. *The Church Monitor, A Magazine Advocating Catholic Doctrine & Practice* 1 (August 1866): 6 (PH 9906).

94. Brandreth, *Dr. Lee of Lambeth,* 46.

95. *Hymnal of the Protestant Episcopal Church in the United States of America, 1940* (New York: Church Pension Fund, 1943).

96. On the movement's contribution to hymnody, see Donovan, *After the Tractarians,* 117–24, and Morse-Boycott, *They Shine Like Stars,* 126–28.

97. A perusal of the biographical sketches appended to the Joint Commission on the Revision of the Hymnal, *Hymnal 1940 Companion,* 3d ed. (New York: Church Pension Fund,

1951), 365–608, makes this point plainly.

98. Quoted in Morse-Boycott, *Secret Story*, 122.

CHAPTER 4

1. Charles John Ellicott, *Ritualism. A Sermon Preached in Bristol Cathedral, Sunday, November 4, 1866* (1866; PH 10266).

2. For an intelligent discussion, see John Kent, *Holding the Fort: Studies in Victorian Revivalism* (London: Epworth Press, 1978), 289–90.

3. See, for instance, W. S. F. Pickering, "Anglo-Catholicism: Some Sociological Observations," in *Tradition Renewed: The Oxford Movement Conference Papers*, ed. Geoffrey Rowell (London: Darton, Longman and Todd, 1986), 165-66 (quotations from 165). Pickering was actually speaking of present-day Anglo-Catholics, who are true to their heritage in this respect. He notes that they "often seem to rejoice in their sectarianism," and points out the irony of "adopt[ing] a sect-like position in the name of catholicism." See also W. S. F. Pickering, *Anglo-Catholicism: A Study in Religious Ambiguity* (London: Routledge, 1989), especially chapter 7.

4. William Allen Whitworth, *Churchman's Grievances* [etc.] (1881; PH 2234).

5. "H. J.," *Concerning the Theory and Truth of Ritualism* (1867; PH 10053).

6. J. G. Lockhart, *Charles Lindley, Viscount Halifax* (London: Centenary, 1935), 1:84.

7. G. Wakeling, *The Oxford Church Movement. Sketches and Recollections* (London: Swan Sonnenschein, 1895), 60.

8. *A Letter to the Bishops of the Church of England on the Necessity of Liturgical Adjustment Arising from the Principles and Practice of the School of Tractarian Theology* (London: Seeley, Burnside, and Seeley, 1843), 14.

9. From the first edition of *Masters's Guide* (1849), quoted in Wakeling, *Oxford Church Movement*, 61.

10. See appendix 1.

11. [Masters, Joseph], *Masters's Guide to the Churches Where the Daily Prayers are Said in England, Wales, Scotland, and Ireland*, 28th ed. (London: Joseph Masters, 1860); *Mackeson's* (1870).

12. Ibid.

13. *Mackeson's* (1870).

14. W. Vincent, *Report of the Proceedings at the Ecclesiastical Art Exhibition, Held at York, on the 9th, 10th, 11th, & 12th October, 1866* (1866; PH 12880); A. J. B. Beresford Hope, *Hints toward Peace in Ceremonial Matters* (1874; PH 1642).

15. E. H. Bickersteth, *Evangelical Churchmanship and Evangelical Eclecticism* (London: Sampson Low, Marston, Searle, & Rivington, 1883).

16. *Correspondence on the Subject of Innovations Introduced in the Celebration of Divine Worship in St. John's Chapel, Torquay* [etc.] (1845; PH 5853).

17. Lockhart, *Charles Lindley, Viscount Halifax* 1:132.

18. Quoted in G. R. Balleine, *A History of the Evangelical Party in the Church of England*, new ed. (London: Church Book Room Press, 1951 [1908]), 175.

19. Bickersteth, *Evangelical Churchmanship*.

20. Figures are from *Mackeson's* (1884), 171; quotation from C. Maurice Davies, *Orthodox London: or, Phases of Religious Life in the Church of England*, rev. ed. (London: Tinsley Brothers, 1876), 29. See also appendix 1. For a defense of the gown, published by the Church Association, see William Fleming, *The Gown in the Pulpit* (n.d.; PH 10963).

21. Presbyter Protestans, *The "English Church Union"... A Romanizing Confederacy* (London: John F. Shaw, 1877), 33.

22. Balleine, *History of the Evangelical Party*, 192–93; *Mackeson's* (1869).

23. W[illiam] Bright, *Evening Communions Contrary to the Church's Mind, and Why* (1870; PH 7221).

24. H. P. Liddon, *Evening Communions Contrary to the Teaching and Practice of the*

Church in All Ages [etc.] (1876; PH 7227).

25. For the Evangelical argument, see Hely Smith, *The Real Ritual Reason Why* (London: Simpkin, Marshall, 1878); for the reply, see A Priest of the Diocese of London, *Are Evening Communions Scriptural?* (n.p., [1873]).

26. *Mackeson's* (1884), 171.

27. Bourchier Wrey Savile, *Hard Speeches and Gentle Words* (1879; PH 71832).

28. *Non-fasting Communions. S. Joseph Tracts No. 2* (n.d., but ca. 1870; PH 10463).

29. W. J. Conybeare, "Church Parties," *The Edinburgh Review* 98 (October 1853): 315.

30. George Worley, *The Catholic Movement of the Nineteenth Century* (London: Elliot Stock, 1894), 147.

31. Conybeare, "Church Parties," 315.

32. Worley, *Catholic Movement*, 147.

33. Ibid.; Michael Reynolds, *Martyr of Ritualism: Father Mackonochie of St. Alban's, Holborn* (London: Faber and Faber, 1965), 68–69.

34. J. Embry, *The Catholic Movement and the Society of the Holy Cross* (London: Faith Press, 1931), 9, 30–31.

35. Wakeling, *Oxford Church Movement*, 148; the beard and wife belonged to the Reverend C. J. LeGeyt, of St. Matthias, Stoke Newington, an ardent Ritualist to whom no other objections could have been made. "Smooth chins" from "Adam Bede," *The Natural History of Puseyism: With a Short Account of the Sunday Opera at St. Paul's, Brighton* (Brighton: G. Smart, [1860]), 5n; emphasis added.

36. *Progress of Ritualism and the Designs of Popery* (London: John Kensit, [1886]).

37. Quoted in Reynolds, *Martyr of Ritualism*, 112.

38. Conybeare, "Church Parties," 315.

39. Francis Paget's *Milford Malvoisin*, quoted in Joseph Ellis Baker, *The Novel and the Oxford Movement*, Princeton Studies in English, No. 8 (Princeton: Princeton University Press, 1932), 14; Conybeare, "Church Parties," 315.

40. A Benighted Layman, *Gropings in Search of the Church of England* (London: George John Stevenson, 1867), 7–8.

41. A. Clifton Kelway, *George Rundle Prynne: A Chapter in the Early History of the Catholic Revival* (London: Longmans, Green, 1905), 66.

42. Quoted in S. C. Carpenter, *Church and People, 1789–1889: A History of the Church of England from William Wilberforce to "Lux Mundi"* (London: SPCK, 1933), 221.

43. Quoted in Andrew L. Drummond, *The Churches in English Fiction* (Leicester: Edgar Backus, 1950), 78.

44. Marcus Donovan, *After the Tractarians* (London: Philip Allan, 1933), 6.

45. Embry, *Catholic Movement and Society of the Holy Cross*, 122–25.

46. Quoted in Baker, *Novel and Oxford Movement*, 14.

47. Benighted Layman, *Gropings in Search of the Church*, 8.

48. A. Metcalfe, *Crosses, Crucifixes and Musical Services* (London: John Kensit, [n.d., but 1889–1890]), 4.

49. Donovan, *After the Tractarians*, 6.

50. Quoted in Baker, *Novel and Oxford Movement*, 14.

51. Quoted in Drummond, *Churches in English Fiction*, 78.

52. *By This Thou Shalt Conquer* (n.d., but ca. 1850?; PH 14123). For a tract explaining and urging genuflection, see *Genuflexions. S. Joseph Tracts No. 3* (n.d., but ca. 1870; PH 10464). Other tracts in the same series (PH 10462–65) treated confession, fasting reception of communion, and "The Cultus of Our Lady."

53. Worley, *Catholic Movement*, 147.

54. This episode at St. Andrew's, Wells Street, is reported in Wakeling, *Oxford Church Movement*, 26.

55. Bernarr Rainbow, *The Choral Revival in the Anglican Church, 1839–1872* (London: Barrie & Jenkins, 1970), quotation from 277. See also Walter Lee Hillsman, "Trends and Aims

in Anglican Church Music 1870–1906 in Relation to Developments in Churchmanship" (D. Phil. thesis, Oxford University, 1985) for the later period. Hillsman examines in detail the practices of a number of churches, including St. Alban's, Holborn.

56. Drummond, *Churches in English Fiction*, 78n.

57. Quoted in David Newsome, *Godliness and Good Learning: Four Studies of a Victorian Ideal* (London: John Murray, 1961), 208.

58. See chapter 6.

59. James Bateman, *The Church Association: Its Policy and Prospects, Considered in a Letter to the Chairman* (2d ed., 1880; PH 4031).

60. Donovan, *After the Tractarians*, 6.

61. G. Bayfield Roberts, *The History of the English Church Union, 1859–1894* (London: Church Publishing, 1895); William Jesse Fong, "The Ritualist Crisis: Anglo-Catholics and Authority with Special Reference to the English Church Union, 1859–1882" (Ph.D. thesis, University of Toronto, 1978).

62. Embry, *Catholic Movement and Society of the Holy Cross*.

63. Ibid., 7–9, 71, 73.

64. Ibid., 67, 128.

65. Roberts, *History of the English Church Union*, 404–5.

66. E.C.U. *Report* for 1875–1876, cited in Presbyter Protestans, *"English Church Union" A Romanizing Confederacy*, 2.

67. English Church Union, *Annual Directory, 1892*.

68. Computed from information in *The Ritualistic Conspiracy* (23d ed., 1877; PH 6018). S.S.C. members who did not belong to the English Church Union were often Scottish.

69. Roberts, *History of the English Church Union*, 81–83.

70. Ibid., 42, 48.

71. Worley, *Catholic Movement*, 143–44.

72. Embry, *Catholic Movement and Society of the Holy Cross*, 97, 102–5; quotation from 103.

73. John B Dykes, *Eucharistic Truth and Ritual: A Letter to the Right Reverend the Lord Bishop of Durham* [etc.] (2d ed., 1874; PH 1631).

74. Embry, *Catholic Movement and Society of the Holy Cross*, 125.

75. Ibid., 103.

76. For accounts of these controversies, see, for instance, Reynolds, *Martyr of Ritualism*, 178, 211–27.

77. Desmond Morse-Boycott, *They Shine Like Stars* (London: Skeffington & Son, [1947]), 197.

78. Ibid., 117–18.

79. See, for instance, Thomas Howard Gill, *A Letter to the Right Reverend the Lord Bishop of Manchester, Touching "Ritualism"* (London: Hatchards, 1878), 4–5.

80. *The Rock*, an ultra-Protestant paper, first published a list of S.S.C. members, supplied by "some unknown friend," in the 23d edition of *The Ritualistic Conspiracy* (1877). Earlier editions had contained lists of priests-associate of the Confraternity of the Blessed Sacrament, clerical members of the E.C.U., and signatories to the petition of 1873. Many similar lists were later compiled and circulated, e.g., Church Association, *Society of the Holy Cross. With List of Members* (1897; PH 8555); *The Ritualistic Clergy List, Being a Guide for Patrons and Others to Certain of the Clergy of the Church of England; Containing a List of Some 9600 Clergymen Who Are Helping the Romeward Movement in the National Church*, 2d ed. (London: Church Association, 1902); and *The Clerical Ritualistic Who's Who, with an Account of the Ritualistic Conspiracy* [etc.] (London: Protestant Truth Society, [1908]).

81. A. M. D. G., *Some Account of the Consultative Meetings of Priests of the Catholic Party in the Church of England Held During Congress Week in Brighton* (1875; PH 7758).

82. Walter Walsh, *The Secret History of the Oxford Movement* (London: Swan Sonnenschein, 1897), 64.

83. Walsh's book, ibid., is a good example of the response.

84. Presbyter Protestans, *"English Church Union" A Romanizing Confederacy*, 1.

85. Worley, *Catholic Movement*, 130.

86. See chapter 8.

87. *Constitutions of the Society for the Maintenance of the Faith* (1876; PH 2180); *Ritualistic Conspiracy* (1877). One more, Archdeacon Denison, joined the next year.

88. *Rules of the Society of S. Alphege, Abp. & M.* (n.d.; PH 4629).

89. *Society of S. Alphege, Abp. & M. List of Associates. Corrected up to May 1, 1868* (1868; PH 4646).

90. Society of St. Alphege, Abp. & M., *Offices for the Society* [etc.] (n.d.; PH 4631).

91. *Rules of the Society of S. Alphege; Society of S. Alphege. List of Associates.*

92. *Ritualistic Conspiracy* (1877).

93. Thomas W. Perry, *The Church of England's Claim to Primitive and Catholic Ceremonial* (1874; PH 7750).

94. It is difficult to be more precise, because at this time the organization was still "semisecret." No listing of lay associates exists, and priests-associate could elect to be omitted from that list. In 1894, the C.B.S. claimed 13,444 lay and 1,682 clerical members (*Annual Report*, cited in Walsh, *Secret History*, 210).

95. Computed from *Ritualistic Conspiracy* (1877).

96. On the Anglo-Catholic ecumenical impulse, see Fong, "Ritualist Crisis," 47–58.

97. "Plaster" in Shane Leslie, *The Oxford Movement, 1833 to 1933* (London: Burns, Oates & Washbourne, 1933), 61; Henry R. T. Brandreth, *Dr. Lee of Lambeth: A Chapter in Parenthesis in the History of the Oxford Movement* (London: S.P.C.K., 1951), 90–93.

98. For this bizarre story, see Brandreth, *Dr. Lee of Lambeth*, 118–45; also Brandreth's *Episcopi Vagantes and the Anglican Church* (London: S.P.C.K., 1947), 64–65, and Peter F. Anson, *Bishops at Large* (London: Faber and Faber, 1964), 57–90.

99. Ibid., 132; [Society of the Holy Cross], *A Statement by the Society of the Holy Cross Concerning the Order of Corporate Reunion* (1879; PH 4097). Estimates of the number of clergymen who availed themselves of the O.C.R.'s services range up to eight hundred (by an ex-Ritualist who had become a Roman Catholic priest, reported in Walsh, *Secret History*, 161), but the most sober guess is by Brandreth, in *Dr. Lee of Lambeth*, 139, who doubts that the total reached a hundred.

100. *The Anglican Crusade* (n.d., but bound with 1885; PH 2361).

101. Morse-Boycott, *Secret Story*, 172; Bateman, *Church Association*.

102. On the "constellation of manufacturers gathered round the Ecclesiological Society" and for illustrations of some of their wares, see Victoria and Albert Museum, *Victorian Church Art: Exhibition November 1971–January 1972* (London: H.M.S.O., 1971), quotation from xvi.

103. On publishing houses connected with the movement, see Wakeling, *Oxford Church Movement*, 293–302.

104. Bateman, *Church Association*.

105. Vincent, *Proceedings at the Ecclesiastical Art Exhibition, York*.

106. *Church Times*, April 14, 1866.

107. *Church Times*, August 16, 1866.

108. Robert Brown, *Ritualism at Barton-on-Humber* [etc.] (London: Marlborough, 1867). For a similar complaint from Doncaster, almost thirty years later, see Charles Alford, *"Stand Fast" or, Contention for the Common Salvation against the Inroads of Ritualism a Christian Duty* (London: Simpkin, Marshall, Hamilton, Kent, [1895]), 4–5.

109. "A High Churchman of the Old School," *Quousque? How far? How long?* (1873; PH 5998).

110. Joyce Coombs, *One Aim: Edward Stuart, 1820–1877* (London: Stanhope Press, 1975), 31.

111. *Mackeson's*, annual after 1866, gave detailed descriptions of the services at all Anglican churches in the metropolis. A competitor with a somewhat Evangelical tinge evident in its

advertisements, *The London Church of England Directory and Guide* (London: Office of the London Church of England Directory, 1879 *et seq.*), began publication some years later.

112. *Mackeson's* (1870).

113. Wakeling, *Oxford Church Movement*, 237.

114. Kelway, *George Rundle Prynne*.

115. *Father Pollock and His Brother: Mission Priests of St. Alban's, Birmingham* (London: Longmans, Green, 1911), 18–22.

116. J. Carne Waram, *Tourist's Church Guide, 1877*, 7th ed. (London: G. J. Palmer, 1877), 28. Waram listed only those churches with communion services at least weekly.

117. J. F. Briscoe and H. F. B. MacKay, *A Tractarian at Work: A Memoir of Dean Randall* (London: A. R. Mowbray, 1932), 156.

118. For descriptions of several of these churches, including some of those mentioned here, see R. W. Franklin, *Nineteenth-Century Churches: The History of a New Catholicism in Württemberg, England, and France* (New York: Garland Publishing, 1987), 272–339.

CHAPTER 5

1. "Adam Bede," *The Natural History of Puseyism: With a Short Account of the Sunday Opera at St. Paul's, Brighton* (Brighton: G. Smart, [1860]), 4.

2. This despite the fact that most Tractarian incumbents served small-town and village parishes, particularly in the rural South (George William Herring, "Tractarianism to Ritualism: A Study of Some Aspects of Tractarianism Outside Oxford, from the Time of Newman's Conversion in 1845, until the First Ritual Commission in 1867" [D. Phil. thesis, Oxford University, 1984], 46–48). Clerical Tractarianism was strong where the Church of England was strong, in other words, with exceptions that can be largely explained by the attitudes of bishops.

3. The figures for St. Pancras are from Roger Lloyd's discussion in *The Church of England, 1900–1965* (London: SCM Press, 1966), 74–76.

4. See, for instance, M. H. Port, *Six Hundred New Churches: A Study of the Church Building Commission, 1818–1856, and its Church Building Activities* (London: S.P.C.K., 1961).

5. An early historian of the movement pointed to the important distinction "between the introduction of a high ritual into a new church or a district church, and into the one old parish church of the place" (J. H. Overton, *The Anglican Revival* [London: Blackie & Son, 1897], 209).

6. Harry Jones, *East and West London: Being Notes of Common Life and Pastoral Work in Saint James's, Westminster and in Saint George's-in-the-East* (London: Smith, Elder, 1875), 47 ff.; quotations from 59–60.

7. Ibid., 59–60.

8. E. B. Pusey, *The Proposed Ecclesiastical Legislation. Three Letters to "The Times"* [etc.] (1874; PH 8063).

9. A. H. Mackonochie, *Remonstrance: A Letter to the Bishop of London* (1875; PH 1694).

10. Information on parish sizes and services from *Mackeson's* (1882). On St. Margaret Pattens, see J. Embry, *The Catholic Movement and the Society of the Holy Cross* (London: Faith Press, 1931), 50.

11. Marcus Donovan, *After the Tractarians* (London: Philip Allan, 1933), 75–76.

12. James Bentley, *Ritualism and Politics in Victorian Britain: The Attempt to Legislate for Belief* (Oxford: Oxford University Press, 1978), 21 (quoting F. Burnard).

13. Desmond Morse-Boycott, *They Shine Like Stars* (London: Skeffington & Son, [1947]), 164.

14. Unless otherwise indicated, this account is taken from the *Church Times*, October 13 and 20, 1866.

15. [W. Vincent], *Catalogue of the Ecclesiastical Art Exhibition, Castlegate House, York, October 9th, 10th, 11th, and 12th, 1866* (1866; PH 10089).

16. W. Vincent, *Report of the Proceedings at the Ecclesiastical Art Exhibition, Held at York,*

on the 9th, 10th, 11th, & 12th October, 1866 (1866; PH 12880).

17. *The York Congress and Church Rites* (1867; PH 1321).

18. Robert Douglas, *Is It Expedient? A Question for Loyal Churchmen on Going to Church Congresses* (London: Simpkin, Marshall, [1879]), 6; J. C. Ryle, *Shall We Go?* (London: William Hunt, 1878), 19.

19. S. A. Walker, *No! An Answer to Canon Ryle's Tract "Shall We Go?"* [etc.] (London: Elliot Stock, n.d.).

20. Newman quoted in [Charles Wood], Viscount Halifax, *The English Church Union: Its Future Viewed in the Light of Its Past* (1901; PH 8487); Oakeley in Owen Chadwick (ed.), *The Mind of the Oxford Movement* (Stanford, Calif.: Stanford University Press, 1961), 56.

21. See, for instance, C. S. Grueber, *"Omission" Not "Prohibition": A Letter to His Grace the Archbishop of Canterbury* (1869; PH 1428) and *Decisions on Ritual: An Appeal to the People of the Church of England* (1874; PH 1649); *Disputed Ritual Ornaments and Usages* [etc.] (1866; PH 7877); Hooker Wix, *Ritualism; or, Ritualistic Worship: Ordained by God Himself, Practiced by the Early Christian Church, strictly legal in the Church of England, Conducive to the Glory of God, and the Edifying of the Congregation. Being an Address to his Congregation* (n.d., but 1866; PH 10029).

22. See, for instance, the quote from Charles Walker, *The Ritual Reason Why,* in Robert Eden, *Our Church Troubles: Their Root, and a Suggestion of the Cure* (London: W. MacIntosh, [1875]), 9; Arthur A. Dawson, *Sacrifice: Patriarchal, Jewish, Christian* (1873; PH 1599).

23. See, for instance, Richard Frederick Littledale, *The North-side of the Altar: A Liturgical Essay* (1865; PH 72868).

24. See Owen Chadwick,"The Established Church under Attack," in *The Victorian Crisis of Faith,* ed. Anthony Symondson (London: S.P.C.K., 1970), 112.

25. Quoted in M. W. Mayow, *Remarks upon the First Report of the Royal Commission on Ritual* [etc.] (1868; PH 7858).

26. Eden, *Our Church Troubles.*

27. Chadwick, "Established Church under Attack," 118 ff. Charles John Ellicott, bishop of Gloucester and Bristol, however, clearly believed that changes in the rubrics would also be required, and forthcoming (*Future Prospects* [1874; PH 7572]).

28. Sir Lewis Dibden, quoted in S. C. Carpenter, *Church and People, 1789–1889: A History of the Church of England from William Wilberforce to "Lux Mundi"* (London: SPCK, 1933), 226.

29. John Conroy, *Mr. Green's Case* (1881; PH 73313).

30. Michael Reynolds, *Martyr of Ritualism: Father Mackonochie of St. Alban's, Holborn* (London: Faber and Faber, 1965), 125.

31. *The Church Association versus Rev. S. F. Green, B.A.* (n.p., 1881) is simply a reprint of the association's bill of costs, presumably distributed by an Anglo-Catholic source. The British Library's copy is the sixth edition.

32. See, for instance, F. W. Puller, *The Duties and Rights of Parish Priests and the Limits of the Obedience due from them to their Bishops* [etc.] (London: Rivington's, 1877), 35.

33. English Church Union, *Report of the President and Council of the English Church Union on the course to be adopted by the Union* [etc.] (1867; PH 10062).

34. Reynolds, *Martyr of Ritualism,* 155.

35. Peter F. Anson, *Fashions in Church Furnishings, 1840–1940* (London: Faith Press, 1960), summarizes the complex and conflicting legal decisions in a table, 213–14.

36. Shane Leslie, *The Oxford Movement, 1833 to 1933* (London: Burns, Oates & Washbourne, 1933), 75. On incense, see R. F. Littledale, *Incense. A Liturgical Essay* (1866; PH 9910).

37. Quoted in J. T. Coleridge, *Remarks on Some Parts of the Report of the Judicial Committee in the Case of "Elphinstone against Purchas"* [etc.] (1871; PH 4209).

38. John Jebb, *The Ritual Law and Custom of the Church Universal* (1865; PH 1962).

39. By the turn of the century this view was widely accepted among extreme Anglo-

Catholics. See Alan Wilson, "The Authority of Church and Party among London Anglo-Catholics, 1880–1914, with Special Reference to the Church Crisis, 1898–1904" (D. Phil. thesis, Oxford University, 1988), 178–226, which draws heavily on the *Acta* of the Society of the Holy Cross.

40. Puller, *Duties and Rights of Parish Priests*, 34–35.

41. Letter to the *Church Times*, March 20, 1874. By January of the next year Denison had apparently changed his mind (see his *Prohibited Ceremonial. What Is the Priest to Do?* [1875; PH 7260]), but he returned to his initial opinion before 1877 (see below).

42. [George Anthony Denison], *The Charge of the Archdeacon of Taunton at his Visitation, April 1877* (Oxford: James Parker, 1877), iv.

CHAPTER 6

1. W. J. Conybeare, "Church Parties," *The Edinburgh Review* 98 (October 1853): 302. Although not entirely reliable, this article presents a convenient, sardonic, and highly quotable anatomy of the Church parties and their constituent factions at mid-century.

2. N. Dimock, *The Crisis in the Church of England: Its History and Present Position* (London: Elliot Stock, 1899), 41, 44.

3. Anthony Trollope, *Barchester Towers* (London: J. M. Dent & Sons, 1977 [1857]), 461.

4. Conybeare, "Church Parties," 301.

5. Ibid., 329.

6. Desmond Bowen, *The Idea of the Victorian Church: A Study of the Church of England, 1833–1889* (Montreal: McGill University Press, 1968), 45–48; quotations from 45, 47.

7. Trollope, *Barchester Towers*, 461.

8. Conybeare, "Church Parties," 306.

9. Owen Chadwick, *The Victorian Church*, 3d ed. (London: Adam & Charles Black, 1971), 1:309–24.

10. For what it is worth, Conybeare ("Church Parties") estimated that the High Church comprised some 39 percent of the Church of England in the 1850s: 14 percent "High and Dry," 19 percent "Anglican" (or moderate), and only 6 percent "Tractarian."

11. Ibid., 302.

12. Richard Frederick Littledale, "The First Report of the Ritual Commission," in *The Church and the World: Essays on Questions of the Day in 1868*, ed. Orby Shipley (London: Longmans, Green, Reader, and Dyer, 1868), 29–30.

13. John B. Dykes, *Eucharistic Truth and Ritual: A Letter to the Right Reverend the Lord Bishop of Durham* [etc.] (2d ed., 1874; PH 1631).

14. Presbyter Anglicanus, *How the Church of England May Be Preserved* (London: William MacIntosh, [n.d., but 1875]), 13.

15. Dimock, *Crisis in the Church*, 41, 44.

16. G. Albert Rogers, *The Real Presence the Basis of Ritualism* (n.d., but ca. 1867; PH 10055).

17. *Church Times*, November 10, 1866.

18. Quoted, in Michael Hill, *The Religious Order: A Study of Virtuoso Religion and Its Legitimation in the Nineteenth-Century Church of England* (London: Heinemann Educational Books, 1973), 182. For complaints that Wilberforce was protecting Anglo-Catholics in his diocese can be found in *The Charge of the Bishop of Oxford in 1866, and Ritualism* (1867; PH 10006) and Causidicus, letter in *Christian Observer* (1867; PH 10007).

19. Quoted in Walter Walsh, *The Secret History of the Oxford Movement* (London: Swan Sonnenschein, 1897), 88.

20. Quoted in Nigel Yates, *The Oxford Movement and Parish Life: St Saviour's, Leeds, 1839–1929*, Borthwick Papers No. 48 (York: University of York, Borthwick Institute of Historical Research, 1975), 12.

21. *What is the Anglo-Continental Society?*, 2d ed. (London: Rivington's, 1879).

22. J. Embry, *The Catholic Movement and the Society of the Holy Cross* (London: Faith Press, 1931), xxxv–xxxvi.

23. Perry Butler, *Gladstone: Church, State, and Tractarianism* (Oxford: Clarendon Press, 1982), 112–21.

24. When John Mason Neale circulated a petition protesting Gobat's activities, nearly every prominent Tractarian signed, but other High Church luminaries were conspicuously absent (*Protest against the Proselytism Carried on by Bishop Gobat* [n.d.; PH 159]).

25. See, for instance, the call for disestablishment by Causidicus (letter in *Christian Observer* cited above).

26. The three laymen were among the organization's seventy-one vice-presidents, most of them noblemen or prelates; the president was the archbishop of Canterbury (*The Church Defence Institution: An Association of Clergy and Laity for Defensive and General Purposes* [n.d.; PH 73720]). James Dunn, *The Honesty of Our Position: A Paper Read before the Clifton Branch of the E.C.U.* (London: Pickering, 1878), 6. On "church defense," see also M. A. Crowther, *Church Embattled: Religious Controversy in Mid-Victorian England* (Newton Abbot, Devon: David & Charles, 1970), 186–218. William Jesse Fong, "The Ritualist Crisis: Anglo-Catholics and Authority with Special Reference to the English Church Union, 1859–1882" (Ph.D. thesis, University of Toronto, 1978), has an extensive treatment of the establishment question (see 94–113).

27. W. Vincent, *Report of the Proceedings at the Ecclesiastical Art Exhibition, Held at York, on the 9th, 10th, 11th, & 12th October, 1866* (1866; PH 12880).

28. *Correspondence Concerning the Celebration of Holy Communion on Good Friday in the Church of England* (London: George Bell & Sons, 1883).

29. Katherine Warburton reported that the sacrament was reserved at St. Margaret's when she arrived in 1858 (*Memories of a Sister of S. Saviour's Priory* [Oxford and London: A. R. Mowbray, 1903], 35).

30. Edward Meyrick Goulburn, *The Confession of a Reticent Dean* [etc.] (1881; PH 2654).

31. E. B. Pusey, *The Proposed Ecclesiastical Legislation. Three Letters to "The Times"* [etc.] (1874; PH 8063).

32. Littledale, "First Report of the Ritual Commission," 18–19.

33. In 1879, the earl was a vice president of the Anglo-Continental Society (*What Is the Anglo-Continental Society?*).

34. *Report of the Council of the English Church Union Relative to the Preparation of the Memorials on Ritual, and of Their Presentation* [etc.] (1866; PH 7872).

35. *The Bishop of Manchester on the Rulings of the Purchas Judgment* (n.d.; PH 4210).

36. Quoted in J. T. Coleridge, *Remarks on Some Parts of the Report of the Judicial Committee in the Case of "Elphinstone against Purchas"* [etc.] (1871; PH 4209).

37. Pusey, *Proposed Ecclesiastical Legislation.*

38. Malcolm MacColl, *My Reviewers Reviewed, in a Preface to the Third and Revised Edition of* Lawlessness, Sacerdotalism, and Ritualism (1875; PH 3365).

39. The Author of "The Rector and His Friends," *The Ritual Difficulty. An Eirenicon* (London: George Bell and Sons, 1877), 21, 22.

40. [George Anthony Denison], *The Charge of the Archdeacon of Taunton at his Visitation, April 1877* (Oxford: James Parker, 1877), ii.

41. Goulburn, *Confession.*

42. Quoted, ibid.

43. Quoted in Thomas Howard Gill, *A Letter to the Right Reverend the Lord Bishop of Manchester, Touching "Ritualism"* (London: Hatchards, 1878), 30–31.

44. Edward Garbett, *What are Our Duties in the Present Circumstances of the Church?* (London: William Hunt, 1867), 27.

45. [Charles Wood], Viscount Halifax, *The English Church Union: Its Future Viewed in the Light of Its Past* (1901; PH 8487).

46. *The Archbishop's Legacy: Will the Church Accept* It? (1883; PH 2303).

47. A Curate [H. W. Holden], *An Humble Expostulation and Appeal for Forbearance* [etc.] (1875; PH 1693).

48. T. T. Haverfield, *A Letter to a Layman, on the Recent Changes in the Manner of Performing Divine Service in the Metropolitan Churches* (1843; PH 5845).

49. Philip Freeman, *Rites and Ritual; A Plea for Apostolic Doctrine and Worship* (1866; PH 7875).

50. E. W. Sergeant, *Ritualism: How Far Reasonable?* (n.d., but ca. 1879; PH 3975).

51. H. M. Luckock, *The Ritual Crisis: How It May be Turned to the Best Account* (1899; PH 7193).

52. Richard Frederick Littledale, *Why Ritualists Do Not Become Roman Catholics: A Reply to the Abbe Martin* (n.d., but 1879; PH 1799).

53. G. Albert Rogers, *The Real Presence the Basis of Ritualism* (n.d., but ca. 1867; PH 10055).

54. John W. Burgon, *The Oxford Diocesan Conference; and Romanizing within the Church of England: Two Sermons Preached at St. Mary-the-Virgin's, Oxford, Oct. 12th and 19th, 1873* (Oxford: James Parker, 1873), 5. *Misconceptions of "Ritualist" Teaching: or, Are We Unfaithful?* (1873; PH 11839) by "An Oxford 'Ritualist' Clergyman" is a contemporary reply. For a later and more sympathetic view of these differences, see Darwell Stone, *The Faith of an English Catholic* (London: Longmans, Green, 1926), 17–19.

55. "Presbyter Anglicanus," Utum Horum: *The Book of Common Prayer, or, the* Directorium Anglicanum *in the Administration of the Holy Communion?* (1866; PH 1258).

56. Quoted in W. J. Sparrow Simpson, *The History of the Anglo-Catholic Revival from 1845* (London: George Allen & Unwin, 1932), 78.

57. Ibid., 79.

58. *Church Times*, December 8, 1866.

59. J. M. Neale, *Extreme Men. A Letter to A. J. B. Beresford Hope* (1865; PH 6002).

60. *Caught Napping* (3d ed., 1866; PH 7853).

61. "The Editor of the Protestant Churchman," *Ritualist Caricature of the Bishops* (n.d., but ca. 1866; PH 10088).

62. A Curate, *Humble Expostulation*.

63. *The Moral Effect of Irregularities in the Ritual of the Church* (1843; PH 5995).

64. Orby Shipley, *A Specimen of Recent Anglican Controversy with Rome: A Letter to the Rev. Dr. Pusey, D.D.* (London: Privately printed, 1880), 9.

65. Malcolm MacColl, *Tractarianism and Ritualism* (1881; PH 4033).

66. *Guardian* of July 14, 1875, quoted in Orby Shipley, *Ought We to Obey the New Court...?* (1875; PH 8064).

67. Coleridge, *Remarks on "Elphinstone against Purchas."*

68. One of those resigning explained his reasons and paraphrased the warden in Vernon W. Hutton, *Reasons for Leaving the English Church Union* (1877; PH 10902).

69. Quoted in J. G. Lockhart, *Charles Lindley, Viscount Halifax* (London: Centenary Press, 1935), 1:201–2.

70. *A Memorial of Nine Hundred and Ten Priests, Presented to Both Houses of the Convocation of the Province of Canterbury* (1871; PH 6506).

71. *An Alphabetical List of the Signatures to a Remonstrance Addressed to the Archbishops and Bishops of the Church of England On Occasion of the Report of the Judicial Committee of the Privy Council* in re *Hebbert* v. *Purchas* (1871; PH 1516). Four years later, even more clergymen signed an opposing petition, *Clerical Address to the Prelates Against Legalising the Eastward Position and a Distinctive Eucharistic Dress; with the Names of 5376 Clergymen by Whom it Was Signed* [etc.] (London: Seeley, Jackson, & Halliday, 1875). It appears that nearly ten thousand clergymen signed one petition or the other.

72. *Declaration: 1874* (1874; PH 1643).

73. *The Prayer-book and Eucharistic Ceremonial* (1874; PH 4817).

74. A. M. D. G., *Some Account of the Consultative Meetings of Priests of the Catholic Party*

in the Church of England Held During Congress Week in Brighton (1875; PH 7758).

75. Pusey, *Proposed Ecclesiastical Legislation.*

76. E. B. Pusey, letter to *The Times* (July 1874; PH 74155).

77. Sergeant, *Ritualism.*

78. John Edward Field, *Some Principles of Christian Ceremonial* (1874; PH 71691).

79. Sergeant, *Ritualism.* Even George William Herring, who insists on the discontinuity between Tractarians and Ritualists, concludes that "it seems clear that by the 1870s the Ritualists had won over a considerable portion of the Tractarians to their cause and that doctrine and Ritual would sink or swim together" ("Tractarianism to Ritualism: A Study of Some Aspects of Tractarianism Outside Oxford, from the Time of Newman's Conversion in 1845, until the First Ritual Commission in 1867" [D. Phil. thesis, Oxford University, 1984], 347).

80. *Declaration on the Doctrine of the Holy Eucharist* (1867; PH 5747).

81. *Declaration Concerning Confession and Absolution* (1873; PH 7257). Pusey quoted in Paul Thureau-Dangin, *The English Catholic Revival in the Nineteenth Century* (New York: E. P. Dutton, n.d.), 1:504.

82. Pusey, letter to *Times* cited above.

CHAPTER 7

1. W. J. Conybeare, "Church Parties," *The Edinburgh Review* 98 (October 1853): 302.

2. Hensley Henson, cited in Roger Lloyd, *The Church of England, 1900–1965* (London: SCM Press, 1966), 125. Henson was by then no friend of the movement, so both figures may have been underestimates, but there is little reason to question the ratio of one kind of support to the other.

3. Andrew Martin Fairbairn, *The New Sacerdotalism and the New Puritanism: A Discourse Delivered before the Congregational Union of England and Wales* (London: Hodder and Stoughton, [1868]), 11–12.

4. John Kent, *Holding the Fort: Studies in Victorian Revivalism* (London: Epworth Press, 1978), 283.

5. See, for instance, *Church Reform: and the Report of the Royal Commission on Ritual, being the second annual Report of the Church of England Laymen's Defense Association; together with a Note on Sacerdotalism* (London: W. MacIntosh, [1868]), 14.

6. Quoted in Orby Shipley, (ed.), *The Church and the World: Essays on Questions of the Day in 1866,* 3d ed. (London: Longmans, Green, Reader, and Dyer, 1867), 545.

7. Quoted in G. Kitson Clark, *Churchmen and the Condition of England, 1832–1885* (London: Methuen & Co, 1973), 83. Clark offers a good study of changing relations between Church and nation.

8. Lloyd, *Church of England,* 74. See also M. H. Port, *Six Hundred New Churches: A Study of the Church Building Commission, 1818–1856, and its Church Building Activities* (London: S.P.C.K., 1961).

9. K. S. Inglis, *Churches and the Working Classes in Victorian England* (London: Routledge and Kegan Paul, 1963), 40, 38.

10. Anthony Trollope, *Clergymen of the Church of England* (Leicester: Leicester University Press, 1974 [1866]), 59–60. See also Paul A. Welsby, "Anthony Trollope and the Church of England," *Church Quarterly Review* 163 (April–June 1962): 213. On clerical education, see also M. A. Crowther, *Church Embattled: Religious Controversy in Mid-Victorian England* (Newton Abbot, Devon: David & Charles, 1970), 219–40.

11. Inglis, *Churches and the Working Classes,* 41; Lloyd, *Church of England, 1900–1965,* 75–76. The social standing of bishops was declining as well; see D. H. J. Morgan, "The Social and Educational Background of Anglican Bishops—Continuities and Changes." *British Journal of Sociology* 20 (September 1969): 295–310 (table on 298).

12. Inglis, *Churches and the Working Classes,* 38.

13. J. E. T. Rogers, "University Extension," in *The Church and the World: Essays on Ques-*

tions of the Day in 1866, ed. Orby Shipley, 3d ed. (London: Longmans, Green, Reader, and Dyer, 1867), 4.

14. Quoted in Shipley, *Church and World: 1866*, 537.

15. Richard Frederick Littledale, "The First Report of the Ritual Commission," in *The Church and the World: Essays on Questions of the Day in 1868*, ed. Orby Shipley (London: Longmans, Green, Reader, and Dyer, 1868), 32.

16. John Henry Hopkins, *The Law of Ritualism* (1867; PH 10673).

17. "Adam Bede," *The Natural History of Puseyism: With a Short Account of the Sunday Opera at St. Paul's, Brighton* (Brighton: G. Smart, [1860]), 14. A.

18. Littledale, "First Report of the Ritual Commission," 52–53.

19. A Priest of the Church of England, *The Form of Godliness: Being Some Remarks on Catholic Ritual* (London: J. Masters, 1867), 5.

20. Richard Frederick Littledale, *Why Ritualists Do Not Become Roman Catholics: A Reply to the Abbe Martin* (n.d., but 1879; PH 1799).

21. Littledale, "First Report of the Ritual Commission," 67.

22. See appendix 2.

23. George William Herring, "Tractarianism to Ritualism: A Study of Some Aspects of Tractarianism Outside Oxford, from the Time of Newman's Conversion in 1845, until the First Ritual Commission in 1867" (D. Phil. thesis, Oxford University, 1984), 45, reports that a majority of the 192 converts in his sample of 958 Anglo-Catholic clergymen were curates.

24. Unless otherwise noted, information in the following paragraphs is taken from G. Bayfield Roberts, *The History of the English Church Union, 1859–1894* (London: Church Publishing, 1895), a year-by-year chronology.

25. The Lower House of the Convocation of Canterbury included only forty-four parish clergymen, but ninety-nine cathedral clergy. See G. R. Balleine, *A History of the Evangelical Party in the Church of England*, new ed. (London: Church Book Room Press, 1951 [1908]), 213.

26. Roberts, *History of the English Church Union*, 56.

27. Quoted from *Church Review*, May 30, 1868, in Charles Dallas Marston, *The Position of the Laity in the Church* (London: W. Hunt, 1868), 7.

28. Desmond Bowen, *The Idea of the Victorian Church: A Study of the Church of England, 1833–1889* (Montreal: McGill University Press, 1968), 352. On Gladstone's ambivalent relations with the movement, see Perry Butler, *Gladstone: Church, State, and Tractarianism* (Oxford: Clarendon Press, 1982), especially 157–94.

29. Quoted in the *Church Times*, January 18, 1868. This quotation was a favorite of the ritualists' opponents; see, for instance, Presbyter Protestans, *The "English Church Union"... A Romanizing Confederacy* (London: John F. Shaw, 1877), and Walter Walsh, *The Ritualists: Their Romanising Objects and Work* (London: James Nisbet, 1900), 29.

30. Quoted in Edwin Hodder, *The Life and Work of the Seventh Earl of Shaftesbury, K.G.* (London: Cassell, 1886), 3:228; variant in Earl of Shaftesbury, *Speech in the House of Lords ... on moving the Second Reading of the Clerical Vestments Bill* (London: Church Association, 1867), 20.

31. Hodder, *Life and Work of Shaftesbury* 2:407. For the equally forthright Erastian views of Lord Selbourne see, for instance, Edmund S. Grindle, *Canon or Statute. A Correspondence on the Public Worship Regulation Act between the Right Honourable Lord Selbourne and a Sussex Priest* (1875; PH 1634). Low Churchmen in general, including Low Church clergy, opposed the revival of convocations; see Peter Toon, *Evangelical Theology, 1833–1856: A Response to Tractarianism* (London: Marshall, Morgan & Scott, 1979), 95–96.

32. Quoted in W. J. Sparrow Simpson, *The History of the Anglo-Catholic Revival from 1845* (London: George Allen & Unwin, 1932), 215.

33. Quoted in *Church Reform*, 14; also in Marston, *Position of the Laity*, 7. The first of these sources is a polemic, the second a scholarly defense of lay participation in church governance.

34. See, for instance, Walter Farquhar Hook, *Hear the Church. A Sermon Preached at the*

Chapel Royal, in St. James's Palace [etc.] (London: J.G. and F. Rivington, 1839).

35. *Rev. J. Keble and the Ritual Question* (1865; PH 5738).

36. Quoted in Sparrow Simpson, *History of the Anglo-Catholic Revival*, 190; remarks on the American church from E. B. Pusey, *Habitual Confession Not Discouraged by the Resolution Accepted by the Lambeth Conference* (Oxford: James Parker, 1878), 34.

37. Quoted in Presbyter Protestans, *"English Church Union" A Romanizing Confederacy*, 11.

38. Quoted in Sparrow Simpson, *History of the Anglo-Catholic Revival*, 207.

39. Ibid., 207.

40. Henry R. T. Brandreth, *Dr. Lee of Lambeth: A Chapter in Parenthesis in the History of the Oxford Movement* (London: S.P.C.K., 1951), 92. Lee's support was characteristically quirky; see his *Beati pacifici. The Need of Spiritual Authority* [etc.] (1882; PH 7587), an 1882 sermon to mark the twenty-fifth anniversary of the Association for the Promotion of the Unity of Christendom and the fifth of the Order of Corporate Reunion.

41. Michael Reynolds, *Martyr of Ritualism: Father Mackonochie of St. Alban's, Holborn* (London: Faber and Faber, 1965), 210.

42. J. Embry, *The Catholic Movement and the Society of the Holy Cross* (London: Faith Press, 1931), 55.

43. On Gladstone's views, see Reynolds, *Martyr of Ritualism*, 206. George Anthony Denison, *The Episcopate with Two Voices* (Oxford: James Parker, 1874), 54.

44. Reynolds, *Martyr of Ritualism*, 207.

45. Stanton quoted in Presbyter Protestans, *"English Church Union" A Romanizing Conspiracy*, 11; Mackonochie in Reynolds, *Martyr of Ritualism*, 149 (see 194–210 for a good discussion of Anglo-Catholics' attitudes toward disestablishment).

46. That a movement begun in defense of the Establishment should in time provide the major Anglican opposition to it is one of several ironies discussed in W. R. Matthews, "By the Dean of Exeter," in Lord Hugh Cecil, the Dean of Exeter [W. R. Matthews], F. R. Barry, and Canon Wilfred L. Knox, *Anglo-Catholicism Today* (London: Philip Allan, 1934), 23–42.

47. See, for instance, E. R. Wickham, *Church and People in an Industrial City* (London: Lutterworth Press, 1957), 110–16, 142–43.

48. On the campaign against pew-rents, see Inglis, *Churches and the Working Classes*, 48–57.

49. See, for instance, A. G. Lough, *John Mason Neale—Priest Extraordinary* (Newton Abbot, Devon: privately published, [1975]), 25–28; James F. White, *The Cambridge Movement: The Ecclesiologists and the Gothic Revival* (Cambridge: Cambridge University Press, 1962), 106–9.

50. See also Paget's *St. Antholin's* (Andrew L. Drummond, *The Churches in English Fiction* [Leicester: Edgar Backus, 1950], 52ff).

51. See above, chapter 2.

52. *The Church and the People. An Address to Churchmen upon the Pew System and the Weekly Offertory* (London: Thomas Bosworth, 1865), 5.

53. White, *Cambridge Movement*, 107.

54. *Church Restoration and Church Arrangement. Being an Extract from the Speech of the Lord Bishop of Lincoln, after Reopening the Church at Newark* (London: Bell & Daldy, 1855).

55. Walter A. Gray, *The Symbolism of Churches and their Ornaments* (1857; PH 9224).

56. In *The Church and the World: Essays on Questions of the Day in 1867*, ed. Orby Shipley (London: Longmans, Green, Reader, and Dyer, 1867), 545.

57. W. Vincent, *Report of the Proceedings at the Ecclesiastical Art Exhibition, Held at York, on the 9th, 10th, 11th, & 12th October, 1866* (1866; PH 12880).

58. David L. Edwards, *Leaders of the Church of England, 1828–1944* (London: Oxford University Press, 1971), 85.

59. Quoted in Raymond Chapman, *Faith and Revolt: Studies in the Literary Influence of the Oxford Movement* (London: Weidenfeld and Nicolson, 1970), 175.

60. A. G. Lough, *The Influence of John Mason Neale* (London: S.P.C.K., 1962), 27.

61. Ibid., 28.

62. Drummond, *Churches in English Fiction*, 52n.

63. *Free and Open Churches. Facts and Opinions from Five Hundred Parishes in Town and Country*, 2d ed. (London: London Free and Open Church Association, 1876).

64. Among the prominent Ritualists who did so were "Mother Kate" Warburton, Richard Littledale, and Arthur Stanton ([Katherine Warburton], *Memories of a Sister of S. Saviour's Priory* [Oxford and London: A. R. Mowbray, 1903], 309). See also chapter 8, below.

65. Walsh, *The Ritualists*, 30.

66. White, *Cambridge Movement*, 98–102.

67. G. R. Portal, *On Some of the Prevalent Objections to Ritual Observances. A Sermon Preached in S. Barnabas' Church, Pimlico* [etc.] (1854; PH 11955).

68. *Ritual: A Plea in Its Behalf, Grounded on Scripture and Reason. By One Who Has Viewed Both Sides of the Questions* (n.d.; PH 70681).

69. *Stand Up, or Sit Down* (n.d.; PH 13696).

70. Reynolds, *Martyr of Ritualism*, 66.

71. *Malleus Ritualistarum; or, the Ritual Reason Why Not* (1872; PH 10918).

72. Nigel Yates, *Kent and the Oxford Movement: Selected Documents*, Kentish Sources VII, Kent Archives Office (Gloucester: Alan Sutton, 1983), 61–66.

73. *Church Times*, January 17 and 31, 1873.

74. E. Garbett, *Extreme Ritualism* (1866; PH 72876).

75. Letter of 1841, quoted in C. P. S. Clarke, "The Genesis of the Movement," in *Northern Catholicism: Centenary Studies in the Oxford and Parallel Movements*, ed. N. P. Williams and Charles Harris (New York: Macmillan, 1933), 31.

76. C. P. S. Clarke, *The Oxford Movement and After* (London: A. R. Mowbray, 1932), 107; Pusey quoted, 108.

77. Quoted against the movement in Bourchier Wrey Savile, *A Letter to the Rev. Dr. Pusey … on the "Catholic" Practice of Auricular Confession* (London: Hatchards, 1877), 64.

78. Trollope, *Clergymen of the Church of England*, 26.

79. C. H. Davis, *Remarks upon the Ritualistic "Memorial" of 12th. January, 1869* (1869; PH 1442).

80. Littledale, "First Report of the Ritual Commission," 20.

81. Brandreth, *Dr. Lee of Lambeth*, 135.

82. A Layman of the Diocese [of Chicester], *Things Indifferent* [etc.] (London: J. T. Hayes, 1877), 1.

83. Ibid., 4.

84. An Ex-Member of the Congregation of S. Bartholomew's, Brighton, *Are You Safe in the Church of England? A Question for Anxious Ritualists* (London: R. Washbourne, 1878), 23. Notice the capitalization of Roman "Bishops" and lower-casing of Anglican "bishops."

85. E. B. Pusey, *The Proposed Ecclesiastical Legislation. Three Letters to "The Times"* [etc.] (1874; PH 8063).

86. A. H. Mackonochie, *Remonstrance: A Letter to the Bishop of London* (1875; PH 1694).

87. Littledale, "First Report of the Ritual Commission," 27.

88. John B. Dykes, *Eucharistic Truth and Ritual: A Letter to the Right Reverend the Lord Bishop of Durham* [etc.] (2d ed., 1874; PH 1631).

89. Embry, *Catholic Movement and Society of the Holy Cross*, 121.

90. Lloyd, *Church of England*, 121.

91. Balleine, *History of the Evangelical Party*, 211–12.

92. Littledale, *Why Ritualists Do Not Become Roman Catholics*.

93. Archbishop Lang repeated the story; he is quoted in J. G. Lockhart, *Charles Lindley, Viscount Halifax* (London: Centenary Press, 1935), 2:220–21.

94. George Anthony Denison, *The Law of God and the Law of Man* [etc.] (1875; PH 2144).

95. C. S. Grueber, *Does the Bishop of London Obey his Own Judgment?* (1876; PH 1720).

96. R. W. Enraght, *Not Law, but Unconstitutional Tyranny* [etc.] (n.d., but 1877?; PH 1652).

97. *Church Union Gazette*, quoted in Presbyter Protestans, *"English Church Union" A Romanizing Confederacy*, 19.

98. James Parker, *The Ornaments Rubric: Its History and Meaning. A Series of Papers Contributed to the "Penny Post"* [etc.] (1881; PH 7329).

99. Embry, *Catholic Movement and Society of the Holy Cross*, 4. For Roman Catholic observations, see, for instance, William Maskell, *Protestant Ritualists* (1872; PH 1584); W. H. Anderson, *Is Ritualism Honest?* (n.d.; PH 73771), and An Ex-Member of the Congregation of S. Bartholomew's, *Are You Safe?*.

100. J. Woolley, *Clergy Discipline: Its Relation to Doctrine, Ritual, and Morals* (1881; PH 73312).

101. Quoted in Clarke, *Oxford Movement and After*, 108.

102. Quoted in Reynolds, *Martyr of Ritualism*, 62.

103. Dykes, *Eucharistic Truth*.

104. An Ex-Member of the Congregation of S. Bartholomew's, *Are You Safe?*, 5.

105. Quoted in Darwell Stone, *The Faith of an English Catholic* (London: Longmans, Green, 1926), 68.

106. *Malleus Ritualistarum*. On the role of missionary bishops in the movement, see Geoffrey Rowell, *The Vision Glorious: Themes and Personalities of the Catholic Revival in Anglicanism* (Oxford: Oxford University Press, 1983), 158–87.

107. Arthur Tilney Bassett, *S. Barnabas', Oxford: A Record of Fifty Years* (London: A.R. Mowbray, 1919), 43.

108. A. Clifton Kelway, *George Rundle Prynne: A Chapter in the Early History of the Catholic Revival* (London: Longmans, Green, 1905), 134–35.

109. Embry, *Catholic Movement and Society of the Holy Cross*, 33; Reynolds, *Martyr of Ritualism*, 114.

CHAPTER 8

1. *Puseyism in London* (1843; PH 5852).

2. Church Association, *Ritualism Rampant in East London* [etc.] (n.d., but ca. 1893; PH 8452).

3. For popular sketches of these and other prominent figures, see, for instance, B. C. Boulter, *The Anglican Reformers* (London: Philip Allan, 1933); Desmond Morse-Boycott, *Lead, Kindly Light: Studies of the Saints and Heroes of the Oxford Movement* (London: Centenary Press, 1932); Bertram C. A. Windle, *Who's Who of the Oxford Movement* (New York: Century, 1926). Good general treatments of Ritualism in the slums are Desmond Bowen, *The Idea of the Victorian Church: A Study of the Church of England, 1833–1889* (Montreal: McGill University Press, 1968), 285–311, and Geoffrey Rowell, *The Vision Glorious: Themes and Personalities of the Catholic Revival in Anglicanism* (Oxford: Oxford University Press, 1983), 116–40. All of these figures have been subjects of biographies and memoirs; two excellent recent ones are Michael Reynolds, *Martyr of Ritualism: Father Mackonochie of St. Alban's, Holborn* (London: Faber and Faber, 1965), and L. E. Ellsworth, *Charles Lowder and the Ritualist Movement* (London: Darton, Longman and Todd, 1982). For an extensive bibliography on Anglo-Catholic parishes and clergymen, see Francis Penhale, *The Anglican Church Today: Catholics in Crisis* (London: Mowbray, 1986), 159–60.

4. Quoted in J. Embry, *The Catholic Movement and the Society of the Holy Cross* (London: Faith Press, 1931), 2.

5. Ibid., 2.

6. See, for instance, J. S. Pollock, "Ritual: Its Influence on the Young and on the Poor," in W. Vincent, *Report of the Proceedings at the Ecclesiastical Art Exhibition, Held at York, on the 9th, 10th, 11th, & 12th October, 1866* (1866; PH 12880).

7. Quoted in Orby Shipley, (ed.), *The Church and the World: Essays on Questions of the Day in 1866*, 3d ed. (London: Longmans, Green, Reader, and Dyer, 1867), 524–25.

8. Richard Frederick Littledale, "The Missionary Aspect of Ritualism," in ibid., 33.

9. Ibid., 39.

10. Earl of Shaftesbury, *Speech in the House of Lords ... on Moving the Second Reading of the Clerical Vestments Bill* (London: Church Association, 1867).

11. Littledale, "Missionary Aspect of Ritualism," 39.

12. Richard Frederick Littledale, "The First Report of the Ritual Commission," in *The Church and the World: Essays on Questions of the Day in 1868*, ed. Orby Shipley (London: Longmans, Green, Reader, and Dyer, 1868), 24.

13. A Priest of the Church of England, *The Form of Godliness: Being Some Remarks on Catholic Ritual* (London: J. Masters, 1867), 8.

14. Reynolds, *Martyr of Ritualism*, 36. For a defense of ritual as a teaching device (and a less successful attempt to base it on scripture), see John Eddowes, *The New Testament and Ritual: A Lecture* (1877; PH 7681).

15. A Priest of the Diocese, *Pictorial Crucifixes. A Letter to the Lord Bishop of Chichester* (1852; PH 5862).

16. A. T. Gilbert, *Pictorial Crucifixes. A Letter to the Rev. Arthur D. Wagner, M.A.* (1852; PH 5861).

17. Quoted in Reynolds, *Martyr of Ritualism*, 29.

18. T. S. F. Rawlins, *A Sermon Preached in the Parish Church of Clifton Campville* (1858; PH 71130).

19. J. MacCartie, *Ritualism and Symbolism Obstructive to the Clear Light of Completed Revelation. A Sermon Preached in Christ Church, Carlisle, on Wednesday, 21st March, 1866* (1866; PH 9923); Littledale, "Missionary Aspect of Ritualism," 50.

20. A Priest of the Church of England, *Form of Godliness*, 8.

21. N. P. Williams, "The Theology of the Catholic Revival," in *Northern Catholicism: Centenary Studies in the Oxford and Parallel Movements*, ed. N. P. Williams and Charles Harris (New York: Macmillan, 1933), 138. Cf. Roger Lloyd, *The Church of England, 1900–1965* (London: SCM Press, 1966), 136–37.

22. Charles A. Bury, *The Church Association* (1873; PH 5995).

23. Percy Alden, "The Problem of East London," in *The Religious Life of London*, ed. Richard Mudie-Smith (London: Hodder and Stoughton, 1904), 37.

24. *Mackeson's* (1882) lists 908 Anglican churches in greater London and gives a variety of information about each. Charles Booth, *Life and Labour of the People in London*, vol. 2: *Streets and People Classified* (London: Macmillan, 1892) has a good discussion of London's class structure (20–21) and an account of the color-coding of his maps (40–41). The seven volumes of Booth's *Life and Labour of the People in London. Third Series: Religious Influences* (London: Macmillan, 1902) give block-by-block maps of the economic situation of Londoners and show parish boundaries.

25. *The Religious Census of London. Reprinted from "The British Weekly"* (London: Hodder and Stoughton, 1888). Unless otherwise indicated, attendance figures are from this source. The census-takers counted the October 24, 1886, congregations at the principal morning service and at the evening service, at every known place of worship in London. For a discussion and a comparison to the *Daily News* census of 1902 and 1903, see Hugh McLeod, *Class and Religion in the Late Victorian City* (Hamden, Ct.: Archon Books, 1974), 23–41. For discussions of an earlier effort, see D. M. Thompson, "The 1851 Religious Census: Problems and Possibilities," *Victorian Studies* 11 (September 1967), 87–97, and W. S. F. Pickering, "The 1851 Religious Census—A Useless Experiment?" *British Journal of Sociology* 18 (1967), 382–407.

26. See chapter 1.

27. Octavius J. Ellis, *Some Time among Ritualists*, 3d ed. (London: Hatchards, 1868), 11.

28. On its early history, see, for instance, Ellsworth, *Charles Lowder and the Ritualist Movement*, 13–20. Nigel Yates indicates that the same situation obtained even at St. Saviour's,

Leeds (*Leeds and the Oxford Movement: A Study of "High Church" Activity in the Rural Deaneries of Allerton, Armley, Headingley and Whitkirk in the Diocese of Ripon, 1836–1934*, Publications of the Thoresby Society, 55, no. 121 [Leeds: Thoresby Society, 1975], 66). For an early statement of the Ritualists' evangelical theory by the senior curate of St. Barnabas, see James Skinner, *Why Do We Prize Externals in the Service of God?* [etc.] (1856; PH 10036).

29. "The principal Clergy of London classified according to their opinions on the great Church question of the day" (1844), Bodleian MS. Add. C 290.

30. J. G. Lockhart, *Charles Lindley, Viscount Halifax* (London: Centenary, 1935), 1:80, 85–87.

31. Charles Mackeson, *A Digest of the Evidence Given Before the Commissioners appointed to Inquire into the Rubrics, Orders, and Directions for Regulating the Course and Conduct of Public Worship* [etc.] (London: James Parker, 1867), 12–15. The vicar was G. Cosby White.

32. On this church, see especially Reynolds, *Martyr of Ritualism*.

33. John Martin, *St Alban's, Holborn. Facts and Figures versus Fiction* (1867; PH 10104).

34. He added, though, that "one would consent to be like a plum pudding, if one could get the poor to Church" (Lockhart, *Charles Lindley, Viscount Halifax* 1:109).

35. This exchange is given in more detail in Reynolds, *Martyr of Ritualism*, 103.

36. Martin, *St Alban's, Holborn*.

37. C. Maurice Davies, *Orthodox London: or, Phases of Religious Life in the Church of England*, rev. ed. (London: Tinsley Brothers, 1876), 24.

38. Booth, *Life and Labour: Third Series* 2:104–5. This is the same area studied more recently by Michael Young and Peter Willmott, in *Family and Kinship in East London* (Baltimore: Penguin Books, 1962); see 17–30 for historical background.

39. Brett is mentioned in Marcus Donovan, *After the Tractarians* (London: Philip Allan, 1933), 64, 136; in G. Wakeling, *The Oxford Church Movement. Sketches and Recollections* (London: Swan Sonnenschein, 1895), 143–47; and in [Katherine Warburton], *Memories of a Sister of S. Saviour's Priory* (Oxford and London: A. R. Mowbray, 1903), 288–91 (where his nickname is given). Brett's funeral was reported extensively in the *Church Times*, February 13, 1874.

40. Stephen Gaselee, "The Aesthetic Side of the Oxford Movement," in Williams and Harris (eds.), *Northern Catholicism*, 433–40. See also W. K. Lowther Clarke, *A Hundred Years of Hymns Ancient & Modern* (London: William Clowes & Sons, 1960), 19–21. For a Protestant critique of *The Hymnal Noted*, see *Ultra-Ritualism. Extracts from the Hymn Books Used in St. Alban's, Holborn, London* (1867; PH 10077).

41. *Free and Open Churches. Facts and Opinions from Five Hundred Parishes in Town and Country*, 2d ed. (London: London Free and Open Church Association, 1876).

42. James F. White, *The Cambridge Movement: The Ecclesiologists and the Gothic Revival* (Cambridge: Cambridge University Press, 1962), 85–93. See also Peter F. Anson, *Fashions in Church Furnishings, 1840–1940* (London: Faith Press, 1960), 44–74, 236–37.

43. *The Ritualistic Conspiracy* (3d ed., 1877; PH 6018). Walters is not shown as a member of the S.S.C. on this list, but does appear as one twenty years later (*Society of the Holy Cross. With List of Members* [1897; PH 8555]).

44. Booth, *Life and Labour: Third Series* 2:93.

45. *Ritualistic Conspiracy* (1877).

46. Booth, *Life and Labour: Third Series* 2:89–95.

47. See Warburton, *Memories of a Sister*.

48. "Ritualistic Theatricals at Shoreditch." *Punch*, September 21, 1867, 121.

49. Church Association, *Ritualism Rampant in East London* [etc.] (n.d., but ca. 1893; PH 8452).

50. Booth, *Life and Labour: Third Series* 2:131.

51. Morrison's novel is dedicated to the vicar of Holy Trinity, who appears in it, thinly disguised.

52. Booth, *Life and Labour: Third Series* 2:74–75.

53. Listings for an earlier period are available in the *ABC (London and Suburban) Church*

and Chapel Directory (London: Robert Banks, 1862 *et seq.*). In addition to Church of England and Protestant places of worship, the *Directory* listed edifying public buildings and exhibitions.

54. Booth, *Life and Labour: Third Series* 2:94.

55. Ibid., 89.

56. The most comprehensive recent treatment is McLeod, *Class and Religion in the Late Victorian City*, 101–31 are devoted to Bethnal Green.

57. Nearly twenty years later, the *Daily News* census estimated the percentage of "twicers" (the percentage of the morning congregation who were also counted in the evening) at 39 percent for "Inner" (non-suburban) London. See Richard Mudie-Smith (ed.), *The Religious Life of London* (London: Hodder and Stoughton, 1904), 450.

58. See, for instance, *Religion in London. Statistics of Church and Chapel Accommodation in 1865* [etc.] (London: Jackson, Walford, and Hodder, n.d.).

59. Figures on seats from *Mackeson's* (1882).

60. Morning attendance of 891, compared to 1210 at the same churches nearly twenty years before, and evening congregations of 787, down from 930 (Mudie-Smith, *Religious Life of London*, 55–61).

61. Ibid., 281. Jeffrey Cox shows a similar pattern for Anglo-Catholic churches in Lambeth (*The English Churches in a Secular Society: Lambeth, 1870–1930* [New York: Oxford University Press, 1982], 296).

62. I have used *Mackeson's* (1882) to characterize these churches. "Ritualist" churches were those we have examined, where the eucharistic vestments were in use. "Low" churches were those where the eastward position was not taken or where evening communion was celebrated.

63. Booth, *Life and Labour: Third Series* 3:123. St. Mary Magdalene's drew large congregations, but Booth reports that they came from outside the parish.

64. Alden, "Problem of East London," 37.

65. Booth, *Life and Labour: Third Series* 2:93–94.

66. Ibid., 57.

67. *Father Pollock and His Brother: Mission Priests of St. Alban's, Birmingham* (London: Longmans, Green, 1911), 39.

68. S. C. Carpenter, *Church and People, 1789–1889: A History of the Church of England from William Wilberforce to "Lux Mundi"* (London: SPCK, 1933), 224.

69. Booth, *Life and Labour: Third Series* 2:90.

70. Mudie-Smith, *Religious Life of London*, 49. The 1886 census did not record the sex and age of the members of congregation.

71. Lucy Menzies, *Father Wainwright: A Record* (London: Longmans, Green, 1947), 62–63.

72. Mudie-Smith, *Religious Life of London*, 266–71. Dissenting congregations generally showed a higher proportion of adults in the morning and children in the evening than Anglican churches in the same area. Thus, for Bethnal Green and Shoreditch, the percentage of children among all churchgoers was 54 percent in the morning and 43 percent in the evening.

73. Quoted in W. J. Sparrow Simpson, *The History of the Anglo-Catholic Revival from 1845* (London: George Allen & Unwin, 1932), 70.

74. *Church Times*, December 24, 1874. For a similar case at St. Anne's, Willenhall, in the Diocese of Lichfield, see Church of England Working Men's Society, *Summary of Proceedings At the Meeting of Delegates on the Second Anniversary of the Society* [etc.] (1878; PH 8109).

75. Booth, *Life and Labour: Third Series* 1:174–75.

76. Bowen, *Idea of the Victorian Church*, 302–3.

77. *Church Times*, January 18, 1868.

78. Church of England Working Men's Society, *Summary of Proceedings*; Indoctus [James Welton], *The Past, Present, and Future of the Church of England Working Men's Society* (n.d., but ca. 1880; PH 8111).

79. Church of England Working Men's Society, *Authorised Report of the Speeches Delivered*

by Delegates ... in Connection with the Fourth Anniversary [etc.] (1880; PH 8110); *Minutes of Proceedings of the Meeting of Delegates* [etc.] (1888; PH 8340); and *Official Declaration of the Objects and Principles of the Church of England Working Men's Society* (1888; PH 8341).

80. Church of England Working Men's Society, *Authorised Report.*

81. *Church Times*, January 19, 1877.

82. James Bateman, *The Church Association: Its Policy and Prospects, Considered in a Letter to the Chairman*, 2d ed. (1880; PH 4031).

83. *Church Times*, January 12, 1877.

84. *Church Times*, January 19, 1877.

85. *Church Times*, July 23, 1875.

86. *Church Times*, February 23, 1877. The delegation from St. Cyprian's was identified in the issue of February 9.

87. Joyce Coombs, *Judgment on Hatcham: The History of a Religious Struggle, 1877–1886* (London: Faith Press, 1969), 79–80.

88. Church of England Working Men's Society, *Authorised Report.*

89. Ibid.

90. *Report of the Council of the English Church Union Relative to the Preparation of the Memorials on Ritual, and of Their Presentation* [etc.] (1866; PH 7872).

91. Quoted in Reynolds, *Martyr of Ritualism*, 128.

92. Church of England Working Men's Society, *Authorised Report.*

93. Quoted in E. A. Down, "Pastoral Ideals and Methods of the Movement: The Tractarian Tradition," in Williams and Harris (eds.), *Northern Catholicism*, 283 (emphasis added).

94. Ibid., 282.

95. Charles E. Osborne, *The Life of Father Dolling* (London: Edward Arnold, 1903), 18.

96. Alden, "Problem of East London," 37–38.

97. Quoted in Reynolds, *Martyr of Ritualism*, 107.

98. Armytage, N. Green. *Temperance* (1894; PH 11710).

99. Osborne, *Life of Father Dolling*, 134.

100. Warburton, *Memories of a Sister*, 313–18.

101. Ibid., 159–60.

102. Osborne, *Life of Father Dolling*, 18.

103. Alden, "Problem of East London," 37–38.

104. The comparison is suggested in Carpenter, *Church and People*, 224.

105. Harry Jones, *East and West London: Being Notes of Common Life and Pastoral Work in Saint James's, Westminster and in Saint George's-in-the-East* (London: Smith, Elder, 1875), 60.

106. "Principal Clergy of London classified."

107. Reynolds, *Martyr of Ritualism*, 51.

108. Quoted in Henry R. T. Brandreth, *Dr. Lee of Lambeth: A Chapter in Parenthesis in the History of the Oxford Movement* (London: S.P.C.K., 1951), 21.

109. Bryan King, *The S. George's Mission, with the S. George's Riots and their Results* (London: Rivington's, 1877), 6.

110. Ellsworth, *Charles Lowder and the Ritualist Movement*, from which these paragraphs are adapted.

111. Quoted in Carpenter, *Church and People*, 224.

112. Booth, *Life and Labour: Third Series* 2:90.

113. Ibid., 92.

114. Bowen, *Idea of the Victorian Church*, 303.

115. Charles John Ellicott, *Ritualism. A Sermon Preached in Bristol Cathedral, Sunday, November 4, 1866* (1866; PH 10266).

116. Ellis, *Some Time among Ritualists*, 5, 4.

117. The Author of "The Rector and His Friends," *The Ritual Difficulty. An Eirenicon* (London: George Bell and Sons, 1877), 29.

118. J. G. Norton, *A Plea and Plan for the Toleration of Ritualists* (1881; PH 4265).

CHAPTER 9

1. Quoted in Mary Cathcart Borer, *People of Victorian and Edwardian England* (London: MacDonald, 1969), 94. L. E. Elliott-Binns, *Religion in the Victorian Era* (London: Lutterworth Press, 1936), 234, also suggests that many of the slum poor were too ignorant to be seriously anti-Roman.

2. G. Wakeling, *The Oxford Church Movement. Sketches and Recollections* (London: Swan Sonnenschein, 1895), 160–61, lists distinguished members of the St. George's Church Defense Association; see 274–92 for a list of other socially prominent Anglo-Catholics.

3. Richard Frederick Littledale, "The Missionary Aspect of Ritualism," in Orby Shipley, (ed.), *The Church and the World: Essays on Questions of the Day in 1866*, 3d ed. (London: Longmans, Green, Reader, and Dyer, 1867), 33–36.

4. This is essentially the distinction identified in Hugh McLeod, "Class, Community and Region: The Religious Geography of Nineteenth-Century England," in *A Sociological Yearbook of Religion in Britain*, vol. 6, ed. Michael Hill (London: SCM Press, 1973), 34, as that between the middle class and "gentlemen," one of the two great social divides in the Victorian city. (The other fell between artisans, on the one hand, and clerks and shopkeepers, on the other.) On the nobility and gentry connections of early E.C.U. council members, see William Jesse Fong, "The Ritualist Crisis: Anglo-Catholics and Authority with Special Reference to the English Church Union, 1859–1882" (Ph.D. thesis, University of Toronto, 1978), 242.

5. Littledale, "Missionary Aspect of Ritualism," 40.

6. *Society of S. Alphege, Abp. & M. List of Associates. Corrected up to May 1, 1868* (1868; PH 4646).

7. Paul Thureau-Dangin, *The English Catholic Revival in the Nineteenth Century* (New York: E. P. Dutton, n.d.), 2:530.

8. Henry Browne, *The Oxford Movement* (London: Catholic Truth Society, n.d.), 32–33.

9. Edward George Kirwan Browne, *Annals of the Tractarian Movement, from 1842 to 1860*, 3d ed. (London: Privately published, 1861).

10. W. Gordon Gorman, *Converts to Rome: Since the Tractarian Movement to May 1899* (London: Swan Sonnenschein, 1899); quote from x.

11. Characterization from N. Dimock, *The Crisis in the Church of England: Its History and Present Position* (London: Elliot Stock, 1899), 32.

12. *Liverpool Mercury*, quoted in James Bentley, *Ritualism and Politics in Victorian Britain: The Attempt to Legislate for Belief* (Oxford: Oxford University Press, 1978), 26; "Adam Bede," *The Natural History of Puseyism: With a Short Account of the Sunday Opera at St. Paul's, Brighton* (Brighton: G. Smart, [1860]), 14.

13. Richard Frederick Littledale, "The First Report of the Ritual Commission," in *The Church and the World: Essays on Questions of the Day in 1868*, ed. Orby Shipley (London: Longmans, Green, Reader, and Dyer, 1868), 7.

14. W. J. Sparrow Simpson, *The Contribution of Cambridge to the Anglo-Catholic Revival* (London: S.P.C.K., 1933), especially 23–32. See also James F. White, *The Cambridge Movement: The Ecclesiologists and the Gothic Revival* (Cambridge: Cambridge University Press, 1962).

15. See appendix 2. Cf. George William Herring, "Tractarianism to Ritualism: A Study of Some Aspects of Tractarianism Outside Oxford, from the Time of Newman's Conversion in 1845, until the First Ritual Commission in 1867" (D. Phil. thesis, Oxford University, 1984), which examined 958 Tractarian clergymen ordained before 1870 and found 431 Oxford graduates to 327 Cambridge ones (41); the imbalance decreased with time, but was still evident in the 1860s.

16. Gorman, *Converts to Rome*, xi–xiii.

17. From 1845 to 1849, new matriculations at Oxford averaged 421 per year; from 1844

to 1848, those at Cambridge averaged 527 per year (*Parliamentary Papers* 42 [1850], 450–52).

18. See appendix 3.

19. Bentley, *Ritualism and Politics*, 26.

20. Charles Williams became principal of Jesus in 1857. *The Clergy Directory and Parish Guide* (London: Thomas Bosworth, 1875) shows him as a Church Association subscriber.

21. Bentley, *Ritualism and Politics*, 27, 78.

22. *Society of S. Alphege. List of Associates.*

23. *Church Times*, May 19, 1866.

24. Raymond Chapman, *Faith and Revolt: Studies in the Literary Influence of the Oxford Movement* (London: Weidenfeld and Nicolson, 1970), 204.

25. [William Kelly], *Ritualism* (London: W. H. Broom, [1876?]); J. C. Wetherell, *Ritualism: Thoughts on the Question of the Day* [etc.] (1866; PH 1963).

26. See chapter 11.

27. An account of that remarkable family can be found in Jo Manton, *Sister Dora: The Life of Dorothy Pattison* (London: Methuen, 1971), 48 ff.

28. Francis Lyne, *Archdeacon Denison and Dr. Pusey. A Circumstance Followed Up* [etc.] (London: W. Pole, 1878), 15, 20, 10. See also the elder Lyne's *Popery: The Bishop of London and Dean Lake* and *The Bishop of London. An Appeal to His Grace the Archbishop of Canterbury* (both London: E. W. Allen, 1887).

29. J. G. Lockhart, *Charles Lindley, Viscount Halifax* (London: Centenary, 1935) 1:104. Wood resigned his position in the prince's household in 1877 so as not to cause embarrassment as president of an organization defying the courts (1:213).

30. W. J. Conybeare, *Perversion: or, the Causes and Consequences of Infidelity* (London: Smith, Elder, 1856), 1:345–61; quotation from 361.

31. Octavius J. Ellis, *Some Time among Ritualists*, 3d ed. (London: Hatchards, 1868), 6.

32. G. A. Denison, *Loyalty to the Church of England. A Letter to the Lord Bishop of Bath and Wells* [etc.] (1873; PH 7258).

33. Littledale, Richard Frederick. *Ritualists not Romanists* (n.d.; PH 1504).

34. Quoted in James S. Pollock, *Romanizing. The Substance of a Lecture delivered in the Town Hall, Birmingham, January 23, 1867* (London: Masters, 1867), 18–19.

35. Ibid.

36. For lists of converts to Roman Catholicism brought up as Evangelicals, see Pollock, *Romanizing*, 18–19, and Sabine Baring-Gould, *The Church Revival: Thoughts Thereon and Reminiscences* (London: Methuen, 1914), 335.

37. Robert H. Greenfield, "Attitude of the Tractarians to the Roman Catholic Church, 1833–1850" (D. Phil. thesis, Oxford University, 1956), 494. On this point, see also Peter Benedict Nockles, "Continuity and Change in Anglican High Churchmanship in Britain, 1792–1850" (D. Phil. thesis, Oxford University, 1982), 605.

38. Littledale, "Missionary Aspect of Ritualism," 40.

39. W. J. Conybeare, "Church Parties," *The Edinburgh Review* 98 (October 1853): 305. See also *Animadversions by Distinguished Divines and Others, on the False Position of the Ritualistic Clergy in the Church of England* (London: Hamilton, Adams, 1882), 19–20.

40. J. K. Tucker, *The Duty of Clergymen to Prevent the Disestablishment of the Church of England, and the Means to be Employed to that End* (London: William Hunt, 1871).

41. Ellis, *Some Time among Ritualists*, 11.

42. E. Garbett, *Extreme Ritualism* (1866; PH 72876).

43. W. E. Gladstone, *The Church of England and Ritualism* (1875; PH 10836).

44. *Ceremonial and Christian Religion* (London: William MacIntosh, 1875), 14–15, 13.

45. See, for instance, George Anthony Denison, *The Law of God and the Law of Man* [etc.] (1875; PH 2144).

46. Owen Chadwick, *The Victorian Church*, 2d ed. (London: Adam & Charles Black, 1972), 2:310.

47. Advertisement appended to F. G. Lee, *The Manuale Clericorum* (London: John Hogg, 1874).

48. For this distinction, see Wilfrid L. Knox, *The Catholic Movement in the Church of England*, 2d ed. (London: Philip Allan, 1930), 231–39; also Stephen Gaselee, "The Aesthetic Side of the Oxford Movement," in *Northern Catholicism: Centenary Studies in the Oxford and Parallel Movements*, ed. N. P. Williams and Charles Harris (New York: Macmillan, 1933), 430–31.

49. Barbara Pym, *A Glass of Blessings* (London: Jonathan Cape, 1977 [1958]), 207.

50. E. A. Knox, *The Tractarian Movement, 1833–1845*, 2d ed. (London: Putnam, 1934), 137.

51. *Puseyism in London* (1843; PH 5852).

52. "The Author of the 'Autobiography' in the 'Church and the World,'" *Protestantism and the Prayer Book* (1867; PH 7910).

53. The characterization is Shane Leslie's, from *The Oxford Movement, 1833 to 1933* (London: Burns, Oates & Washbourne, 1933), xiii.

54. E. R. Norman, *Church and Society in England, 1770–1970* (Oxford: Clarendon Press, 1976), 167–220, especially 175. See also Robert J. Bocock, "Anglo-Catholic Socialism: A Study of a Protest Movement within a Church," *Social Compass* 20 (1973): 31–48, and Peter d'A. Jones, *The Christian Socialist Revival, 1877–1914: Religion, Class, and Social Conscience in Late-Victorian England* (Princeton: Princeton University Press, 1968), especially 85–163.

55. Quoted in Marcus Donovan, *After the Tractarians* (London: Philip Allan, 1933), 156.

56. Quoted in Richard Frederick Littledale, *Why Ritualists Do Not Become Roman Catholics: A Reply to the Abbe Martin* (n.d., but 1879; PH 1799).

57. On Yonge, see Andrew L. Drummond, *The Churches in English Fiction* (Leicester: Edgar Backus, 1950), 77; on Howard, see Joseph Ellis Baker, *The Novel and the Oxford Movement*, Princeton Studies in English, No. 8 (Princeton: Princeton University Press, 1932), 22–23.

58. R. W. Franklin, *Nineteenth-Century Churches: The History of a New Catholicism in Württemberg, England, and France* (New York: Garland Publishing, 1987), 286–87. Franklin identifies a number of frequent contributors to Anglo-Catholic projects, and asserts that Gladstone was "spokesman" for the group.

59. Quoted in Paul Thompson, "All Saints Church, Margaret Street, Reconsidered," *Architectural History* 8 (1965): 74, 80.

60. Advertisements for R. Washbourne and for F. Wyndham & Co., in Lee, *Manuale Clericorum* (1874).

61. *Malleus Ritualistarum; or, the Ritual Reason Why Not* (1872; PH 10918).

62. Quoted in Drummond, *Churches in English Fiction*, 99.

63. *Church Times*, May 19, 1866.

64. J. C. Ryle, *What Do We Owe to the Reformation?* (London: John F. Shaw, 1877), 20.

65. John Kent, "The Victorian Resistance," *Victorian Studies* 12 (December 1968): 145. See also the chapter on "Ritualism and Re-enchantment" in Francis Penhale, *The Anglican Church Today: Catholics in Crisis* (London: Mowbray, 1986), 46–68.

CHAPTER 10

1. S. A. Walker, *Tracts against Treason* (London: Hamilton, Adams, 1874) 3:14.

2. On the religious virtuoso as a type, with particular reference to the rise of Anglican sisterhoods, see Michael Hill, *The Religious Order: A Study of Virtuoso Religion and Its Legitimation in the Nineteenth-Century Church of England* (London: Heinemann Educational Books, 1973), especially 2–3.

3. John Charles Chambers, "Private Confession and Absolution," in *The Church and the World: Essays on Questions of the Day in 1867*, ed. Orby Shipley (London: Longmans, Green, Reader, and Dyer, 1867), 229.

4. *Report of the Council of the English Church Union Relative to the Preparation of the*

Memorials on Ritual, and of Their Presentation [etc.] (1866; PH 7872).

5. A. H. Mackonochie, *Remonstrance: A Letter to the Bishop of London* (1875; PH 1694); Maurice Davies, *Orthodox London: or, Phases of Religious Life in the Church of England*, rev. ed. (London: Tinsley Brothers, 1876), 24.

6. Octavius J. Ellis, *Some Time among Ritualists*, 3d ed. (London: Hatchards, 1868), 10–11.

7. *Church Reform: and the Report of the Royal Commission on Ritual, being the second annual Report of the Church of England Laymen's Defense Association; together with a Note on Sacerdotalism* (London: W. MacIntosh, [1868]), 8.

8. James H. Rigg, *Oxford High Anglicanism, and Its Chief Leaders* (London: Charles H. Kelly, 1895), 339.

9. Richard Frederick Littledale, "The Missionary Aspect of Ritualism," in *The Church and the World: Essays on Questions of the Day in 1866*, ed. Orby Shipley, 3d ed. (London: Longmans, Green, Reader, and Dyer, 1867), 35.

10. Figures in the following paragraphs computed from returns reported in Richard Mudie-Smith (ed.), *The Religious Life of London* (London: Hodder and Stoughton, 1904), 97–126.

11. Thomas Jay Williams, *Priscilla Lydia Sellon: The Restorer after Three Centuries of the Religious Life in the English Church* (London: S.P.C.K., 1950), 62.

12. *Bombastes Religioso or The Protestant Pope of 1899* (London: Simpkin Marshall Hamilton Kent, [1899]), 29.

13. E. H. Bickersteth, *Evangelical Churchmanship and Evangelical Eclecticism* (London: Sampson Low, Marston, Searle, & Rivington, 1883).

14. Ellis, *Some Time among Ritualists*, 9.

15. Quoted in Michael Reynolds, *Martyr of Ritualism: Father Mackonochie of St. Alban's, Holborn* (London: Faber and Faber, 1965), 106. This broadside was taken from the collection maintained by the clergy of St. Alban's. Another item was a ticket that read: "Admit the Bearer and one friend to see the Winking Virgin and the Bleeding Saints."

16. A Layman and Magistrate of that County [Oxford], *A Watchman's Remarks upon a Pamphlet entitled "Thoughts on Church Matters in the Diocese of Oxford"* (London: Arthur Hall, Virtue, 1859), 11–12. A similar analysis was offered a generation later in Alfred Greenhill, *Guy Faux in the Protestant Church: A Lecture* (Exeter: "Devon Weekly Times" Office, 1874), 11.

17. Margaret Maison discusses fictional treatments of Anglo-Catholicism's allure for women in *Search Your Soul, Eustace: A Study of the Religious Novel in the Victorian Age* (London: Sheed and Ward, 1961), 71–88.

18. "Will O' the Wisp," *A Paper Lantern for Puseyites* (1843; PH 5846).

19. *Society of S. Alphege, Abp. & M. List of Associates. Corrected up to May 1, 1868* (1868; PH 4646).

20. Henry Ritson, *The "Ritual" of S. Mark's* (1873; PH 10704).

21. *Church Association Lectures: Delivered at St. James's Hall* [etc.] (London: William MacIntosh, 1867), vii.

22. For an explicit statement of this proposition by a twentieth-century Anglo-Catholic woman, however, see Sheila Kaye-Smith, *Anglo-Catholicism* (London: Chapman and Hall, 1925), 151–52.

23. "A Lady," *La Femme Dévote. Reprinted from the "Church Review"* (1876; PH 11831).

24. A. M. Allchin, *The Silent Rebellion: Anglican Religious Communities, 1845–1900* (London: SCM Press, 1958), 117.

25. Hill, *Religious Order*, 274.

26. On the demographic underpinnings of the rise of Anglican sisterhoods, see ibid., 296–309.

27. Quoted in ibid., 300. See also 308n.

28. These figures and those following (unless otherwise indicated) calculated from data for England and Wales in B. R. Mitchell, *Abstract of British Historical Statistics* (Cambridge: Cam-

bridge University Press, 1962), 6, 12, 16.

29. Hill, *Religious Order*, 308n.

30. Mitchell, *Abstract of Historical Statistics*, 60. These figures are for Great Britain as a whole. Labor force figures do not include those for prostitutes, whose numbers were also widely regarded as growing rapidly. By one contemporary estimate there were 80,000 in London alone (Michael Pearson, *The Age of Consent: Victorian Prostitution and Its Enemies* [Newton Abbot: David and Charles, 1972], 25). For comparison, the third largest official category, clothing workers, numbered 229,000 in all of Britain in 1851.

31. A good selection of contemporary documents is found in Patricia Hollis, *Women in Public: The Women's Movement, 1850–1900* (London: George Allen & Unwin, 1979).

32. Quoted in James F. White, *The Cambridge Movement: The Ecclesiologists and the Gothic Revival* (Cambridge: Cambridge University Press, 1962), 109.

33. *Church Times*, February 28, 1863.

34. *Free and Open Churches. Facts and Opinions from Five Hundred Parishes in Town and Country*, 2d ed. (London: London Free and Open Church Association, 1876). In 1876 all of the West London Ritualist churches mentioned earlier except St. Thomas, Regent Street, did so, but it is not clear what the practice was at the time of the religious census. A notable exception in East London was Charles Lowder's church of St. Peter's, London Docks.

35. *Church Times*, February 7, 1873.

36. *Church Times*, June 18, 1875.

37. *Free and Open Churches.*

38. *Church Times*, June 18, 1875.

39. *Church Times*, February 14, 1873.

40. *Church Times*, June 11, June 18, and July 9, 1875.

41. *Church Times*, June 25, 1875.

42. *Church Times*, June 18, 1875.

43. Ibid.

44. Charles J. Eliot, *Ritual Explanations. A Sermon* (1868; PH 10384).

45. One example among many is Robert Rodolph Sheffield, *Five Letters on a Conversion to Roman Catholicism* (n.d.; PH 11181).

46. T. T. Carter, *The Freedom of Confession in the Church of England. A Letter to His Grace the Lord Archbishop of Canterbury* (London: Rivington's, 1877), 24.

47. *The Armoury: A Magazine of Weapons for Christian Warfare* 5 (1877–79): 98; *Extracts from a Ritualistic Publication, entitled The Priest in Absolution, and Dedicated to the Masters, Vicars, and Brethren of the Society of the Holy Cross* [etc.] (n.p.: [n.d., but ca. 1876]).

48. F. D., *A Plea for St. Barnabas. The Confessional versus the Social Evil* (London: Alfred William Bennett, 1858), 7. This concern was shared by Gladstone, whose "nightwalks" continued even after he became prime minister and earned him, unfairly, the nickname "Old Gladeye" (E. J. Feuchtwanger, *Gladstone* [London: Allen Lane, 1975], 69).

49. Quoted in G. W. Soltau, *A Letter to the Working Classes on Ritualism* (1873; PH 12502).

50. *Watchman's Remarks*, 12.

51. *Malleus Ritualistarum; or, the Ritual Reason Why Not* (1872; PH 10918).

52. See chapter 2.

53. A Graduate of the University of Cambridge, *The Ritualist's Progress: A Sketch of the Reforms and Ministrations of Our New Vicar, The Rev. Septimius Alban, Member of the E.C.U., Vicar of St. Alicia, Slumbertown, as They Appeared to a Bewildered Parishioner* (London: Weldon, [1878]). For a similar, but less indulgent, verse treatment, see *The Stray Kitten* (n.d.; PH 10903)). An advertisement in *The Bewildered Bishop* (n.d.; PH 10905) indicates that at least 10,000 copies of *The Stray Kitten* were printed. The same author's anti-Ritualist *Dream of a Church Mouse* (n.d.; PH 10745) went through at least sixteen thousands, and was popular enough to provoke a response, *The Dream of a Chapel Mouse* (n.d.; PH 10904)).

54. Quoted in Reynolds, *Martyr of Ritualism*, 178; *Armoury* 5 (1877–79): 202.

55. Quoted in Soltau, *Letter to the Working Classes.*

56. *Armoury* 5 (1877–79): 98.

57. Ibid., 201.

58. The archdeacon is cited in Samuel Smith, *Speech to the House of Commons* (1898; PH 72220). "Fountain of filthiness" is from *Ritualistic Teaching Exposed*, a pamphlet directed against the vicar of Christ Church, Belper, quoted in A Layman of the Church of England, *The Church and the Bible. The True Teaching of the Rev. E. E. Hillyard* [etc.] (London: G. J. Palmer, 1877). For accounts of the evils of the Roman confessional, sometimes virtually disordered, see, for instance, Sheffield, *Five Letters*; Soltau, *Letter to the Working Classes*; Walker, *Tracts against Treason*, vol. 2; *"The Priest in Absolution." A Criticism, A Protest, & A Denunciation* [etc.] (London: J. Francis Bursill, 1877); H. J. Brockman, *"The Confessional Unmasked." A Military as well as Moral Plea for abolishing the Confessional* (London: Protestant Evangelical Mission and Electoral Union, n.d.); R. T. McMullen, *Priestly Pretensions, and God's Word* (London: Elliot Stock, 1885).

59. Walker, *Tracts against Treason* 2:14–15. See *Confession a Help to Heaven. Part I* (1869; PH 11667) for an Anglo-Catholic response to this sort of accusation.

60. Walker, *Tracts against Treason* 2:15, 4.

61. Quoted in *Animadversions by Distinguished Divines and Others, on the False Position of the Ritualistic Clergy in the Church of England* (London: Hamilton, Adams, 1882), 46.

62. John C. Miller, in *Church Association Lectures*, 1867), 32.

63. Quoted in Desmond Morse-Boycott, *They Shine Like Stars* (London: Skeffington & Son, [1947]), 197.

64. Smith, *Speech to the House of Commons.*

65. Thomas S. L. Vogan, *Remarks on Catholic Practice, Confession, and the Real Presence, as Advocated in a Late Petition to Convocation* (1873; PH 1595).

66. "The Last Thirty Years in the English Church: an Autobiography," in Shipley (ed.), *The Church and the World: 1866*, 250. The essay is anonymous, but an inked note in the Pusey House copy says "Mrs. J. W. Lea née Russell."

67. Quoted in Shipley (ed.), *Church and World: 1866*, 523.

68. This account is taken from A. G. Lough, *John Mason Neale—Priest Extraordinary* (Newton Abbot, Devon: privately published, [1975]), 107–8 (quotation from 108).

69. Quoted in Soltau, *Letter to the Working Classes.*

70. Quoted in *"The Priest in Absolution": A Criticism*, 7.

71. Quoted in Thomas Howard Gill, *A Letter to the Right Reverend the Lord Bishop of Manchester, touching "Ritualism"* (London: Hatchards, 1878), 15.

72. "Lord Sandon on Sacerdotalism" (Church Association handbill; n.d., but 1867).

73. Andrew L. Drummond, *The Churches in English Fiction* (Leicester: Edgar Backus, 1950), 100–101.

74. F. D., *Plea for St. Barnabas*, 7.

75. *Bombastes Religioso*, 26–27.

76. Carter, *Freedom of Confession*, 15–16.

77. See, for example, an exchange between T. T. Carter and Bishop Wordsworth on the subject of vows: Christopher Wordsworth, *On Sisterhoods and Vows. A Letter to the Ven. Sir George Prevost, Bart.* (1878; PH 8032), and T. T. Carter, *Are "Vows of Celibacy in Early Life" Inconsistent with the Word of God?* (1878; PH 7402).

78. Jo Manton, *Sister Dora: The Life of Dorothy Pattison* (London: Methuen, 1971), 175.

79. Walter Walsh, *The Secret History of the Oxford Movement* (London: Swan Sonnenschein, 1897), 162–201.

80. *The Phantom Railway* was by the author of *Three Years' Captivity as a Nun.* The advertisements are appended to *The Stray Kitten.* Verse from *Armoury* 7 (1881–84): 15.

81. The exchange is quoted in "Sisterhood Life," in Shipley (ed.). *The Church and the World: 1867*, 170–71.

82. Quoted in Peter F. Anson, *The Call of the Cloister: Religious Communities and Kin-*

dred Bodies in the Anglican Communion (London: S.P.C.K., 1955), 378.

83. *Malleus Ritualistarum.*

84. Allchin, *Silent Rebellion.* Allchin's interpretation, adopted wholesale here, has been extended and reinforced in Hill, *Religious Order,* especially 228–300.

85. Manton, *Sister Dora,* 50–67 (quotation from 50).

86. Quoted in Anson, *Call of the Cloister,* 378.

87. Quoted in Hill, *Religious Order,* 279.

88. Manton, *Sister Dora,* 53.

89. This continuation of the account is adapted from Lough, *John Mason Neale,* 108–12.

90. Quoted in Anson, *Call of the Cloister,* 378.

91. Quoted in Hill, *Religious Order,* 279.

92. Alice Horlock Bennett, quoted in ibid., 273.

93. Quoted in Allchin, *Silent Rebellion,* 115.

94. *Malleus Ritualistarum.*

95. Williams, *Priscilla Lydia Sellon,* 120–27, 200–3.

96. Ibid., 123. In this she was like her contemporary, Florence Nightingale, with whom she shared many other characteristics, including (significantly) a family that gave her at least ambivalent support.

97. This correspondence is reprinted in full in George W. E. Russell, *Arthur Stanton: A Memoir* (London: Longmans, Green, 1917), 153–70.

98. See the chapter on Yonge in Raymond Chapman, *Faith and Revolt: Studies in the Literary Influence of the Oxford Movement* (London: Weidenfeld and Nicolson, 1970), 58–88.

99. Allchin, *Silent Rebellion,* 119.

100. Hill, *Religious Order,* 276.

101. Allchin, *Silent Rebellion,* 120.

102. The estimate is Allchin's (ibid., 120). S. L. Ollard's estimate, "at least 1300" by 1912, suggests how imprecise our information is (Hill, *Religious Order,* 280). In any case, the growth had been substantial.

103. Quoted in Allchin, *Silent Rebellion,* 115.

CHAPTER 11

1. Richard Frederick Littledale, *Catholic Ritual in the Church of England Scriptural, Reasonable, Lawful* (1865; PH 1075).

2. *Ritual: A Plea in Its Behalf, Grounded on Scripture and Reason. By One Who Has Viewed Both Sides of the Questions* (n.d.; PH 70681).

3. Quoted in Michael Reynolds, *Martyr of Ritualism: Father Mackonochie of St. Alban's, Holborn* (London: Faber and Faber, 1965), 103.

4. Maurice Davies, *Orthodox London: or, Phases of Religious Life in the Church of England,* rev. ed. (London: Tinsley Brothers, 1876), 24.

5. [William Kelly], *Ritualism* (London: W. H. Broom, [1876?]), 16; John Ashley, *Sequel to the "Church of the Period" with the Author's Reasons for Leaving the Church of England* (London: W. H. Guest, 1876), 31; "Tekel," *The Views of a Church of England Layman Relative to the Church of England Clergy* (1866; PH 1256).

6. Kelly, *Ritualism,* 19; *Malleus Ritualistarum; or, the Ritual Reason Why Not* (1872; PH 10918).

7. Quoted in Andrew L. Drummond, *The Churches in English Fiction* (Leicester: Edgar Backus, 1950), 63.

8. Ashley, *Sequel to "Church of the Period,"* 31.

9. *Fraser's* quoted in *The Church and the World: Essays on Questions of the Day in 1866,* ed. Orby Shipley, 3d ed. (London: Longmans, Green, Reader, and Dyer, 1867), 536; "Adam Bede," *The Natural History of Puseyism: With a Short Account of the Sunday Opera at St. Paul's, Brighton* (Brighton: G. Smart, [1860]), 5.

10. Lothair, *Ritualism: Its Practices and Tendency* (London: Charing Cross, 1877), 37.

11. Quoted in David Newsome, *Godliness and Good Learning: Four Studies of a Victorian Ideal* (London: John Murray, 1961), 209.

12. Owen Chadwick, *The Founding of Cuddesdon* (Oxford: Oxford University Press, 1954), 98.

13. Ibid., 92–93.

14. Sabine Baring-Gould, *The Church Revival: Thoughts Thereon and Reminiscences* (London: Methuen, 1914), 334.

15. A South Australian Lay Reader, *Incense and Ritualism in the Church of England* [etc.] (1873; PH 1600).

16. *Church Review*, quoted in Bourchier Wrey Savile, *Hard Speeches and Gentle Words* (1879; PH 71832).

17. John Henry Newman, *Loss and Gain: The Story of a Convert* (London: Burns & Oates, 1962 [1848]), 31.

18. Ibid., 49–50.

19. Shane Leslie, *The Anglo-Catholic* (London: Chatto & Windus, 1929), 117.

20. Compton Mackenzie, *Sinister Street* (London: MacDonald, 1949 [1913]), 187. For a more recent (and more outrageous) portrait, see A. N. Wilson, *Unguarded Hours* (London: Secker & Warburg, 1978).

21. Quoted (whether with glee or disgust it is impossible to say) in Walter Walsh, *The Secret History of the Oxford Movement* (London: Swan Sonnenschein, 1897), 393.

22. *Ceremonial Detail. Hints to Those Who Assist at Processions or in Quire* (1868; PH 8787).

23. Edward Garbett, *What are Our Duties in the Present Circumstances of the Church?* (London: William Hunt, 1867), 25.

24. The Author of "The Rector and His Friends," *The Ritual Difficulty. An Eirenicon* (London: George Bell and Sons, 1877), 27–28.

25. *Malleus Ritualistarum.*

26. Harry Jones, *East and West London: Being Notes of Common Life and Pastoral Work in Saint James's, Westminster and in Saint George's-in-the-East* (London: Smith, Elder, 1875), 97–98.

27. The boy was D. M. Dolben (Raymond Chapman, *Faith and Revolt: Studies in the Literary Influence of the Oxford Movement* [London: Weidenfeld and Nicolson, 1970], 248).

28. James Bateman, *The Church Association: Its Policy and Prospects, Considered in a Letter to the Chairman*, 2d ed. (1880; PH 4031).

29. N. Dimock, *The Crisis in the Church of England: Its History and Present Position* (London: Elliot Stock, 1899), 22.

30. *The Archbishop's Legacy: Will the Church Accept it?* (1883; PH 2303).

31. A. Clifton Kelway, *George Rundle Prynne: A Chapter in the Early History of the Catholic Revival* (London: Longmans, Green, 1905), 216.

32. Compton Mackenzie, *The Altar Steps* (Bath: Cedric Chivers, 1970 [1922]), 159.

33. Clifton Kelway, *The Story of the Catholic Revival. 1833–1933*, 4th ed. (London: Philip Allan, 1933), 71 ff.; Reynolds, *Martyr of Ritualism*, 100.

34. See, for instance, *Malleus Ritualistarum.*

35. *Directorium Puritanicum, Being a Manual of Directions for the Proper Performance of Divine Service according to the use of the Church of England, and for the Avoidance of Any Perversion of the Book of Common Prayer, in the Direction of Puseyism, or Popery.* (n.d.; PH 4627).

36. Advertisements for Aylen's Carte-de-Visite Gallery, Brighton, *Church Times*—e.g., May 12, 1866.

37. Author of "The Rector and His Friends," *Ritual Difficulty*, 28.

38. Octavius J. Ellis, *Some Time among Ritualists*, 3d ed. (London: Hatchards, 1868), 5.

39. The article, by "A Solicitor," appeared in *The Armoury: A Magazine of Weapons for Christian Warfare* 6 (1880): 15–18.

40. "The Baptistry," in Owen Chadwick (ed.), *The Mind of the Oxford Movement* (Stanford, Calif.: Stanford University Press, 1961), 189.

41. John Jebb, *The Principle of Ritualism Defended. A Sermon Preached in the Church of St. Michael and All Angels* [Tenbury, etc.] (1856; PH 1847).

42. Littledale, *Catholic Ritual in the Church of England*. For similar views on the religious uses of "sensuality," see F. G. Lee, *The Beauty of Holiness. Ten Lectures on External Religious Observances* (2d ed., 1866; PH 10564) and John Eddowes, *The New Testament and Ritual: A Lecture* (1877; PH 7681).

43. On the connections between Anglo-Catholicism and aestheticism, see Margaret Maison, *Search Your Soul, Eustace: A Study of the Religious Novel in the Victorian Age* (London: Sheed and Ward, 1961), 287–306 (Shorthouse quoted, 294).

44. Quoted in ibid., 291.

45. Peter F. Anson, *The Call of the Cloister: Religious Communities and Kindred Bodies in the Anglican Communion* (London: S.P.C.K., 1955), 48–49.

46. See Maison, *Search Your Soul*, 295–306; Thomas Wright, *The Life of Walter Pater* (London: Everett, 1907). A. Dwight Culler, *The Victorian Mirror of History* (New Haven: Yale University Press, 1985) treats Pater's use of history (241–78), as well as the Pre-Raphaelites' (218–40).

47. Wright, *Life of Pater* 2:28–48, 75–76, 143–47.

48. Quotations from Maison, *Search Your Soul*, 299. See *Marius the Epicurean: His Sensations and Ideas* (Garden City, N.Y.: Doubleday, Doran, 1935 [1885]), 250–52, for Pater's views on ritual.

49. W. H. Mallock, *The New Republic* (London: Chatto and Windus, 1889), 273–74.

50. Ibid., 277, 279.

51. Mackenzie, *Sinister Street*, 244.

52. Quoted in Shipley (ed.), *Church and World: 1866*, 546.

53. W. S. Gilbert, "Patience," in *The Complete Plays of Gilbert and Sullivan* (New York: Modern Library, n.d.), 200, 196–97.

54. Richard Frederick Littledale, "The First Report of the Ritual Commission," in *The Church and the World: Essays on Questions of the Day in 1868*, ed. Orby Shipley (London: Longmans, Green, Reader, and Dyer, 1868), 30; Wright, *Life of Pater* 2:38.

55. Rudyard Kipling, "The 'Mary Gloster'" (1894), in *Rudyard Kipling's Verse: Definitive Edition* (London: Hodder and Stoughton, 1940), 132.

56. Quoted in Newsome, *Godliness and Good Learning*, 199. See 195–239 on the Victorian ideal of manliness.

57. Ibid., 207–8. For a similar view, from 1895, see James H. Rigg, *Oxford High Anglicanism, and Its Chief Leaders* (London: Charles H. Kelly, 1895), 109–10.

58. Summary and quotations from Robert Bernard Martin, *The Dust of Combat: A Life of Charles Kingsley* (London: Faber and Faber, 1959), 107.

59. Quoted in Chapman, *Faith and Revolt*, 105; for Kingsley's magnanimous appreciation of Anglo-Catholics' redeeming qualities, see 110–11.

60. Martin, *Dust of Combat*, 71–73, 207–9.

61. See chapter 1.

62. J. Embry, *The Catholic Movement and the Society of the Holy Cross* (London: Faith Press, 1931), 7; [Katherine Warburton], *Memories of a Sister of S. Saviour's Priory* (Oxford and London: A. R. Mowbray, 1903), 164–65.

63. J. G. Lockhart, *Charles Lindley, Viscount Halifax* (London: Centenary, 1935) 1:255. On celibacy, see N. Green Armytage, *Clerical Marriage and Celibacy. Boston Leaflets II* (1893; PH 11711); the same author's *Clerical Marriage and Celibacy. Anglo-Catholic Essays No. 1* (1894; PH 11189); and many other pamphlets at Pusey House.

64. R. W. Church, *The Oxford Movement: Twelve Years, 1833–1845*, 3d ed. (London: Macmillan, 1892), 321.

65. Newman, *Loss and Gain*, 198.

66. G. Wakeling, *The Oxford Church Movement. Sketches and Recollections* (London: Swan Sonnenschein, 1895), 148.

67. Newsome, *Godliness and Good Learning*, 196.

68. Martin, *Dust of Combat*, 107.

69. David Hilliard, "UnEnglish and Unmanly: Anglo-Catholicism and Homosexuality," *Victorian Studies* 25 (Winter 1982): 181–82. Richard Dellamora cites Hilliard and places his article in a larger context, in *Masculine Desire: The Sexual Politics of Victorian Aestheticism* (Chapel Hill: University of North Carolina Press, 1990), 148. W. S. F. Pickering addresses the question of the twentieth-century association in *Anglo-Catholicism: A Study in Religious Ambiguity* (London: Routledge, 1989), 184–206. See also Francis Penhale, *The Anglican Church Today: Catholics in Crisis* (London: Mowbray, 1986), 75–76, 147–48.

70. Nigel Yates, *The Oxford Movement and Parish Life: St Saviour's, Leeds, 1839–1929*, Borthwick Papers No. 48 (York: University of York, Borthwick Institute of Historical Research, 1975), 12.

71. Arthur Calder-Marshall, *The Enthusiast: An Enquiry into the Life, Beliefs and Character of The Rev. Joseph Leycester Lyne alias Fr. Ignatius, O.S.B., Abbot of Elm Hill, Norwich, and Llanthony, Wales* (London: Faber and Faber, 1962), 110–14 (letter quoted, 113). Other episodes are recounted on 120 and 160.

72. Ibid., 160.

73. Ibid., 203–4; quotation from 204.

74. Thomas Jay Williams and Allan Walter Campbell, *The Park Village Sisterhood* (London: S.P.C.K., 1965), 67–69.

75. An article from *The Globe*, quoted under the headline "Too True," *Church Times*, January 17, 1873.

76. Geoffrey Faber, *Oxford Apostles: A Character Study of the Oxford Movement* (New York: Charles Scribner's Sons, 1934), ventures an interpretation of one of Newman's dreams, and of much else besides, in essentially Freudian terms. G. F. A. Best hails these efforts as the sort of interpretation needed to advance our understanding, in "New Bearings on the Oxford Movement," *The Historical Journal* 12 (1969): 709–10, and suggests that many other aspects of the movement would yield to similar psychological analysis. But Piers Brendon, *Hurrell Froude and the Oxford Movement* (London: Paul Elek, 1974), warns against interpreting religious phenomena exclusively in terms of psychopathology (60–61).

77. Chapman emphasizes this point (*Faith and Revolt*, 105).

CHAPTER 12

1. R. W. Enraght, *Not Law, but Unconstitutional Tyranny* [etc.] (n.d., but 1877?); PH 1652).

2. *A Layman's View of Ritualism* (1879; PH 3974).

3. Shane Leslie, *The Oxford Movement, 1833 to 1933* (London: Burns, Oates & Washbourne, 1933), 72.

4. See W. J. Conybeare, "Church Parties," *Edinburgh Review* 98 (October 1853), 273–342, quoted extensively in chapter 6, above. A good description of the parties can be found in M. A. Crowther, *Church Embattled: Religious Controversy in Mid-Victorian England* (Newton Abbot, Devon: David & Charles, 1970), 13–39.

5. This and the following quotations are from *Layman's View of Ritualism*.

6. Tract 3, quoted in Charles E. Raven, *Christian Socialism, 1848–1854* (London: Macmillan, 1920), 18.

7. Quoted in ibid., 20.

8. P. T. Marsh, *The Victorian Church in Decline: Archbishop Tait and the Church of England, 1868–1882* (London: Routledge & Kegan Paul, 1969), 16.

9. On the early history of that opposition, see Peter Toon, *Evangelical Theology, 1833–1856: A Response to Tractarianism* (London: Marshall, Morgan & Scott, 1979). Toon

argues (e.g., 76) that Low Churchmen even sought an alliance with old-fashioned High Churchmen against the Tractarians, a contention disputed by Peter Benedict Nockles, "Continuity and Change in Anglican High Churchmanship in Britain, 1792–1850" (D. Phil. thesis, Oxford University, 1982).

10. Mr. Droop is mentioned in Malcolm MacColl, *My Reviewers Reviewed, in a Preface to the Third and Revised Edition of* Lawlessness, Sacerdotalism, and Ritualism (1875; PH 3365).

11. Samuel Smith, *Speech to the House of Commons* (1898; PH 72220).

12. Quoted in N. Dimock, *The Crisis in the Church of England: Its History and Present Position* (London: Elliot Stock, 1899), 44.

13. Introduction to the French edition of *Apologia pro Vita Sua* (1866), translation included as an appendix to John Henry Newman, *Apologia pro Vita Sua: An Authoritative Text*, ed. David J. DeLaura (New York: Norton, 1968), 365–66.

14. Quoted in A. Clifton Kelway, *George Rundle Prynne: A Chapter in the Early History of the Catholic Revival* (London: Longmans, Green, 1905), 46.

15. Quotations in Andrew L. Drummond, *The Churches in English Fiction* (Leicester: Edgar Backus, 1950), 54n, and Joseph Ellis Baker, *The Novel and the Oxford Movement*, Princeton Studies in English, No. 8 (Princeton: Princeton University Press, 1932), 14.

16. "Lord Sandon on Sacerdotalism" (Church Association handbill; n.d., but 1867).

17. J. C. Ryle, *What Do We Owe to the Reformation?* (London: John F. Shaw, 1877), 19.

18. John M. Clabon, *The Church Rights of the Laity Briefly Considered* [etc.] (1869; PH 3657).

19. A Benighted Layman, *Gropings in Search of the Church of England* (London: George John Stevenson, 1867), 7.

20. Both are listed as S.S.C members in *The Ritualistic Conspiracy* (23d ed., 1877; PH 6018).

21. *The Church and the World: Essays on Questions of the Day in 1866*, ed. Orby Shipley, 3d ed. (London: Longmans, Green, Reader, and Dyer, 1867), 523–54.

22. Maurice Davies, *Orthodox London: or, Phases of Religious Life in the Church of England*, rev. ed. (London: Tinsley Brothers, 1876), 371.

23. Charles James LeGeyt, "On the Symbolism of Ritual," in *The Church and the World: Essays on Questions of the Day in 1867*, ed. Orby Shipley (London: Longmans, Green, Reader, and Dyer, 1867), 524.

24. Roger Lloyd, *The Church of England, 1900–1965* (London: SCM Press, 1966), 127.

25. Unless otherwise noted, material following is from D. Wallace Duthie, *The Church in the Pages of "Punch"* (London: Smith, Elder, 1912). See also A. L. Drummond, *The Churches Pictured by "Punch"* (London: Epworth Press, 1947).

26. Quoted in Lloyd, *Church of England*, 127.

27. The count is from ibid., 127.

28. Quoted in Peter F. Anson, *Fashions in Church Furnishings, 1840–1940* (London: Faith Press, 1960), 206.

29. Verse quoted in Drummond, *Churches in English Fiction*, 61.

30. Richard Frederick Littledale, "The Missionary Aspect of Ritualism," in Shipley (ed.), *Church and World: 1866*, 26.

31. This and subsequent quotations from the *Times* from Malcolm MacColl, *Tractarianism and Ritualism* (1881; PH 4033).

32. Quoted in Shipley (ed.), *Church and World: 1866*, 545–46.

33. Quoted in M. W. Mayow, *Remarks upon the First Report of the Royal Commission on Ritual* [etc.] (1868; PH 7858).

34. *Times*, May 1, 1874, quoted in E. B. Pusey, *The Proposed Ecclesiastical Legislation. Three Letters to "The Times"* [etc.] (1874; PH 8063).

35. Quoted in MacColl, *Tractarianism and Ritualism*.

36. *Layman's View of Ritualism*; "Lord Sandon on Sacerdotalism."

37. Maxwell Julius Blacker, "Religious Toleration," in Shipley (ed.), *Church and World: 1867*, 253.

38. Quoted in James S. Pollock, *Romanizing. The Substance of a Lecture delivered in the Town Hall, Birmingham, January 23, 1867* (London: Masters, 1867), 34.

39. Anthony Trollope, *Clergymen of the Church of England* (Leicester: Leicester University Press, 1974 [1866]), 48.

40. Lothair, *Ritualism: Its Practices and Tendency* (London: Charing Cross, 1877), 4; *Pall Mall Gazette* quoted in the *Church Times*, October 10, 1868.

41. Michael J. F. McCarthy, *Church and State in England and Wales, 1829–1906* (Dublin: Hodges, Figgis, 1906), 6. For an almost identical passage see Lothair, *Ritualism*, 41.

42. *Layman's View of Ritualism*.

43. James Dunn, *The Honesty of Our Position: A Paper Read before the Clifton Branch of the E.C.U.* (London: Pickering, 1878), 3.

44. *Layman's View of Ritualism; Animadversions by Distinguished Divines and Others, on the False Position of the Ritualistic Clergy in the Church of England* (London: Hamilton, Adams, 1882), 10.

45. A Benighted Layman, *Gropings in Search of the Church*, 8.

46. Quoted in William J. E. Bennett, *A Defense of the Catholic Faith* (1873; PH 1615). See also Edward Garbett, *What are Our Duties in the Present Circumstances of the Church?* (London: William Hunt, 1867), 24–25.

47. Quoted in L. E. Elliott-Binns, *Religion in the Victorian Era* (London: Lutterworth Press, 1936), 231.

48. See chapter 4, above.

49. Walter Walsh, *The Secret History of the Oxford Movement* (London: Swan Sonnenschein, 1897), vi.

50. C. H. Wainwright, *The Secrets of Ritualism. A Word of Warning*, 2d ed. (London: William Hunt, 1877), 19.

51. Quoted in Walsh, *Secret History*, 74.

52. Richard Frederick Littledale, "The First Report of the Ritual Commission," in *The Church and the World: Essays on Questions of the Day in 1868*, ed. Orby Shipley (London: Longmans, Green, Reader, and Dyer, 1868), 68.

53. *Church Times*, September 15, 1866.

54. See E. R. Norman, *Anti-Catholicism in Victorian England* (London: George Allen & Unwin, 1968).

55. Perry Butler, *Gladstone: Church, State, and Tractarianism* (Oxford: Clarendon Press, 1982), 142.

56. John G. Hubbard, *A Letter to the Venerable Edward Bickersteth, D.D.* (1874; PH 73147).

57. For an excellent recent treatment, with much discussion of Anglo-Catholicism, see D. G. Paz, *Popular Anti-Catholicism in Mid-Victorian England* (Stanford, Calif.: Stanford University Press, 1992).

58. An Anglican Layman, *The End of Modern Ritualism* (London: Longmans, Green, [1874]), 4, 8.

59. Paraphrased in W. H. Anderson, *Is Ritualism Honest?* (n.d.; PH 73771).

60. Quoted in Lloyd, *Church of England*, 125–26.

61. Quoted in Shipley (ed.), *Church and World: 1866*, 538.

62. Quoted in Michael Reynolds, *Martyr of Ritualism: Father Mackonochie of St. Alban's, Holborn* (London: Faber and Faber, 1965), 50.

63. Quoted in W. J. Sparrow Simpson, *The History of the Anglo-Catholic Revival from 1845* (London: George Allen & Unwin, 1932), 142.

64. Quoted in Reynolds, *Martyr of Ritualism*, 180.

CHAPTER 13

1. The Anglo-Catholic petition was signed by "communicants" only, however, as the *Guardian* pointed out (G. Bayfield Roberts, *The History of the English Church Union, 1859–1894* [London: Church Publishing, 1895], 167).

2. *Anarchy: An Appeal to Members of the English Church* (London: Rivington's, 1867), 9–10.

3. See William Jesse Fong, "The Ritualist Crisis: Anglo-Catholics and Authority with Special Reference to the English Church Union, 1859–1882" (Ph.D. thesis, University of Toronto, 1978), 246–344.

4. C. L. Wood, *The President's Address to the Ordinary Meeting of the English Church Union on Thursday, December 9, 1875* (1875; PH 6544).

5. Paul Thureau-Dangin, *The English Catholic Revival in the Nineteenth Century* (New York: E. P. Dutton, n.d.), 2:529. See also Roberts, *History of the English Church Union*, 404–5. Membership in the S.S.C. did suffer in the mid–1870s, especially after the controversy over *The Priest in Absolution*; it declined from 397 in 1877 to 227 in 1879 (J. Embry, *The Catholic Movement and the Society of the Holy Cross* [London: Faith Press, 1931], 128).

6. Quoted in S. C. Carpenter, *Church and People, 1789–1889: A History of the Church of England from William Wilberforce to "Lux Mundi"* (London: SPCK, 1933), 225.

7. Quoted in W. J. Sparrow Simpson, *The History of the Anglo-Catholic Revival from 1845* (London: George Allen & Unwin, 1932), 132.

8. Nicholas Pocock, *The Ritual Commission. A Paper Read at Bristol in November, 1870* [etc.] (1872; PH 3819). The author was commenting on the recommendations of the "Ritual Commission," later incorporated in the PWRA.

9. Sparrow Simpson, *History of the Anglo-Catholic Revival*, 131; F. H. Deane, *Two Speeches Delivered at the Lincoln Diocesan Conference, 1874 and 1876, on Church Difficulties* [etc.] (London: G. J. Palmer, 1877), 4. On who is to be accounted an "aggrieved parishioner," see also *The "Anti-Ritual" Report. A Sermon for General Distribution* (1867; PH 1939).

10. Roberts, *History of the English Church Union*, 157–58; quotation from 178.

11. W. J. Sparrow Simpson, "The Revival from 1845 to 1933," in *Northern Catholicism: Centenary Studies in the Oxford and Parallel Movements*, ed. N. P. Williams and Charles Harris (New York: Macmillan, 1933), 73–74.

12. "A Priest," *The Coming Campaign: How It Will Be Won* (1874; PH 6005). James Bentley identifies the author as H. W. Holden (*Ritualism and Politics in Victorian Britain: The Attempt to Legislate for Belief* [Oxford: Oxford University Press, 1978], 81n). Holden was a member of the E.C.U. and a brother of the Society of the Holy Cross (*The Ritualistic Conspiracy* [23d ed., 1877; PH 6018]).

13. Roberts, *History of the English Church Union*, 185–95 (Keble quoted, 191).

14. Quoted in Arthur Tilney Bassett, *S. Barnabas', Oxford: A Record of Fifty Years* (London: A.R. Mowbray, 1919), 58–59.

15. Michael Reynolds, *Martyr of Ritualism: Father Mackonochie of St. Alban's, Holborn* (London: Faber and Faber, 1965), 205.

16. [Chapman, Horace], *The Bishop of Salisbury and the Public Worship Regulation Act* (Salisbury: Brown, [1878]).

17. Three of the five clergymen were members of the S.S.C. in 1877; all five were members of the E.C.U (*Ritualistic Conspiracy* [1877]).

18. Reynolds, *Martyr of Ritualism*, 204. For a detailed account of Tooth's case, see Joyce Coombs, *Judgment on Hatcham: The History of a Religious Struggle, 1877–1886* (London: Faith Press, 1969).

19. Roberts, *History of the English Church Union*, 244–45.

20. Quoted in L. E. Elliott-Binns, *Religion in the Victorian Era* (London: Lutterworth Press, 1936), 236.

21. Quoted in *The Imprisonment of Mr. Tooth* (1877; PH 6554).

22. Charles John [Ellicott], *Future Prospects* (1874; PH 7572).

23. Quoted in Reynolds, *Martyr of Ritualism*, 238.

24. J. G. Lockhart, *Charles Lindley, Viscount Halifax* (London: Centenary, 1935) 1:239.

25. George Rundle Prynne, *Treachery; or, Ritualism and Evangelicalism Brought to the Standard of the Teaching of the Church of England. Dedicated to the Church Association* (London: Masters, 1870), 28.

26. Quoted in Sparrow Simpson, *History of the Anglo-Catholic Revival*, 149.

27. Charles Alford, *"Stand Fast" or, Contention for the Common Salvation against the Inroads of Ritualism a Christian Duty* (London: Simpkin, Marshall, Hamilton, Kent, [1895]), 9, 14.

28. Quoted in Carpenter, *Church and People*, 221.

29. In 1853, W. J. Conybeare had also estimated that the High Church and Low Church parties were about evenly balanced (W. J. Conybeare, "Church Parties," *Edinburgh Review* 98 [October 1853], 273–342).

30. *Memorial to His Grace the Archbishop of Canterbury* (1881; PH 71907). Tait called for the creation of a royal commission on the ecclesiastical courts; it reported in 1883, but no one acted on its recommendations.

31. Richard Frederick Littledale, "The First Report of the Ritual Commission," in *The Church and the World: Essays on Questions of the Day in 1868*, ed. Orby Shipley (London: Longmans, Green, Reader, and Dyer, 1868), 29–30.

32. Estimates are from figures in *Mackeson's*. See appendix 1.

33. Computed from data in Bishop of Lincoln [Christopher Wordsworth], *Results of an Inquiry on Ritual* (1875; PH 6010).

34. Quoted in Sparrow Simpson, *History of the Anglo-Catholic Revival*, 102.

35. J. G. Norton, *A Plea and Plan for the Toleration of Ritualists* (1881; PH 4265).

36. For a description of this impasse and its resolution, see Owen Chadwick, *The Victorian Church*, 2d ed. (London: Adam & Charles Black, 1972), 2:348–49.

37. Roberts, *History of the English Church Union*, 251.

38. Ibid., 278–79. On Ryle's career, see below; also Peter Toon and Michael Smout, *John Charles Ryle: Evangelical Bishop* (Cambridge: James Clark, 1976); the Bell-Cox case is treated on 87–90.

39. Quoted in Chadwick, *Victorian Church* 2:349n.

40. Quoted in Sparrow Simpson, "Revival from 1845 to 1933," 57.

41. The Author of "The Rector and His Friends," *The Ritual Difficulty. An Eirenicon* (London: George Bell and Sons, 1877), 26.

42. Quoted in Carpenter, *Church and People*, 218–19.

43. John B. Dykes, *Eucharistic Truth and Ritual: A Letter to the Right Reverend the Lord Bishop of Durham* [etc.] (2d ed., 1874; PH 1631).

44. J. F. Briscoe and H. F. B. MacKay, *A Tractarian at Work: A Memoir of Dean Randall* (London: A. R. Mowbray, 1932), 146.

45. William J. E. Bennett, *Obedience to the Lesser; Disobedience to the Greater* (London: J. T. Hayes, n.d.), 21.

46. Alford, *"Stand Fast,"* 9, 11. Alford had "lost" two sisters, first to Ritualism, then to Roman Catholicism.

47. Quoted in Briscoe and MacKay, *Tractarian at Work*, 143.

48. J. C. Ryle, *What Do We Owe to the Reformation?* (London: John F. Shaw, 1877), 16, 19, 23, 3.

49. Author of "The Rector and His Friends," *Ritual Difficulty*, 21–22.

50. Ibid., 28.

51. Quoted in Thureau-Dangin, *English Catholic Revival* 2:580.

52. Edward Harold [Browne], *The Position and Parties of the Church of England* (1875; PH 10838).

53. Wordsworth, *Results of an Inquiry* and *Senates and Synods, Their Respective Functions*

and Uses [etc.] (1874; PH 1622)). Wordsworth was a former headmaster of Harrow and a longtime supporter of the Sisterhood of S. John the Evangelist (see his *On Sisterhoods and Vows. A Letter to the Ven. Sir George Prevost, Bart.* [1878; PH 8032]).

54. [Christopher Wordsworth], *Charge of the Bishop of Lincoln on the Ornaments Rubric* (1879; PH 7268).

55. Church of England Working Men's Society, *The Bishop of Ely on the Persecution* (n.d., but ca. 1880; PH 8124).

56. J. Woolley, *Clergy Discipline: Its Relation to Doctrine, Ritual, and Morals* (1881; PH 73312).

57. Norton, *Plea and Plan*. Gamaliel is also cited in [F. Bingham], *The Ritual Question: An Appeal to Members of the Church of England and Others* (London: A. R. Mowbray, [1907]).

58. A. N. Bates, *The Ritual Question Briefly Explained* (1899; PH 8842).

59. Quoted in Roger Lloyd, *The Church of England, 1900–1965* (London: SCM Press, 1966), 120.

60. Letter reprinted in Alford, *"Stand Fast,"* 7.

61. J. W. Grover, *Pagans Ancient and Modern; or, the Antiquities of Ritualism* (London: Hatchard, 1868), 5.

62. For that phrase, see, for instance, James Bateman, *The Church Association: Its Policy and Prospects, Considered in a Letter to the Chairman*, 2d ed. (1880; PH 4031).

63. Quoted in G. R. Balleine, *A History of the Evangelical Party in the Church of England*, new ed. (London: Church Book Room Press, 1951 [1908]), 185.

64. E. H. Bickersteth, *Evangelical Churchmanship and Evangelical Eclecticism* (London: Sampson Low, Marston, Searle, & Rivington, 1883). On the Anglo-Catholic origins of these observances, see Marcus Donovan, *After the Tractarians* (London: Philip Allan, 1933), 128–29.

65. Edward Bickersteth, *Counsels of Peace for the Church of England. An Address to the Clergy of the Rural Deanery of Handsworth, delivered at Smethwick, July 23, 1877* (London: Rivington's, 1877), 8, 11, 12.

66. Ryle, *What Do We Owe?*, 17, 18, 21–22, 23 (emphasis added).

67. J. C. Ryle, *Shall We Go?* (London: William Hunt, 1878), 22. Emphasis in original.

68. Balleine, *History of the Evangelical Party*, 231.

69. The *Church Times* (January 28, 1870) reported that stamp returns since 1858 showed a "regular and considerable annual decrease" in the circulation of both the *Record* and the *Rock*, and a "rather more than proportionable increase" for the High Church *Guardian*.

70. Balleine, *History of the Evangelical Party*, 231–32.

71. Ibid., 232–33.

72. Quoted in Elliott-Binns, *Religion in the Victorian Era*, 236.

73. Balleine, *History of the Evangelical Party*, 232.

74. Quoted in ibid., 231.

75. Bateman, *Church Association*.

76. See above, chapter 5.

77. Balleine, *History of the Evangelical Party*, 214–15.

78. S. A. Walker, *No! An Answer to Canon Ryle's Tract "Shall We Go?"* [etc.] (London: Elliot Stock, n.d.), 16.

79. Bateman, *Church Association*.

80. Quoted in Donovan, *After the Tractarians*, 79.

81. *Church Times* and *Morning Post* quoted in Bateman, *Church Association*.

82. See appendix 1.

83. Quoted in Elliott-Binns, *Religion in the Victorian Era*, 236.

84. Quoted in Church of England Working Men's Society, *Rev. R. W. Enraght in Warwick Jail* (n.d.; PH 8125).

85. J. T. Tomlinson, *A Review of Canon J. W. Knox-Little's "Answer to Archdeacon Farrar"* [etc.] (London: Church Association, n.d. [ca. 1894]); Owen Chadwick, *Hensley Henson:*

A Study in the Friction between Church and State (Oxford: Clarendon Press, 1983), 194.

86. Quoted in Lockhart, *Charles Lindley, Viscount Halifax* 1:250.

87. Something of the flavor can be gathered from the title: Thomas Berney, *An Address Shewing by Indubitable Evidence and by Revelations of the Holy Spirit, the "Treachery" and "Offense" unto God, and Extreme Danger to Our Queen, Our Church and Our Country, of the Church Patronage Bill, and a New Edition of the Book of Common Prayer* (n.p., 1895).

88. Roberts, *History of the English Church Union*, 226.

89. Church of England Working Men's Society, *Summary of Proceedings At the Meeting of Delegates on the Second Anniversary of the Society* [etc.] (1878; PH 8109).

90. Chadwick, *Victorian Church* 2:352–53.

91. A Retired Rector, *Babylon in St. Paul's: or, the Eviction of Protestants from the Metropolitan Cathedral. A Letter of Protest and Rebuke to the Bishop of London* (London: John Kensit, [1888]); complaint quoted in Roberts, *History of the English Church Union*, 325.

92. Chadwick, *Victorian Church* 2:352–53.

93. Ibid., 353–54. See also John Newton, *Search for a Saint: Edward King* (London: Church Literature Association, 1983), 97–103.

94. Donovan, *After the Tractarians*, 149. For a sketch of King's episcopate, see Geoffrey Rowell, *The Vision Glorious: Themes and Personalities of the Catholic Revival in Anglicanism* (Oxford: Oxford University Press, 1983), 141–57.

95. *A Grave Crisis in the Church of England. What is to be Done?* (London: John Kensit, n.d.), 6.

96. Quoted in Lockhart, *Charles Lindley, Viscount Halifax* 2:23.

97. Quoted in Balleine, *History of the Evangelical Party*, 235.

98. See [E. H. Bickersteth], Bishop of Exeter, *Pastoral Letter* (1899; PH 73486).

99. *The Ritualistic Clergy List, being a Guide for Patrons and Others To certain of the Clergy of the Church of England; containing a List of some 9600 Clergymen who are helping the Romeward Movement in the National Church*, 2d ed. (London: Church Association, 1902).

100. Lloyd, *Church of England*, 121–41; see also Chadwick *Victorian Church* 2:354–58. An extensive treatment of the extreme Anglo-Catholic response is Alan Wilson, "The Authority of Church and Party among London Anglo-Catholics, 1880–1914, with Special Reference to the Church Crisis, 1898–1904" (D. Phil. thesis, Oxford University, 1988).

101. Royal Commission on Ecclesiastical Discipline, "Reports from Commissioners, Inspectors, and Others," *Parliamentary Papers* 33–34 (1906); conclusion quoted in Lloyd, *Church of England*, 141.

102. Andrew Martin Fairbairn, *The New Sacerdotalism and the New Puritanism: A Discourse Delivered before the Congregational Union of England and Wales* (London: Hodder and Stoughton, [1868]), 282.

103. *Bombastes Religioso or The Protestant Pope of 1899* (London: Simpkin Marshall Hamilton Kent, [1899]), 3–5, 33, 6, 14–15.

CHAPTER 14

1. F. G. Lee, *Directorium Anglicanum*, 4th ed. (London: John Hogg, 1879), li.

2. See appendix 1.

3. Quoted in Thomas Howard Gill, *A Letter to the Right Reverend the Lord Bishop of Manchester, touching "Ritualism"* (London: Hatchards, 1878), 9.

4. Presbyter Protestans, *The "English Church Union"… A Romanizing Confederacy* (London: John F. Shaw, 1877), 31–33, quotes extensively from the *Church Union Gazette*.

5. G. Bayfield Roberts, *The History of the English Church Union, 1859–1894* (London: Church Publishing, 1895), 286; annual report cited in *The Ritualistic Clergy List, being a Guide for Patrons and Others To certain of the Clergy of the Church of England; containing a List of some 9600 Clergymen who are helping the Romeward Movement in the National Church*, 2d ed. (London: Church Association, 1902), 163.

6. J. Embry, *The Catholic Movement and the Society of the Holy Cross* (London: Faith Press, 1931), 51.

7. See W. R. Matthews, "By the Dean of Exeter," in Lord Hugh Cecil, the Dean of Exeter [W. R. Matthews], F. R. Barry, and Canon Wilfred L. Knox, *Anglo-Catholicism Today* (London: Philip Allan, 1934).

8. Alf Hardelin, "The Eucharist in the Theology of the Nineteenth Century," in R. E. Clements, Austin Farrer, *et al.*, *Eucharistic Theology Then and Now* (London: S.P.C.K., 1968), 83.

9. Quotations from G. R. Balleine, *A History of the Evangelical Party in the Church of England*, new ed. (London: Church Book Room Press, 1951 [1908]), 181, and Roberts, *History of the English Church Union*, 19.

10. Quoted in William J. E. Bennett, *Obedience to the Lesser; Disobedience to the Greater* (London: J. T. Hayes, n.d.), 23.

11. *Thoughts on Some Questions of the Day* (1869; PH 3656).

12. *The "Anti-Ritual" Report. A Sermon for General Distribution* (1867; PH 1939), from which the quoted phrase comes, was one of many such appeals; see also, for instance, William J. E. Bennett, *A Plea for Toleration in the Church of England* [etc.] (1868; PH 8198).

13. Charles Walker, *Pax Super Israel. An Irenicon, Respectfully Addressed to the Consideration of the Royal Commission on Ritual* (1867; PH 4621). Emphasis in original.

14. A Layman of the Diocese [of Chicester], *Things Indifferent* [etc.] (London: J. T. Hayes, 1877), 19.

15. Quoted in L. E. Elliott-Binns, *Religion in the Victorian Era* (London: Lutterworth Press, 1936), 231.

16. S[abine] Baring-Gould, *Protestant or Catholic? A Lecture Originally Delivered at Cambridge and Elsewhere* (London: J. T. Hayes, 1872).

17. Owen Chadwick, *The Victorian Church*, 2d ed. (London: Adam & Charles Black, 1972), 2:101–4.

18. "An English Catholic," *Monsignore Capel and the Ritualists* (1875; PH 6009).

19. Robert H. Greenfield, "Attitude of the Tractarians to the Roman Catholic Church, 1833–1850" (D. Phil. thesis, Oxford University, 1956), documents the early ascendancy of this wing of Tractarianism, and its continuing dominance under Pusey's leadership.

20. Roberts, *History of the English Church Union*, 80.

21. C. R. Chase to the S.S.C. (1887), quoted in Alan Wilson, "The Authority of Church and Party among London Anglo-Catholics, 1880–1914, with Special Reference to the Church Crisis, 1898–1904" (D. Phil. thesis, Oxford University, 1988), 24.

22. Richard Frederick Littledale, *Why Ritualists Do Not Become Roman Catholics: A Reply to the Abbe Martin* (n.d., but 1879; PH 1799) and *Ritualists not Romanists* (n.d.; PH 1504). See also Littledale's *Plain Reasons against Joining the Church of Rome* (London: Society for Promoting Christian Knowledge, 1880), and "Was the British or Anglo-Saxon Church Roman Catholic?" (cited in *Church Defense Handy Volume*, 6th ed. [London: Church Defense Institution, 1892], as article no. 87). Littledale's strictures on the Roman Church were protested by Orby Shipley, a former S.S.C colleague who had become a Roman Catholic; see Shipley's *A Specimen of Recent Anglican Controversy with Rome: A Letter to the Rev. Dr. Pusey, D.D.* (London: Privately printed, 1880) and *Truthfulness and Ritualism*, first series (London: Burns and Oates, 1879). On Shipley's secession, see William Jesse Fong, "The Ritualist Crisis: Anglo-Catholics and Authority with Special Reference to the English Church Union, 1859–1882" (Ph.D. thesis, University of Toronto, 1978), 431–32.

23. *The Church in England Catholic Defense Tracts* 2 (London: J. Masters, [1891]).

24. *Ritual Conformity: Interpretations of the Rubrics of the Prayer-Book agreed upon by a Conference Held at All Saints, Margaret-Street, 1880–1881* (1881; PH 71906).

25. Quoted in J. F. Briscoe and H. F. B. MacKay, *A Tractarian at Work: A Memoir of Dean Randall* (London: A. R. Mowbray, 1932), 200–201.

26. The other S.S.C. members were C. L. Courtenay and James Baden Powell;

Wordsworth and W. J. Blew were not listed as E.C.U. members in 1877 (*The Ritualistic Conspiracy* [23d ed., 1877; PH 6018]).

27. James H. Rigg, *Oxford High Anglicanism, and Its Chief Leaders* (London: Charles H. Kelly, 1895), 324.

28. Charles F. G. Masterman, "The Problem of South London," in *The Religious Life of London*, ed. Richard Mudie-Smith (London: Hodder and Stoughton, 1904), 205.

29. Andrew L. Drummond, *The Churches in English Fiction* (Leicester: Edgar Backus, 1950), 99.

30. The Author of "The Rector and His Friends," *The Ritual Difficulty. An Eirenicon* (London: George Bell and Sons, 1877), 28.

31. These are churches where *Mackeson's* (1882) shows the eucharistic vestments in use. *Mackeson's* also reported their use in seven churches outside the metropolis altogether, in Shepperton, Richmond, and Beckenham.

32. *Mackeson's* (1882).

33. Charles Booth, *Life and Labour of the People in London. Third Series: Religious Influences* (London: Macmillan, 1902) 5:191.

34. Booth, *Life and Labour: Third Series* 6:41–43; quotation from 43.

35. Masterman, "Problem of South London," 190.

36. Peter F. Anson, *The Call of the Cloister: Religious Communities and Kindred Bodies in the Anglican Communion* (London: S.P.C.K., 1955), 439–40. The story of St. Augustine's is largely the history of two sisterhoods associated with it from its early days, the Community of St. Peter and the Sisters of the Church (385–93, 439–46).

37. G. Wakeling, *The Oxford Church Movement. Sketches and Recollections* (London: Swan Sonnenschein, 1895), 143–48; on LeGeyt, see Charles Mackeson, *A Digest of the Evidence Given Before the Commissioners appointed to Inquire into the Rubrics, Orders, and Directions for Regulating the Course and Conduct of Public Worship* [etc.] (London: James Parker, 1867), 10.

38. The median for the slum churches was 23 percent; for the suburban churches, 65 percent.

39. Masterman, "Problem of South London," 205.

40. A. Clifton Kelway, *George Rundle Prynne: A Chapter in the Early History of the Catholic Revival* (London: Longmans, Green, 1905), 72–108, 140, 144–45, 155, 159.

41. J. H. Overton, *The Anglican Revival* (London: Blackie & Son, 1897), 199–200.

GLOSSARY

Ecclesiastical Terms[1]

ABSOLUTION Pronouncement by a priest, following confession, that a penitent's sins have been forgiven; also refers to the "Declaration of Absolution" following General Confession in the daily offices and Communion service.

ACOLYTE Assistant minister, usually a lay man or boy, whose duties include lighting and carrying candles, preparing wine and water for the Eucharist, etc.

ALB Eucharistic vestment of white linen, long-sleeved and ankle-length, worn over cassock and amice.

AMICE Rectangular vestment of white linen, covering the neck and shoulders, worn under alb.

APOSTOLIC SUCCESSION Method by which the Church's ministry is held to be derived from the original apostles, to whom bishops are linked by an unbroken series of valid consecrations.

ARCHDEACON Clergyman with administrative authority for all or part of a diocese delegated to him by the bishop of the diocese.

ATHANASIAN CREED Profession of faith beginning "Whosoever will be saved, before all things it is necessary that he hold the Catholick Faith"; thought by some to be unduly harsh in its "damnatory clauses."

BAPTISMAL REGENERATION Doctrine that baptism remits original sin and effects a spiritual rebirth.

BENEDICTINES Monks and nuns who follow the Rule of St. Benedict (established ca. 529), a central part of which is choral celebration of the Divine Office (q.v.).

BENEDICTION Commonly refers to various forms of priestly blessing, e.g., at the end of the Communion service. "Benediction of the Blessed Sacrament" refers to various Roman Catholic observances in which the congregation is blessed with the consecrated wafer

BIRETTA Square cap (black for priests), with three ridges on the top and sometimes a tuft in the middle.

CANON Generally, a clergyman attached to a cathedral, especially one of the salaried staff, although there are also "honorary" or "non-residentiary" canons.

CASSOCK Ankle-length, long-sleeved underdress, usually black.

---

[1] Adapted from *A Catholic Dictionary;* ed. Donald Attwater (New York: Macmillan, 1941); Iris Conlay and Peter F. Anson, *The Art of the Church* (London: Burns and Oates, 1964); *Dictionary of the English Church* (London: Wells Gardner, Darton, & Co., 1881); *The Oxford Dictionary of the Christian Church*, 2d ed., ed. F. L. Cross and E. A. Livingstone (London: Oxford University Press, 1974); and *A Dictionary of English Church History,* ed. S. L. Ollard and Gordon Crosse (London: A. R. Mowbray and Co., 1912).

CENSING Burning incense before a person or thing, as a mark of honor.

CHANCEL The part of a church between altar and nave; includes the choir and the sanctuary (around the altar).

CHANCEL SCREEN Semi-open screen of wood or stone, separating chancel from nave; called a rood-screen when surmounted by a large crucifix, or "rood."

CHASUBLE Outermost eucharistic vestment, worn by the celebrant; hangs from the shoulders, front and back, and is usually ornamented.

CHIMERE Upper robe worn by a bishop, to which lawn sleeves are generally sewn.

CHURCH MILITANT PRAYER The prayer before Communion "for the whole state of Christ's Church" on earth.

CHURCHING OF WOMEN The form of thanksgiving by women after childbirth, provided by the Prayer Book office of that name.

CINCTURE Girdle of a cassock or similar garment.

CLERK, PARISH Lay functionary whose duties include reading responses, lessons, psalms, etc.

COMPLINE The last "hour" of the Divine Office.

CONFESSION, AURICULAR Private confession of a penitent to a priest.

CONFESSOR A martyr; also a priest who hears confessions (see "Spiritual Director").

COPE Vestment in the form of a mantle reaching to the heels, open in front and fastened at the breast, often highly ornamented, with a cape covering the shoulders; worn in processions and at solemn occasions other than the Eucharist.

COTTA A short surplice.

CREDENCE A small shelf or table near the altar, on which the Communion elements are placed before consecration.

CURATE Properly a clergyman who has the charge or "cure" of a parish, but the word has come to mean "assistant curate," i.e., one who assists or substitutes for a rector or vicar.

DALMATIC Ankle-length robe with wide, short sleeves, worn by a deacon.

DEACON The ministerial rank below and usually antecedent to that of priest, not allowed to celebrate the Eucharist or pronounce absolution

DEAN The clergyman who heads a cathedral's or a collegiate church's clerical staff and oversees its services and property.

DIVINE OFFICE The daily public prayer of the Church, especially the monastic "hours" (q.v.), but also the parochial services of morning and evening prayer.

EASTWARD POSITION The practice of celebrating the Eucharist facing the altar, back to the congregation, instead of at the "north end" of the altar, as directed by the Prayer Book.

EPISCOPUS VAGANS Someone consecrated bishop in an irregular or clandestine manner, or excommunicated by the Church that consecrated him, and in communion with no recognized bishop.

EVENSONG Common name in medieval times for the monastic hour of Vespers; also applied to the Prayer Book service of evening prayer.

EXPOSITION Exhibition of the consecrated Host for the purpose of devotion; the form of service is similar to Benediction.

ERASTIANISM Strictly, the subordination of the Church to the secular power in ecclesiastical matters, but has come to mean any tendency in that direction.

FALDSTOOL Properly a folding seat, but the term is frequently, if erroneously, applied to the litany desk (q.v.).

FRONTAL Hangings or panel in front of an altar, usually highly ornamented.

GENUFLECTION Bending of the right knee to touch the ground, done before the consecrated Host and on a few other occasions.

GIRDLE The cord around the waist securing the alb, usually of white cotton.

GOWN (GENEVAN) Long black robe worn by some clergymen as a preaching vestment.

HIGH MASS A Mass celebrated with the assistance of deacon and subdeacon, usually also with a choir and a number of acolytes, and with such distinctive features as the use of incense.

HOURS, MONASTIC The eight divisions of the Divine Office, so called because prescribed for certain times.

LITANY The Prayer Book form of "general supplication," read responsively; its use is called for after morning prayer three days a week and on other occasions.

LITANY DESK Small low desk at which the litany is read, generally placed in the middle of the choir.

LOW MASS A simplified form of the Mass, not sung, requiring only a celebrant and a single acolyte.

MANIPLE A band of silk of the color of the day, worn over the left forearm by ordained clergy at the Eucharist.

MATINS The first of the monastic hours; also applied to the Prayer Book service of morning prayer, an abridgment of the hours of matins, lauds, and prime.

MENSA Properly the flat stone top of a fixed altar, but commonly applied to the top of any altar.

METROPOLITAN In Roman Catholic and Eastern churches, an archbishop who presides over a province consisting of several dioceses; similar to primate.

MIXED CHALICE Practice of mixing water with wine at the Eucharist, largely discontinued by the Church of England in the sixteenth century.

MONSTRANCE A vessel of golden or silver rays with a glass or crystal window in the center through which the consecrated Host may be seen; often used in Benediction and Exposition.

NAVE The body of a church, accommodating the lay congregation, between the rear and the chancel.

NAVICULA An incense boat, or container.

OCTAVE The eighth day after any festival Observance is sometimes extended from the festival to the octave, as in the Prayer Book provisions for Easter, Christmas, and Ascension.

OFFERTORY The portion of the Communion service in which the congregation presents its "alms and oblations"; sometimes improperly applied to any offering or collection.

OFFICES, DAILY Usually the Prayer Book services of morning and evening prayer, but may also refer to the monastic hours (q.v.).

ORPHREY Band of embroidery sewn on a vestment or frontal.

PENANCE, SACRAMENT OF The forgiveness of post-baptismal sin through confession and priestly absolution (see "Sacraments").

PISCINA Stone basin near altar, with drain to carry off water in which priest has washed his hands and rinsed the chalice.

PRIE DIEU Kneeling desk, often covered with a hanging.

REAL PRESENCE The doctrine that Christ's body and blood are present truly, not merely symbolically, in the Eucharist.

RECTOR A clergyman in charge of a parish who is entitled to the tithes of the parish (see "Vicar" and "Curate").

REREDOS Ornamented screen of wood or stone, or a painting, behind an altar.

RESERVATION Setting aside the consecrated bread from the Communion service, originally for the sick and others who could not attend, although well before the Reformation the reserved Sacrament had become the object of devotion.

ROCHET White linen garment similar to surplice, but longer and with close sleeves, worn by bishops under the chimere.

ROOD SCREEN See "Chancel Screen."

RUBRICS The Prayer Book's ritual or ceremonial instructions, so called because originally printed in red.

RURAL DEAN Clergyman appointed by the bishop to oversee a group of parishes within a diocese; subordinate to archdeacon (q.v.).

RURIDECANAL Of or pertaining to a rural dean or deanery.

SACERDOTALISM Belief in the necessity for mediating priests; more generally, an emphasis on the authority of the priesthood.

SACRAMENT, THE Commonly refers to the consecrated communion wafer.

SACRAMENTS There are seven sacraments in Roman Catholic doctrine, but Article 25 of the Prayer Book denies that "five commonly called sacraments" — confirmation, ordination, marriage, penance, and extreme unction — are "sacraments of the Gospel," restricting that term to baptism and the Eucharist.

SACRISTAN The person in charge of a church's vestments, etc.; the sexton.

SACRISTY The place in which a church's vestments, etc., are kept; the vestry.

SEDILIA Seats, usually three and often elaborately carved, within the rail of the sanctuary, for the use of clergy.

SPIRITUAL DIRECTOR One who guides the spiritual life of others; usually, though not always, the priest to whom one regularly confesses.

STOLE A swath of cloth hanging from the shoulder to the feet, worn by parish priests over the surplice and by other ordained clergy over the alb at the Eucharist.

SURPLICE White linen garment of variable length, with full sleeves, usually worn over a cassock.

TABERNACLE Box-like receptacle of wood, stone, or metal in which the consecrated bread is reserved on an altar.

TENEBRAE In Roman Catholic practice, special services for Thursday, Friday, and Saturday of Holy Week, in which successive candles are extinguished until the service concludes in darkness.

THURIBLE Vessel, carried by three chains, in which incense is burned; a censer

THURIFER Acolyte who has charge of a thurible.

TUNIC, TUNICLE Garment similar to the dalmatic, worn by ordained clergy assisting at the Eucharist.

UNCTION Anointing with oil, as at baptism and confirmation. The sacrament of extreme unction refers to a priest's anointing, with specially blessed oil, a person near death (see "Sacraments").

VICAR A clergyman in charge of a parish who does not receive the tithes of the parish, or receives only some of them.

VIGIL Day preceding certain feasts, observed as preparation, sometimes with special services or fasting; eve.

ZUCCHETTO In Roman Catholic use, the skullcap of a dignitary.

WORKS CITED

ABC (London and Suburban) Church and Chapel Directory. London: Robert Banks, 1862 *et seq.*

Abercrombie, Nigel. "Some Directions of the Oxford Movement," *Dublin Review* 193, no. 386 (July–September 1933): 74–84.

Absalom, Francis. "The Anglo-Catholic Priest: Aspects of Role Conflict." In *A Sociological Yearbook of Religion in Britain*, vol. 4. Edited by Michael Hill. London: SCM Press, 1971.

"Adam Bede." *The Natural History of Puseyism: With a Short Account of the Sunday Opera at St. Paul's, Brighton*. Brighton: G. Smart, [1860].

Adams, Pauline A. "Converts to the Roman Catholic Church in England, *circa* 1830–1870." B.Litt. thesis, Oxford University, 1977.

Alden, Percy. "The Problem of East London." In *The Religious Life of London*. Edited by Richard Mudie-Smith. London: Hodder and Stoughton, 1904.

Alford, Charles. *"Stand Fast" or, Contention for the Common Salvation against the Inroads of Ritualism a Christian Duty*. London: Simpkin, Marshall, Hamilton, Kent & Co., [1895].

Allchin, A. M. *The Silent Rebellion: Anglican Religious Communities, 1845–1900*. London: SCM Press, 1958.

Anarchy: An Appeal to Members of the English Church. London: Rivington's, 1867.

An Anglican Layman. *The End of Modern Ritualism*. London: Longmans, Green, and Co., n.d. [1874].

Animadversions by Distinguished Divines and Others, on the False Position of the Ritualistic Clergy in the Church of England. London: Hamilton, Adams, & Co., 1882.

Anson, Peter F. *Bishops at Large*. London: Faber and Faber, 1964.

———. *Building Up the Waste Places: The Revival of Monastic Life on Medieval Lines in the Post–Reformation Church of England*. Leighton Buzzard: Faith Press, 1973.

———. *The Call of the Cloister: Religious Communities and Kindred Bodies in the Anglican Communion*. London: SPCK, 1955.

———. *Fashions in Church Furnishings, 1840–1940*. London: Faith Press, 1960.

The Armoury: A Magazine of Weapons for Christian Warfare V–VII (1877–1884).

Ashley, John. *Sequel to the "Church of the Period" with the Author's Reasons for Leaving the Church of England*. London: W. H. Guest, 1876.

Association for Promoting the Revision of the Prayer-Book. *The Confessional and the Prayer-Book*. London: Wyman & Sons, 1877.

Attwater, Donald. *Father Ignatius of Llanthony: A Victorian*. London: Cassell and Company, 1931.

———, ed. *A Catholic Dictionary*. New York: Macmillan Company, 1941.

The Author of "The Rector and His Friends." *The Ritual Difficulty. An Eirenicon*. London:

George Bell & Sons, 1877.

Baker, Joseph Ellis. *The Novel and the Oxford Movement*. Princeton Studies in English, No. 8. Princeton: Princeton University Press, 1932.

Balleine, G. R. *A History of the Evangelical Party in the Church of England*. New ed. London: Church Book Room Press, 1951 [1908].

Baring-Gould, Sabine. *The Church Revival: Thoughts Thereon and Reminiscences*. London: Methuen & Co., 1914.

———. *Protestant or Catholic? A Lecture Originally Delivered at Cambridge and Elsewhere*. London: J. T. Hayes, 1872.

Barry, Alfred. *The Church Questions of the Day* [etc]. London: Longmans, Green & Co., 1868.

Bassett, Arthur Tilney. *S. Barnabas', Oxford: A Record of Fifty Years*. London: Mowbray, 1919.

Bell, Mackenzie. *Christina Rossetti: A Biographical and Critical Study*. 3d ed. London: Hurst and Blackett, 1898.

A Benighted Layman. *Gropings in Search of the Church of England*. London: George John Stevenson, 1867.

Bennett, William J. E. *Obedience to the Lesser; Disobedience to the Greater*. London: J. T. Hayes, n.d.

Bentley, James. *Ritualism and Politics in Victorian Britain: The Attempt to Legislate for Belief*. Oxford: Oxford University Press, 1978.

Berney, Thomas. *An Address Shewing by Indubitable Evidence and by Revelations of the Holy Spirit, the "Treachery" and "Offense" unto God, and Extreme Danger to Our Queen, Our Church and Our Country, of the Church Patronage Bill, and a New Edition of the Book of Common Prayer*. N.p., 1895.

de Bertouch, Beatrice. *The Life of Father Ignatius, O.S.B. The Monk of Llanthony*. London: Methuen & Co., 1904.

Best, G. F. A. "New Bearings on the Oxford Movement." *The Historical Journal* 12 (1969): 707–10.

Bickersteth, E. H. *Evangelical Churchmanship and Evangelical Eclecticism*. London: Sampson Low, Marston, Searle, & Rivington, 1883.

———. *Counsels of Peace for the Church of England. An Address to the Clergy of the Rural Deanery of Handsworth, delivered at Smethwick, July 23, 1877*. London: Rivington's, 1877.

[Bingham, F.] *The Ritual Question: An Appeal to Members of the Church of England and Others*. London: Mowbray, [1907].

Bishop Butler An Avowed PUSEYITE, & suspected CATHOLIC. n.p., 1842.

Blacker, Maxwell Julius. "Religious Toleration." In *The Church and the World: Essays on Questions of the Day in 1867*. Edited by Orby Shipley. London: Longmans, Green, Reader, and Dyer, 1867.

Bocock, Robert J., "Anglo-Catholic Socialism: A Study of a Protest Movement within a Church." *Social Compass* 20 (1973): 31–48.

Bombastes Religioso or The Protestant Pope of 1899. London: Simpkin Marshall Hamilton Kent & Co., [1899].

Bonham, J. W. *The Great Revival in the Church of England*. New York: T. Whittaker, 1875.

Booth, Charles. *Life and Labour of the People in London*, vol. 2 (Streets and People Classified). London: Macmillan and Co., 1892.

———. *Life and Labour of the People in London. Third Series: Religious Influences*. 7 vols. London: Macmillan and Co., 1902.

Borer, Mary Cathcart. *People of Victorian and Edwardian England*. London: MacDonald and Co., 1969.

Borsch, Frederick Houk. "Ye Shall Be Holy: Reflections on the Spirituality of the Oxford Movement." In *Tradition Renewed: The Oxford Movement Conference Papers*. Edited by Geoffrey Rowell. London: Darton, Longman and Todd, 1986.

Boulter, B. C. *The Anglican Reformers.* London: Philip Allan, 1933.

Bowen, Desmond. *The Idea of the Victorian Church: A Study of the Church of England, 1833–1889.* Montreal: McGill University Press, 1968.

Boyce, Edward Jacob. *A Memorial of the Cambridge Camden Society.* London: G. Palmer, 1888.

Brandreth, Henry R. T. *Dr. Lee of Lambeth: A Chapter in Parenthesis in the History of the Oxford Movement.* London: SPCK., 1951.

———. *Episcopi Vagantes and the Anglican Church.* London: SPCK., 1947.

Brendon, Piers. "A High Road to Anglican UDI?" *Church Times,* July 9, 1983, 6.

———. *Hawker of Morwenstow: Portrait of a Victorian Eccentric.* London: Jonathan Cape, 1975.

———. *Hurrell Froude and the Oxford Movement.* London: Paul Elek, 1974.

———. "Newman, Keble and Froude's *Remains,*" *English Historical Review* 87 (October 1972): 697–716.

Brilioth, Yngve. *The Anglican Revival: Studies in the Oxford Movement.* London: Longmans, Green and Co., 1933.

Briscoe, J. F., and H. F. B. MacKay. *A Tractarian at Work: A Memoir of Dean Randall.* London: Mowbray, 1932.

Brockman, H. J. *"The Confessional Unmasked." A Military as well as Moral Plea for abolishing the Confessional.* London: Protestant Evangelical Mission and Electoral Union, n.d.

Brown, Robert. *Ritualism at Barton-on-Humber* [etc.]. London: Marlborough & Co., 1867.

Browne, Edward George Kirwan. *Annals of the Tractarian Movement, from 1842 to 1860.* 3d ed. London: privately published, 1861.

Browne, Henry. *The Oxford Movement.* London: Catholic Truth Society, n.d.

Burgon, John W. *The Oxford Diocesan Conference; and Romanizing within the Church of England: Two Sermons preached at St. Mary-the-Virgin's, Oxford, Oct. 12th and 19th, 1873.* Oxford: James Parker and Co., 1873.

Butler, Perry. *Gladstone: Church, State, and Tractarianism.* Oxford: Clarendon Press, 1982.

Calder-Marshall, Arthur. *The Enthusiast: An Enquiry into the Life, Beliefs and Character of The Rev. Joseph Leycester Lyne **alias** Fr. Ignatius, O.S.B., Abbot of Elm Hill, Norwich, and Llanthony, Wales.* London: Faber and Faber, 1962.

Campbell, Colin. "Accounting for the Counter Culture," *Scottish Journal of Sociology* 1 (1980): 37–51.

Carpenter, S. C. *Church and People, 1789–1889: A History of the Church of England from William Wilberforce to "Lux Mundi".* London: SPCK, 1933.

Carter, T. T. *The Freedom of Confession in the Church of England. A letter to His Grace the Lord Archbishop of Canterbury.* London: Rivington's, 1877.

"Centenary of the Oxford Movement, 1833 to 1933." Supplement to *St. Thomas the Martyr Parish Magazine* [Oxford], June 1933.

Ceremonial and Christian Religion. London: William MacIntosh, 1875.

Chadwick, Owen. "The Established Church under Attack." In *The Victorian Crisis of Faith.* Edited by Anthony Symondson. London: SPCK., 1970.

———. *The Founding of Cuddesdon.* Oxford: Oxford University Press, 1954.

———. *Hensley Henson: A Study in the Friction between Church and State.* Oxford: Clarendon Press, 1983.

———, ed. *The Mind of the Oxford Movement.* Stanford, Calif.: Stanford University Press, 1961.

———. *The Victorian Church.* 2 vols. London: Adam & Charles Black: 1971, Part I, 3d ed.; and 1972, Part II, 2d ed..

Chambers, John Charles. "Private Confession and Absolution." In *The Church and the World: Essays on Questions of the Day in 1867.* Edited by Orby Shipley. London: Longmans, Green, Reader, and Dyer, 1867.

[Chapman, Horace]. *The Bishop of Salisbury and the Public Worship Regulation Act.* Salisbury:

Brown & Co., n.d. [1878].

Chapman, Raymond. *Faith and Revolt: Studies in the Literary Influence of the Oxford Movement.* London: Weidenfeld and Nicolson, 1970.

The Church and the People. An Address to Churchmen upon the Pew System and the Weekly Offertory. London: Thomas Bosworth, 1865.

Church Association. *Annual Report of the Association. 1875.* London: Church Association, 1876.

———. *Appeal of the Council of the Church Association to Electors, Members of the United Church of England and Ireland.* Undated handbill.

Church Association Lectures: Delivered at St. James's Hall [etc.]. London: William MacIntosh, 1867.

The Church Association versus Rev. S. F. Green, B.A. 6th ed. n.p., 1881.

Church Defence: Report of a Conference on the Present Dangers of the Church. London: R. Washbourne, 1873.

Church Defense Handy Volume. 6th ed. London: Church Defense Institution, 1892.

The Church in England Catholic Defense Tracts. 5 tracts. London: J. Masters & Co., [n.d., but 1891].

Church of England Working Men's Society. *The Church of Our Fathers,* June 1892–July 1893.

Church Reform: and the Report of the Royal Commission on Ritual, being the second annual Report of the Church of England Laymen's Defense Association; together with a Note on Sacerdotalism. London: W. MacIntosh, [1868].

Church Restoration and Church Arrangement. Being an Extract from the Speech of the Lord Bishop of Lincoln, after Reopening the Church at Newark. London: Bell & Daldy, 1855.

Church Times, Supplement to 6,000th Number, February 10, 1978.

Church Union Gazette. London: English Church Union, 1870 *et seq.*

Church, R. W. *The Oxford Movement: Twelve Years, 1833–1845.* 3d ed. London: Macmillan and Co., 1892.

Clark, G. Kitson. *Churchmen and the Condition of England, 1832–1885.* London: Methuen & Co, 1973.

Clarke, C. P. S. "The Genesis of the Movement." In *Northern Catholicism: Centenary Studies in the Oxford and Parallel Movements.* Edited by N. P. Williams and Charles Harris. New York: Macmillan Co., 1933.

———. *The Oxford Movement and After.* London: Mowbray, 1932.

Clarke, W. K. Lowther. *A Hundred Years of Hymns Ancient & Modern.* London: William Clowes & Sons, 1960.

The Clergy Directory and Parish Guide. London: Thomas Bosworth, 1875.

Clerical Address to the Prelates Against Legalising the Eastward Position and a Distinctive Eucharistic Dress; with the Names of 5376 Clergymen by Whom it was Signed [etc.]. London: Seeley, Jackson, & Halliday, 1875.

The Clerical Ritualistic Who's Who, with an Account of the Ritualistic Conspiracy [etc.]. London: Protestant Truth Society, [1908].

Cobb, Peter. *Doctor Pusey.* London: Church Literature Association, 1983.

Conybeare, W. J. "Church Parties," *The Edinburgh Review* 98 (October 1853): 273–342.

———. *Perversion: or, the Causes and Consequences of Infidelity.* 3 vols. London: Smith, Elder & Co., 1856.

The Congregation in Church: A Plain Guide to Reverent and Intelligent Participation in the Public Services of Holy Church, with Brief Information Concerning the Six Points [etc.]. London: Wyman and Sons, [1885].

Conlay, Iris, and Peter F. Anson. *The Art of the Church.* New Library of Catholic Knowledge 11. London: Burns & Oates, 1964.

Coombs, Joyce. *Judgment on Hatcham: The History of a Religious Struggle, 1877–1886.* London: Faith Press, 1969.

———. *One Aim: Edward Stuart, 1820–1877.* London: Stanhope Press, 1975.

Correspondence Concerning the Celebration of Holy Communion on Good Friday in the Church of England. London: George Bell & Sons, 1883.

Correspondence Relating to Cuddesdon Theological College, in Answer to the Charges of the Reverend C. P. Golightly, and the Report of the Commissioners Thereon. Oxford: J. Vincent, 1858.

Cox, Jeffrey. *The English Churches in a Secular Society: Lambeth, 1870–1930.* New York: Oxford University Press, 1982.

Crockford's Clerical Directory for 1883: Being a Statistical Book of Reference for Facts Relating to the Clergy and the Church. London: Horace Cox, 1883.

Cross, F. L., and E. A. Livingstone (eds.). *The Oxford Dictionary of the Christian Church.* 2d ed. London: Oxford University Press, 1974.

Crowther, M. A. *Church Embattled: Religious Controversy in Mid-Victorian England.* Newton Abbot, Devon: David & Charles, 1970.

Culler, A. Dwight. *The Victorian Mirror of History.* New Haven: Yale University Press, 1985.

Davies, C. Maurice. *Orthodox London: or, Phases of Religious Life in the Church of England.* Revised ed. London: Tinsley Brothers, 1876.

Davies, G. C. B. *Henry Phillpotts, Bishop of Exeter, 1778–1869.* London: SPCK, 1954.

Deane, F. H. *Two Speeches Delivered at the Lincoln Diocesan Conference, 1874 and 1876, on Church Difficulties* [etc.]. London: G. J. Palmer, 1877.

Dellamora, Richard. *Masculine Desire: The Sexual Politics of Victorian Aestheticism.* Chapel Hill: University of North Carolina Press, 1990.

[Denison, George Anthony]. *The Charge of the Archdeacon of Taunton at his Visitation, April 1877.* Oxford: James Parker and Co., 1877.

Denison, George Anthony. *The Episcopate with Two Voices.* Oxford: James Parker and Co., 1874.

Dickinson, Bickford H. C. *Sabine Baring-Gould: Squarson, Writer and Folklorist, 1834–1924.* Newton Abbot, Devon: David & Charles, 1970.

Dictionary of the English Church, Ancient and Modern. London: Wells Gardner, Darton, & Co., 1881.

Dilworth-Harrison, T. *Every Man's Story of the Oxford Movement.* London: Mowbray, 1932.

Dimock, N. *The Crisis in the Church of England: Its History and Present Position.* London: Elliot Stock, 1899.

Donovan, Marcus. *After the Tractarians.* London: Philip Allan, 1933.

Douglas, Robert. *Is It Expedient? A Question for Loyal Churchmen on going to Church Congresses.* London: Simpkin, Marshall and Company, [1879].

Down, E. A. "Pastoral Ideals and Methods of the Movement: The Tractarian Tradition." In *Northern Catholicism: Centenary Studies in the Oxford and Parallel Movements.* Edited by N. P. Williams and Charles Harris. New York: Macmillan Co., 1933.

Drummond, Andrew L. *The Churches in English Fiction.* Leicester: Edgar Backus, 1950.

———. *The Churches Pictured by "Punch".* London: Epworth Press, 1947.

Dunn, James. *The Honesty of Our Position: A Paper Read before the Clifton Branch of the E.C.U.* London: Pickering and Co., 1878.

Duthie, D. Wallace. *The Church in the Pages of "Punch".* London: Smith, Elder & Co., 1912.

Eden, Robert. *Our Church Troubles: Their Root, and a Suggestion of the Cure.* London: W. MacIntosh, [1875].

Edwards, David L. *Leaders of the Church of England, 1828–1944.* London: Oxford University Press, 1971.

Elliott-Binns, L. E. *Religion in the Victorian Era.* London: Lutterworth Press, 1936.

Ellis, Octavius J. *Some Time among Ritualists.* 3d ed. London: Hatchards, 1868.

Ellsworth, L. E. *Charles Lowder and the Ritualist Movement.* London: Darton, Longman and Todd, 1982.

Embry, J. *The Catholic Movement and the Society of the Holy Cross.* London: Faith Press, 1931.

English Church Union. *The E.C.U. Church Guide for Tourists and Others.* London: Mowbray, 1924.

An Ex-Member of the Congregation of S. Bartholomew's, Brighton. *Are You Safe in the Church of England? A Question for Anxious Ritualists.* London: R. Washbourne, 1878.

Extracts from a Ritualistic Publication, entitled The Priest in Absolution, and Dedicated to the Masters, Vicars, and Brethren of the Society of the Holy Cross [etc.]. n.p.: [n.d., but ca. 1876].

F.D. *A Plea for St. Barnabas. The Confessional versus the Social Evil.* London: Alfred William Bennett, 1858.

[Faber, F. W.]. *St. Wilfrid, Bishop of York.* James Toovey, 1844.

Faber, Geoffrey. *Oxford Apostles: A Character Study of the Oxford Movement.* New York: Charles Scribner's Sons, 1934.

Fairbairn, Andrew Martin. *Catholicism: Roman and Anglican.* 3d ed. London: Hodder and Stoughton, 1899.

———. *The New Sacerdotalism and the New Puritanism: A Discourse Delivered before the Congregational Union of England and Wales.* London: Hodder and Stoughton, [1868].

Fairweather, Eugene R., ed. *The Oxford Movement.* New York: Oxford University Press, 1964.

Father Pollock and His Brother: Mission Priests of St. Alban's, Birmingham. London: Longmans, Green and Co., 1911.

Feuchtwanger, E. J. *Gladstone.* London: Allen Lane, 1975.

A Few Words on the Prayer for the Church Militant. n.p.: [n.d., but 1864].

Flindall, R. P., ed. *The Church of England, 1815–1948: A Documentary History.* London: SPCK, 1972.

Fong, William Jesse. "The Ritualist Crisis: Anglo-Catholics and Authority with Special Reference to the English Church Union, 1859–1882." Ph.D. thesis, University of Toronto, 1978.

Forrester, David. "Dr Pusey's Marriage," *Ampleforth Journal* 77 (1973): 33–47.

Franklin, R. W. *Nineteenth-Century Churches: The History of a New Catholicism in Württemberg, England, and France.* New York: Garland Publishing, 1987.

———. "Pusey and Worship in Industrial Society." *Worship* 57 (September 1983): 386–412.

Free and Open Churches. Facts and Opinions from Five Hundred Parishes in Town and Country. 2d ed. London: London Free and Open Church Association, 1876.

Fuller, Reginald H. "The Classical High Church Reaction to the Tractarians," in *Tradition Renewed: The Oxford Movement Conference Papers.* Edited by Geoffrey Rowell. London: Darton, Longman and Todd, 1986.

Garbett, Edward. *What are Our Duties in the Present Circumstances of the Church?* London: William Hunt and Company, 1867.

Gaselee, Stephen. "The Aesthetic Side of the Oxford Movement." In *Northern Catholicism: Centenary Studies in the Oxford and Parallel Movements.* Edited by N. P. Williams and Charles Harris. New York: Macmillan Co., 1933.

Gilbert, W. S. "Patience." In *The Complete Plays of Gilbert and Sullivan.* New York: Modern Library, [n.d.].

Gill, Thomas Howard. *A Letter to the Right Reverend the Lord Bishop of Manchester, touching "Ritualism".* London: Hatchards, 1878.

Golightly, Charles P. *A Solemn Warning Against Cuddesdon College.* London: Simpkin, Marshall, & Co., [n.d., but 1879].

Gorman, W. Gordon. *Converts to Rome: Since the Tractarian Movement to May 1899.* London: Swan Sonnenschein & Co., 1899.

A Graduate of the University of Cambridge, *The Ritualist's Progress: A Sketch of the Reforms and Ministrations of Our New Vicar, The Rev. Septimius Alban, Member of the E.C.U., Vicar of St. Alicia, Slumbertown, as They Appeared to a Bewildered Parishioner.* London: Weldon & Co., [1878].

A Grave Crisis in the Church of England. What is to be Done? London: John Kensit, [n.d.].

Greenacre, Roger. *Lord Halifax.* London: Church Literature Association, 1983.

Greenfield, Robert H. "Attitude of the Tractarians to the Roman Catholic Church,

1833–1850." D. Phil. thesis, Oxford University, 1956.

Greenhill, Alfred. *Guy Faux in the Protestant Church: A Lecture*. Exeter: "Devon Weekly Times" Office, 1874.

Grover, J. W. *Pagans Ancient and Modern; or, the Antiquities of Ritualism*. London: Hatchard & Co., 1868.

Grueber, Charles Stephen. *What is the First and Chief Object of Public Worship, or, Why Do You Go to Church?* Oxford and London: Parker & Co., 1894.

Hammond, Peter C. *The Parson and the Victorian Parish*. London: Hodder and Stoughton, 1977.

Hardelin, Alf. "The Eucharist in the Theology of the Nineteenth Century," in R. E. Clements, Austin Farrer, *et al.*, *Eucharistic Theology Then and Now*. London: SPCK, 1968.

Herring, George William. "Tractarianism to Ritualism: A Study of Some Aspects of Tractarianism Outside Oxford, from the Time of Newman's Conversion in 1845, until the First Ritual Commission in 1867." D. Phil. thesis, Oxford University, 1984.

A High Churchman. *Common Sense: About the Church*. London: Hatchard and Co., 1860.

Hill, Michael. *The Religious Order: A Study of Virtuoso Religion and Its Legitimation in the Nineteenth-Century Church of England*. London: Heinemann Educational Books, 1973.

Hilliard, David. "UnEnglish and Unmanly: Anglo-Catholicism and Homosexuality," *Victorian Studies* 25 (Winter 1982): 181–210.

Hillsman, Walter Lee. "Trends and Aims in Anglican Church Music 1870–1906 in Relation to Developments in Churchmanship." D. Phil. thesis, Oxford University, 1985.

Hodder, Edwin. *The Life and Work of the Seventh Earl of Shaftesbury, K.G.* 3 vols. London: Cassell & Company, 1886.

Hollis, Patricia. *Women in Public: The Women's Movement, 1850–1900*. London: George Allen & Unwin, 1979.

Hook, Walter Farquhar. *Discourses Bearing on the Controversies of the Day*. London: John Murray, 1853.

———. *Hear the Church. A Sermon Preached at the Chapel Royal, in St. James's Palace* [etc.]. London: J.G. and F. Rivington, 1839.

Father Hugh, S.S.F. *Nineteenth Century Pamphlets at Pusey House: An Introduction for the Prospective User*. London: Faith Press, 1961.

Hymnal of the Protestant Episcopal Church in the United States of America, 1940. New York: Church Pension Fund, 1943.

Inglis, K. S. "Patterns of Religious Worship in 1851," *Journal of Ecclesiastical History* 11 (1960): 74–86.

———. *Churches and the Working Classes in Victorian England*. London: Routledge and Kegan Paul, 1963.

Isaacs, Albert Augustus. *The Rubrics and Ritual of the Church of England*. London: W. MacIntosh, 1869.

Jay, Elisabeth, ed. *The Evangelical and Oxford Movements*. Cambridge: Cambridge University Press, 1983.

Joint Commission on the Revision of the Hymnal. *The Hymnal 1940 Companion*. 3d ed. New York: Church Pension Fund, 1951.

Jones, Harry. *East and West London: Being Notes of Common Life and Pastoral Work in Saint James's, Westminster and in Saint George's-in-the-East*. London: Smith, Elder, & Co., 1875.

Jones, Peter d'A. *The Christian Socialist Revival, 1877–1914: Religion, Class, and Social Conscience in Late-Victorian England*. Princeton: Princeton University Press, 1968.

Kaye-Smith, Sheila. *Anglo-Catholicism*. London: Chapman and Hall, 1925.

[Kelly, William]. *Ritualism*. London: W. H. Broom, [1876?].

Kelway, A. Clifton. *George Rundle Prynne: A Chapter in the Early History of the Catholic Revival*. London: Longmans, Green, and Co., 1905.

————. *The Story of the Catholic Revival. 1833–1933.* 4th ed. London: Philip Allan, 1933 [1st ed., 1914].

Kent, J. H. S. "The Role of Religion in the Cultural Structure of the Later Victorian City," *Transactions of the Royal Historical Society,* 5th series, 23 (1973): 153–73.

Kent, John. *Holding the Fort: Studies in Victorian Revivalism.* London: Epworth Press, 1978.

————. "The Victorian Resistance," *Victorian Studies* 12 (December 1968): 145–54.

————. "The Study of Modern Ecclesiastical History Since 1930." In J. Daniélou, A. H. Couratin, and John Kent, *Historical Theology. Pelican Guide to Modern Theology,* vol. 2. Baltimore: Penguin Books, 1969.

Kershaw, J. F. *The Reunion of Christendom. The Anglican and the Eastern Churches.* London: J. Masters & Co., 1896.

King, Bryan. *The S. George's Mission, with the S. George's Riots and their Results.* London: Rivington's, 1877.

Kipling, Rudyard. "The 'Mary Gloster'" (1894). In *Rudyard Kipling's Verse: Definitive Edition.* London: Hodder and Stoughton, 1940.

Knox, E. A. *The Tractarian Movement, 1833–1845.* 2d ed. London: Putnam, 1934.

Knox, Wilfrid L. *The Catholic Movement in the Church of England.* 2d ed. London: Philip Allan & Co., 1930.

"The Last Thirty Years in the English Church: an Autobiography." In *The Church and the World: Essays on Questions of the Day in 1866.* Edited by Orby Shipley. 3d ed. London: Longmans, Green, Reader, and Dyer, 1867.

A Layman and Magistrate of that County [Oxford]. *A Watchman's Remarks upon a Pamphlet entitled "Thoughts on Church Matters in the Diocese of Oxford".* London: Arthur Hall, Virtue & Co., 1859.

A Layman of the Diocese [of Chicester]. *Things Indifferent* [etc.]. London: J. T. Hayes, 1877.

A Layman of the Church of England. *An Address to the Laity of the Church of England upon the Errors and Abuses which exist in that Church, with Suggested Reforms.* London: Effingham Wilson, 1860.

A Layman of the Church of England. *The Church and the Bible. The True Teaching of the Rev. E. E. Hillyard* [etc.]. London: G. J. Palmer, 1877.

Lee, F. G. *Directorium Anglicanum.* 4th ed. London: John Hogg & Co., 1879.

————. *The Manuale Clericorum.* London: John Hogg & Co., 1874.

LeGeyt, Charles James. "On the Symbolism of Ritual." In *The Church and the World: Essays on Questions of the Day in 1867.* Edited by Orby Shipley. London: Longmans, Green, Reader, and Dyer, 1867.

Leslie, Shane. *The Anglo-Catholic.* London: Chatto & Windus, 1929.

Leslie, Shane. *The Oxford Movement, 1833 to 1933.* London: Burns Oates & Washbourne, 1933.

A Letter to the Bishops of the Church of England on the Necessity of Liturgical Adjustment Arising from the Principles and Practice of the School of Tractarian Theology. London: Seeley, Burnside, and Seeley, 1843.

Lindsay, Colin. "The Ritual Law of the Church of England." In *The Church and the World: Essays on Questions of the Day in 1867.* Edited by Orby Shipley. London: Longmans, Green, Reader, and Dyer, 1867.

Littledale, Richard Frederick. "The First Report of the Ritual Commission." In *The Church and the World: Essays on Questions of the Day in 1868.* Edited by Orby Shipley. London: Longmans, Green, Reader, and Dyer, 1868.

————. "The Missionary Aspect of Ritualism." In *The Church and the World: Essays on Questions of the Day in 1866.* Edited by Orby Shipley. 3d ed. London: Longmans, Green, Reader, and Dyer, 1867.

Littledale, Richard Frederick. *Plain Reasons against Joining the Church of Rome.* London: Society for Promoting Christian Knowledge, 1880.

Lloyd, Roger. *The Church of England, 1900–1965.* London: SCM Press, 1966.

Lockhart, J. G. *Charles Lindley, Viscount Halifax.* 2 vols. London: Centenary Press, 1935.

The London Church of England Directory and Guide. London: Office of the London Church of England Directory, 1879 *et seq.*

"Lord Sandon on Sacerdotalism" (Church Association handbill; n.d., but 1867)

Lothair. *Ritualism: Its Practices and Tendency*. London: Charing Cross Publishing Company, 1877.

Lough, A. G. *Dr. Pusey—Restorer of the Church*. Newton Abbot, Devon: A. G. Lough, 1981.

———. *The Influence of John Mason Neale*. London: SPCK, 1962.

———. *John Mason Neale—Priest Extraordinary*. Newton Abbot, Devon: privately published, [1975].

Lyne, Francis. *Archdeacon Denison and Dr. Pusey. A Circumstance Followed Up* [etc.]. London: W. Pole, 1878.

[———]. *The Bishop of London. An Appeal to His Grace the Archbishop of Canterbury*. London: E. W. Allen, 1887.

———. *Popery: The Bishop of London and Dean Lake*. London: E. W. Allen, 1887.

McCarthy, Michael J. F. *Church and State in England and Wales, 1829–1906*. Dublin: Hodges, Figgis & Co., 1906.

Mackenzie, Compton. *The Altar Steps*. Bath: Cedric Chivers, 1970 [1922].

Mackenzie, Compton. *The Parson's Progress*. London: MacDonald, 1958 [1923].

———. *Sinister Street*. London: MacDonald, 1949 [1913].

Mackeson, Charles. *A Digest of the Evidence Given Before the Commissioners appointed to Inquire into the Rubrics, Orders, and Directions for Regulating the Course and Conduct of Public Worship, &c., according to the Use of the United Church of England and Ireland; with their First Report*. London: James Parker & Co., 1867.

———. *A Guide to the Churches of London and its Suburbs [for 18—]*. London: Metzler & Co., 1866 *et seq.*

McLeod, Hugh. *Class and Religion in the Late Victorian City*. Hamden, Connecticut: Archon Books, 1974.

———. "Class, Community and Region: The Religious Geography of Nineteenth-Century England." In *A Sociological Yearbook of Religion in Britain*, vol. 6. Edited by Michael Hill. London: SCM Press, 1973.

McMullen, R. T. *Priestly Pretensions, and God's Word*. London: Elliot Stock, 1885.

Maison, Margaret. *Search Your Soul, Eustace: A Study of the Religious Novel in the Victorian Age*. London: Sheed and Ward, 1961.

Mallock, W. H. *The New Republic*. London: Chatto and Windus, 1889.

Manton, Jo. *Sister Dora: The Life of Dorothy Pattison*. London: Methuen & Co., 1971.

Marsh, P. T. *The Victorian Church in Decline: Archbishop Tait and the Church of England, 1868–1882*. London: Routledge & Kegan Paul, 1969.

Marston, Charles Dallas. *The Position of the Laity in the Church*. London: W. Hunt & Co., 1868.

Martin, Brian W. *John Keble: Priest, Professor and Poet*. London: Croom Helm, 1976.

Martin, Robert Bernard. *The Dust of Combat: A Life of Charles Kingsley*. London: Faber and Faber, 1959.

Masterman, Charles F. G. "The Problem of South London." In *The Religious Life of London*. Edited by Richard Mudie-Smith. London: Hodder and Stoughton, 1904.

[Masters, Joseph]. *Masters's Guide to the Daily Prayers of England, Wales, & Scotland*. 4th ed. London: Joseph Masters, 1850.

[———]. *Masters's Guide to the Churches Where the Daily Prayers are Said in England, Wales, Scotland, and Ireland*. 28th ed. London: Joseph Masters, 1860.

Matthews, W. R. "By the Dean of Exeter." In Lord Hugh Cecil, the Dean of Exeter [W. R. Matthews], F. R. Barry, and Canon Wilfred L. Knox, *Anglo-Catholicism Today*. London: Philip Allan, 1934.

May, J. Lewis. *The Oxford Movement: Its History and its Future, A Layman's Estimate*. New York: Dial Press, 1933.

Mayow, M. W. *A Letter to the Right Reverend the Lord Bishop of Worcester*. London: James

Parker and Co., 1873.

Menzies, Lucy. *Father Wainwright: A Record*. London: Longmans, Green and Co., 1947.

Metcalfe, A. *Crosses, Crucifixes and Musical Services*. London: John Kensit, [n.d., but 1889–90].

Mitchell, B. R. *Abstract of British Historical Statistics*. Cambridge: Cambridge University Press, 1962.

Molyneux, Capel. *The Bennett Judgment. Our Duty: What is It?* London: William Hunt and Company, 1872.

Morgan, D. H. J. "The Social and Educational Background of Anglican Bishops — Continuities and Changes." *British Journal of Sociology* 20 (September 1969): 295–310.

Morrison, Arthur. *A Child of the Jago*. Leipzig: Bernhard Tauchnitz, 1897.

Morse-Boycott, Desmond. *Lead, Kindly Light: Studies of the Saints and Heroes of the Oxford Movement*. London: Centenary Press, 1932.

———. *The Secret Story of the Oxford Movement*. London: Skeffington & Son, 1933.

———. *They Shine Like Stars*. New ed., revised, of *The Secret Story of the Oxford Movement*. London: Skeffington & Son, [1947].

Mudie-Smith, Richard, ed. *The Religious Life of London*. London: Hodder and Stoughton, 1904.

[Neale, John Mason]. *Collected Hymns, Sequences and Carols of John Mason Neale*. London: Hodder and Stoughton, 1914.

Newman, John Henry. *Apologia pro Vita Sua: An Authoritative Text*. Edited by David J. DeLaura. New York: W. W. Norton & Company, 1968 [1864].

———. *Loss and Gain: The Story of a Convert*. London: Burns & Oates, 1962 [1848].

Newsome, David. *Godliness and Good Learning: Four Studies of a Victorian Ideal*. London: John Murray, 1961.

———. "Newman and the Oxford Movement." In *The Victorian Crisis of Faith*. Edited by Anthony Symondson. London: SPCK, 1970.

———. *The Parting of Friends: A Study of the Wilberforces and Henry Manning*. London: John Murray, 1966.

Newton, John. *Search for a Saint: Edward King*. London: Church Literature Association, 1983.

Nockles, Peter Benedict. "Continuity and Change in Anglican High Churchmanship in Britain, 1792–1850." D. Phil. thesis, Oxford University, 1982.

———. "The Oxford Movement: Historical Background, 1730–1780," in *Tradition Renewed: The Oxford Movement Conference Papers*. Edited by Geoffrey Rowell. London: Darton, Longman and Todd, 1986.

Norman, E. R. *Anti-Catholicism in Victorian England*. London: George Allen & Unwin, 1968.

———. *Church and Society in England, 1770–1970*. Oxford: Clarendon Press, 1976.

O'Connell, Marvin R. *The Oxford Conspirators: A History of the Oxford Movement, 1833–45*. London: Macmillan Company, 1969.

Oakeley, Frederick. *Historical Notes on the Tractarian Movement*. London: Longman, Green, Longman, Roberts, & Green, 1865.

Ollard, S. L. *A Short History of the Oxford Movement*. 2d ed. 1932. Reprint, London: Faith Press, 1963.

Ollard, S. L., and Gordon Crosse (eds.) *A Dictionary of English Church History*. London: A. R. Mowbray and Co., 1912.

Osborne, Charles E. *The Life of Father Dolling*. London: Edward Arnold, 1903.

Overton, J[ohn] H[enry]. *The Anglican Revival*. London: Blackie & Son, 1897.

Pater, Walter. *Marius the Epicurean: His Sensations and Ideas*. Garden City, N.Y.: Doubleday, Doran & Company, 1935 [1885].

Paz, D. G. *Popular Anti-Catholicism in Mid-Victorian England*. Stanford, California: Stanford University Press, 1992.

Pearson, Michael. *The Age of Consent: Victorian Prostitution and Its Enemies.* Newton Abbot: David and Charles, 1972.

Penhale, Francis. *The Anglican Church Today: Catholics in Crisis.* London: Mowbray, 1986.

Pickering, W. S. F. *Anglo-Catholicism: A Study in Religious Ambiguity.* London: Routledge, 1989.

———. "Anglo-Catholicism: Some Sociological Observations," in *Tradition Renewed: The Oxford Movement Conference Papers.* Edited by Geoffrey Rowell. London: Darton, Longman and Todd, 1986.

———. "The 1851 Religious Census — A Useless Experiment?" *British Journal of Sociology* 18 (1967): 382–407.

Pollock, James S. *Romanizing. The Substance of a Lecture delivered in the Town Hall, Birmingham, January 23, 1867.* London: Masters & Co., 1867.

Port, M. H. *Six Hundred New Churches: A Study of the Church Building Commission, 1818–1856, and its Church Building Activities.* London: SPCK, 1961.

Presbyter Anglicanus. *How the Church of England May Be Preserved.* London: William MacIntosh, [n.d., but 1875].

Presbyter Protestans. *The "English Church Union". . . A Romanizing Confederacy.* London: John F. Shaw & Co., 1877.

Prestige, Leonard. *Pusey.* New ed. 1933. Reprint. London: Mowbray, 1982.

A Priest of the Church of England. *The Form of Godliness: Being Some Remarks on Catholic Ritual.* London: J. Masters, 1867.

A Priest of the Diocese of London. *Are Evening Communions Scriptural?* n.p., [1873].

Progress of Ritualism and the Designs of Popery. London: John Kensit, [1886].

Prynne, George Rundle. *Treachery; or, Ritualism and Evangelicalism Brought to the Standard of the Teaching of the Church of England. Dedicated to the Church Association.* London: Masters, 1870.

Puller, F. W. *The Duties and Rights of Parish Priests and the Limits of the Obedience due from them to their Bishops* [etc.]. London: Rivington's, 1877.

Purcell, William. *Onward Christian Soldier.* London: Longmans, Green and Co., 1957.

Pusey, E. B. *Habitual Confession Not Discouraged by the Resolution Accepted by the Lambeth Conference.* Oxford: James Parker & Co., 1878.

Pym, Barbara. *A Glass of Blessings.* London: Jonathan Cape, 1977 [1958].

Rainbow, Bernarr. *The Choral Revival in the Anglican Church, 1839–1872.* London: Barrie & Jenkins, 1970.

Raven, Charles E. *Christian Socialism, 1848–1854.* London: Macmillan and Company, 1920.

Reich, Charles A. *The Greening of America.* New York: Random House, 1970.

Religion in London. Statistics of Church and Chapel Accommodation in 1865 [etc.]. London: Jackson, Walford, and Hodder, n.d.

The Religious Census of London. Reprinted from "The British Weekly". London: Hodder and Stoughton, 1888.

The Report of the Conference of the Church Association. . . held in Willis's Rooms, London, on 26th and 27th November, 1867. London: Church Association, 1867.

A Retired Rector. *Babylon in St. Paul's: or, the Eviction of Protestants from the Metropolitan Cathedral. A Letter of Protest and Rebuke to the Bishop of London.* London: John Kensit, [1888].

Reynolds, Michael. *Martyr of Ritualism: Father Mackonochie of St. Alban's, Holborn.* London: Faber and Faber, 1965.

Rigg, James H. *Oxford High Anglicanism, and Its Chief Leaders.* London: Charles H. Kelly, 1895.

Ritualism: and What is it?. London: Simpkin, Marshall & Co., 1868.

"Ritualistic Theatricals at Shoreditch." *Punch,* September 21, 1867, 121.

The Ritualistic Clergy List, being a Guide for Patrons and Others To certain of the Clergy of the Church of England; containing a List of some 9600 Clergymen who are helping the

Romeward Movement in the National Church. 2d ed. London: Church Association, 1902.

The Ritualistic Conspiracy. 3d ed. London: *The Rock,* 1873.

Roberts, G. Bayfield. *The History of the English Church Union, 1859–1894.* London: Church Publishing Company, 1895.

Rogers, J. E. T. "University Extension." In *The Church and the World: Essays on Questions of the Day in 1866.* Edited by Orby Shipley. 3d ed. London: Longmans, Green, Reader, and Dyer, 1867.

Roszak, Theodore. *The Making of a Counter Culture.* Garden City, N. Y.: Doubleday & Company, 1969.

Rowell, Geoffrey. *The Vision Glorious: Themes and Personalities of the Catholic Revival in Anglicanism.* Oxford: Oxford University Press, 1983.

Royal Commission on Ecclesiastical Discipline. *Report of the Royal Commission on Ecclesiastical Discipline* and *Minutes of Evidence Taken before the Royal Commission on Ecclesiastical Discipline.* 3 vols. London: H.M.S.O., 1906.

———. "Reports from Commissioners, Inspectors, and Others". *Parliamentary Papers* 33–34 (1906).

Russell, George W. E. *Arthur Stanton: A Memoir.* London: Longmans, Green and Co., 1917.

———. *Saint Alban the Martyr, Holborn: A History of Fifty Years.* London: George Allen & Company, 1913.

Ryle, J. C. *Shall We Go?* London: William Hunt and Company, 1878.

———. *What Do We Owe to the Reformation?* London: John F. Shaw & Co., 1877.

Savage, Stephen, and Christopher Tyne. *The Labours of Years: The Story of St. Saviour's and St. Hilda's Leeds.* Cowley: Bocardo & Church Army Press, [n.d.].

Savile, Bourchier Wrey. *A Letter to the Rev. Dr. Pusey. . . on the "Catholic" Practice of Auricular Confession.* London: Hatchards, 1877.

Schaefer, Paula. *The Catholic Regeneration of the Church of England.* London: Williams & Norgate, 1935.

Shaftesbury, Earl of. *Speech in the House of Lords. . . on moving the Second Reading of the Clerical Vestments Bill.* London: Church Association, 1867.

Sharp, Richard. "New Perspectives on the High Church Tradition: Historical Background, 1730–1780," in *Tradition Renewed: The Oxford Movement Conference Papers.* Edited by Geoffrey Rowell. London: Darton, Longman and Todd, 1986.

Shipley, Orby. *A Specimen of Recent Anglican Controversy with Rome: A Letter to the Rev. Dr. Pusey, D.D.* London: Privately printed, 1880.

———. *Truthfulness and Ritualism.* First series. London: Burns and Oates, 1879.

———, ed. *The Church and the World: Essays on Questions of the Day in 1866.* 3d ed. London: Longmans, Green, Reader, and Dyer, 1867.

"Sisterhood Life." In *The Church and the World: Essays on Questions of the Day in 1867.* Edited by Orby Shipley. London: Longmans, Green, Reader, and Dyer, 1867.

Smelser, Neil J. *Theory of Collective Behavior.* New York: Free Press, 1962.

Smith, B. A. *Dean Church: The Anglican Response to Newman.* London: Oxford University Press, 1958.

Smith, Hely. *The Real Ritual Reason Why.* London: Simpkin, Marshall, & Co., 1878.

Smith, Phillip T. "The London Police and the Holy War: Ritualism and St. George's-in-the-East, London, 1859–1860," *Journal of Church and State* 28 (1986): 107–19.

Sparrow Simpson, W. J. *The Contribution of Cambridge to the Anglo-Catholic Revival.* London: SPCK, 1933.

———. *The History of the Anglo-Catholic Revival from 1845.* London: George Allen & Unwin, 1932.

———. "The Revival from 1845 to 1933." In *Northern Catholicism: Centenary Studies in the Oxford and Parallel Movements.* Edited by N. P. Williams and Charles Harris. New York: Macmillan Co., 1933.

Spurgin, John. *Intoning the Services in Parish Churches Contrary to the Directions of the Church of England.* n.p.: [n.d., but 1864].

Stewart, Herbert Leslie. *A Century of Anglo-Catholicism.* London: J. M. Dent & Sons, 1929.

Stone, Darwell. *The Faith of an English Catholic.* London: Longmans, Green and Co., 1926.

Tavard, George H. *The Quest for Catholicity: A Study in Anglicanism.* New York: Herder and Herder, 1964.

"The Priest in Absolution." A Criticism, A Protest, & A Denunciation [etc.]. London: J. Francis Bursill, 1877.

Thompson, D. M. "The 1851 Religious Census: Problems and Possibilities," *Victorian Studies* 11 (September 1967): 87–97.

Thompson, Paul. "All Saints Church, Margaret Street, Reconsidered," *Architectural History* 8 (1965): 73–94.

Thureau-Dangin, Paul. *The English Catholic Revival in the Nineteenth Century.* 2 vols. New York: E. P. Dutton & Co., [n.d.].

Tomlinson, J. T. *A Review of Canon J. W. Knox-Little's "Answer to Archdeacon Farrar,"* [etc.]. London: Church Association, n.d. [ca. 1894].

Toon, Peter. *Evangelical Theology, 1833–1856: A Response to Tractarianism.* London: Marshall, Morgan & Scott, 1979.

Toon, Peter, and Michael Smout. *John Charles Ryle: Evangelical Bishop.* Cambridge: James Clark & Co., 1976.

[Trench, Maria]. *Charles Lowder: A Biography.* 5th ed. London: Kegan Paul, Trench & Co., 1882.

Trollope, Anthony. *Barchester Towers.* London: J. M. Dent & Sons, 1977 [1857].

———. *Clergymen of the Church of England.* Leicester: Leicester University Press, 1974 [1866].

[Troughton, E. J.] "E.J.T." Letter in the *Examiner,* January 21, 1860.

Tucker, J. K. *The Duty of Clergymen to Prevent the Disestablishment of the Church of England, and the Means to be Employed to that End.* London: William Hunt and Company, 1871.

Turner, Ralph H., and Lewis M. Killian. *Collective Behavior.* 2d ed. Englewood Cliffs, N.J.: Prentice-Hall, 1972.

"Twelve Reasons for Refusing to Join the English Church Union" (undated handbill, ca. 1871).

Victoria and Albert Museum. *Victorian Church Art: Exhibition November 1971–January 1972.* London: H.M.S.O., 1971.

Vicinus, Martha. *Independent Women: Work and Community for Single Women, 1850–1920.* Chicago: University of Chicago Press, 1985.

Voll, Dieter. *Catholic Evangelicalism: The Acceptance of Evangelical Traditions by the Oxford Movement during the Second Half of the Nineteenth Century.* London: Faith Press, 1963.

Wainwright, C. H. *The Secrets of Ritualism. A Word of Warning.* 2d ed. London: William Hunt and Company, 1877.

Wakeling, G. *The Oxford Church Movement. Sketches and Recollections.* London: Swan Sonnenschein & Co., 1895.

Walker, S. A. *No! An Answer to Canon Ryle's Tract "Shall We Go?"* [etc.]. London: Elliot Stock, n.d.

———. *Tracts against Treason 1–3.* London: Hamilton, Adams, & Co., 1874.

Walsh, Walter. *The Secret History of the Oxford Movement.* London: Swan Sonnenschein & Co., 1897.

———. *The Ritualists: Their Romanising Objects and Work.* London: James Nisbet & Co., 1900.

Waram, J. Carne. *Tourist's Church Guide, 1877.* 7th ed. London: G. J. Palmer, 1877.

[Warburton, Katherine ("Mother Kate")]. *Memories of a Sister of S. Saviour's Priory.* Oxford and London: Mowbray, 1903.

Welsby, Paul A. "Anthony Trollope and the Church of England." *Church Quarterly Review*

163 (April–June 1962): 210–20.

Westhues, Kenneth. *Society's Shadow: Studies in the Sociology of Countercultures.* Toronto: McGraw-Hill Ryerson, 1972.

What is the Anglo-Continental Society? 2d ed. London: Rivington's, 1879.

White, James F. *The Cambridge Movement: The Ecclesiologists and the Gothic Revival.* Cambridge: Cambridge University Press, 1962.

Wickham, E. R. *Church and People in an Industrial City.* London: Lutterworth Press, 1957.

The Widow of a Clergyman. *Ritualism and the Touchstone.* Southampton: A. Randle, 1877.

Wild, Ronald. "Community, Communion and the Counter-culture." *Australian and New Zealand Journal of Sociology* 17 (November 1981): 27–34.

Wilkinson, John. "Tradition in Worship." In *Catholic Anglicans Today.* Edited by John Wilkinson. London: Darton, Longman & Todd, 1968.

Williams, N. P. "The Theology of the Catholic Revival." In *Northern Catholicism: Centenary Studies in the Oxford and Parallel Movements.* Edited by N. P. Williams and Charles Harris. New York: Macmillan Co., 1933.

Williams, Thomas Jay. *Priscilla Lydia Sellon: The Restorer after Three Centuries of the Religious Life in the English Church.* London: SPCK, 1950.

Williams, Thomas Jay, and Allan Walter Campbell. *The Park Village Sisterhood.* London: SPCK, 1965.

Wilson, A. N. *Unguarded Hours.* London: Secker & Warburg, 1978.

Wilson, Alan. "The Authority of Church and Party among London Anglo-Catholics, 1880–1914, with Special Reference to the Church Crisis, 1898–1904." D. Phil. thesis, Oxford University, 1988.

Windle, Bertram C. A. *Who's Who of the Oxford Movement.* New York: Century Co., 1926.

Wolfe, Arthur. *A Plea for Revision of the Prayer-Book and of the Authorized Version of the Bible.* Cambridge: Deighton, Bell, and Co., 1866.

Woodgate, M. V. *Father Benson, Founder of the Cowley Fathers.* London: Geoffrey Bles, 1953.

A Worcestershire Vicar. *The Church as it is* [etc.]. London: Whittaker and Co., [1864].

Worley, George. *The Catholic Movement of the Nineteenth Century.* London: Elliot Stock, 1894.

Wright, Thomas. *The Life of Walter Pater.* 2 vols. London: Everett & Co., 1907.

Yates, Nigel. *Kent and the Oxford Movement: Selected Documents.* Kentish Sources VII (Kent Archives Office). Gloucester: Alan Sutton, 1983.

——. *The Oxford Movement and Anglican Ritualism.* General Series 105. London: Historical Association, 1983.

——. *The Oxford Movement and Parish Life: St Saviour's, Leeds, 1839–1929.* Borthwick Papers No. 48. York: University of York, Borthwick Institute of Historical Research, 1975.

——. *Leeds and the Oxford Movement: A Study of "High Church" Activity in the Rural Deaneries of Allerton, Armley, Headingley and Whitkirk in the Diocese of Ripon, 1836–1934.* Publications of the Thoresby Society, vol. 55, no. 121. Leeds: Thoresby Society, 1975.

——. *Ritual Conflict at Farlington and Wymering.* Portsmouth Papers no. 28. Portsmouth: Portsmouth City Council, 1978.

Yinger, Milton. *Countercultures: The Promise and the Peril of a World Turned Upside Down.* New York: Free Press, 1982.

Young, Michael, and Peter Willmott. *Family and Kinship in East London.* Baltimore: Penguin Books, 1962.

PAMPHLETS AT PUSEY HOUSE 341

PAMPHLETS AT PUSEY HOUSE, OXFORD UNIVERSITY
(showing Pusey House catalogue number at end of citation)

"A Catholic Priest." *An Explanation of the Parts of a Catholic Church, and the Ornaments and Ceremonies used in the Holy Sacrifice* (1866). 10096.

"A Churchman of the Reformation." *Tractarian Practices in Protestant Churches: Three letters reprinted from the "Christian Guardian"* [etc.] (1850). 5851.

A Curate [H. W. Holden]. *An Humble Expostulation and Appeal for Forbearance* [etc.] (1875). 1693.

"A High Churchman of the Old School." *Quousque? How far? How long?* (1873). 5998.

Akers, George. *A Letter to My Late Flock* (1868). 8587.

"A Lady." *La Femme Dévote. Reprinted from the "Church Review"* (1876). 11831.

A.M.D.G. *Some Account of the Consultative Meetings of Priests of the Catholic Party in the Church of England Held During Congress Week in Brighton* (1875). 7758.

An Alphabetical List of the Signatures to a Remonstrance addressed to the Archbishops and Bishops of the Church of England On Occasion of the Report of the Judicial Committee of the Privy Council in re Hebbert v. Purchas (1871). 1516.

Anderson, W. H. *Is Ritualism Honest?* (n.d.). 73771.

"An English Catholic." *Monsignore Capel and the Ritualists* (1875). 6009.

The Anglican Crusade (n.d., but bound with 1885). 2361.

"An Oxford 'Ritualist' Clergyman." *Misconceptions of "Ritualist" Teaching: or, Are We Unfaithful?* (1873). 11839.

The "Anti-Ritual" Report. A Sermon for General Distribution (1867). 1939.

A Priest of the Diocese. *Pictorial Crucifixes. A letter to the Lord Bishop of Chichester* (1852). 5862.

"A Priest" [H. W. Holden]. *The Coming Campaign: How It Will Be Won* (1874). 6005.

"A Provincial." *The Helston Case: Twelve Letters on the Rubric and Ritual Innovations. Reprinted from The Standard.* (n.d., but ca. 1844). 70690.

The Archbishop's Legacy: Will the Church Accept it? (1883). 2303.

Are Choral Services in Parish Churches Lawful? (1867). 10144.

Armytage, N. Green. *Clerical Marriage and Celibacy. Anglo-Catholic Essays No. 1* (1894). 11189.

———. *Clerical Marriage and Celibacy. Boston Leaflets II* (1893). 11711.

———. *Dr. Littledale's Place in the Catholic Revival* (1890). 11180.

———. *Temperance* (1894). 11710.

A South Australian Lay Reader. *Incense and Ritualism in the Church of England* [etc.] (1873). 1600.

Authorized Report of the Meetings in Defense of the Athanasian Creed (1873). 7596.

"The Author of the 'Autobiography' in the 'Church and the World.'" *Protestantism and the Prayer Book* (1867). 7910.

Barry, H. *Letter to Lord Wharncliffe, on Innovations in the Services of the Church* (1845). 9254.

Bateman, James. *The Church Association: Its Policy and Prospects, Considered in a Letter to the Chairman*, 2d ed. (1880). 4031.

Bates, A. N. *The Ritual Question Briefly Explained* (1899). 8842.

Bennett, William J. E. *A Defense of the Catholic Faith* (1873). 1615.

———. *A Plea for Toleration in the Church of England* [etc.] (1868). 8198.

Beresford Hope, A. J. B. *Hints toward Peace in Ceremonial Matters* (1874). 1642.

The Bewildered Bishop (n.d.). 10905.

[Bickersteth, E. H.], Bishop of Exeter, *Pastoral Letter* (1899). 73486.

The Bishop of Manchester on the Rulings of the Purchas Judgment (n.d.). 4210.

Bright, W[illiam]. *Evening Communions Contrary to the Church's Mind, and Why* (1870). 7221.

[Browne], Edward Harold, Bishop of Winchester. *The Position and Parties of the Church of England* (1875). 10838.

Bury, Charles A. *The Church Association* (1873). 5995.

By this thou shalt conquer (n.d., but ca. 1850?). 14123.

Carter, T. T. *Are "Vows of Celibacy in Early Life" Inconsistent with the Word of God?* (1878). 7402.

Caught Napping (3rd ed., 1866). 7853.

Causidicus. Letter in *Christian Observer* (1867). 10007.

Ceremonial Detail. Hints to Those Who Assist at Processions or in Quire (1868). 8787.

The Charge of the Bishop of Oxford in 1866, and Ritualism (1867). 10006.

Church Association. *Church Hymnals. The Special Need of Care in Selection* (n.d.). 10909.

——. *Ritualism Rampant in East London* [etc.] (n.d., but ca. 1893). 8452.

The Church Defence Institution: An Association of Clergy and Laity for Defensive and General Purposes (n.d.). 73720.

The Church Monitor, A Magazine Advocating Catholic Doctrine & Practice I, 6 (1866). 9906.

Church of England Layman's Defense Association. *The Layman's Remedy against Ritualism* [etc.] (n.d., but ca. 1867). 10050.

Church of England Purity Society. *Second Annual Report* (1885). 2357.

Church of England Working Men's Society. *Authorised Report of the Speeches Delivered by Delegates . . . in Connection with the Fourth Anniversary* [etc.] (1880). 8110.

——. *The Bishop of Ely on the Persecution* (n.d., but ca. 1880). 8124.

——. *Doctrine and Ritual* (n.d.). 8130.

——. *Minutes of Proceedings of the Meeting of Delegates* [etc.] (1888). 8340.

——. *Official Declaration of the Objects and Principles of the Church of England Working Men's Society* (1888). 8341.

——. *Rev. R. W. Enraght in Warwick Jail* (n.d.). 8125.

——. *Summary of Proceedings At the Meeting of Delegates on the Second Anniversary of the Society* [etc.] (1878). 8109.

Church Reform: and the Report of the Royal Commission on Ritual [etc.] (1868). 10254.

Clabon, John M. *The Church Rights of the Laity Briefly Considered* [etc.] (1869). 3657.

Clerical Declaration on the Athanasian Creed (1872). 1562.

Clipping: *House of Lords—Thursday 20 June* (1867). 5748.

Close, Francis. *Ritualism and Scepticism, Being Two Sermons* [etc.] (1866). 9905.

Codd, Alfred. *Easter Decorations. A Letter to the Parishioners of Beaminster* (1859). 12687.

Coleridge, J. T. *Remarks on Some Parts of the Report of the Judicial Committee in the Case of "Elphinstone against Purchas"* [etc.] (1871). 4209.

Committee on Religious Statistics, Diocese of London. *Provision for Public Worship Made by the National Church and by "The Evangelical Free Churches"* [etc.] (1901). 11582.

Confession a Help to Heaven. Part I (1869). 11667.

Conroy, John. *Mr. Green's Case* (1881). 73313.

Constitutions of the Society for the Maintenance of the Faith (1876). 2180.

Correspondence on the Subject of Innovations Introduced in the Celebration of Divine Worship in St. John's Chapel, Torquay [etc.] (1845). 5853.

The Cultus of Our Lady. S. Joseph Tracts No. 4 (n.d., but ca. 1870). 10465.

Davis, C. H. *Remarks upon the Ritualistic "Memorial" of 12th. January, 1869* (1869). 1442.

Dawson, Arthur A. *Sacrifice: Patriarchal, Jewish, Christian* (1873). 1599.

Declaration Concerning Confession and Absolution (1873). 7257.

Declaration on the Doctrine of the Holy Eucharist (1867). 5747.

Declaration on the Inspiration of the Word of God and the Eternity of Future Punishment (1864). 1134.

Declaration: 1874 (1874). 1643.

Denison, G. A. *Loyalty to the Church of England. A Letter to the Lord Bishop of Bath and Wells* [etc.] (1873). 7258.

————. *Prohibited Ceremonial. What Is the Priest to Do?* (1875). 7260.

Denison, George Anthony. *The Law of God and the Law of Man* [etc.] (1875). 2144.

Directorium Puritanicum, Being a Manual of Directions for the Proper Performance of Divine Service according to the use of the Church of England, and for the Avoidance of any Perversion of the Book of Common Prayer, in the Direction of Puseyism, or Popery. (n.d.). 4627.

Disputed Ritual Ornaments and Usages [etc.] (1866). 7877.

A Dissertation on the 32d Article of the Church of England Prayer Book (n.d., but 1890s). 7336.

The Dream of a Chapel Mouse (n.d.). 10904.

The Dream of a Church Mouse (n.d.). 10745.

Dykes, John B. *Eucharistic Truth and Ritual: A Letter to the Right Reverend the Lord Bishop of Durham* [etc.] (2d ed., 1874). 1631.

Ebury, Lord. *Quis Custodiet Custodes? or, 'Tis Twelve Years Since* (1877). 4245.

Eddowes, John. *The New Testament and Ritual: A Lecture* (1877). 7681.

"The Editor of the Protestant Churchman." *Ritualist Caricature of the Bishops* (n.d., but ca. 1866). 10088.

Edwards, John. *Catholic Ritual the Exponent of Catholic Truth* (1867). 11809.

Eliot, Charles J. *Ritual Explanations. A Sermon* (1868). 10384.

Ellicott, Charles John. *Ritualism. A Sermon Preached in Bristol Cathedral, Sunday, November 4, 1866* (1866). 10266.

[————], Lord Bishop of Gloucester and Bristol. *Future Prospects* (1874). 7572.

English Church Union. *Report of the President and Council of the English Church Union on the course to be adopted by the Union* [etc.] (1867). 10062.

————. *Third Annual Report* (n.d., but 1862). 72807.

Enraght, Richard. W. *Bible-Ritualism Indispensibly Necessary for Purposes of Instruction & of Worship. A Sermon* (2d ed., 1866). 11841.

————. *Not Law, but Unconstitutional Tyranny* [etc.] (n.d., but 1877?). 1652.

Field, John Edward. *Some Principles of Christian Ceremonial* (1874). 71691.

Fleming, William. *The Gown in the Pulpit* (n.d.). 10963.

Freeman, Philip. *Rites and Ritual; A Plea for Apostolic Doctrine and Worship* (1866). 7875.

Garbett, E. *Extreme Ritualism* (1866). 72876.

Genuflexions. S. Joseph Tracts No. 3 (n.d., but ca. 1870). 10464.

Gilbert, A. T. *Pictorial Crucifixes. A Letter to the Rev. Arthur D. Wagner, M.A.* (1852). 5861.

Gladstone, W. E. *The Church of England and Ritualism* (1875). 10836.

Goulburn, Edward Meyrick. *The Confession of a Reticent Dean* [etc.] (1881). 2654.

Grantham, George Peirce. *A History of Saint Saviour's, Leeds* (1872). 13499.

Gray, C. N. *A Statement on Confession, Made by Request, in the Church of St. John Baptist, Kidderminster, on Sunday, November 15, 1868* (1870). 6145.

Gray, Walter A. *The Symbolism of Churches and their Ornaments* (1857). 9224.

Grindle, Edmund S. *Canon or Statute. A Correspondence on the Public Worship Regulation Act between the Right Honourable Lord Selbourne and a Sussex Priest* (1875). 1634.

Grueber, C. S. *Decisions on Ritual: An Appeal to the People of the Church of England* (1874). 1649.

————. *Does the Bishop of London Obey his Own Judgment?* (1876). 1720.

————. *"Omission" not "Prohibition": A Letter to His Grace the Archbishop of Canterbury* (1869). 1428.

————. *A Primitive and Catholic Ritual with Primitive and Catholic Usage the Inheritance of the Church of England* [etc.] (1874). 1621.

————. *A Reply to the "Remarks" of the Rev. C.A. Heurtley* [etc.] (1868). 1336.

"H. J." *Concerning the Theory and Truth of Ritualism* (1867). 10053.

Halifax, [Charles Wood,] Viscount. *The English Church Union: Its Future Viewed in the Light of Its Past* (1901). 8487.

[———]. *The Present Position of the Ritual Question* (1898). 11153.

Harper, Thomas Norton. *A Plea for Simple Toleration. A Letter to the Lord Bishop of London, in Defense of Those Rites and Doctrines which have been condemned in his last Charge* (1851). 9712.

Haverfield, T. T. *A Letter to a Layman, on the Recent Changes in the Manner of Performing Divine Service in the Metropolitan Churches* (1843). 5845.

Hopkins, John Henry. *The Law of Ritualism.* New York: Hurd and Houghton, 1867. 10673.

[Howley], William, Lord Archbishop of Canterbury. *A Letter Addressed to the Clergy and Laity of his Province* [etc.] (1845). 5849.

Hubbard, John G. *A Letter to the Venerable Edward Bickersteth, D.D.* (1874). 73147.

Husband, Edward. *What Will Dr. Newman Do? A Letter to the Very Rev. J. H. Newman, D.D.* (1870). 8080.

———. *Why I Left the Church of England* (1869). 8586.

Hutton, Vernon W. *Reasons for Leaving the English Church Union* (1877). 10902.

The Imprisonment of Mr. Tooth (1877). 6554.

Indoctus [James Welton], *The Past, Present, and Future of the Church of England Working Men's Society* (n.d., but ca. 1880). 8111.

Intoning: or the Possibility of "Saying" Prayers Without making "a slow protracted Noise," duly considered [etc.] (1852). 5860.

Is Our Minister a Puseyite? A Dialogue for the Unlearned (n.d., but ca. 1845). 5569.

Jebb, John. *The Principle of Ritualism Defended. A Sermon Preached in the Church of St. Michael and All Angels* [Tenbury, etc.] (1856). 1847.

———. *The Ritual Law and Custom of the Church Universal* (1865). 1962.

Landels, W. *Ritualism: A Speech Delivered at the Autumnal Meeting of the Baptist Union of Great Britain and Ireland* (1873). 71618.

A Layman's View of Ritualism (1879). 3974.

Lee, Frederick George. Beati pacifici. *The Need of Spiritual Authority* [etc.] (1882). 7587.

———. *The Beauty of Holiness. Ten Lectures on External Religious Observances,* 2d ed. (1866). 10564.

Liddell, Robert. *On the Daily Celebration of Holy Communion* (1868). 8206.

Liddon, H. P. *Evening Communions Contrary to the Teaching and Practice of the Church in All Ages* [etc.] (1876). 7227.

Littledale, Richard Frederick. *Catholic Ritual in the Church of England Scriptural, Reasonable, Lawful* (1865). 1075.

———. *Incense. A Liturgical Essay* (1866). 9910.

———. *Innovations: A Lecture Delivered in the Assembly Rooms, Liverpool, April 23, 1868* (1868). 1363.

———. *The North-side of the Altar: A Liturgical Essay* (1865). 72868.

———. *Ritualists not Romanists* (n.d.). 1504.

———. *Why Ritualists Do Not Become Roman Catholics: A Reply to the Abbe Martin* (n.d., but 1879). 1799.

Luckock, H. M. *The Ritual Crisis: How It May be Turned to the Best Account* (1899). 7193.

M'Donnell, Carlile. *Are We Ritualists?* (1898). 8841.

MacCartie, J. *Ritualism and Symbolism Obstructive to the Clear Light of Completed Revelation. A Sermon Preached in Christ Church, Carlisle, on Wednesday, 21st March, 1866* (1866). 9923.

MacColl, Malcolm. *My Reviewers Reviewed, in a Preface to the Third and Revised Edition of Lawlessness, Sacerdotalism, and Ritualism* (1875). 3365.

———. *Tractarianism and Ritualism* (1881). 4033.

Mackonochie, A. H. *Remonstrance: A Letter to the Bishop of London* (1875). 1694.

Malleus Ritualistarum; or, the Ritual Reason Why Not (1872). 10918.

Martin, John. *St Alban's, Holborn. Facts and Figures versus Fiction* (1867). 10104.

Maskell, William. *Protestant Ritualists* (1872). 1584.

May We Ask the Saints to Pray for Us? St. Bartholomew's Church Tracts No. 36 (n.d., but 1890s). 11188.

Mayow, M. W. *Remarks upon Certain Principles of Ritual* (1872). 1566.

———. *Remarks upon the First Report of the Royal Commission on Ritual* [etc.] (1868). 7858.

———. *A Reply to a Memorial on the Subject of Ritual* (1872). 1556.

A Memorial of Nine Hundred and Ten Priests, Presented to Both Houses of the Convocation of the Province of Canterbury (1871). 6506.

Memorial of the Churchwardens of the Parish of Westbourne, to the Right Reverend the Lord Bishop of Chichester [etc.] (1851). 5859.

Memorial Protest by Evangelical Clergy of the Church of England to the Lord Bishop of London, against His Lordship's Institution of the Rev. A. H. Mackonochie to the Benefice of St. Peter's, London Docks [etc.] (1883). 4988.

Memorial to Convocation (n.d.). 3837.

Memorial to His Grace the Archbishop of Canterbury (1881). 71907.

Memorial to the Most Reverend the Archbishops and the Right Reverend the Bishops of the Provinces of Canterbury and York (1850). 158.

The Moral Effect of Irregularities in the Ritual of the Church (1843). 5993.

Neale, J. M. *Extreme Men. A Letter to A. J. B. Beresford Hope* (1865). 6002.

Nevins, Willis. *Why I Left the Church of Rome* (n.d., but ca. 1870). 8082.

The Newspaper Religious Census and Its Lessons (1882). 8362.

Non-Confessing Catholics. S. Joseph Tracts No. 1 (n.d., but ca. 1870). 10462.

Non-fasting Communions. S. Joseph Tracts No. 2 (n.d., but ca. 1870). 10463.

Norton, J. G. *A Plea and Plan for the Toleration of Ritualists* (1881). 4265.

Observance of the Rubrick — Burial of Schismatics, &c. Report of Proceedings under a Commission Issued by the Lord Bishop of Exeter to Inquire into Certain Charges Preferred against the Rev. Walter Blunt, Curate of Helston [etc.] (n.d., but 1844). 5855.

Oldknow, J. *Anti-Ritual Proceedings: A Letter to the Reverend the Clergy of the Rural Deanery of Birmingham* [etc.] (1866). 9924.

Ormiston, James. *Hymns Ancient and Modern, and Their Romanizing Teaching. Church Association Tract No. XXI* (n.d.). 12498.

———. *A Protest against the Ritualists' Confessional* [etc.] (n.d., but probably 1867). 6144.

Parker, James. *The Ornaments Rubric: Its History and Meaning. A Series of Papers Contributed to the "Penny Post"* [etc.] (1881). 7329.

Perry, Thomas W. *The Church of England's Claim to Primitive and Catholic Ceremonial* (1874). 7750.

Pocock, Nicholas. *The Ritual Commission. A Paper Read at Bristol in November, 1870* [etc.] (1872). 3819.

Portal, G. R. *On Some of the Prevalent Objections to Ritual Observances. A Sermon Preached in S. Barnabas' Church, Pimlico* [etc.] (1854). 11955.

Powell, Charles. *Seven Reasons of Working Men of the Parish and Congregation of St. Alban's, Holborn, Why the Bishops should Refuse to allow the late Decisions of the Judicial Committee of the Privy Council to be used against their Clergy* (1875). 10906.

Powell, J[ames] B[aden]. *On Processions* (1876). 7759.

The Prayer-book and Eucharistic Ceremonial (1874). 4817.

"Presbyter Anglicanus." Utum Horum: *The Book of Common Prayer, or, the Directorium Anglicanum in the Administration of the Holy Communion?* (1866). 1258.

Protest against the Communion of a Unitarian in Westminster Abbey on June 22, 1870 (1870). 1468.

Protest against the Proselytism Carried on by Bishop Gobat (n.d.). 159.

Protestant Evangelical Mission and Electoral Union. *Ritualists and Ritualism* (n.d.). 8134.

Pusey, E. B. Letter to *The Times* (July 1874). 74155.

———. *The Proposed Ecclesiastical Legislation. Three Letters to "The Times"* [etc.] (1874). 8063.

Puseyism in London (1843). 5852.

Rawlins, T. S. F. *A Sermon Preached in the Parish Church of Clifton Campville* (1858). 71130.

Reasons for Ritual. Christ Church, Wolverhampton, Leaflet No. 7 (n.d., but 1876). 3379.

Report of the Council of the English Church Union Relative to the Preparation of the Memorials on Ritual, and of their Presentation [etc.] (1866). 7872.

Rev. J. Keble and the Ritual Question (1865). 5738.

Ritson, Henry. *The "Ritual" of S. Mark's* (1873). 10704.

Ritual Conformity: Interpretations of the Rubrics of the Prayer-Book agreed upon by a Conference Held at All Saints, Margaret-Street, 1880–1881 (1881). 71906.

Ritual: A Plea in Its Behalf, Grounded on Scripture and Reason. By One Who Has Viewed Both Sides of the Questions (n.d.). 70681.

The Ritualistic Conspiracy (23rd ed., 1877). 6018.

Rogers, G. Albert. *The Real Presence the Basis of Ritualism* (n.d., but ca. 1867). 10055.

Rules of the Society of S. Alphege, Abp. & M. (n.d.). 4629.

Russell, John Fuller. *Obedience to the Church in Things Ritual: A Sermon* (1847). 11923.

S. Bartholomew's Church Tracts. Nos. 1–30 (n.d., but ca. 1895). 14131–60.

Savile, Bourchier Wrey. *Hard Speeches and Gentle Words* (1879). 71832.

Sergeant, E. W. *Ritualism: How Far Reasonable?* (n.d., but ca. 1879). 3975.

Shaw, Benjamin. *Ritualism and the Ecclesiastical Law* (n.d.). 9888.

Sheffield, Robert Rodolph. *Five Letters on a Conversion to Roman Catholicism* (n.d.). 11181.

Shipley, Orby. *Ought We to Obey the New Court . . . ?* (1875). 8064.

The Sign of the Cross Defended (1875). 14076.

Skinner, James. *A Plea for the Threatened Ritual of the Church of England* (1865). 7871.

———. *Why Do We Prize Externals in the Service of God?* [etc.] (1856). 10036.

Smith, Samuel. *Speech to the House of Commons* (1898). 72220.

Society of S. Alphege, Abp. & M. List of Associates. Corrected up to May 1, 1868 (1868). 4646.

Society of St. Alphege, Abp. & M. *Offices for the Society* [etc.] (n.d.). 4631.

[Society of the Holy Cross]. *A Statement by the Society of the Holy Cross concerning the Order of Corporate Reunion* (1879). 4097.

Society of the Holy Cross. With List of Members (1897). 8555.

Soltau, G. W. *A Letter to the Working Classes on Ritualism* (1873). 12502.

Stand Up, or Sit Down (n.d.). 13696.

Statistics of Church of England Schools for the Poor in England and Wales (1867). 71411.

The Stray Kitten (n.d.). 10903.

"Tekel." *The Views of a Church of England Layman Relative to the Church of England Clergy* (1866). 1256.

Thompson, H. *Ritualism: A Plea for the Surplice* (1866). 9919.

Thompson, Henry L. *Religious Symbolism* (1878). 13498.

Thoughts on Some Questions of the Day (1869). 3656.

To the Most Reverend the Archbishop of Canterbury, Primate of All England, &c. (1867). 5746.

Ultra-Ritualism. Extracts from the Hymn Books Used in St. Alban's, Holborn, London (1867). 10077.

[Vincent, W.] *Catalogue of the Ecclesiastical Art Exhibition, Castlegate House, York, October 9th, 10th, 11th, and 12th, 1866* (1866). 10089.

———. *Report of the Proceedings at the Ecclesiastical Art Exhibition, held at York, on the 9th, 10th, 11th, & 12th October, 1866* (1866). 12880.

Vogan, Thomas S. L. *Remarks on Catholic Practice, Confession, and the Real Presence, as Advocated in a Late Petition to Convocation* (1873). 1595.

Walker, Charles. *Pax Super Israel. An Irenicon, Respectfully Addressed to the Consideration of the Royal Commission on Ritual* (1867). 4621.

Westerton, Charles. *A Letter to the Right Reverend the Lord Bishop of London, on the Popish Manner in which, Contrary to the Rubrics, Divine Service is Performed on Sunday Mornings at the Parish Church of St. Paul's, Wilton Place, Knightsbridge* (1853). 5863.

Wetherell, J. C. *Ritualism: Thoughts on the Question of the Day* [etc.] (1866). 1963.

Whitworth, William Allen. *Churchman's Grievances* [etc.] (1881). 2234.

"Will O' the Wisp." *A Paper Lantern for Puseyites* (1843). 5846.

Wilson, R. J. *Correspondence on the Subject of Altar Cards, between His Grace the Archbishop of Canterbury and the Rev. R. J. Wilson* (1874). 4330.

Wix, Hooker. *Ritualism; or, Ritualistic Worship: Ordained by God Himself, Practiced by the Early Christian Church, strictly legal in the Church of England, Conducive to the Glory of God, and the Edifying of the Congregation. Being an Address to his Congregation* (n.d., but 1866). 10029.

Wood, Charles L. *A Paper Read at the Church Congress at Derby . . . on Liturgical Improvement* (1882). 7731.

———. *The President's Address to the Ordinary Meeting of the English Church Union on Thursday, December 9, 1875* (1875). 6544.

Woodward, F. B. *Remarks on a Petition Presented to Her Majesty, for a Revision of the Liturgy* (1860). 651.

Woolley, J. *Clergy Discipline: Its Relation to Doctrine, Ritual, and Morals* (1881). 73312.

[Wordsworth, Christopher]. *Charge of the Bishop of Lincoln on the Ornaments Rubric* (1879). 7268.

———. *On Sisterhoods and Vows. A Letter to the Ven. Sir George Prevost, Bart.* (1878). 8032.

———. *Senates and Synods, Their Respective Functions and Uses* [etc.] (1874). 1622.

[———], Bishop of Lincoln. *Results of an Inquiry on Ritual* (1875). 6010.

The York Congress and Church Rites (1867). 1321.

INDEX

JOHN SHELTON REED

A distinguished scholar, essayist, and humorist, John Shelton Reed is William Rand Kenan, Jr. Professor of Sociology and the Director of the Institute for Research in Social Science at the University of North Carolina. He has also served as Pitt Professor of American History and Institutions at Cambridge University. Much of the research for this book was carried out during a year in England as a Guggenheim Fellow. Author of *One South: An Ethnic Approach to Regional Culture; Southern Folk, Plain and Fancy;* and *Whistling Dixie: Dispatches from the South,* among other notable books, Reed also serves as editor of the journal *Southern Cultures.* He attends the Chapel of the Cross (Episcopal), in Chapel Hill.

GLORIOUS BATTLE

was composed electronically using
Galliard types, with
display types in Castellar.
The book was printed on acid-free,
Glatfelter Supple Opaque Recycled paper,
with 80-pound Rainbow endsheets,
Smyth sewn, and bound over 88-point binder's boards
in Kingston cloth, with dust jackets printed in three colors
by Thomson-Shore., Inc.
Book and jacket designs are the work of Gary Gore.
Published by Vanderbilt University Press
Nashville, Tennessee 37235